This book examines the vital role of market towns in the medieval economy. It focuses on Exeter, and how it served as an important link in a marketing chain that connected local, regional, and overseas trade.

Although small by most standards (the population stood at around 3,100 in 1377), Exeter was the largest town in south-western England and had long played a central role in the marketing hierarchy of the region. Its functions can be illustrated through prosopographical analysis, a methodology which creates "collective biographies" of specific groups of traders, thereby revealing the identity – status, occupation, residence – of buyers and sellers, the goods they exchanged, where they traded, and how they marketed their goods. Such an approach also helps to characterize the town's regional networks of trade and hinterland, an area defined by the distance travelled by traders or goods, the direction of exchange, and the types of trade channelled through the urban center from the different agricultural regions. The growing prosperity of Exeter's late medieval hinterland, which covered much of Devon and extended well into Somerset, helps to explain Exeter's own economic and demographic growth in a period when many other urban centers experienced stagnation or decline.

Local markets and regional trade in medieval Exeter

Local markets and regional trade in medieval Exeter

MARYANNE KOWALESKI

Fordham University, New York

Published by the Press Syndicate of the University of Cambridge
The Pitt Building, Trumpington Street, Cambridge CB2 1RP
40 West 20th Street, New York, NY 10011-4211, USA
10 Stamford Road, Oakleigh, Melbourne 3166, Australia

First published 1995

Printed in Great Britain at Redwood Books, Trowbridge, Wiltshire

A catalogue record for this book is available from the British Library

Library of Congress cataloguing in publication data
Kowaleski, Maryanne.
Local markets and regional trade in medieval Exeter/Maryanne Kowaleski.
p. cm.
Includes bibliographical references.
ISBN 0 521 33371 7
1. Exeter Region (England)–Commerce–History. 2. Exeter Region (England)–Industries–History. 3. Markets–England–Exeter Region–History. 4. Exeter (England)–Economic conditions. 5. Commerce–History–Medieval, 500-1500. I. Title.
HF3520.E95K68 1995
381′. 18′0942356–dc20 94-8396 CIP

WV

For my parents,
Edward and Marguerite Kowaleski

Contents

Figures

Tables

Acknowledgments

Projects that are over fifteen years in the making inevitably incur many debts. To J. Ambrose Raftis of the Pontifical Institute of Medieval Studies I owe thanks for his guidance and support when I was a graduate student, and for his idea that medieval economic systems might profitably be studied through collective biography, or prosopography. As a student, I was also fortunate to receive training in medieval economic history from John Munro and Andrew Watson of the University of Toronto. To John Munro I especially extend thanks for his interest, helpful criticisms, and encouragement at an early stage; he more than anyone else is responsible for the path my research interests have taken. I also acknowledge the financial assistance I received as a student for this project from the Pontifical Institute, the University of Toronto, the Social Science Research Council, and the Fulbright Scholarship program. Since then I have also been fortunate to receive funds to finance research in the British archives from the National Endowment for the Humanities, the American Council of Learned Societies, the American Philosophical Society, and Fordham University.

To my friends in Devon I owe a particularly heavy debt. First and foremost, I thank the county archivist, Margery Rowe, and the staff of the Devon Record Office who generously provided practical and cheerful assistance during my many visits to Exeter. My debt to Margery Rowe is particularly large. I am also grateful to the staff of the Exeter Cathedral Library and especially Audrey Erskine for her guidance through the intricacies of the dean and chapter archives. Nicholas Orme also kindly advised me on cathedral records and on the clerical population of medieval Exeter. To Joyce Youings I owe special thanks for sharing her comprehensive knowledge of Devon history with me and for providing scholarly encouragement from the time of my first visit to Exeter as a postgraduate. I also benefited from discussions on southwestern maritime matters with her and with Todd Gray. My considerable debt to Devon archaeologists for showing me other sources of evidence and ways of thinking about medieval trade should also be noted. I thank Chris Henderson in particular for providing Figure 5.1, as well as access to the collection of translated Exeter documents built up by the staff of the Exeter Archaeological Field Unit. I also profited from discussions of archaeological evidence with John Allan, Chris Henderson, Stuart Blaylock, Frances Griffith, and Shirley Simpson. The hospitality they and others in Devon extend me during visits to the county is also much appreciated. Most of all, however, I am deeply grateful to John Allan for guiding me around numerous Devon sites and answering my many questions with patience and insight.

Fellow medievalists on both sides of the Atlantic generously provided advice and assistance at crucial points. Above all I profited from long and pleasant discussions with Harold Fox who shared his extensive knowledge of medieval Devon with me and drew my attention to sources I had not first thought to employ. Discussions on several occasions with Bruce Campbell, Richard Britnell, and Vanessa Harding helped me to sharpen my thinking on key issues. David Farmer, John Hatcher, and Jenny Kermode also answered queries and kindly provided me with copies of some of their work in advance of publication. For sharing their knowledge of maritime trade and quickly responding to my queries I thank Wendy Childs and Richard Unger. My students, Marilyn Oliva and Judy Ann Ford, graciously checked references for me when I was unable to travel to England, as did my colleague at Fordham, Mary Erler. Special thanks are due to Derek Keene who read several chapters and offered welcome criticisms that challenged me to refine my arguments; his encouragment and willingness to talk over numerous points of urban history made this study considerably better. But it is to Judith Bennett that I owe my greatest debt for her intellectual as well as emotional support over the course of a very long project. She read drafts of the entire book at several stages and offered excellent advice on the more practical aspects of writing a monograph, along with helpful suggestions to improve the arguments contained in each chapter. To her friendship and her scholarship I owe much.

New York City M.A.K.

Abbreviations

BL	British Library
DCNQ	*Devon and Cornwall notes and queries*
DCO	Duchy of Cornwall Record Office
DRO	Devon Record Office
EcHR	*Economic history review*
PDAS	*Proceedings of the Devon archaeological society*
PRO	Public Record Office
TDA	*Transactions of the Devonshire association*

Abbreviated titles of manuscripts and works cited in the notes are given in the Bibliography.

A note on dating

Dates given in the form 1377/8 refer to the fiscal or office year from Michaelmas to Michaelmas. Dates given in the form 1377–8 imply a period from some time in 1377 to some time in 1378.

Introduction

In his ambitious survey of the economic history of pre-industrial Europe, *Civilization and Capitalism*, Fernand Braudel divides his study into three parts, likening these parts to the floors of a house.[1] The bottom floor represents material civilization: the structural underpinnings or context of everyday life, comprised of the sources of population, subsistence, energy, and money. The uppermost storeys represent capitalism and the action of more sophisticated economies within a world sphere. In between these two levels lie the first stages of market exchange. Since this middle storey contains the very roots of modern capitalism, it critically holds the house together; but it is also a "shadowy zone" because its intermingling of the lower natural economy and the capitalist economy involves mechanisms not yet fully explored. In order to understand the genesis of modern capitalism, therefore, historians need to focus attention on this crucial middle stage. Only detailed studies of the fundamental structures and instruments of exchange in pre-industrial economies will allow us to analyze fully this critical conjuncture of economic systems.

While Braudel's analogy presents a handy way to conceptualize the evolutionary stages of the modern economy, his application is flawed. Because the operation of pre-industrial markets is most obvious between major merchants and major cities, Braudel and other historians have tended to focus their efforts on an upper level of trade conducted over relatively long distances, and on early modern rather than medieval trade. Their perspective, however, does not give due consideration to the vital function of local markets and the links between these markets and wider networks of exchange. As Rodney Hilton has recently suggested, the emergence of a capitalist economy was probably fueled as much by the spread of simple commodity production in market towns as it was by the growth of merchant capital in the larger cities and ports.[2] Since

[1] Braudel 1981–84.

[2] Hilton 1985. Britnell (1981b) also concludes that local trade between agricultural producers, craftspeople, and traders was the most important factor in promoting economic growth in the high middle ages.

the transition from subsistence production to a profit-based commercial economy began in the middle ages, it is particularly essential to acknowledge the significance of local markets and domestic trade in the medieval economy. Only after we have traced the inner workings of the fundamental building blocks of the medieval economy – local markets and regional trade – can we begin to explain the crucial shifts that had moved western society towards a capitalist economy by the end of the middle ages.

This volume takes up this challenge by examining the local markets and regional trade of the south-western town of Exeter during the middle ages. The aim is twofold: to explore the crucial role of the urban center in linking local, regional, and international trade, and to determine how medieval marketing systems worked by analyzing their organization, participants, and mechanics of exchange. This approach also makes it possible to analyze the role played by local markets and regional trade in the relative prosperity of late medieval Devon and Exeter, both of which experienced considerably more economic growth than other late medieval English counties and towns. "Local markets" refers to the buying and selling that took place within Exeter between its resident consumers or traders and their suppliers (most of whom also resided in the town). "Regional trade" refers to transactions that brought together buyers and sellers of different settlements, or transferred goods to Exeter or beyond its environs. The distinctions between these two types of trade do not necessarily make them mutually exclusive; indeed, one of the central points of this study is that regional networks of trade were often comprised of overlapping networks of local trade. A similar observations can be made about the dividing line between regional and international trade, since the import or export of foreign goods at Exeter depended heavily on coastal trade which exploited regional links via maritime rather than overland routes.

Local markets in medieval England have usually been discussed in the "economy" chapter of a book on a particular town or village. On occasion these studies also examine economic links with the surrounding region or overseas,[3] but regional trade has usually been explored via studies of "internal" trade which are more common for the early modern than the medieval period. Overseas trade, particularly the export market, has received a disproportionate share of scholarly attention, in part because the national records of port customs are so quantifiable. This focus, however, has tended to emphasize unduly the role of long-distance trade and the export market in explaining the evolution and growth of

[3] Two recent works are noteworthy here: Keene 1985 and Britnell 1986b.

the medieval English economy, even though the home market played the more significant role in terms of employment, demand, and the evolution of commercial techniques and organization. Scholarly neglect of domestic trade has also led us to undervalue the economic contributions of artisans and retailers in favor of merchants and distributors, even though the latter represented a minority (albeit a powerful minority) of medieval people.[4] This study does not neglect the powerful role played by merchants in the medieval economy, but it does dwell longer than most studies on the commercial functions and activities of artisans and retailers, groups whose economic contribution was evident in small villages, market towns, seaports, and regional capitals alike.

In stressing the commercialization of the medieval English economy, this study follows a recent trend in English historiography.[5] Historians of agrarian economy and society in medieval England, for example, have increasingly focused on the penetration of medieval agriculture by market forces, as seen in patterns of peasant indebtedness, differentiated and consolidated landholding, and agricultural specialization geared to the market.[6] Several scholars have traced the pace and distribution of this commercialization in the proliferation of markets and the emergence of hierarchies of markets catering to different types of consumers.[7] Because of their role as centers of distribution and/or consumption, the central places in these hierarchies have received particular scrutiny.[8] Marketing connections between town and country have also been explored in studies of the spatial and temporal aspects of the regional marketing system, an approach that draws attention to the models developed by geographers and anthropologists to explain the economic ties that linked peasant villages and market towns together.[9] The applicability of some of these theoretical models (based on such diverse societies as highland Ecuador, late imperial China, and tribal Africa) to the medieval European system is open to debate. While they are helpful in pointing out the importance of specific factors that ordered a hierarchy of markets within regions, their causal explanations often fail to take into account the peculiarities of the pre-industrial situation.

[4] Swanson 1989 has done much to rectify this imbalance.

[5] See especially Britnell 1993.

[6] See especially Clark 1981; Biddick 1985, 1987; Campbell 1988 and forthcoming; McIntosh 1986; Farmer 1991a.

[7] See especially Britnell 1981b; Dyer 1989a, 1992.

[8] Britnell 1986b; Keene 1989a; Campbell, Galloway, Keene and Murphy 1993.

[9] For example, Unwin 1981 and Biddick 1987. Useful introductions to regional analysis may be found in Smith 1974 and (ed.) 1976. One of the few attempts (Russell 1972) to apply central-place theory to the medieval period has met with mixed success. A more recent attempt (Hohenberg and Lees 1985: esp. 4–6, 47–73) suggests a model based on a dual perspective derived from central-place theory and network theory.

The study presented here adds to this growing body of evidence on the commercialization of medieval England by concentrating primarily on the participants in trade, the mechanics of exchange, and the commercial ties that linked local, regional, and overseas commerce. The ancient city of Exeter in Devon serves as the focus of this exploration. With a population of about 3,100 in 1377, Exeter was not big enough to affect patterns of agrarian production in its hinterland, but its gateway position to the south-western peninsula and easy access to both maritime and overland routes helped make it the administrative, ecclesiastical, and economic center of south-western England by the eleventh century. It served as the seat of a diocese that included all of Devon and Cornwall and presided over a commercial hinterland that stretched throughout Devon and well into the neighboring counties of Somerset and Dorset.

Part 1 examines the regional economy of medieval Devon, exploring how the county's agricultural diversity, geographical situation, and seaward orientation promoted commercialization. The hierarchy of markets, fairs, and towns established by the twelfth and thirteenth centuries provides one reflection of this process. Part 2 focuses on the local markets of Exeter. Although long-term economic trends are examined, much of the analysis centers on the late fourteenth century when a particularly good body of evidence allows us to trace the urban occupational and political structure in an unusually precise and comprehensive manner. Through a variety of indices compiled to measure wealth, status, economic privilege, and commercial activities, these chapters analyze the commercial orientation of different occupational and political groups. Part 3 examines in three chapters the commercial networks that linked local and regional trade. The first discusses arrangements within the economic infrastructure, such as municipal regulation, tolls, extension of credit and debt enforcement, that either reduced or raised the costs of doing business for both residents and outsiders. The second employs the unusually detailed local customs of the port of Exeter to trace the town's commercial links by sea, especially the vastly understudied coastal trade which in Exeter accounted for about 70 per cent of all maritime trade. Most importantly, the inland distribution of imports is analyzed to illustrate the dynamic relationship between a distributive center and its hinterland. The last chapter attempts to characterize the hinterland by identifying the occupations, status, commercial activities, regional orientation, and distance from Exeter of regional traders. Two detailed case studies are offered to illustrate the complexity of the networks of trade that linked Exeter to its surrounding regions: one on the meat, livestock, hide and skin trade and the other on the fish trade.

Much of this study relies heavily on a prosopographical methodology that analyzes data from diverse sources to study the characteristics of particular groups within a population.[10] By creating collective biographies of specific groups of traders active in medieval Exeter, this methodology makes it possible to address questions regarding the identity (status, occupation, residence) of buyers and sellers, the goods they exchanged, where they traded, and how they marketed their goods. Some of the groups analyzed in this way include the members of Exeter's merchant oligarchy, the 525 identifiable Exeter householders in 1377, the over 9,000 creditors and debtors who appeared in the Exeter borough courts in 1378–88, the roughly 1,500 importers active at the port of Exeter in the early and late fourteenth century, and the some 190 dealers in fish and 200 dealers in hides and skins at Exeter in 1370–90. Since many of these traders resided outside of Exeter (for example, 20 per cent of the debt litigants, 80 per cent of the fish dealers, and 85 per cent of the importers), this methodological approach also sheds much light on regional networks of trade centered on Exeter.

While this study offers an analysis of the local markets and regional trade of only one town, the sources and methodology employed here might fruitfully be used in studying networks of exchange elsewhere in medieval England. Comparisons with other towns are increasingly possible because of the recent interest in small towns and new publications on larger towns such as Colchester and Winchester.[11] This study's findings on the operation and significance of coastal trade also need to be incorporated into our understanding of the role of maritime trade in the economies of port towns and of medieval England as a whole. Indeed, the conclusions which emerge from this analysis regarding the internal organization of Exeter's local markets, the structure of its inland trade networks, and its role as a center of exchange can in large part be extended to many other provincial towns. In its emphasis upon the significance of local markets, the dynamic relationship between town and country, and the focus on regional networks of trade, it is hoped that this study also suggests some profitable lines of inquiry for historians of the medieval English economy.

[10] See Appendix 1 for a longer discussion of this methodology and the sources employed in this study. Appendix 3 presents the data at the heart of the prosopographical analyses in Part 2.

[11] For small towns, see Hilton 1982, 1984, 1985, and Raftis 1982, 1990; for larger towns, see Keene 1985; Britnell 1986b; Rosser 1989; Bonney 1990; Shaw 1993.

Part 1

The regional economy of medieval Devon

1 Agriculture, industry, and trade

County-focused discussions of the pace of development in Devon from the eleventh through fourteenth centuries usually paint a dismal picture of unimpressive economic gains and slow demographic growth. Devon is listed last in comparisons of assessed wealth from 1086 to 1334, showing the least amount of change of any English county during this period.[1] In the 1334 lay subsidy, Devon ranked thirty-second out of thirty nine counties in assessed wealth per square mile.[2] A comparison of population levels in Domesday with the 1377 poll tax shows that Devon's population increased by a ratio of only 1.26, the lowest for any county. During the same period, the county's ranking in population density fell from eighteenth to twenty-seventh (out of thirty eight counties).[3] Devon's poor showing in this period has been credited primarily to its large tracts of infertile soils and wasteland and its slow rate of colonization after 1086, but other factors, such as its remote location and the devastations caused by war and piracy, have also been noted.[4]

This traditional picture relies heavily on sources that are better at measuring arable productivity and inland open-field villages than economic diversity, dispersed settlements, and populations that could avoid taxation through special exemptions or outright evasion.[5] By reassessing some old evidence and considering some new evidence, the next two chapters reexamine the economic implications of Devon's ostensibly poor record in agricultural production and population. The discussion focuses in particular on the agricultural, industrial, and commercial diversity of the regional economies of medieval Devon which both shielded the county from the worst excesses of the agrarian

[1] Darby, Glasscock, Sheail, and Versey 1979.
[2] Glasscock 1973: 141.
[3] Russell 1948: 132, 313.
[4] Hoskins 1952: 219–20; Hallam 1981: 165–9; Hatcher 1988: 238.
[5] Whether tinners were exempted from the subsidies and poll taxes and the possible impact of such exemptions remain a subject of debate; see Schofield 1965: 494, n. 6; Hatcher 1970.

crises in the fourteenth and fifteenth centuries and promoted economic growth in the county during the fifteenth and sixteenth centuries. In stark contrast to the dismal standing of Devon in scales of demographic and economic prosperity in the high middle ages, the county's performance in comparisons of wealth between 1334 and the early sixteenth century place it first in economic growth; its overall ranking in assessed lay wealth rose from thirty-fourth in 1334 to eighteenth in 1515.[6] Developments in both the agricultural and industrial sectors, particularly the expansion of cloth manufactures, played a central role in this growth.

Agriculture

Devonshire is a hilly county of many deep, steep-sided valleys interspersed with a few broader valleys along the Exe, Creedy, and Culm rivers. The granite mass of Dartmoor dominates the central portion of the county and separates the poor soils of the Culm Measures in north and mid Devon from the lighter, more fertile soils of the South Hams in south Devon (Figure 1.1).[7] The vast moorlands of Dartmoor and Exmoor, along with the hilltops of such ranges as the Blackdown Hills on the Devon and Somerset border and the Haldon Hills between the Exe and Teign rivers, account for the large proportion of wasteland in the county. Well favored with rivers and streams, Devon possesses two long and distinct coastlines and serves as the gateway to the southwestern peninsula. The climate is mild but humid; Devon is one of the wettest regions in England.

The variety and contrast in the county's topography make for distinct regional differences evident as early as the Domesday Book survey of 1086. These regional variations are all too often subsumed in county-wide generalizations that characterize eleventh-century Devon as underpopulated and poor in comparison to other counties, even though

[6] Schofield 1965: 504–6; Darby, Glasscock, Sheail, and Versey 1979: 258–9.

[7] The regions noted in Figure 1.1 correspond, with two exceptions, to the agricultural regions described by Fox 1991. I have enlarged Fox's Dartmoor region to include the borderlands to the north and east of Dartmoor and a smaller portion of the borderlands to the south (including Tavistock) because the commerce of these areas was so dependent on Dartmoor. For the purpose of this study, which concentrates above all on trade, the commercial relationship between the moorlands of Dartmoor and the surrounding border parishes is more significant than their agricultural differences (which, in any case, were not that marked). The proximity of the northern and eastern border areas to Exeter, the chief market town of the county and the focus of this study, is also a significant factor. Similarly, Exmoor (a separate region in Fox) has been included in north and mid Devon because both their commercial ties and their distance from Exeter were similar.

Figure 1.1 Regions in late medieval Devon

large areas of Devon clearly did not fit this pattern.[8] The density of population and plough teams in the fertile "Red Devon" region of rich, red soils located in the Vale of Exeter, but stretching from Tor Bay to the Somerset border along the Exe, Creedy, and Culm rivers, was higher than that of any other area in the five counties of the West Country. Only slightly less fertile and populous were the northern lowlands of the Taw and Torridge rivers which, together with the third most populous region – the South Hams between the Erme river and

[8] For example, Darby, Glasscock, Sheail, and Versey 1979: 250–5. For the following, see Morgan 1940; Welldon Finn 1967: 223–95; Darby 1977: 90–1, 126, 164, 168–9.

the mouth of the Teign – boasted particularly high numbers of demesne sheep and swineherds in Domesday Book. In contrast, demesne sheep were scarcer around Dartmoor while the population densities of the regions around Dartmoor, Exmoor, and the north-west border near Cornwall were extremely low.

The early fourteenth-century lay subsidies show similar regional contrasts.[9] While Devon certainly had more than its fair share of impoverished and underpopulated parishes, it also contained very prosperous parishes such as Ottery St Mary (taxed at 40*s* per 1,000 acres in 1334) in east Devon; other wealthy and populated regions lay in the lowlands of the Taw and Torridge rivers in the north and the South Hams region in the south. The distribution of population in 1377 tells much the same story. Large stretches of mid Devon, Dartmoor, Exmoor, and their bordering parishes were very lightly populated (only between one and fifteen people per 1,000 acres), but south Devon, particularly the coastal parishes around Tor Bay and Start Bay, had far denser populations (around ninety people per 1,000 acres).[10] Similar population densities were evident in some of the parishes bordering the mouth of the Taw and Torridge rivers in north Devon. These results suggest that the inclusion of Devon's vast moorlands in calculations of county prosperity and population density misleadingly skews our view of the county when compared with other English shires.

The Domesday returns and lay subsidy assessments might also be accused of giving a one-sided picture, one that does not adequately take into account the profitable potential of non-arable lands and diversified economies.[11] Despite Devon's appearance of agricultural backwardness and demographic stagnation, the county largely escaped the agricultural crisis that beset so many of the Midland counties in the late thirteenth and early fourteenth centuries. Its abundant waste and pastureland, even though of marginal quality, could be used for grazing or drawn into cultivation as demand for grain grew. The early leasing of demesnes and the dispersed pattern of settlement also eased the pressure on land. Devon residents also largely insulated themselves from the consequences of overpopulation and bad harvests because of the light demand for labor services in the county, as well as the

[9] See Morgan 1940: 321 which maps the assessments for the lay subsidy of 1334. See also *Lay subsidy 1334*: 49–66 and Hoskins 1952, for this and the following.

[10] This and the following are based on an analysis of the surviving Devon poll tax returns (PRO E179/95/34–55, 240/258–9). For the small size of Devon boroughs at this time, see below, Table 2.1.

[11] Similar accusations have been levelled by Bailey 1989; Hatcher 1969.

numerous sources of alternative income from occupations related to mining or the sea.[12]

Indeed, one of the distinctive features of the medieval agrarian economy in Devon was its flexibility, due in large part to the prevailing system of convertible husbandry. Under this system fields were cropped continuously for a number of years and then allowed to revert to fallow or, more commonly, used for pasture. These leys could be lengthened or shortened depending on the demand for grain while the relatively large amount of land under grass at any one time accommodated extensive pastoral interests.[13] The county's reliance on this system helps explain the surprisingly strong arable element in all periods, particularly before the plague when demand for food crops was higher. Even in the demographically stagnant late middle ages arable farming accounted for two-thirds or more of land use in the regions of south and east Devon. The weaker emphasis on nucleated villages and the open-field system in Devon may also have allowed the county to adjust more easily to the changes wrought by the demographic devastations of the Black Death in 1348–9.[14] Although settlements contracted and more lands were enclosed in response to the decline in population, the Devon landscape had always contained many dispersed hamlets, individual farms, and enclosed lands; these features may have helped protect Devon from some of the worst effects of the late-medieval agrarian crisis.[15]

Devon agriculture was also characterized by crop diversity. Orchards and gardens in south and east Devon, where the climate was suitably mild, allowed demesnes and peasants alike to profit from the sale of apples and cider.[16] Gardens and orchards bearing apple, pear, and plum were especially numerous in the area around Exeter and even within the city itself.[17] The chief demesne crop, however, was oats, a grain well suited to a damp climate and poor soil. As H.S.A. Fox points

[12] Ugawa 1962; Finberg 1969: 70–85; Hallam 1981: 169; Hatcher 1988: 383–98, 675–85.

[13] Fox 1991: 154–9, 303–11; Ugawa 1962: 635–8; Finberg 1969: 104–7; Alcock 1970: 168; Fox 1972: 89–99; Fox 1975: 185; Hatcher 1988: 387, 398.

[14] Finberg 1952b: 265–88; Fox 1972; Fox 1975; Fox 1991: 722–33.

[15] For the ability of areas of dispersed settlements better to withstand the effects of the late-medieval crisis, see Dyer 1990.

[16] Ugawa 1962: 652; Alcock 1970: 150; Fox 1991: 322–3. For peasant profits from the sale of apples, see the tithe accounts for Woodbury manor in ECL V/C 3351, 3352.

[17] For orchards and large gardens in Exeter, see Book 53A, ff. 88, 90v; MCR 1321/2, m. 35d; 1355/6, m. 22d; 1381/2 m. 3, 1386/7 m. 52; PCR 1–23 Ric. II, m. 46; BL Add. Ch. 27595; Marshall 1796: vol. II, 119. For the sale of fruit, cider, perry, and mead in Exeter, see also EQMT 1392, 1393; NQMT 1393; MT passim; Hoskins 1972: 94.

out, the prevalence of oats in medieval Devon indicated not the backwardness but the sensible adaptability of Devon farmers.[18] Although much less profitable and much less esteemed than wheat as a crop (one twelfth-century chronicler noted contemptuously that Exeter men and beasts fed on the same grain),[19] oats were nonetheless ideal for the local soil and climate. The predilection for oats extended even to brewing for it was the preferred grain for ale in much of medieval Devon.[20] Wheat was the second most important crop in south and east Devon but rye was more favored on the demesnes of north and mid Devon, and to a lesser extent in east Devon. Barley was a significant part of demesne agriculture only in south Devon, and nowhere did legumes represent much more than 1 per cent of arable land use. Peasant and demense crops were similar except in south Devon where wheat appears to have been the more important grain crop for peasants. Grain yields could be remarkably high, even on the poorer soils of west Devon where the conscientious estate management of the monks of Tavistock abbey produced significant yields. The widespread use of special fertilizing techniques, such as beat-burning and the application of sea sand, along with the ready supply of manure from the county's abundant livestock, also played a part in the successes of Devon agriculture.[21]

These regional differences in crop specialization, arable/pasture balance, and settlement became more marked with the demographic and economic changes of the late middle ages.[22] The spread of livestock husbandry, for instance, while noticeable everywhere in late medieval Devon, became particularly prevalent in mid and much of north Devon as arable land use and population declined sharply. Dominated by the infertile, wet, and heavy soils of the Culm Measures, this region grew oats and rye but increasingly turned to cattle rearing except in the more fertile and arable-oriented lowlands of the Taw and Torridge rivers.[23] Livestock husbandry also increased in the region of Dartmoor and its border parishes. On the Tavistock abbey manor of Hurdwick, income from dairy and wool sales reached its height in the fifteenth century. The high rents paid for demesne grassland here also point to

[18] Fox 1991: 303–7.

[19] *Chronicle of Richard of Devizes*: 66.

[20] Fox 1991: 303–7. For oat malt used by Exeter brewers, see MCR 1373/4, m. 18; PCR 1–23 Ric. II, m. 14.

[21] Ugawa 1962: 635–80; Finberg 1969: 88–115; Fox 1972: 92; Hatcher 1988: 390–3; Fox 1991: 303–7. Demesne yield ratios for oats, rye, and wheat in late medieval Devon were on average higher than for most other areas in England; see Fox 1991: 308–15.

[22] Fox 1991: 152–63, 315–20.

[23] Fox 1991: 157–9, 305–6, 316–18. Unfortunately, there has been little work done on the agriculture of north Devon so that the nature of late medieval changes in the lowlands around Barnstaple is not clear.

the growing pastoral interests of tenant farmers.[24] Arable agriculture did not decline as sharply on the moorlands as it did in mid and north Devon, due in part perhaps to the sustained demand for grain from tinworkers.[25] Indeed, the stannaries kept this region relatively prosperous throughout the late middle ages. In the mid fifteenth century when many claims of poverty reduced the amount of subsidies due, the stannary towns were less hard hit than most: three of the four Devon boroughs with the smallest reductions in 1445 were stannary towns on the fringes of Dartmoor.[26]

In contrast, the south Devon rural economy may not have fared as well after the Black Death. Demographic decline was felt more severely here in the form of vacant holdings, emigration, and perhaps falling arable production.[27] Yet agriculture in south Devon more than in any other region retained its arable emphasis into the late middle ages. The natural fertility of the South Hams, easy access to such fertilizers as sea sand, and the presence of well-populated markets and towns, particularly along the coast, must have encouraged arable agriculture here at a time when most other Devon regions turned increasingly to pastoral husbandry. Nonetheless, even in south Devon the trend to pastoralism can be seen in the growing emphasis on dairying in the late middle ages.[28]

East Devon, which contains both the rich soils of the broad valleys of the Creedy, Exe, and Culm rivers, and the somewhat less fertile hill-and-valley countryside east of the Otter valley, prospered more than any other Devon region in the late middle ages. Settlement did not contract as much in this region and demand for land remained fairly buoyant. When reductions in lay subsidy payments were granted in 1445, east Devon, particularly the easternmost section, received significantly fewer reductions than areas in south Devon.[29] As elsewhere in the county, arable farming remained important, particularly in the late fourteenth and early fifteenth centuries. But the trend towards pastoralism was evident even then. East Devon demesnes possessed the largest flocks in Devon and both sheep farming for wool and dairy farming were prominent in the regional economy. The expanding cloth industry was another important component of the region's prosperity in the late middle ages.[30]

24 Finberg 1969: 139–58.
25 Fox 1991: 154, 158–60.
26 Hoskins 1952: 231.
27 Fox 1975: 189–92, 196–8.
28 Hallam 1981: 388; Fox 1991: 154–5, 169, 306–7, 316.
29 Fox 1975: 195–8.
30 Fox 1991: 154–7, 306, 316–19, 741–2; Alcock 1970: 158–66; Fox 1972; Fox 1975: 192–202.

Comparisons of lay and clerical wealth between the subsidies of 1334 and 1535 show that the Devon economy grew more rapidly than that of any other English shire.[31] Although some areas (notably east Devon) may have benefited most, all regions in Devon shared in this remarkable increase in prosperity. The phenomenal rebuilding in fifteenth-century Devon reflected one aspect of this prosperity; stone bridges were repaired or built anew, church naves expanded, church towers erected or heightened, and new rood screens constructed in parishes throughout the county.[32] Domestic buildings – from small manor houses, to urban merchants' dwellings, to farmhouses – also proliferated, particularly in the late fifteenth and early sixteenth centuries.[33] Devon's neighboring counties of Cornwall and Somerset also shared in this late-medieval economic growth and prosperity which was, unlike that in many other areas of England, experienced in both rural and urban locations. Demographic decline certainly occurred in these counties, but its effects do not appear to have fostered either severe agrarian depression or wholesale abandonment of holdings.

Improvements in the rural economy account for much of late medieval Devon's prosperity. By the 1470s landholding had stabilized and demand for land was up.[34] Agricultural productivity was also high; arable farming in Devon benefited from very high animal ratios, enclosed fields, and careful management. Demand for the products of Devon's increasingly pastoral economy was stimulated by the diversification of livestock husbandry into dairy farming, stock rearing, and sheep farming; this last development also enabled the county to meet the demand for wool from its growing cloth industry. By the sixteenth century Devon agriculture was earning the kind of praise never heard in the pre-plague period.[35] This progress was magnified, moreover, because of the seemingly slow rate of growth in much of the county during the high middle ages; W. G. Hoskins has pointed to the late colonization and under-exploitation of the county's agricultural resources even in the early fourteenth century.[36] Then too Devon's landscape and system of convertible husbandry made simpler the late medieval conversion to pastoral husbandry. Besides agricultural developments, however, the steady and even growing employment in non-agricultural sectors in Devon helped maintain demand for foodstuffs and land at a fairly high

[31] Above, n. 6.
[32] Hoskins 1952: 233–41. For an idea of the scope of rebuilding in fifteenth-century Devon, see the gazetteers in Hoskins 1972: 317–520 and in Cherry and Pevesner 1989.
[33] Portman 1966:1–22; Alcock 1966; Laithwaite 1971; Morley 1983; Fox 1991: 172, 733–5.
[34] See Fox 1991: 171–74, 723–43 for this and the following.
[35] Thirsk 1967: 74–5; Hoskins 1972: 93–8; Blake 1915.
[36] Hoskins 1952: 219, 233–47.

level. The county's tin, silver, and lead mines provided employment, the peculiarities of rural landholding and farming in certain regions promoted the expansion of the cloth industry, and Devon's long coastlines furnished job opportunities in fishing, trade, transport, and other related activities.[37]

Industry and trade

Lead and silver mines, located at Bere Alston and Bere Ferrers (in south Devon bordering the Tamar river) and at Combe Martin on the north Devon coast, provided only occasional employment in medieval Devon. Usually exploited directly by the king, output from the south Devon (Birland) mines reached its peak from 1290 to 1340; in the 1290s hundreds of miners from Wales and the Peak District had to be recruited to supplement the local labor force. But profits in the late middle ages did not match earlier levels, even at their late-medieval height in the mid fifteenth century. By the sixteenth century, many of the mines had probably been abandoned.[38] Less is known about the lead and silver mines at Combe Martin although they appear to have been most profitable in the reign of Edward I when orders went out to augment the local labor force with over 300 men from Derbyshire. The mines were productive throughout the fourteenth and fifteenth centuries but were probably closed from about 1490 until 1586 when a rich new lode was discovered.[39] Considering the low profits of these mines in the late fourteenth century (only nine pounds of silver were produced at Combe Martin in 1379–81),[40] they can scarcely have provided significant employment outside of the immediate neighborhood.[41]

The Devon tin fields on Dartmoor provided substantially more employment than the silver and lead mines. Although Devon tin production in the late middle ages was a fraction of its former height in the

[37] The arguments of John Hatcher (1969) concerning the diversified economy of late medieval Cornwall and Mark Bailey (1989) on the East Anglian breckland could also be applied to many Devon regions; see also Fox 1991: 735–43. For the suitability of east Devon farming and social structure to the growth of a rural cloth industry, see Fox 1975: 194–8.

[38] Lewis 1908: 192–7; Salzman 1950: 68–83; Salzman 1964: 51–66. In the early fourteenth century, very small quantities of copper and gold were also mined in Devon; Salzman 1950: 85–6. The king continued to lease gold mines in Devon in the late fourteenth century; see, for example, *CCR 1354–60*: 663–4.

[39] Lewis 1908: 192; Salzman 1950: 83–4; Hoskins 1972: 136–7.

[40] PRO E101/263/17.

[41] Note, however, that an account written in 1619 by a gold and silver refiner who had access to an earlier account book for Bere Ferrers and Combe Martin claims that 1,000 people were employed at these mines in 1485; Lewis 1908: 192, n. 1; Chope 1912b: 54–7.

mid twelfth to early thirteenth centuries,[42] the industry's concentration in and near Dartmoor in a period of reduced population levels meant tin production continued to have a significant economic impact there. Over 1,000 Devon men claimed exemption from subsidy assessments in the 1370s based on their involvement in the tin industry; most resided in the Dartmoor region.[43] Minor production booms in the late fourteenth and early fifteenth centuries also created relative prosperity in tin-producing areas. Since stannary production in Devon was concentrated in the hands of many small operators (even more so than in Cornwall), the boom probably improved employment throughout the Dartmoor region, particularly among the many farmers who sought by-employment as tin miners.[44] In the largely pastoral economy of late medieval Dartmoor, farming could easily be combined with occasional mining.

Tin mining may have more positively affected eastern than western Dartmoor in the late fourteenth and fifteenth centuries. In 1373 about 70 per cent of the tinners awarded tax exemptions were affiliated with the stannary towns of Ashburton and Chagford on the eastern edge of Dartmoor.[45] Although the profits enrolled in the coinage rolls (which recorded the amount of tin brought to the stannary towns to be weighed, assayed, and taxed) could fluctuate widely during this time, Ashburton and Chagford generally accounted for well over two-thirds of the tin coined.[46] Tavistock on the western edge of Dartmoor usually ranked third and sometimes second in coinage, while Plympton, which only became a stannary town in 1328, always trailed the others.

[42] Hatcher 1973: 152–63. After a boom period of production in the late fourteenth and early fifteenth centuries, production levelled off by the 1420s and slumped through the 1460s, rising again in the 1470s and then jumping to new highs in the early sixteenth century.

[43] PRO E179/95/28, 29, 30, 31, 32, 33. These rolls were produced in response to complaints that those who were not true tinners unjustly claimed exemption from the 1373 lay subsidy; see also PRO E159/150 Trinity view of accounts, mm. 3–3d. The subsidies name the "true tinners," defined as people who continually worked in the stannaries in the year of the subsidy. It is clear, however, that many burgesses (presumably tin merchants) and substantial landowners (presumably of land where tin was worked) also claimed this status. Moreover, a number of the 1,042 names listed in E179/95/33 (which seems to miss the Lifton tinners enumerated in E179/95/31) are entered more than once on the roll; most were landowners claiming separate exemptions in the different parishes in which they held property. See also Fox (forthcoming) who maps the distribution of these tinners and Salzman 1950: 89–91 for similar disputes in the early fourteenth century.

[44] Hatcher (1973: 76, 156–63) notes the prevalence of small-scale operators in the Devon tin trade. Fox (1991: 739) also points to the presence of many itinerant laborers and craftsmen amongst late-medieval tinworkers. See also Hatcher 1974, and Blanchard 1972, 1974 for the debate concerning the relationship between mining and agricultural pursuits.

[45] PRO E179/95/33.

[46] Calculations based on the figures in Finberg 1969: 188–9.

Even more important than mining in the economy of late medieval Devon was the expanding cloth industry. Woollen cloth manufacture was already thriving in Exeter, Totnes, and other boroughs in the late twelfth and thirteenth centuries.[47] Rural manufactures were also evident in the proliferation of rural fulling mills and cloth sales by villagers.[48] In the early fourteenth century, the Devon ports of Exeter and Plymouth regularly exported cloth overseas,[49] and by the mid fourteenth century (when cloth export figures become more reliable) exports from Devon represented some 15 per cent of all English cloth exports.[50] In general, the fortunes of the Devon cloth export trade followed the national trends observed in the enrolled accounts. Devon, like England as a whole, shared in the export boom of the 1350s and 1360s[51] and suffered setbacks in the 1370s when outbreaks of heavy fighting in Gascony disrupted the county's main markets overseas.[52] Similarly, the stagnation of national exports in the 1410s, the growth of the trade from the 1420s

[47] Exeter men paid 10 marks to avoid the new restrictions of the cloth assize of 1196 (*Pipe Roll*, vol. 51: 253; Bridbury 1982: 106–7). The bishop of Winchester's accounts record the purchase of much cloth at Exeter in 1215/16 (Hunt 1957: 91) while the large fines paid by Exeter drapers in 1238 point to an established trade (*Devon eyre*: 121); the presence of cloth merchants in South Molton (p. 54) and Barnstaple (p. 60), weavers in Plympton (p. 91), and a wool carder at Modbury (p. 95) point to cloth production in these towns as well. In 1253 Totnes men sold russet cloth to the royal household; *CCR 1253–4*: 176. Numerous disputes involving cloth, dyestuffs, weavers, dyers, and tailors were recorded in the early Exeter court rolls; see, for example, MCR 1264/5 mm. 1, 2, 4d, 5.

[48] For rural fulling mills, see Carus-Wilson 1941: 39–60; and Fox forthcoming. *Devon eyre*: 17 records the death of a man from Colyton hundred on his way to Exeter to sell cloth.

[49] PRO E122/40/7A/3, 7B/2, 7B/4.

[50] Carus-Wilson and Coleman 1963: 75. The customs jurisdicition of Exeter included all ports in Devon and Cornwall until 1404 when Plymouth and Cornish exports were listed separately. Carus-Wilson and Coleman (p. 175) believe that the Cornish ports accounted separately in the Duchy of Cornwall account, and they list sums under the port of Fowey, extracted from the Duchy accounts, at the bottom of their tables of cloth exports (pp. 79–107) in 1373–1480. But particular accounts (PRO E122/104/14, 40/16, 40/26) cite exports from Cornish ports in the Exeter jurisdiction in the 1380s and 1390s, suggesting that Cornish exports were also included in the Exeter figures on the enrolled accounts in the late fourteenth century. The Plymouth exports for this period also probably include many cloths manufactured in Cornwall. Cornish exports, however, were minuscule compared to Devon exports, never accounting for more than 5 per cent of the two counties' exports in the particular accounts (PRO E122/102/14, 40/16, 40/26); throughout the fifteenth century Fowey exports averaged fewer than thirty cloths per year (Carus-Wilson and Coleman 1963: 175, n. 3). But Hatcher (1970: 170) does note that the Cornish share of the trade may have been somewhat higher in the 1410s through 1430s.

[51] The cloth exports in the 1360s were even more impressive than stated in the enrolled accounts since the 2,220 cloths of color and 2,050 packs of cloth exported by four Devon men with special export licences in 1364 were probably not included in the enrolled account for that year (which registered only 602 cloths exported in 1363/4 and 1,213 in 1364/5); *CPR 1361–65*: 496, 510, 521.

[52] Carus-Wilson 1967d; James 1971: 1–37.

through the 1440s, followed by the decline of the 1450s and 1460s, the eventual rise in the 1470s and take-off in the closing decades of the fifteenth century, all match the general pattern of cloth exports from Devon.[53] One divergence may have occurred: the upward movement of national cloth exports in the 1380s and 1390s was not experienced in Devon while the slight decrease in national exports in the first decade of the fifteenth century was felt even more severely in the trade from Devonshire ports.

This divergence from national cloth export trends was, however, probably more a product of record-keeping than reality. Lone particular accounts from this period all noted substantially larger cloth exports than the enrolled figures for these decades would suggest, even though cloth exports from Exeter itself were not even noted one year (Table 1.1). In 1398–9 a particular account covering only nine and one-half months reported 904 cloth exports but the enrolled account covering twelve months registered only 163 cloths. If, as is more likely, the particular accounts more closely reflected actual exports, then the county's average of exports probably hovered around 1,000 cloths per year in the 1390s and 1400s, indicating a more profitable trade commensurate with national trends. Several factors might have been responsible for the underestimation of Devon cloth exports in the enrolled accounts: administrative changes in customs jurisdictions, customs fraud, and the exclusion of "straits," Devon's primary cloth export, from at least some of the enrolled accounts.

Administrative changes must have caused some disruption; the Devon customs were farmed from 1371 to 1390, and around 1404 the customs jurisdiction (centered on Exeter) was split so that Plymouth and Cornwall henceforth accounted separately.[54] The extremely large size of the customs jurisdiction headed by Exeter also made it difficult to administer and easy to commit fraud. As the only county with two separate and discontinuous coastlines, Devon was part of the largest customs jurisdiction in medieval England (encompassing all of Devon and Cornwall). Customs evasion or administrative fraud was thus probably a more common feature of customs collection in Devon, particularly in the 1390s when massive fraud occurred at Barnstaple, then the center of the county's main cloth-producing area.[55] The prominence of coastal

[53] Carus-Wilson and Coleman 1963: 138–9.

[54] Carus-Wilson and Coleman 1963: 79–89; further disruptions occurred when the ports under Exeter jurisdiction were temporarily included with Bristol.

[55] PRO E159/170 Michaelmas recorda, mm. 3–6; the fraud also extended to the port of Ilfracombe. Exports and imports by about 135 people were noted in the Memoranda Roll inquisition but only thirty entries were included in the particular account for 1391/2 (PRO E122/40/26). For customs fraud elsewhere in Devon, see below, pp. 225–6.

Table 1.1. *Cloth exports (in cloths of assize) from Devon during the late middle ages*

Year	No. of years with data	Annual average in enrolled accounts	Annual average in selected particular accounts	Total Devon exports	% of total English exports[a]
1350s	(6)	647		3,882	12.1
1360s	(10)	913		9,126	7.1
1369–71	(2)	1,262		2,681	8.2
1377–79[b]	(2)		782	1,563	5.5
1383/84[c]	(1)		[679]	[679]	[2.7]
1390s	(7)	304		2,126	0.8
1398–99[d]	(1)		904	904	3.1
1400s	(10)	303		3,031	0.9
1410s	(10)	667		6,670	2.4
1420s	(10)	672		6,720	1.7
1430s	(10)	1,738		17,376	4.1
1440s	(10)	2,841		28,409	5.3
1450s	(10)	1,636		16,358	4.4
1460s	(10)	1,235		12,353	3.7
1470s[e]	(9)	1,601		14,408	3.7
1480s	(10)	3,638		36,378	7.0
1490s	(10)	3,990		39,896	6.9
1500s	(10)	9,282		92,823	11.5

Sources and notes: Figures from enrolled accounts were extracted from Carus-Wilson and Coleman 1963: 75–113 for those years which include all Devon ports. Cornish exports (normally very few) were usually included in the fourteenth-century and some fifteenth-century figures. Other sources are as follows:

[a] Based on totals calculated from Bridbury 1982: 118–21; only figures for years covered by extant Devon accounts were used.

[b] Exeter customs were farmed from 1371/2–90. Figures given here from particular accounts in PRO E122/40/8, 158/34.

[c] PRO E122/102/14; this particular account lists cloth exports to the value of £1,358; estimated cloth amounts were derived by assuming that one cloth was worth £2 (as in Gray 1924: 25, n. 6). The total is almost certainly an underestimation since no Exeter exports were included in this account.

[d] PRO E122/40/23 (covers nine months from 2 December 1398 to 15 September 1399); the enrolled account for the whole year lists only 163 cloths.

[e] There are eight months missing from the Exeter account for 1475/6 so the totals from Exeter and Plymouth were omitted for that year; Carus-Wilson and Coleman 1963: 105.

trade in the county (particularly in east and north Devon) must also have reduced Devon's cloth export figures. With the possible exception of Dartmouth and Plymouth, Devon ports usually exported goods via coastal craft, thereby escaping detection in royal customs accounts which only recorded trade on overseas routes. As a result, many of the county's exports would have been registered in the accounts of its larger and busier neighboring ports, Southampton and Bristol.[56] The official figures for Devon cloth exports would have been further reduced by the exclusion from customs enumeration of smaller cloths such as kerseys and the "straits" or "dozens" in which Devon specialized; this problem was particularly acute in the last three decades of the fourteenth century when Devon exports on the surface seem to have suffered a significant decline.[57]

Devon exports were largely coarse, rough woollens called "dozens" or "straits" because they were much narrower than the standard broadcloth. Narrow dozens measured only 12 × 1 yards; four narrow dozens were reckoned to equal one cloth of assize.[58] Made of short wool, flocks, and lamb's wool, these primarily russet, grey, and white cloths sold cheaply for about 4*d* per yard in the 1390s.[59] Such coarse, almost hairy cloths were the natural product of the poor-quality Devonshire wools.[60] The market for Devon's cheap cloths both at home and abroad (in Brittany, Normandy, Gascony, and Spain) was relatively buoyant because the main customers – wage earners and other poorer people – had relatively greater earning power in the late middle ages.[61] From the mid fifteenth century, the manufacture of dozens was increasingly replaced by the production of kerseys, particularly in east Devon. Kerseys were a light cloth of somewhat better quality that also measured 12 × 1 yards but needed only three cloths to equal one cloth of assize.[62] It was the growing popularity and production of this type of cloth in the fifteenth century that accounted for the rising fortunes of the east Devon cloth industry.

Devon's concentration on the production of smaller cloths that did not easily compare with the cloths of assize used to calculate official sums may be partly responsible for the underestimation of the county's exports, but it does not explain why its woollen cloth manufacture has

[56] This process also inflated the export figures of Dartmouth and Plymouth; see below, pp. 232–3.

[57] For the exclusion of kerseys, see Gray 1924: 27–8; Carus-Wilson 1967d: 263. For straits, see PRO E122/40/8, 40/23, 102/14, 158/34; and Childs 1992: 79.

[58] Broad dozens measured 12 × 2 yards and were also manufactured in Devon. Cornish dozens measured 24 × 1 yards.

[59] Carus-Wilson 1963: 18–19; Finberg 1969: 152; Chope 1912a: 577. Britnell 1986b: 55–6 discusses the appearance of russet-colored cloth and notes its association with the lower orders.

[60] For the poor quality of Devonshire wool, see Chope 1919: 290–1; Youings 1965: 70–2; Finberg 1969: 146–7; Munro 1978: esp. 130, 140; Fox 1991: 320–1.

[61] For rising standards of living, see Bridbury 1975; Dyer 1989b.

[62] Chope 1912a: 556; Gray 1924: 28; Carus-Wilson and Coleman 1963: 14; Finberg 1969: 152–3; elsewhere kerseys often measured 18 × 1 yards. For cloth *de kerseto* purchased by the Courtenay household (of Tiverton) in this period, see CR 488.

also been seriously underestimated. The aulnage statistics computed by H. L. Gray, for example, state that average annual cloth production in Devon and Cornwall in 1394–8 was 1,461 cloths, but in fact Devon production alone was closer to 2,500 cloths each year because Gray omitted the cloths sealed in Exeter.[63] Even these corrected figures, however, probably underestimate actual cloth production in the county since aulnage collection in Devon was also subject to widespread fraud. Exchequer inquisitions concerning collection in the 1390s, for example, reveal that the aulnager missed hundreds of cloths in and near Ottery St Mary, Totnes, and Dartmouth.[64] Excessive hostility to aulnage collection may have accounted for some of these lacunae; the aulnage collector at Dartmouth barely escaped from a mob with his life while threats on the life of a collector at Crediton supposedly made him unable to seal 600 marks-worth of cloth there.[65] Fraud was particularly pervasive in Exeter during these years and became even worse in 1399–1403 when the aulnager was Thomas Wandry, an Exeter merchant who, although responsible for the entire county during this roughly three-year period, sealed only 374 cloths, most sold by Exeter merchants in suspiciously small amounts.[66] The accounts for these years and others in the fifteenth century are thus unfortunately useless for the calculation of cloth production of Devon.

Although efforts to derive exact figures of cloth production from the aulnage accounts are problematic, the accounts can yield insights into the regional distribution of the trade in late medieval Devon. In the late fourteenth century, cloth sales were highest in north and mid Devon, particularly at the ancient borough of Barnstaple on the north

[63] Gray 1924: 34; these are repeated in Bridbury 1982: 114. Presumably Gray derived his figures from PRO E101/338/11, mm. 1–6d which cover the years 1394–7 (although using his methods I calculated about 1,860 cloths for Devon alone in this period). Unfortunately, these accounts excluded the city of Exeter where an annual average of 632 cloths were sealed in this period; these latter figures are included in the enrolled aulnage accounts (PRO E358/8, mm. 1d, 2d, 4d). Cornwall sealed an average of only sixty two cloths per year during this period.

[64] PRO E159/179 Easter recorda, m. 7. The appointment of special commissions (*CPR 1381–5*: 143; *1385–9*: 392) to investigate the false sealing of cloth in Devon also suggests these same problems occurred earlier. For similar fraud elsewhere, see PRO E179/173 Michaelmas recorda, mm. 3d–4 (at Tiverton, Honiton, Totnes, Ashburton, and Chagford); and C258/27/17 which, among other accusations, singles out the Somerset aulnager for sealing cloth in Devon. For the problem of fraud generally in the fifteenth-century aulnage accounts, see Carus-Wilson 1967a.

[65] *Chronicon Adae de Usk*: 61, 184; PRO E159/171, Hilary recorda, m. 14; E159/172, Trinity recorda, mm. 2, 5. For threats at South Zeal, see E159/171, Trinity recorda, m. 2d.

[66] PRO E101/338, mm. 8–11; Chope 1912a. See also PRO E159/181, Trinity recorda, m. 6.

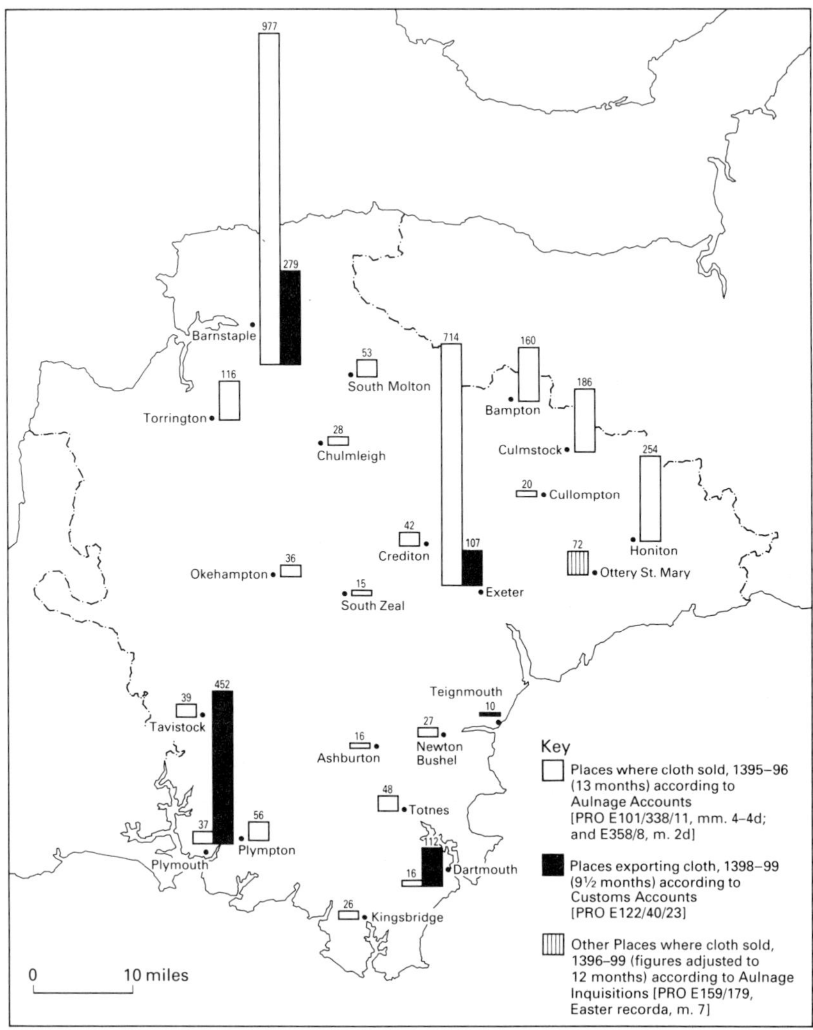

Figure 1.2 Cloth sales and exports in Devon, 1395–98 (in cloths of assize)

coast (Figure 1.2 and Table 1.2). The concentration of cloth production in this region is difficult to explain, and several factors need to be considered. The agrarian structure of north and mid Devon was not particularly suitable for cloth manufacture, nor were there many fulling mills there compared to other regions in the county.[67] Cloth manufacture therefore probably occurred in the towns rather than in the countryside, a trend also seen in the dominance of cloth sellers from Barnstaple and the prevalence of surnames denoting textile occupations in the records of the small boroughs of this region.[68] It is also possible that the figures for Barnstaple were artificially inflated by cloth manufactured in Somerset west of Taunton or in the northerly regions of the Exe valley near Bampton. These producers may have favored Barnstaple because of its easy coastal connections to Bristol, one of the country's major exporters of cloth in this period.[69] Given the propensity for fraud in the Devon aulnage accounts, it is also possible that the region's impressive cloth trade was less an indication of strong production in north Devon than a result of greater fraud elsewhere.[70] Whatever the source of north and mid Devon's cloth in the late fourteenth century, cloth manufacture elsewhere rose more rapidly in the fifteenth century and by the mid fifteenth century overshadowed north and mid Devon's previous dominance.

East Devon cloth sales ranked only slightly behind north and mid Devon in the fourteenth century if Exeter's sales are included (Table 1.2). Late medieval cloth production grew most rapidly in this region; by the 1460s, more than 50 per cent of Devon's cloth was sold from locations in east Devon, including Exeter. Because of east Devon's prominence as the center of Devon's early modern cloth industry, much more is known about woollen manufacture there.[71] Exeter functioned as the commercial hub of the region and also possessed its own significant cloth-finishing industry; the emergence of powerful guilds of tailors, weavers, fullers, and shearmen in the mid fifteenth century was one

[67] Fox forthcoming.

[68] For the Barnstaple sellers, see Chope 1912a. The aulnage accounts (see Figure 1.2) also suggest production in the boroughs of Torrington, South Molton, and Chulmleigh as do the surnames of Draper, Taillor, Touker, and Webber in the extant borough court rolls of South Molton (PRO SC2/168/27), Combe Martin (SC2/166/32), and Holsworthy (SC2/167/34) in this period. Similar surnames are noticeable in the 1329 and 1332 lay subsidies for Barnstaple, Newport, South Molton, and Torrington (PRO E179/95/6, mm. 31d–32d, 33; *Lay subsidy 1332*: 116–19). For licences to export cloth purchased by Chulmleigh merchants, see *CPR 1361–4*: 480.

[69] For caveats about conflating the place of sale with the place of production, see Bridbury 1982: 47–82. For Barnstaple and Bristol, see Kowaleski 1992: 64–7; Carus-Wilson 1967c.

[70] North and mid Devon were the only regions not specifically noted as practicing fraud in the aulnage inquisitions (above, notes 64, 65).

[71] For example, Hoskins 1935; Stephens 1958: 3–7, 40–55, 131–44; Carus-Wilson 1963: 17–22; Youings 1968; Seward 1970; Fox 1991: 741–73.

Table 1.2. *Regional distribution of cloth sales and exports in late medieval Devon*

Region and ports	Exported Cloths		Aulnaged Cloths	
	% of cloths 1398–9 (N=960)[a]	% of cloths 1383–99 (N=£2,871)[b]	% of cloths 1395–7 (N=£5,582)[c]	% of cloths 1467–8 (N=940)[d]
East Devon			41	51
Exeter	12	9	(23)	(20)
Teignmouth	1	1		
South Devon			10	36
Dartmouth	11	25		
Plymouth	47	37		
North and mid Devon			46	13
Barnstaple	29	27		
Ilfracombe		1		
Dartmoor and Borders			3	0
Total	100	100	100	100

Sources and notes: See Figure 1.1 for regions.
[a]PRO E122/40/23.
[b]PRO E122/102/14 (1383/4); 40/16; 40/26 (1391–2); 40/23 (1398–9). Customs fraud at Barnstaple in the 1390s (PRO E159/170 Michaelmas recorda, mm. 3–6) means that its cloth exports for 1383–99 are probably underestimated. Percentages based on value of cloths.
[c]PRO E101/338/11, mm. 4–6d (two accounts covering twenty four months); Exeter aulnage figures from PRO E358/8 mm. 2d, 4d (for twenty six months from 1395–7 but here adjusted to a twenty-four month period); the figures in parentheses show the portion of east Devon cloths marketed in Exeter.
[d]PRO E101/338/14.

notable effect of this concentration.[72] A great deal if not most of the region's cloth, however, was produced in rural villages and small towns. Crediton, Honiton, and Bampton were very small boroughs, while Culmstock, Cullompton, and Ottery St Mary were largely rural parishes (Figure 1.2). As H.S.A. Fox has described, the social structure and farming system of east Devon were ideally suited to the formation and growth of a rural cloth industry.[73]

Cloth production around the Dartmoor borders was on a small scale, important mainly around the market towns of Okehampton and Tavistock (Figure 1.2 and Table 1.2). Cloth from this region accounted for only 3 per cent of Devon's total production in the late fourteenth

[72] Below, pp. 93–4, 156.
[73] Fox 1975: 192–200.

century. In south Devon, the manufacture of cloth was scattered throughout the region and was probably concentrated in the towns more than in the countryside. Plympton and Totnes were the most active centers of cloth sales. Totnes, as has been noted, had a thriving industry in the thirteenth century; by the end of the fifteenth century it was known as one of the foremost centers of cloth manufacture in the West Country and was primarily responsible for south Devon's improved showing in the cloth sales figures of 1467/8.[74]

The most striking aspect of the south Devon trade in the late fourteenth century was the large percentage of cloth exports that passed through its ports of Dartmouth and Plymouth (Figure 1.2 and Table 1.2) even though the region produced only 10 per cent of the county's cloth according to the aulnage accounts. Cloth meant for export was diverted to Dartmouth and Plymouth because they were the county's main export centers. Cloth arrived at these ports via overland transport from their own south Devon hinterlands, as well as from Dartmoor and its border areas and the Cornish part of the Tamar valley (which stretched from Saltash to Launceston).[75] Even larger amounts for export arrived by coastal craft from Exeter, east Devon, Dorset, and Somerset.[76] With their excellent deep harbors and access to the quickest shipping routes from the important export market in Gascony, these two ports were favored by the bigger ships plying the overseas trade routes. The favorable military and political relationship of these ports with the Crown during the Hundred Years War also made them a popular embarkation point for all sorts of overseas business.[77] Barnstaple may have sealed more cloth, but the inconvenience of its port on the north Devon coast for markets abroad, combined with the competition it probably faced from its very successful neighboring port of Bristol, must have deterred to some extent the growth of north Devon's export market.

The seemingly small role played by Exeter in the export trade reflected its greater orientation to the home market and the tendency for its exports to be sent via coastal trade to Dartmouth, Plymouth, and Southampton.[78] Located ten miles from the open sea and four miles from its outport at Topsham, Exeter enjoyed access to overseas trade routes but focused more on trade with its hinterland, particularly east

[74] Nicholls 1960: 121–2; Russell 1964: 33–4. See also PRO E159, Easter recorda, m. 7.
[75] For the cloth trade in eastern Cornwall, see Hatcher 1970: 169–71, 224–5.
[76] For their role as export-bulking centers, see below, pp. 232–3.
[77] Kowaleski 1992.
[78] This and the following arguments are made at greater length in Chapters 6 and 7, below.

Devon. The city's status as the administrative and ecclesiastical center of the south-western peninsula, as well as its good overland communications with mid Devon, east Devon, and parts of Somerset, also promoted greater sales in domestic rather than export markets. The trade figures yielded by the national port customs accounts, moreover, tell only part of the story; some 70 per cent of Exeter's import trade, for example, came via coastal not foreign trade routes, thus escaping altogether enrollment in the national port customs accounts. Exeter and east Devon cloth bound for overseas markets was probably shipped via coastal craft to more suitable overseas ports (such as Southampton, Dartmouth, and Plymouth), thus escaping registration in Exeter. Despite this diversion, however, it is clear that both east Devon cloth production and exports rose substantially during the fifteenth century; by the end of the fifteenth century, Exeter was responsible for the majority of Devon cloth exports and ranked behind only Bristol and Southampton as a center of provincial cloth exports in all of England.[79]

Equally if not more important to the prosperity of the late medieval Devon economy were activities associated with the sea. As the only shire with two distinct non-continuous coasts, Devon enjoyed maritime links to the Bristol Channel, Wales, and Ireland in the north, and to southern England and Atlantic Europe in the south. The county also possesses more coastline than any other English shire and thus probably had more commercial and fishing ports than most counties. These features endowed Devon with an enormous stock of ships and boats which were used in a wide variety of ventures, including overseas and coastal trade; the transport of pilgrims, crusaders, and troops; service in the royal navy; fishing, privateering, and piracy. These activities employed thousands of Devon inhabitants as mariners, fishers, traders, and shipbuilders. In wartime, particularly during the Hundred Years War (1337–1453), service in the royal navy also engaged many Devon men and ships. When the king assembled a fleet to take him to Antwerp in 1338, thirty ships and 968 men represented Devon even though the fleet assembled at the opposite end of the kingdom in Yarmouth.[80] The fleet involved in the siege of Calais in 1346 included ninety three ships and 1,985 men from Devon.[81] Even the

[79] By the sixteenth century, Exeter ranked behind only Southampton as a provincial cloth exporter (Carus-Wilson and Coleman 1963: 108–19).

[80] *Wardrobe book:* cii–civ, 363–86. For Devon ships levied by the king at other times, see Oppenheim 1968: 4–23.

[81] *Dartmouth*: 359; Watkin incorrectly included ships and men from Lynn in his totals for Devon.

Table 1.3 *Devon's shipping fleet in the fourteenth century*

Home ports	Ships in royal service 1324–1402[a] (No.)	%	Wine ships at Bordeaux 1372–86[b] (No.)	%	All ships in 1390–99[c] (No.)	%
Axmouth	(6)	1	(1)	½	(10)	5
Sidmouth	(12)	3	–	–	(3)	2
Ottermouth	(5)	1	(1)	½	(11)	6
Exmouth	(34)	7	(10)	5	(18)	10
Teignmouth	(23)	5	(9)	5	(12)	6
Torbay	(6)	1	(1)	½	(6)	3
Dartmouth	(213)	46	(79)	40	(57)	31
Portlemouth	(14)	3	(1)	½	(9)	5
Plymouth	(137)	29	(96)	48	(40)	21
North Devon	(20)	4	–	–	(21)	11
Total	(470)	100	(198)	100	(187)	100

Sources:

[a]Each incidence of service counted once: PRO E101/28/21; 29/1, 32/3, 32/36, 32/9, 32/22, 34/26, 36/20, 39/25, 40/19, 40/21, 40/40, 41/2, 41/27, 41/29–32, 41/37–38, 41/40, 42/5–8, 42/18, 42/21–22, 531/31, 676/32; BL Add. Ms. 26891; DRO Deeds M/196, 214; *CCR 1341–3*: 629, 651, 664, 668–90, 700; *1343–6*: 84, 129–31; *1346–9*: 308; *1354–60*: 657; *1360–4*: 27, 416; *1381–5*: 523; *1396–9*: 330; *CPR 1377–81*: 356, 405; *CIM*, vol. 3: 150–1; *Wardrobe book*: 365–72; *Dartmouth*: 355, 374–5; Hewitt 1966: 182–4.

[b]Each voyage counted once: PRO E101/179/10, 182/5–6, 183/11, 184/9.

[c]Each ship counted only once in this decade: based on 940 references to Devon ships in 1390–9 in PRO E122 (all accounts for Devon and Cornwall and selected accounts for other ports); E101 naval accounts (as above, n. a). E101 Bordeaux wine accounts (as above, n. b); E101 Butlerage accounts; E159 Memoranda rolls; SC6 Duchy havener's accounts; DCO Minister's accounts; *CCR*, *CFR*, *CPR*, *CIM*; Exeter local port customs accounts (PCA); and miscellaneous other sources.

tiny fishing village of Budleigh could claim in 1347 that continual maritime service to the king had cost its residents three ships, twelve boats, and 141 men.[82]

The port of Dartmouth on the south Devon coast played the most prominent role in fourteenth-century Devon shipping (Table 1.3). Although only half the size of Exeter and Plymouth,[83] Dartmouth's fleet of ocean-going vessels was substantially larger than that of any other port in Devon, and Dartmouth provided more ships for the fourteenth-century war effort against the French than any other single

[82] *Rotuli Parliamentorum*, vol. ii: 203.

[83] See Table 2.1, below.

port in England.[84] Dartmouth vessels also took a central role in England's seaborne carrying trade, particularly in the Bordeaux wine trade and the Iberian trade.[85] Although small, its own commercial hinterland included the prosperous small town of Totnes, the stannary town of Ashburton, and other tin-working areas on Dartmoor.[86] Since Dartmouth's hinterland was hemmed in by the granite mass of Dartmoor to its north and the hinterlands of Exeter to the east and Plymouth to the west, the port's residents turned their attention to the sea. At least 39 per cent of Dartmouth householders in 1377 had first-hand experience at sea as mariners, merchants, shipowners, or shipmasters.[87] Piracy and high-risk ventures at sea also attracted a disproportionate number of Dartmouth ships and sailors in the late middle ages. Men such as the infamous John Hawley, mayor of the town fourteen times (and perhaps the model for Chaucer's Shipman), gained national prominence and tremendous wealth through their piratical exploits at sea.[88] The line between outright piracy and privateering, when Devon shipowners and mariners received official sanction for their attacks on enemy shipping, was all too frequently blurred, particularly during the late fourteenth and fifteenth centuries when such activities made West Country mariners notorious throughout the land.[89] The fortunes of Hawley and other Dartmouth residents may actually have been promoted by the Hundred Years War. Trade and shipping routes were interrupted, but the War brought ships, pilgrims, and troops about to depart for France or Spain, as well as new opportunities for royal favor, privateering, and other profitable ventures.[90]

Although both Dartmouth and Plymouth were used as ports of embarkation for pilgrims and military expeditions, Plymouth increas-

[84] Runyan 1986: 94–6. Dartmouth was well rewarded for its contribution by grants of new political and economic privileges from the Crown in 1341; see *CChR* 1341–1417: 3–4, 338–9; *Dartmouth*: 38–41.

[85] For the wine trade, see Table 1.3. For Dartmouth's involvement in the Iberian trade, see *Cal. P & MR London, 1381–1412*: 194–7; *CCR, 1343–6*: 218–19; *1364–8*: 158; *1396–9*: 328–9; *CPR, 1377–81*: 631; *CIM*, vol. 7: no. 220; Childs 1978: 31, 45, 127, 156, 179.

[86] In 1390 Dartmouth was granted a monopoly of tin exports for three years in recognition of the port's service to the crown; *CPR 1388–90*: 38. See also Hatcher 1973: 92, 110–15, 174; Kowaleski 1992: 63–6.

[87] Kowaleski 1992: 68.

[88] Russell 1950: 13–18; Gardiner 1966; Pistono 1979. For the piracy and privateering of Dartmouth men in the last twenty years of the fourteenth century, see PRO C47/6/4; *W.C. Chancery proc*: passim; *CCR 1377–81*: 292–3, 318, 413, 424, 464; *1381–5*: 403, 509; *1385–9*: 145–6, 226–7, 271, 328, 349, 518; *1389–92*: 379, 410; *1392–6*: 174–5, 324.

[89] Appleby 1992; Kingsford 1925: 78–106; Mace 1925a: 110–15.

[90] Kowaleski 1992 and below, p. 235.

ingly assumed the more important role in the expeditions during the late middle ages.[91] Its fine deep harbor and the Prince of Wales' administrative interests in the Duchy of Cornwall, to which the port of Plymouth (called Sutton Pool) belonged, considerably advanced the interests of the growing town.[92] The port of Dartmouth also belonged to the Duchy but Plymouth seems to have been favored by the Black Prince and others because of the hospitality and "pliable" borough administration of its lord, Plympton priory, compared to that offered by "such magistrates-cum-privateers as the mayors of Dartmouth."[93] The town's commercial growth was stimulated in large part by the business turned its way via the Hundred Years War. Over the course of the fourteenth century, for example, Plymouth ships docking at Exeter multiplied five times, from less than 3 to almost 17 per cent.[94]

Plymouth's growth in the fourteenth century was also prompted by its more extensive overland connections compared to Dartmouth. Although limited by the proximity of Dartmoor and by competition from Dartmouth, Plymouth's hinterland was enlarged by the navigability of the Tamar river and enriched by the fertile lands of the South Hams and coastal Cornwall. Plymouth was the county's second largest borough in the late fourteenth century and probably its biggest overseas port since it enjoyed a 41 per cent share of Devon's foreign trade and dominated the county's wine trade with Bordeaux (Table 1.3).[95] Unlike Exeter and Barnstaple, whose exports were almost entirely limited to cloth, exports from Plymouth (and Dartmouth to some extent) were more varied, including tin, hides, skins, shoes, cheese, and above all fish (especially hake) which in some years even approached cloth exports in total value.[96]

The north Devon ports were oriented towards Wales, Ireland, or coastwise to Bristol, traffic that has left few traces in the extant customs

[91] For pilgrims, see Childs 1992: 83–4.

[92] Hewitt 1958: 14–42; Gill 1966: 50–1, 66–9, 75–81; Kowaleski 1992.

[93] Russell 1950: 14.

[94] They accounted for eight of the 311 Devon ships in *Local PCA 1266–1321*: Table 1 and thirty-seven of the 217 Devon ships in PCA 1381/2–1390/1. Dartmouth ships at Exeter went from under 12 per cent to 30 per cent during this same period.

[95] See below, Table 2.1 and Kowaleski 1992: esp. Tables 7.2, 7.4; Childs 1992: esp. Table 9.4. Despite Plymouth's high percentage of foreign trade, it was not as commercially prominent or active as Exeter.

[96] For tin exports, see Hatcher 1973: 112–15, 174–5; PRO E159/175, Hilary recorda, m. 5. For others, see PRO E122/158/25, 102/14, 40/7A, 40/23, 40/16, 40/26 (the last two being years of high fish exports). Plymouth exports were also occasionally specified in the havener's accounts for the Duchy of Cornwall; PRO SC6 Duchy accounts and DCO Minister's Accounts, passim.

accounts.[97] Barnstaple was the region's main overseas port; with Ilfracombe it accounted for about 11 per cent of the value of Devon's overseas trade in the late fourteenth century.[98] Foreign trade in north Devon ports was probably inhibited by the powerful presence of Bristol across the Bristol Channel, as well as by the sparsely settled and poor regions of north and mid Devon that made up these ports' hinterlands. Only the Taw and Torridge lowlands in Barnstaple's immediate neighborhood were well populated. Other small ports were located at the boroughs of Bideford and Combe Martin; they along with the even smaller ports of Clovelly, Appledore, and Northam focused on fishing and some coastal trade. North Devon ships were generally smaller than those from south or east Devon, played little role in naval levies (except for troop transport to Ireland) and did not appear at all in the wine-carrying trade from Bordeaux (Table 1.3).[99]

Teignmouth in east Devon was the most noteworthy of the smaller Devon ports, particularly in the thirteenth and early fourteenth centuries when it usually ranked fourth in naval levies at Devon ports.[100] Its importance diminished during the late middle ages due to a devastating French raid it suffered in 1340, the insufficiency of its shallow harbor, competition from its neighboring ports of Exeter and Dartmouth, and the lack of investment by its ecclesiastical lords. Other east Devon ports, such as Sidmouth, Seaton, and Ottermouth, also lacked the deeper harbors of the south Devon ports and in the late middle ages their shipping was increasingly confined to fishing and coastal trade, especially the transport of limestone from quarries at Beer and Branscombe and greenstone from Salcombe Regis.[101] The smaller south Devon ports in Torbay and Portlemouth also profited mainly from fishing although a number of Portlemouth ships were large enough to engage regularly in overseas trade (Table 1.3). Portlemouth ships also transported via coastal trade vast numbers of roofing tiles and stone from

[97] For this trade, see PRO E122/102/14, 40/16, 40/26, 40/25/1, 40/23, 1/1; PRO E159/170 Michaelmas recorda, mm. 3–6; E159/181 Easter recorda, m. 20; PRO JUST1/195, mm. 2d, 4–4d; NDRO Barnstaple CR 441; *Barnstaple records*, vol. I: 150, 252; *W.C. Chancery proc.*: 56–7, 64, 66, 92–5; Mace 1925a: 117–19; Carus-Wilson 1967c: 5–7; *Bristol*; 90, 118–19, 134–5, 205; Childs 1992.

[98] See Kowaleski 1992, (esp. Table 7.2) for this and the following.

[99] Oppenheim 1968: 5–23; Kowaleski 1992: esp. Table 7.4. They occasionally transported pilgrims (*CPR 1388–92*: 387; Childs 1992: 83).

[100] Oppenheim 1968: 6–17. See Kowaleski 1992: 67 and below, p. 241 for this and the following.

[101] Kowaleski 1992. For their naval levies, see Oppenheim 1968: 4–23. They too made fewer appearances at Exeter over the course of the fourteenth century, dropping from almost 12 per cent (*Local PCA 1266–1321*: 71–186) to 3 per cent of the Devon ships there (PCA 1381/2–1390/1). For the quarries and transport of stone, see Hoskins 1972: 259 62; Erskine 1983: xiii–xv; *Fabric accounts*: passim; Allan 1991.

the slate quarries of south Devon, unloading this cargo at ports all along the coast of southern England.[102]

Although coastal trade has left little trace in the extant records, it probably represented well over half of all traffic in and out of Devon ports; only Dartmouth and Plymouth probably relied more on overseas trade. At Exeter, which possesses an unusual series of extant local port customs accounts that allows us to trace both coastal and overseas commerce, coastal trade accounted for about 70 per cent of all incoming traffic in the late fourteenth and early fifteenth centuries.[103] The port of Exeter, usually called Exmouth because it included all landing places in the Exe estuary, never possessed the shipping interests of either Dartmouth or Plymouth although its fleet was the third largest in fourteenth-century Devon (Table 1.3). Despite the lesser number of ships originating there, Exeter was the most commercially active of all the Devon ports because of the value of its coastal trade. Besides being the largest town in the county, it was also the administrative and ecclesiastical capital of Devonshire. Unlike Plymouth and Dartmouth, its hinterland stretched far inland, eastwards to Somerset, northwards up the Exe valley to Tiverton and Bampton, and westwards to the borders of Dartmoor and Okehampton. Its central location in Devon, moreover, gave it easy access to most of the county's regions; situated at the southern end of the Exe valley it also enjoyed good communications to the Clyst, Culm, and Creedy river valleys. The nature, extent, and impact of Exeter's trade in local, regional, and maritime markets will be discussed at length in the following chapters.

Although shipping, maritime trade, and the spoils of privateering and piracy contributed greatly to the medieval Devon economy, fishing may have employed the greatest number of people in Devonshire coastal areas. The customs of the manor of Stokenham on the south Devon coast, for example, recorded that every year from February until the second week after Easter, three teams of nine villeins each had to station themselves by rocks on the seashore to watch for schools of fish (particularly mullet), ready with their own boats and tackle to put out to sea; the lord expected to receive one-third of their catch.[104] The lord of the manor of Stoke Fleming, just north of Stokenham on Start Bay, derived similar profits from his villeins' capture of plaice, bream, skate, conger, salmon, and porpoise.[105] Some of this fish was shipped overseas or by coast to other ports; some was also carried overland to Exeter

[102] PCA passim; Jope and Dunning 1954; Allan 1984: 300–4; Holden 1989.
[103] This and the following points are elaborated below, pp. 224–31.
[104] Finberg 1950: 69–70.
[105] 902M/M2/2, mm. 1–2 (1382–3 Stoke Fleming court roll).

for sale.[106] Tithes of fish from Devon coastal parishes also attest to the ubiquity and profitability of fishing in medieval Devon. The fish tithes at Sidmouth and Otterton on Devon's east coast were worth over £13 in 1408.[107] Similar tithes listed in the *Valor ecclesiasticus* of 1535 indicate that the most profitable fisheries lay in Tor Bay with Brixham (including Kingswear) the most lucrative, followed by Paignton and St Marychurch, and then by Plymouth, Dawlish, and Seaton.[108]

Many of the coastal villages and towns possessed fishing fleets that regularly exploited the rich fishing grounds off the south Devon coast; hake, cod, and herring were the most common catches although pilchard became increasingly important in the fifteenth century, especially in the Plymouth area.[109] Much fish was also exported overseas, ranking after only cloth and tin as the county's most important exports. Both Cornwall and Devon early on acquired a reputation for the export of fresh, salted, and dried fish, particularly to Gascony.[110] Although the scale of this trade is difficult to measure, it is clear that fish exports from both Devon and Cornwall grew tremendously in the late middle ages and eventually outstripped the previously prominent fish trade in eastern and south-eastern England.[111] The south-western fish trade differed from the older eastern fish trade in several ways. It was more varied, including cargoes of hake, pilchards, herring, and rays; it was largely in the hands of local merchants and fishermen; it was usually linked with other exports such as cloth and tin; and it was less seasonal in nature, with small loads exiting from ports all during the year.

The abundant rivers and streams of Devon also provided good fishing and provoked continual disputes over the ownership of fishing rights and profits. An inquiry in 1389 concerning manorial rights near the mouth of the Erme river listed salmon, trout, ray, mullet, bass, mussels, cockles, spratt, *peles*, *log*, and *beyt* among the fish available there.[112] The abbot of Buckland's on-going dispute with the tenants of Meavy concerned their capture of salmon, roach, perch, and other fish worth

[106] See below, pp. 312–16.

[107] Hockey 1968: 8. See also the Sidmouth court rolls (BL Add. Ch. 27285–89) which had special sections noting forestallers and regrators of fish.

[108] Russell 1951: 282.

[109] Russell 1951; Gill 1987; and Chapter 7, below.

[110] *Rotuli de oblatis et finibus*: 191; *CPR 1361–4*: 496; *1364–7*: 7, 11, 32, 50; *1370–4*: 181.

[111] Litler 1979: 245–9 for this and the following; see also Chapter 7, below and PCA passim.

[112] PRO E159/168 Hilary recorda, mm. 19–21. For fish (and similar disputes) in the Exeter region, see Chapter 7, below.

£40 at the Bickleigh weir on the Plym river.[113] Particularly productive salmon fisheries existed in the Torridge river in north Devon, and in the Plym, Avon, Dart, and Exe rivers near the south coast.[114] Such fisheries had a long history in Devon; Domesday Book recorded sixteen places with fisheries in Devon, the most for any county in the South-west.[115]

The sea also provided economic opportunities in shipping and related activities. While the thirteenth through fifteenth centuries were in general periods of prosperity and growth for Devon shipping and overseas trade, both the Black Death and the Hundred Years War prompted significant disruptions. The depopulation caused by the Black Death and subsequent plagues reduced the traffic and profits of ports in the middle decades of the fourteenth century but thereafter Devon and Cornwall seem to have escaped further severe visitations of the plague.[116] The effect of the Hundred Years War on Devon shipping and trade is harder to gauge. A French fleet harassed the southern coast of England as early as 1337, burning ships and buildings in Plymouth; in 1340 a similar fleet burned Teignmouth.[117] The unusual absence of Devon ships from the Bordeaux wine fleet of 1339/40 may well have been the result of these coastal disturbances and destruction. In 1350 and 1377 the French again attacked Plymouth but were repulsed with little damage. The threat of harm was quite real to port town residents, however, since Dartmouth, Exeter, Kingswear, and Plymouth all built or strengthened their fortifications during the late fourteenth or early fifteenth century.[118] More severe raids occurred from 1399 through 1404; part of Plymouth's suburbs were burned in a raid in 1403 when Salcombe was also attacked, but Dartmouth residents successfully beat off a major Breton assault in 1404. This raid was the last direct French attack on Devon soil. Thereafter the effects of the War were apparent mainly at

[113] PRO CP40/497, mm. 360–360d.

[114] Welldon Finn 1967: 269–71; Beale 1969. For the Exe fisheries, see also below, pp. 319–20.

[115] Welldon Finn 1967: 269–71, 433.

[116] Their effect is seen clearly in the sharply declining profits of the neighboring ports of the Duchy of Cornwall which the Duchy's accounts attributed to the pestilence; see PRO SC6/817/1; 817/3, m. 17; 817/6, m. 10; 817/7, m. 10; 818/8, m. 6; DCO Ministers' accounts 31/17, 31/20. Major visitations of the plague in Exeter were noted in 1349–50 and 1361 (Pickard 1947: 22–28; MCR 1349/50; 1360/1, 1361/2; MT 1348–1350, 1361, 1362).

[117] The timing, location, and severity of these French raids are discussed in Gill 1966: 75–94; Oppenheim 1968: 13–23; Russell 1950: 42–7.

[118] *CPR 1374–7*: 25, 476, 486, 502; *1377–81*: 3–4, 81; *1381–5*: 83; *CCR 1385–9*: 537–8; *Reg. Stafford*: 294–5; *Register of the Black Prince*, vol. 2: 36; Burrow 1977; Russell 1950: 42–7, 51; Gill 1966: 84–94.

sea in the form of piracy and retaliatory seizures of ships and goods – activities in which Devon shipmasters and mariners were enthusiastic participants.

The profits Dartmouth and Plymouth accrued from their activities during the Hundred Years War probably outweighed the damage to their local economies from the French raids which were, at any rate, intermittent and concentrated in the late fourteenth century. While ships and mariners were often compelled into naval service, the transport of troops or supplies could be conducted in the off-season when fishing and the wine trade were at a low ebb; such duties could also pay well if bonuses were included.[119] These lump-sum payments of wages and bonuses, along with the crown's purchases of supplies and other services, poured hard cash into the port towns. Plymouth in particular benefited from the many military and diplomatic expeditions that sailed from its port. The influx of ships, sailors, soldiers, gentry, and merchants at these times must have been truly impressive. In 1348, a fleet of forty ships assembled at Plymouth to accompany Princess Joan to Bordeaux, and in 1355 the Black Prince's expedition to France gathered a retinue of some 2,600 men at Plymouth, which itself only had a population of about 2,500. Even after the expeditions had left, Plymouth profited from the victuals and other supplies it gathered and shipped to English forces abroad in the second half of the fourteenth century.[120]

Although outbreaks of fighting in Gascony could severely disrupt the wine trade and consequently the export of English cloth, the wine trade at Exeter remained remarkably steady over the course of the late fourteenth and early fifteenth centuries.[121] Indeed, Devon ships heightened and then maintained a strong presence in the late fourteenth- and early fifteenth-century Bordeaux carrying trade, spurred on in part by the declining presence of ships from eastern England. Before the War began, Devon ships accounted for only 8 per cent of all vessels at Bordeaux; by the second half of the fourteenth century their share had

119 The thirty Devon ships that served the king for twenty one days in July–August 1338 were paid very well for their efforts in a season when demand for their services was low; *Wardrobe book*: 365–72. For similar payments to Devon mariners and shipmasters for voyages to France and Spain in the fourteenth century, see PRO E101/29/1, 32/22, 676/32, 36/20, 39/25, 40/19, 40/40, 41/2, 4/7, 41/38, 42/5, 42/18, 42/21, 42/22. For expeditions to Ireland (which involved a larger proportion of north Devon ships), see E101/41/29–33, 42/5–8, 531/31.

120 Hewitt 1958: 14–42, 92–4, 141, 148–9; Hewitt 1960; Gill 1966: 78–81. See also Tuck 1985 for a discussion of how warfare stimulated the economy of northern counties in the Anglo-Scottish conflicts. For purveyance supplies assembled at Devon ports, see PRO E101/555/14, 555/20, 555/32B–38.

121 Touchard 1973; below, pp. 228–9. For the fluctuations in the Gascon trade, see James 1951, 1971; Carus-Wilson 1967c: 28–49, and 1967d.

more than doubled to 18 per cent, and increased again in the first half of the fifteenth century to 22 per cent.[122] Their representation in the English wine fleet was even larger; in some years, such as 1372/3, Devon ships accounted for over 30 per cent of all English vessels exporting wine from Bordeaux.[123]

This is not to say that the late medieval war effort left the economy of Devon untouched. Obviously the French raids or even the threat of them imposed both a financial and psychological toll upon the population while the defensive measures they engendered had to be paid for largely out of local funds. It is also quite likely that the War diverted a greater proportion of the relatively smaller population of coastal communities to the navy than inland towns and villages contributed to the army.[124] This burden, along with the diversion of shipping, fell heavily upon the port towns of Devon. Purveyance also took its toll, as it did in other counties.[125] The loss of English territory in Gascony in 1451, moreover, not only closed off the wine trade, but also halted the military and supply expeditions that had so profited Dartmouth and Plymouth. All indications are that after a period of prosperity lasting throughout the late fourteenth and early fifteenth centuries, the fortunes of Exeter, Plymouth and Dartmouth suffered some setbacks in the 1450s and 1460s, although this period was also one of depression for most other English ports as well.[126]

From the 1470s, however, Devon overseas trade grew tremendously, particularly in Exeter which became one of the country's leading provincial ports in the Tudor period.[127] In the last quarter of the fifteenth century Devon tin production also surged[128] and cloth production mounted significantly at such places as Plympton, Totnes, Tiverton, and other places in east Devon.[129] In the closing decades of the fifteenth century, the ports of Devon and Cornwall also emerged as the country's most important exporters of English fish, overtaking the previously dominant east coast ports.[130] Devon ports were thronged with ship traffic from all over Europe. Visits by ships from the Channel Islands increased from the 1460s as the bulk of that trade passed from its

[122] Percentages calculated from figures in Childs 1992: Table 9.1.
[123] PRO E101/179/10; see also James 1971: 99–104.
[124] Sherborne 1967: 167–73 makes this argument.
[125] Hewitt 1966: 170; PRO E101/555/8, 14, 17, 18, 22, 32B, 33–5.
[126] Carus-Wilson 1963: 8–9; Childs 1992.
[127] Carus-Wilson and Coleman 1963.
[128] Hatcher 1973: 158–98. Much was shipped through Plymouth but Exeter's share of this trade also grew dramatically.
[129] PRO E101/338/14; Nicholls 1960: 121–2; Carus-Wilson 1963.
[130] Litler 1979: 230–6, 245–8.

previous center in Southampton to the more westerly ports of Poole, Exeter, and Dartmouth.[131] Devon ports also shared in the expansion (evident by the 1470s) of Castilian trade to England.[132] As the fifteenth century ended and the sixteenth century began, the growth of industry and trade in the county had catapulted Devon from its previous lowly position among English counties into the fastest growing economy in the entire realm.

While the economic and commercial growth of Devon at the end of the fifteenth century was remarkable, developments in the late fourteenth and early fifteenth centuries set the stage for and frequently even anticipated this later take-off. Long-established agricultural and settlement patterns almost certainly allowed Devon to adapt more readily than other counties to the late medieval demographic crisis. As H.S.A. Fox points out, the flexible system of convertible husbandry allowed farmers to continue labor-intensive techniques of fertilization and supervision at a time when labor was not plentiful, and thus to maintain relatively high levels of arable productivity.[133] The trend towards early enclosure in Devon, combined with the system of convertible husbandry and the abundance of waste and pasture in the county, also facilitated the movement towards less labor-intensive pastoral farming at a time when labor was in short supply. The reduced population levels of the late middle ages, moreover, did not lead to deserted villages and wholesale abandonment of holdings in Devon. Instead, the dispersed pattern of settlement that prevailed in the South-west eased the adjustment to population loss in comparison with the experience of the nucleated and open-field villages of the Midlands.[134] Devon had never been an over-populated county; it suffered no "Malthusian crisis" in the late thirteenth and early fourteenth centuries.[135] While the Black Death was no less severe in Devon than elsewhere, its effects on the landscape and settlement there were not as harsh since the changes did not wreak havoc with a region already characterized by scattered hamlets, farmsteads, and a few larger villages. Similarly, the prevalence of freehold and the less demanding servile tenure in the South-west may have ameliorated the seigneurial reaction and landlord–tenant hostilities experienced in other English regions during the late fourteenth century.

[131] Childs 1986.
[132] Childs 1978: 52–65, 156, 88–90, 135, 179, 204.
[133] Fox 1991: esp. 303–23.
[134] Fox 1991: 722–42.
[135] Hallam 1981: 169; Hatcher 1988.

Labor shortages could also have been eased by steady immigration to the county in the late fourteenth and fifteenth centuries. Such immigration would have been stimulated by the commercial opportunities offered by Devon's diversified economy (in cloth manufacture, mining, fishing, shipping, and maritime trade), as well as by the growing use of Devon ports for military, diplomatic, and pilgrimage expeditions during this period. The hundreds, even thousands of people who passed through the county every year on their way to join the Black Prince, to accompany diplomats and members of the royal family on voyages abroad, to set sail for Santiago, to sell supplies or bring victuals to royal purveyors, to accompany their ships to assemblies of naval levies or wine fleets, to sail into Devon ports with cargoes from abroad, or to buy tin in Dartmoor or imports and other goods in Exeter,[136] swelled the population of late fourteenth- and early fifteenth-century Devon, stimulated demand, and must have encouraged emigration. Certainly the profusion of residents with French and Flemish names in southern port towns and the prevalence of Welsh and Irish names in north Devon ports during this period suggest that at least some of the overseas visitors chose to stay.[137] Denizen licences were granted to men like Edmund Arnold who claimed he was born in Gascony but had resided in Dartmouth for the past twenty years and was now married with children; as a wealthy merchant he went on to serve Dartmouth as mayor.[138] His fellow merchant and another burgess, William Saundre, had been born in Ireland.[139] Other immigrants did not rise to such exalted positions; a Breton man labored for an Exeter smith and another was accused of assaulting the wife of an Exeter dyer, while three

[136] For example, merchants and girdlers came from Bristol and Coventry to buy tin at Ashburton, Chagford, and Tavistock; *CPR 1327–30*: 367, 379. See also Hatcher 1973: 89–117, 136–46. Visitors to and from Cornwall also passed through Devon unless they went by sea. For the frequent presence of outsiders in Exeter markets, see chapters 5–7, below.

[137] See the names of Dartmouth (Kowaleski 1985) and Exeter residents in 1377 (Table A3.1, below). For other Flemish immigrants to Devon during the late fourteenth century, see PRO JUST3/15/3 m. 3 rider; SQMT 1365, WQMT 1366; for Irish immigrants, see *CCR 1381–5*: 433. The most comprehensive listing of immigrants to Devon is in the alien subsidy of 1440 (PRO E179/95/100); almost 70 per cent were of French origin (including Normans, Bretons, and Gascons), 15 per cent of Irish background (mostly in north Devon), and 11 per cent of Flemish or Dutch origin. Most were concentrated in coastal communities, particularly in south Devon and around the Exe estuary. Devon ranked eighth among thirty-five English counties in the number of aliens (or sixth if the largely Scottish populations of two northern counties are excluded); see Thrupp 1957.

[138] *CPR 1388–92*: 23; PRO SC6/827/7; *W.C. Chancery proc.*: 2, 15; *CIM*, v. 7: 129. For such licences in 1436 alone, see R.B.M. 1929.

[139] *CCR 1381–5*: 432–3.

children of a poor Norman family were sent to work in Brixham.[140] By 1523, no fewer than 21 per cent of the taxpayers assessed for the lay subsidy in Dartmouth were aliens (mostly French).[141]

Devon undoubtedly suffered from labor shortages, vacant holdings, and other effects of the late-medieval population decline. Agrarian depression was not unknown. But the scale of the crisis in Devon (and much of Cornwall) did not match that noted elsewhere in England, and the opportunities for recovery existed at hand. The county's diversified economy provided employment and stimulated demand while its natural geography, farming system, and tenurial structure eased the consequences of population decline.[142] Political factors also spurred the development of Devon ports. The growth of English interests in France, particularly in Gascony, worked to the advantage of Devon ports because the shortest sea trip from Bordeaux to England went via Plymouth and Dartmouth. The regular maritime business conducted by the crown and others benefited Devon greatly because of its position on shipping routes with easy access to areas of Brittany, Gascony, and Spain, regions whose political and commercial affairs were much intertwined with England's in the late middle ages. Accidents of geography and politics, therefore, worked together to lay a foundation for relative prosperity in late medieval Devon.

[140] PRO CP 40/490, m. 135d; *W.C. Chancery proc.*: 14–15; *Cases before the king's council*: 118–20.

[141] Nicholls 1964: 118.

[142] The arguments put forth by Hatcher (1969) on the diversified economy of Cornwall and by Bailey (1989) and Dyer (1989c, 1990) concerning "marginal" lands are relevant here. The Devon economy, particularly in upland and maritime regions, was better equipped to deal with the agrarian crisis of the late middle ages than predominantly arable economies elsewhere in England.

2 Markets, fairs, and towns

Medieval Devon was characterized by an unusually high number and density of markets, fairs, and boroughs, institutions which scholars usually view as the outward signs of commercialization. This phenomenon, in light of the low population, poverty, and backwardness depicted in the county's medieval tax assessments, requires further explanation. By examining economic development through the spatial and temporal distribution of these marketing centers, the following discussion points to how the regional diversity noted in the previous chapter stimulated commercial exchange. For a variety of reasons, Devon's particular bundle of resources placed a premium on places of exchange compared to areas like the Midlands where resources were less diverse and exchange more localized. This regional dimension can also be explored in tracing the emergence of a hierarchy of marketing centers and boroughs in the county.

Markets and fairs in Devon

Markets and fairs provided the main venues for the sale and purchase of goods throughout the middle ages. Local and retail trade predominated at markets (weekly gatherings of a single day's duration) while wholesale and regional trade was more common at fairs (annual meetings lasting about three days). The privilege of holding specific markets and fairs was usually granted by the king to lords (and sometimes to the inhabitants of vills or towns) who profited from the tolls and justice they administered at these meetings. "Private" trade obviously took place outside of these officially sanctioned markets and fairs, particularly in the late middle ages when inns and shops became more favored locations for commerce.[1] But much trade, particularly in victuals, manufactured items, and livestock, occurred at fairs and markets. By furnishing traders with secure surroundings, access to a steady stream of

[1] Dyer 1989a, 1992: 149–50.

customers, quick adjudication of disputes by means of law merchant, and facilities and services for storage, display, and transport, fairs and markets provided structure and organization for a great deal of commercial activity in the middle ages.

Historians have, not surprisingly, assumed that a strong relationship existed between the grants of fairs and markets and the development of the commercial or market economy. As a result, much scholarly effort has been put into identifying fair and market grants, using the county as the basis of most comparisons.[2] By outlining the chronological, spatial, and temporal distribution of these foundations, scholars have explored the various factors that influenced the origin, development, and success of the markets and fairs of particular counties. No one has yet surveyed systematically the markets and fairs of any south-western county, a regrettable omission since Devon, Somerset, and Cornwall had the highest number of boroughs and planted towns in medieval England.[3] Medieval Devon, in fact, had seventy one boroughs, more than twice as many as the next highest-ranked county of Somerset. The link between the proliferation of boroughs, and markets and fairs, is immediately obvious in Devon's case since the county also had an extremely high number of fairs and markets. Only the far more densely populated county of Norfolk and the far bigger county of Yorkshire possessed more markets than the 108 identified in medieval Devon before 1349 (and 113 before 1500).[4] And few counties served as the site for as many fairs (150 by 1500) as those identified in medieval Devon.[5] The sheer size of Devon obviously explains in part this abun-

[2] Britnell 1981b; Tupling 1936 (Lancashire); McCutcheon 1940 (Yorkshire); Coates 1965 (Derbyshire); Palliser and Pinnock 1971 (Staffordshire); Reed 1978 (Buckinghamshire); Britnell 1981a (Essex); Unwin 1981 (Nottinghamshire); Postles 1987 (Oxfordshire); Goodfellow 1988 (Northamptonshire).

[3] Britnell (1981b) relied solely on Devon markets for his regional category of "South Western." Beresford and Finberg 1973: 38, 48–9, and Beresford 1981 identify seventy five boroughs in Devon but only seventy one will be counted in the following discussion because Little Totnes was the same as North Ford, Sutton Prior the same as Plymouth, and Marlborough and Moretonhampstead were not termed boroughs before the seventeenth century. For planted towns, see Beresford 1967: 277–80, 417–26.

[4] Britnell (1981b: 210) identified market grants for twenty one counties before 1349, including ninety four for Devon. For the Devon markets, see Appendix 2, below.

[5] The fairs are listed in Appendix 2, Table A2.1, below. The study of fairs has not progressed as far as that for markets so there is less scope for comparison here. Certainly Devon had more fairs than the fifty in Lancashire before 1500 (Tupling 1936); the sixty one in Gloucestershire before 1500 (Finberg 1957: 86–8); the twenty eight chartered in Derbyshire before 1350 (Coates 1965); the thirty medieval fairs identified in Herefordshire (O'Donnell 1971); the sixty three known for Buckinghamshire from 1200 to 1500 (Reed 1978); or the sixty nine for Northamptonshire before 1500 (Goodfellow 1988). McCutcheon (1940: 161–71) listed grants from the Calendar of Charter Rolls for 158 different fairs in Yorkshire up to 1500 but Yorkshire was a far larger county than Devon.

dance of markets and fairs, but such an explanation does not completely account for the county's density of markets and fairs which was also greater than that in most other counties.[6] It is possible that south-western lords more actively solicited official recognition of their boroughs and commercial marts than lords elsewhere because of the region's "insecure urban life."[7] But this explanation, by focusing on the supposed backwardness of the South-west, also ignores the possibility that other factors, such as the area's regional diversity or the difficulties of transport, may have played a significant role in the proliferation of boroughs, markets, and fairs in medieval Devon.

Recent scholarship has related the pattern of markets and fairs to population density and the diversification of the economy. R. H. Britnell, for example, has shown that the proliferation of markets before 1349 was due in large part to agricultural development.[8] Agricultural expansion in the twelfth and thirteenth centuries spurred population growth (or vice versa) which in turn promoted rising demands for food, manufactures, and services. Other factors also moved the economy towards increased monetization and stimulated the type of formal trade that took place at markets and fairs; non-agricultural occupations multiplied (in part because market exchange allowed for a greater number of landless workers and smallholders), more people received cash wages (especially in the multiplying towns), and lords and governments sought to extract a growing proportion of their rents, fines, and taxes in coin. Landlords responded to these factors by founding markets and fairs, although it was primarily the consumer demand and market surplus of the peasantry which underlay this commercial growth.

The proliferation of markets and fairs in Devon seems to have followed the same general pattern observed elsewhere in England. The majority of the county's markets and fairs were founded in the most densely populated districts, notably along the southern coast and in east Devon (Figures 2.1 and 2.2). The continued establishment of Devon markets even into the fourteenth century, when the pace of

[6] Using the figures provided by Britnell (1981b: 210) for markets founded before 1349, Farmer (1991a: 331) ranked Devon eleventh of twenty one counties in market density; using the 108 markets identified in Appendix 2, Devon ranked ninth. Figures for density of fairs are harder to come by. Of the seven counties for which medieval fairs have been identified (n. 5, above), Buckinghamshire (one fair for every 7,619 acres) and Northamptonshire (one per 9,130 acres) had a greater density of fairs than Devon (one per 11,000 acres). Devon's figure is deceptive, however, since so much acreage in Devon was uninhabited moorland.

[7] Dyer 1992: 151 suggests this as a possible explanation for the high density of boroughs in the region. Lordship as a factor in the foundation of markets and fairs is discussed further below, pp. 51–3.

[8] Britnell 1981b. See also Coates 1965; Unwin 1981.

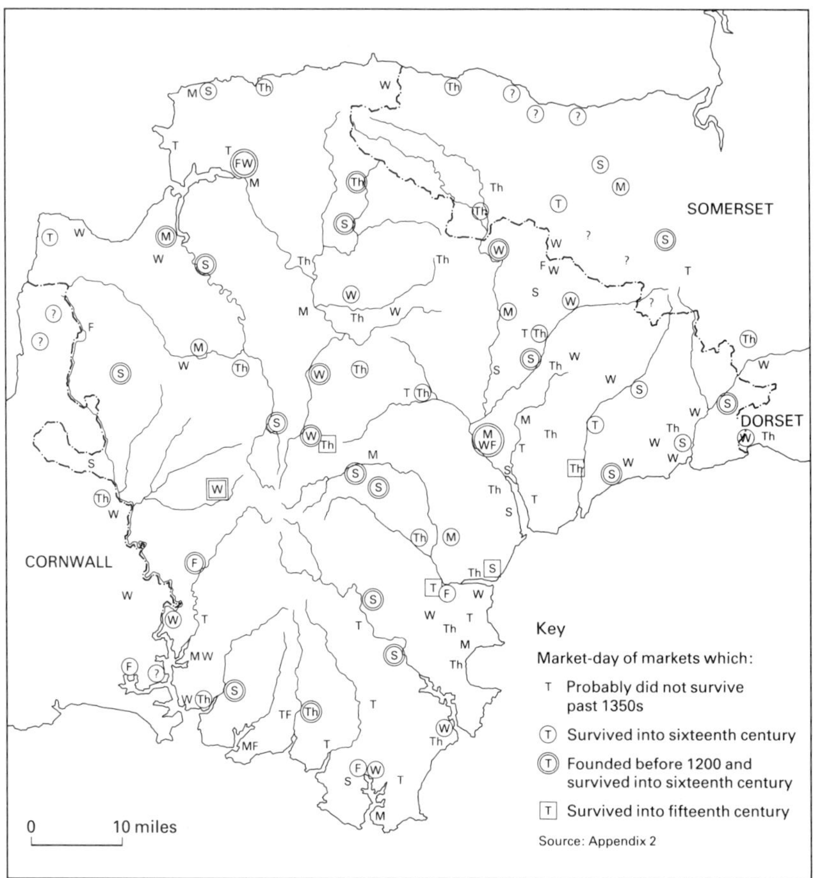

Figure 2.1 Markets in medieval Devon before 1400

foundation had slowed in most other counties, illustrates the extent to which the county's relatively late agricultural expansion was linked to the multiplication of markets. And the diversified economy of Devon, which emphasized mining, fishing, shipping, and other maritime activities, clearly promoted occupational specialization and stimulated consumer demand and trade.

But beneath the general pattern lay trends, peculiar to Devon, which require further elucidation. Thus the stress upon population density and agricultural development cannot be carried too far in a county ranked near the bottom of all counties in population density in 1377 and characterized by one of its most famous historians, W. G. Hoskins, in 1334 as "agriculturally one of the most backward counties of England . . . the county as a whole presents a picture of a rather poor peasantry, without much in the way of moveable goods."[9] The abundance of markets and fairs in Devon must also be related to the extraordinary number of planted towns and boroughs founded in the county: twice as many as were established in any other county.[10] What factors, then, were responsible for these signs of vital economic exchange in a county which at first glance does not fit the model of an agriculturally prosperous and densely populated county?

To begin with, we must be careful not to equate prosperity and commercialization solely with a corn-rich economy. While arable farming enjoyed a higher profile in pre-plague Devon than is usually assumed, the county's vast stretches of moorland and considerable upland acreage in all its regions ensured that the pastoral economy always played an important role. This pastoral emphasis was particularly crucial in promoting inter-regional trade through transhumance, transfers of estate flocks between manors, the urban demand for meat, and the diversified industrial and food uses of livestock and livestock by-products.[11] Indeed, the market economy, as K. Biddick's innovative study of thirteenth-century lay subsidies illustrates, had more thoroughly penetrated the peasant livestock economy than the arable economy in parts of medieval England.[12]

Certainly the seasonal distribution of fairs in Devon represents one reflection of how the county's pastoral and commercial interests were intertwined. The percentage of fairs during the autumn months, when cattle could be sold to drovers and graziers for fattening before slaughter, or flocks culled before the harsh winter months, was higher in Devon than elsewhere.[13] This pattern is particularly noticeable around Exmoor

[9] Hoskins 1952: 219.

[10] Beresford 1967: 277; Beresford and Finberg 1973: 38–54; Beresford 1981.

[11] See, for example, E. Power's (1941) comments on the *collecta* system which are suggestive in this regard, and Biddick's (1989) comments on the pastoral economy of Peterborough Abbey estates. See also the discussion of the hide trade and its links with urban meat consumption in Kowaleski 1990, and below, pp. 298–307. Farmer (1989, 1991a: 342–7) noted that fairs played little role in the grain trade, but were more important as the site of exchange for pastoral products, particularly livestock and hides. For the importance of livestock, hides and skins, and wool at the bigger English fairs, see Moore 1985: 47–59, 197, 269–70, 284. For transhumance, see McDonnell 1988, although he does not explore the commercial ramifications of the system he describes.

[12] Biddick 1985 and 1987. For an example of how specialized livestock production formed the basis of local exchange at an even earlier date, see Gilchrist 1988.

[13] Before 1400, 28.4 per cent of Devon's fairs and fair days occurred in the fall compared with 15.7 per cent of all English fairs and 21 per cent of the fairs of northern counties. I am grateful to David Farmer for providing me with the data he collected concerning fair grants in medieval England (Farmer 1991a: 341).

and Dartmoor where successful fairs occurred, for example, at Bampton in October and at Ashburton and Moretonhampstead in November.[14] Fully 40 per cent of the fair days in the Dartmoor region occurred in the autumn months, compared to 28 per cent for the county as a whole. This pastoral influence could also extend to fairs at places bordering the moorland region. Crediton, for example, perched just above the Dartmoor border region and located on a thin spit of productive "red Devon" land projecting into the pastorally oriented (and much less fertile) Culm Measures, became especially well known for its livestock fairs. During the fourteenth century, Exeter men and Exeter cathedral supervisors purchased horses at Crediton's May and August fairs; the reeve of Holcombe Rogus bought two oxen there; men from Sampford Courtenay acquired sheep; and manorial officials at Bishop's Clyst both sold cattle and bought cows at Crediton.[15] Crediton's role in this livestock trade was due in part to its crucial geographic position near the meeting point of three regions: Dartmoor, east Devon, and mid Devon.[16]

While pastoral interests help explain some of the anomalies in the pattern of markets and fairs in Devon, the influence of mining, particularly in the Dartmoor region, also played an important role. Consumer demand on the part of tinners must have promoted the growth of both markets and fairs. Periods of expansion in the tin industry, particularly in the late twelfth and early fourteenth centuries, coincided with both periods of colonization and the institutional establishment of markets and fairs in Devon.[17] Surely it is no coincidence that the Dartmoor border region contained fewer unsuccessful fairs than any other region in Devon (Figure 2.2), or that the bulk of early markets in Devon formed a neat ring around Dartmoor (Figure 2.1).[18] Many of these early markets on the margins of Dartmoor, moreover, probably predated the Conquest; J. R. Maddicott has recently linked renewed exploitation of tin on Dartmoor to very high levels of commercial prosperity in tenth- and eleventh-century Wessex, particularly in the towns of Exeter,

[14] Appendix 2; see also Lysons 1822: xxxv, xxxvii; Hoskins 1972: 327, for the continued success of these fairs and their importance in the livestock trade.

[15] MCR 1308/9, m. 45; 1348/9, m. 12d; DD 22279, 54878; *Fabric Accounts*, 108, 131, 140, 149 (*Pridie* refers to the St Lawrence fair at Crediton); Alcock 1970: 166–7.

[16] See Figure 1.1 for these regions. Unlike the rest of the large rural parish of Crediton, the southern portion did not lay in the fertile "red Devon" area and could more accurately be considered part of the Dartmoor border region. Coates 1965: 104 has also noted the tendency for certain markets to appear in Derbyshire "at the junction of areas with marked contrast in physical environment."

[17] Hatcher 1988: 244–5, 684; Appendix 2.

[18] Overall, 40 per cent of Devon's fairs founded before 1400 survived into the fifteenth century while 67 per cent of the Dartmoor fairs survived; see Appendix 2.

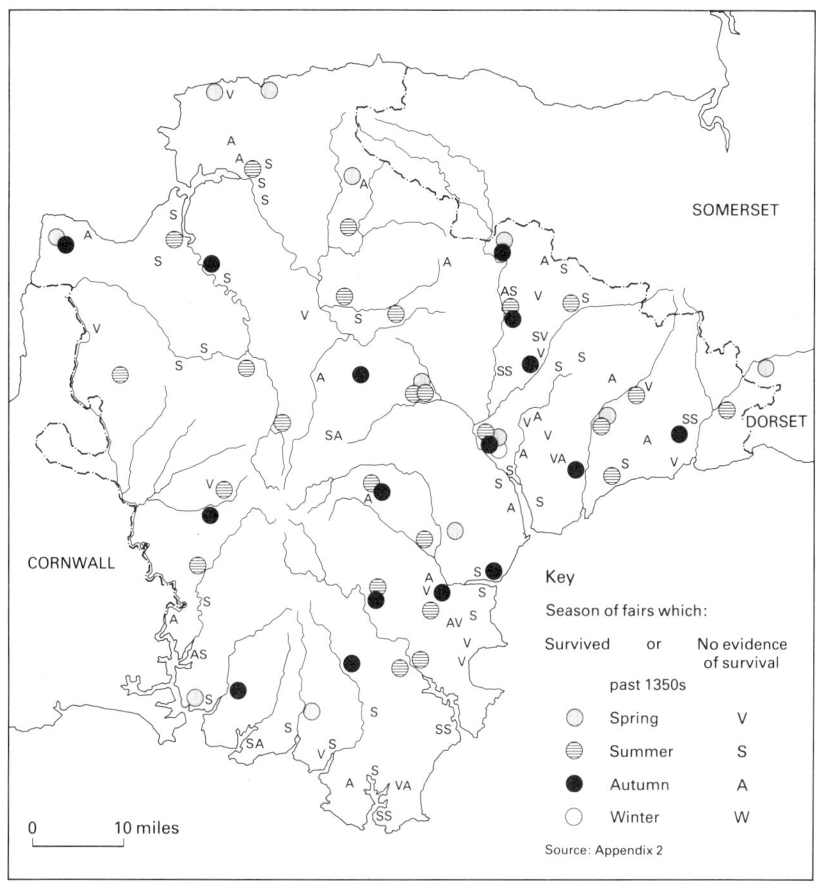

Figure 2.2 Timing of fairs in medieval Devon before 1400

Totnes, and Lydford, all of which had mints in this period and benefited as market centers for Dartmoor tin.[19]

The effect of the sea on the founding and success of markets and fairs in Devon is harder to gauge. At first glance, the impact seems impressive since almost one-third of all markets occurred in places with easy access to the sea. Obviously foreign and coastal trade promoted market exchange and facilitated urban growth in port towns with suitable harbours and larger agricultural hinterlands (Barnstaple, Bideford,

[19] Maddicott 1989: esp. 22–38. See also Appendix 2 for a discussion of markets and fairs active before officially sanctioned by charter.

Exeter, and Plymouth). Ports with access to valuable raw materials, such as the tin-rich uplands of Dartmoor (Dartmouth, Plymouth, Plympton, Totnes), silver and lead mines (Bere Alston, Combe Martin), or slate and limestone quarries (Kingsbridge, Portlemouth, Seaton), also had distinct advantages. For many smaller coastal villages, fishing constituted an important element of their commercial prosperity. Casual fish markets, like the unchartered ones at Exmouth, Alphington, and Ashprington, undoubtedly existed in many coastal areas, particularly in the Exe, Plym, and Taw estuaries.[20] But the strong relationship between ports and markets in medieval Devon may have had as much to do with the sheer length of Devon's coastline as it did with the favorable economic climate of fishing villages and port towns. Indeed, the survival rate of markets in these ports was actually slightly less than the average for the county as a whole. Maritime activities, moreover, barely affected the distribution or success of fairs in medieval Devon. Fish was more commonly sold at markets, not fairs, and no fairs in Devon ever lured foreign traders from overseas.

While the maritime orientation of Devon's coastal communities undoubtedly stimulated trade and encouraged the founding of markets, fairs, and boroughs at many of these locations, the influence of the sea mattered little away from the coast. Large areas in north and mid Devon, east Devon, and the Dartmoor region were miles away from the sea or even navigable rivers. Although the county was richly endowed with rivers and streams, river transport was rare in Devon aside from short stretches of the Dart (about 8 miles between Dartmouth and Totnes), the Tamar (about 24 miles up from Plymouth), and the Torridge (less than 5 miles through Bideford to Weare Giffard).[21] In the inland regions, communications overland thus took on a greater consequence. These communications were not made easy by the alternating hills and valleys, numerous tidal estuaries, large stretches of waste, high moorland, and rainy climate which characterized Devon. Travel through the county had obviously not improved much even by the sixteenth century when the antiquarian John Hooker wrote that the county was

> full of waste, heath, moor; uphill and downhill among the rocks and stones, and the pinnacled, long crags; and very painful for man or horse to travel, as

[20] Appendix 2. For unauthorized fish markets elsewhere in England, see Benton 1934: 137–9. For a more detailed discussion of fish markets and the fish trade centered around Exeter and the Exe estuary, see below, pp. 308–10.

[21] Lysons 1822: cclix. Fishing weirs and mill dams also prevented much river travel in Devon; see, for example, *CPR 1381–5*: 355 (Taw river between Barnstaple and Molland); Jackson 1972 (Exe river).

all strangers travelling the same can witness, for be they ever so well mounted upon their fine and dainty horses out of other counties, after they have travelled in this county but one journey, they can forbear the second.[22]

Devon's arduous terrain and difficult inland transport have been singled out by M. Beresford and H.P.R. Finberg as a major influence on the surprisingly large number of borough foundations in Devon; towns proliferated in the county because of the need for "more frequent nodal resting places."[23] The profusion of markets and fairs in Devon may also have been the product of the inconveniences of transport since peasants, in seeking quick trips to local markets or fairs, must have favored those markets within easy reach. The incommodious roads were also largely responsible for the reliance upon packhorses instead of carts and wagons in transporting goods to market.[24] Horse-drawn carts, the best means of transporting goods in bulk, were scarce in Devon.[25] In 1346, Bishop Grandisson responded to the Black Prince's request for horses and carts by writing that, "as your people who know this country are well aware, there are but few chariots nor such horses in this country, for all the transporting that we do here we do on pack-horses or bullock-carts because of the mountains and valleys and bad ways which are here."[26] Thus both the difficulties of road transport and the inefficiencies of packhorse haulage probably made peasants and other traders especially eager to do business at the nearest markets and fairs.

Road networks also had a significant impact on trading patterns and the distribution of markets and towns, particularly in the hinterlands.[27] Certainly the success of inland market towns located in thinly populated districts, such as Bow, Crediton, Hatherleigh, Holsworthy, Okehampton, Sheepwash, South Molton, and South Zeal, was due in large part to their position on major roadways.[28] The map of the medieval road network in Devon also strikingly illustrates the centrality of Exeter in the road and communications system of the south-western peninsula.

[22] Blake 1915: 336; I have modernized the spelling and added punctuation.

[23] Beresford and Finberg 1973: 54. See also the questions raised by Beresford (1967: 347) concerning the proliferation of planted towns in regions of inefficient transport.

[24] MCR 1373/4, m. 31; *Brokage Book of Southampton, 1439–40*: 104; Coleman 1960: xx, xxxiv; Langdon 1986: 73, 227, n. 164. For the inefficiencies of packhorse haulage, see Seebohm 1952: 206; Langdon 1986: 116–17, 226–7.

[25] Langdon 1984: 50, 60–3; 1986: 33, 41, 44, 88, 90, 144–7, 178, 205. The South-west was the only region with more ox- than horse-hauled vehicles in Langdon's sample of demesnes.

[26] Rose-Troup 1928: 259.

[27] Coates 1965: 105–7; Beresford 1967: 104–19; Willan 1976: 1–14; Chartres 1977: 39–43; Britnell 1981a: 18–20; Unwin 1981: 247–8.

[28] For maps and discussions of the road system in medieval Devon, see Sheldon 1928: 40–58; Joce 1912, 1918; Hoskins 1972: 145–56; Hindle 1976; Toulson 1983: 15–19.

Overlooking the lowest crossing point of the Exe river, the borough's site was the meeting place of ridgeway routes and valley-bottom roads along the Exe, Culm, and Creedy rivers. The two main routes from the east converged at Exeter; the London road went through Salisbury, Shaftesbury, Crewkerne, and Honiton to Exeter, and the Bristol road passed through Taunton, the Brendon and Blackdown Hills, and then down through either Tiverton or Cullompton into Exeter. The chief roads westwards into the rest of the county and Cornwall also began in Exeter. The two most travelled western routes lay along the northern edge of Dartmoor through Okehampton or along the southern border of Dartmoor through Newton Abbot, Totnes, Dartmouth, and Plymouth.[29]

Although location on roadside sites was an important factor in determining the success of medieval markets, fairs, and towns, historians have shown that early date of foundation was even more crucial in predicting survival.[30] Early foundation was particularly important for the survival of markets; 95 per cent of pre-1200 markets in Devon lasted into the early modern period, but only 30 per cent of those founded between 1200 and 1349 endured, with the survival rate declining in each half century.[31] Newer markets and fairs had a harder time competing with the established markets because the earlier marts were more embedded in the infrastructure; they had the more advantageous sites, better facilities, and a larger pool of customers. The early fourteenth-century foundations also faced a less hospitable economic climate since they were granted at a time when the pace of agricultural expansion was beginning to slow. Devon differed from other counties, however, in that the overall success ratio of markets in Devon was greater than in most other counties; 42 per cent of markets founded before 1349 survived into the sixteenth century and the success ratio for the early fourteenth-century foundations was higher than for any other county.[32] The vigor with which lords in Devon continued to found markets,

[29] Aside from the sources cited above, n. 28, see the itinerary followed by municipal officials from Exeter and local gentry on their way to London in: Misc. Roll 6, mm. 19d–20; CRA 1433/4; CR 1466. See also the routes travelled by William Worcestre in *Itineraries*: 13–17, 39–40, 111–13; and Leland in *Itinerary*, vol. I: Map II.

[30] Britnell 1981b: 219–20 (markets); Beresford 1967: 263–70 (planted towns); Reed 1978: 567, 574–6 (markets and fairs). Much less is known about the factors involved in the success ratio of fairs.

[31] Appendix 2. See also Britnell 1981b: 219–20. Some 39 per cent of Devon fairs founded by 1349 survived into the fifteenth century, compared to 65 per cent of the seventeen fairs founded by 1220.

[32] Appendix 2; Britnell 1981b: 219. Note, however, that Britnell's figures need to be treated with caution; for example, he uses three Devon examples (Bovey Tracey, Combe Martin, and Newton Abbot as on p. 219, n. 69) to show that markets founded in the 1260s and 1270s could survive into the early modern period, yet these three were actually established many decades earlier (Table A2.1, below).

fairs, and towns attests to the healthiness of the county's early fourteenth-century economy while the relatively high survival rate of markets into the sixteenth century may be one more indication that Devon avoided the worst effects of the late-medieval agrarian contraction. The regional variations in the success of fairs also illustrates the relationship between economic prosperity and the continued success of markets and fairs. By the fifteenth century, for example, east Devon's share of fair days grew as south Devon's share declined, a trend which correlates with the relatively greater depopulation and agrarian decline experienced in late-medieval south Devon as compared to the eastern portions of the county.[33] The expansion of the east Devon cloth industry and the vitality of its pastoral economy were largely responsible for that region's commercial prosperity in the late middle ages.

The distribution and success of markets and fairs (as for boroughs) could also have been affected by the status and social prestige of their lords and founders. Measuring their impact is, however, a difficult exercise. Most lords who paid the five marks usually charged by the king for the privilege of holding a market or fair, or who granted a borough charter to the residents of one of their manors, must have had potential profits in mind when they set up such enterprises. Tolls, rents, and court fines represented an immediate cash return while future profits could be realized if additional settlers were drawn to the lord's borough or village. Beresford and Finberg have pointed to variations between counties in the proportion of lay seigneurial lords who founded boroughs and planted towns; Devon stands out as the county where their influence was most notable since almost 70 per cent of the boroughs in Devon were established by lay lords, compared to under 40 per cent for the country as a whole.[34] This trend was partly if not largely a consequence of the later foundation of towns in Devon since the entrepreneurial activity of lay lords became increasingly important after 1250. But little difference existed in the status of grantees of fairs and markets between counties; in most places, lay seigneurial lords founded

[33] East Devon had 41 per cent of the fairs and 43 per cent of the fair days in Devon and enjoyed 48 per cent of the successful fairs and about 53 per cent of the successful fair days (i.e., those that lasted into the fifteenth century and later); these figures reflect the commercial prosperity and occupational diversity of this region. In contrast, south Devon had 25 per cent of the fair grants and fair days but only 13 per cent of the successful fairs and 14 per cent of the successful fair days. For the differing pace of agrarian development in these two regions, see Fox 1972, 1991.

[34] Beresford and Finberg 1973: 41. For "planted" towns the percentage was even higher; almost 77 per cent (of the seventeen) in medieval Devon were founded by lay seigneurial lords, compared to 45 per cent for all of England (Beresford 1967: 100, 417–26). These trends also reflected the pattern of land ownership in Devon since less land was in the hands of ecclesiastical lords there.

about two-thirds of all these enterprises.[35] The proportions in Devon were only marginally higher than in most other counties.

The status of the founder, particularly his or her social prestige, did have a slightly greater effect on the success or longevity of individual markets and fairs.[36] Lay seigneurial lords experienced more failures than the other founders, particularly in their fairs, which failed almost 20 per cent more often than those owned by ecclesiastical lords. These abortive fairs and markets were most often founded by provincial but enterprising lay lords who were faced with the double handicap of late foundation and inhospitable site. In 1333, for example, John de Langford, owner of the tiny sub-manor of Langford in Cullompton, obtained a grant for a Thursday market and a three-day fair in July. Neither of these ventures ever got off the ground. A successful Thursday market had been active in Cullompton itself for almost eighty years and at least ten other places within 10 miles of Langford claimed similar summer fairs.[37] In 1292, Henry de Ralegh, lord of another small manor called Strete Raleigh in the parish of Whimple, also obtained a grant for a fair (in May) and a market (on Thursday). Faced with competition from two other Thursday markets in nearby Newton Poppelford and Cullompton, as well as several other springtime fairs in the neighborhood, Ralegh's ventures also failed.[38]

In contrast, fairs and markets owned by the earls of Devon, the most powerful lay lords in south-western England, enjoyed a higher rate of success; 53 per cent of their thirteen markets and almost 57 per cent of their fifteen fairs survived into the fifteenth century or later.[39] The earls of Devon owned more markets and fairs than any other single

[35] In Devon, 72 per cent of markets and 67 per cent of fairs established before 1500 were founded by lay lords. Similiar proportions were calculated for other counties (based on the lists of grants given in the works cited in n. 2, above). Only Nottinghamshire, where lay lords received 75 per cent of the market grants, ranked higher than Devon. The proportions of royal foundations varied more widely from county to county but will not be considered here since so few markets, fairs, or towns in Devon were royal foundations (see Table A2.1).

[36] For brief discussions of the role of lordship, see Coates 1965: 100–1; Palliser and Pinnock 1971: 57; Reed 1978: 568–71; Britnell 1981a: 218–221; Unwin 1981: 248–9; Masschaele 1992.

[37] See Figure 2.2 and Appendix 2. There is no trace of either the fair or market in the 1356/7 Langford manorial account roll in Corpus Christi College, Oxford, Kn. 3/1.

[38] Appendix 2; and see Figures 2.1 and 2.2.

[39] Overall 41 per cent of fairs founded before 1500 survived including about 55 per cent of those owned by ecclesiastical lords and just under 36 per cent of those held by lay lords. Markets owned by ecclesiastical lords survived into the sixteenth century 42 per cent of the time while only 36 per cent of the markets with lay lords did so. Fairs and markets owned wholly or in part by the earls (the Vernons, de Redvers, and Courtenays) have the Grantee field of Table A2.1 marked in bold. They also set up five boroughs (Beresford 1967: 68; Beresford and Finberg 1973: 86–101).

lord in south-western England. Their five fairs at Tiverton, the main residence of the Courtenay earls, were outnumbered only by the seven fairs in Exeter. Their Tiverton fairs were further distinguished by the fact that only one was sanctioned by charter, perhaps an indication of the great influence and power enjoyed by the earls in Devon.[40] The earls, however, were rather unusual; none of the great ecclesiastical lords, such as the bishop of Exeter, enjoyed higher success ratios for their ventures, nor did any other noble or gentry family rival the earls (particularly the Courtenays) in the number of their foundations. The earls' success with markets and fairs also owed much to their placement, at a relatively early date, in good-sized settlements on important roadways where the earls had built a castle or residence. Overall, the founding lord's wealth, social prestige, and political influence were probably not as crucial to the success of markets and fairs as were other factors such as early foundation date and advantageous site. Even the rich and powerful Courtenays experienced failure when they tried to challenge long-established markets and fairs.[41]

The dynamics of the medieval marketing system – the competition between particular markets and fairs, as well as the reasons why some failed and others survived – can best be seen in the legal disputes that occurred during the early thirteenth century when royal law increasingly compelled lords to acquire formal charters for their markets and fairs. Lords, anxious to protect their investments and augment their profits, came to the king's courts to defend or extend their markets and fairs. This litigation brought about a greater elaboration of the law regarding market rights, as well as greater protection for owners of officially sanctioned markets.[42] A dispute in 1220 between rival market owners in Chagford and Moretonhampstead, two villages lying less than 4 miles apart on the Dartmoor border, shows how previously informal markets could be obliged to acquire royal charters in order to legitimize their existence when challenged by a rival. The defendant's market at Chagford had grown out of an informal assembly held on Sundays, as were many early markets since they provided a ready-made group of customers attending church services. Under pressure from the Church, however, these market meetings were forced to abandon Sundays in

[40] Appendix 2. The absence of charters could also have been due to the early origin of the fairs or the loss of the charters; but the coincidence of four early fairs or four lost charters in the same location is unprecedented and especially unlikely given the small size of Tiverton. Two new fairs were granted in 1615 (Youings 1967: 161).

[41] For example, their abortive markets and fairs at Kennford and Topsham (Table A2.1).

[42] Salzman 1928 and 1931: 121–60; Britnell 1978; Singer 1980. Masschaele (1992: 84) downplays the number of cases concerning market rights in the central courts, arguing that local institutions handled most of the problems.

favor of another day. The defendant, Hugh de Chagford, switched his market to Saturdays but apparently did not get a charter sanctioning either the move or the market and so ran foul of the lord of Moretonhampstead who had the foresight to acquire a charter when he changed his market from Sunday to Saturday.[43] Similar complaints were lodged by other lords in Devon. Fulk de Bréauté, owner of a chartered Saturday (but once Sunday) market at Honiton, sued the lord of Sampford Peverel, 13 miles to the north, and the lord of Sidmouth, about 9 miles to the south, for harming his market by arbitrarily setting up Saturday markets without proper authorization.[44] The Sampford Peverel market was also cited in a complaint by the owner of a chartered Saturday market at Bradninch, 8 miles to the south, while the Sidmouth market was also challenged by William Brewere, owner of a Saturday (but previously Sunday) chartered market at Axminster over 15 miles away. At the same time, Brewere sued the lords of Lyme Regis, about 5 miles away across the border in Dorset, for injuring his market at Axminster.[45]

These disputes, which all occurred within a two-year period, illustrate the growing competition of market owners within a relatively small area of east Devon. Equally important, the disputes show how concerned lords were about the temporal and spatial distribution of nearby markets, a topic that has also engaged the attention of scholars in more recent times. How close did a new market need to be in order to be considered harmful to an existing market? This question has been considered at length by many historians and geographers because answering it would also give clues as to the size of an individual market's hinterland and the relationship beween market distribution, population density, and agrarian development. Many have pointed to the guidelines set down in the legal treatise (attributed to Henry Bracton) that advised in the thirteenth century that markets be spaced no closer than six and two-thirds miles apart, especially if occuring on the same day or within a few days of one another. This advice was based on the premise that a day's journey of 20 miles, when divided by three to account for the

[43] In his defense, Hugh claimed his market was much older than the one at Moretonhampstead although the plaintiff disputed this. No resolution is given in the case, but both markets survived (*Curia regis*, vol. 8: 267–9; also discussed in Salzman 1928: 126, Hoskins 1947: 21–2, and Flower 1944: 334). For efforts to prohibit Sunday markets, see Cate 1938. Sunday markets continued, however, as did the practice of holding markets and fairs in churchyards as the warnings issued by the bishops of Exeter against these practices in the fourteenth and fifteenth centuries attest (*Reg. Brantingham*: 507; *Reg. Stafford*: 85–6; *Reg. Lacy*, vol. I: 143). For a seventeenth-century Devon market held on Sunday, see Walker 1972: 201.

[44] *Curia regis*, vol. 9: 305–6, 330; vol. 10: 96, 109, 177; vol. 13: 530, vol. 14: 1.

[45] *Curia regis*, vol. 13: 530; vol. 14: 1; vol. 8: 212.

journey there, time spent in the market, and the journey back, amounted to six and two-thirds miles.[46] Although the emphasis upon distance and travel time is significant (particularly the assumption that visitors to a market intended to return home the same day), there is no evidence that the courts or contemporaries ever cited this advice or took it seriously. As the disputes noted above indicate, medieval lords could consider markets over 15 miles away almost as threatening as those within 4 miles distance. And markets less than one mile away from each other, such as those at Dodbrooke and Kingsbridge, or Newton Abbot and Newton Bushel, could also co-exist.[47] Distance was important, but other factors, such as the size and economic orientation of the market settlement and immediate hinterland, as well as lords' interests in pursuing legal rights, also had a significant effect on the temporal and spatial distribution of markets.

The complaints voiced by one of the owners of the Axminster market about the injurious nature of the Lyme Regis market across the border in Dorset raises the issue of whether the administrative boundary of the county was also considered an economic boundary. Did medieval market and fair goers tend to limit their trips to places within their own county? This issue is important because almost all studies of markets and fairs, including this one, take the county as their unit of analysis. Certainly some contemporaries thought that the county border mattered; in 1227 the abbot of Ramsey defended his market at St Ives from complaints by an owner of a neighboring market by noting, among other factors, that they took place in different counties.[48] On occasion, customary carrying services were also specifically limited to places within county boundaries.[49] But such provisions were primarily a reflection of the limited marketing area for grain, rather than a recognition that the county boundary served as any kind of economic border. Non-grain-carrying services often specified more distant markets with known specialties; some Taunton and Stogumber customary tenants, for example, were required to fetch wine, herring, or salt from the port of Exeter.[50]

46 *Bracton*, vol. III: 198–9. Unwin, 1981, provides the best discussion of Bracton and of the whole issue of the spatial and temporal distribution of markets. If Bracton did write these comments, he may have been influenced by his own familiarity with Devon; he was a native of Devon and served as the chancellor of Exeter cathedral. See also below, p. 285 for the relevance of "Bracton's" comments.

47 Beresford 1967: 134, 244–6, 300, 422–4; Weddell 1985; Appendix 2.

48 *Curia regis*, vol. 13: 88–9.

49 Postles 1984: 4–7, 12.

50 Siraut 1985: 184; *Customs of the manors of Taunton*: 32; grain was also carried to Exeter by these tenants but wine seems to have been the primary lure. See also Campbell, Galloway, Keene, and Murphy 1993: 54–5, 62–3 for how the customary carrying services around London did not respect county boundaries.

Only a few scholars have recognized this problem concerning county and economic borders, usually by noting the particular physical features, such as rivers, that often served as both a county boundary and an impediment to travellers.[51] But the extent to which such physical features actually acted as barriers to trade needs to be assessed more carefully. Small rivers easily forded or crossed by a variety of bridges near major market centers were not much of an obstacle to trade. Larger rivers and estuaries which could be crossed only by ferry, such as the long stretches of the Tamar river which separated Devon and Cornwall, were more likely to deter peasants and casual traders from attending markets on the other side of the river.[52] The open sea and vast expanses of moorland could also be effective barriers to the local trade that occurred at markets. Devon, bordered on the north and south by the sea, and on much of its western border by the Tamar river, probably could claim coterminous administrative and economic borders more easily than most other counties, particularly those in the Midlands. The county's eastern border was more porous to trade although even here Exmoor, the Brendon Hills, and the Blackdown Hills could have represented a substantial deterrent to casual travel. Only on the southernmost eastern border between Dorset and Devon – in exactly that area between Axminster and Lyme Regis where market rivalries developed – was the county boundary little more than an administrative convenience.[53]

Although the physical features that marked Devon's county boundaries served as a fairly effective barrier to market trade between Devon and its neighboring counties, hilly terrain and wide rivers were much less noticeable deterrents to fair goers, who were more likely to travel longer distances for commercial purposes. Fairs in east Devon and west Somerset were particularly likely to draw visitors from each other's region. Traders from Exeter, for example, visited fairs in Lopen, Merriott, South Petherton, Tintinhull, and St Decuman,[54] while Somerset inhabitants frequented fairs in Devon at Bampton and Exeter.[55] Fairs in south-western Devon, especially at Tavistock and Plymouth, drew Cornish residents from Launceston and Morval.[56] Exeter merchants also

[51] Coates 1965: 102–4; Palliser and Pinnock 1971: 55, 61; Unwin 1981: 240.

[52] For the ferries across the Tamar, see Misc. Roll 2 m. 27; *Rotuli hundredorum*, vol. I: 76–7, 81; *Min. Accts. Cornwall*, vol. 2: 237, 242; *IPM*, vol. 3: 457–8. But see below, p. 294, for visits by Devon bailiffs to Cornish fairs.

[53] This informal interchange is exemplified by the Devon man who got into trouble on his way back from an ale-feast in Dorset (*Devon eyre*: 18).

[54] *Placitorum abbreviatio*: 121; *Fabric Accounts*, passim (for Lopen and South Petherton); *Somerset pleas*: 325; MCR Roll 1, m. 28; 1303/4, m. 10d; 1318/19, mm. 4d, 22d.

[55] *Somerset coroner's roll*: 468; Misc. Roll 40.

[56] Peter and Peter 1885: 101; *Rotuli parliamentorum*, vol. 6: 35–6.

travelled long distances to attend the great cloth fairs in Winchester, Boston, and Lincoln.[57] Intra-county travel to trade at fairs could also cover substantial distances; Exeter men attended fairs at Holsworthy, Lydford, Totnes, and Crediton, traders from South Tawton travelled to Tavistock fair, and a Newton Poppelford man sold cloth at the Colyton fair.[58]

Aside from the longer distances traders were willing to travel, fairs differed from markets in other significant ways. Unlike markets, which normally convened once a week except in the bigger towns like Exeter and Barnstaple, fairs were held only once a year for a predetermined length of time. Most fairs in Devon, as elsewhere in England, met for three days on the vigil, feast, and morrow of some particular saint's day. Many lords deliberately asked for fairs on the feast day of the local parish's patron saint in order to take advantage of pre-exisiting celebrations on those days. Thirty seven per cent of the Devon fairs coincided with the feast days of locally prominent saints and an even greater proportion (59 per cent) of the pre-1220 fairs occurred on such holidays, suggesting that many of the early fair charters merely bestowed official sanction on long-established gatherings.[59] Less than 28 per cent of the fairs founded after 1300 were set up on locally prominent feast days. Instead, owners of these later fairs often sought to take advantage of, or even deliberately to subvert, successful fairs in the neighborhood. For example, shortly after he acquired the manor of Cockington in south Devon, Walter de Wodeland, one of the Black Prince's retainers, secured a market and a three-day fair on the feast of the Holy Trinity for his new manor. This fair must have been set up to compete directly with the bishop of Exeter's successful Trinity fair at Paignton, only one and a half miles away.[60] In a similar fashion, the acquisition in 1309 of a fair lasting from 29 October to 2 November at Newton Bushel was probably designed to forestall and capitalize on the business that came to the much older fair (on 5–7 November) of the adjacent borough of Newton Abbot.[61] Some lords, in their quest for greater profits, even sought to take advantage of fairs they already owned. In 1300, Hugh

[57] MCR Roll 1, m. 18; 1302/3, m. 7; 1305/6, m. 16d; Keene 1985: 1117; Erskine 1983: xvii; PRO SC8/232/11588.

[58] Holsworthy: MCR 1288/9, m. 41d. Lydford: MCR 1360/1, m. 7. Totnes: MCR 1285/6, mm. 21, 27. Crediton: MCR 1308/9, m. 45; 1348/9, m. 12d; PRO E159/171 Hilary recorda, m. 14; Colyton; PRO E159/171 Trinity recorda, m. 2d; Tavistock: Lega-Weekes 1903: 507.

[59] See Appendix 2.

[60] For these fairs, see Appendix 2. For Wodeland, see Russell 1960: 122, 133. For similar strategies in north Devon, see below, pp. 69–70.

[61] Table A2.1. The lord of Newton Bushel may have tried this ploy before since his previous claim to a fair there had been rejected (*Quo warranto*: 180).

Courtenay, earl of Devon, obtained a charter for two July fairs, one at his manor of Topsham from 19–21 July and another at Kennford, only 4 miles away, on 21–22 July.[62] In positioning these fairs so closely together, the earl probably hoped to encourage fair goers to travel on a circuit, starting out at Topsham, then going on to Kennford, and ending up at the famous Lammas fair in Exeter which began on 31 July. Since the earl was also part-owner of the Lammas fair, he would directly benefit from promoting such a circuit.

Fairs also differed from markets in the goods sold there and in the traders who attended. Ellen Moore has discussed at length the merchants who frequented the great English cloth fairs before their decline in the early fourteenth century.[63] Although visited by many traders from nearby villages and small towns, these fairs were primarily distinguished by the number of royal agents and foreign merchants who came great distances to trade. Cloth from all over England and Europe was the major commodity sold at these fairs, but transactions for wine, metals, livestock, hides, and furs were also common.[64] Unfortunately, very little work has been done on the many smaller regional fairs all over England so their history is much less well known than that of the great cloth fairs. We do know that, unlike the international cloth fairs, regional fairs lasted only a few days rather than several weeks, drew traders from a much more limited area, rarely attracted foreign merchants, and witnessed commercial transactions on a considerably smaller scale. But the goods sold at both types of fair tended to be the same. Livestock, hides, skins, wool, farming equipment, metals, ironmongery, and cloth were important items at the regional fairs of the fourteenth and fifteenth centuries; grain, dairy products, and meat were not.[65] Merchandise sold at fairs in late medieval Devon shows a concentration on the same types of products: horses, sheep, hides, skins, and cloth.[66] In the fifteenth century, for example, the bailliffs of Ashwater manor in mid Devon (near the Cornish border) sold livestock at Devon fairs in Holsworthy, Brent Tor, and Tavistock, and at Cornish fairs in Launceston and

[62] *CChR*, vol. 2: 488. A previous earl had obtained a charter for a similar July fair at Topsham in 1257 (*CChR*, vol. 2: 2) but it probably failed because of heavy opposition from the citizens of Exeter (*CCR, 1259–61*: 218; Jackson 1972: 59). Exeter also protested unauthorized fish markets at Kennford and Alphington in the late fourteenth century; see below, pp. 308–10.

[63] Wedemeyer [Moore] 1970; Moore 1985: 63–92, 249–78.

[64] Moore 1985: 24–62. See also *Law merchant*, vols. 1–2: passim; Keene 1985: 1091–32; Salzman 1931: 142–60.

[65] *Law merchant*, vol. I: 107–36; Dendy 1905; McCutcheon 1940: 127–31; Erskine 1983: xvii; Farmer 1989, 1991a: 342–7, 379–85.

[66] See above, notes 15, 54, 55, 58, and Misc. Rolls 40 and 52, m. 7.

Week St Mary; at these fairs they purchased pitchforks, locks, halters, and herring.[67]

Just as regional fairs differed in size and scale from the few international fairs in England, similar variations also existed between the various regional fairs. These differences were most obvious in the revenues the fairs generated for their owners. At one end of the scale in Devon were small localized fairs, such as the two owned by the bishop of Exeter at Ottery St Mary which together generated less than 3*s* profit in 1382/3, or the fair at Bradninch which produced only 12*d*–18*d* profits annually in the late fourteenth century, or the tiny St Giles fair at Sidmouth which accounted for a paltry 6*d* in revenues in 1374/5.[68] Medium-sized fairs were fewer in number but drew upon a wider clientele and therefore reaped larger gains. In the late fourteenth century, the early July fair of Bovey Tracey on the Dartmoor border yielded profits of 10*s* while the fairs at South Molton on the Exmoor border and Holsworthy in mid Devon probably generated even larger amounts.[69] The biggest fairs in the county were those at Barnstaple in early September and the Exeter fairs at the beginning of Lent, early August, and early December. While Exeter's St Nicholas fair was the biggest moneymaker in the late fourteenth century with annual revenues as high as £7, the city's Lenten fair was the more successful in the fifteenth century, with average annual profits of about £4. These revenues, when compared to the sums of more than £10–30 that the great fair at Winchester was still collecting in its declining years during the late middle ages, do not seem particularly impressive.[70] But it is important to remember that the profits from the Exeter fair and, indeed, from many of the regional fairs, probably did not decline as precipitously as did those of the great cloth fairs from the late thirteenth century onwards.[71] The absence of any severe agrarian depression in Devon, combined with the rise of rural and urban industry and the diversification of occupations, may have promoted fair-going in late medieval Devon by generating a relatively large body of customers willing to trek a few miles to partake in the commercial and social activities offered by a town or village fair. Then too some regional fairs may have reduced or abandoned altogether the collection of tolls at fairs in

[67] 4088M/Ashwater bailiff's accounts for 1418–20, 1463/4, 1467/8, 1468/9, 1476/7, 1477/8; I am grateful to Harold Fox for pointing me towards these accounts.

[68] BL Add. Ch. 13973; DCO Min. Accts. 32/22, 32/25, 33/29; PRO SC6/829/13.

[69] PRO SC2/165/53, m. 2; 168/27, m. 5d; *CIM*, vol. 7: 47, 50.

[70] Keene 1985: 1125–7. For Exeter fair revenues, see CRA passim.

[71] For the decline of the great fairs, see Moore 1985: 204–22; Keene 1985: 1113–29; Titow 1987. For the continuing strength of late medieval regional fairs, see Farmer 1991a: 346–7.

order to encourage greater attendance. This arrangement decreased the fair profits enrolled in account rolls, but was a step willingly taken by towns such as Exeter in order to attract more fair goers and their cash.

Markets and fairs in Exeter

It is no surprise that the city of Exeter had both the most and the biggest markets and fairs in the county; its large, well-populated and prosperous hinterland, its geographic position on the major roads through the south-western peninsula, its role as a headport for Devon and Cornwall, and its own substantial population gave it tremendous commercial advantages over the other towns and ports in the county. As the ecclesiastical and administrative center of both Devon and Cornwall, it attracted merchants, gentry, farmers, and clergy as both visitors and residents, thereby providing a ready-made group of traders and customers for the local fairs and markets. It was the only town in south-western England to possess three market days each week, itself an indication of the scale of commerce that occurred there. Another mark of its dominant position in the hierarchy of marketing centers was the way neighboring markets avoided having market days that conflicted with the Monday, Wednesday, or Friday market days of Exeter (Figure 2.1). By the late fourteenth century, the closest viable Monday market was in Chudleigh, 9 miles away across the Exe river and on the other side of the steep Haldon Hills. To reach the nearest Wednesday market, a trader would have to travel about 16 miles up the Culm river valley to Uffculme, or 17 miles in the opposite direction to North Tawton. On Friday, probably its biggest market day, Exeter had no competition at all in east Devon; only Barnstaple in north Devon, Tavistock on the other side of Dartmoor, and Newton Abbot, 14 miles away in south Devon, possessed rival Friday markets.[72]

Exeter's seven fairs, all of which survived into the sixteenth century, also underline the city's premier status within the county's marketing network. Four of the city's fairs had no competition whatsoever in the county; from the beginning of December until the beginning of April the only successful fairs in medieval Devon were the four that took place in the city of Exeter. The oldest fair in Exeter, perhaps the oldest fair in all of Devon and Cornwall, was the three-day fair around the

[72] Unwin 1981: 238, 242–4, 250 discovered a somewhat similar, although not as striking, pattern in Nottinghamshire where smaller towns avoided holding markets on Saturday, the major market day of Nottingham and the two other most important urban settlements in the county. Kingsbridge in south Devon also had a Friday market which may have been changed to a Saturday (below, Table A2.1, n.12).

feast of St Nicholas in early December. Profits and lastage (a toll) due to the king, owner of the fair, appeared on the earliest extant pipe roll of 1130.[73] For the next two centuries, the fair remained in the hands of the king, although the farm of the fair was often assigned with the city fee farm and other properties in Devon to the queen regnant.[74]

The fair was obviously linked to the Benedictine priory of St Nicholas in Exeter, both by commemorating the priory's patron saint, and by location since the thirteenth-century city custumal specifically noted how payments of toll altered when mercers left the precincts of the priory during the fair.[75] This relationship also caused tension in the 1320s when the city complained that the prior of St Nicholas had constructed a house on a piece of land he had appropriated between the priory and the city's own marketplace at the Carfoix.[76] The building was probably put up to serve as a market hall since the city claimed that the prior's "house" had diverted trade away from both the St Nicholas fair and the weekly markets, so much so that the city had not been able to afford to pay for three years the annual farm it owed the Crown. Yet this dispute and others between the city and the priory over St Nicholas fair only concerned particular fair tolls and privileges; there is no evidence that the priory ever owned any part of this fair.[77]

The biggest dispute over the ownership of this fair involved the Crown and the city. In 1332 the city acquired a new charter regranting them the fee farm, along with its related responsibilities and privileges, in return for an increased annual payment.[78] The citizens clearly believed that this charter gave them rights over St Nicholas fair since they issued new regulations governing the fair and began recording revenues from

[73] *Magnus rotulus scaccarii*: 153.

[74] Payments of £6 from the fair and lastage appear on the pipe rolls almost every year; see *Pipe roll, 1155–58*: 48, 75, 159 (the lastage was farmed to Nicholas son of Floer in these years); *Pipe roll, 1188–89*: 130; *Rotulus cancellarii*: 16; and *Pipe roll*, vols. 1–85: passim. No fair payments appear for the periods from about 1190 to 1193 when Devon was one of the counties in the hands of John, and from 1205 to c. 1217 when the fair formed part of several farms granted to Queen Isabella. Although the fair was regularly granted out (along with roughly seven other "farms" in Devon) to various members of the royal family, in most years the sheriff of Devon continued to render account for the fair. Reichel (1897: 461) mistakenly identified this fair as Crolditch (Lammas) fair.

[75] *Anglo-Norman custumal*: 30.

[76] BL Cotton Vit. D. ix, f. 171.

[77] Note also the article of complaint in an arbitration between the priory and the city in 1352 (Misc. Roll 55) when the prior claimed that merchants located on the porch of the priory on the feast of St Nicholas did not owe toll. Those who claimed that King John gave this fair to the priory (Clarke 1912: 196; Mace 1925b: 202; Parry 1960: 9) were probably confused by similar claims by the city concerning the priory's ownership of Lammas fair; see below, p. 62.

[78] Exeter city charter no. 19; *CChR*, vol. 4: 259–60.

the fair in the city's accounts.[79] It took some time for the Crown to object to what it viewed as a confiscation, probably because the fee farm had been granted in 1337 to Edward, the Black Prince, as duke of Cornwall; by 1347, however, the Crown had initiated proceedings to recover arrears on the fair revenues.[80] Although both the duke and the sheriff were discharged of payment because the profits were said to belong to the city by virtue of its fee farm, the Crown again brought suit in 1394, this time claiming arrears on the fee farm and the fair revenues from the city since the death of the Black Prince in 1376. A very long court battle ensued in which Exeter claimed that rights to the fair were included in those rights granted with the fee farm.[81] After paying considerable legal expenses, the city finally won its case in 1411 when the king recognized its right to the profits of the fair.[82]

The conflict over St Nicholas fair pales in comparison, however, to the prolonged battle over the rights to the Lammas fair which ran for three days around the feast of St Peter's Chains on August 1st. Also called "Crolditch fair" after a pasture outside the city wall where the fair took place,[83] the early history of the fair is obscure. The citizens of Exeter claimed in 1274/5 that they once owned the fair along with the king but that the earls of Devon had somehow acquired one-half of the fair and the priory of St Nicholas had been granted the other half by King John.[84] Actually, it had been John's widow, Isabella, who granted the fair to St Nicholas priory in about 1217.[85] The earl of

79 The regulations, dating from 1331/2, are printed in *Citie of Excester*: 851–2. Profits from the fair do not appear in the first extant receiver's account (CRA 1304–6), but do appear in the next surviving account (CRA 1339/40), and in all subsequent accounts. From the 1330s on, the MCR also recorded the annual profits on the dorse of the membrane dated in the week of the fair (usually mm. 10d or 11d).

80 *CCR, 1337–9*: 198; and n. 81, below. Copies of all these proceedings were also kept by the city (Misc. Rolls 83–90, 98).

81 PRO E159/171 Michaelmas recorda, m. 44; E358/167 Michaelmas communia, mm. 35–36d (printed in Madox 1726: 263–9). Although the name of the fair was never given in any of these proceedings, nor in the pipe roll accounts, the chronological correlation between the city's new fee farm in 1332, its issuance of new regulations for the fair in 1331/2, its new enrollment of profits from St Nicholas fair in the same period, and the antiquity of the connection between St Nicholas priory, the city, and the fair, all suggest that the proceedings refer to the St Nicholas fair; also see below, n. 85.

82 CRA 1406/7, 1410/11. For the settlement, see PRO E358/167 Michaelmas communia, m. 36d; Exeter city charter no. 23.

83 Much of this land was in present-day Southernhay; see Lega-Weekes 1914.

84 *Rotuli hundredorum*, vol. I: 70, 95. *Citie of Excester*: 852–3 claims that the whole fair had belonged to the city since the Conquest but that John acquired one-half, then the whole of it, after which he granted a moiety to the prior of St Nicholas.

85 *Rotuli chartarum*: 128; *Rotuli litterarum clausarum*, vol. II: 51, 120, 193; BL Cotton Vit. D. ix, ff. 65–65v. These references imply that the whole fair, not half of it, was given to St Nicholas but the Hundred rolls and all subsequent documents make it clear that the priory only enjoyed one-half of the revenues of the fair. Isabella actually

Devon's interest in the fair is less certain, although his title may have been of even more ancient date.[86] In any case, there is little evidence that the city of Exeter ever enjoyed the revenues of the Lammas fair. Even around 1240, the city's custumal carefully noted that the city had to give up collection of the town customs to the bailiff of the fair between the hours of noon on the first day and noon on the last day of the fair.[87]

As their continual claims to this fair indicate, however, city residents were clearly never happy about what they perceived as loss of their revenue and jurisdiction.[88] Yet their claims were never successful and the dispute only escalated; in 1322 violence broke out and fair booths

held two fairs of Exeter as part of her dower; one was the St Nicholas fair referred to above, and the other was a fair, called *ferie que fuit Willelmi de Heliun*, which escheated to the Crown in 1163/4 (*Pipe roll*, vol. 7: 19). In 1169/70, a house associated with William de Helion also came into the hands of the Crown (*Pipe roll*, vol. 15: 97). All subsequent references, in the pipe rolls and in the legal disputes concerning the city's rights in these fairs (see above, notes 81–2), group the two fairs together. Although the documentary references to these fairs never give the dates of the fairs, there are several reasons for believing that the fair of William Helion was the same as the Lammas fair: (1) since St Nicholas priory never claimed any fair but the Lammas fair, the grant by Isabella to the priory must refer to the Lammas fair; (2) the older and larger fair that Isabella also held brought in five times as much as the fair of William Helion, a proportion which roughly matches the revenues garnered by the much more profitable St Nicholas fair and poorer Lammas fair in the fourteenth and fifteenth centuries when their revenues can be compared (see below, pp. 65–7); (3) the earl of Devon's claim to one-half of the Lammas fair can be traced to a connection with William Helion (see below and n. 86); (4) the other, richer fair can be identified as the St Nicholas fair, for the reasons outlined in n. 81, above. One anomaly remains, however; in 1332 the city included both fairs in its claim that its new fee farm encompassed rights over fair lastage and stallage, but only the St Nicholas fair was actually taken into its control. The earl's stubborn defense of his privileges in Lammas fair, along with the relatively low profits that fair yielded compared to the St Nicholas fair may account for the city's failure to win control of the fair during the middle ages. The other possibility is that the fair of William Helion was the Whitsuntide fair (see below).

86 Jackson 1972: 59, n. 10, citing *Pipe roll*, vol. 28: 15, traces the earl's claim to the *40s de feria Exonie* collected by Richard, earl of Devon in 1178/9. Actually, the earl enjoyed this fair revenue from 1175/6 (*Pipe roll*, vol. 25: 153), the sum varied from 25*s*–40*s* (equaling at most but one-quarter of the profits of just the one fair), and all the profits of these fairs later came back into the hands of the king according to the entries on the pipe rolls. Another clue to the earl's one-half ownership of Lammas or Crolditch fair lies in the survey of the earl's barony of Plympton compiled around 1340 (Brooking-Rowe 1906: 12–15) in which one-half of the fair of "Curledeche" was associated with the manor of Farway and its advowson. Since the estate of Whitleigh in Farway was owned by the de Helion family from 1086 into the thirteenth century (Reichel 1934b: 349–51), it is likely that the earl's claim was in some way based on his feudal overlordship of this estate (*Feudal aids*, vol. 1: 330, 428). It is thus certainly possible that the earls retained a one-half interest in the fair of William Helion that escheated to the crown in 1163/4.

87 *Anglo-Norman custumal*: 30.

88 *Rotuli hundredorum*, vol. I: 70, 95; Exeter city charter no. 21; *CPR 1364–7*: 84–5.

were torn down after the city's bailiffs demanded stallage from merchants setting up booths in the fairgrounds of Crolditch on the day before the fair officially began.[89] In the ensuing legal action brought by the earl and prior, the citizens tried to show that the owners of the fairs had only limited rights to collect tolls and rents but the court sided with the earl and prior, confirming their extensive privileges of jurisdiction and customs. No goods could be sold anywhere in the city for the duration of the fair except in the fair grounds and all merchandise exposed for sale in shops or houses within an arm's length of a door or window could be forfeited to the bailiffs of the earl and prior. While the fair lasted, the city courts were supposed to be suspended and all grievances settled at the Tollbooth before the stewards of the fair, who possessed stocks for punishing offenders. This judicial decision did not settle the quarrel, however, since similarly violent confrontations and prolonged legal battles occurred in the 1330s, 1380, and 1392, usually over the forceful efforts of unruly Exeter residents to impede the earl and prior's bailiffs of the fair as they tried to collect toll or enforce justice at the fair.[90]

These endless battles over rights and profits during the Lammas fair illustrate how important a major fair could be to the commercial life and prestige of a medieval city. The on-going disputes also show the tension which could erupt when two powerful opponents – in this instance, the city of Exeter and its only effective rival, the earls of Devon, representatives of the most influential family in south-western England – clashed over commercial privileges. Indeed, the quarrels over Lammas fair were but one part of a longstanding commercial conflict between the city and the earls which also involved the earl's ownership of the property outside the city's west gate, rights to fishing in the Exe river, and control over the manor of Topsham, the out-port of the city of Exeter.[91] It is also hard to escape the conclusion that the earls may have won most of the legal battles but were probably losing the war, at least as far as fair profits were concerned. The amount of money the earls had to spend on legal fees, as they continually initiated legal proceedings against the city, must have far outweighed the actual profits they collected from some of these enterprises. During the late fourteenth century, for example, the earl's share of the Lammas fair profits was

[89] BL Add. MS. 49359, ff 55, 59–60v (Courtenay Cartulary); Misc. Rolls 55, 79. Hooker also described this dispute and the others which followed, along with the rights of the owners of the fair, in *Citie of Excester*: 396–405, 854–8 and Book 51, ff. 56–9.

[90] For the disputes in the 1330s, see Misc. Roll 78; Book 51, ff. 57–9; *CCR 1334–8*: 354. For the dispute in 1380, see PRO CP40/480, m. 68, and for the conflict in 1392, see Misc. Roll 79 and *Citie of Excester*: 405.

[91] Jackson 1972; Kowaleski 1993: 1–7.

rarely more than 10*s*; in some years, as in 1377 when rainy weather interfered with the fair, profits fell to under 3*s*.[92] And the earls' victories in court were often ignored by the citizens. They continued to convene the mayor's court during fairtime and even had the temerity to run their own pie-powder court in 1415 when they administered justice right in the middle of the Lammas fair.[93] Indeed, the hostelers, victuallers, and merchants of Exeter probably reaped many times the profits of the earl or prior from the business generated by traders and visitors attracted to the fair. Their formal victory was solidified in the mid sixteenth century when the city purchased the prior's rights in the fair and effectively took control of most of the fair.[94]

The city's third fair, at Whitsuntide or Pentecost in late May, had an even more chequered history. Dating from before 1240,[95] the fair seems to have gone into decline by 1291 when the mayor and councillors made a special attempt to promote this fair by sending a messenger to Crediton (less than 7 miles away) during that town's early May fair.[96] The messenger was to publicize Exeter's fair, to be held for the next seven years from the vigil of Pentecost to the vigil of Trinity: in other words, for a week in late May when the city hoped to capitalize on the traffic leaving Crediton's fair. In order to attract customers, the city's messenger also promised that anyone coming to the fair was to enjoy freedom from toll, murage, and all other dues. This enticement shows that the civic governors believed that the business generated by the fair was more important than the tolls that could be collected. In this their interests may have differed from most fair-owners who were non-resident lords and probably more interested in the short-term cash profits to be made from tolls and the administration of justice than the long-term and diverse benefits such gatherings generated for the town as a whole. Unfortunately, the Crediton authorities did not appreciate the messenger's proclamation or the potential competition; his horse

92 PRO SC6/827/39 shows a 17*s* profit for the earl from the fair in 1286/7; for 1377, see *IPM*, vol. 14: 311. For the prior's 10*s* share of the profits in 1476/7, see Misc. Roll 52, f. 1.

93 Misc. Roll 40; see also MCR Roll 1, m. 19; 1290/1, m. 40d; 1291/2, m. 39d for other examples of the citizens' resistance to the earl's prerogatives during Lammas fair.

94 *Citie of Excester*: 417, 847–58. The earl's half of the fair remained attached to the manor of Topsham and continued to be fought over by rival claimants to the manor (DD 23290). The Lammas fair endured until the last decade of the eighteenth century.

95 The *Anglo-Norman custumal*: 30 noted the tolls to be collected by the city from mercers who attended the Whitsuntide fair.

96 MCR 1291/2, m. 18d; the special efforts of the city to promote this fair and the messenger's claim that "he had in his possession letters from the king concerning the fair" suggest that the fair had lapsed and that this was a new attempt to make the fair a going concern. Note also that this is the earliest reference to a Crediton fair which did not receive a charter until 1309 (*CChR*, vol. 3: 133).

was attacked and he was forcibly detained and brought before the local court.

The city's efforts to promote this fair do not seem to have achieved any notable success; except for a reference to a special stall and shop rentals in Pentecost week of 1309, this fair was never mentioned in the fourteenth century.[97] In 1404, however, the city reinstituted the fair on Whitmonday. This most likely represented a new venture on the part of the city because the city accounts began recording its revenues, collecting only 13*d*, hardly the amount typical of an already established fair. Although never as prosperous as the Lenten fair, the Whitmonday fair achieved some success, particularly at the end of the fifteenth century when revenues rose to over 21*s* in some years.[98] Its lower revenues may have been due to the keen competition from other Whitsuntide fairs in Devon or perhaps to the city's continued policy of charging no or few tolls at the fair. The fair lasted into the seventeenth century and was later always referred to as the "Whitsuntide fair."

Exeter's enterprise in refounding its old Whitsuntide fair was not the first time the city took such initiatives without the authority of the king. Given the disputed ownership of Exeter's two oldest fairs, it was perhaps not surprising that the burgesses decided to start their own fairs in which they would retain sole rights. In 1374 the burgesses began another new fair on Ash Wednesday. Called the "Carniprivium" or "new" fair, it was cleverly situated at the beginning of Lent and thus had no county competition in the two months preceding and following it.[99] There is some evidence that the city's "foundation" merely institutionalized a large Lenten market for fish which already took place in Exeter at this time.[100] Special tariffs drawn up for the

97 MCR 1308/9, m. 30d. The first (CRA 1304–6) and subsequent (CRA 1339/40 on) city accounts do not mention this fair, nor do the court rolls. While the fair's freedom from tolls might explain such an absence, it is likely that the absence of related fair matters (e.g. the city's purchase of boards and trestles, profits from the administration of justice and leasing of stalls at the fair, or incidental references to the fair such as survive for all of the city's other fairs) in the extant records means that the fair had lapsed.

98 CRA 1403/4–1495/6; in these accounts it was usually termed "the fair on the Monday after Pentecost." For a pie-powder court entry for this fair, see MCR 1418/9, m. 37. MacCaffrey 1975: 79 notes that the Whitsuntide and St Nicholas fairs were the most important fairs in mid-sixteenth-century Exeter.

99 MCR 1373/4, m. 20d; CRA 1373/4. For the rising profits of the fair, see CRA 1373/4 and onwards. For references to it as the "new fair," see MCR 1378/9, m. 1, 1379/80, mm. 17, 19, 50.

100 For example, CRA 1339/40 records that carpenters were hired in the week of Ash Wednesday to make tables and trestles (the standard items used to display fish, as noted in other city accounts for the fish market). For other evidence of Exeter's

fair in later years certainly indicate the fair's prominence as a supplier of fish.[101] These tariffs may have been partly responsible for the rapid rise in revenues from this fair; within twenty years, earnings topped £5 and the Lenten fair went on to become the most profitable fair in fifteenth-century Exeter.

Only two years after the city began collecting revenues from the Whitmonday fair, it also enrolled profits from an entirely new fair on the feast of St Thomas the Apostle (December 21). Like the Whitmonday fair, profits started low, amounting to only 18*d* the first year, but rising to about 8*s* by the end of the century.[102] It is difficult to understand why the city initiated a new fair only two weeks after its own longstanding St Nicholas fair. Perhaps the city fathers, almost all of them merchants, may have wanted to cater to the Christmas trade and to take advantage of the lack of any other winter fairs in Devon. But this strategy was shortsighted since the St Thomas fair eventually cut into the profits of the St Nicholas fair; the latter's revenues fell precipitously from the time the new December fair began. Indeed, the St Nicholas fair had been the most substantial source of commercial income for the city in the late fourteenth century, garnering over £7 in some years (for example, 1376) and averaging about £4 in the early fifteenth century. By the 1450s, however, the profits from the St Nicholas fair had dropped tremendously, generally averaging less than £1 in the following years.[103] Nor did the relatively small profits of the new fair compensate for the losses sustained by the older fair. Yet it is also possible that the reduced revenues reflected a new city policy of lower tolls or more exemptions, a strategy the Exeter rulers had adopted almost two hundred years earlier with the Whitsuntide fair.

What is perhaps most remarkable about these new fairs is that there is no evidence that the citizens of Exeter ever bothered to obtain a charter for any of these enterprises. Nor did they obtain one for another fair they began about thirty years later in 1431. The fair took place on Good Friday; this timing was probably well thought out in that it occurred right at the end of Lent (a period when no fairs were staged), but before the big round of Whitsuntide and Trinity fairs. The revenues from the Good Friday fair were unimpressive, averaging about 5*s* annually. But the city continued with the fair nonetheless, even extending

increasingly prominent role in the regional fish trade at this time, see below, pp. 310–12.

[101] *Citie of Excester*: 553–4, 567, recorded a list of special tariffs for the Lenten fair that clearly shows the predominance of fish supplies there. For a pie-powder court from this fair, see MCR 1384/5, m. 23.

[102] CRA 1405/6–1500/1.

[103] CRA passim.

it to Wednesday and Thursday in 1500/1, suggesting once again that fair revenues might not be the best indication of the success of late medieval fairs.[104] Low revenues also did not discourage the city from founding yet another new fair in 1463. This time the municipal leaders went to the trouble of acquiring a proper charter for the fair which was to take place on the vigil and feast of St Mary Magdalene (21–22 July).[105] When the city leaders chose this date, they may well have been interested in forestalling the trade of the earl and prior's Lammas fair in Exeter which took place only a week or so later. The city leaders also followed a policy of charging no tolls at this fair either; all the fifteenth-century account-roll entries recorded nil profits and the city council at a meeting in 1522 noted that the annual Magdalene fair was a free fair at which no tolls were charged.[106]

There was probably no other city in medieval England that started five new fairs between the 1370s and the 1460s, a period generally considered one fraught with difficulties for most English towns. That only one of these new fairs was sanctioned by a charter is in itself also quite remarkable considering the legal challenges that could be offered by owners of previously existing fairs in the neighborhood. And the fact that all five new fairs, plus the two older existing fairs, were successful enough to survive into the sixteenth and, in some cases, the eighteenth century, is also an impressive feat. It seems fair to conclude that these new fairs, mostly unchartered, were a reflection of the city's confidence and healthy economic state in the late middle ages, an outlook in stark contrast to the economic depression that so many other English towns seem to have suffered in this period.[107]

Markets, fairs, and late medieval boroughs

We are fortunate to have so many extant records to tell us the history of the fairs in medieval Exeter. Unfortunately, such documentation does not exist for the other major towns in Devon, in part because their fairs did not enjoy the kind of regional renown possessed by the fairs

[104] CRA 1430/1 to 1500/1 passim. The timing of the fair also seems to be audacious since Good Friday was one of the holiest days on the Christian calendar.

[105] *CPR, 1461–7*: 275; Exeter City Charter no. 29. The fair was granted in return for the city's agreement to abandon claims to rights in the bishop's fee.

[106] CRA 1480/1–1500/1; *HMCR*, vol. 73: 303. For the continuation of the Magdalene fair into the sixteenth century, see also MacCaffrey 1975: 79.

[107] It is possible, of course, that the charters for these five new fairs are simply missing; but considering the fullness of both the Exeter documentation and central government records in this period, this seems doubtful. For a recent summary of the debate on late medieval urban decay, see Dyer 1979.

of the county capital. After Exeter, Barnstaple, located in north Devon at the head of the Taw estuary, was the next most important town in the marketing hierarchy in medieval Devon. Like Exeter, Barnstaple was an Anglo-Saxon *burh* and Domesday borough, but unlike Exeter it was loosely controlled by a series of largely absent seigneurial lords.[108] As the most important port on the north coast of Devon, its trade was more oriented towards the Bristol Channel, Wales, and Ireland than to the French or Iberian Atlantic regions served by Exeter and the other southern coastal ports.[109] Its prominent commercial position, recognized as early as the tenth century when it served as a mint, was due in large part to the agrarian prosperity of its immediate hinterland in the Taw and Torridge lowlands and to the cloth produced in its larger hinterland which stretched to the Exmoor borders and well into mid Devon. Its hinterland's cloth manufactures made Barnstaple the leading exporter of cloth in late fourteenth-century Devon.[110]

Barnstaple's role as a small regional entrepôt was also reflected in the vitality of its fairs and markets; aside from Exeter, it was the only town in Devon that enjoyed more than one successful market day. The Friday market day, which possessed no rivals in north and mid Devon, was the town's most frequented market. Its Wednesday market, founded later, was still strong enough to induce nearby Bideford, one of Barnstaple's chief competitors as a port and market center, to change its market day from Wednesday to Monday in 1272.[111] The competition between Bideford and Barnstaple went back many years. In 1218, for example, the owners of Bideford's Friday market changed to a Wednesday market day, probably to avoid direct competition with the more popular Friday market in Barnstaple.[112] And when the Barnstaple burgesses tried to start up a new fair in the 1340s, they deliberately selected a four-day fair from 21–24 July which would interfere with Bideford's own fair on 19–23 July.[113] In this instance, Barnstaple was the aggressor and took the commercial initiative (and lost since its July fair never got off the ground), but more commonly it was Barnstaple's neighboring communities that tried to cut into Barnstaple's own commercial sphere.

108 Reynolds 1969; Haslam 1984: 251–6.
109 Kowaleski 1992.
110 See above, pp. 23–5.
111 Although the grant of the Monday market to Bideford in 1272 did not specifically state that it replaced the Wednesday market founded in 1218, the Hundred rolls of 1274/5 and 1275/6 noted only a market on Monday (*Rotuli hundredorum*, vol. I: 64, 95; see also below, Table A2.1 and Figure 2.1). This grant of a new market on Monday also provides evidence that Barnstaple's Wednesday market dates back to at least 1272, even though it was not formally recorded until 1344.
112 *Litterarum clausarum*, vol. I: 169.
113 *Barnstaple records*, vol. I: 141; *CChR*, vol. 2: 181.

Thus in 1344 Pilton priory attempted to establish a two-day fair from 21–22 September in its own community of Pilton, a suburb of Barnstaple. These dates conveniently placed the Pilton fair between two of the most popular fairs in north Devon: Barnstaple's own fair on 7–8 September and Great Torrington's fair on 28–30 September.[114] The prior may have hoped to take advantage of the increased traffic passing through the area for these two well-known fairs. The owner of the fair (established in 1293) to take place on 28–30 September at Marwood, about 2 miles north of Barnstaple, probably had the same objective in mind. None of these later fairs survived; indeed, it is doubtful that they were ever much more than paper entries in the charter rolls, representing the frustrated commercial expectations of ambitious medieval lords.

Neither of the two other important boroughs in Devon, Plymouth and Dartmouth, had the same impact on the regional marketing network as did Barnstaple and Exeter, even though late medieval Plymouth was twice as big and Dartmouth was almost the same size as Barnstaple (Table 2.1). Neither Dartmouth nor Plymouth had particularly successful fairs and their markets did not have the same kind of effect on neighboring markets that Barnstaple and Exeter exercised. There are several reasons for this anomaly. Probably the most significant factor is that Barnstaple and Exeter were much older towns than Dartmouth and Plymouth. The marketing network visible in the late fourteenth century was largely a product of a much earlier period, as indicated in the substantially higher survival rate of twelfth-century foundations. Since Plymouth was little more than a fishing village before the thirteenth century and did not even acquire an official market until 1254, it played a smaller role in the formative stages of the county's commercial network. Dartmouth too had a relatively late start compared to Exeter and Barnstaple, growth being stimulated only from the mid twelfth century as its fine harbor became a point of assembly for fleets setting sail for the Crusades or the newly acquired English territories in southern France. Dartmouth was also at a disadvantage because of the competition offered by the ancient and wealthy borough of Totnes, only 10 miles north of Dartmouth on the navigable Dart river. An Anglo-Saxon *burh*, Totnes was much older than Dartmouth and its lords actively worked to protect their market privileges in Totnes once Dartmouth began to grow. In 1233 and 1242, the lords of Totnes complained that the market at Dartmouth harmed their market because ships were now stopping at Dartmouth and paying customs rather than going up the river to

[114] See Appendix 2 and Figure 2.2 for these fairs.

Table 2.1. *Wealth and population of fourteenth-century Devon taxation boroughs*

Taxation borough	Lay subsidy valuations in £			1377 poll tax		
	1327	1332	1334	Lay	Clerical	Total population
Exeter[a]	389	307	406	1,666	185	3,101
Plymouth[b]	263	311	400	1,549	18	2,729
Barnstaple[c]	241+	162+	207	788	17	1,396
Dartmouth[d]	139+	118	185	683	13	1,208
Totnes[e]	139	82	84	303	10	540
Crediton[f]	34+	31+	46	291	25	534
Ashburton	30	26	33	277	7	492
Gt Torrington	107	68	79	[262?]	5	[464?]
Plympton	60	41	43	240	26	446
South Molton[g]	82	53	63	[231?]	5	[409?]
Tavistock	120	82	90	[221?]	18	[405?]
Kingsbridge	42	32	35	[216?]	2	[380?]
Modbury	42	31	35	210	8	376
Bideford	60	50	60	150	2	265
Honiton[h]	<45	<27	28	[116?]	2	[205?]
Dodbrooke	39	15	22	114	2	202
Bradninch[i]	<50	<35	28	[80?]	2	[142?]
Tiverton	26	18	20	[75?]	3	[135?]
Okehampton	20	15	16	[54?]	2	[97?]
Lydford	12	10	12	[25?]	1	[45?]

Sources: Lay subsidies: PRO E179/95/6; *Lay subsidy 1332; Lay subsidy 1334;* Lay poll taxes: PRO E179/95/34–55; PRO E401/528. Clerical population: all figures are estimates only, based on PRO E179/24/9, 10a, 10b, 33, 80, 96, 98, 99, 317, 319. Exeter's clerical population includes thirty "lay servants of the bishop"; see below, p. 371.

Notes: Total population figures derived by multiplying lay taxpayers by 1.75, to account for those under fourteen years of age and for evasion, then adding the estimated clerical population. Poll tax populations in brackets are *very* rough estimates only, calculated by deriving ratios between subsidy returns for a borough and its manor (or hundred in some cases) and then using this figure to estimate the borough's population from the known tax return for the manor (or hundred) in 1377.

[a]See Appendix 3, pp. 371–5 for Exeter's population in 1377.

[b]Plymouth figures for the lay subsidy include Sutton Prior as well as the largely agricultural tithings of Sutton Vautort and Sutton Rauf; the 1377 figure is from PRO E401/528.

[c]Barnstaple figures exclude its suburbs of Pilton (sixty one taxpayers in 1377) for 1327 and its suburb of Newport (estimated forty seven taxpayers in 1377) for 1332.

[d]Dartmouth figures include its suburb of Southtown (177 taxpayers in 1377), except for the lay subsidy of 1327.

[e]Totnes figures exclude its small suburb of Bridgetown Pomeroy (which probably had fewer than fifty inhabitants in 1377).

[f]Crediton figures for 1327 and 1334 exclude Canon's Fee.

[g]The South Molton figures are deceiving since the borough was coterminous with its large parish (almost 6,000 acres); the genuinely "urban" population of South Molton was probably fewer than 200 people.

[h]Honiton figures for 1327 and 1332 include both the manor and borough.

[i]Bradninch figures for 1327 and 1332 include both the manor and borough.

Totnes.[115] Even though the market at Totnes was held on Saturday and that of Dartmouth on Wednesday, the jury suppressed the Dartmouth market because both ships and livestock were being diverted to Dartmouth's market. The Dartmouth Wednesday market was only reinstated in 1244 when certain tolls were promised to the lords of Totnes.[116]

The location of Dartmouth and Plymouth in south Devon also helps explain why neither town had much of an impact on regional marketing networks. Although the coastal portions of the region were among medieval Devon's most populated and urbanized areas, the hinterlands of Dartmouth and Plymouth were not as extensive as those surrounding Exeter and Barnstaple. The commercial traffic passing through Dartmouth and Plymouth was always oriented more towards their seaward than their inland connections. Dartmouth in particular had a small hinterland, hemmed in by physical features like the sea and the granite mass of Dartmoor, as well as by competition from Totnes, the Torbay towns, and Newton Abbot. Plymouth's hinterland was larger although it too was restricted by both Dartmoor and the sea. The extent of Plymouth's influence up the navigable Tamar river is harder to determine. The stannary town of Tavistock, with one of the oldest markets and fairs in all of Devon, must have provided stiff competition, particularly since the monastic lords of Tavistock owned so many of the surrounding estates.[117] Markets and fairs across the Plymouth Sound at Saltash, St Germans, and Trematon also vied with Plymouth for customers, particularly in the region's thriving fish trade.[118] Dartmouth and Plymouth had to contend, moreover, with the old, established markets and fairs of the Dartmoor border region, as the rivalry between Dartmouth and Totnes indicates. The stannary towns of Ashburton and Chagford (both near Dartmouth) and Plympton and Tavistock (near Plymouth) also jealously guarded their prerogatives. All four of these towns had markets and three even had fairs dating from the twelfth century. Exeter and Barnstaple were also in the middle of heavily populated coastal districts but their antiquity and early mercantile stature gave them the competitive edge over the commercial pretensions of neighboring towns.

Despite their low profile in an earlier period, both Dartmouth and Plymouth prospered greatly during the fourteenth and fifteenth centur-

[115] *Curia regis*, vol. 15: 52–3, 319–20; vol. 17: 90–1, 331.

[116] *Devon fines*: 193–4; *Totnes*: 146. Totnes was also quick to complain about the Thursday markets set up in nearby Ipplepen and Paignton; see *Totnes*: 194.

[117] Finberg 1952a, 1969.

[118] For their fairs and markets, see *CChR*, vol. 2: 258; vol. 3: 183; Beresford 1967: 410–13; Figures 2.1, 2.2. For the fish trade and competition there, see *Rotuli hundredorum*, vol. I: 76–7; *Min. Accts. Cornwall*, vol. 1: 237–8; *IPM*, vol. 3: 457–8.

ies, benefiting from the business they attracted in their capacity as favorite embarkation points for troops and supplies sent to the Continent during the Hundred Years War. As their maritime interests grew and they took advantage of English commercial and military interests in the Atlantic regions, the two ports began to attract more business in their hinterlands. Their growing influence was particularly noticeable in their significant role as exporters of cloth and in the new political and economic privileges they received.[119] The lord of Dartmouth's (probably unsuccessful) bid to add an extra market day and start a new fair in 1302 may have been an early attempt to exploit the port's growth. Plymouth's addition of an extra market day and two new fairs in 1440 when the borough incorporated was slightly more successful; the market survived but the fairs may not have.[120]

Although the markets and fairs of Exeter, Barnstaple, Dartmouth, and Plymouth exercised a differing impact, these towns still had much in common and together represent the first tier of boroughs in medieval Devon. As Table 2.1 illustrates, these four seaports were the largest and wealthiest towns in fourteenth-century Devon. Exeter, at the top of the hierarchy, was particularly distinguished by the size of its clerical population which included a bishop's household; a secular cathedral chapter with resident canons, annuellers, secondaries, choristers, vicars choral, and their servants; a Benedictine priory, Dominican and Franciscan friaries; two small hospitals, twenty parishes, and a large number of chantries.[121] Plymouth had many fewer ecclesiastical establishments and did not, moreover, possess Exeter's administrative functions. Although Plymouth had grown rapidly in the fourteenth century, its large population was much less commercially and industrially oriented than was Exeter's.[122]

Ranging in size from slightly over 500 to just under 400 residents in 1377, inland market towns predominated in the second group of taxation boroughs in Devon. Totnes, one of the oldest towns in Devon, had lost much of its earlier prominence by the fourteenth century as Dartmouth's growth cut into its commercial sphere of influence.[123] Yet Totnes, along

[119] For Plymouth, see Gill 1966: 45–104; for Dartmouth, Russell 1950: 4–47. For their growing economic profile in the late middle ages, see Kowaleski 1992 and above, pp. 29–31, and Tables 1.1, 1.2, and 1.3.

[120] See Appendix 2.

[121] For the clerical community at Exeter, see below, p. 371.

[122] The Plymouth tax totals usually included the large suburban jurisdictions of Sutton Valletort and Sutton Rauf where many if not most residents pursued largely agricultural occupations.

[123] Russell 1964; Kowaleski 1992. The history of the town can also be traced through the documents collected by Watkin (*Totnes*).

with Great Torrington, an important market town near the fertile and populous Torridge lowlands in north Devon, and Tavistock, a stannary town on the western edge of Dartmoor, were the wealthiest of the second-rank boroughs. Two other stannary towns were also included in this group: Ashburton, on the eastern edge of Dartmoor, and Plympton in south Devon. Much more stannary business passed through Ashburton than Plympton.[124] Although Plympton was a prominent twelfth-century town and had access to the sea, it had become overshadowed in the fourteenth century by its more powerful neighbor, Plymouth, located only a few miles away. The other seaport in this group, Kingsbridge, was like Plympton in that it bordered the fertile South Hams region, but Kingsbridge was a more viable port since it lay at the head of the Portlemouth estuary and dominated the rich quarries of blue slate and other building stone in this region.[125] With Kingsbridge must also be considered its neigboring borough of Dodbrooke; together the two boroughs constituted an urban area which numbered almost 600 persons.

The remaining boroughs in this second group were all agricultural market towns. Crediton lies in east Devon but its proximity to mid Devon and Dartmoor helped to make it an important market town, particularly for the sale of livestock.[126] Modbury was also an old and lively market town; situated in the middle of the arable farming region of the south Hams, it had one of the region's most important fairs.[127] The borough of South Molton in north Devon was co-terminous with its large parish (almost 6,000 acres) so its standing in Table 2.1 is rather misleading; the genuinely "urban" population of South Molton was probably less than 250 people.[128]

The third and last group of taxation boroughs included very small market towns located far inland, except for Dodbrooke which lay immediately east of the port of Kingsbridge, and Bideford which had access to the sea by virtue of its position on a navigable portion of the Torridge river. Honiton and Bradninch were both part of larger rural manors, although Honiton was noteworthy because of its position on the main road linking London with the South-west. Tiverton, Okehampton, and Lydford, though tiny, nonetheless possessed important castles, markets, fairs, and small groups of merchants who engaged in

[124] See above, p. 18.
[125] Born 1986; and see above, p. 32.
[126] Crediton had three fairs, two of nine days' duration (Table A2.1). For its prominence as a livestock market, see above, p. 46.
[127] See Appendix 2. Modbury Local History Society 1971; Hoskins 1972: 435–6.
[128] See also the borough court roll in PRO SC2/168/27, and Worth 1894.

regional and even overseas trade. Okehampton possessed the only Devon castle and borough with a market specifically mentioned in Domesday book; as the head of the barony of Okehampton, its castle also hosted important administrative functions.[129] Tiverton castle, built in the twelfth century, became the favored residence of the Courtenay earls of Devon. Although small in population, Tiverton possessed more fairs than any other borough in Devon but Exeter; in the fifteenth and sixteenth centuries, moreover, Tiverton grew very prosperous from the woollen cloth industry.[130]

The list of twenty taxation boroughs does not reflect the twenty largest boroughs in the county. Ilfracombe, Moretonhampstead, Newton Abbot (with its neighbor, Newton Bushel), Paignton, Sidmouth, and Teignmouth were probably as large or larger than the taxation boroughs of Honiton and Bradninch. All but Moretonhampstead and Newton Abbot/Newton Bushel were port towns whose ships were active in fishing fleets, coastal trade, and even the overseas carrying trade.[131] Their failure to qualify as taxation boroughs probably had more to do with the vagaries of lordship than with their size or commercial function. The three smallest taxation boroughs (Tiverton, Okehampton, and Lydford), for example, were all Saxon settlements and enjoyed the support of particularly influential lords. Lydford, a royal borough, was the site of an Anglo-Saxon mint, one of the four Anglo-Saxon *burhs* of Devon, and its castle served as the administrative center for stannary and Dartmoor forest courts. Okehampton, like Lydford, was a Domesday borough; it and Tiverton both served as sites of substantial Norman castles and were the two most important seats of the county's most powerful lords, the earls of Devon. Patronage from their prominent lords and an early date of foundation thus propelled Tiverton, Okehampton, and Lydford to borough status while settlements of similiar or greater size never achieved this mark of distinction.

The small size of Devon towns may also have been in part due to the availability of so many markets and fairs in Devon and its neighboring counties. Devon consumers and traders had more choice than most English people in deciding where to bring their business, a factor that may have prevented the emergence of larger urban centers. Borough population and taxation figures for Devon may also be lower than they actually were because of the ease of tax evasion in the county. With more coastline than any other English shire, Devon's seafaring population was highly mobile and absent for long periods of time. Tax exemptions

[129] Young 1931: 28–43; Higham 1977: 11–14; Higham, Allan, and Blaylock 1982.
[130] Carus-Wilson 1963: 18–19; Youings 1967; Welsford 1984.
[131] Kowaleski 1992.

allowed for tinners also may have reduced the final taxation figures. In 1374–5 there were at least thirty seven tinners awarded such exemptions in the borough of Ashburton, twelve in Tavistock, ten in Plympton, ten in Plymouth, nine in Modbury, six in Okehampton, six in Lydford, five in Totnes, three in Torrington, eight in Crediton, two in Tiverton, and even one in Exeter.[132] The practice of allowing such exemptions, combined with Devon's position on the periphery of the kingdom, may well have encouraged substantially greater tax evasion in medieval Devon than in most other counties.

Despite their small size, the number of boroughs in Devon was impressively high; its seventy one medieval boroughs numbered twice as many as found in the second-ranked county, Somerset.[133] Even the county's biggest towns, however, did not stand out for their wealth or size. In 1334, the county's two largest towns, Exeter and Plymouth, ranked below more than twenty other English towns in assessed wealth, and in 1377 Exeter's population of just over 3,000 placed it behind twenty two other boroughs.[134] Over half of the boroughs in Devon possessed a population of less than 400 in 1377, smaller than places classified as villages elsewhere in England. Yet these tiny boroughs were consistently identified as such by local tax collectors, by the eyre courts, and even in parliamentary returns; in the estimation of local Devon people, these places clearly had an urban character.[135] This estimation was probably based on the trading activities of these places; all of the taxation boroughs in Devon had their own markets and fairs.[136] Although Devonians might have possessed different standards for classifying places as towns than residents of other counties, it is more likely that they were genuinely reacting to the presence of regular commerce and industry in the places they labeled boroughs.

The large number of boroughs, planted towns, markets, and fairs in medieval Devon might also have been merely a product of the intervention of Devon lords; in a county usually portrayed as backward and poor, lords might have gone to more trouble to support new foundations with the official sanction of royal charters.[137] Lordship certainly did

[132] PRO E179/95/28–32; these lists were drawn up in an attempt to ferret out false claims to tinners' status.

[133] Above, n. 3.

[134] Glasscock 1973: 184; Russell 1948: 142; Russell's figures for Plymouth's population are incorrect (Hoskins 1952: 226); for the correct figure, see PRO E401/528. The figure for Exeter in Table 2.1 includes Exe Island (Exeter's western suburb owned by the earl of Devon), which neither Glasscock or Russell counted.

[135] Willard 1933.

[136] Appendix 2; Willard 1933: 424.

[137] Dyer 1992: 151 makes this suggestion concerning the large number of boroughs in the South-west and Wales.

have an effect on the status of the small boroughs of Tiverton, Okehampton, and Lydford, as we have seen. Yet the diversity of the regional Devon economy, its relatively greater emphasis upon pastoral agriculture, its poorer inland transport, and the longer period over which commercial development occurred offer perhaps more compelling arguments to explain the high density of commercial marts in the county. The poorness of Devon in tax assessments offers but a one-sided view of regions that ill fit the traditional medieval picture of open-field arable agriculture. The county's regional diversity was probably the more important factor in stimulating commercial exchange, as seasonal and spatial distribution of markets and fairs illustrates. The proliferation of towns, markets, and fairs in Devon – a proliferation that exceeded that of most other English counties – was in part a response to particularly high levels of commercial pressure, which in turn was stimulated by a greater degree of regional specialization in the county, as well as by the difficulties of negotiating its difficult terrain. Although the agrarian sector clearly played a significant role in generating these commercial pressures, it was the mining, maritime, and pastoral specializations that set Devon apart from most other counties. Determined by regional geography, these specializations stimulated the foundation of new marketplaces and the creation of new markets for the producers, consumers, and traders involved in the exchange of raw materials and products within and between regions.[138]

[138] See also above, Chapter 1 and below, pp. 293–318 and Table 7.7 for this regional diversity and inter-regional exchange.

Part 2

The economy of medieval Exeter

3 Economy and government in medieval Exeter

Economic developments

When the Romans built a legionary fortress in the middle of the first century to secure control over the South-west, they chose a hill overlooking the first low bridging point of the Exe river. Although a settlement may have already existed on this site, it was the Romans' construction of a forum, basilica, public baths, and other stone buildings that gave Exeter an urban character.[1] The Romans also surrounded the roughly 90-acre site with stout stone walls and made the city, called Isca Dumnoniorum, their administrative capital for all of present-day Cornwall, Devon, and western Somerset. This area corresponded to the canton of the Dumnonii, a Celtic people who continued to use Exeter as their tribal capital after the Romans withdrew early in the fifth century.

While Exeter was probably not completely deserted in the fifth and sixth centuries, neither archaeological nor documentary evidence suggests much urban continuity.[2] During this period the Saxons expanded their control westwards so that by the end of the seventh century most of Devon lay within the kingdom of Wessex.[3] A Saxon minster, where Boniface received his early education, was founded at Exeter at the end of the seventh century.[4] But it was not until the late ninth century when King Alfred established a mint in Exeter and refortified the city's defences that Exeter showed definite signs of urban occupation and commercial activity.[5] J. R. Maddicott has argued, in fact, that Exeter became Wessex's major seaport in the tenth century.[6] Sustained by

[1] Bidwell 1979, 1980; Henderson 1988. For contrasting views on whether the site was already inhabited, see Hoskins 1963b: 1–4, and Todd 1987: 205–6, 214–16.

[2] Bidwell 1980: 86–7; Allan, Henderson, and Higham 1984: 409–10.

[3] The timing and process of this expansion are still a matter of debate; see, for example, Hoskins 1970 and Todd 1987: 267–75.

[4] Henderson and Bidwell 1982.

[5] Shiel 1980; Allan, Henderson, and Higham 1984.

[6] Maddicott 1989, esp pp. 23–35 for this and the following. See also his reply (1992: 176–88) to the criticisms of Nelson (1992: 151–9) concerning Exeter's prominence in this period.

trade with France and Ireland as well as by its central role as an exporter of Dartmoor tin, Exeter enjoyed great prosperity in the tenth and early eleventh centuries. The city's status was marked, moreover, by special corporate privileges; obligated to pay geld only when London, York, and Winchester did so, Exeter also benefited from a very low fee farm and light military services. Another indication of the city's growing status was the transfer of the bishop's see from Crediton to Exeter by Leofric in 1050.[7]

In his account of William the Conqueror's siege of the city in 1068, Orderic Vitalis described Exeter as a "wealthy and ancient city built in a plain, strongly fortified."[8] Although the town walls resisted the Norman attack, the city eventually surrendered to William who solidified his victory by building a royal castle on the highest point within the town, demolishing as many as fifty one houses in the process. Domesday Book recorded 399 houses in Exeter, suggesting a population of over 2,000 in 1086.[9] These houses included 114 held by lords of rural manors, an indication that Exeter already played a significant role as the regional capital of Devon. Similarly, the minster at Exeter served as a religious focal point for people from surrounding villages, some as far as 15 to 20 miles away. Members of the Anglo-Saxon prayer guild at Woodbury, for example, offered regular payments to the minster at Exeter for obits and masses.[10]

William of Malmesbury described Norman Exeter as "magnificient and wealthy, abounding in every kind of merchandise."[11] Recent analysis of pottery evidence suggests that the city's overseas trading links were indeed fairly extensive, oriented in particular to northern France.[12] Large fines paid to the Crown by the vintners of Exeter and those involved in the marketing of dyed cloths also attest to the impressive scale of the city's trade in the late twelfth and early thirteenth centuries.[13] Pointing to its prominence in fishing and maritime trade, the author of the *Gesta Stephani* claimed Exeter was the fourth largest town in England.[14] This assessment was more moderately echoed in the city's contributions to twelfth- and early thirteenth-century royal aids and tallages in which Exeter usually ranked sixth or seventh among English

[7] Barlow 1972; Blake 1974.
[8] *Ecclesiastical history*: II, 211.
[9] Welldon Finn 1967: 280–2.
[10] *Diplomatarium anglicum aevi saxonici*: 608–10; Barlow 1979: 196–8; Gross 1890: I, 181–3.
[11] *English Historical Documents* 277–83.
[12] Allan 1984: 3–18; Hodges and Mainman 1984: 13–18.
[13] *Pipe roll*, vol. 48: 196; vol. 53: 253; vol. 59: 74.
[14] *Gesta Stephani*: 32–3.

cities.[15] Exeter's twenty nine churches in the late twelfth century (thirty two by the early thirteenth century) also testify to the city's standing (only five other English towns possessed more).[16]

Exeter's fortunes declined, however, in the thirteenth century as the city lost its prominent position in tin exporting and as the eastern towns and ports of England assumed more dominant roles in both the cloth industry and export trade.[17] By 1334 Exeter ranked below at least twenty English towns in wealth assessed by the lay subsidy. Yet Exeter's "decline" was probably more a reflection of the faster pace of commercial development elsewhere than an indication of crisis in Exeter's economy. Certainly the population continued to expand during this period; the number of locative surnames in Exeter rose over the thirteenth century and increasing population was probably responsible for the thirteenth-century subdivision of previously cultivated areas within the walls into tenements.[18] The city also retained its importance as a regional market center and port, although it was no longer one of the leading entrepôts of England. When the system of national port customs developed in the late thirteenth century, however, Exeter was still prominent enough to be selected as the headport for all of Devon and Cornwall.[19] Overseas trade links were maintained with Normandy, Picardy, Brittany, and Gascony while the substantial importation of dyestuffs and wine and export of woollen cloth indicated a thriving commercial life.[20] In 1326 Exeter was also named one of nine places where a wool staple was fixed. Aside from these marks of commercial importance, Exeter also functioned as the premier religious and administrative center of south-western England. Most of the abbots and abbesses of Devon monasteries had town residences in Exeter from which the bishop ruled a see encompassing all of Devon and Cornwall.[21] With a royal castle and gaol conveniently at hand, Exeter served, moreover, as the county's main meeting place for itinerant justices at eyres, sessions of the peace, assizes, and gaol deliveries. Gentry families, such as

[15] Barlow, Biddle, von Feilitzen, and Keene 1976: 501. In 1204 Exeter also ranked with London and Winchester in its contribution to royal almsgiving; see *Rotuli de liberate ac de misis et praestitis*: 95–6.

[16] Rose-Troup 1923; Allan, Henderson, and Higham 1984: 397–8; Maddicott 1989: 23.

[17] Maddicott 1989: 23–50.

[18] Postles 1994: 253–9; Devon Archaeological Society 1990: 8–9. See also Fox 1986: 166 for subdivision of tenements c. 1300.

[19] Carus-Wilson and Coleman 1963: 7–8, 36ff.

[20] *Local PCA 1266–1321*; Table 3.2; and below, pp. 234–5 for a longer discussion of maritime trade during this period.

[21] *Cartulary of Canonsleigh abbey*: xxvii, 66–76; Youings 1952: 125–6; Oliver 1864, passim.

the earls of Devon, also owned residences and other properties in Exeter.[22]

As a regional capital, Exeter attracted rural and small-town migrants from throughout south-western England. An analysis of the place-name surnames of newly admitted freemen from 1284 to 1349 offers a rough guide to the migratory pull exerted by the town (Table 3.1).[23] The non-ambiguous locative surnames (representing uniquely named places) provide the best indication of the distances travelled by immigrants to Exeter. The city's primary catchment area extended a radius of 20 miles, a figure similar to York, but less than the larger towns of London, Winchester, and Bristol; Leicester, Norwich, and Nottingham all had somewhat smaller catchment areas.[24] This hierarchy was maintained for migration at most distances although for the very long distances (over 100 miles) Exeter's figure matched that of Winchester and was only 3 per cent behind the numbers London drew from that range. In contrast, Exeter's ability to draw from the middle distances (35 to 60 miles) was markedly less than might be expected considering its position in the hierarchy at the other mileages. Here the town's proximity to the sea and position at the gateway to a peninsula probably created a "dead" zone from which no migrants could arrive. Other natural features like the granite mass of Dartmoor, or the Blackdown Hills and Exmoor to the northeast, lie within this zone and may also have had a negative impact which was largely absent in towns with more low-lying hinterlands.

Not surprisingly, given the size of Devon and Exeter's central location in the county, 75 per cent of the new freemen came from

[22] For residential properties owned by Devon gentry in fourteenth-century Exeter, see: BL Add. Ch. 27593 (Pomeroy); 64183 (Courtenay); ED/M/276 (Poltymore); /420 (Crewys and Cammynon); /510, 518 (Chuddelegh); DD 245 (Botreaux); MCR 1351/2, m. 33 (Ralegh); 1362/3, m. 24 (Deneys); 1388/9, m. 40 (Courtenay), m. 53 (Stapeldon); 1389/90, m. 38 (Herle); 1397/8, m. 38 (Bonvill and Audley); 1398/9, m. 17 (Courtenay).

[23] *Exeter freemen*: 1–29. Gentry and clergy were omitted from the analysis which may still include some who resided outside of Exeter since restrictions on non-residents in the freedom were not always enforced in this period. There are several drawbacks to relying on freedom entries to indicate rural–urban migration; freedom entrants were likely to be better off than the bulk of rural migrants, and some of the locative surnames had already become hereditary by this time and thus not truly indicative of recent migration; see also Postles 1944: 258–63 for further analysis of the freemen's surnames.

[24] Figures for this comparison and those following are from: McClure 1979: 178 (Leicester, London, Norwich, Nottingham), 181 (York freedom entries, 1272–1327); Penn 1983 (Bristol); Keene 1985: 371–9 (Winchester). For Westminster, whose migration fields were similar to those for London, see Rosser 1989: 182–90.

Table 3.1. *Immigration to Exeter, as indicated by place-name surnames and stated origins of freemen, 1284–1349*

Distance in miles	Non-ambiguous surnames % (N=95)			Nearest-place surnames % (N=110)			Origin stated with surname % (N=30)			Total % (N=235)		
1–5	11			13			3¼			11		
		25			27			16½			25	
6–10	14			14			13¼			14		
			52½			61			33½			54
11–15	19			21			10			19		
		27½			34			17			29	
16–20	8½			13			7			10		
21–25	8½			11			13¼			10		
		15½			16			26½			17	
26–30	7			5			13¼			7		
			26½			25			39½			27
31–35	7			6			10			7		
		11			9			13			10	
36–40	4			3			3			3		
41–45	1			1			7			2		
		2			2			10			3	
46–50	1			1			3			1		
			3			2			13			4
51–55	0			0			3			½		
		1			0			3			1	
56–60	1			0			0			½		
61–100	5			2			7			4		
		18	18		12	12		14	14		15	15
>101	13			10			7			11		
Total	100	100	100	100	100	100	100	100	100	100	100	100

Source: Exeter Freemen: 1–29. This analysis follows the guidelines suggested by McClure 1979. Non-ambiguous surnames refer to uniquely named places; nearest-place surnames refer to more than one place but are identified as the place closest to Exeter. The places noted in the column "origins stated" were specifically noted as the freeman's origin and were thus not derived from surnames; 60 per cent of these places were non-ambiguous. This table excludes thirty one unidentified place-name surnames.

Devon itself.[25] By far the largest number (38 per cent) of migrants came from east Devon, Exeter's own region. Nineteen per cent came from north or mid Devon, 15 per cent from south Devon, and 14 per cent from the region of Dartmoor and its borders. The relatively

[25] These and the following figures are based on the non-ambiguous names although the ambiguous surnames show similar patterns, differing primarily in the larger number of names from east and south Devon. See also Figure 21 in Postles 1994.

small number of migrants from south Devon, a highly populated and urbanized region of the county, probably reflected the alternatives available in other towns. The south Devon boroughs of Totnes, Dartmouth, and Tavistock were all substantial market towns by the thirteenth century; Dartmouth and Plymouth in particular experienced marked growth from the late 1330s because of their role as embarkation points and suppliers of ships for troops and supplies during the Hundred Years War.

One-quarter of the new freemen in Exeter before the plague came from outside of the county. About half of these came from Somerset and Dorset whose westernmost regions were effectively an extension of the east Devon region; these regional patterns directly reflect the direction of trade in Exeter's hinterland.[26] Only two migrants in the sample were identified as Cornish, but this figure is clearly a gross underestimation. Unlike most migrants, those from Cornwall tended to be identified by their county of origin, rather than a specific place. The different language of Cornwall in particular would have marked out Cornish people and prompted Devonians to label them all similiarly. Surnames like "Cornisshe" or "de Cornwall" were common in Exeter, but since locative surnames referring to whole counties are excluded in the analysis of place-name surnames,[27] the Cornish surnames (and thus Cornish migration) are undercounted in this survey.

Although the evidence is slim and hardly definitive, there is little to suggest that migration into Exeter slowed much before the onslaught of the Black Death in 1348–9. Entries to the freedom of the city were higher in the half century before the Black Death than at any other time in the middle ages (Table 3.2). Increased levels of sales and consumption in Exeter's local markets were evident in the almost doubling of the town customs on the sale of fish between 1304 and 1348; customs from the sale of ale, bread, and other goods also increased during this period.[28] While the amount collected from the meat custom actually declined in the early fourteenth century, this trend may indicate decreased urban meat consumption in the face of rising pressure on arable production at the expense of livestock husbandry. For Exeter, as has been shown recently from an entirely different type of record for Norwich, urban demographic expansion, fed largely by migration,

[26] These patterns are discussed in Chapters 6 and 7, below, and mapped in Postles 1994: Figures 2, 4, 21.

[27] McClure 1979: 174.

[28] CRA passim; those for 1304–35 are printed in *Receiver's accounts*. Customs figures for years when the CRA do not survive were drawn from sales of customs farms noted in the MCR (usually mm. 1d–2d).

probably continued well into the first half of the fourteenth century.[29]

The Black Death, however, considerably reduced the population of mid-fourteenth-century Exeter. Clerical mortality in Devon was over 60 per cent, and in Exeter itself about 50 per cent of the parochial clergy died.[30] Lay mortality in Exeter was at least 30 per cent and perhaps considerably higher. The number of testaments recorded in the mayor's court rolls, which had averaged only four per year in the 1330s and 1340s, shot up to fifty five in 1348/9. At least five extra elections had to be held that year to replace a recently deceased mayor, steward, two coroners, and three bailiffs.[31] Five of the city's ten major bakers disappeared from the regular enrollments of the assize of bread and there was a 30 per cent drop in the number of people who brewed.[32] Pleas recorded in the mayor's court slowed to a trickle, vast numbers of rents, fines, and court amercements were noted as uncollectable, city officials were only paid for part of the year, and the town customs collected that year fell by over two-thirds.[33] When another plague hit the city in 1361 the effects were less severe but still noticeable. Clerical mortality averaged just under 27 per cent in this second plague, business in the mayor's court slowed once again and the provosts' court was suspended "on account of the pestilence."[34]

The plague left Exeter with two long-term problems: vacant tenements and a consistent shortage of labor. The late fourteenth-century account rolls of the city and other institutional landowners such as Exe Bridge, the dean and chapter, and the vicars choral, listed many defective rents or rents which had to be "allowed" because of unoccupied tenements. Shops and tenements in the suburbs constituted the bulk of vacant properties although some plots of pasture also went unused "because no one buys it." In this regard, Exeter was no different than other provincial towns that struggled with a slumping property market in the late middle ages.[35] Labor shortages were also troublesome. Throughout

[29] Rutledge 1988.

[30] Gasquet 1908: 100–3, 199–200; Pickard 1947: 25–6.

[31] MCR 1348/9, mm. 14d, 15d, 32d, 35d, 38d, 41.

[32] For bakers, see: MCR 1348/49, mm. 3d, 7d, 16d, 22d, 24d, 29d, 37d, 39d, 46d, 47d; 1349/50, mm. 3d, 12d, 52d. For brewers, see MT 1348–49; there were 222 brewers in 1348 but only 153 in 1349 and 151 in 1350.

[33] CRA 1348/9; Rowe and Draisey 1989: xxii.

[34] Pickard 1947: 27–8; MCR 1360/1, m. 48. Superscripts of *obiit* also appeared more often over people's names in the mayor's tourn and fifteen wills were recorded in MCR 1361/2 compared to what had previously been a yearly average of fewer than three.

[35] For example, Butcher 1979b. City rents were noted in the CRA, those of Exe Bridge in the EBW, the manor of Duryard in DRA, the dean and chapter in ECL D&C 5150–56, the vicars choral in ECL V/C 3331, 22282, and the chapel of Clyst St Gabriel in W1258/G3/11.

most of the 1350s, proceedings under the Statute of Laborers surfaced in the mayor's court, and individual suits brought by employers against servants, apprentices, or those who lured them away became a regular feature of the late fourteenth-century courts.[36]

The demand for labor in late medieval Exeter, however, did not go unheeded in the surrounding countryside. The jurors of the manor of Pinhoe, only a few miles north of the city, specifically noted in 1390/1 that several villeins had fled to Exeter.[37] When representatives of the dean and chapter visited their rural manors in 1381, residents in those manors closest to Exeter (such as Stoke Canon and Ide) vociferously complained about the unsanctioned departure of villeins to Exeter.[38] With its solid industrial base in cloth and leather, large service sector, and busy construction industry, Exeter must have attracted many peasants to the city in search of economic opportunity.[39] The regular entry to the fifteenth-century freedom by young apprentices from Cornish towns, Plymouth, Dartmouth, and Barnstaple, as well as from such surrounding rural villages as Kenn, Hennock, and Colaton Raleigh, also testifies to the wide appeal of work in Exeter.[40] Immigration to Exeter was so plentiful in the fifteenth century that Exeter grew from a town of slightly over 3,000 residents in 1377 to about 7,000 in the 1520s, rising from the twenty-first to perhaps the fourth largest provincial town in England.[41] Much of this demographic growth probably took place in the middle and later decades of the fifteenth century, a period normally characterized by urban historians as one of decline.[42] No other provincial city in England grew so fast in the fifteenth century.

The urban property market in late medieval Exeter also betrays little evidence of urban crisis after the initial adjustment to the population decline that immediately followed the plague. Despite the vacant tenements listed in account rolls, most institutional landowners embarked on new building programs and spent large sums maintaining their older properties. The wardens of Exe Bridge, for example, built a large new

[36] See in particular the dorses of MCR 1352/3.

[37] PRO SC2/168/1, m. 12.

[38] ECL D&C 2857.

[39] See Chapter 4, below, for the city's industrial and service sectors. For female immigrants, see Kowaleski 1986: 153–4. For similar immigration to Canterbury, see Butcher 1984: 93–9. See also Postles 1994: 253, 258–63 on this point.

[40] *Exeter freemen*: 41–61 passim.

[41] For estimates of 8,000, see Hoskins 1963a: 72 MacCaffrey 1975: 11. Dyer 1991: 72, estimates a population of only 6,825 for this period.

[42] The town population was clearly much bigger by 1489 when a partial list of those paying the tenth (*Tudor Exeter tax assessments*: 1–5) included 450 taxpayers compared to the 420 listed in the murage tax of 1377, a tax that cast a far bigger net than the tenth of 1489; see Rowe 1977 for the 1489 tax and below, Appendix 3, for the 1377 tax.

house and two new shops on the bridge in the 1360s, while the city receiver spent more than £10 on a new row of shops at Bolehill Street in 1358/9 and over £11 on rebuilding the town's meat market, called the Fleshfold, in 1380/1.[43] These substantial investments by the city, along with the enormous sums spent upgrading the town's defences from the 1360s through 1420s (over £200 alone in 1402–6) indicate a city able to meet its financial obligations with little difficulty.[44] The construction of new mills also points to a growth in industrial investment. New corn mills were constructed in 1364/5 in the western suburb at Crikelpit and two new fulling mills were built in the northern suburb of Duryard in 1390/1.[45] Estate owners in the neighborhood made similar investments; the lord of the western suburb of Exe Island constructed two new houses, a new corn mill, and at least one new fulling mill sometime in the first two decades of the fifteenth century.[46]

It appears that from 1350 to the 1410s Exeter made a surprisingly easy adjustment to the demographic devastation of the plague and its early recurrences. The population decline, reflected in labor shortages and empty tenements, was not paralleled by decline in the city's prosperity. Indeed, Exeter enjoyed a kind of commercial boom during this period. Although wine imports were severely curtailed by disruptions in the wine-producing regions and on the high seas during the Hundred Years War, the annual average number of ships visiting Exeter's port remained relatively steady and increased greatly from the 1390s (Table 3.2). Town revenues from the St Nicholas fair soared, reaching a peak of over £7 in 1376 and averaging just under £5 in the 1390s. Profits from the new Lenten fair founded in 1374 also grew quickly during this period, amounting to over £5 in its peak year of 1399.[47] The city governors started two more new fairs in 1404 and 1405; both were successes, lasting well into the sixteenth century. Town customs from the sale of meat, fish, bread, and ale also rose during the late fourteenth and early fifteenth centuries.[48] Particularly noticeable was the rise in

43 EBW 1361/2–1363/4; CRA 1358/9, 1359/60, 1380/1. For a new house built in the 1390s by the dean and chapter in the High Street, see D&C 3550, f. 94v.

44 CRA passim; Misc. Roll 6. See also Juddery, Staniforth, and Stoyle 1989 for an account of the enormous expenditures on the city defences from the 1360s through 1420s.

45 EBW 1364/5; DRA 1390/1. The city also built new corn mills at Duryard in the early 1370s after the old ones burned down; DRA 1370/1 *et seq.*

46 PRO SC6/1118/6; in 1388 there were only two mills there; see PRO CP40/509, m. 438.

47 CRA passim. See also above, pp. 60–8 for these fairs.

48 CRA passim and MCR, m. 1–2 passim. These customs were farmed every year, presumably to the highest bidder, so they offer a rough indication of the expectation of profits from commerce. Although there were fluctuations from year to year, the trend was

the tolls collected on the sale of ale (brewgavel) from unenfranchised brewers (many probably recent immigrants) and the increasing number of brewers fined for breaking the assize of ale or selling drink (Table 3.2). The number of those fined for brewing and selling ale was actually slightly higher in the late fourteenth century than before the plague when the population of Exeter was certainly larger.[49] This suggests that rising consumption fueled the brewing industry in the late fourteenth century; either people were drinking more (rising living standards), or there were more people (population growth), or both.[50]

These signs of economic recovery and commercial prosperity in Exeter are similar to those found in other late fourteenth-century towns.[51] By the second decade of the fifteenth century, however, indications of decline and strain became evident in almost all English towns, a decline which worsened in many cities as the century wore on. To one degree or another, falling or stagnating populations, widespread epidemics, dwindling urban revenues, difficulties meeting payments on the city farm, petitions from townspeople claiming poverty, reduced urban building programs, and a weak property market characterized English towns in the fifteenth century.[52] Exeter residents did not entirely escape the woes that beset so many other English towns in this period. The difficulties of the 1420s and 1430s are evident in the decline of marketing fines for the sale of ale and drink, a fall in wine imports, and setbacks in the export of cloth (Table 3.2).[53]

generally upward, particularly for fish (see below, pp. 311–12). From the mid-fifteenth century, however, the farms of customs are less useful as indices of economic trends since some were farmed for a term of years or left in the hands of the city receiver.

[49] From the 1300s through 1340s, there was an annual average of 188 brewers although in some years (1319) over 250 different brewers were named. From the 1370s through 1390s, the average was 193 and reached as high as 230 in some years (MT passim). These figures should be treated cautiously, however, since the variable wording of the presentments before the 1350s and the practice of noting the suburban populations in separate tourns for some of these early years make direct comparisons difficult. For similar trends among sellers of ale, see Table 3.2.

[50] See Britnell 1986b: 88–91 for Colchester where the number of ale brewers had doubled by 1405 when compared to the pre-plague period. See also pp. 193–203 for his comments on the use of brewing statistics as evidence of economic and demographic change.

[51] For this and the following, see Britnell 1986b: 159–60, for Colchester and references to similar trends in Coventry, Norwich, Salisbury, and York; Holt 1985, for Gloucester; Keene 1985: 86–105, 299–318 for Winchester; and Palliser 1988 and Dyer 1991 for recent summaries.

[52] N. 51, above. For arguments to the contrary, see Bridbury 1975.

[53] Note that the marketing fines for ale and drink were affected by the introduction of beer (which cut into the market for ale), and by administrative changes in the MT when the city lost jurisdiction over its eastern suburb owned by the dean and chapter (Curtis 1932). The institutional decline of the MT (which disappeared altogether in 1460) was also responsible for the decreasing number of marketing fines in the 1450s.

But the degree of difficulties experienced by Exeter inhabitants in the first half of the fifteenth century was relatively mild; there was little contraction in the hosteling business, the number of ships visiting the port remained steady in the early fifteenth century and shot up tremendously in the 1440s, and cloth exports increased substantially by the early 1430s (Table 3.2). Revenues from the three new fairs, although modest, also rose in value, with the biggest increases coming after the 1440s.[54] In 1463 the city felt confident enough to acquire another new fair which also survived into the next century. The aggressive course pursued by the city through the 1440s to bring under its control the separate jurisdictional fees owned by the dean and chapter and by the bishop may also be considered an expression of an assured and relatively prosperous city.[55] Although largely unsuccessful, the lengthy and expensive litigation in which Exeter engaged for this purpose was not characteristic of towns in deep economic crisis.

Another indication of the healthy state of Exeter's economy was the city's ability to meet its financial obligations to the Crown and other creditors throughout the fifteenth century. Despite the heavy drains on the municipal budget (occasioned by the city's dispute with the cathedral authorities in the 1440s, payments in the 1450s to the rival gentry factions of the Courtenays and Bonvilles, legal fees and other expenses in the continuous conflicts with the Tailors Guild from the late 1460s on, and the royal visit by Richard III in 1483) Exeter almost always managed to balance its budget.[56] In the middle and late decades of the fifteenth century the city also invested in a series of expensive building projects, including work on the conduits for the underground water system in 1441 and 1461 and extensive rebuilding of parts of the Guildhall in the late 1460s and mid 1480s.[57] And unlike many other English cities during this time, Exeter did not regularly beg for tax relief or seek reductions on its fee farm. Besides paying a much lower fee farm (£45) than other large cities, Exeter also consistently paid less

Wine imports were also probably affected more by wartime disruptions in the supplying regions than by declining demand or financial difficulties in Exeter.

54 CRA passim. See above, pp. 67–8 for these fair profits and the low tolls or absence of tolls charged there to attract visitors.

55 Curtis 1932.

56 CRA passim. For more on these various expenses, see Curtis 1932, esp. 62–71; Cherry 1981; Radford 1903, 1912; and pp. 100–1 below for the disputes with the Tailors Guild.

57 Misc. Roll 7; Morris 1932; Blaylock 1990; Stoyle, Juddery, and Staniforth forthcoming.

Table 3.2. *Indices of economic trends in medieval Exeter (in decennial averages)*

Years	Marketing fines for selling:[a] 1. Ale	2. Drink	3. Oats	Freedom entries[b]	No. of ships docking[c]	Wine imports[d] (in tuns)	Cloth exports[e] (cloth of assize)
1300–09	187 (4)			15.7	47 (3)	1,275 (3)	
1310–19	194 (4)			17.6	47 (7)	865 (7)	
1320–29	238 (2)			11.7	50 (8)	1,181 (7)	
1330–39	177 (9)			16.4	56 (8)	1,031 (8)	
1340–49	186 (9)			19.8	53+ (8)	968 (7)	
1350–59	151 (1)	166 (4)		5.0	50 (6)	663 (6)	647 (6)
1360–69	140 (4)	169 (9)	32 (1)	6.5	41 (7)	522 (7)	913 (10)
1370–79	167 (8)	169 (8)	35 (8)	6.6	43 (3)	313 (3)	1,262 (2)
1380–89	205 (10)	216 (10)	52 (10)	7.6	32 (9)	481 (9)	– –
1390–99	208 (10)	237 (10)	72 (10)	6.6	75 (9)	795 (9)	304 (7)
1400–09	162 (10)	247 (10)	79 (10)	7.9	84 (10)	545 (10)	303 (10)
1410–19	130 (10)	258 (10)	92 (10)	11.7	80 (10)	573 (10)	457 (10)
1420–29	112 (5)	203 (5)	86 (5)	19.7	71 (9)	475 (9)	367 (10)
1430–39	111 (5)	210 (6)	97 (6)	8.2	73 (3)	408 (3)	998 (10)
1440–49	85 (5)	205 (7)	93 (7)	5.3	113 (4)	460 (4)	1,868 (10)
1450–59	67 (2)	165 (3)	74 (10)	12.0	114 (5)	321 (5)	1,146 (10)
1460–69				8.3	129 (6)	426 (6)	1,017 (10)
1470–79				9.3	122 (5)	453 (4)	1,323 (9)
1480–89				11.9	116 (6)		2,926 (10)
1490–99				14.5	133 (5)		3,474 (10)
1500–09				11.6	126 (4)		8,479 (10)

Sources and notes: Figures in round brackets represent number of years with extant data.
[a]MT 1303–1459; the totals generally include all areas of the city except the suburb outside the west gate; only sellers actually found liable were counted. All three sets of "fines" were essentially licensing fees to carry on these retailing activities. Although the MT survive for almost every year before the 1420s, the variable wording of the presentments or incomplete tourns for certain quarters means that complete data are not always available. By the late 1440s the MT was in decline; the last MT was held in 1459. *Column 1:* fines for brewing and selling ale against the assize. From 1351 to 1364 ale brewers were not distinguished from sellers of drink. The drop in brewing fines in the fifteenth century was partly due to the introduction of beer (which was excluded from the fines). *Column 2:* fines for selling ale, cider, mead, wine, and other liquors in false measures. *Column 3:* fines for selling oats in hostels (inns) in false measures: paid annually by all hostelers in the city.

[b]*Exeter freemen:* 1–65. Data extant for every year except 1383/4. Entries for 1300–19 and some plague years (1348–50) were probably under-recorded.

[c]PCA 1302–1508.

[d]PCA 1302–1480. Wine imports for subsequent years remain to be counted.

[e]Carus-Wilson and Coleman 1963: 75–113. Up to 1405, the Exeter customs jurisdiction included all of Devon and Cornwall; thereafter Plymouth and Cornwall were noted separately. The Exeter customs were farmed from 1372–90. See Table 1.1 and pp. 20–1 above for the customs fraud and other problems in this period that make the export figures for the 1370s–1390s suspiciously low.

to the Crown in the form of loans and other debts than towns of similar standing – towns which, unlike Exeter, were experiencing demographic loss and economic difficulties.[58] Exeter had fewer obligations and met them easily.

Much of Exeter's fifteenth-century prosperity was based on its expanding cloth industry, particularly in cloth-finishing. New fulling mills were built outside the western gate at Crikelpit in 1452/3 and rents from the "rakkys" where cloth hung to dry became an increasingly important item in city accounts.[59] Fulling mills were also constructed in nearby manors, such as Ide, Stoke Canon, and Exe Island, all within one mile of the city.[60] Shearing and dyeing were also important finishing industries in Exeter.[61] The city's growing reliance on the textile trades is evident in the appearance of formal craft organizations in the fifteenth century. Although the Cordwainers, Skinners, Bakers, and Smiths all possessed some sort of craft organization before the 1430s,[62] it was the two cloth guilds of the Tailors and the Weavers, Tuckers (fullers) and Shearmen that became most prominent in the city. The Tailors were the only guild strong enough to challenge the entrenched city oligarchy; in 1466 they went over the head of the city authorities when they acquired a royal charter of incorporation by letters patent.[63] Their attempt to bypass city control led to almost twenty years of acrimonious litigation and disputes, sometimes violent, which only ended in 1482 when the city managed to have the charter annulled. The ability of the Tailors to carry on this challenge reflected the successes of the local cloth trade; the guild was largely made up of wealthy merchant tailors and drapers whose profits in this period of rapidly expanding cloth exports surely helped fuel their ambitions. The Weavers, Tuckers, and Shearmen also established a guild sometime before 1460 when their dispute with the Cordwainers over precedence in city processions was settled by the city governors.[64] In 1471 the guild acquired the site

[58] Attreed 1984: Tables 5–11c shows Exeter's healthier fiscal position compared to Norwich, Nottingham, and York in the fifteenth century.

[59] EBW 1452/3; for the racks, see EBW 1470/1 on, and Carus-Wilson 1963: 22–3. For tenter racks in private hands, see Fox 1986. For racks rented in Exe Island, see PRO SC6/1118/6.

[60] ECL D&C 3550, f. 92v; DD 5139. For the four fulling mills in the western suburb of Exe Island in 1422/3, see PRO SC6/1118/6. For the proliferation of fulling mills in fifteenth-century Devon, see Fox forthcoming.

[61] Carus-Wilson 1963: 22–3; Youings 1968.

[62] See below, pp. 99–100.

[63] For this and the following, see *English gilds*: 299–330; Green 1894: II, 167–89; Rose-Troup 1912: 422–7.

[64] MCR 1459/60, m. 29d. Exeter's sixteenth-century town chamberlain declared the Weavers and Tuckers the "more auncient" craft; see Youings 1968: 9–17 for this and the following. For their ordinances, which date from 1483, see Youings 1970.

where even today stands Tucker's Hall, a lasting monument to the influence and prosperity of this group of artisans and cloth dealers.

The emergence of prominent cloth guilds in fifteenth-century Exeter also reflected the rapid expansion of the regional cloth industry. The port customs accounts show how the dramatic rise in cloth exports from Devon contributed crucially to the prosperity of fifteenth-century Exeter. Devon cloth exports registered at the customs headport of Exeter mounted significantly in the 1430s and 1440s; the pace slowed in the 1460s through mid 1470s, but thereafter there was spectacular growth into the sixteenth century (Table 3.2). Exporting a cheaper and lightweight woollen cloth popular among the wage-earners and artisans whose buying power had increased in the labor-short decades of the late middle ages, Devon ports increased their cloth exports more than tenfold over the course of the fifteenth century. As the headport for the county, much of this increase was channelled through Exeter.[65] Local Exeter and Devon merchants, moreover, retained control of the bulk of this trade; up until the 1480s, only 10 per cent or less of the county's cloth exports was handled by alien merchants.[66]

The county's economic growth was also reflected in the rising number of wine imports handled by Devon ports, their triumph over the east coast ports as centers of the fishing industry, and their increasing share of the tin export trade, particularly in the last three decades of the fifteenth century.[67] These trends in overseas trade were paralleled by developments in the coastal trade which provide, it might be argued, an even more sensitive gauge of the city's fortunes. The average number of ships that carried goods to Exeter rose dramatically in the 1390s, fell slightly in the 1420s, then rose steadily again to the end of the century with some setbacks in the 1480s (Table 3.2). By the 1490s, an average of over 130 ships docked at Exeter each year compared to an annual average of about forty in the four decades after the Black Death.

The striking appreciation in Exeter's maritime trade was due primarily to the remarkable expansion of the cloth industry in south-western England. Although Exeter shared in this manufacturing boom, particularly in its cloth-finishing industry, it was the city's role as the regional market center of Devon and much of south-western England that really must be emphasized. Exeter's fifteenth-century prosperity can only be understood when placed in the context of developments in its surround-

[65] Carus-Wilson 1963: 11, n. 11; Childs 1992.

[66] Hoskins 1952: 244; Carus-Wilson 1963: 16, especially n. 20; Child 1992: 85–6.

[67] James 1971: 99–104, for wine; Hatcher 1973: 174–93, for tin; Litler 1979: 230–6, 245–8, for fish; see also below, pp. 235–8 for a longer discussion of trends in maritime trade, and pp. 310–12 for the fish trade.

ing regions, particularly in its hinterland. The burgeoning cloth industries of small towns such as Cullompton and Tiverton in east Devon and Taunton and other places in western Somerset employed Exeter as an export and marketing center.[68] Other industrial and agricultural developments in Devon during this period, such as the expansion of the Dartmoor tin industry and trade and growing agricultural specialization (especially pastoral husbandry) also promoted regional prosperity and prompted commercial growth in the county's chief inland entrepôt.[69] The debate over the nature and extent of the "urban crisis" of the late middle ages could profit by turning more attention to regional developments in urban hinterlands, rather than focusing so much on the internal urban developments that currently dominate the issue.

Government and the merchant oligarchy

Little is known about the governing structure of Exeter during the prosperous years of the tenth and eleventh centuries. An Anglo-Saxon guild was active during this time, but its functions were primarily religious and social.[70] By the twelfth century there was a merchant guild in Exeter, governed by stewards who also controlled the considerable revenues from the city's manor of Duryard outside the northern town wall.[71] Only members of the guild could trade in Exeter or its suburbs; they were also exempt from tolls and customs throughout England and Normandy, and enjoyed all the liberties accorded to London's citizens. The functions of this merchant guild were probably absorbed by the expanding civic institutions of the thirteenth century. By 1205 the office of mayor had been introduced into Exeter and soon after the merchant guild's monopoly on trade had been assumed by the organization of the "freedom" or "liberty" of the city.[72]

[68] Carus-Wilson 1963. For a more extended discussion of how regional developments affected Exeter's trade, see below, Chapters 6 and 7.

[69] See above, Chapter 1, for these developments.

[70] *Diplomatarium anglicum aevi saxonici*: 613–14; Brentano 1870: xviii; Gross 1890: I, 181–3.

[71] The earliest reference to the guild occurs in 1179/80 (*Pipe roll*, vol. 29: 93) although a grant of 1141 referred to "our steward" in connection with Duryard (Easterling 1931: xvii–xviii, and 1938: 464–5). The "Gilthalla" was first mentioned c. 1160 (Parry 1936: 1). For the 1228/9 charter confirming the merchant guild's privileges, see BL Cotton Claudius D, ii, 131, f. 134.

[72] Easterling 1938: 466; Rowe and Cochlin 1964: v–vii. The merchant guild was last mentioned in the confirmation charter of 1228/9 (above, n. 71); a similar confirmation charter of 1300 (BL Cotton Claudius D, ii, 131, ff. 129–132v) omits any mention of the merchant guild. The freedom organization was fully operational by c. 1240 when Exeter's custumal was composed; see *Anglo-norman custumal*: 26, 29, 31, 33–5.

Access to civic power in medieval Exeter was determined first and foremost by admission to the freedom of the city. Only members of this exclusive group were full-fledged citizens and could vote or stand for high city office. In addition to political perquisites, freedom members received numerous economic privileges, chief among them the right to trade at retail.[73] These privileges, detailed in the Anglo-Norman custumal of Exeter compiled around 1240, also included exemptions from market tolls in Exeter and other English towns, as well as monopolies in the cloth, wool, and woad trades, and in all trade in merchandise sold "by weight" or "by measure," except for victuals. Freedom members also enjoyed pledging and essoin rights within the local courts. Compared to similar freedom organizations in other provincial towns, Exeter's freedom was highly selective; no more than 21 per cent of all householders and a mere 4 per cent of the total population of Exeter in 1377 actually belonged to this privileged group.[74] Eventually some 34 per cent of the householders in 1377 joined the freedom but this figure was still significantly lower than the roughly 54 per cent of York householders in 1377 who became members of that city's freedom.[75]

Entry into the freedom could be gained in a variety of ways: by patronage, patrimony, fine, gift, service, and apprenticeship. In the thirteenth century, admittance by patronage, "at the instance of" particular individuals whom the city wished to reward, was by far the most common means of entry, followed by patrimony, whereby men inherited the place of their fathers or male next-of-kin (Table 3.3). Both these types of admission, along with that by gift (when the mayor and/or community in their corporate capacity bestowed admission), declined in the fourteenth century as entry into the Exeter freedom became increasingly restricted. By the mid-fourteenth century, admittance by patrimony or succession was limited to the eldest son.[76] Younger sons enlisted either by apprenticeship or upon payment of a fine. Concern about the excessive number of freedom members was probably the impetus behind the restriction on the number of sons and male kin entering by succession.

[73] *Anglo-Norman custumal of Exeter*; Rowe and Jackson 1973.

[74] The figure drops to less than 20 per cent if the unidentified households in Exe Island in 1377 are included; see Appendix 3, pp. 373–4. For other freedom organizations, see Goldberg 1992: 53–4; Veale 1933: 21–4 (Bristol); Britnell 1986b: 36 (Colchester); Hill 1965: 302–3 (Lincoln); Hudson and Tingey 1910: II, xxxiii–xxxix (Norwich); Dobson 1973: 1–22 and Swanson 1989: 108–10 (York); Woodward 1970: 89–95.

[75] For York: Legett 1972: 130; for Exeter, see Table A3.1, below.

[76] Rowe and Jackson 1973: xiv; see also MCR 1334/5, m. 38d for the city's efforts to limit membership to only one male heir.

Table 3.3 *Entries to the freedom of Exeter, 1284–1499*

	Percentage entering in:				
Type of entry	1284–99	1300–49	1350–99	1400–49	1450–99
Patronage	45	29	2	½	¼
Patrimony	23	17	7	4	3½
Fine	16	44	77	75	45
Gift	14	9	5	2½	4
Service	–	1	½	1	¼
Apprenticeship	–	–	8	17	25
Unidentified	2	–	½	–	22
Total	100	100	100	100	100
Total no.	185	809	313	532	567

Source: Exeter freemen: 1–63. Entries by patronage were granted "at the instance of" named individuals; on occasion these individuals were being rewarded for services to the city. Entries by gift were granted by the mayor and/or community in a corporate capacity. Either type of entry could entail payment of a fine although many of the fines were waived in full or in part. Most of the "Unidentified" entries in 1450–99 were probably made by fine. This table replaces that in Kowaleski 1984: 357.

Complaints also arose in the 1340s regarding the number and quality of men admitted.[77] The greatest outcry centered on the practice of nominating candidates "at the instance of" prominent men who were often subsequently rewarded for their patronage. In 1308, for example, Walter Tauntefer, a one-time mayor of Exeter, received £3 for sponsoring Thomas de Rewe's application for membership.[78] Another widespread patronage custom was to admit men at the request of influential outsiders, such as the countess of Devon, bishop of Exeter, and members of the local gentry.[79] The city also gave freedom membership to certain individuals at reduced rates or free of charge, while allowing others to nominate a candidate in return for service they had rendered the city. Most of these practices were halted in response to the complaints of the 1340s; regulations passed in 1345 required the consent of the council of twelve before anyone was admitted by patronage or by fine. As a result, entry by patronage practically ceased after 1345, while the number of men admitted by "gift" also dropped (Table 3.3). But the "reforms" of the 1340s also worked to give the

77 For the text of the complaints, see Wilkinson 1931: 71–4.
78 Rowe and Jackson 1973: xv.
79 *Exeter freemen*: 1–27, passim, for this and the following.

town's ruling elite more control over who was admitted because the agreement of a majority of the council of twelve was necessary to admit new members.[80] Income minimums were set for those seeking the highest offices and future mayors were required to have served for at least a year as a steward of the city. Those disagreeing with these and similar ordinances were deemed to be "rebels and enemies of the city," liable for expulsion from the freedom or made ineligible for office. In this way the higher ranking members of the town administration solidified their control over both entry into the freedom and the governing of the town.

As a result of these restrictions, the number of men admitted to the freedom fell. In 1339–41 an average of twenty seven men per year entered; in 1342–7 this figure was almost halved, to thirteen entrants per year.[81] In the first half of the fourteenth century, the number of men admitted to the freedom was two and one-half times the number who entered in the second half of the century (Table 3.3). Declining population, indicated in the reduction in the number of men entering by patrimony after the Black Death, was partially responsible for the decrease in freedom entrants. Yet the restriction on the number of sons entering the freedom by succession remained, although the citizenry was obviously experiencing difficulties replacing itself after the damage wrought by the plague. Nor did the increasingly powerful council of twelve show any desire to welcome more entrants to make up for the reduced ranks of the freedom; the annual average of entrants in the six decades following the Black Death never rose above eight men although immigration to the city must still have been plentiful (Table 3.2). Few of the immigrants, however, were likely to possess the financial resources or status the elite believed necessary to gain admittance to this exclusive organization.[82] It is also unlikely that eligible men eschewed membership because of the price of admission or a decline in the value of the freedom privileges. When the city needed to raise funds to meet extraordinary expenditures, for example, it suddenly

[80] Wilkinson 1931: 71–3; Rowe and Jackson 1973: xv–xvii.

[81] *Exeter freemen*: 24–8. The high figure for entrants in the 1340s (Table 3.2) was also due to the sixty three men admitted in 1348–9; this jump in admissions obviously reflected an effort to replace members lost during the Black Death. Under-recording of admissions was mostly a problem before the 1320s and during plague years; see Rowe and Jackson 1973: xvii, and below, Table A3.1 for the relatively low number of missed entries discovered among the householders of 1377.

[82] Entry fines ranged from £1 to £5; almost 75 per cent of entrants paid £1. The higher fees were assessed on wealthy individuals and those from outside of Exeter; see *Citie of Excester*: 788–9. Presumably those immigrants willing to wait, establish a thriving business, and gain the respect of freedom members would be allowed entry for the lower sum.

allowed large numbers of men to enter in order to collect the admission fees, implying that there was always a large pool of applicants ready to join if allowed.[83] But the more rigid control over the selection process, combined with a reduced urban population, worked to make the freedom of late fourteenth-century Exeter an increasingly exclusive organization.

While entry by patronage, patrimony, and gift declined greatly in the second half of the fourteenth century, entry by fine and apprenticeship increased. In the hundred-year period following the Black Death, admittance by fine constituted about three-quarters of all freedom entries (Table 3.3). This situation indicates both the replacement problems of the old citizenry following the plague and the still fledgling state of the apprenticeship and craft institutions before the mid fifteenth century. Although the first recorded admission by apprenticeship only occurred in 1358 and the next did not take place until 1380, disputes and contracts enrolled in the mayor's court indicate that the practice of taking on apprentices had begun earlier.[84] But the institution was still developing in Exeter; from 1380 to 1400, only twenty five men entered the freedom via apprenticeship and most served masters who were major merchants or were politically prominent in the borough. Only after the last decade of the fourteenth century, when the practice had become established, did apprentices serving artisans regularly enter the freedom.[85] During the fifteenth century, apprenticeship became more common, accounting for at least one-quarter of all freedom entries by the end of the middle ages.

The slow development of apprenticeship and the craft guilds in Exeter was probably a product of the tremendous civic power vested in the town's freedom and its members' desire to restrict competition from rivals. Throughout the fourteenth and early fifteenth centuries there were only hints of loose craft affiliations. In 1329, for example, glovers were accused of making certain agreements among themselves and contributing to a common fund for burials and other such things.[86] In

[83] For example, the twenty nine admissions in August–September 1378 and seventeen in November 1380 were probably linked to massive expenditures on the city defences; see Misc. Rolls 6, 79; CRA 1376/7–1379/80. The high numbers admitted in the 1420s were probably due to particularly high expenditures on the construction of new shops and the lawsuit against the dean and chapter; Rowe and Jackson 1973: xvii.

[84] For early references to apprentices, see MCR 1309/10, m. 23; 1352/3, m. 50d; 1361/2, mm. 7, 8, 27; 1363/4, m. 3d; 1364/5, m. 29d. Few of these apprentices were ever mentioned again in the records so perhaps they died or left Exeter before their terms were up. For the high rate of attrition among apprenticeships even in a later period when the institution was more secure, see Rappaport 1991: 253–9.

[85] See below, pp. 169–70.

[86] MCR 1328/9, m. 44d. The glovers were not formally incorporated until 1560; see *Citie of Excester*: 892.

1352 Bishop Grandisson railed against the wanton behavior of townspeople towards the shoemakers' craft (whose high prices had raised the ire of the citizenry).[87] By 1413, crafts like the skinners were organized enough to take responsibility for specific pageants within the annual Corpus Christi play.[88] The skinners' sense of solidarity was also evident in their lease of the charnel chapel for religious services in 1426–31, although they were not formally incorporated until 1462.[89] Trade conspiracies among the "*Arte de Bakers crafte*" also points to some organization among the bakers even though their guild ordinances were not formally enrolled until 1483.[90] Other groups elected wardens or *custodes* well before they were formally recognized as craft guilds. The earliest such wardens were the butchers elected to supervise the town's meat market (the Fleshfold) in 1384.[91] By 1387 the shoemakers and tanners were electing two wardens; the smiths were doing the same by 1410.[92] All those chosen to fill these offices acted at the sufferance of the mayor and councillors; their duties rarely extended beyond the surveillance of quality and price control, tasks the oligarchic clique in power was probably quite happy to hand over.[93]

The efforts of Exeter's ruling elite to keep a tight grip on craft associations was particularly evident in the city's long-running dispute with the Tailors Guild, the wealthiest and most powerful of the craft groups in Exeter. When the Tailors bypassed the city authorities in 1466 by acquiring a charter of incorporation from the king, the mayor and council fought vigorously for almost two decades to have the charter annulled. They eventually succeeded, and the Tailors, like all the other craft guilds that received formal recognition from the 1480s on, had to recognize the ultimate superiority of the mayor and council over the

87 *Reg. Grandisson*, vol. 2: 1120; see also Wassom (ed.) 1986 (*Devon*): 11–12, 323–5, 439–40.

88 MCR 1413/14, m. 38d (printed in Wassom [ed. 1986, *Devon*]: 82–3, 357–8; see also pp. 106–10 for extracts from the CRA concerning payments to the skinners for this play).

89 Orme 1991: 166; Rose-Troup 1912: 421–2.

90 MCR 1428/9, m. 13; Book 51, ff. 303, 482v; *English gilds*: 333–7; see also below, pp. 140–1.

91 MCR 1384/5, m. 2d and below, p. 188, n. 45 for the butchers' reluctance to fill this position. See also below, Chapter 5, n. 61 for supervisors of the sale of fish, meat, poultry, and woad appointed in the early fourteenth century; their duties, however, seem to have involved mainly the collection of toll for the city.

92 MCR 1387/8, m. 9d; 1410/11, m. 2. The reference to the *custodes sutorum et frunctorum* was probably the source of Hooker's oft-quoted comment that the cordwainers were the first guild to "incorporate" in Exeter (Book 51, f. 290).

93 The early gild ordinances also illustrate the limited purview of the craft officers; see *English gilds*: 299–37.

guild leadership.[94] The late-fifteenth-century guilds in Exeter were required to seek justice in the mayor's court, to split fines with the city, and even, in one case, to surrender all the powers of the guild to the city authorities once a year, receiving these rights back only upon payment of a fine.[95] By such means the ruling elite retained ultimate political and economic control in Exeter.

The ruling elite exerted power through a mayor assisted by four stewards, one of whom was the town receiver and, as such, was responsible for the city's annual accounts.[96] The mayor presided over the main borough court (the mayor's court), while the stewards oversaw the provosts' court which primarily heard pleas of debt. The so-called "common" council of twelve of the "better and more discreet men" or *meliores* of the borough advised the mayor on all important business.[97] Originally the council had been designed to check the abuses of the mayor and stewards, but, in practice, the members of the common council came from the same pool of wealthy citizens as did the mayor and stewards and the interests of both groups were identical. Over the course of the fourteenth and fifteenth centuries, the power of the council grew considerably. Besides controlling freedom admissions, the council also had to give its consent before any bonds, letters of pension, or acquittances were to be sealed by the city.[98]

Re-elected year after year, the eighteen men who held the highest ranking offices in late fourteenth-century Exeter (mayor, four stewards, recorder or town lawyer, and twelve councilors – hereafter called Rank A) made up less than 1 per cent of the city's total population. In 1377, only 6 per cent of the city's 525 known householders had ever held one of these powerful positions (Table 3.4). These men were distinguished not only by their political power, but also by their wealth. None would have failed to meet the income minimum for a mayoral

[94] This conflict is described in some detail in Green 1894: II, 167–89. See also *English gilds*: 299–330; Rose-Troup 1912: 422–7.

[95] *English gilds*: 299–337; Youings 1970. The evidence concerning Exeter's guilds supports the argument of Swanson (1988) regarding the ultimate power of urban mercantile elites over craft guilds. For the tendency of sixteenth- and seventeenth-century guild members to opt out of freedom membership, see Rowe and Jackson 1973: xxiii–xxv.

[96] For the early history of Exeter's town government, see Easterling 1931; and Wilkinson 1931; *Citie of Excester*: 801–45.

[97] Along with Bristol, Exeter possessed the first recorded common council in medieval England (Tait 1936: 330–3). The ordinances of 1345 permanently established the council in Exeter but such a group had appeared sporadically from the 1260s on. For this and the following, see Easterling 1931; Wilkinson 1931; and Misc. Roll 2, no. 54.

[98] In the late 1430s and early 1450s there were (ultimately unsuccessful) attempts by the larger body of the freedom to make the common council share some power with representatives of the "community"; see Parry 1941: 42.

Table 3.4. *Political rank, commercial activity, and wealth of Exeter householders in 1377*

Political rank	Total householders (no.) %	No. in freedom (no.) %	Average murage tax	In seaborne trade (no.) %	Average no. of servants
A	(32) 6	(32) 100	53.8*d*	(24) 75	1.53
B	(34) 6	(34) 100	24.7*d*	(11) 32	1.24
C	(31) 6	(8) 26	12.4*d*	(1) 6	0.97
D	(428) 82	(38) 9	8.4*d*	(21) 5	0.61
Total	(525) 100	(112)		(58)	
Average		21	13.0*d*	11	0.73

Source: Table A3.1. All columns represent the situation in 1377 except for those on seaborne trade (from all available years) and servants (data mostly from 1370–90). Averages based on totals for each category.

candidate (100*s*-worth of property) set by the ordinances of the 1340s. In the murage roll of 1377, which taxed all heads of household according to property wealth, all but one of the eleven most highly assessed taxpayers had served as mayor, steward, or councillor.[99] In view of their tight control over the freedom and civic government, their greater wealth, and their small numbers, this group can justifiably be characterized as an oligarchy: government by the few.

The mayor, stewards, and councillors were elected annually at Michaelmas by a body of thirty six electors. These electors were chosen yearly by an elaborate selection process that favored the *meliores* or *maiores*. The first four electors, chosen from men who had already served in high office (Rank A men), nominated the remaining thirty two electors. Middling men were, however, included in this group; in 1267, for example, twelve of the electors were specifically labelled *mediocres*.[100] A comparision of the wealth and mercantile orientation of Rank A officeholders with those who never served in any office higher than elector (here termed Rank B) also shows the gap that separated the two groups. Rank B officeholders all belonged to the freedom, but their wealth, as indicated by the average murage tax they paid or the average number of servants they hired, was clearly less than that enjoyed by Rank A men (Table 3.4). Occupational standing also differed between

[99] Misc. Roll 72; see Table A3.1. The one exception was Robert Dene who served as a bridge-warden, and as an elector over twenty times, thus making him a prominent member of the B Rank oligarchy.

[100] Easterling 1931: xxiv–xxxii. See also *Citie of Excester*: 789–801 for a discussion of the election reforms of 1497 in which he cites the old way of electing city officials.

the two groups. About three-quarters of the Rank A men were merchants who regularly traded by sea, three were prominent lawyers, and only two can be identified as artisans (a skinner and a corveser). In contrast, less than one-quarter of Rank B men were merchants while almost two-thirds were wealthy artisans or hostelers. When Rank B men did engage in maritime trade (as almost a third of them did), their commercial activities were normally on a much smaller scale. It is significant, however, that four of the eight Rank B men in 1377 who eventually reached the Rank A group were merchants by occupation.[101]

Politically, the influence of Rank B citizens remained more tenuous as well. While Rank A men appeared in office year after year, sixteen of the thirty four Rank B men had only served three or fewer times in office by 1377 and nine never served more than four times during their whole career. But because Rank B men voted in the electoral process, could hold lower-level (but still influential) offices such as bridge-warden, bridge-elector, or warden of the Magdalene hospital, they had some political power and must be counted as members of the "oligarchy." This two-tiered elite may also have reduced political tensions within Exeter because it allowed substantial artisans a voice in city government and a share of civic responsibilities, as well as the possibility of movement from the lower to the higher echelons (Rank B to Rank A) of public power.[102]

Below the Rank B offices of electors and wardens were a host of minor municipal offices, such as aldermen (who in the fourteenth century were only wardsmen with few powers),[103] gatekeepers (one for each of the four gates into the city), bailiffs (four officers with police powers), and assorted market officials. Together these men formed a third group of officeholders (called Rank C) whose offices did not require freedom membership and who held no real political power because they had little say in either the city elections or the civic decision-making process. The duties of their offices were, however, often crucial to the everyday functioning of the town (notably in terms of police control) and they were thus endowed with a certain measure of civic responsibility. Rank C men occupied a middle position between the wealthier oligarchy and poorer residents who never held any civic office (Table 3.4).

101 See Table A3.1.

102 It is striking that a similar two-tiered elite existed in eighteenth-century West Country towns; see Triffit 1983.

103 In the late fourteenth century there were six aldermen, two for each of the suburbs outside the north, east, and south gates. Earlier in the century there had also been two aldermen for the western suburb but those offices disappeared when the earl of Devon asserted his rule over this area, called Exe Island.

At the bottom of the scale of municipal power and responsibility were those residents who held no offices at all (called Rank D). Their only voice in town government came through occasional appearances as jury presentors in borough courts. In 1377, 82 per cent of the Exeter householders had never served in any of the available eighty seven civic offices (Table 3.4). Social mobility out of this group was possible, but not particularly common since only 12 per cent of Rank D householders in 1377 ever managed to be elected to municipal office. Nine reached the most powerful level of Rank A offices, nineteen attained Rank B, and twenty four were elected to a Rank C position. Only 9 per cent Rank D people in 1377 ever belonged to the freedom and their wealth was considerably lower than that possessed by men in the higher ranks. Table 3.4 shows the high correlation between political office, wealth, and commercial privilege (as represented by membership in the freedom) among Exeter heads of household in 1377. As one's personal wealth rose, so too rose one's chances of attaining economic and political privilege. In some few cases, the economic privileges of freedom membership could have preceded personal wealth, but this was unlikely considering the selective nature of admittances and the emphasis placed on ability to pay the entrance fee. More often than not, political power, economic privilege and personal wealth went hand-in-hand in late fourteenth-century Exeter.

The privileges of high political rank in Exeter worked to favor the commercial dealings of highly placed civic officials in several ways. Politically active citizens received preferential treatment in both financial assessment and the allocation of borough business to private contractors. The yearly city receiver's accounts, for example, regularly condoned the amercements and fines of the more powerful members of the oligarchy. Rents were also excused for some of the wealthiest men of the town. Thus the wardens of Exe Bridge noted in their 1381/2 account that John Talbot's rent of 40*s* for a garden in Paulstreet "could not be raised" even though Talbot ranked as the second wealthiest man in the 1377 murage tax.[104] Members of the oligarchy also habitually obtained first choice of the profitable farms of the customs of the city (for sales on such items as fish, meat, brewing, and baking) and had first selection of the city-owned pastureland. From 1372 to 1392, a small group of forty six people controlled all (a total of 132) of the customs farms in Exeter.[105] The oligarchy was responsible for 57 per cent of these farms

[104] EBW 1381/2; Misc. Roll 72; and see Table A3.1.

[105] The customs were listed each year in the MCR, mm. 1d–2d, immediately following the annual municipal elections, thereby suggesting that the customs were bid upon or handed out when the town's most powerful officials were present and could reserve the customs for themselves, or influence who received the farms.

even though the group represented less than 13 per cent of the householders in 1377. Business generated by civic activities frequently passed to the oligarchy as well. Wine and ale sent as gifts and bribes to influential officials were invariably purchased from members of the oligarchy as were most materials bought for the building or repair of city property.[106] The major merchants in town were undoubtedly the most likely candidates for such business, but their close association with the town government assured that all such trade was funnelled their way.

Members of the oligarchy, particularly those in Rank A, were also chosen, and paid handsomely, to supervise such civic projects as the building of the city wall and ditch, the repair of mill leats and weirs, and the construction of the city barge, even though such activities were rarely directly related to the commercial dealings of the appointed merchants. Richard Bozoun, for example, a wealthy overseas merchant and four-time mayor of Exeter, received the princely sum of £20 for "supervising" the new construction work on the city wall in 1387, the same year he was first elected mayor.[107] Such extra "tasks" greatly augmented the income of already powerful and wealthy men. Indeed, the assignment of these positions undoubtedly hinged on political influence.

The power of the Exeter oligarchy was also substantially reinforced by frequent appointments to such royal offices as controller, customer, havener, and aulnager.[108] The appointments, generally available only to Rank A members of the oligarchy, endowed their holders not only with political pull, but also with additional opportunities for financial gain. No fewer than four former mayors of the city were indicted and convicted (although two were ultimately pardoned) of fraud in the collection of customs.[109] These problems did not discourage the king, however, since such appointments allowed him to build a local political base while at the same time he could rely on these merchants' experience and knowledge of local commerce. Several members of the oligarchy repaid the king by serving him on expeditions to such troublesome

[106] The purchases were enrolled each year in the CRA under *Dona et exhennia* and *Expensi necessari*. See also the DRA under mill expenses; the EBW under mill expenses and bridge repairs; Misc. Roll 6 for the accounts for the city barge (mm. 17, 25–28), expenses on city weirs, walls, ditches, gates, the pillory, and the new Duryard mill (mm. 1–5, 8–12, 22–24, and 29–34).

[107] CRA 1386/7.

[108] For appointments as port customs officials, see the relevant PRO E122 national customs accounts, as well as the *CFR* and *CPR*. Aulnager appointments are in PRO E101/338/11 and E358/8, 9.

[109] They were Roger Plente, John Grey, Richard Bozoun, and Robert Noble; *CPR 1367–70*: 52; *1391–6*: 234; *CFR 1356–69*: 98.

spots as Ireland, or by loaning him money for his overseas wars.[110] Ties between the central government and the Exeter oligarchy were also reinforced in attendance at Parliament (again, a perquisite of Rank A men).[111]

Many members of both A and B Ranks of the oligarchy also served in minor royal offices, primarily at the county level. As tax collectors, commissioners on special inquisitions, coroners, and escheators, the Exeter oligarchy participated in the political and economic life of the Devon county community, brushing shoulders with the local gentry who also served in these offices.[112] These royal and county appointments thus fostered close ties that linked members of the urban elite with the local aristocracy and gentry. Such powerful and wealthy citizens as John Grey, Robert Wilford, and John Webber numbered among the "esquires" of the earl of Devon's retinue in 1384.[113] Members of oligarchic families remembered local gentry as friends in their wills, provided masses for their souls, appointed them executors, stood as mainprise in purchases of land or in debt suits – and were the recipients of similar favors in turn.[114] Oligarchic merchants formed similar strong relationships with the leading merchants of towns such as London, Dartmouth, and Plymouth.[115] These relationships were facilitated by Exeter's pre-eminent position in the South-west as the regional market town, port, merchant staple, ecclesiastical center, and administrative center, functions that helped compel both gentry and non-Exeter merchants like Humphrey Passour of Plymouth to own land or tenements in Exeter.[116] Thus personal relationships, fostered through common interests, political ties, commercial connections, and even intermarriage, built associations that further bolstered the high status of Exeter's ruling elite.[117]

[110] *CPR 1350–4*: 143 (Robert Noble and Robert de Brideport); *1396–9*: 390 (Richard Bozoun); *1399–1401*: 234 (Walter Thomas); *Issue roll of Thomas de Brantingham*: 187 (Robert Wilford).

[111] Kowaleski 1984: 267–8.

[112] For positions shared by the Exeter oligarchy and the local landed gentry, see, for example, *CPR 1354–58*: 494; *1381–5*: 143; *1385–9*: 392; *CFR 1369–77*: 390; *1377–83*: 55, 231; Misc. Roll 6, m. 17; Alexander 1928: 201–5; Cherry 1979: 71–90.

[113] BL Add. Ch. 64320; Cherry 1979: 73, 82, 85–7.

[114] Kowaleski 1984: 365–6.

[115] Kowaleski 1984: 366–7.

[116] For gentry holdings in Exeter, see above, n. 22. For Passour, see MCR 1360/1, m. 4. For other city properties held by non-Exeter merchants, see MCR 1378/9, m. 32, 1395/6, m. 23; ED/M/460.

[117] For intermarriage between the gentry and oligarchy, see Alexander 1928: 203–7. Only the richest and most powerful of the oligarchic families, such as the Wilfords and Talbots, formed such alliances. For instances of the oligarchy benefiting from their ties with the local gentry, see MCR 1387/8, m. 6; Tyldesley 1978: 17–18.

While the political status of the Exeter oligarchs gave them further opportunities for financial, social, and political gain, it also engendered responsibilities and burdens. The demands of office took time, distracting the merchant or craftsman from his regular business. Much time and effort were expended on elections, council meetings, civic expeditions to London or other towns on city business, entertainment of visiting justices and dignitaries, and the innumerable arrangements required for the repair and upkeep of city property. More onerous than these duties, however, were those associated with keeping the peace and administering justice in the town. The mayor and stewards spent at least one day a week presiding in court, the receiver and wardens of Exe Bridge collected rents and compiled annual accounts, and all members of the oligarchy frequently served as jurors in the borough courts. High-ranking officials were also subject to financial liabilities by virtue of their civic office. The outgoing mayor, for example, was required to give a feast for all the most prominent town officers at his own expense on election day.[118] Special projects, such as the construction of a barge for the naval service, the rebuilding of a burned city mill, or the repair of the city wall, could only be met by loans from wealthy citizens.[119] The oligarchy's bequests for public projects such as the construction of a water conduit "for the easement of the whole community," or the foundation of almshouses and hospitals for the poor and sick of the community, also show how civic responsibility went hand in hand with wealth.[120] Members of the oligarchy considered themselves the most qualified directors of borough affairs not only because their position as merchants allowed them to dominate the urban economy and government, but also because their wealth enabled them to bear the substantial burdens of public office.[121]

It was the wealth and commercial clout of the oligarchy that formed the basis of their municipal political power; indeed, commercial success was crucial for anyone who aspired to urban political office. To understand fully the tight civic control of town elites, it is necessary to recognize the commercial power that laid the foundation for political hegemony. The pre-eminence of the oligarchy within the local markets

[118] *Citie of Excester*: 914.

[119] Misc. Roll 6, m. 16. For other loans to the city by members of the oligarchy, see Misc. Roll 6, mm. 16 and 20; and CRA 1393/4, 1396/7.

[120] EBW 1369/70, 139½; MCR 1420/21, m. 52; *Citie of Excester*: 858–9; *Reg. Stafford*: 397, 401.

[121] Exeter's oligarchy expressed this sentiment at election time (MCR 1305/6, m. 4d) and in the regulations of 1345 (Wilkinson 1931: 71). For a discussion of class distinctions in medieval London and the right of the merchant oligarchy to rule, see Thrupp 1948: 14–27.

Table 3.5. *Creditors and debtors in Exeter by political rank*

Political rank	% Householders in 1377 (N=525)	% Creditors 1378–88 (N=3,886)	% Debtors 1378–88 (N=3,389)	% of all litigants (N=7,275)
A	6.1	21.7	4.5	13.7
B	6.5	12.0	5.8	9.1
C	5.9	11.5	11.1	11.3
D	81.5	54.8	78.6	65.9
Total	100	100	100	100

Source: Table A3.1; MCR and PCR debts 1378–88; MCR election returns, 1340–1405.

of Exeter can be illustrated through an analysis of debt cases in the borough courts.[122] Supplemented by information on occupations and political ranks from the voluminous and detailed Exeter records of this period, the type and extent of commercial participation by individuals in Exeter's local markets can be broadly measured by the frequency and nature of their appearances in these debt cases.

Members of the oligarchy, who accounted for less than 13 per cent of the total population, nonetheless were responsible for almost 23 per cent of the commercial activity represented in the debt cases that dominated the business of the borough courts (Table 3.5). Their more frequent appearance as creditors (they were almost four times as likely to come into court as creditors than as debtors) emphasizes their financial solvency in the community. In contrast, members of Rank D (and, to a lesser extent, Rank C), who generally lacked freedom membership and exercised little or no political influence, were often at a disadvantage in their commercial dealings, surfacing as debtors 24 per cent more often than they showed up as creditors. The less frequent appearances overall of Rank D debt litigants compared to their greater numbers within the urban population also illustrate their relative inactivity in commerce. As artisans, laborers, or servants, they did not engage as often in the types of commercial exchange that brought so many oligarchic merchants into court.

The economic strength of the oligarchy resulted largely from the wholesale and distributing functions its members played in local, regional, and international markets. No less than 75 per cent of Rank A and 32 per cent of Rank B oligarchs actively traded by sea compared to a mere 5 per cent for the non-oligarchic householders (Table 3.4).

[122] For a full explanation of this analysis, which includes data on 4,638 creditors and 4,711 debtors in 1378–88, see below, pp. 347–9.

Even artisans like Nicholas Bynnecote of Rank A, who never traded overseas, were nonetheless involved at the distributing end of their business, as shown by Bynnecote's sale of furs to the county gentry and his dealings with skinners as far away as London.[123] Within Exeter's own local markets, oligarchic traders served as the most important middlemen, selling either to retailers or directly to consumers. For example, Richard Bozoun imported large quantities of wine, herring, figs, oil, iron, bowstaves, boards, wainscot, and other goods, while exporting primarily cloth and small amounts of wool and hides. He sold lead "*in grosso*," as well as consignments of madder and woad. He also retailed smaller amounts of goods such as malt, oats, ale, wine, and building stone.[124] Other members of the oligarchy specialized; John Aisshe, termed both "vintner" and "merchant" in the records, regularly imported and then sold large quantitites of wine to taverners, although he also retailed wine, ale, mead, and wood himself. Like many oligarchs, he also exported cloth, acting as a middleman between textile producers and overseas merchants.[125]

Maritime trade required large amounts of capital, the ability to take financial risks, and good commercial connections. Membership in the freedom also helped since members were exempt from port customs and had sole access to certain types of retail and wholesale activities. Only 11 per cent of the Exeter householders in 1377 ever engaged in the port trade (Table 3.4); at any one time, less than 5 per cent of the householders actually carried on such trade.[126] Oligarchs, moreover, made up 97 per cent of those traders whose maritime activities were most intense.[127] This small group of prominent merchants controlled over one-third of the import trade at Exeter and as much as 44 per

123 PCR 1–23 Ric. II, mm. 27, 63, 66; MCR 1382/3, m. 4d; BL Add. Ch. 64317 (under the name Nicholas Pees).

124 Maritime activities: PCA 1371/2, 1372/3, 1382/3, 1383/4, 1385/6, 1386/7; PRO E122/158/31, 193/23, 40/8, 40/6, 40/18. Wholesale: MCR 1388/9, m. 52; PCR 1–23 Ric. II, m. 73; PRO E101/338/11/6; ECL D&C 2708. Retail: SQMT 1374–88; CRA 1380/1, 1386/7; PCR 1-23 Ric. II, m. 65. Bozoun's debts extended from just over 2*s* to £51 (PRO E159/173, m. 13), another indication of the range of his commercial activities.

125 MCR 1376/7 m. 44, 1382/3 m. 18, 1390/1 m. 8; PCR 1–23 Ric. II mm. 10, 63; NQMT 1373–74, 1376, 1383, 1386; CRA 1386/7; PCA 1365/6 to 1372/3, 1381/2, 1383/4–84/5; PRO E122/158/24, 40/8, 193/23. See below, pp. 234, 250–4 for a further discussion of the role of the oligarchy in the port trade.

126 Because the Exeter port accounts do not survive for the period 1373/4 to 1380/1, it is impossible to know exactly which of the householders in 1377 traded by sea before that date although what slim evidence there is shows that fewer than twenty of the householders in 1377 (4 per cent) were active in maritime trade before 1373.

127 These importers are marked "++" in Table A3.1. Those with lesser involvement are marked "+"; 30 per cent of these maritime traders never reached the ranks of the oligarchy.

Table 3.6. *Debt amounts of Exeter creditors and debtors by political rank, 1378–88*

		Per cent of political rank paying debts of						
Political rank	Average debt	1*d*–1*s*	1–5*s*	5–10*s*	10*s*–£1	£1–5	>£5	Total
Creditors								
Oligarchy (N=527)	17*s* 7*d*	5.7	46.7	20.5	13.5	10.0	3.6	100
Ranks C and D (N=1,062)	8*s* 3*d*	15.9	53.0	16.0	8.2	6.0	0.9	100
Debtors								
Oligarchy (N=126)	28*s* 10*d*	8.7	31.0	21.4	15.1	15.9	7.9	100
Ranks C and D (N=1,461)	9*s* 2*d*	11.3	51.7	18.9	10.1	6.6	1.4	100

Sources: MCR and PCR debt cases, 1378–88; MCR election returns, 1340–1405. The oligarchy includes political ranks A and B.

cent of the valuable wine import trade at the same time as they dominated the cloth export trade.[128] The oligarchy's predominance as distributors also made them the natural middlemen for non-Exeter importers who wanted to wholesale their goods in Exeter. Obviously control of the profitable and commercially prestigious port trade contributed to the ruling elite's domination of the local markets through the wealth and commercial advantages such trade generated.

The concentration and dominance of the oligarchy in the town's local markets may also be seen in the cash value of the debts they contracted which were for far higher amounts than other Exeter residents (Table 3.6). Although lower-ranking residents outnumbered those of Ranks A and B in the local markets, the oligarchy compensated for its small numbers by controlling the high end of the trade in these markets. Major trade, moreover, required major expenditures; high debts were the natural offshoots of such ventures. The average amount owed by oligarchic debtors was more than three times as large as the sums owed by non-oligarchic debtors. These heavy debts stress the potentially risky nature of some of the oligarchy's commercial ventures. While they expected higher returns on their greater investments, so too they had to accept potentially greater losses, although the financial resources at their disposal made such risks manageable.

The risks undertaken by the merchants of the oligarchy were revealed most dramatically in overseas and coastal trade. The dangers of such trade were well known to Exeter merchants; storms at sea, pirates, and

[128] For this and the following, see below, Chapter 6, esp. Tables 6.4–6.7.

the constant threat of war all combined to present real hazards to the merchant willing to embark on such ventures.[129] The financial risks and cash-flow problems associated with both overseas and wholesale trade could be eased, however, by forming financial partnerships.[130] The Exeter evidence suggests that partnerships for maritime trade were particularly beneficial to those beginning a commercial career who lacked the requisite capital (or experience). Both John Talbot and Thomas Estoun, for example, began their sea-trade activities by importing wine in partnership with well-established merchants.[131] At the time, neither enjoyed freedom membership or oligarchic status, but both men went on to attain entry into the freedom, great wealth, and Rank A status in the oligarchy. While their success underlines the important role that maritime trade investment played in attaining commercial and political power, it also shows how partnerships with wealthier, established merchants could mitigate the high risks of initial forays into overseas trade.[132]

The sources of mercantile capital for these risky commercial ventures are difficult to identify although landowning was clearly important. Landed property served both as a source of capital for mercantile activities and as a repository for commercial profits.[133] As a general rule, the wealthier the man, the more intense his participation in the land market. Robert Wilford, the richest inhabitant of Exeter in 1377, owned dozens of properties scattered throughout the town, including shops, cellars, solars, houses, messuages, gardens, and pasture.[134] The investment represented by these properties could be considerable; in 1384, for example, Wilford and his wife Elizabeth paid £40 for just one tenement in Exeter.[135] All but one of the references to Wilford's property transactions concerned acquisitions. The position of Wilford and other oligarchs as important landlords in Exeter was reflected in their more frequent appearance as creditors than debtors (47 creditors,

[129] For such hazards experienced off the south Devon coast, see *CPR 1361–4*: 83; *1377–81*: 356; *1396–9*: 584–5; *CCR 1354–60*: 32, 83, 87; *W.C. Chancery proc.*: passim.

[130] Postan 1973b: 65–91; James 1971: 206–7; Thrupp 1948: 104, 108, 111.

[131] Talbot: PCA 1372/3; Estoun: PCA 1384/5.

[132] For other examples of such partnerships, see Kowaleski 1984: 375 and below, pp. 209–12.

[133] Scholars disagree as to the extent that urban rents or property represented a source of mercantile capital; see Hilton 1967; Butcher 1979b: 14–18; Keene 1989b: 217–23; Rosser 1989: 95–6.

[134] CRA 1376/7, 1377/8; Book 53A, fols. 29, 63, 75; EBW 1386/7, 1390/1; Misc. Roll 4, m. 3v; ED/M/520; MCR 1377/8, m. 25; 1380/1, mm. 39, 40; 1382/3, m. 1; DCR 2–22 Ric. II, m. 30d; ECL D&C 119, 121 (D&C Deeds); 4858 (SCR 20 April 1392); 5155–6 (D&C Rent Rolls); Lega-Weekes 1912: 484, 490, 505–7.

[135] MCR 1384/5, m. 12. For the one property Wilford sold, see ED/M/546.

thirteen debtors) in rent disputes. Fully 60 per cent of the creditors in cases concerning unpaid rent were members of the oligarchy, even though they accounted for less than 13 per cent of all householders in 1377.[136]

Mercantile wealth was also tied up in commercial ventures and stock. Roger Plente, a wealthy merchant who served as mayor four times, died holding goods and chattels worth £1,000, 60 per cent of which was tied up in trading stock (60 tuns of wine, 50 quarters of salt, iron, tin, lead, spices, and cloth) and £80 in a ship with its freight.[137] He also possessed £200 in "counted money of gold and silver," household items worth £100, and livestock valued at £20. From this amount must be subtracted his debts, including sums like the 59*s* 8*d* his executors had to pay for cloth he had purchased.[138] Although the legal suit recording his assets did not enumerate his landed property, it is unlikely that his rental income even approached the sums he had invested in commercial stock. He inherited some lands from his father, but Roger probably earned more through his own efforts; Walter never served in any office higher than elector and ranked near the middle of Exeter taxpayers in 1332.[139] Among the properties Roger held were tenements in Northgate Street and Southgate Street, a vacant lot near High Street, a shop and solar, and one acre outside the north gate.[140]

Oligarchic interests in commercial ventures were also evident in the diversity of their commercial activities. Sales debts represented one-half of all debts tried; oligarchic creditors were slightly more likely to be involved in such cases than other creditors, but oligarchic debtors showed a more varied pattern. Only 35 per cent of the oligarchy (and 25 per cent of Rank A alone) were involved in sales debts compared to 52 per cent of Ranks C and D. Oligarchic litigants also appeared more frequently in cases involving cash loans and bonds.[141] Such data

[136] Information on type of debt is based on responses for 796 creditors and 819 debtors; 95 of the total 778 cases involved money owed for rent or property purchases. Oligarchic debtors were also more likely to appear in these rent disputes (21 per cent as opposed to only 13 per cent of non-oligarchic debts), a further indication of their heavy involvement in the city's property market.

[137] *Year books of Richard II. 13 Richard II*: 11–12.

[138] MCR 1374/5, m. 15.

[139] His father was Walter Plente; *Lay subsidy 1332*: 110; MCR election returns 1317/18–1344/5; *Exeter freemen*: 29. Walter's wife, Claricia Plente, also survived Roger and held some of Walter's estate (ED/M/356, 426, 438; NQMT 1373–5; DRA 1383/4).

[140] ECL V/C 3158, D&C 23; MCR 1370/1, m. 38; MCR 1382/3, mm. 46–7.

[141] The oligarchy (which represented 12.6 per cent of householders in 1377) represented 44 per cent of creditors and 22 per cent of debtors of bonds; for cases concerning cash loans they made up 29 per cent of creditors and 13 per cent of debtors. Information based on fifty three cases concerning loans and thirty one cases involving bonds (including *obligationes*). For their interest in bonds, see also below, pp. 213–14.

Table 3.7. *Court results for Exeter creditors and debtors by political rank, 1378–88*

Political rank	Percentage of cases resolved by						
	Guilty verdict	Plea not pursued	Licence of concord	False query	Failure to wage law	No information	Total
Creditors							
Oligarchy (N=1,307)	30	23	15	4	2	26	100
Ranks C and D (N=2,557)	26	33	14	7	4	16	100
Debtors							
Oligarchy (N=348)	19	33	14	8	2	24	100
Ranks C and D (N=3,041)	32	27	14	6	4	17	100

Source: MCR and PCR debt cases, 1378–88; MCR election returns, 1340–1405. The oligarchy includes political ranks A and B.

corroborate the patterns already established for the oligarchy. As the wealthiest men in the borough, the oligarchic citizens were the natural moneylenders at the same time as their personal and business connections by sea and throughout Devon made them rely heavily on the commercial bonds made under statute merchant or statute staple.

The immense power and influence of the Exeter oligarchy affected even the administration of justice in the community; oligarchic creditors and debtors received more favorable judgments than their counterparts of lower political rank (Table 3.7). Oligarchic debtors, for instance, were judged guilty ("in mercy") in only 19 per cent of their cases, but debtors of lesser ranks were convicted 32 per cent of the time. Oligarchic creditors also won more guilty verdicts against their debtors. Similarly, members of the oligarchy obtained *non prosequitur* verdicts (in which the creditor was fined for failing to pursue the case) less frequently as creditors but more often as debtors when this decision became advantageous. The same trends occurred in the false query decisions (when plaintiffs were fined for bringing a false complaint) and cases ending with the defendant's failure to wage law.[142] Little difference, however,

[142] See below, pp. 217–19 for the ramifications of this court decision and others. The substantially larger number of oligarchic cases with no recorded outcome ("no information" in Table 3.7) was probably due to the greater number of non-Exeter residents involved in the oligarchy's debts; these outsiders either did not show up in court, or their case was removed to a higher court; see below, p. 220, n. 201.

appeared in cases resolved by mutual agreement (licence of concord). In most cases, those of the highest group of the oligarchy, Rank A, received better verdicts than any other group. Only 15 per cent of Rank A debtors, for instance, were convicted of debt and only 4 per cent of Rank A creditors were found guilty of bringing a false complaint. These results show that members of the oligarchy possessed a distinct advantage in the local courts; their wealth and power encouraged them to pursue suits at the same time that such advantages discouraged their opponents.[143]

Although the substantial power wielded by the oligarchy within urban politics and the economy was always confined to a small number of wealthy men in Exeter, the oligarchy was not a permanently closed system of government. Social mobility was made possible by a variety of factors that encouraged recruitment into the ranks of the oligarchy. The vicissitudes of commercial life, the failure to produce heirs, and the occasional drain of the wealthy urban elite to the rural gentry combined with the constant flow of immigration to the town, entrepreneurship, simple good fortune, and advantageous marriages, to ensure that the town's oligarchy was not restricted to the same pool of oligarchic families; the oligarchic pool remained small but not stagnant. In Exeter as in other towns, demographic failure to produce heirs dealt the most devastating blow to oligarchic fortunes.[144] Less of a factor in Exeter than in the larger towns was the loss of oligarchic families to the ranks of the landed gentry.[145]

Financial and commercial risks also weakened the ability of some oligarchic families to survive. The accumulated misfortune of men like the oligarchic Rank A merchant Walter Fouke illustrates the dangers. Walter participated in both local and overseas trade but in 1377 was considerably less wealthy than other members of the elite, paying only 18*d* in murage compared to the 4*s* 6*d* average for other Rank A citizens.[146] His lack of commercial success is evident in the large debts he owed, including 16 marks to Henry Martyn of Chulmleigh, 50*s* to the spicer John Seyneet, more than 36*s* to Thomas Canun, and £16 to the merchant Robert Wilford.[147] His own actions as a creditor were equally unfortunate. One of his debtors, Thomas Webber, died without

143 Similar trends were evident in rural England; see Hanawalt 1979: 53, who notes that primary villagers were convicted less often than poorer villagers in criminal cases.

144 Thrupp 1948: 191–206; Platt 1976: 98–102; Kowaleski 1984: 379.

145 Kowaleski 1984: 381–2; Thrupp 1948: 279–87; Platt 1973: 63.

146 PCA 1365/6 to 1371/2. Fouke was elected steward in 1371 and 1375 and served as elector twelve times from 1366 to 1381. See Misc. Roll 72 and Table 3.4 for murage payments.

147 MCR 1374/5, m. 24; 1375/6, m. 51; PCR 1–23 Ric. II, mm. 13, 16.

paying the £10 debt Fouke had been trying to recoup from him. Walter then approached Webber's widow, Helewisia, but she put him off saying that she had decided to marry again. After the wedding, Fouke once again tried to claim the debt but Helewisia and her new husband continued to stall. To complicate matters, Webber had died intestate and his affairs took years to settle, so Fouke had to spend much time pursuing the matter in the Exeter courts.[148] Other misfortunes also befell Fouke. His house was burglarized in 1375 and goods valued at 26*s* were stolen. In 1378 several malefactors forcibly entered his house and then set it afire to the damage of £20. He also failed to meet a custom payment and suffered the distraint of his goods to cover the cost of the debt.[149] When Fouke died in 1381, his widow Christine was immediately sued by numerous creditors, including at least one former business partner of her husband.[150] This post-mortem debt litigation continued to plague Christine for nearly a decade; as late as 1390 a Somerset merchant claimed she owed him 5 marks as Fouke's widow and executor. All this evoked sympathy for Christine; in 1393 the city receiver pardoned her court fines with the comment "because she is a pauper."[151] Whether Fouke's misfortunes were due to a lack of business acumen, an unpleasant personality, personal tragedy, or just plain bad luck, we will never know. While his continuous financial difficulties underline the problems and risks that faced Exeter's merchants, the wealthiest merchants rarely suffered such unrelenting financial disasters. Secure in their business dealings and landed wealth, and acknowledged as the governors of the town, the more prosperous members of the Exeter oligarchy reigned supreme within their provincial setting.

These weaknesses in the oligarchic class (failure of heirs, the occasional elevation of urban merchants to the landed gentry, and commercial or financial disaster) required that the ranks of the ruling elite be bolstered periodically with new members. Those born into a lower political rank, as well as new immigrants to the town, could still hope to climb the urban ladder to commercial, political, and social success. Opportunities came in several different forms. Some, like the goldsmith John Russell, received money, property, and a head start in their chosen occupation as a reward for faithful service to a childless master.[152] Others, like John Talbot and Thomas Estoun, appear to have succeeded through

[148] PCR 1–23 Ric. II, m. 7; MCR 1378/9, mm. 35, 36.
[149] PCR 1–23 Ric. II, m. 45; MCR 1374/5, m. 43; 1378/9 m. 6.
[150] MCR 1382/3, mm. 15, 20; 1385/6, m. 46; 1390/1, m. 10 for this and the following.
[151] CRA 1392/3.
[152] Kowaleski 1984: 379.

commercial risk-taking and business acumen, using maritime trade as a stepping stone to freedom membership and oligarchic status.[153] Such opportunities for upward mobility may actually have been greater in the underpopulated decades immediately following the Black Death. The shrinking demographic pool of the later middle ages may also have raised the number of men who gained access to the merchant elite through marriage to a wealthy woman. Such marriages boosted the fortunes of Philip Seys, John Holm, and Richard Kenrigg, who all attained entry to the Exeter freedom the same year they married wealthy widows of the oligarchy.[154] All three men went on to obtain oligarchic status.

Although such examples show that upward social mobility was certainly possible in medieval Exeter, the combination of wealth, commercial success, and political power necessary for entry into the higher echelons of the oligarchy was not attained easily or frequently. Birth was still the best path to success in medieval town life and the families of the Exeter oligarchy tried at all times to maintain their status in the borough. The oligarchic class always remained a small, tight-knit community united by wealth, social ties, business connections, and common political aims. Only thirty seven of the 459 non-oligarchic householders in 1377 went on to join the oligarchy and they were twice as wealthy as those who were not elevated to the ruling elite.[155] The distinctions in wealth and commercial activity between Ranks A and B also remained firm. Of those reaching Rank A, 64 per cent participated in overseas trade while only 12 per cent of the future Rank B citizens did so. Rank A always remained more selective; only eighteen of the heads of household in 1377 went on to join this elite rank (and seven had already reached Rank B by 1377). It must have been fairly clear to Exeter inhabitants that the chances of boosting themselves into the oligarchy were slim without a background of wealth.

The less privileged inhabitants of Exeter undoubtedly noted the immense gap that separated them from the oligarchy. Reports of abuses of power by the oligarchy and of the resulting resentment of the general populace were not that uncommon. This resentment, however, rarely went beyond the stage of heated words and accusations, and usually the troublemakers were successfully prosecuted by the oligarchy in

[153] See above, p. 111. For other examples, see Kowaleski 1984: 382.

[154] *Exeter freemen*: 34–5; MCR election returns, 1379–90; PCR 1–23 Ric. II, m. 7; MCR 1381/2, m. 42; 1382/3, m. 15.

[155] Their average murage was 18*d* compared to 8.7*d* paid by those who remained in Ranks C and D (Table A3.1, below).

court. For assaulting Peter Hadlegh, one of the city's chief stewards, and tearing up his cloak in the presence of the mayor, William Knyght, an unenfranchised retailer, was fined 3*d* and made to pay one-half mark damages.[156] This did not silence William, however; eight months later he was fined 40*d* for his contemptuous actions in the presence of the mayor and councillors and for creating a disturbance at the election of the new mayor. John Cole, a skinner who held no political offices but did belong to the freedom, was sued by William Rok, a wealthy merchant of Rank A, for calling William a false juror in the city court.[157] William and Stephen Boghewode, two well-off butchers who never held political office, were also charged fines of 20*s* apiece for acting in a contemptuous manner in the presence of the civic governors.[158]

Many of the most direct challenges to the authority of the oligarchy came from lower-ranking members of the oligarchy itself. Thus Robert Plomer, a successful craftsman and marginal member of Rank B (he served as elector only once), was presented by twelve sworn men in the mayor's court because he "maliciously and falsely said openly that Robert Wilford, recently mayor of Exeter, had sealed a charter of Felicia Kirton with the seal of the mayor against her will."[159] Other accusations of fraud and deceit in town government came from men such as Robert Coble who accused John Talbot, then mayor of Exeter, of unjustly fining a woman in the mayor's court when she was not present. Apparently Coble accompanied this accusation with a rude gesture, for Talbot became angry and cautioned Coble that as mayor he represented the king in court and should not be insulted in such a manner. Coble answered back that the office of mayor stood for nothing since Talbot maintained prostitutes and other *lurdicos* in the city, as well as forestalling and regrating wine, herring, and other merchandise. Talbot promptly called Coble a liar, arrested him, and threw him into prison.[160] At the time of his arrest Coble had served in no civic office; within two years, however, he was chosen an elector and four years later was himself elected a steward, thus placing him in the Rank A oligarchy.[161] His quarrel with the sitting mayor may have thus reflected

156 MCR 1378/9, mm. 20, 24; and Table A3.1 for both. For the following see MCR 1379/80, m. 1.

157 MCR 1382/3, m. 15; and Table A3.1 for both.

158 MCR 1367/8, m. 22; and Table A3.1 for Stephen. Accusations of slander were far more frequent in the late thirteenth and early fourteenth centuries which may indicate greater oligarchic power and thus more "class" tensions at that time.

159 MCR 1389/90, m. 6; and Table A3.1.

160 MCR 1396/7, m. 43d.

161 MCR election returns 1398/9, 1403/4.

his own aspirations, although the outrage he expressed over Talbot's particular abuses suggests that his claims were more than just the hot words of a young, up-and-coming rival.

These incidents underline contemporary awareness that members of the Exeter oligarchy could and did manipulate public office to their own advantage. But the oligarchy's firm grip on municipal government and justice prevented most residents from expressing this awareness or proffering accusations openly. Indeed, with the exception of the (failed) attempt by the Tailors Guild to acquire a larger share of public power in the 1460s and 1470s, the Exeter oligarchy never experienced organized overt challenges to its authority, nor did "class" disputes in Exeter reach the level of bitterness seen in other English towns.[162] While there are hints that some of the political tensions in Exeter stemmed from factionalism among the ruling elite,[163] other complaints levelled against the elite suggest that economic disparity and a genuine anger by the less privileged at oligarchic manipulation of public office also provoked such tensions. Political tensions in medieval Exeter were evident primarily in the complaints of individuals censured and fined by Rank A oligarchs in the mayor's court; further research may reveal incidences when personal hatreds and/or resentment of the economic and political abuses of the Rank A oligarchs coalesced and led to more virulent and widespread quarrels.

The lack of such virulent quarrels between the privileged and less privileged groups of society in Exeter may have been due to several factors. The gap between rich and poor, franchised and unenfranchised, was not as large in Exeter as in the bigger, more commercially active towns of Bristol and London. Then too the evidence for relative prosperity in late medieval Exeter may have dampened some hostilities because of the greater range of economic opportunities. Perhaps more important was Exeter's electoral system, which allowed men of more moderate means to have some say in local government, and which created a buffer zone or "middle class" (Ranks B and C) between the truly wealthy and the poorer majority, thus easing social and political tensions within the town. It is also possible that the early, constitutionally reinforced grip of the oligarchy on the freedom and all high political offices, backed up by their dominance of local commerce, allowed the elite to mute most challenges to their power. It does appear that as the economy of fifteenth- and sixteenth-century Exeter grew more vigorous

162 In Bristol, for example, a riot by townspeople angry with the way fourteen members of the oligarchy had coopted the customs of the port and market for themselves forced the fourteen to flee the city for over a year; see Green 1894: 266–8.

163 For examples of such factionalism elsewhere, see Barron 1970; Dobson 1984.

and the town emerged as a major market center, the authority of the oligarchy expanded.[164] Similar movements occurred in other English towns; as trade grew more complex and profitable and the wealth of individual merchants increased, town governments became more elaborate and subject to the control of a select few.[165]

[164] Wilkinson 1931: 24–9; Parry 1941: 43–7.
[165] Green 1894: 280–7; Reynolds 1977: 175–7.

4 Commerce and the occupational structure

Historians have long relied on occupational surveys to discern the economic development, specialization, and prosperity of pre-modern towns. Analyses of occupational structures can not only indicate broad trends within urban economies, but also depict the place of individual commercial and industrial activities within urban society. For medievalists and early modernists, however, the problems involved in dealing with limited and recalcitrant sources, grouping individual skills into occupational categories, or merely identifying what is meant by a particular occupational designation have themselves engendered a significant body of scholarly work.[1] While freemen's rolls, wills, records of property-holding, and poll tax returns have all been employed to help determine urban occupational structures, these sources can have drawbacks when used by themselves.[2] Freedom organizations, for example, usually allowed only a fraction of urban residents to join while the poll taxes of 1379 and 1381 suffered from widespread evasion.[3] More successful have been efforts that employ several different sources, particularly the richly detailed material found in borough court rolls; annual presentments in these rolls have, for example, allowed scholars to trace

1 For recent discussions of these problems, see the essays in Corfield and Keene (eds.) 1990, especially those by the editors; Pound 1966; Patten 1977; Palliser 1983: 237–65, 392–3.

2 For freedom rolls, see Woodward 1970; Dobson 1973; Butcher 1979a; Pound 1981. Swanson 1989, 1990 employs both freedom rolls and craft ordinances. For wills and inventories, see Pound 1988. For records of property-holding, see Kelly, Rutledge, and Tillyard 1983; Keene 1985 (who also relies on court rolls and other sources). For poll taxes, see Goldberg 1990a: 209–13.

3 For freedoms, see above, n. 2. Goldberg (1990a: 109) effectively uses poll taxes to compare occupational structures of different towns, but includes only the "economic" population of towns (excluding as much as half of the urban population in some instances). His use of surnames to identify occupations is also problematic; in Exeter there was no correspondence between occupational surname and occupational group 37 per cent of the time in 1377 (based on eighty four householders with occupational surnames whose occupations are also known; below, Table A3.1).

broad demographic and economic developments over the course of several centuries.[4]

The occupational analyses offered in this chapter provide a somewhat different perspective on urban occupational structure by focusing primarily on the commercial involvement of the various occupations within the local markets. They also aim to circumvent some of the problems implicit in reliance on one or two sources by including data drawn from diverse sources and by compiling a variety of indices to measure the wealth, status, and commercial activity of different occupations.[5] The methodology employed in the quantitative analyses is essentially prosopographical and draws upon the tremendous depth and range of the Exeter documentation to facilitate comparisons between occupations. This type of analysis, however, requires concentration on a short span of years, thus precluding a study of how Exeter's occupational structure changed over time. The following quantitative analyses therefore concentrate mostly on one decade in the fourteenth century (1378–88), although the general discussion employs material dating from roughly 1285 to 1415 to elucidate the participation of various groups in the local markets. The narrower focus also helps to avoid some of the problems associated with changes in occupational terminology and perceptions of work that plague many studies of medieval occupations.

The starting point is a prosopographical analysis of the 420 householders listed in the murage tax roll of 1377, supplemented by the addition of 105 householders who escaped enumeration in the tax for one reason or another.[6] These 525 households represented about 94 per cent of Exeter's households in 1377; only some thirty six households resident in the exempt jurisdiction of Exe Island (outside the west gate) and perhaps another 390 or so persons too poor or too mobile to leave much trace in the extant records were not included.[7] Firm occupations were established for over 75 per cent of the identified households.[8] The political offices, freedom membership, maritime trade, brewing, and servants of these householders were also identified to

[4] Britnell 1986b; Keene 1985: 249–365.

[5] See below, Appendix 1 for these sources and pp. 344–5 for a discussion of how they were employed to identify occupations.

[6] For the methods and sources used to compile this list, see below, Appendix 3, esp. Table A3.1 which lists all 525 householders and much of the information on which the following discussion is based.

[7] See below, Appendix 3 for the calculations behind these estimates. Five of the forty one Exe Island householders were included in Table A3.1; the other missing persons were probably servants or boarders; very few would have been householders.

[8] The guidelines employed to determine occupations are discussed below in Appendix 1, pp. 344–5, 350–2.

illustrate other aspects of their commercial activities. The second prosopographical analysis employed here surveys 7,547 Exeter litigants involved in all (4,536) debt cases before the borough courts in 1378–88.[9] Occupations could be attributed to 75 per cent of these resident creditors and debtors, and all could be identified in terms of political rank. Because the vast majority of debt cases concerned commercial matters, this latter analysis provided much valuable information on the nature and degree of involvement of various occupations in the local markets.

Three problems that hinder all investigations of medieval occupational structures had to be confronted in these analyses. The first concerns the varying coverage afforded different occupations. In this study, six occupational groups were well documented: the merchants, hostelers, professions/administrative group and those in the leather/fur, metal, and building trades.[10] The relative proportions of these occupational categories in the following tables are thus fairly accurate. The data for the remaining three occupational groups – the victuallers, clothing/textile trades, and miscellaneous trades – are less complete; most of those in the Unidentified group probably belong to one of these categories. The "miscellaneous trades" (the service sector, wood crafts, and other trades) are the most under-represented because few were included in the systematic presentments of marketing and craft offenses in the mayor's tourn and because their lower commercial profile meant they less frequently appeared in debt litigation and freedom entries. Domestic and craft servants went unrecorded even more often because of their poverty, mobility, youth, gender, and lack of householder status. For the victualling trades the problem of coverage was less serious since the more prominent occupations (bakers, brewers, butchers, cooks, fishmongers) fell under the purview of regular presentments of the assizes of ale and bread, or the "fines" assessed in the mayor's tourn on their commercial

[9] This analysis is discussed at length, below, pp. 347–9. For the impact of political status on these commercial matters, see above, pp. 108–14.

[10] Merchants were easily identifed because of their visibility in the freedom entries, election returns, local port customs accounts, and debt cases concerning commercial matters; documents recording these items survive with few gaps for this period (see below, pp. 337–41). Identifications of hostelers and those in the leather/skin trades were also fairly reliable because of the regular enrollment of "fines" (in effect, licencing fees) assessed on them in the MT (see below, p. 339). The clerks, lawyers, and bailiffs who comprised the professional/administrative groups frequently appeared in the abundant administrative and legal sources extant for medieval Exeter (below, pp. 337–42). Those in the building and metal trades were identified largely with the aid of the cathedral fabric rolls (ECL D&C 2636–57), building accounts for the city walls and institutional properties (esp. in CRA, EBW, DRA, Misc. Roll 6 and ECL D&C 5150–56), and debt litigation concerning building contracts (MCR, PCR passim).

activities.[11] But the poorer victuallers, especially the food hawkers who staffed market stalls, roamed the streets, and retailed foodstuffs for the more substantial victuallers, often escaped notice because of the part-time nature of their work and the presence of large numbers of women and poorer people in their ranks.

Part-time and female workers in the clothing and textile trades were also difficult to identify, although the municipal authorities' desire to regulate unenfranchised clothworkers meant that many were subjected to annual fines in the mayor's tourn.[12] More substantial members of the freedom, however, made clothing or cloth with less interference and may be under-represented here; most were identified by explicit statements of their occupation in the documents or by references to their activities in court cases. It is also important to note that this analysis grouped many at the top end of the clothing/textile trades (drapers, mercers, clothiers) with the merchants because of their emphasis upon distributive trade, maritime trade, and their regular marketing of unrelated commodities (especially imported goods like wine, iron, salt, and herring).[13]

The second problem with occupational classifications concerns the multiple income-generating interests of medieval townspeople. Individuals often practiced more than one occupation; within households diverse economic interests were the rule rather than the exception. This problem is further aggravated by the traditional occupational classifications that group trades according to the raw material used and goods produced. John Somerforde of Exeter, for example, fulled and sold cloth, often purchased untanned skins and hides, and also retailed dairy products, poultry, and meat.[14] Because of the frequency of his appearances in activities related to fulling, and because fulling was a more highly skilled task that brought in greater income than his victualling or the resale of a few cured skins every year, Somerforde's primary occupation has been identified as that of fuller. His secondary occupation selling eggs, cheese, and poultry may have actually been carried on largely by his wife (since women represented the bulk of food hawkers in the city).

[11] These presentments are listed below, p. 339.

[12] These fines were for retailing cloth without freedom membership, washing cloth with urine, or adulterating cloth by adding inferior materials.

[13] Merchants heavily involved in the textile/clothing trades are identified in the Occupation column of Table A3.1, below. In this study, merchants were identified mainly by their regular involvement in maritime trade (see below, Chapter 6) and the diversity of their distributive interests; see Thrupp 1948: 6–12 on this point.

[14] PCR 1–23 Ric. II, m. 10; MCR 1374/5, m. 40, 1391/2, m. 1; SQMT 1372, 1374–93.

Somerforde's case also points to the third problem that undermines attempts to pin down urban occupational structures. The administrative preference in Exeter and most other towns to hold the head of household responsible for the activities of all other household members often obscures the different activities of husbands, wives, and adolescent and grown children, as well as the nature of the wife's contribution to the household economy. Heads of households, not individuals, were generally listed in tax assessments, were eligible for entry to the freedom, or participated in elections to civic office. As a result, this study, like most others, concentrates more on the primary occupations of the heads of households, rather than the multiplicity of occupations in which household members might have engaged. The extant records' emphasis upon householders' occupations tends to under-represent in particular the victualling, clothing, textile, and domestic service occupations that provided employment for many women and poorer people.[15]

Several efforts have been made here to address the problems of multiple occupations and emphasis upon householders rather than individuals. One, which highlights the brewing that many households (particularly via women and servants) carried on, will be discussed shortly in the section on victualling. Another involves the care taken to distinguish how occupations were designated. The correlation between those occupations explicitly stated in the surviving documents and those surmised from the activities pursued by individuals helps to illustrate which tasks or occupations contemporaries perceived as most important.[16] In addition, the analysis of commercial debt litigation includes many servants, wage-earners, and women omitted from the occupational analysis of households, allowing us to examine the commercial activities of many who belonged to households rather than headed them.[17]

An attempt was also made to analyze the frequency with which certain occupational groups practiced other trades (Table 4.1).[18] The two groups

[15] For women in these trades, see Kowaleski 1986; Goldberg 1986a, 1986b, 1990b; Swanson 1989: 9–52; Roberts 1990.

[16] See below, Table A3.1 under "Occ—Fl." This exercise also helped to determine which occupations were better covered than others and how frequently occupational surnames described the actual pursuits of individuals (see above, n. 3).

[17] There were ninety five people singled out as "servants" in these debt cases; many craft servants and apprentices were included under the occupational group with which they were most strongly identified. There were also 332 different women involved in this litigation.

[18] Keene's (1985: 326–7) evidence of combinations of trades among Winchester property-holders shows basically the same trends as appear in Table 4.1 for Exeter; the mercantile and innkeeping trades led the way in multiple occupations. Note, however, that Keene's approach is less conservative than the one adopted here because he counted occupations within the same occupational group (such as baker and cook) and I did not. Note

Table 4.1. *Multiple occupations in Exeter, c. 1377*

Occupational group	Primary occupation (no.)	%	Known occupations: Primary occupation %	Primary and other occupation (no.)	%	Those with >1 occupation (no.)	%
Distributive	(43)	8	11	(54)	11	(25)	58
Victuallers	(82)	16	21	(97)	20	(11)	13
Hostelers	(35)	7	9	(56)	12	(17)	49
Clothing and textiles	(56)	11	14	(68)	14	(7)	13
Leather and furs	(74)	14	19	(78)	16	(9)	12
Metal	(37)	7	9	(38)	8	(4)	11
Building	(40)	8	10	(41)	8	(2)	5
Miscellaneous	(18)	3	4	(33)	7	(2)	12
Professional and administrative	(12)	2	3	(17)	4	(5)	42
Unknown	(129)	24					
Total	(525)	100	100	(482)	100		
Average						(82)	21

Source and note: See Table A3.1. The last column indicates the number and percentage of people within that group who practiced an occupation outside of the occupational group, with the exceptions noted in Appendix 1, p. 350. Table A1.1 lists the specific occupations within each occupational group. The ale-brewing done by householders was not considered here in counting other occupations; see Table 4.4.

with the most active participation in other occupations were the merchants and retailers in the distributive trades (58 per cent) and hostelers (49 per cent). This finding is hardly surprising since by definition merchants, retailers, and hostelers (the Exeter term for innkeepers) were distinguished by the wide-ranging nature of their commercial activities. Unlike most of the other occupations, which were characterized by their relationship to particular products or raw materials, the distributive trades and hostelers were noted for their dealing more than for their specialization in one type of good. The professions and administrative occupations also tended to conduct business in other trades, with those at the high end often engaged in mercantile activities while the petty officials (such as the town bailiffs) at the lower end sometimes pursued other trades at the same time they were serving the city.[19]

also that his table is based on property-holders while the Exeter one is based on heads of household.

[19] Since this study in effect freezes occupations at one moment in time, it places certain civic officials (notably clerks and bailiffs) in the professional/administrative grouping if they were in office during 1377 or when they appeared in debt litigation. Most of the men treated in this way, however, served the city for long periods of time.

In the end, no completely satisfactory method of dealing with the multiple occupations of both individuals and households can be devised. Although the following discussion attempts to shed further light on the problem, most of the quantitative analyses by necessity focus on the primary occupations of the heads of households (here called householders). We are constrained not only by the statistical difficulty of juggling multiple occupations, but also by medieval prejudices that maintained the fiction of "one man, one trade" and underplayed the economic contributions of women.[20] Nonetheless, the picture presented here is as accurate as possible in that the primary occupations represent those tasks that brought in the greatest amount of household income and upon which the householder probably expended the greatest amount of time.

The distributive trades

The distributive trades comprised two groups: merchants (who accounted for 78 per cent of the category) and retailers (such as chapmen, brokers, and chandlers). While some merchants might have been noted for a particular specialization (for example, those called "draper" or "cutler"), their commercial activities were characterized more by diversity than by specialization. All those with strong distributive functions and wholesaling interests who participated in maritime trade have therefore been designated as merchants in these analyses.[21] These merchants stood at the apex of civic society; they all belonged to the freedom, traded overseas and served in the oligarchy (Table 4.2). Their wealth, as indicated by both their mean murage tax and number of servants, was significantly greater than that possessed by any other occupational group. Indeed, the gap that separated the merchants from other occupations was actually a chasm. As a group the merchants paid almost four times the average murage tax and made up almost 60 per cent of traders by sea even though they represented a very small group of householders. The commercial and political ramifications of their control over the freedom and municipal government were outlined in some detail in the previous chapter. Their domination of the port trade and regional trade is treated more extensively in later chapters.[22]

[20] For the medieval legislation that maintained this fiction, see Lipson 1959: 357–9. For women, see especially Swanson 1989: 6–7; Goldberg 1992: 82–157.

[21] Not all those who participated in seaborne trade were labelled merchants, however; see Table A3.1. For the guidelines generally employed here to determine who were merchants, see Thrupp 1948: 6–12.

[22] See below, Chapter 6.

The extraordinary influence of the Exeter merchants within the local markets can be seen in their high profile as creditors. Although they made up only 8 per cent of all householders in 1377, merchants appeared as creditors in almost 20 per cent of all debts.[23] Unlike most occupational groups who actually arrived in court more often as debtors than creditors, merchants showed up owing money in fewer than 4 per cent of the cases, five times less often than they acted as creditors. Their dominance, moreover, went beyond the frequency of their appearance; as creditors their mean debt was twice that of all creditors (Table 4.3). Although they appeared less frequently as debtors, the sums they owed were four times the average debt of 11.2*s*. As noted earlier in the discussion of the merchant oligarchy, mercantile commerce could entail heavy obligations and risk as well as great profits.[24]

The distributive trades also included retailers who focused primarily on the resale of a variety of relatively inexpensive items. Thomas Cardmaker, for example, dealt in ale, boards, lathes, nails, arrows, cloth, livestock, and other "diverse things." He also loaned money to fellow residents (as did other retailers like William Knyght) and regularly did business with outsiders in the local markets, pursuing debts against men from Silverton, Thorverton, Crediton, and even London.[25] The category of retailers is admittedly a somewhat artificial one, designed to distinguish distributors who rarely if ever engaged in wholesale and maritime trade from those who regularly did so. Contemporaries may not have coined the term "retailer" but they did recognize the smaller scale of their commercial activities. Richard Lovel and William Knyght, for example, were both called "common merchants."[26] As a group, retailers were considerably less wealthy and powerful than their fellow merchants; their mean murage tax was about the same as the overall average of 13*d*, none of them ever traded overseas, and only three gained entry to the ruling elite, and then only as electors or bridge wardens in the B rank of the oligarchy (Table 4.2). The retailing privileges endowed by freedom membership must have proved attractive, however, since five of the ten entered the organization. As indicated by their frequent appearance in debt suits, they too were heavily involved in the local markets, acting as creditors 70 per cent of the time (Table 4.3). Like merchants, their

[23] They represented 659 of the 3,386 Exeter lay creditors and 130 of the 3,359 lay debtors; see also Table 4.3.

[24] See above, pp. 110–15.

[25] Retailing activities: MCR 1373/4, m. 24, 1386/7, m.9, 1387/8, m. 9, 1389/90, m. 24, 1390/1, mm. 21, 24; PCR 1–23 Ric. II, mm. 36, 37, 47; EQMT 1390. Moneylending: MCR 1390/1, mm. 27, 33 and PCR 1–23 Ric. II, m. 31. Debts with non-Exeter residents: PCR 1–23 Ric. II, mm. 16, 17, 23, 30, 37, 68.

[26] MCR 1379/80, m. 50.

Table 4.2. *Indices of wealth, servants, commercial activity, and political rank of occupational groups in late fourteenth-century Exeter*

Occupational group	Had as primary occup. in 1377	Average murage tax in 1377	Average no. servants in c. 1370–90	Those in group who eventually: Entered freedom (no.)	%	Traded by sea (no.)	%	Were in oligarchy (no.)	%
Distributive	(43)	41.2*d*	1.72	(38)	88	(34)	79	(36)	84
Merchants	(33)	49.1*d*	1.85	(33)		(33)		(33)	
Retailers	(10)	13.1*d*	1.30	(5)		(1)		(3)	
Victuallers	(82)	12.0*d*	0.49	(21)	26	(1)	1	(10)	12
Bakers	(13)	11.9*d*	0.69	(2)		(0)		(2)	
Butchers	(14)	20.2*d*	0.86	(10)		(0)		(5)	
Cooks	(6)	5.0*d*	0	(0)		(0)		(0)	
Fishmongers	(14)	9.1*d*	0.57	(2)		(0)		(0)	
Millers	(19)	6.7*d*	0.16	(0)		(0)		(0)	
Spicers	(2)	18.0*d*	3.00	(2)		(0)		(2)	
Taverners	(4)	17.0*d*	0.25	(1)		(1)		(1)	
Others	(10)	10.5*d*	0.10	(4)		(0)		(0)	
Hostelers	(35)	14.5*d*	0.94	(18)	51	(5)	14	(9)	26
Clothing and textiles	(56)	8.3*d*	1.05	(19)	34	(4)	7	(4)	7
Dyers	(3)	19.0*d*	1.67	(1)		(2)		(0)	
Fullers	(11)	6.8*d*	1.55	(2)		(0)		(0)	
Shearmen	(2)	3.0*d*	1.00	(0)		(0)		(0)	
Tailors	(14)	7.5*d*	0.57	(4)		(0)		(0)	
Weavers	(15)	8.0*d*	1.00	(6)		(0)		(1)	
Others	(11)	11.3*d*	1.09	(6)		(2)		(3)	
Leather and furs	(74)	11.6*d*	0.95	(34)	46	(3)	4	(17)	23
Curriers	(2)	15.0*d*	0	(2)		(0)		(0)	
Furriers/skinners	(23)	13.6*d*	1.35	(12)		(2)		(9)	
Glovers	(6)	6.4*d*	0.33	(2)		(0)		(1)	
Shoemakers	(20)	12.6*d*	1.15	(11)		(1)		(3)	
Saddlers	(9)	7.5*d*	1.00	(5)		(0)		(2)	
Tanners	(2)	21.0*d*	0	(1)		(0)		(1)	
Others	(12)	8.7*d*	0.42	(1)		(0)		(1)	
Metal	(37)	11.1*d*	1.22	(17)	46	(5)	14	(8)	22
Braziers	(2)	30.0*d*	2.00	(2)		(0)		(2)	
Goldsmiths	(7)	10.5*d*	0.57	(3)		(0)		(1)	
Pewterers	(2)	6.0*d*	1.50	(1)		(1)		(1)	
Plumbers	(3)	8.0*d*	2.00	(2)		(0)		(1)	
Smiths	(17)	12.1*d*	1.47	(8)		(4)		(3)	
Others	(6)	6.5*d*	0.50	(1)		(0)		(0)	
Building	(40)	6.4*d*	0.63	(3)	8	(1)	3	(1)	3
Carpenters	(22)	6.7*d*	0.59	(1)		(0)		(0)	
Glaziers	(3)	8.7*d*	1.33	(1)		(1)		(1)	
Masons	(7)	5.6*d*	0.71	(1)		(0)		(0)	

Table 4.2. *cont.*

Occupational group	Had as primary occup. in 1377	Average murage tax in 1377	Average no. servants in c. 1370–90	Those in group who eventually: Entered freedom (no.)	%	Traded by sea (no.)	%	Were in oligarchy (no.)	%
Roofers	(3)	5.0*d*	1.00	(0)		(0)		(0)	
Others	(5)	4.0*d*	0	(0)		(0)		(0)	
Miscellaneous	(17)	14.1*d*	0.73	(4)	23	(2)	12	(1)	6
Barbers	(2)	18.0*d*	2.50	(1)		(0)		(0)	
Bowyers/fletchers	(3)	14.0*d*	0.67	(1)		(1)		(1)	
Farmers/graziers	(6)	15.0*d*	0.33	(0)		(0)		(0)	
Others	(6)	9.0*d*	0.33	(2)		(1)		(0)	
Professional and administrative	(12)	18.7*d*	0.83	(10)	83	(3)	25	(10)	83
Bailiffs	(5)	12.0*d*	0.60	(3)		(2)		(3)	
Lawyers	(4)	12.0*d*	0.75	(4)		(0)		(4)	
Others	(3)	32.0*d*	1.33	(3)		(1)		(3)	
Unidentified	(129)	6.2*d*	0.16	(11)	9	(0)	–	(7)	5
Total	(525)			(175)		(58)		(103)	
Averages		13.0*d*	0.74		33		11		20

Source and note: Table A3.1. Figures for the murage tax based on taxes for 418 residents; the median tax was 6*d*. The total number of servants counted was 387.

debts as creditors were also relatively costly compared to the other trades. But unlike merchants, the sums they paid as debtors were significantly smaller than the amounts they sought as creditors, a sign of the lower investment necessary for retail trade. On occasion, however, retailers could operate on a larger scale. Cardmaker once made a recognizance for £10 and Richard Lovel sued a cleric for £45 for cloth he had sold to him.[27] Such large transactions remind us that the line between retailers and wholesalers is not easily drawn.

The victualling trades and hostelers

As in most medieval towns, victuallers represented the single largest occupational group. In Exeter victuallers represented 21 per cent of the known occupations in 1377, and almost 30 per cent when hostelers are included (Table 4.1). This figure is close to the 26 to 33 per cent of

[27] MCR 1389/90, m. 6 (under the name of Newman); PCR 1–23 Ric. II, m. 47, for Lovel.

Table 4.3. *Debt suits and debt amounts of Exeter creditors and debtors by occupational group, 1378–88*

Occupational group	Primary occup. in 1377 %	All debt suits %	% of creditors in group	Average debt as creditors (No.)	Amt.	Average debt as debtors (No.)	Amt.
Distributive	10.8	19.4	79.5	(343)	23.4*s*	(110)	27.6*s*
Merchants	8.3	13.5	83.6	(261)	25.7*s*	(55)	44.3*s*
Retailers	2.5	5.9	70.0	(82)	15.9*s*	(55)	10.9*s*
Victuallers	20.6	28.2	50.1	(367)	8.3*s*	(389)	10.1*s*
Bakers	3.3	1.6	58.3	(25)	5.4*s*	(23)	7.5*s*
Butchers	3.5	14.5	62.2	(246)	8.3*s*	(143)	13.3*s*
Cooks	1.5	0.9	16.0	(3)	3.7*s*	(23)	4.3*s*
Fishmongers	3.5	4.9	36.4	(48)	6.8*s*	(94)	5.8*s*
Millers	4.8	2.4	16.8	(7)	5.8*s*	(47)	3.3*s*
Spicers	0.5	1.7	53.5	(20)	10.5*s*	(22)	27.1*s*
Taverners	1.0	1.0	58.6	(9)	30.9*s*	(5)	46.8*s*
Others	2.5	1.2	28.7	(9)	3.7*s*	(32)	12.3*s*
Hostelers	8.8	6.8	66.5	(110)	7.6*s*	(71)	10.2*s*
Clothing and textiles	14.2	12.1	39.7	(135)	4.8*s*	(204)	9.9*s*
Dyers	0.8	1.2	45.6	(15)	4.9*s*	(16)	12.9*s*
Fullers	2.8	2.0	33.9	(22)	4.4*s*	(47)	9.8*s*
Shearmen	0.5	0.3	15.0	(2)	1.3*s*	(11)	4.4*s*
Tailors	3.5	2.8	45.1	(34)	3.2*s*	(39)	4.6*s*
Weavers	3.8	3.6	29.7	(25)	3.9*s*	(75)	5.1*s*
Others	2.8	2.2	53.2	(37)	7.2*s*	(16)	46.1*s*
Leather and furs	18.7	12.4	46.7	(125)	8.2*s*	(177)	7.9*s*
Curriers	0.5	0.4	81.8	(7)	11.9*s*	–	–
Furriers/ skinners	5.8	3.7	41.2	(34)	6.7*s*	(54)	7.0*s*
Glovers	1.5	0.4	28.6	(2)	10.1*s*	(8)	3.0*s*
Saddlers	2.3	0.9	57.4	(10)	3.3*s*	(13)	13.3*s*
Shoemakers	5.0	5.0	58.3	(62)	9.7*s*	(55)	8.7*s*
Tanners	0.5	0.3	52.6	(3)	10.0*s*	(2)	25.2*s*
Others	3.1	1.7	14.1	(7)	3.5*s*	(45)	6.5*s*
Metal	9.4	7.3	56.5	(103)	8.0*s*	(108)	11.1*s*
Braziers	0.5	0.1	50.0	(1)	1.3*s*	(2)	3.3*s*
Goldsmiths	1.8	1.5	28.4	(9)	8.3*s*	(36)	8.8*s*
Pewterers	0.5	0.1	75.0	(1)	2.3*s*	–	–
Plumbers	0.8	0.6	52.9	(10)	4.4*s*	(9)	49.3*s*
Smiths	4.3	3.9	66.4	(68)	9.9*s*	(51)	6.8*s*
Others	1.5	1.1	27.2	(14)	2.2*s*	(10)	8.7*s*

Table 4.3. *cont.*

Occupational group	Primary occup. in 1377 %	All debt suits %	% of creditors in group	Average debt as creditors (No.)	Amt.	Average debt as debtors (No.)	Amt.
Building	10.1	3.1	35.4	(25)	13.1*s*	(46)	5.1*s*
Carpenters	5.5	1.4	35.8	(12)	21.8*s*	(22)	3.5*s*
Glaziers	0.8	0.4	13.6	(1)	2.0*s*	(10)	4.8*s*
Masons	1.8	0.8	38.6	(5)	2.5*s*	(4)	17.2*s*
Roofers	0.8	0.3	50.0	(5)	8.4*s*	(5)	5.1*s*
Others	1.2	0.2	57.1	(2)	4.8*s*	(5)	3.9*s*
Miscellaneous	4.3	3.4	41.4	(36)	10.3*s*	(48)	7.0*s*
Barbers	0.5	0.4	72.0	(5)	7.7*s*	–	–
Bowyers/ fletchers	0.8	0.7	57.1	(10)	10.8*s*	(3)	29.7*s*
Farmers/ graziers	1.5	0.2	10.0	(1)	1.0*s*	(7)	9.7*s*
Servants	–	1.5	36.0	(15)	3.4*s*	(24)	3.3*s*
Others	1.5	0.6	22.9	(5)	4.6*s*	(14)	4.3*s*
Professional and administrative	3.1	7.3	86.9	(144)	9.7*s*	(26)	24.0*s*
Bailiffs	1.3	3.2	78.5	(69)	11.0*s*	(19)	23.1*s*
Lawyers	1.0	1.2	79.5	(23)	3.4*s*	(5)	33.1*s*
Others	0.8	2.9	94.7	(52)	11.3*s*	(2)	9.3*s*
Total	100.0	100.0		(1,388)		(1,179)	
Average			57.9		12.5*s*		11.2*s*
Unidentified	24.0	19.4	35.8	(205)	7.5*s*	(141)	25.1*s*
Clergy		2.9	43.9	(42)	25.9*s*	(30)	7.3*s*

Source and note: Table A3.1; MCR and PCR debt cases, 1378–88. See Table 4.2 for numbers of householders in 1377 in each primary occupation and occupational group. The total number of creditors and debtors was 5,843; including the unidentified occupations and clergy, it was 7,457.

Winchester occupations that practiced these trades at this time.[28] Yet even these figures underestimate the local market's concentration on victualling since the provision of food and drink also represented the most common secondary occupation of urban residents (Table 4.1). Indeed, almost three-quarters of all households brewed and sold ale;

[28] Keene 1985: 252–3, 362–3 (and see n. 18, above). The poll tax returns show somewhat lower figures (12 to 27 per cent) for other towns in 1377 (Goldberg 1990a: 211). Although some differences could be due to the size and economic orientation of towns (smaller towns and those hosting large numbers of students or visitors might have larger victualling sectors), most of the differences are probably due to under-reporting of these occupations in the tax returns.

29 per cent could be termed commercial brewers since they brewed ten or more times during the period under study (Table 4.4).[29]

Although fines for breaking the assize of ale were usually assessed on heads of household, wives and servants did most of the brewing. Before the lists of brewing fines became standardized, for example, clerks tended to list women as brewers rather than their husbands or the male head of household.[30] Disputes over the payment of brewgavel (a yearly toll paid by unenfranchised brewers) also show female servants, sisters, and wives doing the brewing.[31] Women were also heavily involved in the marketing of malt, and debt litigation involving malted grains drew wives into court more frequently than any other type of obligation.[32] The sudden appearance of widows paying brewing fines in the years immediately following their husbands' deaths also suggests that they, rather than their husbands (who had previously been listed as the household brewer), had probably been brewing (or supervising) all along.[33] Indeed, only one man was ever given the specific occupational designation of "brewer" in late fourteenth-century Exeter.[34] Most brewers were women in their middle married years and most were aided to some degree by servants or family members.[35] Such activities supplemented the family income and, in the case of poorer women (who were probably more often tapsters than brewers), may have contributed a significant amount to the household budget.

[29] Unfortunately, the Exeter records do not reveal how many times a year a household brewed or the size of the batch brewed so it is impossible to specify the economic contribution made by this activity. For this reason, brewing has not been added to the figures for multiple occupations in Table 4.1.

[30] For example, MCR Roll 1 (1264–71), mm. 1d, 5d, 9, 10d, 11, 11d, 18d. Once the brewing fines became standardized and enrolled on the MT in the fourteenth century, the clerical influence on how to list the presentments is evident in the decision of some clerks to list women instead of men; see especially the MT in MCR 1324/5, m. 5d and MT 1345–9 where the multiplicity of clerical hands shows how different clerks chose to enroll presentments in different ways. See also Keene 1985: 265, and Swanson 1989: 21; Goldberg 1992: 28–9, for the under-recording of female brewers in other towns.

[31] MCR 1296/7, m. 21; 1320/1, m. 15d.

[32] See below, p. 205 and Kowaleski forthcoming.

[33] MT 1373–93; forty two of the 150 female brewers in this period first appeared in the brewing lists the year their husbands died; all forty two husbands had been enrolled as brewers the year before they died. See also Goldberg 1988: 116; 1992: 111–13.

[34] John Scarlet: see EQMT 1373–93; MCR 1380/1, m.5. Several women, however, had the surname "Tappistere" or "Brewstere."

[35] The earlier brewing lists (n. 30, above) often distinguished wives, daughters, and *ancilla*. See also the comments of Margery Kempe of Lynn concerning her brewing efforts and the help rendered by her servants (*Book of Margery Kempe*: 9–10). For more on the age and marital status of female brewers see Bennett 1986 and forthcoming; Goldberg 1988: 116–18, and 1990b: 42.

It would be a mistake, however, to see brewing as a mainstay of the poor. Selling ale as tapsters may have been a common pursuit of some poorer, unskilled people, but brewing required a considerable investment in equipment, fuel, and malted grain.[36] Many households had the basic equipment to brew, as suggested by the 71 per cent of households that did so at one time or another, but very few poor households brewed regularly. High grain prices could turn many away; in years when grain became very expensive (such as 1374–5 and 1390–1) the number of households brewing in Exeter dropped by around 15 per cent.[37] The correlation between prosperity and brewing is also obvious in the higher mean murage tax paid by those who brewed more than ten times.[38] These commercial brewing households also enjoyed freedom membership almost twice as often as the average (60 per cent compared to 33 per cent) and belonged to the oligarchy more than twice as often as all households (43 per cent compared to 20 per cent). The average number of servants in such brewing households (1.22) was also much higher than the overall average (0.74) although here the relationship between household wealth and the ability to employ large numbers of servants may take precedence.

Occupation could also influence which households brewed; this was particularly evident for the hostelers who all brewed, and brewed on a more regular basis than any other occupational group (Table 4.4). Obviously the innkeepers of Exeter were able to offer clients drink as well as lodging during their stay. Almost all of the merchant and professional households (including lawyers, bailiffs, and clerks) also brewed; their substantial wealth must have made such activity feasible (Table 4.2). Besides wealth, the roles of servants and wives also may have influenced which occupations regularly engaged in brewing. Households that brewed frequently tended to have more servants; some of this extra labor could easily have been channelled towards brewing. The correlation between frequent brewing and servants is especially apparent in the households of merchants, the metal trades, barbers, and professionals (Tables 4.2 and 4.4). The relative involvement of

[36] Britnell (1986b: 89–90) also found that the Colchester wealthy elite was heavily involved in brewing. For examples of the relatively high cost of brewing equipment in medieval towns, see Goldberg 1988: 116–17; Swanson 1989: 22; *Calendar of Letter Book L*: 232; *London assize of nuisance*: 175 (I am grateful to Judith Bennett for these last two references). Ale and malt were also the most frequent subjects of debt litigation (below, Table 5.2).

[37] Brewing fines were usually assessed in late autumn and reflected brewing for the previous year. The number fined were as follows: 1374 (168 brewers), 1375 (145), 1376 (152), 1376 (no MT), 1377 (205 brewers), 1389 (225), 1390 (219), 1391 (184), 1392 (195). For grain prices see Beveridge 1929: 531; Farmer 1991b: 502–3.

[38] They paid 19*d* compared to the 13*d* average.

Table 4.4. *Brewing activity in Exeter households by occupational group, 1365–93*

Occupational group	% in primary occup. N=520	% of brewing fines N=3,272	% of group brewing: Once N=371	% of group brewing: Ten times N=150	Average no. of brewing fines: brewing HH N=371	Average no. of brewing fines: all HH N=520
Distributive	8.3	13.0	86	54	11.51	9.91
Merchants	6.4	11.5	94	61	11.39	12.13
Retailers	1.9	1.5	60	30	8.33	5.00
Victuallers	15.3	12.3	68	21	7.43	5.01
Bakers	2.3	2.5	83	25	8.20	6.83
Butchers	2.5	3.6	85	46	10.64	9.00
Cooks	1.2	0.2	67	0	1.75	1.17
Fishmongers	2.7	2.6	71	36	8.60	6.14
Millers	3.5	1.0	42	5	3.50	1.47
Spicers	0.4	0.2	100	0	3.50	3.50
Taverners	0.8	1.0	100	25	8.50	8.50
Others	1.9	1.2	40	0	8.00	4.00
Hostelers	6.7	15.7	100	69	14.63	14.63
Clothing and textiles	10.4	8.1	69	15	7.08	4.85
Dyers	0.4	0.2	50	0	6.00	3.00
Fullers	2.1	2.3	91	18	7.40	6.73
Shearmen	0.2	0.2	100	0	5.00	5.00
Tailors	2.7	0.7	57	0	2.75	1.57
Weavers	2.9	1.7	47	13	8.14	3.80
Others	2.1	3.0	91	36	10.89	8.91
Leather and furs	14.2	12.3	69	26	7.96	5.49
Curriers	0.4	0.7	100	100	12.00	12.00
Furriers/skinners	4.4	4.4	74	35	8.53	6.30
Glovers	1.2	0.1	33	0	2.00	0.67
Shoemakers	3.8	3.2	65	20	7.43	5.20
Saddlers	1.7	2.2	100	33	8.00	8.00
Tanners	0.4	0.2	100	0	3.50	3.50
Others	2.3	1.5	45	18	10.00	4.17
Metal	7.1	10.1	76	46	11.86	8.97
Braziers	0.4	1.4	100	100	23.50	23.50
Goldsmiths	1.3	0.9	57	14	7.50	4.29
Pewterers	0.4	0.0	0	0	0.00	0.00
Plumbers	0.6	1.2	100	67	13.30	13.30
Smiths	3.2	5.7	88	65	12.40	10.90
Others	1.2	0.9	67	17	7.25	4.83

Table 4.4. *cont.*

Occupational group	% in primary occup. N=520	% of brewing fines N=3,272	% of group brewing: Once N=371	% of group brewing: Ten times N=150	Average no. of brewing fines: brewing HH N=371	Average no. of brewing fines: all HH N=520
Building	7.7	5.7	78	23	6.03	4.68
Carpenters	4.2	2.6	68	14	5.67	3.86
Glaziers	0.6	0.7	100	67	8.00	8.00
Masons	1.3	1.7	86	43	9.33	8.00
Roofers	0.6	0.5	100	33	5.00	5.00
Others	1.0	0.2	80	0	1.75	1.40
Miscellaneous	3.3	2.4	65	24	7.27	4.44
Barbers	0.4	0.6	100	50	10.50	10.50
Bowyers/fletchers	0.6	0.1	67	0	1.50	1.00
Farmers/graziers	1.2	0.9	67	33	7.75	5.17
Others	1.1	0.8	50	17	8.33	4.17
Professional and administrative	2.4	4.4	92	58	13.09	12.00
Bailiffs	1.0	1.3	80	40	10.50	8.40
Lawyers	0.8	1.4	100	50	11.25	11.25
Others	0.6	1.7	100	100	19.00	19.00
Unidentified	24.6	16.0	59	17	6.86	4.08
Total	100.0	100.0				
Average			71	29	8.82	6.26

Source and note: See Table A3.1. Brewing fines taken from MT 1365–93 (missing years = 1367, 1373, 1377). The five Exe Island households (a baker, butcher, dyer, shearman, and one unidentified) were excluded from this table since they were not within the city's jurisdiction for the assize of ale.

wives in the household business also helped to determine which households brewed more often and on a larger scale. Wives of merchants and professionals, for example, were probably less involved in their husbands' affairs and therefore had more time to engage in brewing than artisanal wives whose labor was crucial to the success of the family business. The relatively high brewing profile of householders in the metal trades (and to a lesser extent the building trades) suggests the same possibility (Table 4.4). These trades were not especially wealthy but they did represent crafts largely carried on by men who did not rely as much on the contribution of their wives and daughters as did those in the clothing, textile, leather, and victualling trades.[39] The demands of the family business may have made it more difficult for women in these latter households to brew ale regularly.

Victuallers were not among the more active brewers, in part because the production and sale of food and drink probably required the full attention of all members of the household. The relatively low level of profits and skill involved in food preparation encouraged victuallers to employ spouses and children to help process, prepare, sell, or deliver foodstuffs. This family participation may also account for the very low number of servants found in victualling households (Table 4.2). It is significant that butchers were the biggest brewers among victuallers (Table 4.4). Their workplace in the Fleshfold was more physically separated from their homes than most, the skills required for their job probably took longer to learn and required more strength, and their wealth was greater than most victuallers; all these factors probably promoted participation in brewing by their wives.[40]

With the exception of butchers and spicers, few victuallers joined the freedom (Table 4.2). The victuallers' focus upon food may have made freedom membership less necessary because sales of foodstuffs for immediate consumption were exempt from tolls in the town. Since only about one-quarter of the victuallers ever joined the freedom, a correspondingly low number (12 per cent) exercised any political power as part of the ruling oligarchy; butchers and spicers were the main exceptions. Only one victualler (a taverner who imported wine) participated in maritime trade.

Although the wealth, political power, and foreign trade of victuallers were limited, their participation in the local markets was not. Since 60 to 80 per cent of medieval incomes went for the expenditure of food, it is not surprising that over half of all debt cases before the Exeter courts involved food and drink.[41] Drink alone (ale, wine, and cider) accounted for 19 per cent of all debts, cereals and cereal products represented another 13 per cent, and meat a further 10 per cent. The dominance of the trade in food and drink was also reflected in the victuallers' share of debt litigation in Exeter; they were involved in about twice as many debt suits (28 per cent) as other occupational groups (Table 4.3). The status of most victuallers may have been low

[39] For the higher profile of women in these trades, see Kowaleski 1986; Swanson 1989.

[40] The brewing activities of fishmongers reflected the predilection for innkeeping among this group (Table A3.1, below) while the brewing by taverners was a natural offshoot of their provision of drink; see Table 4.4.

[41] For food expenditures, see Phelps-Brown and Hopkins 1962; de la Roncière 1976: 413. For food and drink in debt litigation, see below, Table 5.2.

and the value of the individual segments of their trade not particularly high (witness the average sum of their debts in Table 4.3), but their combined share of local trade and representation within the town was impressive.

Within the victualling trades there were wide variations in the status and commercial activities of individual occupations. By far the most prominent in Exeter were the fourteen butchers who headed households in 1377. Paying an average murage of slightly over 20*d*, the butchers also enjoyed freedom membership more often than other victuallers (over 70 per cent belonged) and served in oligarchic offices more frequently. They had an extremely high profile in the local markets, alone comprising some 14 per cent of all Exeter debt litigants and thus outnumbering even the merchants. Yet merchants surpassed them as creditors and in the scale of their trade; the sums paid to and by butchers hardly compared with the much higher amounts owed in mercantile debts (Table 4.3). The butchers' prominence in urban markets may be traced to the value of their products and the diversity of their commercial dealings. Besides profiting from meat sales, butchers marketed several by-products of the animals they slaughtered. In Exeter, as in most other English towns, cattle and sheep carcasses had to be sold with hides and horns attached so butchers possessed a virtual monopoly on the sale of skins, hides, and horns to tanners, other leatherworkers, and horners.[42] Butchers also dominated the sale of tallow to chandlers, soapers, and leatherworkers.[43]

Since the cattle and sheep that constituted the bulk of meat consumed by urban residents were brought to town on the hoof for slaughter, butchers were usually heavily involved in the regional livestock trade, an activity that required a significant initial investment.[44] The rising demand for meat which accompanied the improved standards of living after 1350 also benefited butchers, some of whom extended their interests to include the breeding, fattening, and trading of livestock on a large scale.[45] Exeter butchers showed similar interests by the late fourteenth century in their joint ownership of bulls and their leases of city pastureland on the outskirts of town.[46] Indeed, butchers occupied almost

[42] Those who failed to adhere to this prohibition in Exeter were subject to fines; see, for example, MCR 1360/1, m. 8d, and Kowaleski 1990: 59–60.

[43] See, for example, MCR 1391/2, m. 7; 1392/3, m. 26. See also Jones 1976: 142–3, for London butchers' dealings in tallow and Swanson 1989: 14–17, for the diversity of butchers' dealings in York.

[44] For meat consumption in medieval Exeter, see Maltby 1979 and below, p. 297. For the livestock trade, see below, pp. 293–300.

[45] See below, pp. 294–300. For the similar situation elsewhere, see Dyer 1981: 17–21.

[46] MCR 1384/5, mm. 36, 41, 49; 1392/3, m. 1; 1393/4, m. 1.

70 per cent of the forty eight biggest and most valuable parcels of city-owned pasture and meadow (with annual rents of at least 20*s*).[47] They also went farther afield, leasing pasture and meadow in the neighboring manors of Cowley, Cowick, Heghes, and Topsham, and buying up animals in more distant places such as Woodbury and Chudleigh.[48] These regional networks of trade in meat, including the significant presence of rural butchers in Exeter's markets, are discussed at greater length in Chapter 7.

Fishmongers also participated in regional networks of trade, buying fish at markets near the sea and selling it to fish dealers from inland market towns.[49] Despite the geographic range of their dealings, however, the fishmongers never matched the butchers in wealth or prestige within the city, and no group comparable to the powerful fishmongers of medieval London emerged; merchants rather than specialized fishmongers handled most fish imports and exports in Exeter.[50] Although Exeter fishmongers were often called "fishers" in the extant records, their activities centered almost exclusively on marketing rather than catching fish. Most were rather humble; they paid less than half the average murage of the butchers (7.3*d*), only two ever achieved freedom membership, and none served in the ruling oligarchy. Their 5 per cent share of debt litigation in the borough courts placed them second only to the butchers among victuallers, but the considerably lower value of their debts and their higher profile as debtors (they appeared owing money over 64 per cent of the time) reflects their weaker position within commerce.[51]

Unlike butchers, who devoted their whole attention to butchering and related activities, fishmongers often combined fish marketing with other pursuits, particularly innkeeping, which explains the high profile of some fishmongers in brewing (Table 4.4). As hostelers, fishmongers were well placed to make contact with the fish dealers from Somerset, Dorset, and east Devon who regularly travelled to Exeter to acquire

[47] Based on leases of eighty two parcels of pasture and meadow leased from 1378–82 (DCR 2–22 Ric. II, mm. 8–11, 13; MCR 1378/9–1382/3). Butchers represented thirty five of the total ninety six lessors and thirty three of the lessors of the forty eight biggest parcels (those with rents over 20*s*); oligarchic merchants were also prominent lessors.

[48] PCR 1–23 Ric. II, m. 38 (Cowley); PRO CP40/490, m. 55 (Cowick); ED/M/528, 583; DD 50111, 50113 (Heghes); PRO CP40/463, m. 158d (Floyersheghes); W1258/G2/50 (Topsham); DCO Min. Accts. 42 (Bradninch, under the name of John Shephurd); MCR 1286, m. 8d (Woodbury); PCR 1–23 Ric. II, m. 25 (Chudleigh).

[49] See below, pp. 308–20 for an extended discussion of this regional trade.

[50] For the London fishmongers, see Unwin 1938: 37–43; Thrupp 1948: 60–97.

[51] They ranked eighth among creditors but second among debtors.

fish.[52] The frequent complaints against hostelers who kept "fish markets" in their establishments attests to how convenient local and non-Exeter fishmongers found inns as sites of exchange for their goods. Although rarely heads of households, many women also sold fish and especially shellfish like oysters and mussels. Some of these women may have harvested these shellfish themselves in the waters of the Exe estuary just south of the city, then returned to hawk them in the streets or marketplace.[53] Other women retailed fish from stalls at the fish market near Broad Gate.[54] Although women were an integral part of the fish trade, their marginal role as retailers and shellfish gatherers, combined with their poverty and married state, often obscured them from the view of administrative and other sources so that their contribution to the trade is difficult to measure.

Women also worked on the fringes of the baking trades, making and selling inexpensive horse bread (made of beans and peas and occasionally eaten by poor people), oat bread, and "gruel" bread.[55] Most baking, however, was done by male householders who paid an average murage tax of 12*d* and only occasionally joined the freedom. The only two who belonged to the freedom were also elected to the B Rank oligarchy. Since both had been active years before they gained entry, it appears that the political perquisites of membership were more attractive than the economic benefits which, because of the exemptions from toll granted to much of the trade in food, were of less use to the bakers. These oligarchic bakers (Andrew and Thomas Bakere), along with the other eleven resident bakers, provided the bulk of the city's bread needs during the 1370s and 1380s. There is little trace in Exeter of the "country" bakers found in medieval London until the second half of the fifteenth century when the Exeter authorities promulgated regulations against "foreign" bakers to restrict their activities within the

52 See below, p. 316 for this and the following. These fishmonger/hostelers seem also to have been more involved in the shellfish trade, a pattern also evident in Winchester (Keene 1985: 261).

53 See, for example, MCR 1302/3, m. 4d; 1308/9, m. 21d; 1349/50, m. 21; 1360/1, m. 23; EQMT 1401; WQMT 1405. Women continued these activities for centuries in Devon; see Porter 1984.

54 See the NQMT presentments in the 1390s for leaving fish viscera in the street. The fish shambles was in the NT; see Lega-Weekes 1915: 21–3. For similar "fishwives" in Bristol, see *Great Red Book of Bristol*, vol. 4: 134, 143; for Winchester, see Keene 1985: 261.

55 See, for example, MCR 1317/18, mm. 5d, 20d, 38d which include many women in the assize *panis gruell'*; the regular assize of bread presentments in MCR 1317/18, mm. 3d, 11d, 22d, 26d, 38d, and throughout the fourteenth century, only mention women as bakers of horse bread. Others may have hawked bread for the bakers but no evidence of this survives in Exeter. For this practice elsewhere, see *Little Red Book of Bristol*, vol. 2: 32–3; Swanson 1989: 12.

city.[56] Perhaps it was only then that the population of Exeter became large enough to warrant competition from non-resident bakers.

Two baker's servants (John Holewill and Henry Marchaunt) earned enough to set up their own households. Both were the subject of considerable litigation as rival bakers fought over their services.[57] Such disputes illustrate the keen competition for skilled labor after the Black Death, as well as the civic authorities' determination to penalize those who did not adhere to labor contracts, even if one of the employers was himself a prominent member of the community. It also points to some of the difficulties in determining the occupational structure of any one town since some skilled servants (like John Holewill) set up their own households and thus came under the administrative eye of town records while others (as Henry Marchaunt did for a while) either leased accommodation or lived with their parents or employers, thus escaping the purview of such sources.

Although bakers quarrelled among themselves over servants, they also exhibited considerable solidarity. They were accused of trade conspiracies more than any other occupation, accusations that may have been prompted in large part by their control of a vital foodstuff. Indeed, the assize of bread (taken whenever the price of wheat changed significantly) subjected bakers to heavy quality and price controls. They clearly chafed at these restraints since at least two of the conspiracies involved strikes whereby they refused to bake bread because of disputes about prices or quality.[58] In another strike, four of the major bakers were said to have plotted to monopolize the manufacture and sale of bread for seven leagues around the town.[59] This was one of the few instances when the commercial interests of the bakers went outside the narrow bounds of the city, aside from those times they were accused of buying up supplies of grain from cornmongers before they reached the central marketplace.[60] Such presentments named non-bakers much more frequently than bakers, suggesting that the bakers more often purchased their grain directly from dealers in Exeter, rather than themselves venturing into the agrarian networks of trade. The bakers were also united in their resentment of the municipal ordinance that forced them to grind their grain at the city-owned mills in Duryard while

[56] Thrupp 1933: 56–9; *Citie of Excester*: 874. For similar regulations in York, see Swanson 1989: 12.
[57] MCR 1380/1, mm. 1, 2, 4, 4d. Holewill was also known under the name of John Bakere; see Table A3.1.
[58] MCR 1323/4, m. 13d; 1362/3, m. 7.
[59] SQMT 1356. For an earlier conspiracy, see MCR Roll 1, m. 13d (1266).
[60] For example, MCR 1392/3, m. 21. For more on their role in the grain trade, see Kowaleski forthcoming.

other Exeter residents were free to grind their grain at whatever mill they chose.[61] Fined when caught doing otherwise, the bakers also regularly clashed with the Duryard millers, accusing them of systematically stealing their flour and other offenses.[62]

The Exeter millers were the only pure wage-earners among the victualling occupations; they were paid by the mills' institutional landlords or by the men (usually rich merchants) who farmed or leased them. Some of these millers were well rewarded; John Berie, the master miller at Duryard, made 24*d* per week in the late 1380s for an annual salary of £5 4*s*.[63] Pay rates for his three fellow millers (sometimes called loders) were normally 13*d*–16*d* a week. These sums were far more than those received by any country miller.[64] Wages at the other Exeter mills were less generous than at Duryard.[65] These millers, however, seem to have augmented their income by receiving a share of the multure paid by clients.[66] These perquisites, along with a cloth livery worth up to 8*s*, may have served as the enticement to lure John Berie away from his high-paying job at Duryard to the position of miller at Crikelpit where he only received an annual stipend of one mark, eight times less than his Duryard salary.[67]

The wage-earner status of millers shows up in the low murage rates they paid and their complete absence from the ranks of the freedom and oligarchy (Table 4.2). They rarely acted as employers themselves and their activity within the local markets, as shown by their appearances in debt cases, was not impressive. As debtors their average debt was the lowest of all victuallers (Table 4.3). Their disadvantageous position within commerce was also evident in their propensity to come into court as debtors rather than creditors; 83 per cent of their appearances in debt litigation were as debtors.

Only the cooks of Exeter had a worse creditor/debtor ratio than the millers; a mere 16 per cent of their appearances in court were as creditors (Table 4.3). The other indices of wealth and commercial

[61] Misc. Roll 55, no. iv. In the late fifteenth century, bakers were also allowed to grind their grain at Crikelpit mills (*Citie of Excester*: 844).

[62] For example, MCR Roll 1, m. 20; 1295/6, mm. 7, 29d, 47; 1367/8, m. 32; 1370/1, m. 41d; 1373/4, mm. 15, 22; 1376/7, mm. 24, 25; 1387/8, m. 42; NQMT 1363.

[63] DRA 1384/5–1389/90 for this and the following.

[64] Holt 1988: 92–9, 163 cites annual wages which were rarely over £1.

[65] The master miller at Crikelpit was paid 13*s* 4*d* per year while his assistants earned stipends of only 8*s* (EBW 1379/90–1389/90).

[66] The Courtenay-owned mills outside the west gate allowed millers one loaf of bread for each quarter of grain they ground and two gallons of ale for the grain ground for a brewing (W1258/G4/13). Holt (1988: 92–5) also notes arrangements whereby rural millers' wages were supplemented by a livery of grain or share of tollcorn.

[67] EBW 1389/90–1393/4.

success show a similarly dim picture for the Exeter cooks; their average murage was the lowest among the victuallers, they had no identifiable servants and none of them ever joined the freedom or was elected to any office, not even one of the lower C Rank positions (Table 4.2). Many of these cooks operated with the help of family out of small shops in Cook Row or other streets near the marketplace and center of town.[68] The shops were probably equipped with fireplaces or ovens since cooks were regularly presented in the mayor's tourn for such offenses as selling badly cooked or reheated fish and meat (the latter being dried or chopped up and put into pasties).[69] One of their staples was cooked poultry, an ingredient that led to frequent fines for forestalling poultry, especially geese and capons.

Joining the cooks at the less profitable end of the food and drink trades were the victuallers and hucksters who retailed dairy products, poultry, vegetables, fruit, and flour. While some, like Robert Melbury and Thomas Scare, were prosperous retailers with diversified interests (they may also have run inns), most of these victuallers lived on the edge of poverty, were often "part-time" workers, and many, if not most, were women.[70] Some sold eggs, cheese, and butter from stalls in the marketplace while others hawked fruit, garlic, and onions in the streets.[71] Their numbers were augmented by rural dwellers who brought their produce to the town marketplace for sale. In 1372, for example, the manorial court at Pinhoe, a small village about 3 miles away, fined six villeins because they went to Exeter to sell cheese, butter, eggs, and other victuals without licence from the lord.[72] One of these men also sold geese in Exeter. Other victuallers came from farther away; men from Whimple (about 9 miles north-east of Exeter) and Monkton (almost 20 miles away in the Otter valley) purveyed cheese and butter in Exeter.[73] On the other hand, many of these food items were also

[68] All presentments against cooks were made in SQMT; the marketplace and one side of Cook Row were located in the south quarter. For shops and properties held by cooks in Cook Row, see ECL D&C 21–24, 26 (Robert and Sarra Taverner); Book 53A, f. 85d (William Jon and Hauys Coke). For the family labor employed by cooks, see the example of Robert Taverner whose wife, Sarra (also called Sarra Lyf), and father William were both cooks: DRO 51/1/3/4; SQMT 1378–83; NQMT 1384; PCR 1–23 Ric. II, m. 72.

[69] MCR 1389/90, m. 48; SQMT passim, for this and the following.

[70] See Table A3.1 and Kowaleski 1986: 148–51; Hilton 1990; Swanson 1989: 11.

[71] SQMT passim, for annual presentments concerning dairy products; see also MCR 1349/50, m. 21; EQMT 1360, 1395; WQMT 1360. For flour, see MCR 1376/7, m. 6. For fruit and dairy products see SQMT 1393, EQMT 1392, 1393; for garlic and onions, see *Anglo-Norman custumal*: 26.

[72] PRO SC2/168/1, mm. 10, 12d. For the following, see MCR 1391/2, m. 1.

[73] EQMT 1394.

raised in the gardens of town residents. Many urban households kept their own pigs and fowl, grew herbs, fruits, and vegetables in their gardens or tended gardens and orchards in nearby plots.[74] For this reason, and because the profits and scale of their trade were so low, these victuallers and hucksters were less easy to trace in the records than others in the food and drink trades. Their low profile in the extant documentation, however, should not deceive us into underestimating their numbers or their overall impact on local and even regional markets.[75]

Of all the victualling trades, taverners had the strongest connections to other trades, particularly the merchants and hostelers. All taverners sold wine but the scale of their activities could vary greatly. Taverners like the prosperous John Piers, for example, regularly imported wine from overseas and reached the A Rank oligarchy.[76] Further down the social ladder, Joan Goldsmyth combined her tavern with an inn; she paid only 4*d* murage tax and was accused of maintaining a brothel on several occasions.[77] All the taverners brewed but the wealthier taverners seem to have more often relied on others for their supplies since the lists of those breaking the assize of ale often pointedly excluded taverners from brewing fines but included them in the sections regarding sales. Further generalizations about taverners as an occupational group are hard to make because of the disparity of their income and adjunct commercial functions.[78]

Like taverners, innkeepers also sold drink although they probably dispensed ale more frequently than wine.[79] The alcohol served at these establishments may have helped provoke the brawls and violent quarrels that too often broke out there.[80] Inns and taverns were also often the scene of commercial exchange, an activity that city authorities tried,

[74] In 1378, the year after the murage tax was assessed, 192 households were fined in the MT for straying pigs and sows. For fowl, see Maltby 1979: 67–71. For Exeter gardens, see above, p. 13. For the produce and livestock raised in urban gardens and curtilages, see Keene 1985: 152–4, and McLean 1980: esp. 64–71.

[75] See Hilton 1982, and 1990: 132–42, on this point.

[76] Misc. Roll 72; MCR election returns 1377–89; PCA 1366–93; *Exeter freemen*: 33.

[77] Misc. Roll 72; EQMT 1372; MCR 1376/7, mm. 6, 39.

[78] It is also difficult to identify all the taverners since the Exeter records do not contain the systematic list of fines on taverners or vintners such as are available for towns like Winchester (Keene 1985: 270) and Colchester (Britnell 1986b: 91–2). For those running taverns as a secondary occupation, see Table A3.1.

[79] Keene 1985: 167–9, 274–7, provides a useful discussion of the differences between inns, taverns, and alehouses in Winchester. See also Rosser 1989: 122–33, for a good survey of the same in Westminster.

[80] For example: ECL D&C 3550, f. 67; PRO JUST3/15/6, m. 7; MCR Roll 1, m. 13d; MCR 1285/6, m. 17d; 1318/19, m. 42d; 1328/9, m. 44d.

usually without success, to prohibit.[81] In 1391 and again in 1393, for example, accusations were levelled against several out-of-town fish dealers for selling fish in Henry Archer's tavern and thereby avoiding town custom.[82] This type of "illegal" commercial exchange seems to have taken place more often at inns than at taverns and alehouses. And as the multi-faceted dealings of the Exeter innkeepers illustrate, the hostelers themselves took a very active role in facilitating this exchange.

Innkeepers were involved in several distinct activities that made them easy to identify. They were commonly presented for selling oats in improper measures, presumably for the horses that stayed at the stables attached to most inns. They also appeared frequently in court for baking horse bread (again, for the horses they boarded), for receiving suspicious people or known thieves, and for sheltering prostitutes. They were also the biggest brewers in Exeter; all of the thirty five hostelers in 1377 brewed and almost 70 per cent of them brewed ten or more times (Table 4.4). Another of their distinguishing characteristics was their widespread involvement in occupations outside innkeeping. Almost half of the primary hostelers in 1377 worked in other trades and over twenty households carried on innkeeping as a secondary occupation (Table 4.1). In all, at least fifty six people, representing about 12 per cent of all households, were involved in innkeeping of some type. Trades associated with innkeeping covered the whole spectrum of occupations from bailiffs and cordwainers, to fishers, roofers, and merchants. Their ability to combine such a wide variety of jobs with innkeeping suggests that hostelers depended on servants and family labor, especially that of their wives and daughters, to help run the inns. The strong presence of women amongst the ranks of hostelers, many of them widows who continued to run inns after their husbands died, reinforces this impression.[83] Other inns were probably managed with the aid of servants, particularly those owned by the rich merchants who frequently appeared as hostelers; overall hostelers employed more servants than most Exeter households (Table 4.2). Many of the larger inns in Exeter seem to have been owned by merchants since their names were often attached to inns. "Talbotysyn," "Noblesen," and "Suttonsysyn" were all late fourteenth-century inns associated with A Rank oligarchic

[81] For fish marketing at inns, see below, pp. 316, 320. For trade at inns elsewhere, see Dyer 1992: 149–50; Keene 1985: 277.

[82] MCR 1391/2, m. 1; 1392/3, m. 45.

[83] See Table A3.1. Alice Plomere, Joan Portisham, and Elena Wilde were all widows; John Streyngher's daughter Joan also became an innkeeper. Roughly 10 to 20 per cent of innkeepers in Winchester were women; Keene 1985: 276. For similar patterns in York, see Swanson 1989: 23.

merchants.[84] Local gentry, religious institutions, clerics, and well-off canons also owned inns in Exeter although some of the latter may have limited their clientele to fellow clerics.[85]

On the whole Exeter hostelers were a prosperous group. They ranked behind only merchants and professionals in the murage tax they paid, and in the percentage of their members who entered the freedom (51 per cent) and traded by sea (14 per cent). Those who ran inns as a secondary occupation had an even more impressive profile.[86] This evidence suggests that innkeeping (or perhaps only inn-ownership) may not have lowered one's social status in Exeter to the extent that it did elsewhere, although it should be noted that Rank A status was infrequently achieved by the Exeter hostelers.[87] While it is impossible to tell what proportion of any householder's income came from innkeeping activities, such activities were clearly attractive enough to lure many into the business. Innkeeping in Exeter must also have been promoted by the city's role as the major administrative and ecclesiastical center of the South-west, its position as the headport for two counties, and its crucial location on the road system of the south-western peninsula. Exeter must have hosted more visitors than many towns of comparable size, thus increasing the number of households that accepted paying guests.

Exeter hostelers profited from more than the fees they charged for room, drink, and stabling. As the evidence concerning debt litigation indicates, they were also fully engaged in commercial exchange. About 7 per cent of all debt suits involved hostelers, a proportion that rises

[84] Roger atte Wille owned "Suttonsynyn": *CPR 1377–81*: 596. "Noblesen" was associated with Richard Kenrigg and probably named after a member of the wealthy Noble family: MCR 1389/90, m. 5. "Talbotysyn" was owned by the Hospital of St John in the early fifteenth century: its various owners included wealthy merchants, gentry, and clerics, but not a member of the rich Talbot family for whom it was presumably named: Book 53A, f. 21. See also Dymond: 1880, for more examples. For merchants who ran inns, see also Table A3.1.

[85] Book 53A f. 21; *CCR 1422–9*: 11; Dymond 1880; Lega-Weekes 1915: 180; Hoskins 1963b: 44–5.

[86] There were twenty one householders who ran inns as a secondary activity; they paid a mean murage tax of 20*d*, 71 per cent belonged to the freedom, and 57 per cent to the oligarchy (data compiled from Table A3.1).

[87] Swanson 1989: 23 remarks that few declared it as an occupation because it "was not socially acceptable." A similar silence is observed in Exeter, but it may have been due partly to the tendency for hostelers to be involved in different occupations, a trend Swanson also observes in York. Keene 1985: 266, 274–6 also notes that running an inn was perceived as dishonorable, especially while holding high office. If Swanson and Keene are correct, it may suggest that the oligarchic hostelers and merchant/hostelers of Exeter (Table A3.1) owned but did not run inns. I am reluctant to draw this conclusion, however, since most of these same men were very clearly associated with the distinct activities carried out by hostelers. Obviously this question could bear further scrutiny.

to 14 per cent if those running inns as a secondary occupation are included.[88] Hostelers normally held the upper hand in these debt suits since they appeared as creditors 67 per cent of the time, although the sums involved in their debts suggest they operated mostly as petty retailers (Table 4.3). They often served as middlemen between local and regional traders, in part because the inns over which they presided provided a convenient meeting place for non-residents. Hostelers were the only occupation outside of leather artisans and butchers regularly to purchase hides and skins in Exeter; they played an even more significant role in the regional fish trade.[89]

The diversity of hostelers' commercial interests and their middlemen functions are illustrated in the activities of John Splot, a hosteler who also dabbled in the leather trades. Although he was one of the richer hostelers, paying a 40*d* murage tax, he never joined the freedom and served only twice in the minor (C Rank) office of alderman for the northern suburbs.[90] Like most hostelers, he brewed regularly, hired out horses, provided stabling, and was accused at least once of maintaining a brothel.[91] Up until 1377, he also seems to have worked as a cordwainer but thereafter his forays into the leather trade were restricted to occasional purchases of hides and skins. He sold such varied goods as ale, cloth, dyestuffs, fish, flour, harness, hay, iron, lard, oats, salt, and timber, and purchased ale, fish, horses, madder, and wine.[92] His commercial dealings extended to London grocers (John Hanfeld, Thomas Knolles), coastal fishermen (Nicholas Yealme) and men from the nearby village of Ide (William Webber) and the more distant town of Plymouth (Thomas Stephene). Within Exeter he did business with armorers (John Armener), carpenters (Walter Broun), cordwainers (John Boggebrook, Thomas Wylde), fullers (John Chilton), hostelers (John Bayg), merchants (Thomas Estoun), millwards (William Wylcok), and spicers (John Syneet). He probably carried on some (if not most) of this business within his inn; he was, for example, indicted for selling

[88] To the hostelers listed in Table 4.3 can be added those who ran inns as a secondary activity; they represented 230 creditors and 194 debtors. If such hostelers are added to the householders in 1377 who ran inns as a primary occupation (Table A3.1), the total number of innkeeping households was fifty six; this figure represents 11 per cent of all households and 14 per cent of households with known occupations.

[89] Kowaleski 1990: 60; and see below, pp. 301, 316.

[90] Misc. Roll 72; MCR 1390/1, m. 1; 1391/2, m. 1. John Splot junior, who was probably his son, did join the freedom: *Exeter freemen*: 36.

[91] ECL D&C 2654; PCR 1–23 Ric. II, m. 71; NQMT 1374–75, 1389–93; WQMT 1374–88; MCR 1376/7, m. 6 for this and the following.

[92] MCR 1375/6, m. 51; 1376/7, mm. 8, 17; 1380/1, m. 31; 1382/3, m. 17; 1388/9, mm. 17, 40; 1389/90, mm. 2, 7; 1390/1, m. 14; PCR 1–23 Ric. II, mm. 31, 39, 43, 44, 45, 46, 65, 73; DRA 1394/5; EBW 1393/4; ECL D&C 4858 for this and the following.

fish there.[93] The amount of business conducted in his inn by others may also have been partly responsible for the pledging services he offered to fellow townsmen – services for which he expected remuneration, even if he had to sue for payment.[94]

The textile and clothing trades

The clothing and textile trades are here grouped together since they worked with similar materials and because the distinction between those who only manufactured cloth and those who sold or shaped it was not always clear.[95] Cloth manufacturers and finishers predominated, however, accounting for almost three-quarters of the occupational category. Not included among these cloth manufacturers – but very much a part of their world – were those merchants at the very top of the textile hierarchy, often called "draper" or "mercer," who balanced their imports of wine and other goods with exports of cloth. These merchants (grouped with the distributive trades because of their multifarious dealings) profited from the cloth trade, particularly through their exports, but also in their coordination and capitalization of cloth-workers.[96]

The aulnage accounts allow us to identify many of the cloth sellers in Exeter, although the type of fraud that pervades the surviving accounts makes it impossible to discern with any great precision the scale of their activities or to compare them with other Devon cloth sellers.[97] But the accounts can still give us a rough idea of the economic status of the city's cloth sellers. As in most towns, the market was dominated by a small number of large entrepreneurs; the top five vendors (11 per cent of the total) were responsible for 36 per cent of

93 MCR 1376/7, m. 8.

94 PCR 1–23 Ric. II, mm. 42, 43, 44, 45, 47, 65; MCR 1382/3, m. 49.

95 See, for example, the tailor who made cloth and hose in NQMT 1353. Presentments made against non-freedom members retailing (literally "cutting up") cloth were in every MT and included tailors, shipsteres, mercers, weavers, fullers, and even dyers.

96 Note, however, that householders whose primary occupation was not merchant were not included in the merchant category in the tables; several of these drapers and mercers were included in the "Others" category of the clothing and textile group in Tables 4.2–4.4. For their exporting and importing activities, see below, Chapter 6.

97 Only three particular accounts detail the Exeter cloth sellers (PRO E101/338/11, mm. 8–11). While these accounts purport to cover all of Devon and Exeter, the aulnager (Thomas Wandry, an Exeter merchant/draper) only listed Exeter residents in the accounts. He also grossly undercounted the cloths sold, accounting for only 374 cloths of assize over a thirty-eight month period in 1399–1403, compared to 714 cloths aulnaged in Exeter during just fourteen and a half months in 1395–6 (PRO E358/8, m. 2d). During this three-year period, Wandry charged himself with the sale of only six cloths even though he was one of the city's richest merchant/drapers and leased two of the city's fulling mills. See also Chope 1912a: 581–3 for the central government's discovery of this fraud, and above, p. 23.

the aulnaged cloth.[98] Only eleven vendors (23 per cent) sold more than ten cloths but they accounted for about 58 per cent of all cloths sealed.[99] Small entrepreneurs (those selling three cloths or fewer) represented 32 per cent of cloth dealers but sold only 8 per cent of the cloth.[100]

How did the Exeter cloth trade compare to that of other towns during this period? Colchester had more small entrepreneurs; 44 per cent of the sellers controlled only 9 per cent of the cloth marketed.[101] The concentration of cloth sales among the biggest dealers was also slightly less at Colchester where the top 11 per cent handled about 44 per cent of the cloth sold. But in Winchester the large entrepreneurs were more dominant since just under 8 per cent of the sellers were responsible for 30 per cent of the cloths aulnaged.[102] The most striking contrast appears at York where the biggest cloth dealers exerted a powerful influence over cloth sales; 7 per cent of the vendors sold 52 per cent of the cloth.[103] While these comparisons suggest that mercantile dominance of the cloth market at Exeter did not match that seen at Winchester and York, other evidence regarding the Exeter cloth strongly hints otherwise. The aulnager's fraud in compiling the extant aulnage accounts for Exeter so grossly under-reported cloth sales that the domination of the biggest sellers appears less than it probably was.[104]

Exeter cloth vendors, for example, were much more likely to be involved in the export trade than vendors in these other towns. At least

[98] The three accounts listed sixty eight vendors and 373½ cloths but there were only forty seven different vendors; the top five sold 124 cloths.

[99] Note that the fraud in these accounts distorts the number of cloths sold by each vendor, making it fruitless to compare average cloth sales with figures from other towns. The fraud could also have worked to exclude small entrepreneurs from the accounts, but it is likely that a greater distortion resulted from the aulnager's under-reporting of the sales of the larger vendors (noticeable in particular in the case of the aulnager himself; see above, n. 97).

[100] These figures should be treated with caution since among this group were merchants such as Richard Bozoun, John Russell, and Roger Shaplegh, the merchant/tailor William May, the fuller John Blakelond, and the dyer Roger Hakeworthy. These men possessed substantial wealth and commercial connections (see Table A3.1) and evidence from other sources shows that they were heavily involved in both cloth sales and cloth exports, strongly suggesting that their sales as represented in the aulnage accounts were gross underestimations.

[101] In 1395–7, the eighty three vendors (of a total 189) who aulnaged ten or fewer cloths accounted for 9.5 per cent of the cloth sold; the top twenty one vendors sold 44.4 per cent of the cloth; Britnell 1986b: 78–9.

[102] In 1394–5, twelve of the 159 vendors sold 30 per cent of the 3,390½ cloths; Keene 1985: 309.

[103] In 1394–5, thirty two of the sellers sold 1,734 of the total 3,300 cloths aulnaged; Swanson 1989: 32, 141. Although Swanson does not give the total number of sellers, her figure of 7 per cent implies there were about 457.

[104] See above, notes 97 and 100. Discrepancies between towns could also stem from different aulnaging or marketing practices; see especially Bridbury 1982: 62–83.

34 per cent of the Exeter vendors exported cloth and a minimum of 64 per cent were also active in the import trade.[105] The known cloth exporters controlled at least 27 per cent and probably 54 per cent of cloth sales at Exeter noted in the aulnage accounts.[106] In contrast, Colchester cloth sellers were responsible for only 9 per cent of the cloth sold there while the three Winchester vendors who exported cloth accounted for less than 3 per cent of the aulnaged cloth.[107] Comparable figures for York are harder to come by but what evidence there is suggests that not many of them exported cloth either.[108] Merchants clearly dominated the cloth market in Exeter, accounting for nearly 85 per cent of all cloth sales in the aulnage accounts. The A Rank oligarchy (all but one were merchants) was alone responsible for 78 per cent of all cloth sales.[109] Artisan vendors were fewer and included five clothworkers (two tailors, a weaver, a dyer, and a fuller) as well as two butchers, a skinner, and a chandler. The occupations of the remaining ten vendors are unknown but most were probably artisans as well.

The inferior status of many clothing and textile workers in Exeter also points to mercantile domination of not only the cloth trade but also the cloth manufacturing process. Only artisans in the building

105 At least thirteen of the forty seven vendors listed in the 1399–1403 aulnage accounts showed up exporting cloth in the port customs accounts of 1391–9 (PRO E122/40/16, 26, 18, 23). If the exports of the husbands of three widows who appeared in the aulnage accounts are counted (from PRO E122/40/8 which covers seventeen and a half months in 1377–9), then the total rises to sixteen vendors. At least thirty of the forty seven vendors imported goods by sea in PCA 1381–99; investigation of the early fifteenth century accounts might reveal more.

106 An export account of 1398–9 (PRO E122/40/23 covering eight and a half months immediately before the aulnage accounts began) included seven vendors who sold ninety three cloths (27 per cent of the total) in the aulnage accounts which covered thirty eight months. If aulnage vendors listed as exporting cloth in other customs accounts are included (PRO E/122/40/26, 40/16, 40/18 which covered sixteen and a half months in 1391–3), the total rises to 40 per cent. If the exports of the husbands of the three widowed vendors are included (from PRO E122/40/8 which covered seventeen and a half months in 1377–9) then the total rises to sixteen vendors who together were responsible for 54 per cent of the cloth sales.

107 Britnell (1986b: 78) identifies Colchester cloth exporters from a customs account that covered fourteen months, the first seven months of which overlapped with the aulnage account. Keene (1985: 311–12) identified three Winchester vendors who exported cloth at Southampton; two exported cloth in 1394–5 when they were responsible for about 1.1 per cent of the aulnaged cloth. In 1398–9 one of these exporters and another one accounted for 2.6 per cent of the cloth aulnaged in 1394–5.

108 Swanson 1989: 141 notes that thirty of the sixty six mercers in the York aulnage account of 1394–5 exported cloth in the extant accounts of 1377–99; these thirty mercers represented 7 per cent of all vendors (and were probably responsible for the single largest share of cloths sold; see p. 32). She also notes that a weaver and a bowyer in the aulnage accounts exported cloth.

109 The twenty five A Rank men sold 290 cloths; only Nicholas Boghewode (a butcher) was not a merchant.

crafts ranked consistently lower than the textile and clothing trades in the various indices of wealth and commercial success (Table 4.2). Fullers, shearmen, tailors, and weavers paid very low murage taxes and only one of the forty two householders in these trades in 1377 ever served in the oligarchy. Perhaps most revealing is the relatively low percentage of the group that entered the freedom (29 per cent) despite the fact that only members could retail cloth in the city. Unenfranchised traders who sold cloth were subject to annual fines (ranging from 2*d* to 12*d*) which may not have proved an effective deterrent, but it is hard to believe that the other advantages of membership, such as freedom from toll, legal privileges, and political opportunities, would not have been immensely appealing to any clothing or textile trader who could afford to join. While their relative poverty could have kept many clothworkers out of the freedom, it is also possible that the merchant elite which dominated the freedom deliberately blocked the admission of clothworkers in too great numbers because of its vested interest in subordinating cloth manufacturers and retailers.

Another indication of the subservient position of many clothing and textile workers may be seen in their disadvantageous position in debt litigation (Table 4.3). As a group they appeared more than twice as often as debtors than as creditors; no other occupational category came close to experiencing this type of disparity. Fullers, shearmen, and weavers were particularly burdened by debts. With the exception of the dyers (and the drapers grouped with "others"), the sums that creditors in this group hoped to collect were markedly lower than most other occupations while the sums they were compelled to pay as debtors were usually twice as big. Other occupational groups also paid more as debtors than as creditors, but clothing and textile workers generally had much smaller financial resources upon which to draw than these other trades.

A closer look at the commercial relationship between cloth merchants and clothworkers also suggests that the capitalist clothier so common in the sixteenth and seventeenth centuries had begun to emerge by the late fourteenth century in Exeter.[110] Merchants, for example, often supplied wool yarn to weavers to make cloth as is evident from the prosecutions of weavers who tried to keep some of this yarn for them-

[110] Others also see evidence of such clothiers in the late fourteenth century; see Salzman 1964: 226–8 and Carus-Wilson 1959: 127–46. But Unwin (1927: 266–73), Heaton (1965: 89–101), and Ramsay (1965: 6–22) see the capitalist clothier emerging mainly in the Tudor period. To some extent these differences may reflect changes in the terminology describing drapers and clothiers (and thus historians' notions of what these terms entail) rather than any historical reality; see Keene 1985: 309 for such changes.

selves.[111] These amounts could be considerable; for example, the merchant Richard Swan accused Peter Yurle of replacing 17 pounds of the 51 pounds of white yarn he had given him with weaker yarn, thus damaging Richard's cloth to the tune of 100*s*.[112] Other problems arose over contracts merchants made with weavers concerning the quality and delivery dates of cloth to be woven. In 1390 the wealthy merchant John Grey (who twice served as mayor) prosecuted the weaver Michael Cartere for breaking an agreement to place Grey's cloth in his "le Webtakel" at the time desired by Grey.[113] Another merchant, John Russel, successfully sued the weaver Hugh Webber for failing to weave his cloth to a satisfactory standard.[114] Merchants made similar arrangements to hire the services of fullers. The same John Grey, for example, claimed 40*s* damages from Philip Touker for tearing Grey's cloth during the fulling process.[115] Merchants also delivered cloth over to shearers for processing. When the merchant Robert Noble handed over twelve pieces of grey cloth called "backes" to the shearman Richard Broun, the latter had to make a formal recognizance that he would deliver the cloth to Noble in a marketable state, half at Christmas and the other half at Easter.[116] Dyers also worked for merchants on a contractual basis; Walter Hakeworthy dyed cloths for the merchant John Piers, a member of the town's oligarchy.[117] Merchants also controlled the importation of such dyestuffs as alum, madder, and woad; their regional networks of trade in dyestuffs allowed them to service the needs of dyers scattered throughout east Devon and west Somerset.[118]

This evidence, piecemeal as it is, of the multifaceted involvement of late-fourteenth-century Exeter merchants in the production and sale of cloth sounds remarkably like the well-known descriptions offered of sixteenth-century Devon clothiers, both rural and urban, who supplied capital to weavers to enable them to purchase yarn, sent the cloth to fullers and dyers for finishing, and then marketed or exported the cloth.[119] Few historians agree about when the full-fledged clothier so characteristic of the early modern period first appeared, nor is there really widespread agreement on the extent of these clothiers' control

[111] MCR 1377/8, m. 17; 1391/2, m. 22.
[112] MCR 1413/14, m. 41.
[113] MCR 1389/90, m. 42.
[114] PCR 1–23 Ric. II, m. 12.
[115] PCR 1–23 Ric. II, m. 68; see also MCR 1391/2, m. 17; 1404/5, m. 18d for similar relationships between merchants and fullers.
[116] MCR 1354/5, m. 46d.
[117] He also dyed cloths for the local gentry: MCR 1379/80, m. 4; PCR 1–23 Ric. II, mm. 19, 20.
[118] See below, pp. 272–3.
[119] Blake 1915: 346; Carus-Wilson 1957.

over the industry or why they became visible in some places earlier than others.[120] The evidence presented here suggests that clothiers had emerged in Exeter by the end of the fourteenth century, that they came primarily from a mercantile background, and that they funded and employed cloth artisans whose own opportunities to participate in the large-scale commercial marketing of cloth were limited.

The high profile of merchant clothiers in Exeter's cloth industry does not mean that cloth manufacturers always worked for them or that the latter were completely lacking in entrepreneurship. Weavers, fullers, and dyers were also among the cloth vendors listed in the Exeter aulnage accounts and some of the merchants who appeared in the aulnage and export accounts were probably marketing cloth that they had acquired from these clothworkers. The fullers in particular appear to have ventured beyond just the process of fulling. References to merchants and others who "sold" cloth to fullers imply that it was the fuller who then marketed the fulled cloth, rather than handing it back to the merchant who had hired only his labor.[121] Fullers also employed shearman more often than other occupations while their possession of large numbers of teasels (200 in one case) illustrates their interests in different aspects of the cloth-finishing process.[122] They were also the only textile occupation whose job required them to lease or purchase racks (for stretching and drying cloth), tenter grounds (upon which the racks or tenters stood), and fulling mills.[123] Both weavers and fullers also commonly made arrangements with individuals to weave or full small amounts of cloth, obviously for the personal use of the client.[124] Local gentry and ecclesiastical institutions also contracted with weavers, fullers, and shearmen for their services on particular pieces of cloth.[125] These

[120] See n. 110, above. Britnell 1986b: 77–9, 183–6 notes the emergence by the 1470s in Colchester of rich clothiers, at the expense of the weavers, fullers, and dyers who used to sell cloth. For evidence of clothiers' increasing activities in late fifteenth-century Suffolk, see McClenaghan 1924: esp. 6–9.

[121] For example, MCR 1388/9, m. 42; 1391/2, mm. 7, 8, 49.

[122] See, for example, PCR 1–23 Ric. II, m. 85 where the shearman John Wappelood had to sue the fuller John Halam for his 27*s* stipend. For the 200 teasels of the fuller John Tyngtenhill, see MCR 1391/2, m. 42.

[123] Racks and tenter grounds: Book 53A, f. 34 (which includes a sketch map of the location of racks in Teyytestrete that is discussed in Fox 1986); MCR 1318/19, m. 12d; 1376/7, m. 36; 1404/5, m. 20d; EBW 1383/4; for fulling mills, see below, pp. 154–5.

[124] MCR 1319/20, m. 15d (a chalon weaver was paid 2*s* to make a *tapetum* $4\frac{1}{2}$ yards long); 1360/1, m. 32; 1404/5, m. 27d; PCR 1–23 Ric. II, m. 30

[125] CR 1466 (6*d* paid for shearing of blanket for the Courtenay children); BL Add. Ch. 13972, 64321 (weaving and shearing for the Courtenay household). The weaver Walter Forst was paid 4*d* a day for twelve days for making cloth for the dean and chapter in 1383: ECL D&C 3777, f. 37d.

arrangements, however, still point out the dependence of clothworkers on wages or payments from clients who contracted for their labor, even when they were free of ties to the merchant clothiers.

Although cloth manufacturers relied heavily on task work or piece work, they were themselves amongst the biggest employers in town; only the distributive trades and metalworkers hired more servants (Table 4.2). Unlike the servants of merchants, many of the servants of textile or clothing artisans were more often employed in craft activities than in the domestic sphere. Women constituted an important part of this craft labor force. Their surnames offer some idea of the jobs they performed; Isolda Spinster, Magota Spinster *alias* Lavender, Cecilia Wolbeater, Emma Hosiere, Joan and Cecilia Kemystere (wool combers), and Agnes, Joan, and Julia Shippestere (dressmakers often employed by tailors to cut out patterns) were just a few of the women engaged in the Exeter cloth trade.[126] These female textile workers, like Meliora, wife of the saddler Richard Stoke, who agreed to "work" (most likely to spin or weave) 25 pounds of wool for Peter Coureour, only occasionally appeared in the extant records because they labored (probably "part-time") at occupations different from their husbands, the heads of household.[127] Weavers and tailors hired the largest number of women to help out in their businesses. Although the tasks these women performed demanded skilled labor, their status within the textile and clothing trades was anomalous. For example, the weaver William Wymark called Joan Blakhay his "servant and apprentice" and claimed she had agreed to serve him for five and one-half years.[128] Yet she was one of the few women ever referred to as an apprentice in this period, and it is clear that neither she nor her employer expected that she would follow the customary path of male apprentices and be granted freedom membership. More typical was the case of Alice Greneweye who worked as a weaver for Walter Floit but was simply called his servant.[129]

126 MCR 1290/1, m. 47d; 1328/9, m. 17d; 1370/1, m. 47; 1376/7, m. 38; WQMT 1373–88; EQMT 1385, 1390; SQMT 1376; PCR 1–23 Ric. II, mm. 31, 74; CRA 1376/7, 1397/8. Most of these women were unmarried. For similar tasks performed by urban women elsewhere, see Swanson 1989: 30–1, 35–9, 46, 51; Goldberg 1990b: 42–5, and 1992: 118–24.

127 MCR 1349/50, mm. 19, 21. It is telling that the dispute about the contract was entered under her husband's name, not her own. Another part of the dispute also implies that Meliora's agreement was actually with Peter's wife, not with Peter.

128 MCR 1380/1, m. 9. The only other reference to a female apprentice I have found is for Agnes, daughter of Isabel Cornyssh, in MCR 1403/4, m. 20d who agreed to serve John Chuddelegh, a mason for the cathedral (ECL D&C 2638, 2652, 2653, 2657; Book 53A, f. 32), thus suggesting either that her work was of a domestic nature or that she was apprenticed to Chuddelegh's wife in another trade.

129 MCR 1382/3, m. 20; 1387/8, m. 49. For the employment of female weavers elsewhere, see *Little Red Book of Bristol*, vol. 2: 12; Goldberg 1992: 120–1.

A relatively large number of women, many of them single or widowed, also achieved some independence in the clothing and textile trades, particularly as hosiers and tailors. Emma Taillor (alias Emma Hosiere) paid a 12*d* murage as a head of household in 1377 and regularly retailed cloth.[130] But Emma, like most other women who retailed cloth or made stockings for a living, had to pay an annual fine to carry on this activity because she did not belong to the freedom.[131] The only exceptions were three wealthy oligarchic widows who carried on their husbands' businesses by selling and exporting cloth and thus also continued to enjoy the commercial, but not the political benefits of freedom membership.[132] More typical than the wealthy widows or Emma Taillor was Joan Shippestere. She both retailed and worked cloth for customers such as Walter atte Wode (who accused her of stealing wool, as well as linen and wool cloth from him over a period of three years) and John Stobbe, a smith (who levelled a similar charge against her).[133] Obviously Joan was not as financially secure or commercially successful as Emma Tailor and the three merchants' widows.

While women often worked for weavers and tailors, fullers seem to have preferred to hire men.[134] Much of this work was done on contract. The fuller John Tyngtenhill contracted to do fulling work for oligarchic merchants (John Talbot and Roger atte Hille), as well as for another clothworker (William Skyradon); but at the same time he employed three servants as fullers (one who claimed he had only agreed to make cloth at home, not at the mill), and subcontracted work out to three other fullers.[135] One of these fullers was John Russel who together with John Payn, another fuller, leased the Duryard fulling mills for an annual rent of 40*s*.[136] Their debts and disputes with fellow fullers over the years make it clear that they regularly fulled cloth for these other

130 Misc. Roll 72; WQMT 1373–83.

131 MT, passim. From 1373–93, 10 per cent of these fines were paid by women, all of whom were single or widowed. See also MCR Roll 1, m. 2; 1295/6, m. 28.

132 They were Alice Nymet, Magota Golde, and Elizabeth Wilford. Both Nymet's and Wilford's husbands had served as mayor and Golde's husband Adam had frequently been elected city receiver, the second highest civic office. See Kowaleski 1986: 155.

133 WQMT 1378, 1388; MCR 1376/7, m. 38; PCR 1–23 Ric. II, m. 42.

134 None of the many references to craft work employment by fullers cited women. Fullers also employed more servants on the average (1.55) than all but the dyers; see Table 4.2.

135 MCR 1386/7, m. 42; 1387/8, mm. 35, 49; 1388/9, m. 42; 1391/2, mm. 7, 8, 17; PCR 1–23 Ric. II, mm. 72, 86 For the following, see MCR 1391/2, mm. 17, 42.

136 DCR 2–22 Ric. II, m. 23; Book 53A, f. 75v. The John Russel who aulnaged three cloths in 1399 (PRO E101/338/11, m. 9) has here been identified as the merchant of that name (see Table A3.1) since he also had interests in the cloth trade and was far more prominent than John Russel the fuller in 1399.

fullers.[137] Despite their control of the mills, however, neither Russel nor Payn ever gained entry to the freedom, or appeared as cloth exporters or vendors in the aulnage accounts. The highest political office they achieved was that of alderman for the northern suburb, a C Rank office.[138] Another fuller who leased half of the fulling mill owned by St Nicholas priory for a term of twenty nine years did slightly better. John Blakelond was admitted to the freedom and sold one cloth in the 1401 aulnage account and another in 1402, but he never exported cloth nor reached the ranks of the oligarchy.[139] The only other known fulling-mill lessor was the oligarchic merchant Thomas Wandry who leased the Duryard fulling mills in the late 1390s after Payn and Russel. His interests, however, were clearly those of a merchant capitalist. Unlike Payn and Russel, there is no evidence that he had hands-on experience in fulling.[140] Few fullers could compete with Wandry who was already taxed 24*d* in the 1377 murage roll (at the time he was probably still in his twenties), while the ten fullers paid an average tax of less than 7*d*.

Few of the textile and clothing artisans showed much higher levels of wealth in 1377 (Table 4.2). The average amount of the debts they contracted was correspondingly low, with the shearmen possessing debts of the lowest amounts, followed by the tailors, weavers, and then fullers (Table 4.3). Only the dyers distinguished themselves by higher levels of wealth (19*d* average murage tax), more servants, occasional stints as importers of valuable dyestuffs, and more costly debts than others in the occupational group (Tables 4.2, 4.3).[141] While these figures suggest that dyers enjoyed a higher status than most others in the clothing and textile trades, they could hardly compete with the wealth, political profile, and commercial activity of merchants or butchers. The number of dyers identified, moreover, was very low, partly because some lived in the exempt jurisdiction of Exe Island, and partly because their services were less in demand in this period when so much of the cloth made for export was undyed.[142]

137 MCR 1386/7, m. 33; 1388/9, mm. 3, 27, 37; 1391/2, m. 42; PCR 1–23 Ric. II, mm. 52, 86; WQMT 1389; NQMT 1390–91.

138 MCR election returns, 1392–1401; Russel served twice and Payn at least eight times.

139 ED/SN/61; *Exeter freemen*: 38; PRO E101/338/11, mm. 8–11.

140 He regularly imported a variety of goods (PCA 1385–1400) and was one of the busiest members of the oligarchy (MCR election returns, 1378–1404), serving forty four times in office. For his mill leases, see CRA 1396/7; DRA 1396/7, 1397/8, 1400/1; he also had six cloths aulnaged (PRO E101/338/11, mm. 8–11). See also Misc. Roll 72 and his entry in Table A3.1 for this and the following.

141 The data are rather slim, however; only two dyers were taxed: one at 24*d* and the other at 4*d* so the sample is very small. For dyers' imports, see below, n. 142.

142 The dyers Walter and Roger Hakeworthy lived in Exe Island (Book 53A, f. 85; ED/M/655; Table A3.1). Roger imported woad, madder, and alum (PCA 1395/6,

Tailors were the most visible occupation within the Exeter clothing trades although hatters, shippesters (dressmakers), and hosiers (who worked with leather as well)[143] were also active. But the tailors were no wealthier than others in the cloth industry, paying an average murage of only 7.5*d*. Only four of the group eventually joined the freedom and all but one (who served as a city gatekeeper) never held any civic office (Table 4.2). Their commercial profile was also hardly impressive since they made up less than 3 per cent of all creditors and debtors and their debts were for lower sums than for all but the shearers in their occupational group (Table 4.3). As cloth retailers and garment makers, tailors also faced competition from rural and small-town merchants, drapers, tailors, and other clothworkers who came to Exeter with cloth and clothing to sell.[144] Later in the fifteenth century, however, the tailors did better, forming the only guild that ever challenged the merchant elite in Exeter. Chartered by the king in 1466, the Tailors Guild included many wealthy civic officeholders (many perhaps more akin to drapers than tailors) whose position in the guild allowed them to maintain firm control over the "free sewers" and other wage laborers in the tailoring profession.[145] In any event, the guild's challenge to the merchant oligarchy was shortlived since the city successfully petitioned Parliament to annul the charter and the guild was forced to recognize the jurisdictional superiority of the mayor and city council.

The leather and fur trades

Like the clothing and textile artisans, those in the leather and skin trades concentrated much of their effort on producing garments and other apparel. Leather shoes, boots, hats, gloves, hose, aprons, purses, girdles, scabbards, and raingear were manufactured by shoemakers,

1396/7). Dyers were more numerous and of higher status in pre-plague Exeter when larger amounts of dyestuffs were imported (below, p. 230). This emphasis was reflected in the stricter measures taken to assay imported woad in the thirteenth and early fourteenth centuries (MCR 1319/20, m. 12d; 1328/9, m. 46d; Rowe and Jackson 1973: xii–xiii; and below, p. 263). Philip Tinctor, probably a dyer, served as mayor eight times from 1255/6 to 1262/3 (Rowe and Cochlin 1964: 3). For the similarly high status of pre-plague dyers in Winchester, see Keene 1985: 303–4.

143 Hosiers have usually been grouped with the leather occupations because of the frequency with which they appeared as buyers of hides and leather in the annual MT lists concerning those who purchased such goods outside the sanctioned market. Further evidence might reveal that some hosiers specialized in leather attire while others focused more on making knitted hose.

144 The MT lists of unenfranchised cloth retailers often contained the names of non-Exeter men.

145 For this and the following, see above, pp. 93, 100–1, and their ordinances and selected court proceedings printed in *English gilds*: 312–23.

glovers, hosiers, pursers, girdlers, and other leatherworkers, while furriers and skinners trimmed or lined capes, jackets, robes, dresses, hats, and footgear with fur. Other leather goods included saddles, harness, armour, bottles, and buckets. In Exeter and other medieval towns, leather and skin workers were usually the third most numerous occupational group (after victuallers and the clothing/textile trades); in 1377 they constituted 14 to 19 per cent of primary occupations (Table 4.1).[146] The raw materials and finished products of the leather industry also ranked behind only victuals and clothing and textile items as the subject of debt litigation in Exeter.[147]

The medieval leather industry was generally divided into the heavy and light trades, depending on whether hides or skins were used.[148] In the heavy leather trade, raw hides from larger animals, mainly cattle, underwent a lengthy tanning process of about a year in which prepared hides passed through a series of tannin solutions (usually made from water and oak bark) in various pits. This produced a strong, durable, and waterproof leather for use, once curried or dressed, by shoemakers and saddlers. Calf and sheep skins were also tanned and used in the manufacture of cheaper shoes, although civic authorities tried to restrict this practice.[149] It was more common, however, for skins from smaller animals such as sheep, calves, goats, and pigs to undergo a simpler process of preservation characteristic of the light leather trades. These skins were generally made into leather within a matter of weeks by tawing with alum or with oil and were then used in gloves, leather garments, pouches, laces, and shoe uppers. Furriers and skinners also employed the services of tawyers to dress their skins. While technically not leather, parchment and vellum, made from sheep and calf skins, were subjected to some of the same processes (like dehairing and fleshing) as light leather goods.

As a group the Exeter leather and skin trades ranked at the top of the artisanal occupations in terms of wealth and status in 1377 (Table 4.2) and maintained a steady if not particularly impressive profile in debt litigation (Table 4.3). Within the individual occupations of the leather trades, however, there was significant diversity. Skinners, for example, were at the high end of the group; they paid a slightly higher

[146] For the reasons cited above, n. 10, artisans in this trade were easy to identify. For these artisans in other towns, see also Kowaleski 1990; Swanson 1989: 53–65; Keene 1985: 285–91.

[147] See below, Table 5.2. Livestock was the subject of 13 per cent of debts.

[148] Clarkson 1960: 245–53; Waterer 1946: 136–53.

[149] See the presentments against cordwainers who used tanned sheepskins (called "bazan") in WQMT 1374–6, 1385; EQMT 1389–92. For their use in shoes, see MCR 1319/20, m. 8d. For the practice elsewhere, see Waterer 1946: 66, 80.

than average murage tax, over half joined the freedom and almost 40 per cent were eventually elected to oligarchic office.[150] But within this occupation there were also wide variations. At the top stood skinners like Walter Thomas who paid 42*d* murage, served as an elector seven times and as bridge warden (B Rank offices) once. Some of his commercial transactions took place on an impressively large scale. He purchased over 100 quarters of salt (probably for curing skins) from the oligarchic merchant John Talbot, did business with such London citizens as the skinners William Comberton, John Mannyngton, and Robert Marklee, and had in his inventory Baltic, Italian, and English furs (squirrel, polecat, and rabbit) worth large sums of money.[151] He also owned considerable property in Exeter, including three tenements, three shops, a messuage, a close of two acres, and a garden worth over £6 in rents each year.[152] His wealth was also reflected in the size of his debts, including one of £10 and another of £142 (to a London skinner) that he had difficulty paying.[153] Although these costly imported furs regularly brought Thomas and other skinners into regional and international networks of trade, his indebtedness to London skinners points to how much of the high end of the fur trade had settled in the country's capital by the late fourteenth century.[154] It is telling that fur imports into Exeter trickled in at the rate of fewer than two cargoes a year and that local merchants or foreign traders, not local skinners, were more often responsible for these shipments. Local demand for the most expensive furs was unlikely to be very high, and those who could afford such luxuries – rich merchants and neighboring gentry – were able to do their shopping in London where both quality and variety were undoubtedly superior to what Exeter skinners could offer. Local saddlers experienced much the same sort of problem since the London saddlers virtually monopolized the manufacture of elaborate and expensive saddles for the country's nobility and gentry.[155] This may account for

150 This group includes three men called "furrier" who were considerably less prominent than men termed "skinner"; see Table A3.1.

151 MCR 1374/5, m. 22; 1389/90, mm. 6, 7; 1387/8, m. 44 (furs worth 4 marks); PRO C131/38/21. See also MCR 1382/3, m. 33 for his possession of greywork, the finest Baltic squirrel skins. For fur identifications, see Veale 1966: 215–29. For the extensive geographic range of other skinners' dealings, see below, pp. 304–7.

152 PRO C131/38/22; MCR 1391/2, m. 43.

153 *CPR 1396–9*: 131; PRO C131/38/21, 22. The latter debt was contracted in 1377 but still not wholly paid by 1392; see MCR 1391/2, m. 43.

154 Keene 1985: 285–7, notes an even more marked loss of trade to London furriers by Winchester men in the trade. For the London trade, see Veale 1966: esp. 36–56. Even local furs could make their way to the London market; see MCR 1303/4, m. 8d.

155 The extensive reach of London saddlers is also visible in their debts with gentry from many different counties; see, for example: PRO C131/41/8; PRO C241/158/14, 173/67; PRO CP40/472, m. 76d; 480, m. 317d; 484, mm. 16, 414d; 497, mm. 217d, 297. See also Sherwell 1937: 17–18.

the very low profile of Exeter saddlers in the local markets and the substantially higher sums they owed when debtors (Table 4.3).

Despite the competition Walter Thomas faced from London, he was still much better off than the many skinners at the low end of the trade like John Maiour; he paid only 4*d* in murage and never joined the freedom or served in an elective office. Maiour's more subservient position is evident in the fines he and other unenfranchised skinners suffered for purchasing fells and making furs without benefit of freedom membership, and for taking "excessive salaries" in their work for enfranchised skinners.[156] This relationship helps explain why skinners' debts were so low when the cost of their product could be so high (Table 4.3). Maiour, like most skinners, catered to the less expensive tastes of the urban majority or worked for the small group of wealthy skinners who employed them to taw, dress, or even sew skins.[157] Yet Maiour was probably better off than many of his fellow unenfranchised servant-skinners who worked for the richer skinners; he was the head of a household, held arable and pasture land in the suburbs, employed a servant, and owned several valuable horses and at least thirty geese.[158]

Similar divisions of wealth and commercial activity separated the shoemakers, although the range of prosperity was not so great as that among the skinners. The wealthiest shoemakers were called cordwainers (because of their affiliation with the more valuable cordwain leather) and the poorer were usually termed sutors (who made less costly footwear and repaired old shoes). The city's cordwainers paid an average murage of almost 16*d* but the six sutors paid 6*d* or less. In several indices, in fact, the cordwainers came out ahead of even the skinners; 79 per cent of them joined the freedom, for example, and their average number of servants was 1.64 compared to 1.35 for the skinners.[159] The cordwainers also maintained a more favorable balance within the local markets, collecting more as creditors than they paid out as debtors.[160]

[156] MCR 1379/80, m. 24. See also his entry in Table A3.1.

[157] The skinner Stephen Tapyn tawed lamb skins for the richer skinner Peter Ponte (PCR 1–23 Ric. II, m. 13) and contracted to work for the oligarchic skinner Nicholas Bynnecote for a year: MCR 1379/80, m. 23. The skinner Richard Fogheler (paid 6*d* murage) tawed rabbit skins for both John Bonde and William Whithiel: MCR 1386/7, mm. 19, 20. See also MCR 1379/80, mm. 24, 38 where skinner-servants were fined for taking excessive salaries and were pledged by the richer skinners who were probably their employers.

[158] MCR 1381/2, m. 12; 1382/3, mm. 6, 37, 45 (where he won a suit for theft of his silver ring and 16*d* in silver); 1392/3, mm. 26, 30; PCR 1–23 Ric. II, m. 61.

[159] Table A3.1; based on twenty three servants for fourteen cordwainers and thirty one servants for twenty three skinners.

[160] The fifty one cordwainer creditors paid an average of 10*s* 3*d* while the forty two debtors paid an average of 9*s* 4*d*; sutors had lower debts and their inclusion with shoemakers lowered the overall debt sums for that trade (Table 4.3).

Both cordwainers and sutors, however, appeared as creditors more often than as debtors (Table 4.2).

In contrast to many skinners, shoemakers could count on local supplies and relatively cheap raw materials and also catered to a localized market. The rising standard of living in the post-plague period (which stimulated demand for the relatively inexpensive products of the leather industry), combined with the growing availability of cheap hides and skins as pastoral farming expanded also helps to explain the solid performance of shoemakers and other late medieval producers of relatively inexpensive leather apparel.[161] Shoemakers were also more likely to be independent artisan-retailers who sold products of their own labor, whereas the skinners included a wider range of workers, from rich oligarchic skinner/merchants to poorer laborers who were employed by their more wealthy fellows in the craft.

None of the remaining leather artisans had as big an impact on the local markets as the skinners and shoemakers. Glovers were the poorest of all the leather/skin artisans (Table 4.2) and accounted for a minute proportion of debts in the local courts, as did saddlers and other leather artisans such as girdlers, hosiers, and pouchmakers (Table 4.3).[162] Curriers and tawyers, who finished leather for these artisans, made an even smaller impact on the local commercial scene, perhaps because they were employed mainly by artisans who sold the finished product. Yet curriers may well have had a hand in purchasing raw materials since both the Exeter curriers in 1377 enjoyed freedom membership which carried with it the privilege of dealing in skins and hides customfree (Table 4.2). Their participation in the local markets also operated in their favor, as indicated by their high profile as creditors (Table 4.3).

The tanners were the occupation most involved in the purchase and handling of the basic raw materials of the leather trade. Only two tanners were identified as householders in 1377 but they were among the wealthier artisans and one eventually joined the freedom (Table 4.2). Several tanners may also have lived in the exempt jurisdiction of Exe Island where they would have enjoyed ready access to the water so necessary for the success of their business.[163] The scarcity of tanners within the city itself is not surprising since the annoying smells and pollution generated by the tanning process encouraged boroughs to

[161] This relationship is explained at greater length in Kowaleski 1990.

[162] Hosiers (see above, n. 143) appeared in only one debt, pouchmakers in fourteen, and girdlers in none; they were included among "others" in Tables 4.2–4.4.

[163] Note the payments for hanging hides in the river Exe made to the lord of Exe Island in PRO SC6/1118/6.

restrict the industrial activities of tanners to areas on the fringes of towns.[164] But the low number of tanners in Exeter also reflects the extent to which the supply of tanned hides and skins was in the hands of non-urban tanners who resided in the small towns and villages of Exeter's hinterland. These regional networks of trade which provided the fundamental raw materials of the urban leather industry are examined in more detail in Chapter 7.

The metal and building trades

In terms of wealth, freedom membership, and political activity, the metal trades were similar to the leather and skin crafts, paying a similar murage tax and joining the freedom and oligarchy in roughly the same proportions (Table 4.2). But metalworkers were not as numerous, constituting only 9.4 per cent of the householders in 1377, thereby ranking them behind all the other artisanal occupational groups. Nonetheless, their participation in the local markets was still significant since their appearance in debt cases (7 per cent) was closer to their general numbers within the population than the leather and skin or building crafts. They also enjoyed a higher creditor/debtor ratio than most artisanal groups, an indication of their relatively favorable position within the local markets.

The large sums owed by metalworker debtors (Table 4.3) reflected the substantial value of the metals that formed the raw material of their trade. Many of these metals, such as copper, iron, lead, steel, and tin, came to Exeter via coastal and overseas trade. The necessity of importing much of their basic raw materials accounts for the high profile of metalworkers in seaborne trade; about 14 per cent of the metalworkers imported goods at one time or another, a percentage more than twice that for any of the other artisanal groups (Table 4.2).[165] Smiths represented the largest group of importers in the metal trades, sometimes forming partnerships, as four Exeter smiths did in 1395 when they imported 8 tons of iron. At least three of the partners belonged to the freedom and two were members of the B Rank oligarchy, but the fourth partner, John Doccombe, was assessed only 6*d*. Yet John Doccombe was the only one of the four who appeared again as an importer in the

[164] Kowaleski 1990: 61.

[165] To this figure might also be added the merchant/cutler, John Nymet, who imported iron and tin along with other goods (PCA 1382/3, 1383/4, 1389/90, 1390/1; see also Table A3.1). His wife, Alice, carried on his business and also imported iron and tin (PCA 1391/2, 1392/3, 1393/4, 1398/9).

surviving customs accounts.[166] Smiths and other metalworkers more commonly acquired their raw materials through the oligarchic merchants who dominated the port trade. Even so, the costs of the material could be high for some of the less well-off smiths. Lawrence Spealte, for example, paid the lowest possible murage rate of 2*d* yet still contracted with the oligarchic merchant Raymond Goos for 41*s*-worth of iron.[167]

Like other smiths, John Doccombe both retailed iron and hired himself out to manufacture or repair iron implements and parts.[168] Unlike other smiths, Doccombe seems to have had nothing to do with shoeing horses. But two of his co-importers, Robert Cook and Walter Wylde, leased traves (barred enclosures that held horses being shod) in the High Street.[169] Wylde also had a contract worth 23*s* to shoe the horses attached to Duryard mill for one year and was alternately termed "ferrour" or "marshal" in local records.[170] The different occupational designations for those who worked in iron – ferrours, smiths, marshals, lorimers, and locksmiths – might indicate specialities but did not preclude common tasks and functions.[171] The same blurring occurred between other branches of the metal trades; the spurrier Matthew Ikesbonere worked on armour (helmets and hauberks), although the armourer John Armener dealt in a wider array of armour and weapons (hauberks, helmets, lances, swords).[172] The fact that the far richer Ikesbonere once sued the poorer Armener for transgressing the Statute of Laborers also suggests that Armener either worked for Ikesbonere or lured away one of his employees.[173]

The metal trades employed more servants than all but the distributive trades (Table 4.2). This reliance on servants suggests that family labor may have been less important in the metal crafts, perhaps because the artisan so often worked away from the home or shop at building sites or other places where repairs were needed. Certainly women were never mentioned in connection with the trade in Exeter although elsewhere

166 Their joint appearance was in PCA 1394/5 (Doccombe, Robert Cook, and Walter Wilde were in the murage tax, Ralph Feraunt was not: see Table A3.1). Doccombe's other imports were all of iron (PCA 1390/1, 1392/3, 1398/9).

167 MCR 1368/9, m. 36; and see their entries in Table A3.1.

168 CRA 1379/80, 1381/2, 1386/7; DRA 1384/5; EBW 1393/4; Misc. Roll 6, mm. 3, 10, 30, 32, 34; ECL D&C 2646, 2647, 2648, 2650, 2654, 2655.

169 CRA 1377/8, 1389/90.

170 DRA 1386/7 (under the name Walter Ferrour); MCR 1373/4, m. 20.

171 See the interchangeable designations for metalworkers in Table A3.1; all have been considered smiths in Tables 4.2–4.4. Swanson 1989: 67–9 notes the same phenomenon at York and other towns.

172 Armener: PCR 1–23 Ric. II, mm. 37, 42, 49; MCR 1380/1, m. 32; Ekesbonere: PCR 1–23 Ric. II, m. 41; MCR 1385/6, mm. 4, 6, 16, 46, 48.

173 MCR 1379/80, m. 42. Ikesbonere paid 2*s* in the 1377 murage tax and Armener paid only 4*d*; see Misc. Roll 72 and Table A3.1.

they can be found working with copper wire or even as founders.[174] The very large percentage of commercial brewers among the households of metalworkers (Table 4.4) also implies that the attention of metalworkers' wives and daughters was directed towards other activities. Just as metalworkers themselves were often hired for specific tasks, so too they may have employed their own craft servants for particular jobs over a limited period, rather than retaining servants on annual contracts as was the custom for domestic servants or those in the textile and clothing trades. This pattern of employment was also prevalent amongst the building trades, but both the latter's financial ability to hire servants and their demand for labor may have been lower (Table 4.2).

As in the other occupational groups, there could be great differences both within and between the various occupational designations. The two braziers were the most prominent, followed by the smiths and goldsmiths (Table 4.2). With the exception of the B Rank oligarch John Russel (whose wealth was based on his inheritance from his childless master, Richard Goldsmith), none of the Exeter goldsmiths was very prominent.[175] Only three of the seven belonged to the freedom, and goldsmiths appeared much more frequently as debtors than as creditors (Table 4.3). The ecclesiastical establishment in Exeter provided some with steady employment, however; Robert Cateneys regularly made and repaired such items as chalices, pitchers, chains, and basins for the dean and chapter.[176] The pewterers were even fewer in number although one of them, Richard Peuterer, was also a merchant whose diversified interests in the cloth and wine trade helped to promote him to the A Rank oligarchy.[177] Peuterer was an exception; the majority of the non-smithing metalworkers had limited participation in local commerce, a reflection of their less retail-oriented activities.

The Exeter metalworkers more often appeared purchasing raw materials and working for others (particularly institutions) than selling finished products to consumers. Competition also came from the many metal goods that arrived by sea, from scissors and swords, to batterie-ware and bells.[178] Of all the metalworkers, only the smiths made much of

174 Swanson 1989: 72–4; Goldberg 1992: 127–9. Swanson also notes the large number of servants and apprentices in the metal trades.

175 Richard Goldsmith was in the A Rank oligarchy and left his entire estate to his servant John Russel: MCR 1376/7, m. 12d. Russel served as an elector twice (1382/3 and 1384/5); see also Table A3.1.

176 ECL D&C 3777, ff. 7d, 10, 12, 13d, 32.

177 PRO E101/338/11, m. 8; PCA 1390/1, 1391/2, 1395/6, 1397/8; and see Table A3.1. His activities were largely responsible for the high percentage of appearances by creditors of pewterers (Table 4.3).

178 PCA, passim. No less than forty five bells were imported in the surviving accounts from 1350–99.

an impact in the local markets, in part because they were the single largest group of metalworkers (Tables 4.2, 4.3).[179] Smiths appeared as creditors 66 per cent of the time and their debts entailed cash sums larger than most; they were also one of the few occupations who could expect to be paid larger amounts than they owed (Table 4.3).[180]

At construction sites, metalworkers often worked alongside those in the building trades who constituted 10 per cent of the householders in Exeter in 1377. There was plenty of demand for their services in Exeter; both the stone walls surrounding the city and the town's ecclesiastical establishments (parish churches, a Benedictine priory, two mendicant houses, two hospitals, and the cathedral) provided steady employment to carpenters, masons, and others.[181] Work carried out on the cathedral, however, was the major stimulus to the building trades, and promoted Exeter's ability to accommodate more construction workers than similarly sized non-cathedral towns. Well over half of the householders in the building trades in 1377 worked on the cathedral at one time or another (seven masons, two glaziers, one roofer, and fourteen carpenters and sawyers).[182] Some worked for the cathedral only for a short time, as did the mason John Dalby who was hired for less than two weeks one year and for one day thirteen years later, while others, such as the carpenter Thomas Porter, worked for months at a time over a period of decades.[183] Others served the cathedral for an even longer duration. The master carpenter Walter Gist was retained by the cathedral for

[179] The smiths also include a lorimer/locksmith, a marshal, and a marshal/ferrour; see Table A3.1.

[180] But note that sixty two of the creditor appearances of smiths were made by just one man, Thomas Smytheshegher, an oligarchic smith/merchant; see Table A3.1.

[181] Wage lists for the city's building projects on the wall and gates may be found in Misc. Roll 6, and in CRA, DRA, and EBW; work on the city walls was especially intense in the late fourteenth century. For an example of the mendicants' patronage, see PCR 1–23 Ric. II, m. 34 where the Dominican prior sued William Beste for breaking an agreement to build a wall 40 feet long and 8 feet wide.

[182] Identified from the ECL Cathedral Fabric Accounts, D&C 2636–2657 (1371–1398). The totals would be higher if work performed on other properties within the cathedral close was included. All three heliers appeared in the fabric accounts at least once for roofing or for other tasks like carting, but only William Heliere seems to have worked on the cathedral itself. All (see Table A3.1) but the following carpenters (including sawyers) worked on the cathedral: William Benet, Walter Broun, Hugh Halewill, William Johan, Thomas Lorying, John Pederton, Henry Placy, and John Tolke. The only glazier not to appear was David Glasiere. For a short description of the cathedral workforce from 1279–1326, see Erskine 1983: xviii–xxiv.

[183] Dalby: ECL D&C 2638, 2648; Porter: ECL D&C 2640 (five weeks), 2642 (nine weeks), 2643 (three weeks), 2644 (one day), 2649 (five days), 2650 (five weeks), 2651 (one week), 2652 (sixteen weeks), 2653 (three weeks), 2654 (two days). Both may also have worked during the period 1353–71 when no fabric accounts are extant.

over twenty years with an annual pension of one mark in addition to a daily rate and other payments for specific tasks.[184]

Gist and other carpenters also took on other work. He built one house and repaired many others for the tenants of the dean and chapter's St Sidwell's fee, constructed six new shops in the Fleshfold *ad tascham* (for 48*s*), did repair work on the Guildhall on several occasions, constructed a new pillory over a period of about seven weeks (receiving 40*d* per week), and was the "master carpenter" for work on Exe Bridge (paid 40*d* per week plus a one mark bonus).[185] Gist represented the top end of the carpentry trade; he and three others paid 12*d* in murage when the overall average for the town's carpenters was only 6.7*d* (Table 4.2). Poorer carpenters, like Thomas Porter, received lesser wages and were employed on fewer large-scale and long-term projects.[186] Those who could not count on a steady income from the cathedral or other institutional projects had to solicit their own work from other inhabitants. Such contracts are evident in Luke Carpenter's agreement to build a room (*camera*) for Thomas Lane before Christmas (he still had not done it by February) and the roofer John Golewyr's difficulties in obtaining the balance of his stipend for work done for Walter Mileward.[187]

The building trades in Exeter differed in several ways from the other occupational groups. Although the industry provided work for many occasional laborers, the householders in this occupation were the occupational group least likely to pursue other trades (Table 4.1).[188] Even their involvement in brewing as a secondary source of income reflected this; although they generally brewed more often than other trades, they did so at a lower rate than most households. Almost half (fifteen of thirty one) of these households brewed only three times or less. This rather unusual involvement in commercial brewing (many brewed at least once but few brewed consistently) may have reflected the sometimes

[184] ECL D&C 2636–2657.

[185] ECL D&C 5154, 5155; Misc. Roll 6, mm. 29, 32; CRA 1381/2, 1382/3, 1383/4.

[186] Porter's wages from the cathedral ranged from 1*s* 8*d* to 2*s* 6*d*, depending on the season. His wages also rose slightly over the period of his employment at the cathedral, reflecting either generally rising wages or a recognition of his greater skill. The only city project he worked on was in c. 1372 when he was paid for about four weeks of work on the city wall (at 2*s*–2*s* 2*d* per week): Misc. Roll 6, m. 14.

[187] MCR 1389/90, m. 19; PCR 1–23 Ric. II, m. 24.

[188] Obviously this would be less true for the many laborers and less skilled positions within the industry; those householders involved in the building trade were clearly the more skilled artisans who could expect more steady employment. Note also that Swanson (1989: 92) found that sedentary masons often had secondary sources of income.

erratic or seasonal employment of building workers; investment in brewing by these households might have depended on the amount of income generated by the householder in any one year. Then, too, the scarcer financial resources of building households might also have reduced their opportunities for commercial brewing on a large scale (Table 4.2). With the exception of one glazier (an oligarch who made occasional forays into maritime trade) and a few master carpenters, most construction workers paid very low murage taxes, rarely belonged to the freedom, and did not trade by sea or serve in civic office.[189] The lack of freedom membership is understandable since the retailing privileges and toll exemptions bestowed by membership were of little use to construction workers whose income derived almost wholly from the sale of their labor. Without freedom membership these artisans were not eligible to be elected to the oligarchic offices, although the low level of wealth amongst building workers would also have precluded such office holding.

By and large, construction workers rarely engaged in any craft-related retailing activities. Some of the carpenters sold timber, but their activities were infrequent and on a small scale.[190] Most purchased timber as part of work they had contracted to do, rather than retailing or wholesaling it separately. Glaziers did keep glass on hand for use in the windows they were hired to make or repair, but they mostly acquired their supplies from merchants.[191] On rare occasions, a helier (roofer) appeared as the importer of a cargo of slate tiles.[192] Merchants, foreign shipmasters, and occasionally local gentry and clergy were the major importers of building materials such as boards, building stone, marble, and roofing slates. The wage-dependence and weak commercial involvement of the building trades are evident in their extremely low share of debt litigation in the Exeter courts; they represented 10 per cent of the households but accounted for only 3 per cent of debt suits (Table 4.3).

[189] Thomas Glasiere paid an 18*d* murage tax, served as an elector seventeen times (starting in 1362) and imported herring in PCA 1385/6. He was probably also the Thomas le Glasiere who imported glass in PCA 1357/8; see his entry in Table A3.1. Swanson 1983: 7, 29–31 discusses the similarly low status of the building trades in York.

[190] For examples, see Walter Gist (CRA 1382/3, 1386/7), Henry Placy (Misc. Roll 6, m. 17; EBW 1381/2), and Henry Carpenter (EBW 1382/3; ECL D&C 2644). Swanson (1983: 14–15, 29) cites a few instances when York carpenters acted as timber merchants.

[191] Only one of the six shipments of glass in 1350–99 was imported by a glazier (PCA 1357/8).

[192] Walter Helier, who may have been the same Walter Helier who agreed to serve the dean and chapter in the "office of tiler" (ECL D&C 3550, f. 59v), imported roofing slates in PCA 1396/7. John Helyer of Ottermouth paid for a similar cargo in PCA 1367/8.

Most appeared much more often as debtors than as creditors, another indication of their position within local commerce. The amount of their debts was generally low although the inclusion of sums related to substantial building repairs or construction raised the amounts of some debts (Table 4.3).[193] Nonetheless, the building trades were clearly not major players in the town's local commercial scene.

Other trades and services

Some generalizations about the remaining trades can be made if they are divided into three sub-groups. The first comprises artisan-retailers who all fashioned and sold their own products. They included the wood trades (bowyers, fletchers, and coopers), as well as candlemakers, horners, and ropers. The most prominent among them was the bowyer, Thomas Pye; he paid a murage tax of 24*d*, served once in the B Rank office of elector, and imported goods on several occasions, including bowstaves.[194] As his other imports of wine, woad, tar, and figs imply, he had a very wide range of commercial connections that extended beyond just the manufacture and sale of bows. The sole roper belonged to the freedom and sold cord as well as fixing ropes and cables.[195] Horners also concentrated on manufacturing, using animal horns that they had purchased from butchers or tanners to make such items as combs and lantern leaves.[196] Less specialized and prominent were those who manufactured cheap candles from tallow acquired from butchers. Candle-making was also a secondary occupation for soapers and other occupations; many women were also involved in this craft.[197] But some, such as Thomas Founteyn, made larger profits by supplying wax for candles.[198]

The second sub-group comprises the service sector, including both the service trades (barbers, carters, messengers, musicians, pledgers,

[193] The average debt of mason-debtors, for example, includes an outlier of £7 5*s* which unduly skews the small sample of cases.

[194] He served as elector in 1384; his imports are recorded under the name of Thomas Boghier in PCA 1389/90, 1395/6, 1396/7. See also his entry in Table A3.1.

[195] He was Robert Ropere; see Misc. Roll 6, m. 32; ECL D&C 2653; and Table A3.1, below.

[196] For the activities of the horner William Payn, see MCR 1377/8, m. 17; PCR 1–23 Ric. II, m. 66; Table A3.1. For horners in Exeter see also Levitan 1989: 163–4; for elsewhere, see Swanson 1989: 104–5.

[197] This is clear from the regular MT presentments against those who adulterated candles with inferior fat skimmings; see SQMT 1388; EQMT 1388, 1391, 1393; WQMT 1388; NQMT 1392; MCR 1391/2, m. 26. Most chandlers in Exeter at this period only made candles and are thus included here rather than in the retailer category.

[198] ECL D&C 3777, ff. 21d, 34; see also D&C 3773, f. 10d.

and watercarriers) and servants (apprentices, as well as domestic and craft servants). All these trades were under-represented in the survey of householders; only six such householders could be identified, although references in the debt litigation show others.[199] Little information is available concerning their activities in Exeter. The two identified barbers were clearly prosperous and commercially active (Tables 4.2, 4.3). But neither they nor any of the other barbers in Exeter showed signs of the medical skills medieval barbers are known to have practiced.[200] Most references to medical services concerned leches while medicines were supplied by spicers, taverners, and the clergy.[201] Midwives, who provided vital health-care services to women, would also be included in this service group although they were rarely mentioned in extant records.[202] Also part of the service sector were messengers who, mounted on horseback, carried messages and legal documents for the civic authorities and others.[203] Musicians, such as pipers and at least one "giterner," also appeared.[204] The city waites entertained at official functions and announced important proclamations.[205] None but the barbers played much of a role in the city's commercial life.

Since servants were rarely heads of households, they made little impression on the occupational analysis presented in the foregoing tables and discussion. They were, however, present in great numbers in Exeter and other medieval towns. By a very conservative estimate, at least 40 per cent of the Exeter households employed servants and several had between five and seven servants each.[206] Many of these servants were

199 Table A3.1. Craft servants who showed signs of independent craft activity were counted in that occupational group rather than in the service category, further reducing the figures offered here.

200 Both of the Exeter barbers (John Barber and William Bremelham) dealt in cloth; see PCR 1–23 Ric. II, mm. 11, 46, 62. For barbers' work elsewhere, see Swanson 1989: 100–1.

201 Although active in Exeter at other times, no leches could be definitively identified in 1377. For leches involved in medical matters: PCR 1–23 Ric. II, m. 12; MCR 1349/50, mm. 41, 43d; 1387/8, mm. 33, 37. Sales of medicine: PCR 1–23 Ric. II, mm. 41, 52; MCR 1388/9, m. 48.

202 Seven are named, however, in a gaol delivery case since they had to determine if the female defendant was pregnant or not; see PRO JUST3 221/6, m. 4.

203 These trips were made by the messenger Adam Monte: see CRA 1366/7, 1368/9, 1376/7; MCR 1374/5, m. 4; Misc. Roll 6, m. 18; and his entry in Table A3.1.

204 MCR 1384/5, m. 23; 1392/3, m. 18; 1398/9, m. 2d; PCR 1–23 Ric. II, m. 38.

205 For the election and activities of waites (and other entertainers in Exeter), see Wassom (ed.) 1986; *Citie of Excester*: 821, 945–6.

206 Forty per cent of the households listed in Table A3.1 had at least one servant, a very conservative estimate since servants, who were usually considered dependants rather than full householders, were under-recorded in the extant documentation. In York at this time, one-third of the poll-tax payers had servants and 20 to 30 per cent of taxpayers over fourteen were described as servants; see Goldberg 1986a: 21. See also Goldberg 1990b: 36–40 for the high number of servants in other towns.

young women who migrated to provincial towns (often in greater numbers than did men) in search of economic opportunities.[207] Their low status is evident in the manner in which 160 female servants were identified in the Exeter records from 1373 to 1393; 74 per cent were designated only by their first name and their employer's name; 6 per cent were recorded under the name of a husband or father; and only 20 per cent were called by their own full names.[208] Their vulnerability is also apparent in the number of complaints by female servants of physical abuse by their employers and by the not uncommon association between female servants and prostitution.[209]

While the terms of employment varied, most servants, in this period of high demand for labor, contracted to work for only one year at a time.[210] In exchange for their labor, servants received a predetermined salary and sometimes room and board in their employers' homes. Because the commercial activities of servants were negligible, the vast majority of their court appearances concerned labor disputes (Table 4.3). Servants sued employers for unpaid salaries or unfair treatment while employers sued servants for breaking their contracts by leaving before their term was up or for cheating and robbing them.[211] Not all employer–employee relationships were so acrimonious. One grateful master, Walter Gerveys, bequeathed his servant Margaret Bryan a shop, garden, and one-half acre of land, while others left their servants personal goods and cash.[212] Employers also frequently acted as pledges for their servants and aided them in times of distress.

Apprentices represented the top end of the servant group. They agreed to serve their masters for three to seven years in exchange for training in the craft, upkeep, and occasionally a small stipend.[213] After the apprenticeship was up, masters sponsored their apprentices' entry into the freedom, allowing these men to join the small group of householders who enjoyed the special economic, legal, and political privileges that accompanied full citizenship. Apprenticeship thus served as a means

207 Hilton 1982: 10; Goldberg 1986a, 1986b, 1990b: 39.

208 The basis of this sample is discussed in Kowaleski 1986:147–8, 153.

209 Kowaleski 1986: 154. For a master accused of raping his servant, see MCR 1303/4, m. 5d.

210 Examples of such contracts, which normally begin at Michaelmas, frequently appear in the mayor's court rolls. There is some evidence that early fifteenth-century employers wanted longer terms; see, for example, the five-year terms in MCR 1403/4, m. 17d; 1404/5, m. 52d.

211 The MCR especially are full of such cases.

212 MCR 1399/1400, m. 22; 1413/14, m. 41; ED/M/542.

213 For examples of fourteenth-century apprenticeship agreements, see MCR 1309/10, m. 23; 1352/3, m. 16d; 1361/2, m. 7; 1363/4, m. 3d; 1364/5, m. 29d; Book 55 (Freemen's Book), f. 186.

of social mobility for many young men. Former apprentices such as Thomas Estoun and Peter Sturte, for example, went on to serve as mayors of Exeter.[214] But many apprentices who attained political and commercial prominence were themselves the sons of the civic elite.[215] Moreover, the distinctions between artisans and merchants also applied to their apprentices. Merchants' apprentices were much more likely to achieve political and economic success than were the apprentices of artisans.

Agricultural occupations were in the third group of trades. At least sixteen households in 1377 made some portion of their living from agricultural pursuits although the majority did so as an adjunct to another occupation.[216] Most of these families lived in the suburbs outside the east (St Sidwell's fee) and north (Duryard manor) gates; they along with many of their neighbors grew crops (particularly beans) and/or kept small herds or flocks of cattle, sheep, and poultry. In 1385, the dean and chapter collected great tithes (on crops) worth over £12 from more than thirty individuals in St Sidwell who tilled about 267 acres in this suburb.[217] The northern suburb of Duryard possessed more pasture and meadow (it bordered the Exe river) than arable. Roger Pestour, who later served as the bailiff of Duryard for the city, appeared in the court rolls as the owner of twenty six cattle, two cows, a calf, three horses (including two mares), geese, chickens, and eleven pigs; he also owed money for hay-raking services and leased five different pastures, one of which cost him 100*s* in annual rent.[218] In the city and suburbs some families also tended large orchards.[219] The seasonal rhythm of agricultural work could also affect the urban labor market. In late July of 1376, for example, the city indicted thirteen men and women

[214] *Exeter freemen*: 35–37; Rowe and Cochlin 1964: 7.

[215] For example, John Webber Jr., son of John Webber Sr.; John Scut, son of Adam Scut; and Roger Shaplegh, son of John Shaplegh. See *Exeter freemen*: 35, 36, 37; Rowe and Cochlin 1964: 6–7; MCR and PCR election returns; PCA passim.

[216] See Table A3.1. Many of these men were identified from the sale of their tithes in 1385 in ECL D&C 5235; only those men who paid more than 2*s* in great tithes were assigned an agricultural occupation in Table A3.1. A few others were identified through their appearances in farming-related activities in the DCR and SCR. In any case, the number of households that gained some income through agricultural activities is certainly underestimated in Table A3.1.

[217] See ECL D&C 5235 which breaks down the sale of tithes in St Sidwell's fee according to owner so that it is possible to see the relative amounts of arable held by individuals; see also Kowaleski forthcoming.

[218] DRA 1386/7; MCR 1388/9, m. 35. NQMT 1373, 1378–88; DCR 2–22 Ric. II, mm. 4–24; PCR 1–23 Ric. II, mm. 7, 38; MCR 1375/6, m. 8; 1377/8, m. 47; 1379/80, mm. 5, 49; 1380/1, m. 33; 1381/2, mm. 41, 43; 1382/3, m. 31; 1387/8, mm. 21, 22; ECL D&C 5235.

[219] MCR 1321/2, m. 35d; 1355/6, m. 22d.

who had left their jobs to go "eastwards," presumably to help bring in the harvest of the rural communities surrounding Exeter.[220] Others had more substantial agricultural investments; the clerk John Ponton kept some 200 sheep on lands outside of Exeter and several of the butchers were involved in fattening livestock.[221]

The professions, administrators, and clergy

Those in the professions or administrative posts represented the smallest occupational category; if the many clerical administrators and clerks attached to the city's religious establishments were included, their numbers would be much greater. Not surprisingly for a group that included lawyers and powerful municipal administrators, the professional category was second only to the merchants in wealth (albeit a distant second; see Table 4.2). They also ranked second in the percentage that joined the freedom, traded by sea, and served in the oligarchy. Like the merchants, they were also remarkably prominent in debt litigation, appearing much more frequently as creditors (11 per cent) than as debtors (2.3 per cent), figures made even more impressive when we recall that they represented but 3 per cent of the population (Table 4.3). But their prominence in debt cases reflected not so much their commercial activity as their policing, legal, and administrative functions within the town. At least 64 per cent of their appearances in debt cases, for example, concerned disputes about town custom, rent, and court fines, compared to only 21 per cent for all occupational groups.[222]

Many of these borough officials used their position to commercial advantage, however, by farming city customs and pastures.[223] Bailiffs, lawyers, and clerks also received special treatment in the courts where their fines for such petty offenses as breaking the assize of ale were often condoned by the mayor. The city clerk John Ponton and three of the four lawyers residing in Exeter in 1377 all enjoyed the privileges of freedom membership although no official record of their entry was made.[224] Even more unusual was Ponton's vault to the top of the civic

220 MCR 1375/6, m. 43.

221 PRO E159/173 Hilary recorda, m. 13. For the butchers, see below, pp. 297–9.

222 MCR and PCR debt cases, 1378–88; based on ninety nine responses for the professional and administrative occupational category.

223 Farms of customs were enrolled immediately after the annual elections on mm. 1d and 2d of the MCR. For the oligarchy's control of many of these farms, see above, pp. 104–5.

224 This was an unusual circumstance for Exeter; see Table A3.1 and the explanation under the note for the freedom. The three lawyers were John Bozoun, William Criditon, and John Wille.

ladder; the very first office he held was the city's second most powerful, that of receiver.[225] From that time on Ponton served every year in the city's most influential offices of steward, councillor, and elector; he also became constable of the Exeter staple.[226] Even before he was elected to these official posts, however, Ponton worked for the city as its clerk, writing important city letters and holding the manorial court at Duryard; these duties probably helped convince the mayor to condone all his brewing fines from 1375 to 1382.[227] Ponton's position may also have given him an inside track on acquiring various customs farms and city pasture leases over the years.[228] Ponton appears to have pushed his luck a bit far, however, since he got into deep trouble over large unpaid debts, including 100 marks owed to the king.[229] His illegal confiscation of the city's statute staple seal also caused some problems.[230]

The clergy numbered about 185 in 1377, representing about 6 per cent of the total urban population.[231] Well over half of the clerics were attached to the cathedral as canons, vicars choral, annuellers, secondaries, and choristers. The clergy's impact on the local markets is hard to measure, but some general observations can be made. They were, for instance, very substantial employers; each of the eighteen canons had about six servants attached to his household, at least thirty lay servants served the bishop's household, and others were hired to cater to the cooking and cleaning needs of the minor clergy.[232] The Benedictine priory, two mendicant houses, two hospitals, and twenty parishes must also have provided occasional and full-time employment to a large number of domestic servants. Payments for services rendered by Exeter lawyers like John Bozoun, or bailiffs and rent collectors in St Sidwell's fee, also show the work furnished by the clergy to the professional occupations in the city.[233]

More significant than their role as employers may have been the way clerical consumers fueled demand for food, drink, and clothing, as well

[225] MCR 1383/4, m. 1d.
[226] MCR election returns, 1383–95; PRO C267/6/36–39.
[227] CRA 1373/4. CRA 1376/7 notes a payments to him of 40*s* for his fee as clerk and 15*s* for his robe. For the brewing fines, see WQMT 1375–82; NQMT 1376.
[228] MCR 1377/8, m. 1d; DCR 2–22 Ric. II, mm. 8, 9.
[229] PRO E159/173, Hilary recorda, mm. 13–14d; this debt concerned the forfeiture of cloth and was probably related to work Ponton did for the royal government in Exeter. For his other financial problems, see *CPR, 1401–5*: 188; *CIM*, vol. 6: no. 166; MCR 1390/1, m. 17.
[230] PRO C267/6/33.
[231] See Table 2.1; see Appendix 3 for a discussion of how this figure was derived.
[232] Orme 1986: 41–2; PRO E179/95/34.
[233] See, for example, ECL D&C 3773, ff. 9v, 10v; 3777, ff. 10v, 34.

as for personal luxuries, furnishings, and building materials.[234] Even their liturgical and charitable efforts had an impact on local commerce as indicated by their continual demand for wax and oil for the former and food for the latter (including more than 2,300 eggs in one three-day period for the baking of "flans" for distribution to the poor).[235] Their role as consumers is also evident in their share of the debt litigation in the Exeter courts where they appeared more often as debtors than as creditors (Table 4.3). Also suggestive of their wealth, property ownership, and ready cash for loans is the substantial sums they sued for as creditors (Table 4.3). Clerical creditors sued for cash loans or unpaid cash advances in 48 per cent of their debts while creditors overall only did so 11 per cent of the time; 19 per cent of the clerical creditors sued for rent, compared to 12 per cent of all creditors.[236]

This analysis of the occupational structure of late fourteenth-century Exeter has had two aims: to offer as comprehensive a picture as possible of the relative importance of various trades in the urban economy and to compare the commercial role of these trades in the local markets. The unusually detailed and voluminous records of Exeter have made a more quantitative approach possible at the same time as they have allowed us to identify a much larger percentage of individuals and occupations than other studies of medieval English towns. Particular emphasis has been placed on the construction of a wide variety of indices concerning the wealth, commercial activity, and political rank of individual trades and occupational groups. By viewing occupational structure from diverse angles and sources, rather than depending solely on one type of source such as freedom registers or declared occupations in deeds, wills, and tax rolls, a richer and more accurate representation of the relative importance of different sectors of the urban economy can be attained. The methodologies employed here to exploit these sources are very time-consuming because of their prosopographical basis, but the unusual precision of the analyses suggests that they might be fruitfully applied elsewhere as well.

[234] Orme 1986: 31–42; Portman 1966: 3–22; Erskine 1983: ix–xxxv. Further insights into the cathedral clergy's expenditures in Exeter can be gleaned from the dean and chapter's notebooks of expenses and payments dating from about 1377–1403 in ECL D&C 3773, 3777. See above, p. 163 for the dean and chapter's employment of goldsmiths.

[235] See, for example, ECL D&C 3773, ff. 8v, 10, 10v; 3777, ff. 7, 9v, 12, 17v, 18, 21v, 23v, 24, 29, 32, 34, 35, 37.

[236] Based on data concerning twenty one clerical creditors; see also Table 5.1. For the clergy's role in regional trade, see below, Chapter 7.

Still open to debate is the question of how typical of other towns are the observations and conclusions made here concerning Exeter's occupational structure and the workings of its local markets. Although it might be argued that Exeter was representative of other market towns with similarly sized populations of around 3,000, it is likely that size was not the most important factor here. Despite Exeter's relatively small population, its position as a seaport, regional capital, and cathedral town must have been more influential in determining its occupational structure and commercial orientation. Exeter was more likely to resemble large seaports like Bristol, Southampton, and Newcastle, or provincial capitals and cathedral towns such as Lincoln, Norwich, Winchester, and York, even though these towns were much more populous than Exeter in 1377. Inland market towns of Exeter's size were unlikely to possess its substantial mercantile element and regional influence, nor were non-cathedral towns apt to have as large a building sector.

Although local circumstances helped shape an individual town's occupational structure, urban commerce everywhere shared common features. Many householders, particularly those engaged in distributive or innkeeping businesses, practiced more than one occupation, making money from a variety of seemingly unrelated pursuits. When households rather than individuals are considered, multiple occupations become almost the norm. Spouses, children, and non-kin residents were capable of both helping the householder in a primary occupation and carrying on other types of income-generating tasks, such as brewing or domestic service. The pervasiveness of commercial brewing – over 70 per cent of households brewed at least once and almost 30 per cent did so ten or more times – points to one of the more common types of by-occupations as well as the dominance of the victualling sector within urban economies. Victualling trades represented the single largest occupational group in Exeter, accounting for at least 21 per cent of primary occupations. To this figure should be added not only the 9 per cent of households who ran inns, but also a hefty percentage of the mercantile households since wine, fish, salt, and other victuals represented 74 per cent of the cargoes imported into late fourteenth-century Exeter.[237] When the by-occupations of ale brewers are factored into these figures, it becomes clear that about one-half of urban residents traded food and drink, a figure which accords well with the 49 per cent share of local debt litigation that concerned these same commodities. Local markets

[237] Based on 1,208 different goods (including 625 cargoes of wine) imported in PCA 1381/2–1390/1; see Table 6.2 and Chapter 6 for a more extensive discussion of the role of these commodities within the port trade.

were certainly capable of handling a great variety of goods and services, but the provision of food and drink by a wide margin constituted the single most important sector of local commerce.[238]

[238] This is not to deny that certain manufacturing specialisms could not co-exist with this emphasis; see Nigel Goose (1982) on this point.

Part 3

Local markets and regional networks of trade

5 Transaction costs

The profits that medieval traders hoped to realize from their market exchanges were in large part determined by the costs of using the market. These transaction costs include search costs (finding appropriate buyers and sellers with whom to trade), negotiation costs (agreeing about the quality, amount, and price of a good as well as the time and place of exchange and payment), and enforcement costs (ensuring that the terms of the bargain were kept).[1] In the pre-industrial world, these costs could be lowered (and thus the market made more efficient, commerce stimulated, and profits made potentially larger) in a variety of ways. One of the most important concerned the economies of scale that could be realized when one central marketplace linked local, regional, and long-distance networks of trade. Search costs could be reduced when large numbers of producers, traders, and consumers from diverse places regularly went to the same entrepôt; such market towns (and fairs) offered a wider range of goods and terms of sale to buyers and sellers, thus making their job easier. The concentration of traders in large market towns also made it more likely that buyers and sellers could negotiate favorable exchanges because of the greater variety of goods, regular (and personal) contact with more traders, and greater availability of credit and investment opportunities. These towns also acted in their own best interests when they contributed to a lowering of enforcement costs by providing secure surroundings, consistent trading guidelines, and opportunities for legal redress if problems developed.

The following chapter examines the features of medieval urban trade that most affected the costs of doing business and tries to determine the impact these factors exerted on different groups of traders. Practices that raised transaction costs generally included the authorities' quest for civic revenues, the desire of freedom members to protect their

[1] For transaction costs, see North and Thomas 1973; North 1985. This chapter employs aspects of the transaction-costs approach because of its usefulness in understanding the role of the entrepôt in pre-industrial markets. It does not, however, consider the debate about the North–Thomas theory of economic growth.

monopolies and privileges, the system of tolls, and the difficulties of debt collection; arrangements that worked to lower transaction costs included the regulation of trade, the use of credit and partnerships, and the legal machinery behind debt collection. Distance and transportation were also crucial factors in determining transaction costs, but they are assessed here mainly by focusing on when and how a trader's non-residency influenced the cost of doing business in the town.[2] The city of Exeter's role as a regional entrepôt (a factor associated with reduced search costs) is also discussed at length in the two following chapters. This chapter will thus focus largely on the negotiation and enforcement costs faced by buyers and sellers who traded in Exeter. In so doing, it will point to how transaction costs varied depending on the status and home residence of traders, as well as the conflicting interests of the mercantile elite, other traders, and consumers.

The regulation of trade

Most local ordinances and national statutes regulating markets in the fourteenth century aimed to protect the interests of consumers by providing for low prices, reliable quality, and regular supplies. These aims, however, often conflicted with the interests of producers and middlemen, who sought to make a profit in an unencumbered and unregulated way. This tension between the interests of producers, middlemen and consumers is particularly evident in municipal market legislation. The merchants who controlled town governments often passed self-serving ordinances that restricted competition, nurtured monopolies, and raised prices at the same time as their membership in freedom organizations or guilds gave them special privileges in court and exemptions from tolls and customs. Thus the non-elite ended up financing through their tolls, customs, and court fines much of the city government from which they were excluded.[3] On the other hand, most traders may have considered these charges acceptable in light of the protection, security, and facilities offered by the town to those who frequented its markets. The ease with which many evaded the often ineffective market ordinances may also be seen as a victory by the petty traders over the vested interests of the merchant oligarchy.

[2] Transportation costs and the impact of distance are discussed at greater length above, pp. 000–00, and below, pp. 000–00.

[3] Complaints against the monopolies and favored commercial position of richer burgesses were voiced at one time or another by poorer residents in most towns; Reynolds 1977: 130–9, 182–7; Fraser 1969: 57–8.

Consumer and municipal interests were ensured first of all by regulating the time of commercial transactions. In Exeter and most other fourteenth-century English towns, no buying or selling could occur before the first ringing of the market bell at prime (around dawn) or after the last ringing of the bell in the late afternoon or at nightfall.[4] These rules ensured that all transactions took place openly, in broad daylight, under the supervision of the market wardens and toll collectors. To help enforce this ordinance, the city gates were closed at nightfall and not reopened until the next morning at sunrise. Non-residents sought to avoid these restrictions by bribing the gatekeepers to open the gates and allow them to enter the town early with their goods in order to get an early jump on the market.[5] Regulations against forestalling and regrating also aimed to control the timing of commercial activities. Forestallers intercepted goods coming to town, generally before prime, and then marketed the goods in town at a higher price. Regrators bought goods available legally in the market early in the day but resold them later when shortages drove the price up. Authorities believed both practices led to less competition, unreliable supplies, higher prices, and a loss of toll for the town.[6] Their attempts to halt these common retailing methods met with limited success, however; by the late fourteenth century many if not most offenders clearly preferred to pay the generally low fines (ranging from 3–12*d*) assessed against them in the annual mayor's tourn (the annual market court) rather than forego these profitable practices.

The borough also made efforts to stipulate the locations of legal retailing. Quality and price control, as well as the collection of town custom, were more easily guaranteed when transactions occurred in predetermined locations under the watchful eyes of market wardens and other officials. The officially sanctioned open marketplace in Exeter was called the Carfoix (from *quatre vois*) because it was located at the crossroads of the town's four main streets (Figure 5.1). This area was the only sanctioned marketplace for non-residents to sell their goods, aside from designated locations for the sale of meat, fish, and a few other goods. Like other towns, Exeter tried to channel the trade in particular goods to specific locations. Poultry was sold at the northern

4 MCR 1387/8, m. 22, 1390/1, m. 2; MT passim for fines on those who bought or sold *ante primam*; *Citie of Excester*: 819. For similar rules elsewhere, see *Records of the city of Norwich*: vol. I, 181–3; Salusbury 1948: 167–71, 185–7.

5 MCR 1378/9, mm. 24, 25; 1381/2, m. 52.

6 The MT regularly listed forestallers and regrators. See also Britnell 1987; Mastoris 1986; Salzman 1931: 75–9 for the similar situation elsewhere.

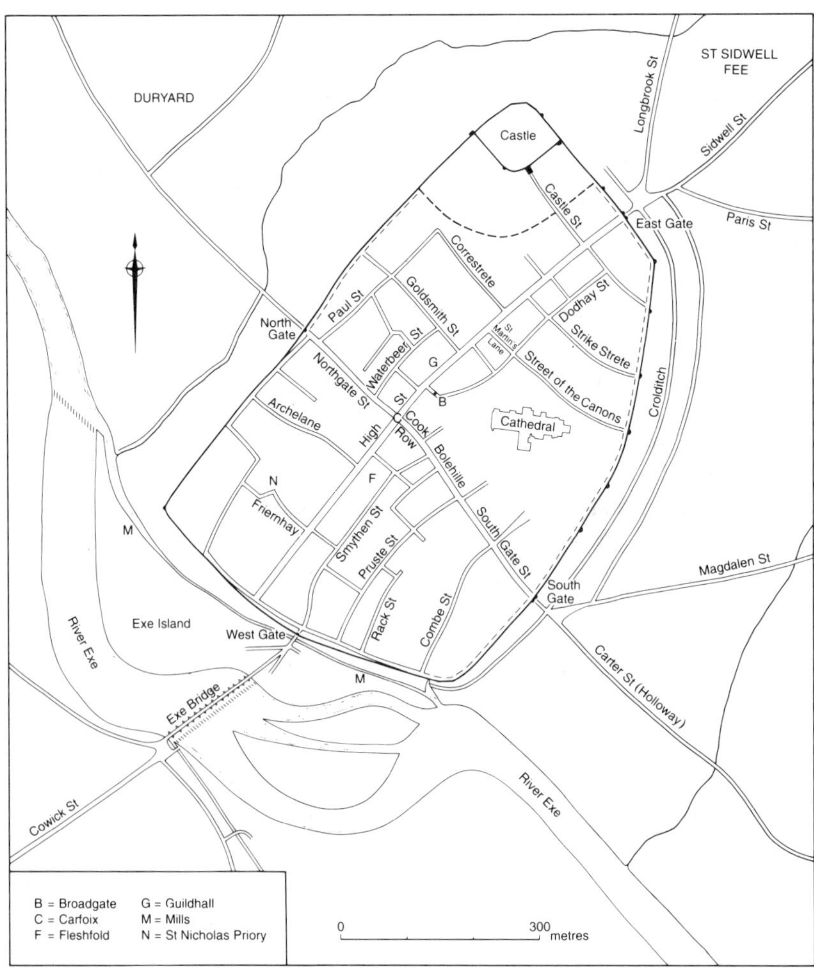

Figure 5.1 Medieval Exeter

end of the Carfoix, reaching up Northgate Street as far as St Kerrian's, while dairy products were concentrated at the southern side of the Carfoix closer to Cook Row which itself was lined with shops, many owned or leased by cooks.[7] A section of the highway south of the Carfoix opposite St George's church was reserved for the sale of oats;

[7] NQMT 1379; Hooker, *Citie of Excester*: 916–17. Market offenses usually appeared in the SQMT since most of the marketing areas of the Carfoix came under that quarter's jurisdiction.

sales of wheat and wool were also confined to a specific site.[8] One of the oldest markets was that for fish, called the "Fishfold" or "Fishshambles," located on the small lane connecting High Street with the Broad Gate leading into the cathedral close. Maintained at the expense of the city, this market consisted of open stalls and simple boards on trestles.[9] Much more elaborate was the city's meat market or "Fleshfold," a partially stone-built, roofed structure secured with a locked door. Up until 1380/1, the Fleshfold contained about twelve shops but in that year the city invested over £11 in an expansion that doubled the number of shops leased out.[10]

The municipal government's efforts to restrict trade in certain goods to specific locations was more vigorous in the late thirteenth and early fourteenth centuries than in the following period.[11] The reduced vigilance was probably linked to its decision to lease (or "farm" out) the collection of most tolls, thereby transferring more responsibility and worry to individual lessors or farmers of the customs.[12] By the late fourteenth century the city's battle to confine trade to the marketplace centered mainly on the sellers of fish, hides, and skins who set up stalls or markets in unsanctioned places like private houses, taverns, inns, and areas just outside the city gates (where they could both obtain first crack at those coming to town and avoid the town custom collectors).[13] The city was fighting a losing battle, however, and trade increasingly occurred in these "private" places during the late middle ages.[14] In Exeter the presentments for selling hides and skins in "private" or "suspicious" places became such a regular feature of the

[8] CRA 1376/7, 1377/8 for oats; MCR 1376/7, m. 50 for wheat. For a *hous lanena*, see PCR 1–23 Ric. II, m. 47.

[9] Lega-Weekes 1915: 21–3; MCR 1317/18, m. 2d. The city's expenses on the upkeep of the market give a good idea of its configuration; see especially *Receivers' accounts*: passim, under "Necessary Expenses"; and CRA 1367/7 to 1376/7, 1386/7, 1387/8, 1390/1, 1395/6, 1396/7. Broad Gate was also called "Fishfoldgate."

[10] See the detailed Fleshfold rentals in MCR 1351/2, m. 1d, and Book 53A, f. 76 (1392) for a comparison. See also the building account for the new Fleshfold in CRA 1380/1 and the regular accounts of shop rentals (normally numbering twenty six) and repairs there in subsequent CRA.

[11] For example, MCR 1290/1, m. 46; 1295/6, m. 46; 1300/1, m. 16; 1301/2, m. 11; 1349/50, m. 2d.

[12] For an example of the city bailiffs collecting brewgavel and bacgavel, see MCR 1326/7, m. 14d. The farming of city customs seems to have become fairly common around the 1330s; see CRA passim; MCR passim (mm. 1d–2d for the farms).

[13] For example, MCR 1318/19, m. 10d; 1374/5, m. 40; 1375/6, mm. 43, 44; 1376/7, m. 7; 1377/8, m. 16; 1378/9, m. 25; 1382/3, m. 20; 1391/2, m. 1; 1393/4, m. 45; 1403/4, m. 38d; 1413/14, m. 50; SQMT 1374, 1375, 1392. The areas outside the south and west gates were the most popular locations for these illicit markets.

[14] Keene 1985: 168; Dyer 1992; Britnell 1993: 161–4.

mayor's tourn by the late fourteenth century that the fines had clearly become merely licensing fees to continue the practice.

Exeter citizens were, of course, allowed to sell in shops: retail outlets usually situated on the ground floor at the front of a building.[15] Many shops also functioned as manufacturing or storage sites and frequently had a solar (an upper room) built on top or cellars below that were used to store merchandise.[16] High Street from the Carfoix to about St Martin's Lane had the densest concentration of shops, followed by Bolehille Street, Cook Row, Northgate Street, and Southgate Street (Figure 5.1). Numerous shops also clustered around the city gates and the lanes leading into the Cathedral close around Broad Gate and St Martin's Lane. Shops were a less common feature of the side streets, however; only Smythen Street which lay in back of the Fleshfold seems to have possessed any great number. None of these shops was very large. One in High Street measured only four feet by five feet while another situated on Castle Street measured twelve feet by fifteen feet and had a solar built above.[17] Rents on these shops varied according to their size as well as their location. In the late fourteenth century, two shops at the front of the Guildhall produced an annual rent of 16*s* (on a twenty-nine-year lease) while the five shops on Exe Bridge yielded annual rents of 3*s* to 10*s*.[18] Presumably small shops off the main access routes were had for smaller rents.[19] Even lower rents were paid by those who retailed goods from stalls (booths for displaying wares) and selds (long narrow rows of booths built on street frontages).[20] The dean and chapter owned four selds near the pillory and two newly built in Northgate Street which it leased for 40*s* per year in the 1380s; the Hospital of St John owned six which were wedged between its building and the city wall.[21]

In the late fourteenth century, oligarchic merchants and most freedom members clearly operated out of shops, selds, or stalls rather than in the open marketplace. Many of the wealthier merchants had shops attached to their residences, some of which they illegally rented out during fair time.[22] Besides domestic accommodation, shops could also

[15] Portman 1966: 3–5, 33; Erskine and Portman 1960; Parry 1936: 4–6. See also the accounts concerning shops owned by the city (CRA, passim), Exe Bridge (EBW, passim), and private citizens (ECL D&C Deeds, Exeter city deeds, passim).

[16] For example, SQMT 1405; MCR 1385/6, m. 36; Book 53A, f. 63.

[17] Book 53A, f. 17; Hoskins 1963b: 45.

[18] ED/M/519; Book 53A, f. 63.

[19] This was the case in Cheapside (Keene 1990: 34).

[20] For selds elsewhere, see Keene 1985: 138, 1098–9, 1109; and Keene 1990.

[21] D&C 5150–56; Book 53A, ff. 19, 63.

[22] MCR 1360/1, m. 11d; 1367/8, m. 11; CRA 1440/1.

be attached to rooms used for storage or manufacture. The hosteler and draper, John Renebaud, conducted business at "Renebaudesshopes" which consisted of two shops and two cellars for storage. He rented these shops from the oligarchic merchant, John Webber senior, who in a rent dispute with Renebaud entered the shops and seized eighteen pounds of white wool and wool thread, one pair of woolcombs, and two casks.[23] Renebaud's mercantile activities were, however, even more varied than his inventory suggests; he also ran an inn and sold malt, oats, ale, cloth and timber.[24] John Grey, who was one of the city's most prominent merchants, may also have operated out of more than one commercial location since he owned at least nine shops with solars and four cellars, one of which he used to store "wine, mead, ale and other liquors and merchandise."[25] Less prominent members of the freedom may have favored selds over the more expensive shops. Robert Waryn, a glover, had a seld in the Fishfold from which twelve pairs of gloves and two locks of wool were stolen.[26]

The freedom members who used shops as their place of business were seldom prosecuted for selling at illegal times and places. Forestalling and regrating fines, for example, were levied almost exclusively on unenfranchised residents or those who lived outside of Exeter.[27] Freedom members and those outsiders engaged in wholesale trade largely escaped the purview of local market ordinances which were designed mainly to control the activities of retailers and middlemen in the open marketplace. The special privileges of freedom members were first outlined in the city custumal compiled around 1240.[28] Only they could engage in retail trade without paying custom duties while certain trades, such as the retailing of cloth, fish, and apples, were reserved exclusively for them. With the exception of victuals sold on market days, freemen enjoyed a virtual monopoly on merchandise sold "by weight" or "by measure," with such goods as wine, spices, salt, dyestuffs, cloth, hides, and skins mentioned most often.[29] But this rigid system of trade restrictions began to slacken in the late thirteenth and early fourteenth centuries. When unenfranchised resident fishers who contributed to the watch and ward

23 MCR 1378/9, m. 18.

24 MCR 1376/7, m. 23; 1387/8, m. 17; 1388/9, m. 52; 1389/90, m. 16; 1392/3, m. 38; PCR 1–23 Ric. II, m. 60; WQMT 1377–1393.

25 Most of these properties were probably leased out; see DD 23130; 51/1/3/7; MCR 1385/6, m. 36 (noting the stored merchandise); and ECL D&C 216.

26 MCR 1318/19, m. 2d; *Exeter freemen*: 24.

27 See, for example, EQMT 1375 where Geoffrey Ammary was quit of a fine for forestalling and regrating dairy products "because he is in the freedom."

28 Schopp 1925: 7–11; *Anglo-Norman custumal*: 28–9.

29 Rowe and Jackson 1973: xii–xiii; see also MCR 1373/4, m. 20 and MT, passim.

of the city were allowed to retail fish and unfree skinners who performed similar civic duties were permitted to sell furs in the city without paying custom.[30] By the late fourteenth century, unfree residents occasionally paid for special licences that enabled them to sell or purchase wine, skins, and hides custom-free.[31] Upon payment of a fine, unenfranchised residents and outsiders who retailed dairy products, fish, poultry, hides, skins, and cloth could also carry on these theoretically illegal activities; these fines represented little more than licensing fees since the same names appeared year after year, often written in the same order.

These annual fines for retailing without freedom membership or for forestalling and regrating are visible signs of the ruling elite's recognition that it was impossible to restrict retailing and middlemen's activities to the small number of men who gained admission to the franchise. The low amount of the fines, which averaged about 3–6*d* and rarely rose above 12*d*, also indicates that the mercantile elite considered such fines to be fees rather than true deterrents. On the other hand, the annual levying of such fees reminded unenfranchised retailers of the controlling interests of the freedom at the same time as it brought tidy sums into the city's treasury. The courts also did not hesitate to impose significantly higher fines (24–40*d*) on traders whose retailing activities clearly led to a rise in prices or challenged the trading monopolies of the freedom.[32] These higher fines, along with the steady accumulation of fines paid over a number of years, may have also been meant to encourage eligible men to seek entry to the freedom. Such was probably the motive behind the unusual compilation of a mid fifteenth-century list of fines assessed on about seventy unenfranchised "Open Shopholders" who were retailing goods without freedom membership. Twelve of the names were crossed through with notations that these shopholders had decided to enter the freedom upon payment of the usual fine of £1; all twelve appeared as new entrants to the freedom within the month.[33] These fines on unenfranchised shopholders may also reflect the authorities' response to the increasing amount of trade channelled through shops rather than the open marketplace in the late middle ages. The fines first appeared in 1454 and were enrolled immediately after the proceedings of the annual mayor's tourn, the market court

[30] Rowe and Jackson 1973: xiii; Easterling 1931: xxi; MCR 1289/90, m. 19d; 1324/5, m. 4d; 1329/30, m. 5d.

[31] For example, MCR 1295/6, m. 16d; 1370/1, mm. 5, 7; 1376/7, mm. 20, 52; see also CRA 1379/80–1400/1 for licences to retail wine.

[32] See, for example, MCR 1370/1, m. 5d, 38d; 1422/3, m. 58d; and MT, passim, for the higher fines assessed on some individuals for forestalling and regrating fish or grain.

[33] MT 1454; *Exeter freemen*: 52.

which had been declining for twenty years and disappeared altogether by 1460. The charges on the shopholders may have been meant to substitute for the fines previously levied in the mayor's tourn. They also served as a reminder that only freedom members had full trading privileges in Exeter, a reminder that continued to be articulated by municipal ordinances well into the sixteenth century.[34]

Although freedom members could escape many of the strictures concerning the time and place of commercial transactions, they were clearly subject to ordinances governing the price and quality of goods sold. These ordinances focused overwhelmingly on the trade in victuals. National legislation was especially prominent in this area as indicated by the universal application of the assizes of bread, ale, and wine which all took place regularly and were locally administered.[35] The prices of ale and bread were set according to the fluctuating price of the grains from which they were made. By the early fourteenth century, however, the annual amercements for breaking the assize of ale had become little more than a type of licensing fee for the privilege of brewing and retailing ale.[36] The authorities stepped in with separate presentments and fines only when the price of ale became excessively high.[37] Problems concerning quality were usually handled in personal pleas in the borough courts. The most frequent complaints concerned the sale of bad or spoiled malt that produced whole batches of undrinkable ale.[38] In contrast, the municipal authorities scrupulously administered the assize of bread via detailed presentments in the mayor's court whenever the price of wheat changed.[39] The assize also regulated the quality of bread, fining bakers for baking bread badly or mixing good grains with gruel.[40] Thus bakers who sold poor-quality bread faced civic prosecution, not personal litigation from offended customers. The different level of enforcement for ale and bread was probably due both to the more essential role played by bread in the medieval diet and to the easier task of regulating some ten professional bakers compared to over 200 part-time brewers.

[34] *Citie of Excester*: 903.
[35] Walford 1880: 81–99, 140–9.
[36] See above, p. 132 and below, p. 339.
[37] For example, MCR 1374/5, m. 17; 1376/7, m. 17; 1392/3, m. 21; NQMT 1364, 1365, 1376.
[38] MCR 1373/4, m. 9; 1386/7, m. 43; 1389/90, m. 22; 1391/2, mm. 38, 47; PCR 1–23 Ric. II, mm. 25, 58.
[39] See also Ross 1956; Beveridge 1929.
[40] For example, MCR 1379/80, m. 1d; 1380/1, m. 1d; 1384/5, m. 11d. For the bakers' resistance to municipal controls and their efforts to establish monopolies, see above, pp. 140–1.

Wine and mead were subject to similar price controls. The courts regularly fined those retailers of mead who sold their product at prices above the going rate.[41] But enforcement of prescribed wine prices as set by the assize of wine was more difficult since the price of wine varied greatly during the fourteenth and fifteenth centuries. National and municipal efforts to stipulate wine prices often failed to keep pace with economic and political realities.[42] Further problems arose because of the different types of wine; prices varied in response to both quality and supply as determined by the changing political scene in the various wine-producing regions on the Continent. Nonetheless, Exeter officials persevered, fining both tavern retailers and wine wholesalers for charging excessive prices or for such quality infringements as selling the dregs of wine casks as first-quality wine.[43]

Although they had no national assize governing their activities, butchers were the most penalized of the victual traders. In all medieval towns, the grave dangers of selling unsound meat and the difficulties of finding acceptable slaughtering and disposal sites generated great concern among consumers and town officials alike.[44] It is no accident that the trade officers most often mentioned in Exeter records before the rise of the guilds in the mid fifteenth century were the two wardens of the Fleshfold who were elected with the rest of the town officers each Michaelmas. Their duties included the supervision of slaughtering, inspection of shops and meat, and the presentment of offenses in the borough courts.[45] Quality was ensured by fining butchers who failed to bait bulls before their slaughter (a practice designed to tenderize the meat as well as provide sport),[46] and by both court presentments and private pleas against butchers for the sale of "measly," "verminous," "fetid," "dried-up," and "corrupt" pork, mutton, beef, and veal.[47] The attention and expense lavished by the city on the Fleshfold also reflected the authorities' eagerness to guarantee the sale of quality meat and to curb sanitation hazards by providing a special marketplace for butchers; at the same time, the city could profit from the rents it charged butchers for maintaining stalls there.

41 MT, passim.

42 James 1971: 1–37; Carus-Wilson 1967b: 271–8; Salzman 1931: 386–405; for Devon in particular, see *CCR, 1354–60*: 111–12, 299.

43 Price: MCR 1374/5, m. 17; 1376/7, mm. 44, 52; 1382/3, m. 9; 1391/2, m. 26. Quality: SQMT 1384; *Citie of Excester*: 938.

44 SQMT passim; for other towns, see Sabine 1933; Jones 1976: 77–87; Keene 1985: 257–8.

45 Hooker, *Citie of Excester*: 818. Butchers did not like to stand for this office and sometimes refused to serve if elected (MCR 1404/5, m. 2).

46 SQMT passim; see also *Citie of Excester*: 821; Keene 1985: 257.

47 MCR 1376/7, m. 39; 1389/90, m. 48; SQMT 1376, 1378, 1382–4; Misc. Roll 55.

The regulation of other foodstuffs was also accomplished by a combination of official jury presentments and private pleas. In Exeter and other towns like Winchester, the fish trade received the most attention because of its economic importance and the large number of outsiders involved.[48] Cooks were regularly fined in the mayor's tourn for forestalling and regrating poultry and other victuals, as well as for selling reheated fish and meat. Although the regularity and low level of these fines suggests that they too had become a type of licensing fee by the late fourteenth century, offenders could be prosecuted by private citizens or civic authorities if their actions posed serious health hazards or raised prices significantly.[49] The trade in grain was controlled mainly through presentments concerning forestalling and regrating; those fined for these practices were accused of raising prices and disturbing the supply of these essential foodstuffs to the city.[50] In times of shortages, particularly in the early fourteenth century, the number and amount of fines increased as did complaints about grain unfairly carried out of the city.[51] Common throughout the period were citations in the mayor's tourn for selling oats, flour, and salt in false measures. Innkeepers and women, several with the surname "Melmanger" (mealmonger), were the retailers regularly fined for these infractions.[52]

The enforcement of proper weights and measures was closely related to the concern for quality and price control. While the right to collect fees for the use of the official measures was leased out, the town itself assumed responsibility for the upkeep of such items as the balance and the purchase of wax for sealing sacks after weighing.[53] Following national statutes, it also held regular assays to ensure that all privately owned measures met proper standards. The assay of 1390 found so many false measures that the thirty three offenders (both rich and poor) not only incurred fines, but had their measures broken and burned.[54] Periodic presentments of gross offenders were also made as when the victualler John Penkerigg was indicted for using deceitful measures: they were

[48] Keene 1985: 259–61; for Exeter, see below, pp. 307–9.

[49] SQMT, passim; MCR 1389/90, m. 48; 1391/2, m. 1.

[50] These results were often expressed in the presentments. MCR 1374/5, m. 17; 1390/1, m. 16; 1392/3, m. 21. NQMT 1390; SQMT 1364, 1365, 1372, 1396; EQMT 1363; WQMT 1363, 1373, 1396.

[51] MCR 1322/3, m. 4d; 1323/4, m. 15d; 1324/5, m. 2d. See also the MT of the 1310s–1325 for the increased number of such presentments.

[52] For example, MCR 1376/7, m. 6; MT passim. For more on the Exeter grain trade, see Kowaleski forthcoming.

[53] CRA 1367/8, 1389/90, 1395/6.

[54] MCR 1389/90, m. 35; CRA 1389/90. For other assays, see MCR 1310/11, m. 10d; 1317/18, m. 2d; 1341/2, m. 22d.

too large when buying and too small when selling.[55] The use of false measures was particularly widespread among petty retailers of ale, wine, mead, oats, flour, and salt. The lengthy annual lists of these offenders in the mayor's tourn attest to the basic ineffectiveness of much of the regulation concerning accurate weights and measures. Yet the city's continual presentments regarding illegal measures and its prosecution of flagrant offenders suggests that it maintained enough vigilance to assure traders that it was attempting to promote the use of standardized measures.

Municipal authorities also regulated local industries though their supervision here was light compared to their concern for the food trades. Candlemakers who mixed grease with tallow or sold candles too dearly were annually fined in the mayor's tourn, as were weavers who adulterated their cloth with poor materials, fullers who cleaned cloth or wool with urine (instead of fuller's earth), and shoemakers who substituted inferior basan leather for cordwain leather.[56] More serious charges were presented in the mayor's court by panels of jurors who accused a bowyer of "producing bad odors with grease, resin and other instruments to the harm of his neighbors" and a weaver of being a "common malefactor and devious in his art" because he fraudulently kept back the wool thread of several customers.[57] Most problems concerning the quality of manufactured goods, however, were settled in personal suits brought before the borough courts.

The city was also content to leave complaints concerning the cost or quality of labor to individual employers and employees. The few exceptions involved presentments against those who left the city during harvest to seek work in the countryside, or those, like the skinners' servants, whose activities threatened a freedom monopoly.[58] During the late fourteenth century employers in Exeter also eagerly welcomed the opportunity to use the new legal weapon provided to them by the Statute of Labourers. Such pleas flooded the courts in the 1350s and 1360s but by the late 1380s had slowed to the extent that they made up only 5 per cent of the cases before the mayor's court.[59] At the same time apprenticeship became a more common means of entry to the

[55] MCR 1376/7, m. 20; see also MCR 1349/50, m. 21 for a similar case.

[56] MT passim. For an assize of candles, see MCR 1327/8, m. 8d.

[57] MCR 1391/2, mm. 1, 22.

[58] Harvest workers: MCR 1375/6, m. 43; for the skinners' servants, see above, p. 159. Higher authorities only made a few incursions (in the 1350s) in Exeter to enforce these statutes; see *CPR, 1354–58*: 494 and PRO JUST1/195 (extracts printed in Putnam 1908: 166–9).

[59] Labor disputes (including cases concerning broken service contracts) accounted for forty five of the 992 cases which appeared in the MCR from 1385/6 to 1387/8.

freedom.[60] The first craft wardens also made their appearance – the wardens of the Fleshfold in 1384 and wardens of the shoemakers and tanners in 1387 – although they were elected by the freedom members as a whole and were expected to report to city officials and in city courts.[61] Only in the mid fifteenth century did the crafts themselves take on significant regulatory powers over the price and quality of goods made by their members.[62] By 1460 the old mayor's tourn, which had served for over 150 years as the city's primary institution for regulating trade and industry, had disappeared.[63] The city continued, however, to issue trade ordinances, taking a special interest in retail trade, the freedom, and the application of tolls and customs.[64] And although the guilds took on greater regulatory powers, the city continued to reap its usual profits from the regulation of trade; most of the new guilds in the fifteenth century were required to give up half of their profits from fines, or try cases in the mayor's court, or even pay a yearly fine to renew their privileges.[65]

Trade regulations lowered transaction costs if they provided reliable trading conditions through quality and price controls, standardized measures, and information about sanctioned locations and times of trade. Yet the amount of non-compliance in Exeter and other medieval towns suggests that government intervention (whether by the city or state) was not particularly successful. From a modern point of view, many of these regulations also lagged considerably behind economic realities in their attempt to dictate that goods be transfered from producers to consumers as directly as possible without the intervention of middlemen (the "forestallers" and "regrators"). It seems likely, however, that the fourteenth-century situation described here shows a system in the throes of transition; both traders' non-compliance and the degeneration of fines

[60] See above, p. 99.

[61] MCR 1384/5, m. 2d; 1387/8, m. 9. *Conservatores* and *custodes* of fish, meat, poultry, hides, and wool were noted earlier but their duties seem to have focused largely on regulating tolls rather than quality; see MCR 1298/9, m. 1; 1301/2, mm. 1d, 12d; 1310/11, m. 1d; 1311/12, m. 1d. Woad assayers were elected in the late thirteenth and early fourteenth centuries; although they were involved in quality control, their job was primarily focused on maintaining the freedom's woad monopolies; see below, p. 263.

[62] *English gilds*: 299–37, esp. 321–3; see also above, pp. 99–101.

[63] See Appendix 1 below, pp. 338–9 for a description of this court. A similar transition in regulatory powers occurred elsewhere too, although perhaps for different reasons; see Britnell 1986b: 134–9, 236–45.

[64] Book 55, esp. ff. 41–41v, 48v–49, 63–64v. *Citie of Excester*: 540–69, focuses on the customs rates and pp. 863–94 abstracts all the ordinances made by the mayor and common council from the mid-fifteenth through the sixteenth centuries.

[65] *English gilds*: 331–7 (Cordwainers and Bakers); Youings 1970: 235–8 (Weavers, Tuckers, and Shearmen).

from punishments to licensing fees might be viewed in this way. These developments cracked open the door that privileged freedom members and civic government tried to keep shut in the face of the vast majority of traders who were unenfranchised, thereby reducing costs for many petty retailers and producers. The municipal government lowered its own enforcement costs by farming out the collection of market tolls in the early fourteenth century and handing over more regulatory powers to the craft guilds in the mid fifteenth century. Trade regulation did not cease, but the thrust of much of the new municipal and national legislation was towards greater control of quality and measures, both of which reduced transaction costs for the majority rather than for the few.[66]

Market revenues and tolls

Market-related revenue (such as tolls, the farms of customs, fines collected from transgressors, and entry fees for membership in the town freedom) made up over half of Exeter's annual income in the late fourteenth century.[67] In Exeter, as in other medieval towns, market legislation seems often to have aimed to fill the town's treasury just as much as to protect consumers and producers. To ensure steady profits and avoid the heavy costs of enforcement, the authorities began leasing out the bulk of Exeter's customs in the second and third decades of the fourteenth century, selling them to the highest bidder after the annual election of officers at Michaelmas, usually to members of the oligarchy or to the city bailiffs who were well placed to enforce collection.[68] These customs farmers sometimes found it difficult to meet their own commitments and were forced to seek allowances on their farms. In 1391, the farmer of the baking and brewing tolls, John Liteljohn, had 13*s* 4*d* of his farm excused because "fewer were brewing that year

[66] Note, for example, the later market ordinances in Exeter; *Citie of Excester*: 546–51, 841–57, 863–947 passim.

[67] CRA, passim. The town's income can be divided into three parts: rents, customs and tolls, and perquisites of the court. In the late fourteenth century fixed rents on city-owned property and for the farm of Duryard manor came to about £40 and should have accounted for 30 to 40 per cent of the town's income. But rents were frequently in default and the farm of Duryard so heavily in arrears that this fixed income often represented less than 30 per cent of the total. Customs and tolls varied more than rents but for the decade 1366–76 averaged about £30. Court fines, amercements, and freedom entries varied widely; freedom entries could bring in nothing or over £18 (CRA 1380/1), the amercements on bakers could fluctuate from nothing to over £4 (CRA 1376/7), while the sale of forfeited goods could bring as much as £9 in some years (CRA 1390/1). "Market-related revenue" includes all items in the customs and tolls category as well as fines from the mayor's tourn, assizes, and freedom entries.

[68] See above, pp. 104–5.

on account of the dearness of grain."[69] Others failed to find the proper security or downpayment and had to forfeit the farm.[70] Still others found their profits reduced by allowances made by city officials to certain individuals, particularly those who claimed poverty.[71]

In the late fourteenth century, the most lucrative market revenues came from the perquisites of the mayor's tourn and the farm of the fish custom, both of which averaged about £11 in the 1380s.[72] Next were the profits of the fairs which netted over £8, followed by the meat and stallage custom of the Fleshfold which brought in just under £8. Stallage actually yielded more than the custom itself (over £5 compared to £2) which, along with the hefty profits garnered from the fish trade, justified the annual sums spent on maintaining the Fleshfold and fish market.[73] The remaining customs brought in lesser amounts; baking and brewing tolls were farmed for £3, petty custom for under £2, flour for 4–8*s*, and measures for 2*s*. The port customs averaged just over £6 in the 1380s but could vary widely from year to year, sometimes reaching amounts of over £20.[74]

All of these customs were part of a larger system of tolls that subjected both buyers and sellers to a wide variety of dues on their transactions. In Exeter and other towns, these tolls varied according to the nature of the transaction (buying or selling), the type of commodity, the amount being traded, the place where exchange occurred, and the status of the trader. Two of the oldest tolls in Exeter were bacgavel and brewgavel, ancient taxes levied on unenfranchised sellers of bread and ale; by the fourteenth century these dues had become standardized into an annual payment of 2*s* 6*d* and were farmed out to an individual who took responsibility for collection.[75] Probably the most universal toll was that paid by sellers for the privilege of selling (or even exposing for sale) goods in the town's marketplaces.[76] While freedom members were not obliged to pay these sales taxes, even they were subject to the daily

[69] CRA 1390/1.

[70] CRA 1387/8, 1390/1.

[71] CRA 1367/8, 1381/2, 1389/90.

[72] MT 1379–1388; CRA 1379/80–1388/89 for this and the following.

[73] CRA passim. Expenses on the Fleshfold were more substantial since it was a large freestanding building which was enlarged in 1381 at a cost of over £11 (CRA 1380/1). Sums expended on the "Fysshamell" usually went for trestles and boards for stalls and rarely exceded 10*s*. Similar amounts were spent for trestles and boards during fair times.

[74] CRA 1399/1400.

[75] *Anglo-Norman custumal*: 30–1; *Citie of Excester*: 552; Rowe and Draisy 1989: xiii. Both tolls appear on the earliest MCR (1264, m. 1d). Each was 15*d* apiece by the fourteenth century; see PCR 1–23 Ric. II, m. 85.

[76] *Anglo-Norman custumal*: 24–37; *Citie of Excester*: 553–69, 878–9, 894–5; Book 55, f. 48v, for this and the following.

rates or annual rents demanded of all who displayed their wares in the fish or meat markets. Most tolls on selling ranged from ¼*d*–½*d* but could reach 4*d* or more when large amounts were sold; lists of rates carefully set out the different charges for each type of commodity and amount. Street hawkers also had to pay special tolls to sell their goods. Custom was even due on exchanges if money changed hands as when Richard Forst swapped his red horse and 2*s* for John Mulleborn's brown horse.[77] The city bore the expense of collecting these tolls until about the 1320s; thereafter they were leased out and collection was usually handled by an employee of the custom farmer who had to bring personal debt pleas against those who failed to make the proper customs payments.[78]

Buyers also had to pay custom on goods they purchased in Exeter although exemptions were allowed for those who bought victuals for their own use or the use of their lord.[79] Thus gentry consumers like Walter Cornu did not have to pay custom on the large amount of wine he bought in Exeter *pro hospicio suo*.[80] Importers of wine at the port of Exeter could also claim small amounts (normally one or two pipes) of wine "for their drink" and thus avoid toll.[81] Indeed, most ordinary food purchases (but not sales) probably escaped custom since they were destined to meet household needs. Considering the dominance of the victual trade in Exeter, the number of transactions liable to this exemption must have been considerable. Buying tolls were levied on purchases of non-essential items, however, and especially targeted unenfranchised retailers and non-resident traders who carried goods (including victuals) outside of Exeter for resale in their own communities or elsewhere.

In the early and mid thirteenth century the unenfranchised could avoid constant custom charges by annually paying chepgavel (a type of fee for retailing) although the payment did not cover the tolls due if the trader carried goods out of the city.[82] Chepgavel disappeared by the fourteenth century and may have been subsumed under the farm of petty custom or perhaps that of bacgavel and brewgavel.[83] But chepgavel may also have been supplanted by different forms of licensing

77 MCR 1317/18, m. 13d.

78 For example, MCR 1375/6, m. 32; 1376/7, m. 3; 1385/6, mm. 31, 36, 41; 1386/7, m. 7; PCR 1–23 Ric. II, mm. 61, 85.

79 *Anglo-Norman custumal*: 29, 34, 36; see also MCR 1319/20, m. 32d.

80 CRA 1405/6.

81 Kowaleski 1993: 13.

82 *Anglo-Norman custumal*: 29, 32, 34–8. Franchised residents may also have paid this toll; see Schopp 1925: 20–1.

83 By 1472 the farm of bacgavel and brewgavel and that of petty custom included several charges that would have come under chepgavel; *Citie of Excester*: 552–3, 878, 894. I have found no trace of chepgavel in the fourteenth-century records nor does it appear that chepgavel was collected as part of the farm of bacgavel and brewgavel.

retail activity by the unfree. By the late thirteenth century, unenfranchised residents who contributed to the watch and ward of the city were allowed to retail such items as skins and fish.[84] In the late fourteenth century, unfree traders occasionally paid for special licences to retail wine and purchase wool-fells and hides custom-free.[85] The annual lists of fines in the mayor's tourn levied on forestallers and regrators or on those selling in unsanctioned places may also have served as a substitute for toll collection, as well as a type of licence for the unfree to conduct retail trade in certain commodities. As such, these fines can be viewed, along with the decision to farm out most of the customs, as the city's pragmatic solution to the very difficult task of pursuing custom evaders and those who infringed the freedom's monopoly on retail trade.

In addition to the regular tolls on buying and selling, towns added special tolls at certain times or locations. Grants of murage and pavage from the king allowed Exeter and other towns to levy extra tolls to pay for repairs to its walls and streets.[86] Exeter enjoyed such grants almost continuously from 1224 through 1374, levying these tolls on items brought to the city for sale and collecting them at the four city gates or at the port when goods coming in by sea were included in the grant.[87] Murage and pavage tolls thus fell more heavily on rural dwellers and others who regularly visited the city to trade; their effect was also more extensive since they were not subject to as many exemptions as town customs. Even so, their returns in the 1360s and 1370s rarely reached £6 per year, a paltry sum compared to the over £28 collected in 1377 when a new system of murage was instigated that levied a tax on resident property-holders, rather than on traders.[88] Thereafter the regular murage and pavage tolls disappeared in Exeter.

Special tolls were also levied by fair owners who had the right to collect all tolls as well as the fruits of justice administered during the days of their fair, a right which yielded large profits and provoked

[84] Easterling 1931: xxi; Rowe and Jackson 1973: xiii.

[85] MCR 1373/4, m. 20; 1376/7, m. 20; 1380/1, mm. 5, 7; CRA 1379/80, 1383/4, 1385/6–1388/9, 1390/1, 1392/3–1400/1.

[86] Turner 1971: esp. 194–5. See also Rowe and Draisy 1989: xviii. For similar grants elsewhere, see Tingey 1911; Fraser 1969.

[87] *Citie of Excester*: 540–3; DRO Transcripts 2013–14, 2020, 2023, 2026; Misc. Roll 6, mm. 14, 16; MCR 1373/4, mm. 3d, 4d, 5d, 39d; *Receivers' accounts*: 93–110. Pavage and murage at the port: PCA 1320/1, 1322/3; 1360/1, 1361/2, 1368/9–1371/2.

[88] For the sums collected, see n. 87 above and CRA 1368/9–1373/4. The amounts collected in an earlier period were much larger; in MCR 1306/7, m. 31d they totaled almost £40. For the new style of grant, see *CPR, 1377–81*: 3; Turner 1971: 39–43. For the new murage at Exeter, see Misc. Roll 72; Kowaleski 1980; and Appendix 3, below.

several virulent disputes among rival fair owners in Exeter.[89] Indeed, the only Exeter tolls never leased out were those gathered at the fairs and at the port, both jealously guarded prerogatives that the city was forced to defend on several occasions.[90] The city was especially anxious to maintain its right to collect customs on all goods landed at its outport in Topsham or anywhere in the Exe estuary (although it had to hand over one-third of the wine custom to the earl of Devon).[91] All foreign and many denizen merchants had to pay local port customs to Exeter, as well as port duties (keelage, cranage, and tronage) to the lord of Topsham, royal customs and subsidies to the king, and the usual sales tolls for selling goods in Exeter or carrying them through the town for sale elsewhere.[92] Such charges were clearly disliked and exemptions frequently sought. The local customs were applicable only to imports, however, and Exeter's port customs were light compared to those of other towns or to the national customs.[93] And even though slightly over half of all importers paid custom in the early 1380s, the average sum paid was only 3*s*, an amount equivalent to the toll on 9 tuns of wine.[94] Some handed over significantly higher amounts (up to 30*s*), but anyone importing on this scale clearly had the wherewithal to manage such sums. In assessing the impact of port customs, it is probably better to stress how exemptions lowered costs for privileged traders than to dwell on the obstacle such customs may have represented for non-privileged importers.

All of these tolls were subject to exemptions. The 21 per cent of Exeter householders who belonged to the freedom benefited from the widest range of exemptions. They not only escaped all tolls in Exeter, but also avoided most tolls outside the city by virtue of exemptions granted in royal charters to Exeter citizens.[95] The value of these exemptions, which must have saved regular traders in the freedom substantial sums of money, encouraged some non-freedom members to claim falsely that they belonged to the freedom in order to avoid tolls in Exeter and at fairs and markets elsewhere.[96] Other problems arose when freedom members "covered" unenfranchised traders by claiming these traders'

[89] See above, pp. 61–5.
[90] For the fairs, see above, pp. 62–7; for the port customs, see Kowaleski 1993: 1–14 and below, pp. 223–4.
[91] Kowaleski 1993: 1–7; see also below, pp. 222–4.
[92] Kowaleski 1993: 7–13.
[93] Kowaleski 1993: 11–12; Touchard 1967a: xxx–xxxi.
[94] Based on a survey of three years (PCA 1381/2–1383/4); 154 of the 296 importers paid custom.
[95] *Anglo-Norman custumal*: 26, 29, 34; MCR 1319/20, m. 32; 1396/7, m. 47; Exeter City Charters nos. 1–7, 14, 15–18, 22.
[96] For example, SQMT 1317; MCR 1318/19, m. 22; 1326/7, m. 7d; EQMT 1350.

transactions as their own or by trading together in such a way that the unenfranchised trader escaped payment of toll. Jordan le Marchal, for example, was accused of covering purchases of horses made by his son William, the oligarchs Ralph de Nyweton and William de Chaggeford covered the transactions of their servants Roger and Stephen, and Thomas Gerveys (a merchant oligarch and ex-mayor) covered the butcher John Veisy for a period of five years before Veisy joined the freedom.[97] Although this offense often involved highly placed freedom members, the borough courts (run by these same freedom members) regularly prosecuted both free and unfree residents who conspired in this way to avoid custom, an indication of their desire to protect the monopolies of the freedom against unenfranchised traders. Coverage of women and other household members also caused difficulties, particularly in the brewing industry since it was not always clear if the female servants, sisters, or widows who did much of the brewing could avoid the brewgavel payment if their employer or head of household enjoyed freedom membership.[98]

Members of the freedoms of other towns and exempt jurisdictions privileged by royal charters (such as tinners and residents of ancient demesne) also avoided toll payments in Exeter.[99] Non-resident merchants who enjoyed such exemptions were quick to point to the basis of their custom-free status and often came equipped with copies of their charters.[100] Others had to find pledges to back up their assertion or wait until their claim could be proved before having the custom assessed on their transaction respited.[101] Some traders, such as those from Okehampton and Lydford, sought to enforce their claims of exemption in the Exeter borough courts, albeit with mixed success.[102] Several residents of Taunton in Somerset even pursued their claims for custom-free status in Exeter through the courts of Chancery.[103] To avoid these problems, Exeter and many other towns kept updated lists of towns whose citizens enjoyed customs exemptions.[104] Excluding additions made after c. 1400,

97 MCR 1318/19, mm. 10d, 22; EQMT 1363–5; NQMT 1362; SQMT 1362.

98 MCR 1296/7, m. 21; 1320/1, m. 15d. See also NQMT 1346 for a woman accused of covering her son's transactions.

99 MCR 1312/13, m. 20; *Rotuli parliamentorum*, vol. 2: 343 (tinners); PRO JUST1/186, m. 52; MCR 1390/1, rider between mm. 18–19 (ancient demesne).

100 These claims were often registered in the margins of the PCA, passim. See also MCR 1285/6, m. 15; 1296/7, m. 19d; 1335/6, m. 3d; 1378/9, m. 3d; 1390/1, rider between mm. 18–19.

101 For example, MCR 1296/7, m. 19d; CRA 1396/7, 1410/11; PCA 1419/20; 1427/8.

102 MCR 1285/6, mm. 10, 15; 1288/9, m. 51d; 1310/11, m. 44d.

103 PRO C1/6/329; Kowaleski 1993: 38–9.

104 *Anglo-Norman custumal*: 24–6, 51–2; *Citie of Excester*: 302–7; Book 51, ff. 223–4 for this and the following. For the lists of other towns, see *Little Red Book of Bristol*,

Exeter's list noted about sixty one different places, at least 80 per cent of which were in Devon.

Residence in a custom-exempt town, however, was not in itself a guarantee of toll-free standing; personal status and the degree of immunity enjoyed by the town were also considerations. Over 70 per cent of the places that appeared on Exeter's list of custom-free places enjoyed exemptions only on purchases for personal use or for sales of their own agricultural produce; most of these places were villages or small towns in Exeter's own hinterland.[105] The remaining places were usually larger towns, but only the "franchised men" who belonged to the freedoms of these towns actually benefited from full exemptions. Similarly, residents of exempt towns not on Exeter's list had to prove they were franchised citizens of these places before they were allowed to forego paying toll on their transactions.

One of the thorniest problems in the application of tolls and customs was the exemptions claimed by the residents of the six separate franchises in Exeter. Two of these, the castle fee and Kalendar fee, were so tiny that they caused few difficulties.[106] A third lay outside the west gate in the manor of Exe Island, owned by the powerful earl of Devon. Although the city once enjoyed considerable jurisdictional powers in this suburb, it lost these rights in the early 1320s and did not regain them until 1550 when Edward VI granted the manor to the city.[107] Even so, the tenants of Exe Island enjoyed minimal customs exemptions in the city of Exeter; if they transacted business within the city, they had to pay one-half mark annually to be quit of custom on the sale of their produce and were required to pay other tolls in full.[108] Similarly, the households of St Sidwell's fee, owned by the dean and chapter and lying outside the east gate in the city's largest suburb, were also quit of custom on the sale of their produce and livestock (albeit without

vol. II: 58, 199, 211–17, 224, 232–5, 240–1, 245; *Oak Book of Southampton*, vol. I: 4–21.

[105] They were noted as "free of their increases"; Book 51, ff. 223–4; *Anglo-Norman custumal*: 24–6, 51–2.

[106] See ECL V/C 3125 and MCR 1319/20, m. 28d for the Kalendar fee exemptions from brewgavel and bacgavel. See also below, p. 373, n. 10 for these fees.

[107] For the earl's usurption of these rights, see Misc. Roll 3, mm. 1–2; *Citie of Excester*: 636–45. The city's rights to hold a MT there also declined; see MCR 1318/19, mm. 21–21d which listed only four jurors and no ale brewers. For the (sometimes violent) disputes that followed, see Book 60h, ff. 22–42v; BL Add. Ch. 49359, ff. 58v–60; *Citie of Excester*: 389–95, 407–11; PRO C260/66/45. The 1377 poll tax listed 106 people there (PRO E179/95/52/46). The city still maintained properties on Exe Bridge and several in Exe Island, however; see EBW passim; Book 53A, f. 63. For the 1550 grant, see *Citie of Excester*: 372–87.

[108] *Anglo-Norman custumal*: 25; Hooker, *Citie of Excester*: 174–89. In 1377 there were about 41 households in the fee (below, p. 374); Curtis 1932.

having to pay the one-half-mark fine), but were subject to all other customs, including bacgavel and brewgavel.[109] The dean and chapter, however, seem always to have been involved in bitter disputes with the city over the rights of their tenants to avoid these and other city impositions.[110] Although the dean and chapter maintained their own court in St Sidwell's (largely for pleas of trespass within the franchise), their tenants in the late fourteenth century just as often sought recourse in the city's courts and were usually included under the jurisdiction of the mayor's tourn for the east quarter.[111]

More extensive customs exemptions were enjoyed by the residents of the other two fees. Tenants of the bishop of Exeter's fee (also called St Stephen's fee and totaling about thirty households in 1377) and those in the fee of St Nicholas owned by the local Benedictine priory (also called Harold's fee and including about twenty six households in 1377) were free of tolls on backgavel, brewgavel, chepgavel, and sales of their own agricultural produce and livestock.[112] The ecclesiastical owners of these two franchises frequently claimed (without much success) further rights and exemptions; in the mid fifteenth century, however, the bishop acquired a royal charter enforcing his prerogatives in the face of what he perceived to be the city's encroachments.[113] Jurisdiction over these two fees was probably made more difficult because both consisted of scattered properties rather than physically distinct fees as was the case with Exe Island and St Sidwell's fee.[114] In the fourteenth century, the city commonly included residents of these two franchises in the mayor's tourn presentments, but then excused the fine either in the tourn or later in special lists in the city receivers' accounts.[115]

[109] *Anglo-Norman custumal*: 25; *Citie of Excester*: 174–89. In 1377 there were about forty nine households in the fee (below, Table A3.1).

[110] Curtis 1932.

[111] For the SCR, see below, Appendix 1, p. 342. For these tenants in the MT, see especially EQMT 1380 which lists the brewing tenants separately; see also the evidence for these residents in Table A3.1 below. From the mid thirteenth century, the city and the dean and chapter split the profits of the assize of bread and ale in St Sidwell's, or the dean and chapter merely farmed them out to one of the city bailiffs; see Rowe and Draisy 1989: xiii; ECL D&C 3550, ff. 85, 89, 96; Curtis 1932: 17–18.

[112] They were also free of distress within their fees; *Anglo-Norman custumal*: 25, 31. See below, Appendix 3, Table A3.1 for the population estimates.

[113] Bishop's fee: Curtis 1932. St Nicholas fee: Misc. Roll 55, nos. 1–2, 5–6, 10; BL Cotton Vitellius D. IX, ff. 177v–179v; and Clarke 1912.

[114] The bishop's properties were located mainly in the south quarter and outside the south gate (*Citie of Excester*: 664–73; Curtis 1932: 88–91) while the priory's holdings lay scattered about in the northern suburb of Duryard and in the western and northern quarters of the city (Misc. Rolls 12, 49; *Citie of Excester*: 410–24, 707–13).

[115] Kowaleski 1980: 218–19. Residents of these franchises also appeared frequently in the city's courts, even if both parties involved in the plea resided in the franchise; see, for example the trespass suit of Joan Goldsmyth vs. Robert Hopere and his wife,

The frequent efforts made to evade tolls show that local and regional traders in Exeter's markets were well aware of their own custom status and the nature of toll exemptions. Some, especially rural dwellers, falsely claimed to be purchasing for their lords or other magnates in order to avoid tolls. When purchasing poultry Richard Arbe pretended to be the buyer of the bishop of Exeter, and Richard Draycote the steward of a local canon; others claimed to be the agents of such magnates as the earl of Devon, William Botreaux, and the prior of Otterton.[116] Some unfree traders also formed partnerships with freedom members in the hopes that they could evade tolls.[117] Poorer people simply tried to evade town customs by stealth, transporting their goods under cover of night or conducting transactions outside the sanctioned markets in private dwellings or immediately outside the city gates.[118] Others adopted more devious strategies but paid the price if caught. John le Hore was fined 10*s* for regularly stopping in the village of Exwick (less than a mile away on the other side of the Exe river) in order to intercept men bringing livestock to Exeter for sale; John then sold the animals in Exeter himself but avoided one toll because the purchase took place outside the city.[119]

Rural and small-town dwellers who traded in Exeter were the most frequent targets of urban trade taxation. Many fewer of them could claim the customs exemptions cited in urban charters, and their financial resources scarcely matched that of the merchant importers. Their frequent visits to Exeter also made them liable to urban tolls more often, particularly before the 1370s when murage or pavage was collected at the city gates. Certainly the many examples of toll evasion suggest that the tolls were burdensome enough that some were willing to risk being caught and paying larger fines. Arguing against this view are the moderate sums most non-residents liable to toll would have paid; a peasant who visited Exeter's market each week was unlikely to pay more than 1–2*d* on each trip, an annual outgoing of 4–8*s*. Complaints by rural residents against urban tolls on trade were also rarely recorded and

Cecilia in PCR 1–23 Ric. II, m. 39; all parties resided in the Bishop's fee (see Table A3.1).

116 NQMT 1353; SQMT 1390, 1392; EQMT 1385, 1386; WQMT 1384. See also MCR 1303/4, m. 8d; 1317/18, m. 27d; 1349/50, m. 7.

117 The city was quick to spot these offenders; see, for example, MCR 1317/18, m. 18d; NQMT 1362; EQMT 1385; *Anglo-Norman custumal*: 26, 29; and above, n. 97.

118 Such evasion was particularly noticeable when the city still had responsibility for collecting customs; see MCR 1303/4, m. 1; 1317/18, m. 18d; 1322/3, m. 2d; MT passim. For trade conducted in illegal places, see above, pp. 181–3.

119 MCR 1321/2, m. 9d.

entries in manorial accounts concerning tolls are few.[120] Did these outsiders merely consider such tolls the price one had to pay to use the market facilities offered by an entrepôt such as Exeter? Were the amounts paid so small (amounting to a penny or less for each trading excursion) that the bite did not seem so harsh? Regular traders to Exeter could also lessen the financial pain and inconvenience of these tolls by making a one-time payment to cover tolls for a week, several months, or a year.[121] It is also possible that the difficulties of administering this complex customs system, coupled with massive evasion, may have lessened the impact of such tolls on outside traders.

Unenfranchised Exeter residents were another matter. They did complain about their disadvantaged state in local trade and often tried to evade tolls.[122] The 80 per cent of Exeter's households who did not enjoy the customs exemptions bestowed by freedom membership were basically at a disadvantage when involved in any type of retailing activity. Freedom members enjoyed a clear advantage in local trade, an advantage they could add to the other economic, legal, and political benefits of freedom membership. Even more significant was the dividend such customs exemptions gave freedom members in regional and port trade; they not only avoided tolls on goods they imported or exported from the city, but also enjoyed immunity from most tolls and customs (including murage and pavage) throughout the rest of England.[123] The value placed on this privilege is evident in the legal action the city initiated against towns that did not acknowledge their customs exemptions or individuals who falsely claimed the freedom of Exeter in order to escape tolls outside the city.[124] The trouble taken by city authorities in Exeter and other towns to keep lists of places custom-free in their towns and to buy charters to extend their own exemptions also shows how conscious they were of the advantages such relief could bring.

[120] Farmer 1991a: 357. For a local example of a 3*d* toll claimed by the Langford (in Cullompton) reeve for purchasing an ox (probably in Exeter since he also claimed expenses for doing the lord's business there), see Corpus Christ College, Oxford, Kn. 3/1.

[121] For such deals in Exeter, see *Anglo-Norman custumal*: 33, 34, 37; MCR 1288/9, m. 43d; 1302/3, m. 13d; 1373/4, m. 31.

[122] See the frequent references in the early MT before the city started farming out the tolls; see also MCR 1396/7, m. 47. Court presentments of those selling outside the sanctioned market areas, or pretending to be buyers for their lord, or even forestalling and regrating often specifically mentioned toll evasion as a motive. For other towns, see Reynolds 1977: 133–5.

[123] Exeter city charters, nos. 1–7, 14, 15–18, 22.

[124] Misc. Roll 2, m. 27; SQMT 1317; *Citie of Excester*: 606–27; Rowe and Jackson 1973: xviii–xix.

These actions, combined with the significantly higher commercial profile and wealth of freedom members, indicates that freedom members at least were well aware of how much such toll exemptions did to enhance their commercial opportunities and cut their transaction costs in Exeter and elsewhere.

Credit and partnerships

Both credit and financial partnerships (including the use of agents) could promote the flow of trade by spreading risk and reducing the cost of using the market. Negotiation costs in particular could be lowered if buyers and sellers could find credit and employ agents easily and under standardized terms. The most direct reflection of the ubiquity of credit in medieval trade was the debt litigation that clogged every borough court as well as the court of common pleas at Westminster. The growing number of debt cases in the Exeter mayor's court and provosts' court in the late fourteenth century and the separation of the rolls of the two courts in 1373/4 suggests that this was a period of rising indebtedness in Exeter.[125] By the second half of the 1380s, debts accounted for 65 per cent of the pleas that came before these two courts. R. H. Britnell observed the same trend in late fourteenth-century Colchester and attributed the increase in debt litigation to economic expansion and the greater availability of credit, rather than to monetary problems occasioned by a reduction in the supply of money.[126] In Exeter, as in Colchester, commercial growth during the prosperous decades following the Black Death made it easier to extend credit at all levels of retail and wholesale trade. In the late fourteenth century the common law courts also greatly improved the legal machinery that governed the enforcement of contracts and obligations.[127] These improvements made it much easier for creditors to compel debtors to pay up, thus reducing transaction costs and alleviating, to some degree, the difficulties caused by reductions in the supply of money during the fifteenth century.

[125] The annual average of debts from 1378/9–1387/8 (henceforth 1378–88) grew from 442 in the first three-year period to 483 in the last three-year period. A strict accounting of debts before this period would be difficult since the provosts' court (which tried 80 per cent of the debt cases in 1378–88) was enrolled in a variety of places, including the membranes of the mayor's court.

[126] Britnell 1986b: 98–108. For the monetarist position, see Munro 1983; Day 1987; Nightingale 1990, although they do not directly address the issue of indebtedness in local courts. For Exeter's prosperity during this time, see above, pp. 89–90. See Kermode 1991 for discussion of credit in a region that suffered more problems.

[127] Palmer 1993: esp. 57–103, 133–51.

Table 5.1. *Types of debts by amount for all litigants, and for non-Exeter litigants, 1378–88*

Debt type	% of all debts (N=778)	Average amount (N=716)	% debts ⩽ 5*s* (N=418)	% non-Exeter debts Creditors (N=143)	% non-Exeter debts Debtors (N=129)
Sale	50	11*s* 7*d*	59	52	52
Rent	12	5*s* 4*d*	71	8	7
Service	10	9*s* 6*d*	60	13	13
Cash loan	7	14*s* 7*d*	35	6	10
Pledge	6	17*s* 7*d*	50	8	6
Custom	5	10*s* 2*d*	68	–	2
Bond	4	54*s* 5*d*	24	11	6
Damages and amercements	4	4*s* 0*d*	76	1	2
Chattel loan	2	8*s* 8*d*	88	1	2
Total	100			100	100
Average		12*s* 7*d*	58		

Source: MCR and PCR debt cases, 1378–88. These figures exclude the 3,578 cases for which no information is available on type of debt. Bonds include all written instruments.

Table 5.1 offers a breakdown of the type of debts incurred in late fourteenth-century Exeter, their average amounts, and relative participation by non-Exeter litigants.[128] One-half of the debts concerned sales in which sellers gave buyers credit on all or part of their purchases. These extensions of credit were common at all levels of trade and ranged from small sums like the 6*d* Henry Wynd owed for apples to larger sums of £3 and more owed to oligarchic merchants for purchases of imports such as wine and madder.[129] Although the average amount of sale debts was about 12*s*, most people owed far smaller sums (59 per cent of these debts were actually 5*s* or less). It is also significant that sales debts involved a greater number of outsiders than any other type of debt, even more than the overall average. Many of the outsiders' debts involved agricultural goods, thus highlighting the pull of the Exeter marketplace for rural dwellers in the town's hinterland. Fairly typical was the suit of John Corbyn of Kingskerswell (a village about 17 miles south of Exeter near Torbay) against Matthew Ekesbonere and

[128] See Appendix 1, pp. 347–9 below, for an explanation of this debt analysis, including the argument that these debts were representative of all commercial transactions, not just those that failed.

[129] PCR 1–23 Ric. II, mm. 53, 73; MCR 1386/7, m. 4. For a general discussion of sale credits, see Postan 1973a: 5–11.

his wife for the 18*s* 4*d* they owed on 12 bushels of malt they had bought from him over two years earlier.[130]

Purchases made on credit were a common feature of local and regional trade and are well illustrated by the transactions of the butchers Stephen Boghewode and his son Nicholas. During the decade 1378–88 they appeared as creditors sixty eight times but as debtors only five times, an indication of their business success and high profile (typical of butchers in general) in the local markets.[131] Not surprisingly, most of their debts involved meat or livestock.[132] But the amounts they sought varied widely depending on the type of sale and customer. Debts for meat sold to consumers averaged only 18*d* but livestock sales averaged over £3 (and ranged from 8*s* to £10). Other butchers figured prominently amongst those to whom the Boghewodes extended credit; no less than 31 per cent of their debts involved fellow butchers. These business debts represented but one link in the larger network of social, economic, and personal connections the Boghewodes had with many different butchers. For example, Nicholas leased pastureland with Benedict Bochere; was involved in land transactions with Thomas Smyth, John Shephurde, and John Batyn; borrowed money with William Lange; served as a warden of the Fleshfold with John Shephurde, Thomas Bailly, and others; rented a stall in the Fleshfold next to over twenty other butchers; twice assaulted Henry Veisy and his wife; fought a suit of trespass brought by Thomas Smyth; married the widow of Nicholas Goldying; and served as the pledge of several other butchers.[133] Obviously the credit extended by the Boghewodes was only one part of a complex web of reciprocal ties that supported social relationships as well as facilitating exchange. Such embedded relationships also lowered transaction costs because they reduced the trouble and expense of negotiating deals and made compliance easier.

[130] PCR 1–23 Ric. II, m. 49. The Ekesbonere household brewed frequently; see Table A3.1.

[131] PCR 1–23 Ric. II, mm. 16, 18, 23–25, 28, 30, 34, 36, 38, 39, 41, 45, 46, 48, 50, 52, 53, 56, 59, 69, 72, 74, 77, 79; MCR 1378/9, m. 15; 1380/1, m. 18; 1384/5, mm. 3, 30, 35, 42, 47, 51; 1385/6, m. 21. For the occupational profile of butchers, see above, pp. 137–8.

[132] Sale items were stated in twelve of their debts; five were concerned with the sale of meat (PCR 1–23 Ric. II, mm. 25, 41, 45, 52, 72), five with livestock (mm. 24, 34, 41, 45) and the others with a horse (m. 52) and tallow (mm. 16, 17).

[133] MCR 1381/2, m. 43; 1384/5, mm. 1, 30, 35, 41; 1397/8, mm. 1, 48; 1398/9, m. 1; 1403/4, m. 3d; PCR 1–23 Ric. II, mm. 52, 79; ED/M/581, 614. Butchers who owed them money were Benedict Bochere, John and Stephen Bolle, John Hood, Henry and John Veisy, Roger Truel, Geoffrey Hopere, Thomas Hore, and William Lange; all of them rented space in the Fleshfold: Book 53A, f. 76. For similar ties of reciprocity and credit in a rural setting, see Clark 1981.

Also conspicuous among the Boghewodes' debtors were six leather workers (who probably purchased hides and skins from them) and six victuallers and hostelers.[134] The latter group included the cook Richard Bakere whose 9*s* debt was supposed to be paid off in installments of 40*d*; one of the butchers, John Hood, was also obliged to pay his 30*s* 6*d* debt in two installments three months apart.[135] These deferred payments were very common for all types of debt and were especially visible in cases specifying that the creditor was seeking the "remainder" of the debt. Like butchers in other towns, the Boghewodes must have kept a kind of running tab for regular customers and then settled up at certain times of the year.[136] The fact that the Boghewodes sued fifteen of their forty nine debtors (and six of the ten butcher-debtors) for debt more than once also suggests longstanding associations with these clients.

The products of butchers and other victuallers dominated the business of the local markets; food, drink, and edible livestock accounted for 54 per cent of all items noted in the debt litigation of 1378–88 (Table 5.2). Particularly prominent were ale and the malt used to brew ale (alone responsible for 20 per cent of debts) and meat and livestock (14 per cent).[137] Women were especially active in the trade of ale, malt, and other foodstuffs; over 70 per cent of their debts involved these commodities compared to only 43 per cent of male debts, an indication of the active participation of women in the victualling trades, especially ale-brewing.[138] Cloth and other items associated with the textile industry were also prominent in the local markets, although clothing was mentioned in relatively few cases, an indication of the lower profile of the clothing compared to the textile trades in late fourteenth-century Exeter.[139] The large number of servants and non-householders employed in the cloth trades, along with the regional importance of the industry, also explains why textiles and clothing were more significant items of trade than the products of the leather and skin trades which ostensibly engaged the attention of more householders. Other manufactured goods,

[134] Skinners: John atte Forde, Peter Ponte, John Toket, John Beyveyn. Cordwainer: Walter Sampforde. Saddlers: Roger Shepton, John Viene. Fisher/hostelers: Walter Horrig, John Streyngher. Cook: Richard Baker. Baker/hosteler: John Brendon. Baker: Alex Baker. Victualler: William Egleshale. Most are listed in Table A3.1, below.

[135] PCR 1–23 Ric. II, mm. 18, 23.

[136] Britnell 1986b: 103.

[137] This excludes horses which were mentioned in disputes about hires as often as sales.

[138] Commodities involved in debts known for seventy two debts involving women and 323 involving men. For women's profile in the victual and brewing trades, see above, pp. 132–44.

[139] See above, pp. 147–67, especially Tables 4.1, 4.2, and 4.3 for this and the following comments on the distribution of trades in Exeter.

Table 5.2. *Commodities involved in Exeter debt cases, 1378–88*

Commodity	(No. of cases)		%
Food and drink		(198)	49
Ale	(51)		
Meat	(39)		
Malt	(29)		
Wine	(23)		
Barley, oats, rye, wheat	(14)		
Fish, herring	(10)		
Bread	(7)		
Other	(25)		
Textiles and clothing		(57)	14
Cloth	(34)		
Cloaks, veils	(6)		
Wool	(4)		
Hose	(4)		
Dyestuffs	(2)		
Other	(7)		
Livestock		(51)	13
Horse, colt	(32)		
Cattle, oxen, cows	(8)		
Sheep, ewes	(8)		
Other	(3)		
Leather and skins		(35)	9
Skins, furs	(15)		
Shoes	(9)		
Hides, leather	(7)		
Saddles, harness	(4)		
Miscellaneous goods		(31)	7
"Diverse things"	(9)		
Lances, arrows, swords	(5)		
Candles, wax	(5)		
Medicine	(4)		
Silver cup, spoons	(3)		
Other	(5)		
Land and hay		(17)	4
Pasture	(10)		
Hay	(6)		
Herbage	(1)		
Raw materials		(16)	4
Iron	(9)		
Timber, boards	(5)		
Coal, silver	(2)		
Total	(405)	(405)	100

Source: MCR and PCR debt cases, 1378–88.

such as candles and metal implements, played a lesser role in commercial transactions, as did such items as pasture and raw materials.

Rent arrears (12 per cent) followed sales as the second most frequent cause of litigation (Table 5.1). The sums involved in such cases were generally low, in part because the ubiquitous practice of making quarterly rent payments meant that landlords usually sued for relatively small amounts unless arrears had mounted over time. Other types of debts involving mostly small sums included suits brought to recover court-awarded damages or amercements (4 per cent of all cases), those to recover unpaid custom (also 4 per cent), and those regarding the loan of a chattel (only 2 per cent); most of these "loans" concerned horse hires. Service debts, the third most common cause of debt litigation, were also fairly small, particularly if employees quickly claimed redress for unpaid wages. Adam Russell waited a week after his stipend was due before suing the fuller John Gibbe for failing to pay him from Easter to Michaelmas, yet when Henry Spycer and his wife Joan sued John Webber they claimed he owed them 45*s* for Joan's salary as his servant for the previous five years.[140] Service debts also brought many in the professions or ecclesiastical posts into court. For example, the priest William Saxeffene sued the clerk William Pyl for his 25*s* stipend for one-quarter of the year; the rector of Stockleigh Pomeroy (for 6*s* 8*d*) and the vicar of Cadbury (12*s* 8*d*) were sued on similar grounds.[141] The involvement of non-residents in service debts was not unusual; over 13 per cent of all such litigants sued for unpaid salaries and stipends, an indication of the regional exchange of labor and services centered on Exeter (Table 5.1).

The substantial ties between Exeter's local markets and the surrounding region are also illustrated by the presence of outsiders in bond debts (which entailed a written instrument or *obligatio*). Although bonds comprised only 4 per cent of all debts, they represented the debts of 11 per cent of the non-Exeter creditors and 6 per cent of non-resident debtors (Table 5.1). Their appearance reflected the town's role as an official staple; bonds made in Exeter or collectable there could be enforced in the city's courts. Bond holders from outside the city may also have found the borough courts' application of law merchant and machinery for enforcement attractive options for securing the value of their bonds. The high sums involved (over four times the average debt) made them riskier ventures; unlike the majority of debts before the courts, however, they were backed up by a written instrument. Cash

140 PCR 1–23 Ric. II, m. 16; MCR 1381/2, m. 22.

141 PCR 1–23 Ric. II, mm. 35, 36, 46.

loans (which made up 7 per cent of all debts) also tended to be for higher sums than other debts although for amounts considerably smaller than for bonds. But like bonds, cash loans also drew in people from outside of Exeter, particularly borrowers who made up 10 per cent of all outside debtors. The circumstances that prompted villagers like Richard Clerc of Halberton to borrow 5*s* 8*d* or William Coryton of nearby Alphington to borrow 40*s* from Exeter residents are unknown, but such debts might suggest that ready cash or liquid capital was more available in Exeter than in these rural locations.[142] It is also possible that these loans represented advance payments for the purchase of goods, as the uneven amount extended to Richard Clerc implies. In these instances, the *mutuum* or *prestitum* represented credit given to the seller by the buyer. A plea of detinue, however, was the more common action taken by buyers when advance payment did not result in the timely delivery of the goods purchased.

Cash loans, commercial credit, and craft affiliation could all work together to create enduring, often reciprocal, client relationships. John Boggebrook, for instance, was a shoemaker who also regularly loaned money to the skinner Thomas Jesse, who borrowed 20*s* from him in 1374 (at 25 per cent interest). Boggebrook's dealings with Jesse continued over the next sixteen years and involved further loans as well as advance payments for hides and skins.[143] Another of Boggebrook's borrowers, also in the leather trade, served as his pledge ten years after Boggebrook loaned him cash.[144] These types of trading ties could help to lower transaction costs by making it possible to extend credit on personal trust alone, rather than requiring pledges and securities.[145] The villagers from Halberton and Alphington who borrowed money from Exeter residents were probably also capitalizing on these types of ties.

The informal nature of so many commercial transactions should not conceal, however, the extent to which traders sought to safeguard their investments. One indication of this system of safeguards may be seen in the frequency with which debts concerning pledges came before the Exeter courts (Table 5.1). In many of these suits, creditors sued to recover trade debts from their debtors' pledges, presumably because the original debtors had not satisfactorily met their obligations. When

[142] MCR 1378/9, mm. 3, 31; PCR 1–23 Ric. II, mm. 44, 50. These debts all refer to a *mutuum*.
[143] NQMT 1374, WQMT 1374; MCR 1373/4, m. 20; 1374/5, m. 16; 1388/9, m. 13; 1389/90, m. 47; PCR 1–23 Ric. II, mm. 33, 47, 74.
[144] The borrower was John Bithewalle: MCR 1374/5, m. 16; 1384/5, m. 51.
[145] On this point, see also Britnell 1986b: 103–4; Clark 1981.

Walter Belstoun and the sister of Walter London failed to pay Walter Sheppe for wool he had sold to them, Sheppe successfully sued their pledge (Walter London) for two payments of 9*s*.[146] As with the extension of credit and cash loans, these pledging duties could entail a complex network of familial, personal, economic, and craft relationships. The interlocking nature of these ties is evident in the dealings of Margery Scarlet who purchased malt for 5*s* 6*d* from Thomas Smyth; when she failed to pay up, Smyth sued her pledges (John Tugg and John Ferlegh) in May 1382. In August of that year, John Ferlegh in turn sued Margery Scarlet for 3*s* as her pledge in the dispute with Smyth; this amount might represent Ferlegh's half of the obligation plus some interest for his trouble. Since Margery also sued Ferlegh for two debts and a trespass from July to September and Ferlegh brought Margery into court as her creditor three times from March 1382 to June 1383, we can assume that they had some type of on-going relationship.[147] This relationship may have been based on craft affiliation since Ferlegh was a tailor and Margery also worked in the cloth trade.[148]

Pledges were necessary for a wide variety of actions: to back up one's ability to deliver goods or pay for items, to allow plaintiffs to proceed with a suit, to ensure that defendants would appear in court, to guarantee the payment of fines, customs, rents, and tithes, and to warrant the good performance of officeholders. Many found such pledges among their family, friends, or business partners and probably did not have to pay for such services because of the reciprocal favors they could extend. But others undoubtedly had to pay for pledging services, thus making broken pledging contracts subject to litigation concerning both debt and covenant. The demand for pledging (a type of insurance that potentially reduced enforcement costs) also led to the development of professional pledgers and brokers; in Exeter, John Jetour's brokering activities also entailed mainprise and attorney services which he extended to various clients.[149]

Some traders went beyond the casual reciprocity embodied in pledging and contracted more formal partnerships with fellow traders. By pooling resources, merchants could afford to finance bigger ventures and thus expect greater profits. Such partnerships took several forms; traders could contribute both capital and labor to an enterprise or one (or

146 PCR 1–23 Ric. II, mm. 45, 46.

147 PCR 1–23 Ric. II, mm. 44, 45, 46, 48, 49, 50, 56.

148 For Ferlegh as a tailor, see MCR 1382/3, m. 30. Margery purchased cards and may have been a woolcarder; see PCR 1–23 Ric. II, m. 53, and her entry in Table A3.1.

149 For example, PCR 1–22 Ric. II, mm. 42, 44, 50, 54, 55, 66, 67; MCR 1384/5, m. 15b; 1385/6, m. 18; see also his entry in Table A3.1.

more) of the partners could restrict participation to just capital or just labor.[150] Both types of partnership were evident in maritime trade. Almost 12 per cent of the cargoes imported at Exeter in the late fourteenth century were owned by partners; most involved shipmasters (who contributed their labor and perhaps some capital) but others involved mariners or merchants.[151] Exeter merchants probably found such associations a convenient way to share the financial burdens and risks of sea trade. Thomas Estoun's first foray into maritime trade began by importing 19 tuns of wine with Thomas Boteler in 1385, four years before Estoun entered the freedom and nine years before he served in town government. Estoun went on to an active career as a merchant and served as mayor three times.[152] Other men may have started off by providing more labor than capital as Henry Forbour probably did when he took wheat, beans, and peas to Gascony for Bartholomew Thomassyn with orders to "make a profit there."[153] Less wealthy artisanal residents also used partnerships to enable them to engage in maritime trade. William Bluet, a clothworker who never held any civic office, imported goods only once. But his lone foray into seaborne trade was done in partnership with two wealthier merchants, John Domet and Henry Hull, both regularly engaged in maritime trade.[154] In this instance, partnership represented a risk-avoidance strategy that reduced transaction costs. But even the richest merchants formed partnerships to their mutual advantage. Oligarchic merchants like Simon Grendon and John Talbot together purchased large quantities of oil, almonds, and figs at Dartmouth and also owned land in common in Exeter.[155] Public service also brought these two men together; they sat together on the powerful city council for at least seventeen years and served together as electors for eight years. Both were elected mayors of Exeter as well: Grendon in 1395/6 and Talbot a year later in

[150] These and other forms of partnership are described in Postan 1973b.

[151] PCA 1381/2–1390/1; eighty one of the 935 cargoes during this time were imported by partners, almost 75 per cent of whom were shipmasters and their *socii* (usually crewmen or foreign merchants).

[152] PCA 1384/5 and passim; *Exeter freemen*: 36; MCR election returns 1393–5, 1399, 1400–2. Boteler was a member of the local gentry and an esquire in the earl of Devon's retinue: Cherry 1983–5: 155.

[153] *CPR 1350–4*: 329. For his imports at Exeter, see PCA 1350/1–1353/4, 1356/7. He came from a wealthy Exeter family and served in public office almost annually until 1391 when he must have been in his seventies.

[154] PCA 1382/3. Domet imported fourteen times in PCA 1388/9–1396/7; Hull imported twenty nine times in PCA 1381/2–1399/1400. See also their entries in Table A3.1. For another example, see above, pp. 161–2.

[155] *CIM*, vol. 7: 129; MCR 1397/8, m. 52; 1413/14, m. 50; ED/M/596.

1396/7 when the outgoing mayor probably had a strong voice in selecting his successor.[156] Their common mercantile interests, property acquisitions, and political duties helped them reduce their costs of doing business by facilitating the establishment of a commercial partnership, easing credit, and promoting them to positions of public (and therefore economic) influence.

One of the rare instances when we can see the particular terms of such partnerships survives for a pair of Dartmouth merchants, Henry Bakleford and John Denebaud.[157] In 1385 Henry delivered £50 to John for their common use in trade (*ad mercandizandum*). This money was to be used only in ventures they both agreed upon and three times annually John would account to Henry for the value of the money and merchandise; John was also charged with finding appropriate storage facilities for the merchandise. With the £50 John purchased cloth that he then sold to the Dartmouth merchant Benedict Bottyshale for £60. John used this sum to buy 15 tons of iron from Benedict which he later sold to John Horewode of Warwick for £5 a ton, thereby gaining a total profit of £15 on the original investment, which he delivered to Henry. This was probably a commenda-type financial partnership in which one partner provided the capital and the other the labor. In this instance, Henry's investment also seems to have been secured by John's transfer of a Dartmouth tenement to him on the same day they sealed their trade contract.[158]

Partnerships were also behind many of the pleas of account in which the primary investing partner sued his counterpart for failing to render account as his bailiff and receiver.[159] John Somaister and Nicholas Taverner, for example, wanted William Focregay to render account for the cloth (valued at £40) and money (£2) they had given him to trade with (*ad mercandizandum*); John and William had also both sold wine to each other on several occasions.[160] Such temporary partnerships in which one or more partners provided either goods or cash to another were a common feature of trade at all levels. The fishmonger Thomas Pode sued Henry Fisshere for failing to render account for a load of fish worth 40*s* while another fish dealer, Thomas Nelgable, made a similar plea of account against three fish dealers, one of whom lived in

[156] MCR election returns, 1382/3–1404/5. Talbot was also mayor in 1383/4 and Grendon in 1398/9 and 1405/6.

[157] DD 60768; summarized in *Dartmouth*: 367.

[158] *Dartmouth*: 68; see Postan 1973b: 72–82 for the features of the commenda-type partnership.

[159] For this action as an indication of partnerships, see Postan 1973b: 72–82.

[160] MCR 1355/6, mm. 2d, 14d; all three men were also importers.

Bradninch about 10 miles away.[161] The amounts exchanged could be relatively small as when John Renebaud and his wife, Alice, brought suit against Roger Pestour, claiming that he did not properly account for 12*s* he had received from Alice to spend on her behalf (*ad mercandizandum*).[162] In another case, Richard atte More, a smith and member of the oligarchy, delivered 2 marks to Roger Monlyssh to purchase 8 quarters of coal; Monlyssh pleaded that he had promised to buy the coal only when the ship carrying this cargo arrived from Swansea.[163] In another case, William Loude of the merchant oligarchy sued Adam Monte, a messenger who worked for both the city and private citizens, for breaking an agreement to do business (*negociis*) for William on his way to Southampton. William complained that Adam transacted business for others when he should have concentrated on William's affairs.[164] In this instance, Adam may have been paid a set fee for his troubles on William's behalf rather than sharing in the profits of the business negotiations as a partner. Such associations, whether formal partnerships or agent–client relationships, eased the cost of doing business by allowing traders to pool capital and labor. The growing popularity of the plea of account in the late middle ages may have reflected the increasing use of such arrangements, as well as the development of a legal mechanism to facilitate collection and thus lower enforcement costs.[165]

Debt collection

The enforcement of commercial contracts represent one of the key elements of transaction costs. To ensure compliance buyers and sellers could themselves come to agreements (often pre-arranged) or they could resort to the coercive power of the government. Most contracts regarding local trade could satisfactorily be settled in the borough courts. But for transactions involving large sums of money or traders whose personal knowledge of each other was diluted by distance and infrequent contact, some opted for the greater security afforded by written instruments, notably bonds or recognizances made under statute staple or statute

[161] Pode: PCR 1–23 Ric. II, m. 18. Nelgable: PRO CP40/490, m. 273. For the fishing activities of these men and the other three (Walter Horrigg, John Frank, and William Andrew of Bradninch), see SQMT 1370–90.

[162] MCR 1384/5, m. 24.

[163] MCR 1387/8, mm. 49, 52.

[164] MCR 1374/5, m. 4.

[165] For the growth of the plea of account in common law courts, see Stoljar 1964; Milsom 1966. For the rise of account cases in Colchester, see Britnell 1986b: 99, 105–6. For legal improvements, see Palmer 1993.

merchant. Under this system, debts were formally registered before the mayor and clerk of the staple in designated towns (of which Exeter was one) and if debtors defaulted, they or their goods could be seized straight away to enforce payment.[166] If the debtors or their chattels and land were not within the town's jurisdiction, then creditors could deposit a certificate of the debt in Chancery which would authorize the issue of process for the imprisonment of debtors and seizure of their chattels and goods. Such statutory bonds thus afforded extra security and easier, more efficient debt collection for large loans and sales credits. The existence of a staple at Exeter would also have attracted traders and others involved in the extension of credit because of the protection the system offered. Unfortunately for our purposes, statutory bonds by the late fourteenth century had increasingly become the territory of non-merchants who used these recognizances to register loans and penal bonds rather than straightforward trading debts.[167]

The declining mercantile importance of statutory bonds is confirmed by an analysis of eighty four certificates of debt for Exeter statutory bonds deposited in Chancery over the decade 1377–87.[168] Although the only bonds with any details concerning their intent (four of them) referred to merchandise purchased, merchants and artisans made up but 52 per cent of the known occupations; clergy, lawyers, gentry, and smaller landowners represented the balance.[169] Not surprisingly, merchants, clerics, and lawyers predominated amongst the creditors while the gentry, yeomen, and artisans were more prominent in the debtor group. What also may be indicative of the decreased commercial use of these bonds was the lower profile of urban residents; 58 per cent of all the participants lived in villages and small towns rather than

[166] For a description of the system, see Rich 1934: 30–63; Beardwood 1939; Conyers 1973.

[167] Postan 1973c: 38–9. The details spelled out in the rare survival of three Exeter bonds from this period (314M/TF45; 1508M/Devon/Moger/80; PRO E159/172, Michaelmas recorda, mm. 35–36d) support Postan's view.

[168] PRO C241/162–175; all certificates that recorded bonds made at the Exeter staple (sixty seven) or that involved Exeter people elsewhere were analyzed (eleven at Westminster, two at Lostwithiel, two at Bristol, and one each at Oxford and Winchester).

[169] There were ninety nine creditors and 105 debtors. They included merchants (thirty two creditors, five debtors); gentry (fourteen creditors, fifteen debtors); clergy (thirteen creditors); crafts/services (eight debtors, seven creditors); lawyers (six creditors, one debtor); and unidentified (twenty six creditors, seventy eight debtors). Specific occupations (or titles) were given for forty four of them but it was possible to provide occupational/status data for another fifty two (usually merchants, Exeter residents, and gentry). Most of the unidentified parties (most of whom were debtors) appear to have been substantial yeomen landowners (below, n. 170).

in urban locales.[170] Yet bigger towns were more likely to be the source of the capital that fueled these investments since fully half of the creditors were urban residents, compared to only 22 per cent of the debtors.

The sums involved in these statutory recognizances far exceeded those which formed the basis of debt litigation in the local courts of Exeter. The latter tried debts which ran from 1*d* to £80 and averaged under 13*s* while the staple debts averaged over £69 and included amounts from £2 to £2,000.[171] The prevalence of penal bonds, which usually carried clauses ordering a return of double the original amount if payments were not made on time, accounts for part of this high amount, the substantial cash loans and bulk sales of regional trade account for the rest. Credit was extended for an average of just under four months although the median was three months and times ranged from three days to just under one year. The amount loaned to the debtor had little effect on the time allowed for repayment; the seventeen bonds that extended credit for six months or more actually averaged only £32, considerably less than the overall average. More diversity is evident in the interval between when the debtor defaulted and when the creditor deposited the certificate in Chancery. Some creditors waited only three or four days before pursuing their debtors but 30 per cent actually postponed their collection efforts more than five years, including eight who waited over twenty years.[172] The death of the creditor may account for about half of these long delays but the reasons behind the other creditors' reluctance to resort immediately to the enforcement mechanism are less obvious. The long-term purpose of many of these investment debts may have been one factor, as perhaps were the difficulties in assigning these debts to others and the challenges posed to creditors by the growth of equity in Chancery.[173]

A more complete picture of specifically mercantile debts handled by the central courts can be obtained from an analysis of debt and account cases involving Exeter residents brought before the court of common

[170] Residences were stated for 138 persons (including thirty four noted by county only) and another thirty three (thus totaling 84 per cent) were deduced by matching data in the certificates with known facts about these people. The predominance of villages and small towns reinforces the impression that smaller landowners or yeomen represented a large proportion of the "unidentified" occupation/status category.

[171] The median debt of the statutory recognizances was £40. The lowest debt amount allowed into the central courts was 40*s*. Without the £2,000 debt (a definite outlier since the next highest debt was £228), the average was just over £46. Minus this outlier, the average of the debts sealed at the Exeter staple was slightly less than £37.

[172] The median was one year.

[173] Postan 1973c: 39–54; see also Bailey 1932: 264–71 on the assignment of debts.

pleas at Westminster.[174] Several of these cases appear to have started in the Exeter borough courts but had obviously not ended to the creditor's satisfaction. John Talbot, the richest merchant in Exeter in 1377, had brought no less than three suits of debt against a non-Exeter trader, Thomas Hustyng, in the local courts over a seven-month period from 1386 to 1387. Although the first ended with a licence of concord, Hustyng must have proven elusive since Talbot sued him twice more. Only a few weeks after the final suit (in which Talbot claimed that Hustyng was evading him) Talbot sued him in the court of common pleas for £10.[175] This sum was very close to the average of £10 16*s* for all these cases, an amount probably more reflective of genuine commercial debts in regional trade than the higher amounts seen in the analysis of statutory bonds. In these disputes, moreover, merchants and artisans represented a much greater proportion (about 80 per cent) of the litigants.[176] Urban litigants were also more numerous (64 per cent); most were from Exeter since that constituted the basis of selection for the analysis.[177] Not surprisingly, the oligarchy represented the bulk of Exeter litigants (65 per cent) and comprised 80 per cent of the Exeter creditors but only 38 per cent of the debtors.[178] Wealthy oligarchic merchants had more reasons to contract large debts with non-residents and thus enter into the type of commercial arrangements which, if they did not work out, could best be resolved through the authority of the central courts.

While Exeter creditors who found it difficult to enforce contracts against debtors often resorted to the coercive powers available to them in the central courts, they paid dearly for these services. The time and expense entailed in the collection of debts in the central courts could be a costly affair at the same time as the common law upheld there was not always as favorable to creditors as borough custom and law merchant.[179] The price paid for writs, attorney fees, travel to London,

[174] All debt (eighty one) and account (twenty two) cases involving Exeter residents in a sample of seven plea rolls were analyzed. All Devon and some London filazers were examined in PRO CP40/463 (Trinity 1377), 472 (Mich. 1378), 480 (Mich. 1380), 484 (Hilary 1382), 490 (Trinity 1383), 497 (Easter 1385), 509 (Easter 1388).

[175] MCR 1385/6, m. 52; 1386/7, m. 38; PCR 1–23 Ric. II, m. 79; PRO CP40/509, m. 36. Hustyng imported wine at Exeter; PCA 1384/5. For Talbot, see Table A3.1.

[176] Occupations known for 160 of the 219 litigants; forty seven were stated in the text and 108 were deduced from other information (largely because 125 litigants resided in Exeter).

[177] The geographical distribution of the non-Exeter litigants is analyzed below, Figure 6.1 and pp. 281–93.

[178] There were 125 Exeter litigants; eighty three creditors and forty two debtors.

[179] For the costs and problems involved in the recovery of debts in the central courts, see Hastings 1947: 157–244; Milsom 1981: 244–6, 253–7, 260; Conyers 1973.

and the loss of the use of the money loaned all added to the expense of doing business. To impatient creditors, the delays that awaited them while the ponderous machinery of justice slowly worked its way to a resolution of the dispute must have seemed endless. And once the creditor secured judgment against the debtor and writs went out ordering sheriffs or bailiffs to seize the debtor's goods and property in order to satisfy the debt, further delays could take place since local bailiffs and local juries were often reluctant to give a full assessment of their neighbor's property in favor of a stranger.[180] Even if debtors were threatened with the ultimate court judgment – outlawry – they could still escape the effects of the decision by purchasing a pardon or making a "gift" of all their goods and property to close friends. Such was the case of John Ponton, clerk and receiver of the city of Exeter, who granted his considerable estate to two wealthy friends several months before he was outlawed for debt.[181] Despite these problems, however, Exeter traders regularly employed the enforcement system available to them in the central courts; they obviously felt the return was worth the extra expense such courts entailed. Enforcement costs were clearly higher for those engaged in regional trade, but these traders were willing (and more able) to pay for effective results.

Debt recovery was much less expensive and time consuming in the local courts.[182] Lawyers were rarely employed there and the fines charged by the court for its decision averaged only 2–3*d*. Borough customary law also endowed burgesses with immense advantages in their own courts, including greater scope for attachments, fewer worries over losing through a legal technicality, and more favorable treatment for burgesses than foreigners.[183] Although recalcitrant debtors could use a series of delaying tactics that forced creditors to wait while the court worked its way through summons, essoins, attachment, and distress, few borough debt pleas in Exeter ever followed this course. Well over two-thirds of the debts tried in the provosts' court were resolved within two sessions of the court (about eight to twelve weeks). Creditors

[180] Hastings 1947: 224–30; Conyers 1973: 5–6, 11–12. The excuses offered by sheriffs who failed to act on the writ, or by juries who reported that the debtor owned nothing (or very little) in their locale, are especially obvious in the Chancery extents for debts (PRO C131). For such a case at Exeter, see PRO E163/6/8 (concerning Robert Nevyle).

[181] *CIM*, vol. 6: 79; he probably did this to escape distraint. For the inquisitions and problems which followed, see PRO C260/114/7; PRO E159/173, Hilary recorda, mm. 13–14d. For such "gifts" elsewhere, see Thomas 1943: xix–xxiii; for pardons and outlawry, see Hastings 1947: 176–82.

[182] Thomas 1924: ix; Thomas 1926: ix.

[183] Thomas 1926: xxiii–xxvii; Bateson 1906: xlii–lxi, cxlix–clv. Burgess defendants also enjoyed greater rights compared to non-residents, particularly in the number of essoins.

responded to the speed of this court by favoring it with about 80 per cent of all debt actions in Exeter.[184] Some debts in the mayor's court also took but one or two weekly sessions to resolve, but others stayed on the plea rolls for as long as nine months. As the court of record in Exeter, the mayor's court was more often sought out for particular types of debts (such as bonds, rent, and custom) and for disputes concerning large sums; debts there averaged three times the amount of those tried in the provosts' court.[185]

Creditors also had little to lose by initiating a debt action in the borough courts since only 8 per cent of the time did they receive an outright unfavorable verdict of false query, in which they lost the case and had to pay a fine (Table 5.3). Creditors won clear judgments against debtors 38 per cent of the time, either because creditors convinced the court or jurors to render a guilty verdict in which the debtor was judged to be "in mercy" or because debtors failed to wage their law.[186] The latter outcome usually resulted when debtors could not find a sufficient number of compurgators to act as character witnesses to support their oath that they did not owe the sum demanded by the creditor.[187] Wagers of law could not, however, be employed when plaintiffs produced a written instrument, tally, or sufficient witnesses to back up the debt. If debtors successfully waged their law by finding the court-dictated number of oath-helpers to attest to their truthfulness, creditors were judged to have brought a false query.[188]

The "winner" in the many cases (35 per cent) when the creditor failed to pursue the debt in court (*non prosequitur*) and had to pay a fine is less clear cut (Table 5.3). Sometimes the creditor backed off from prosecuting because it was clear that the debtor was going to be able to turn up with the requisite number of compurgators.[189] In these

184 Based on the 4,536 cases tried in the MCR and PCR, 1378–88.

185 Overall, 20 per cent of debts were tried in the MCR, compared to 58 per cent of bonds, 45 per cent of rent disputes, and 45 per cent of custom cases. The average debt in the PCR was 9*s* 2*d*, but 27*s* 3*d* in the MCR. For more on the differences in these two courts, see below, pp. 337–40.

186 For pleading and the various means of proof in borough courts, see Bateson 1906: xxvii–xxxiv; Thomas 1924: xxxv–xliii; Henry 1926: 11–178.

187 For compurgation as a means of proof in debt cases, see McGovern 1968 and works cited above in n. 186. For compurgation in Exeter, see *Anglo-Norman custumal*: 32, 34.

188 For cases when the defendant was *ad legem* and a false query judgment resulted, see, for example, PCR 1–23 Ric. II, mm. 11, 12 (Bakere vs. Marshal); MCR 1382/3, mm. 37, 38 (Lane vs. Jurdan); 1387/8, mm. 42, 44 (Boghedich vs. Syde). False queries could also result when the jury ruled against the plaintiff or when the creditor failed to appear at a jury trial (Hastings 1947: 202; although I found no direct evidence for the latter instance in the Exeter debt cases).

189 For examples of the defendant *ad legem* and an outcome of *non prosequitur*, see MCR 1380/1, mm. 51, 52 (Armener vs. Hadlegh); 1382/3, mm. 5, 6 (Boggebrok vs. Truel);

Table 5.3. *Court results by debt amount for all litigants, and for non-Exeter litigants, 1378–88*

Court result	% (N=3,628)	Average amount (N=1,726)	% Debts ≤5*s* (N=1,061)	% non-Exeter debts Creditors (N=663)	Debtors (N=1,233)
In mercy	33.5	12*s* 0*d*	66	29	22
Didn't prosecute	36.7	14*s* 6*d*	54	41	49
Licence of concord	17.8	24*s* 2*d*	46	16	19
False query	8.0	9*s* 4*d*	60	10	7
Failure to wage law	4.0	8 4*d*	64	4	3
Total	100.0			100	100
Average		12*s*	61		
No information	20.0	24*s* 6*d*	60	22	28

Source and note: MCR and PCR debt cases, 1378–88. No-information cases totaled 908. Note that 70 per cent of the information concerning the amount of the debt by result comes from guilty verdicts because of the court's predilection for giving greater details for these cases.

cases, the creditor may have seen the handwriting on the wall and decided not to pursue a case which the debtor would surely win. Other creditors may have chosen not to prosecute because they thought they could obtain a better judgment at a later date or because they wished to settle the dispute privately out of court.[190] But in many other cases that ended with a *non prosequitur*, the creditor probably only brought the suit in the hopes that the threat of legal action would make the debtor pay the sum owed.[191] The inconveniences and costs of litigation for both the plaintiff and defendant also propelled many litigants (18 per cent) to settle their dispute with a licence of concord. The fact that cases resolved in this fashion had the highest average value of all (twice the amount for cases ending with a guilty verdict) may also explain why the litigants were more anxious to end the dispute without risking the final verdict of the court. The defendant usually paid a small fine for the licence (2–3*d*) which suggests that the debt was a legitimate one that the debtor had to pay sooner or later.

1387/8, mm. 38, 39, 40 (Langhe vs. Southle). In this last case, the creditor initiated another debt suit against the debtor two months later in the provosts' court which also ended in *non prosequitur*; PCR 1–23 Ric. II, mm. 87, 88.

190 Hastings 1947: 206.

191 Clark 1981: 253 believes this to be the creditor's motive.

Some of these concords may have been the result of court-ordered arbitration.[192] It is also possible that arbitrations followed upon some of the *non prosequitur* outcomes since the litigants were usually ordered to suspend all actions against each other both during and after the arbitration.[193] In these instances, the litigants themselves usually chose one or more arbitrators each, with an additional man jointly selected by both to serve as referee. The arbitrators were usually merchants or artisans with some knowledge of the business at hand. In a dispute concerning the Dominican prior's refusal to pay a mason for his work on the priory's pavement because the mason had broken the stone, the arbitrators were Thomas Pope, another mason, and Walter Gist, Exeter's premier master carpenter.[194] In some arbitrations, the parties chose a cleric or even a member of the local nobility as the referee to help settle the dispute, hoping perhaps that the prestige of the arbitrator would ensure the success of the process.[195]

The outcomes of these debt actions could be affected by several factors. We have already seen how the wealth and political rank of the Exeter oligarchy positively influenced the conclusions of their cases.[196] Oligarchic creditors won guilty verdicts against their debtors more frequently and less often withdrew before pursuing the plea to the end. The contrast between oligarchic and non-oligarchic debtors was even harsher with the latter being found guilty 13 per cent more often and benefiting from *non prosequitur* outcomes 11 per cent less often. The oligarchy was similarly favored in the other court decisions (although not to as great a degree). Non-residence in Exeter could also affect the judgments awarded to debt litigants although here too the wealthier non-residents (who tended to live farther away) enjoyed better outcomes (Table 5.3).[197] Even so, most non-resident creditors who brought suits in the Exeter courts clearly operated at a disadvantage. They were not as successful in attaining guilty verdicts, their suits were more often deemed to be false queries, and they more frequently had to pay fines for failing to pursue the case.[198] Many of these creditors did not,

192 For arbitration elsewhere, see Thomas 1926: xxix–xxx; Rawcliffe 1991.

193 Clark 1977: 4, 64–66, 79–80 suggests this possibility in her study of debts in seigneurial courts.

194 MCR 1404/5, m. 13d; for Pope's work as a mason, see ECL D&C 2654–55, 2657. For Gist, see above, p. 165.

195 MCR 1403/4, m. 6d (Philip Courtenay, uncle of the earl of Devon, was the umpire elected by both parties); m. 42d (Master Walter Robert was the umpire).

196 See above, pp. 113–14, especially Table 3.7.

197 This is discussed at more length below, p. 292.

198 Compare also with the figures in Table 3.7, above, which show the overall rates for Exeter residents alone and points out even more the differences between residents and non-residents.

however, have a choice about where to plead if their debtors were Exeter citizens since such debtors, like burgesses elsewhere, had the right to be sued only in their own courts.[199] But non-resident debtors did have more of a choice as indicated by how often their creditors had to pay a fine for failing to pursue the suit or the case came to no resolution (Table 5.3).[200] Because they were not compelled to respond to their creditors in a foreign court, debtors from elsewhere could simply not show up; there was no way for the borough court to punish them unless they had goods or property in Exeter upon which distress could be levied.[201] Creditors therefore had to seek them out in their own home courts or initiate action against them in the central courts. Creditors were so eager to use the central courts that they sometimes inflated the amount of their debt in order to meet the 40*s* jurisdictional limit; this suggests that they preferred the relative impartiality and the enforcement mechanisms of central courts over local courts, particularly when their debtors resided outside their home jurisdiction.[202]

Although the urban enforcement of regulations regarding the place, time, prices, and standard weights and measures drew tidy sums into a town's treasury, their main aim was to protect consumers and reduce risks for traders. While the continual fines assessed on transgressors of these regulations might indicate their basic ineffectiveness, the scale of the fines shows that serious infractions were always punished severely, even if high-status traders engaged in such activities. Transaction costs could also be lowered when traders exploited familial, craft, political, and personal ties to acquire credit, find pledges, solicit compurgators, and create partnerships. These informal arrangments were especially crucial in lowering negotiation and enforcement costs and, though difficult to measure, deserve more extended treatment from historians. We also need to direct more attention to the relationship between legal developments and commercial practices; the growing use and complexity of the plea of account, for example, was probably propelled by commercial developments. Borough customary law also lowered enforcement costs, although franchised traders in their home borough accrued the greatest advantages.

199 *Anglo-Norman custumal*: 29.
200 Note also that non-resident debtors suffered guilty verdicts less often than residents. See above, Table 3.7 for Exeter residents.
201 *Anglo-Norman custumal*: 29, 31. The fact that no result was recorded for 28 per cent of cases involving non-Exeter residents is also significant here.
202 Beckerman 1975.

Assessing the exchange infrastructure's negative impact on transactions costs is more difficult because the status and residency of traders become particularly important variables. These factors loom large when examining the effect of forestalling and regrating prohibitions on unenfranchised retailers although such prohibitions seem increasingly to have been relaxed on payment of small fines in the later middle ages. The ruling elite's desire to protect the freedom's monopolies and privileges also interacted with the government's urge to augment revenues to burden unenfranchised traders with a dizzying array of tolls and fines. Widespread efforts to evade such tolls and fines actually helped increase transaction costs because of the risk and the energy such tactics required. This convergence of interests raised transaction costs for the vast majority (the unenfranchised) but reduced them for a minority (the franchised).

The situation for non-residents was even more complex. All traders had to face the expense (in time and money) of enforcing and collecting debts, but those engaged in frequent transactions outside the friendly confines of a home jurisdiction sustained the highest costs. What is striking about the outcomes of local debt litigation, however, is that non-residents were generally no more disadvantaged than the many unenfranchised residents of Exeter.[203] Non-resident debtors, moreover, were actually better off than the unenfranchised Exeter debtors because the latter could be forced to answer plaintiffs through distress levied on their possessions in town. The toll system in Exeter tells much the same story. The unenfranchised residents were subject to the full array of tolls and customs in Exeter while non-residents, particularly the richer urban merchants among them, either enjoyed specific exemptions or had the wherewithal to pay the tolls levied on them when they traded in Exeter. In other words, transactions costs probably weighed relatively more heavily on unenfranchised retailers and artisans than on many outsiders who traded in Exeter because the relative wealth and privileged status of the latter helped smooth their way. Of course, many peasants and small-town residents who visited Exeter for marketing were subject to similar charges and perhaps similarly biased treatment in the borough courts when involved in debt litigation. To assess fully their commercial position in Exeter, we need to know more about who they were, where they came from, and what brought them to the city. Their trading experience with Exeter, as well as that of richer merchants and artisans, will form the subject of the next two chapters.

[203] Compare figures in Table 5.3 with those for Ranks C and D in Table 3.7, above.

6 The port trade and the hinterland

Exeter's important role in the marketing system of south-western England owed much to its position as the region's largest port. Its maritime prominence was recognized in its emergence as the headport of England's largest royal customs jurisdiction and in its designation as one of the staple towns through which all English exports were to be channelled. Located on a river 4 miles from the Exe estuary and over 10 miles from the open sea, Exeter also enjoyed better inland communications than many other ports. The following chapter investigates the extent of this inland penetration and examines the commercial connections that linked coastal and foreign traders with Devon markets and merchants. It also considers the vital role played by coastal trade in Exeter's maritime economy, particularly for the better-documented import trade. These coastal links gave inland Devon and Somerset importers relatively cheap and easy access to neighboring coastal regions and foreign goods. By comparing the import trade in two sample decades in the early and late fourteenth century, we will also trace changes in the regional balance of maritime trade within Devon, and between Devon and its English and foreign trading partners. Although Exeter merchants seemingly lost ground over the course of the century, the much more extensive participation of inland merchants in the port's trade reflected industrial and commercial development in Exeter's relatively large hinterland during the late middle ages. Exeter merchants, we shall see, were well situated to take advantage of these developments.

The port of Exeter

Because Exeter was located far from the open sea, the village of Topsham at the head of the Exe estuary (about 6 miles from the sea and 4 miles south of Exeter itself) served as the outport of Exeter during the middle ages. Smaller boats may once have sailed up the river at high tide to dock at the walls of the city, but the thirteenth-century blocking of the Exe by weirs prevented even this limited traffic from reaching the town proper. Indeed, it is likely that Topsham served as Exeter's port and link to the sea as early as the Roman period.[1] The longstanding relationship between the city and its outport is evident in the early claim by Topsham's lords, the powerful earls of Devon, to one-third of the wine custom collected by Exeter.[2] The relationship was not always a harmonious one. The earls' plans to encourage the commercial growth of their manors at Topsham and at Exminster (which lies across the estuary from Topsham) often directly threatened Exeter's own economic interests in the region. From the mid thirteenth to the early fourteenth century, the earls built weirs on the Exe river to enlarge their fisheries at the expense of Exeter residents; the weirs also effectively blocked even small boats from reaching Exeter and caused periodic flooding.[3] By promoting fairs and markets at Topsham and other estuarine locations, improving the outport's facilities, and attempting to limit Exeter's claims to tolls and jurisdiction in the estuary, the earls also increased their trading profits to the damage of the city.

Exeter citizens defended themselves against these incursions vigorously, through litigation as well as more strong-arm tactics. Against other estuarine rivals, such as the lords of Littleham and Bradham (two manors near the mouth of the Exe), Exeter even acted as the aggressor in pursuing rights over the fish trade and the ferry crossing at Exmouth, going so far as to conduct raids on the communities they felt were transgressing the city's rights. But Exeter met with only limited success in these raids and in its court litigation; although it always claimed to control all trade along the ten-mile length of the estuary from Exe Bridge outside its walls to the mouth of the Exe, the city never enjoyed such extensive powers. Despite these setbacks, however, Exeter's merchants continued to dominate the port trade locally; only a few estuarine merchants in each generation managed to compete with them. Exeter also never lost its right to collect town customs on all goods unloaded at estuarine ports, keeping for itself not only a two-thirds share of the wine custom, but also the whole of the custom on other merchandise.

Although the citizens' endless grievances against the earls tended to focus above all upon the putative loss of trade and shipping caused by the construction of weirs on the Exe, it is unlikely that any but the smallest boats had ever sailed directly up the Exe river to the city. As

[1] Henderson 1988: 92–3.

[2] *Pipe roll*, vol. 28: 15, notes wine custom at Topsham among the earl's dues in 1178/9.

[3] *Citie of Excester*: 32–4, 626–57; Book 51, ff. 43–48v; and Misc. Roll 3 offer copies of most of the original documents concerning the ongoing disputes with the earls of Devon. These are discussed and expanded with additional citations by Jackson 1972. This and the following paragraph are a summary of a longer discussion in Kowaleski 1993: 1–7.

the earls' early claims to Exeter's wine custom suggest, Topsham had probably always served as the outport for Exeter, particularly for the larger ocean-going ships that transported wine from the Continent.[4] The Exeter authorities, moreover, made the earls' promotion of Topsham port facilities work to their advantage. By the end of the thirteenth century, Exeter officials were insisting that all ships unload their saleable cargoes only at Topsham and in the following two centuries collected considerable monies from those seeking licences to discharge elsewhere in the estuary.[5] The jurisdictional unity of the estuarine ports was also reflected in the interchangeable nature of such terms as the "port of Exeter," "port of Topsham," or "port of Exmouth" in the national and local customs accounts. Exeter's jurisdictional control of the port was evident too in the royal writs for naval levies or customs collection which, even if directed to the bailiffs of the port of Topsham or Exmouth, were put into effect by Exeter officials, not the bailiffs of Topsham or the other estuarine manors.[6]

Coastal trade

The city's obligation to deliver to the earl of Devon one-third of the custom on wine shipped into the estuary was in large part responsible for the fortunate survival of a remarkable series of local customs accounts for the port of Exeter. The Exeter accounts are distinguished from other local customs accounts by their early date, high rate of survival, and comprehensive record of all incoming (but not outgoing) ships that unloaded saleable goods in the Exe estuary.[7] Enrolled on the dorses of the mayor's court rolls as early as 1266, they were kept on their own rolls by 1302/3 and survive for two-thirds of all years up to 1500. Unlike the customs accounts of other towns, they list almost every ship's name, home port, and master; the importers, their custom status, and custom owed; and the type and quantities of all goods imported. Of special importance is the accounts' enumeration of the importers and commodities that did not owe custom. The inclusion of these details combined with their extensive survival means that the Exeter accounts furnish an unusually complete record of both the coastal and overseas import trade of this provincial port.

[4] The fact that the earls were leasing out stalls for the sale of wine at Topsham from at least 1225 also suggests a longstanding arrangement; see Ugawa 1962: 662.

[5] Kowaleski 1993: 7–8. See also MCR 1289/90, m. 15; 1301/2, m. 9; 1410/11, m. 3d.

[6] Jackson 1972: 62.

[7] The surviving accounts for 1266–1321 have been edited in *Local PCA 1266–1321*. For a survey of the surviving local customs accounts for medieval England, see Cobb 1973.

These local accounts show clearly what is obscured in royal customs records: the overriding significance of coastal trade to a regional entrepôt like Exeter. Since coastal trade went unrecorded in the national customs accounts, scholars have tended to ignore its importance, focusing instead on the more easily traceable overseas trade with which the national accounts were concerned. Yet coastal trade accounted for about 70 per cent of all shipping activity through the port of Exeter in the late fourteenth and early fifteenth centuries (Table 6.1). Only 20 per cent of the importers and 31 per cent of the ships discharging at Exeter in these years employed direct overseas routes. These figures should warn us against relying on the data in national customs accounts to sketch a picture of the totality of any medieval port's trade.

In assessing the relative weight of coastal and overseas trade, we must also consider the possibility that the comparisons made for Exeter exaggerate the level of coastal trade because of flaws in the national customs accounts. The royal custom collectors appointed for the port of Exeter had a tough job; they not only covered all of Devon and Cornwall, but also were responsible for two distinctly different coastlines, one facing the Bristol Channel, Wales, and Ireland, and the other facing the Atlantic.[8] As no other customs jurisdiction in medieval England encompassed such a large, disparate stretch of coastline, the opportunity for fraud or error may have been proportionately greater. Indeed, direct comparisons between the local and national accounts for alien trade to Exeter in the early fourteenth century show that local officials were more accurate than the royal custom officials who had less to lose if their accounts failed to tally.[9] The inefficiency of the royal customers, however, was not sufficient to negate the usefulness of the national accounts as an index of direct overseas trade, while reforms in the royal customs system in the following years reduced the opportunities for fraud.[10] Irregularities if not outright fraud were certainly a problem in late fourteenth-century Devon, but complaints concerning Barnstaple and Plymouth surfaced much more regularly than for Exeter in these years.[11] Even if we allowed

[8] For the customs jurisdictions of the various headports, see Carus-Wilson and Coleman 1963: 175–93. In the early fifteenth century, Plymouth became the headport of a new customs jurisdiction centered on Cornwall.

[9] Kowaleski 1993: 39–43.

[10] Kowaleski 1993: 31, 39–42; Baker 1961.

[11] For problems with customs collectors at Barnstaple, see PRO E159/169, Easter recorda, m. 53 (wine and wax imports c. 1392); E159/170 Michaelmas recorda, mm. 3–6 (massive fraud in 1391–3) and *CPR 1391–6*: 337 (fraud in 1392–3). For Plymouth, see PRO E159/172 Hilary recorda, mm. 5–6, Easter recorda, mm. 9–23, and Michaelmas recorda, mm. 14–21d (customs evasion and extortions by searcher c. 1394); E159/173 Michaelmas recorda, m. 14 (in 1396, when the problems were minor); E159/174, Michaelmas recorda, mm. 3, 6; E159/175 Michaelmas recorda, mm. 13d, 19, 35, 38d

a generous margin of error for fraud, moreover, the volume of coastal trade would still be significant.[12]

The types of goods carried by coastal trade varied greatly. Native English goods, such as coal, corn, fish, building stone, and roofing slates, were transported exclusively by coastal craft passing to and from their source of supply. The geographic range of these coastal contacts is reflected in the medieval pottery found in Exeter, including wares manufactured as far away as Yorkshire, Lincolnshire, and Nottinghamshire, as well as Dorset, Hampshire, and London.[13] For foreign goods, Exeter relied heavily on the re-export trade from the larger ports of Southampton and London and on the two south Devon ports of Dartmouth and Plymouth.[14] In the 1380s and 1390s, for example, more than 90 per cent of the valuable trade in foreign dyestuffs, linen cloth, canvas, garlic, onions, and spices arrived by coast from such distribution centers.[15] Iron often reached Exeter by re-export from Dartmouth.[16] Wine was the commodity most likely to arrive directly from overseas; 39 per cent of the wine imported at Exeter during these years came via the direct overseas route (Table 6.1). Even so, almost two-thirds of all wine imported at Exeter was unloaded from coastal craft and thus escaped the attention of the national customers at the port. In some years the differential was even greater. In 1383/4, for example, the national accounts only noted 18 per cent of the total Exeter wine imports registered in the local accounts.

Since most imports originated overseas, the wars, epidemics, and agricultural crises that affected Continental markets generally left their mark on the pattern of Exeter maritime trade, regardless of whether

and Hilary recorda, mm. 5, 9 (problems with searcher). For Exeter, see *CPR 1367–70*: 52; PRO E159/169 Easter recorda, m. 38 (concerning wool exports in 1391–2); E159/171 Michaelmas communia, m. 1d (1394 dispute on gauging of wine); PRO E159/171 Easter recorda, mm. 84–84d (customers fail to account for wool exports in 1391–2); *CPR 1391–6*: 234, 337 (pardon to collectors for Devon and Cornwall in 1392–3 for irregularities, especially by their deputy at Barnstaple); *CIM*, vol. 7: 331–2 (concerning ale exports in 1419). Note also the nil accounts delivered for poundage and tunnage in all Dorset, Devon, and Cornish ports but Dartmouth in PRO E122/177/16 (1386–7), perhaps because the customers that year were two Dartmouth men.

[12] Carus-Wilson and Coleman 1963: 19–33, 201–7, also argue against the charge that the national customs accounts missed a substantial portion of overseas trade.

[13] Allan 1984: 22, 30–1, 354.

[14] Touchard 1973: 533, 536; Williams 1951: 278–82. It is significant that overseas trade licences granted to Exeter merchants named Southampton and London first in the list of ports to which they should return with wine; Exeter was only mentioned as a possible port of entry in one of the licences (*CPR 1361–4*: 510, 521). For Dartmouth and Plymouth, see also below.

[15] Based on the comparisons and sources cited in Table 6.1.

[16] Kowaleski 1992: 67.

Table 6.1. *A comparison of coastal and overseas imports at Exeter, 1383–1411*

Month/year and PRO E122 account	SHIPS			IMPORTERS			WINE IMPORTS (TUNS)		
	No. in			No. in			No. in		
	E122	PCA	coastal %	E122	PCA	coastal %	E122	PCA	coastal %
9/1383–9/1384 (102/14, 14A*)	(18)	(47)	62	(33)	(136)	76	(122)	(660)	82
8/1391–6/1392 (40/26*, 40/15 & 40/16*)	(11)	(45)	76	(30)	(137)	78	(263)	(724)	64
1/1393–7/1393 (40/18)	(7)	(32)	68	(22)	(78)	72	(130)	(233)	44
12/1398–9/1399 (40/23, 40/25*)	(18)	(62)	71	(36)	(158)	77	(266)	(437)	39
11/1410–9/1411 (40/30*, 40/30A)	(28)	(83)	66	(43)	(297)	85	(262)	(608)	57
Total	(82)	(269)		(164)	(806)		(1,043)	(2,662)	
Coastal average			69			80			61
Overseas average			31			20			39

Sources and notes: PCA 1383/4, 1391/2, 1392/3, 1398/9, 1410/11; PRO E122 K. R. Customs Accounts as noted above in the first column; particular accounts are starred, controllers' accounts are not; all accounts were for tunnage and poundage. The opening and closing dates of the national accounts (E122) determined the time periods compared although, because of differences in the arrival dates recorded in the two sets of accounts, the first and last ship arrivals in the national accounts were sometimes taken as the beginning and terminal points so as to avoid skewing the comparisons in favor of coastal trade. Use of this method may result in a slight underestimation of coastal trade.

these goods arrived by coastal or direct overseas routes.[17] But coastal trade did not incur many of the risks associated with overseas trade; trade with nearby ports such as Dartmouth and Southampton involved much less of a gamble than overseas trade with Gascony or Normandy. The dangers from piracy, foreign reprisals, and long journeys at sea were fewer while the transaction costs involved were considerably lower.[18] This combination of reduced risk and reduced cost opened up the import trade to a wider range of participants. Artisans and lesser merchants in Exeter who could not have ventured into overseas trade were nonetheless able to acquire foreign goods via coastal trade.[19] The same was true of merchants from such inland towns as Honiton, Cullompton, Tiverton, Okehampton, and Newton Abbot (to name only a few); they too were substantially more active in coastal than overseas trade, particularly in the late middle ages.[20]

Exeter's reliance on coastal trade may also have insulated the city's traders and economy from some of the worst consequences of the crises that ravaged overseas trade in the late middle ages. This is not to say that ports like Exeter escaped the major effects wrought by war and plague on foreign trade because they did not. If military events or other crises limited the annual wine excursions to Bordeaux, then Exeter, like every other port in England, had to make do with fewer wine imports that year. As at all other ports, the volume of trade at Exeter shrank greatly after the demographic devastations of the Black Death and subsequent epidemics severely reduced the number of consumers and producers (Table 6.2). Yet overall the maritime trade of Exeter was remarkably stable during some of the more troublesome decades. When the regions along the Atlantic coast were rocked by various political and economic crises in the 1380s through the 1430s, for example, Exeter remained largely immune. Indeed, this period was one of "golden mediocrity" for Exeter, an age of modest but steady maritime trade.[21] The amount of key imports, such as wine and salt, remained relatively constant over these decades, as did the number of ships visiting each year and the share of shipping traffic handled by Devon, foreign, and other English regions.[22] Other factors that may have pro-

[17] These patterns may be seen in Table 3.2 (above), in the number of ships docking at Exeter and the amount of wine imported.

[18] Compare the overseas and coastal transport costs in James 1971: 151–5.

[19] See below, pp. 250–2.

[20] Very few of the inland merchants active in coastal trade (Table 6.4 and Figure 6.1) appeared in the overseas customs accounts.

[21] The term was coined by Henri Touchard (1973: 533).

[22] See Table 3.2 (above) for the number of ships docking and wine imports; the jump in wine imports during the 1390s was due to the long peace that prevailed then. For

moted such stability – such as the minimal presence of aliens in Exeter's maritime trade, or the strength of the local carrying trade – were also bound up with the reliance of the port on coastal trade.[23]

Was Exeter typical of most headports in its dependence on coastal trade? This question is difficult to address quantitatively since no other medieval English port possesses as comprehensive a set of local custom accounts as Exeter.[24] In particular, the omission of local burgesses and other custom-free English merchants from all but the Exeter accounts makes direct comparisons hazardous.[25] But several factors hint that coastal trade may have been a more dominant factor at Exeter than elsewhere. First, the city's geographic position some 10 miles away from the open sea and its dependence on a sometimes hostile outport might have promoted a more landward-oriented commerce than ports with direct access to the sea and sole ownership of their port facilities. Second, the lack of deep water at the main port at Topsham and the generally inadequate port facilities in the rest of the Exe estuary also may have deterred visits by some of the larger ships on the foreign trade routes. The shallowness and narrowness of the entrance to Topsham put larger vessels at such risk that shipowners and shipmasters sometimes paid large sums for licences to unload at spots lower down in the estuary.[26] Third, the power struggle between Exeter and the earls of Devon for jurisdictional and financial control of the outport at Topsham may have hampered the development of other more suitable landing places in the estuary. Fourth and perhaps most important, the relatively low level of exports from Exeter up until the very end of the fifteenth century gave traders employing ships on the overseas routes few reasons

the share of shipping traffic, compare Table 6.3 with Touchard 1973: 532–3. Salt imports were also remarkably steady during this period; compare the figures in Touchard 1967a: 133 with those in PCA 1381/2–1390/1 (when salt imports averaged 751 quarters per year).

23 For the weak role of aliens at Exeter, see below, pp. 241–3.

24 A comparison between a now lost local account for Hythe in 1393 and the corresponding royal customs account shows that some 80 per cent of the ships arrived via coastal trade (Britnell 1986b: 70).

25 The sole surviving Bristol account (Bush 1828: 17–25) also seems to have included custom-free merchants, but the fifteenth-century local port books of Southampton provide perhaps the best comparison because they recorded much of the coastal trade for wine imports. They show that overseas imports of wine at Southampton were far more important than those coming via coastal trade, unlike the situation at Exeter (Cobb 1961: lxiii–lxvii).

26 See especially *CPR 1364–7*: 169; MCR 1360/1, m. 15d; 1365/6, m. 6d; 1422/3, mm. 6d, 7d. The increasing number of such licences in the fifteenth century suggests that the channel was getting worse; see, for example, CRA 1433/4, 1440/1, 1445/6, 1450/1, 1455/6. For the difficulties in negotiating the estuarine channel, see Clark 1960: 49–72.

Table 6.2. *Goods imported at the port of Exeter in the early and late fourteenth century*

	1302–20			1381–91		
Goods	(No.)	%	Amount	(No.)	%	Amount
Wine	(1,620)	54.4	9,877 tuns	(625)	51.7	4,991 tuns
Foodstuffs		23.5			22.9	
Herring	(223)		432 lasts	(49)		201 lasts
Fish and shellfish	(9)			(43)		
Grain, flour, vetches	(198)		16,849 qtrs	(20)		528 qtrs
Onions and garlic	(119)			(27)		
Salt	(62)			(64)		
Almonds and nuts	(24)			(1)		
Sugar and spices	(28)			–		
Bacons and livestock	(6)			(9)		
Lard, grease, seam	(6)			(1)		
Oil	(7)			(20)		
Figs, raisins, fruit	(11)			(34)		
Other	(8)			(9)		
Dyestuffs and cloth industry		9.4			4.9	
Woad	(125)		7,404 qtrs	(21)		435 qtrs
Weld	(56)			–		
Archil, ochre, copperas	(8)			–		
Madder	–			(18)		
Potash	(55)			(1)		
Alum	(29)		185 cwt	(16)		216 cwt
Other	(8)			(3)		
Raw materials		6.6			13.9	
Iron	(116)		78 tons	(86)		216 tons
Coal/charcoal	(16)			(20)		
Lead, tin, copper, steel	(10)			(7)		
Rosin, pitch, tar	(9)			(10)		
Wax, tallow	(10)			(16)		
Hides, skins, leather	(23)			(13)		
Stone, glass, wood	(8)			(12)		
Other	(3)			(1)		
Manufactured goods		6.1			6.6	
Canvas	(52)			(9)		
Linen cloth	(18)		69 pieces	(50)		549 pieces
Other cloth and mercery	(44)			(2)		
Clothing and domestic linens	(13)			(2)		
Domestic ware	(26)			–		
Horseshoes, spurs	(13)			–		
Millstones, mortars	(5)			(2)		
Soap	(1)			(7)		
Armor, weapons	–			(4)		
Other	(8)			(3)		
TOTAL	(2,977)	100.0		(1,208)	100.0	

Sources and notes: Each period includes ten complete annual accounts (*Local PCA 1266–1321*: 71–186; PCA 1381/2–1390/1). The totals exclude two unidentified goods in 1302–20 and three in 1381–91.

to sail to the port.[27] Ships on the direct overseas routes were more likely to visit Exeter when they could be assured not only of a healthy market for their incoming goods, but also of desirable cargoes for their journey out.

Although the discovery of a substantial coastal trade at Exeter does not threaten our interpretation of the national trends of foreign trade, it should make historians more wary of using royal customs accounts to delineate the maritime trade of individual port towns. In late fourteenth-century Devon, for example, a survey of seaborne trade at the county's major ports would lead one to believe that both the value and variety of foreign goods imported and exported at Plymouth far surpassed what showed up at Exeter and Dartmouth. The national accounts show that Plymouth accounted for 41 per cent, Dartmouth 25 per cent and Exeter 23 per cent of the value of this foreign trade.[28] For wine imports alone, Exeter ranked higher (matching Plymouth's total), but for other foreign goods, Exeter ostensibly captured only 9 per cent of the market compared to Plymouth's 55 per cent and Dartmouth's 27 per cent. If we did not have the Exeter local customs accounts to correct the dismal picture provided by the national accounts, we would be led to believe that the value of maritime trade in Plymouth was almost double what Exeter experienced while tiny Dartmouth, less than one-half the size of Exeter, handled about the same amount of commerce. Even given the probability that coastal trade was also a significant component of the shipping at Plymouth and Dartmouth, demand and production in Exeter and its larger hinterland clearly outstripped that in the smaller, less densely populated, and less prosperous hinterlands of Dartmouth and Plymouth. These two south Devon ports also had good reason to focus on overseas trade. Their deeper harbors, more advantageous positions on trade routes to Gascony and Iberia, and the favor showered upon them by the Crown during the Hundred Years War all promoted their use by ships on the overseas routes, particularly in the later middle ages.[29]

Nevertheless, the factors promoting Exeter's reliance on coastal trade did not preclude the growth of direct overseas trade at the port, as

[27] See below, pp. 235–7.

[28] PRO E122/102/14–14A (1383/4); 40/15–16, 40/26 (1391–2); 40/23, 40/25 (1398–9); wine was valued at £4 per tun. Barnstaple, Teignmouth, and Ilfracombe accounted for the remaining 11 per cent; see also Kowaleski 1992: Table 7.2.

[29] See above, pp. 28–31, 35–7, 73 and Kowaleski 1992 for a longer discussion of these factors. For late fourteenth-century examples of Dartmouth and Plymouth's role in re-exporting goods which arrived there from overseas, see DCO Min. Accts. 5/30 (wine from Plymouth to Fowey); *CCR 1389–92*: 52, 423 (Plymouth to Southampton); PRO E101/555/20 (corn and flour from Dartmouth to Teignmouth).

Exeter's emergence as a major exporting center at the end of the fifteenth century illustrates. Favored by the growing emphasis upon cloth production in its hinterland, as well as by the cessation of the Hundred Years War, the port of Exeter became one of England's most prominent exporters of cloth in the last decades of the fifteenth and first decades of the sixteenth century.[30] Exeter's increasing ability to offer for export a product much in demand throughout Europe meant that ships now had more reason to visit the port. This shifting balance of trade resulted in an increase in direct overseas trade to Exeter while coastal trade held steady, thus reducing the port's relative reliance on coastal trade.[31] This change, however, came only at the very end of the middle ages; for hundreds of years before this period, coastal trade and importing dominated the maritime commerce of medieval Exeter.

The export trade

What was true of the import trade in the fourteenth century was also undoubtedly true for the export trade as well; the paltry 8 per cent share of Devon exports handled by Exeter in the late fourteenth century reflects only the traffic that travelled directly overseas, not goods carried by coastal craft to neighboring ports and reloaded onto other ships for export overseas.[32] The suspicion that Exeter's portion of the export trade was larger than the customs accounts show is reinforced by comparisons with Plymouth and Dartmouth whose share of the county export market in the same period was ostensibly much higher than Exeter's: 41 and 24 per cent, respectively. Yet it is difficult to believe that Exeter, whose hinterland was at least twice as large as that of other Devon ports (stretching well into Somerset and Dorset), produced exports that were three to five times less valuable than those shipped out of the other ports.[33] In the export trade as in the import trade, the maritime advantages of the ports of Dartmouth and Plymouth worked to raise their profile on the direct overseas routes compared to the port of Exeter.

These advantages promoted the use of Dartmouth and Plymouth as collection or bulking centers for exports which probably came originally from Exeter and other Devon and Cornish ports. As detailed in the

[30] Carus-Wilson 1963.

[31] Childs 1992: 84–86.

[32] See n. 28 above for the accounts used to derive this and the following figures. Unfortunately, the local accounts of Exeter did not register outgoing cargoes.

[33] Barnstaple accounted for 25 per cent of the total value of exports from the county. See above, pp. 70–3 for the hinterlands of these ports, and below, pp. 274–7, 280–93 for Exeter's hinterland.

customs accounts, Exeter's exports in the late fourteenth century consisted largely of woollen cloth and very small amounts of wool, hides, and hake.[34] In contrast, exports from Dartmouth and Plymouth were both more substantial and more diversified, including much cloth as well as tin, lead, hides, calf skins, hose, boots, shoes, salt, beans, cheese, ale, and several kinds of fresh, dried, and salted fish.[35] Even the types of cloth ostensibly exported by Exeter paled in comparison to the varieties dispatched through Dartmouth and Plymouth. The two south Devon ports exported the same white and russet narrow dozens and "short" cloths as Exeter but also shipped out narrow cloths "called Tauntons," narrow grey cloths of Cornwall, cloths of Wales, worsteds, embroidered and "English" bedclothes (*lectis anglic'*), colored narrow cloths (including red, green, and black), "large" cloths, and broadcloths.[36] Given the smaller and poorer hinterlands of Dartmouth and Plymouth and the more substantial cloth production in Exeter's hinterland at this time, the differences observed in the volume and diversity of exports can only be explained by the role of the two south Devon ports as bulking centers for exports from other ports.[37] Evidence regarding Exeter's greater share of imported dyestuffs also suggests that many of its cloth exports were recorded in the accounts of other seaports. Although the royal customs value of Exeter's foreign imports at this time was almost three times smaller than the value of such imports at Dartmouth and Plymouth, Exeter's share of dyestuffs directly imported from overseas (excluding the larger amounts shipped in by coastal craft) was seven times what it was at the other two ports.[38] It is therefore reasonable to assume that some of the cloth exported by Exeter and its hinterland exited on coastal craft to re-export centers such as Dartmouth, Plymouth, Southampton, and Bristol, thus escaping detection in the national customs accounts for Exeter.[39]

34 PRO E122/40/8, 40/14 (wool), 40/15–16, 40/18, 40/20, 40/22, 40/23 (hake), 40/24–6, 158/31–32 (wool and hides), 158/33–34; 193/23; *CPR 1396–99*: 83 (wool); *CCR 1385–9*: 166 (hides).

35 PRO E122/40/8, 102/14–14A, 40/16, 40/18, 40/25–26, 158/25–26, 158/34, 190/1. See also the sources in n. 11 above for Plymouth.

36 See especially PRO E122/40/16, 40/23, 158/34, as well as PRO E159/172, Easter recorda, m. 12d; *CIM*, vol. 6: 71 and the sources in n. 11 above for Plymouth.

37 For other late fourteenth-century examples of their role as a collection center for exports, see *CIM*, vol. 3: 151 (Irish goods); *CPR 1354–8*: 406 (Irish wool); and above, pp. 26–7, esp. Table 1.2.

38 Dyestuffs imported into Exeter were valued at £127 while those at Dartmouth and Plymouth were only £18 (PRO E122/102/14–14A, 40/18, 40/23, 40/26). See also Childs 1992: Table 9.2.

39 For Exeter cloths shipped out of Bristol, see Childs 1978: 79; for Southampton's role as re-export center for Devon goods, see PRO E159/173, Michaelmas recorda, m. 21 (tin and cheese); Coleman 1963: 17, 19–20.

Although cloths from Exeter and its hinterland may have been shipped to neighboring ports for export, Exeter merchants rarely showed up as exporters outside their own home port. Their names are conspicuously absent from the surviving late fourteenth-century export accounts of Southampton, Dartmouth, Plymouth, and Bristol, suggesting that Exeter merchants kept a low profile in the export of goods overseas. On their own turf, however, they made a better showing, representing 47 per cent of the overseas exporters and owning 66 per cent of the value of all exports (almost all cloth) at the port of Exeter.[40] Foreigners accounted for only 3 per cent of the exports, Taunton (Somerset) men for 9 per cent, and Devon exporters for the remaining 22 per cent, an indication of the strongly local control of the export trade. The thirty Exeter exporters who can be singled out in the late fourteenth century were among the city's most powerful men; one-third served as mayors and an additional one-third had held the second-highest position of steward.[41] All the exporters were oligarchic merchants and all but four eventually rose to the highest civic offices (A Rank).

The high social and political status of Exeter exporters remained the same throughout the middle ages, but the nature of the export trade itself underwent substantial change. Roughly three phases can be distinguished in the port's export trade. The first, spanning the late thirteenth and early fourteenth centuries, was characterized by a livelier and more diversifed trade than the period that followed (the late fourteenth through early fifteenth centuries). Hides, wool, and tin, for example, were all regularly exported in this earlier period but rarely appeared in the second phase.[42] Cloth was by far the most valuable export, although exact figures in this period before customs accounts registered denizen trade are hard to come by.[43] When such accounts

[40] Based on extant accounts that specified port of export; PRO E122/40/26 (1391), 40/16 (1392), 40/18 (1393), 40/23 and 40/25 (1398–9). Exports were valued at just over £489 and there were fifty exporters in all.

[41] This count includes those in the sources above, n. 40, as well as Exeter men in PRO E122/158/26 (1371–2), 158/31 (1376), 40/8, and 193/23 (1377–9), 158/34 (1379), 177/16 (1386–7), 40/14 (1390–1) which generally do not specify the particular port although other evidence strongly suggests most operated out of Exeter.

[42] For wool, see Carus-Wilson and Coleman 1963: 36–74, 132–33. For the early export of hides, see MCR Roll 1, m. 5; *Rotuli parliamentorum*, vol. I: 312; PRO E122/40/1A, 40/3, 40/5, 156/8, 40/7–7A and 7B; Exeter names dominate especially in the late thirteenth-century accounts when exports reached well over 6,000 hides. For tin, see PRO E122 passim, esp. E122/40/7A for tin exports from Exmouth valued at £61 in 1323/4; Hatcher 1973: 110–17, 174.

[43] PRO E122/40/7A; Childs 1992: 79. Only the cloth exports of aliens were taxed in this period; their fairly low profile in the South-west combined with that region's laxity in taxing them means the few figures available are of questionable use (Lloyd 1982: 36, 59, 210–26).

do become available in the 1350s, they show that some 12 per cent of the country's cloth exports passed through the customs jurisdiction of Exeter, a figure not again matched by the port until the early sixteenth century.[44] The greater quantities and wider variety of foreign dyestuffs brought to Exeter in the early fourteenth century also point to the amount and types of cloth exported by Exeter and its hinterland. Imports of woad (a blue dye) in ten early fourteenth-century accounts amounted to 7,404 quarters, compared to only 435 quarters during a comparable period in the 1380s (Table 6.2). Similar contrasts are visible in the importation of dyestuffs such as archil, weld, and copperas, and mordants like potash which either disappeared or were reduced to a trickle in the second half of the fourteenth century. The vast amount of woad imported by Exeter in the late thirteenth and early fourteenth centuries came mostly from Picardy and occasionally from Normandy; these areas also supplied grain to Exeter during these years.[45] It is likely that these regions, along with Poitou and Gascony which provided enormous amounts of wine to Exeter, served as the most important overseas markets for Devonshire cloth in this first phase.[46]

In the second phase of Exeter maritime trade (c. 1350–1450), the Hundred Years War and shifting political alliances severely affected the export trade of the Devonshire ports with their Continental markets. Cloth exports plunged in the late fourteenth century, reaching a nadir of less than 1 per cent of England's exports in the 1400s, even though Devon exports in that decade had actually increased relative to the previous thirty years.[47] The War cut Devon off from many of its traditional trading partners. Commerce with Normandy and Picardy suffered the most; in the late fourteenth century they accounted for less than 1 per cent of all ships reaching Exeter in contrast to the over 10 per cent of shipping traffic they furnished before 1320 (Table 6.3). The import of woad from these regions also plummeted and by the early fifteenth century had been largely replaced by woad from Languedoc which usually arrived from Gascon ports.[48] South-western France probably served as the principal market for Exeter cloth during this second period. Still controlled by the English, Gascony was also the source of the wine that dominated the import trade at Exeter (Table 6.2). Indeed, the cloth trade was linked closely to the wine import

[44] Table 1.1, above.
[45] Kowaleski 1993: 26–8 and Kowaleski forthcoming.
[46] Note also that Norman and Saintonge pottery dominated the foreign wares found at Exeter in this period (Allan 1984: 17–23).
[47] Table 1.1, above.
[48] Touchard 1967b: xxvi; Carus-Wilson 1953.

trade. Trade licences granted to such Exeter merchants as Roger Plente and Warin Bailly stipulated that they could take local cloth to Gascony and Spain in exchange for wine and other merchandise.[49] The Gascon wine trade was also associated with the south-western trade in fish which increased substantially in the fifteenth century, particularly at the port of Plymouth.[50]

During the late fourteenth and early fifteenth centuries, Brittany and Iberia also developed as markets for Devon cloth. Breton ships had always visited the ports of south-western England because of the convenient overseas routes between the two regions, but Breton commerce at Exeter increased dramatically from the 1390s when political ties between Brittany and England were particularly close.[51] Despite the growing commercial contacts, however, Breton activity at Exeter always focused more on the carrying trade and imports of Breton linen, salt, garlic, and onions than on the purchase of Devon cloth.[52] The situation was slightly different with Spain and Portugal since their products more often reached Exeter through the re-export trade from Bristol, Dartmouth, Plymouth, and Southampton than through direct international trade.[53] Such Iberian products as wines, spices, oil, fruit, and skins usually arrived at Exeter on English ships sailing along the coast; presumably Exeter cloth exports destined for Spain or Portugal travelled similar routes. Iberian arrivals at the port of Exeter itself only became more common in the third phase of Exeter's export trade (the mid fifteenth to early sixteenth centuries) as Exeter itself emerged as a major export center for cloth.

Although the Anglo-French conflicts were largely responsible for the changing markets and reduced exports of Exeter maritime trade in this second phase, the demographic decline brought on by plagues and epidemics also contributed to the fall in cloth exports during the late fourteenth and early fifteenth centuries. Fewer producers and fewer customers inevitably meant reduced exports. Yet the decline in cloth exports, as we have seen earlier, may not have been as severe as the enrolled accounts suggest.[54] The ostensible export figures for the port

[49] *CPR 1361–4*: 510, 521; see also p. 496 for similar licences to Plymouth and Cornish merchants. For Devon cloth in the Toulouse region, see Wolff 1950. For Devon grain shipped to Gascony, see *CPR 1350–4*: 359.

[50] *CPR, 1361–4*: 496; *1364–7*: 7, 11, 32, 50; *1370–4*: 181; PRO E122/40/7A, 102/14, 40/26, 40/16, 40/23; Childs 1992: 80. See also below, pp. 307–12 for the expansion of the fish trade at Exeter.

[51] Touchard 1967a: 111, 393; Touchard 1967b: 362–4.

[52] Breton ships were common but Breton exporters were relatively rare in Exeter (PRO E122 passim; Touchard 1967a: 133–4, 136–7).

[53] Childs 1978: 78–142; Childs 1992: 778, 82–3.

[54] Table 1.1, above, and pp. 19–23; Childs 1992: 79.

of Exeter were lowered by the exclusion of "straits," Devon's primary cloth export, from at least some of the enrolled accounts of the 1390s; by massive fraud at Barnstaple (the county's major cloth exporter) during the same decade; by the farming of Exeter customs for most of the 1370s and 1380s; and by administrative changes from the 1400s as Plymouth and Cornwall were separated from Exeter's customs jurisdiction. Cloth exports certainly fell in the last three decades of the fourteenth century and stagnated through the 1420s, but probably not to the extent the enrolled customs figures suggest. Real recovery, moreover, began by the 1430s and accelerated thereafter despite some setbacks in the 1450s and 1460s. Devon cloth was also well placed to take advantage of the economic shifts that resulted from the late medieval demographic crises. Rising standards of living increased consumer demand for the cheap, light cloths produced by the Devon cloth industry. Costs may also have been kept down by the growing tendency to export white or undyed cloths, a trend reflected in the lagging imports of foreign dyestuffs from the mid fifteenth century on.[55]

The third and last phase of trade, from the late fifteenth through early sixteenth century, witnessed by far the highest level of exports. With the advent of an enduring peace in 1475, exports of Devon cloth skyrocketed while Exeter's share of these exports swelled to two-thirds or more, in stark contrast to the situation over one hundred years earlier.[56] Within Devon, Exeter became the favored port of call for ships on the overseas routes and the value of both its overseas imports and exports for the first time exceeded those of all other south-western ports.[57] Brittany and Gascony were still Exeter's chief trading partners, but exchanges with Iberia also increased while Norman merchants and mariners once again carried on a regular trade at the port.[58] Although cloth dominated the exports shipped out of Exeter, greater variety was visible in the other exports now found in the cargoes of departing vessels: tin, pewter ware, and some hides, lead, and roofing tiles. Imports also became much more diverse, due as much to the greater earning power and rising demand of the town and its hinterland as to the expanding overseas markets for local cloth. The volume of certain imports, such as linen cloth, grew so much that Exeter moved into the ranks of the re-export centers.[59] Devon ports, unlike those in eastern

[55] PCA passim; Childs 1992: 78–9, Table 9.2.

[56] Carus-Wilson 1963: 9–11; Childs 1992: esp. Table 9.4.

[57] Carus-Wilson 1963: 9–16; and compare Childs 1992 (esp. Table 9.4) with Kowaleski 1992 (esp. Table 7.2).

[58] Mollat 1952: 152–3, 481; Childs 1978: 62, 79, 88, 159; Carus-Wilson 1963: 13–16. The pottery evidence confirms this picture (Allan 1984: 20–22, 109–11).

[59] Childs 1992: 81 and Table 9.2; MacCaffrey 1975: 168.

England, also did not succumb to the tough competition from London; led by the upswing in maritime trade at Exeter, business at the Devon ports expanded more than at any other provincial port in this period.[60] What did not change was the relatively low profile of foreign merchants in the port trade and the crucial middleman role played by Exeter merchants who marketed local and regional cloth overseas and imported goods for the town and hinterland.[61] Then, as in the fourteenth century, their wealth derived largely from the pivotal role they played in the distribution of imported goods where they served as the vital link between foreign, regional, and local trade.

The import trade

Exeter's role as a regional entrepôt and its merchants' crucial position in the distribution of merchandise can best be illustrated through an analysis of the import trade, both coastal and overseas. The changes that occurred over the course of the late thirteenth to mid fifteenth centuries can be highlighted in a comparison of trade in two periods with ten extant accounts each at the beginning and near the end of this time span.[62] The first period (1302–20) was typical of the late thirteenth and early fourteenth century (roughly 1280 to 1349), although the grain imported during the sample period was higher than usual because of substantial corn imports during the Great Famine of 1315–22.[63] The second sample (1381–91) was representative of the late fourteenth and early fifteenth centuries (1350 to about 1440), although the intermittent warfare and truces of the Anglo-French conflicts were responsible for some severe short-term fluctuations.[64] Wine imports, for

[60] Childs 1992: 88.

[61] This situation prevailed throughout the sixteenth and seventeenth centuries (MacCaffrey 1975: 160–73).

[62] The first period covers the first ten surviving accounts of the century: 1302/3, 1304/5, 1305/6, 1310/11, 1312/13, 1315/16, 1316/17, 1317/18, 1319/20 (printed in *Local PCA 1266–1321*: 71–186). The account for 1303/4 was excluded because it is incomplete. The second period covers the ten accounts in PCA 1381/2–1390/1.

[63] For the representativeness of the sample years, compare the ship arrivals in Kowaleski 1993: Table 1 (mostly for 1285–1321) with those in Table 6.3. See also the ship arrivals and wine imports in Table 3.2, above. For the grain trade, see Kowaleski forthcoming.

[64] The percentage distribution of ships' homeports, importers' residences, and shipmaster-importers by region in the thirty four surviving accounts in PCA 1350/1–1398/9 and those of 1381–91 were very similar considering the severe short-term fluctuations that occurred. The differences between the two periods never amounted to more than 4 per cent for any single category except for the percentage of shipmaster-importers which tended to be lower for Cornwall (by 14 per cent) and the British Isles (by 6 per cent) in 1350–99, and higher for the Channel Islands (by 6 per cent) and the Continent (by 8 per cent). See also Table 3.2, above, for similarities in the number

example, ranged from a low of 226 tuns in 1372/3 to a high of 1,202 tuns in 1393/4. The number of ships entering the port each year could also vary greatly, from a low of 18 in 1387/8 to 87 only ten years later. Warfare in France or the threat of coastal raids were responsible for the marked downswings, while the relatively rare periods of universal peace prompted sudden jumps in the volume of trade, especially in the 1390s. Such fluctuations were also characteristic of the trade at other English ports during this period.[65]

Although the volume of trade at the port of Exeter decreased significantly over the course of the fourteenth century, the distribution of most imports altered little (Table 6.2). Wine remained the dominant import, albeit at half the tunnage of the earlier part of the century. Imports of foodstuffs were also steady but tended to shift from essential items like grain to more superfluous foods such as oil, figs, raisins, and salt.[66] A greater decline (almost 5 per cent) occurred in the relative standing of cargoes of dyestuffs and mordants for the cloth industry. Within this category emphasis also shifted from woad (a blue dye) to madder (a red dye), and from potash to alum as a mordant. The predominance of undyed and russet (madder-dyed) cloths in the region's late medieval exports reflected these changes in both the amount and type of imported dyes. Increases in the importation of other raw materials compensated for much of the slump in the raw materials imported for the cloth industry; iron from Spain, coal from northern England, roofing slates from south Devon, and boards, pitch, and tar from the Baltic all appeared at Exeter in greater quantitites in the late middle ages. The percentage of manufactured goods also rose slightly, due mostly to the expansion of linen cloth imports from Brittany. While some of these changes in the distribution of imports reflected England's shifting political alliances (for example, the reduction of woad from Picardy and the surge in linen cloth from Brittany), they also indicate how Exeter and its hinterland coped with the demographic and political difficulties of the late middle ages. Total consumption certainly declined following the devastating plagues of the late fourteenth century, but the percentage increases in some foodstuffs and manufactured goods

of ship arrivals and wine imports over the period 1350–1440, and Touchard (1973) for the similarities in 1381–1433. The distribution of wine cargoes also differed for some regions; in 1350–99, estuarine importers owned more such cargoes (by almost 7 per cent) and south Devon importers fewer (by 8 per cent) than in 1381–91.

65 Carus-Wilson 1976b, 1967d; James 1971: 1–69, 104–8.

66 The decline in spice imports is harder to explain. Their high prices and low weight may have made them more suitable for overland transportation, particularly when real demand declined after the Black Death. For the overland transportation to Devon of spices and other light foreign goods, see below, pp. 273–4.

Table 6.3. *Home ports of ships at the port of Exeter in the early and late fourteenth century*

	1302–20			1381–91		
	(No.)	% of known		(No.)	% of known	
Devon			51.4			68.2
Exe estuary[a]	(107)	24.2		(73)	22.9	
East Devon	(88)	19.9		(26)	8.2	
South Devon	(30)	6.8		(118)	37.1	
North Devon	(2)	0.5		–	–	
British Isles			26.4			7.9
Cornwall	(5)	1.1		(11)	3.5	
Dorset	(29)	6.5		(2)	0.6	
Hampshire	(37)	8.4		–	–	
Other counties	(46)	10.4		(11)	3.5	
Wales and Ireland	–	–		(1)	0.3	
Continent			17.2			16.0
Brittany	(23)	5.2		(40)	12.6	
Normandy, Picardy	(46)	10.4		(2)	0.6	
Southern France	(3)	0.7		(6)	1.9	
Spain	(1)	0.2		(1)	0.3	
Other	(3)	0.7		(2)	0.6	
Channel Islands	(22)	5.0	5.0	(25)	7.9	7.9
Total Known	(442)	100.0	100.0	(318)	100.0	100.0
Unidentified	(16)			(31)		
Grand Total	(458)			(349)		

Source: and note: Each period includes ten complete annual accounts (*Local PCA 1266–1321*: 71–186; PCA 1381/2–1390/1). For the Devon regions, see Figure 1.1.
[a]Includes home ports of Exeter, Exmouth, Kenton, Lympstone, Powderham, Pratteshide, and Topsham, locations usually counted as part of east Devon.

point to rising standards of living. The virtual disappearance of some dyes and mordants in the late fourteenth century was offset by switching to other dyes, by exporting cloths undyed, and by shifting imports to other raw materials for domestic industries.

The South-west's adjustment to the shifting political alliances of the late fourteenth and early fifteenth centuries is also visible in the changing profile of ships that visited the port of Exeter (Table 6.3). Except for ships from England's allies in Brittany and the Channel Islands, the percentage of vessels from foreign regions fell at Exeter in the late fourteenth century. The significant decline in ships from English ports was also a by-product of the political problems between England and France. Many of the eastern ports of England suffered greatly from the wartime loss of their most important trading partners in Picardy and Normandy, leaving them with little to carry to Devon ports. The striking reduction in Hampshire and Dorset vessels at Exeter, however, was probably more a product of the strength of the Devon carrying trade than a reflection of poor commercial ties with the county. By the end of the fourteenth century, the share of shipping from south Devon (especially Dartmouth and Plymouth) had multiplied by six times. This extraordinary growth in the south Devon carrying trade was financed in part by the Crown's wartime spending in Dartmouth and Plymouth for naval and transportation services.[67] Shipping in east Devon could not meet this challenge and slumped by some 11 per cent over the course of the century. The failure of its largest port, Teignmouth, to recover from a disastrous French raid in 1340 was responsible for most of the decline; Teignmouth's percentage of Devon shipping at Exeter slipped from 29 per cent in the early fourteenth century to 9 per cent in 1381–91.[68] Its decline was accompanied by the weakening presence of other east Devon ships (from Ottermouth, Seaton, and Sidmouth) at Exeter; the generally inferior harbors and poorer facilities at these ports did not enable them to compete with their more powerful neighbors. Only ships from the Exe estuary (which enjoyed home-port advantages at Exeter) and those from Cornwall (which capitalized on growth in the south-western fishing trade) were able to meet the mounting challenge from south Devon's carrying trade. Nonetheless, the boom in south Devon shipping helped Devon carriers to raise their control of shipping at Exeter to almost 70 per cent by the late fourteenth century, although even in the early part of the century Devon carriers had accounted for over half of the vessels at the port.

The regional distribution of importers at Exeter mirrored many of the same trends that affected the commodities and ships arriving there (Table 6.4). Foreign participation in Exeter's trade, for example, declined over the course of the century and there was a marked shift from Norman and Picard importers in the early fourteenth century to Breton importers in the second half of the century. Norman and Picard

[67] See also Table 1.3 (above) for the south Devon fleet in naval service and among wine carriers. For the strong presence of Dartmouth ships in the carrying trade throughout England and for the effects of wartime spending there and at Plymouth, see Kowaleski 1992.

[68] In 1302–20 there were sixty six Teignmouth ships at Exeter but in 1381–91 there were only seventeen; see also Kowaleski 1992 and 1993: 14–15, 22 and Table 6.2 for Teignmouth's shipping and trade.

Table 6.4. *Residences of importers at the port of Exeter in the early and late fourteenth century*

	% of individual importers[a]		% of all cargoes[b]		% Cargoes owned by mariners and masters[c]	
Residence	1302–20	1381–91	1302–20	1381–91	1302–20	1381–91
Exeter	21.0	11.9	49.6	30.0	–	–
Exe estuary	11.0	5.5	11.8	6.8	38.8	42.9
East Devon	13.1	6.2	10.0	6.2	57.2	26.6
South Devon	4.5	19.6	1.8	17.6	78.6	29.4
Other Devon	0.4	0.9	0.2	0.8	50.0	–
Somerset and Dorset	3.7	3.6	2.0	5.4	44.0	3.6
Cornwall	0.5	1.9	0.2	1.2	80.0	91.7
Other British Isles	7.3	3.4	3.1	2.2	53.8	54.5
Channel Islands	1.7	5.0	0.8	3.2	72.7	90.9
Continent	8.3	11.2	6.0	6.4	21.5	75.8
Unidentified	28.5	30.8	14.5	20.2	2.2	9.2
Total	100.0	100.0	100.0	100.0		
(Sums)	(942)	(581)	(2,551)	(1,022)	(497)	(224)

Source: Each period includes ten complete annual accounts (*Local PCA 1266–1321*: 71–186; PCA 1381/2–1390/1).

Notes: See Figure 1.1 for the Devon regions; the Exe estuary settlements have here been separated from the east Devon region.

[a]Counts each different importer only once regardless of the number of times he or she imported goods during this period.

[b]Each cargo equals all the goods an importer brought in on one ship. Cargoes imported by partners were counted once for each partner, but unnamed partners (such as the mariners or *socii* who imported goods with many shipmasters) were counted as one individual; there were sixty one in 1302–20 and sixty in 1381–91.

[c]Percentage of all importers from that residential group who also served as shipmaster or mariner on the ship carrying their imports. In 1302–20, 19.4 per cent of cargoes were owned by shipmasters or mariners, and in 1381–91, 21.9 per cent. In 1302–20 mariners were identified from their claims to be free of custom because of portage, and in 1381–91, it was assumed that the *socii* partners of shipmasters were mariners.

importers had tended to be wealthy merchants from Abbeville, Amiens, and Rouen involved in the valuable dyestuff and grain trades, but Breton importers were often shipmasters who imported less costly cargoes.[69] Although Breton ships brought in almost all of the salt, about

[69] Kowaleski 1993: 22–3, 26–7. Normans and Picards accounted for about 52 per cent of importers and cargoes in 1302–20 while Bretons accounted for over 60 per cent of the Continental importers and cargoes in 1381–91.

40 per cent of the linen cloth, and about 15 per cent of the wine cargoes in 1381–1433, they actually owned less than 23 per cent of the salt imports and less than 2 per cent of the wine (Tables 6.5 and 6.6).[70] Merchants from Exeter were happy to rely upon the transport services of Breton ships, but they retained ownership of the lion's share of the cargoes these ships carried.[71] In contrast to these changes among northern French importers, the percentage of Gascon wine importers at Exeter remained relatively stable over the century, although the size of their cargoes dropped significantly in the face of growing English competition and wartime difficulties.[72] The alien share of trade at Exeter had in fact always been lower than at most other English ports,[73] because the heavy reliance on coastal trade in Exeter reduced foreign ownership. Little trace survives in Exeter of the hosting regulations that were so common in ports visited by large numbers of foreigners.[74] Even in the later fifteenth century, when Exeter's port trade rose in value and volume and overseas trade became more important, alien merchants never gained much of a foothold there.[75]

Like the Bretons, importers from the Channel Islands (almost all from Guernsey) took advantage of hostile relations between England and her northern French trading partners by increasing their presence as carriers (Table 6.3) and importers at Exeter (Table 6.4). The Islanders were frequent visitors to the stretch of coastline between Plymouth and Chichester, although by the second half of the fifteenth century their activity centered more on Poole, Exeter, and Dartmouth.[76] They dominated the transport of onions and garlic (most from Brittany but some perhaps from the Islands themselves) and that of conger, ray, and mackerel from their own waters.[77] Many agricultural goods, such as cows, oxen, sides of bacon, and quantities of wheat, barley, and beans also arrived on their ships. Their most valuable cargo, however, was linen cloth and canvas (most from Brittany); their share of this carrying trade actually increased from just under 8 per cent in the last decade

[70] Touchard 1973: 537; Touchard 1967a: 136–7. In 1381–91 Bretons imported 68 tuns of wine and 1,693 quarters of salt.

[71] Exeter ownership of Breton cargoes actually increased in the fifteenth century (Touchard 1967a: 133–4, 136–7).

[72] In Table 6.5, their relatively large cargoes of wine account for the steady share of tunnage Continental importers held over the century. For the competition faced by Gascon vintners in England, see James 1971: 70–92.

[73] Lloyd 1982: 59, 211–26; Beardwood 1931: 142–80.

[74] See Ruddock 1946 and Fryde 1976 for these regulations.

[75] Carus-Wilson 1963: 15–16; Power and Postan 1966: 337–9; Childs 1992: 85–6.

[76] Childs 1986.

[77] PCA passim and Childs 1986: 51–2.

of the fourteenth century to over 42 per cent in the 1420s.[78] Even so, their profits came as carriers, rather than owners; only 3 per cent of the late fourteenth-century cargoes were owned by the Islanders and almost all of the importers were shipmasters, not merchants (Table 6.4). As importers, they played a minuscule role in the all-important wine trade, concentrating instead on imports of corn and linen cloth (Tables 6.5 and 6.6).

With only two exceptions, the trade of non-Devon English importers at Exeter, like that of their ships (Table 6.3), decreased over the course of the fourteenth century. Many of the importers from counties east of Devon conducted trade in their capacity as shipmasters (Table 6.4) so that their presence at Exeter declined as their ships found less reason to visit the port (Table 6.3). But even merchant-importers from these counties appeared there less often, a trend particularly noticeable in the diminishing role of the Yarmouth herring traders; by the late fourteenth century, most herring cargoes were owned by Devon importers (Table 6.6).[79] The two exceptions to this pattern of shrinking English activity at Exeter were importers from Cornwall and from Somerset. Cornish importers, most of whom were shipmasters (Table 6.4), became more active at Exeter during the late middle ages because of their prominent role in the expanding fish trade (Table 6.2). Somerset importers, almost all from inland locations, also showed up more often in the late middle ages, unlike the Dorset importers whose activity at Exeter slowed to a trickle, a trend evident in the drastic fall in shipmaster-importers among the Somerset/Dorset importers (Table 6.4). In the early fourteenth century, 80 per cent of the Somerset/Dorset importers resided in Dorset and 44 per cent of their cargoes were owned by either shipmasters or mariners. Yet by the late fourteenth century, 81 per cent of the group resided in Somerset, and merchants, not shipmasters, owned all but two of the cargoes.[80] In 1381–91, Somerset importers may have accounted for only 4 per cent of importers and owned 5 per cent of the cargoes (Table 6.4), but they were responsible for at least 10 per cent of the iron imports, 75 per cent of the alum, 18 per cent of the madder, and 10 per cent of the woad imports (Table 6.6). Their prominence in the importation of dyestuffs is especially striking and stems from the demands of the Somerset cloth industry.[81] This surge in Somerset importing activity stemmed from industrial and commercial expansion in Somerset,

[78] Touchard 1967a: 137, n. 190.

[79] In 1302–20, there were twenty three importers from Yarmouth, fewer than half of whom were shipmasters or mariners; by 1381–91, there were only four such importers and all were shipmasters and their *socii*.

[80] All the cargoes listed in Tables 6.5–6.7 were owned by Somerset merchants.

[81] For the prosperity of the Somerset cloth industry at this time, see Hewitt 1911: 405–15; Gray 1924: 21–2, 30–1; Pelham 1951: 249–53.

Table 6.5. *Wine importers and imports at the port of Exeter in the early and late fourteenth century*

	% of individual wine importers[a]		% of wine cargoes[b]		% of wine tuns imported[c]	
Residence	1302–20	1381–91	1302–20	1381–91	1302–20	1381–91
Exeter	28.6	15.5	55.1	34.6	59.3	43.6
Exe estuary	16.3	5.9	14.8	6.6	6.3	3.3
East Devon	18.8	5.9	13.1	5.9	10.7	4.5
South Devon	6.3	23.9	2.3	18.6	2.7	15.5
Other Devon	0.5	0.8	0.2	0.7	0.1	0.6
Somerset and Dorset	3.0	3.5	1.1	5.1	1.4	3.8
Other British Isles[d]	3.6	2.9	1.3	1.8	2.4	1.6
Channel Islands	–	1.1	–	0.6	–	0.7
Continent	1.6	7.8	1.3	4.4	5.1	7.7
Unidentified	21.1	32.7	10.8	21.7	12.0	18.7
Total	100.0	100.0	100.0	100.0	100.0	100.0
(Sums)	(559)	(373)	(1,671)	(665)	(9,877) (tuns)	(4,991) (tuns)

Source: Each period includes ten complete annual accounts (*Local PCA 1266–1321*: 71–186; PCA 1381/2–1390/1).

Notes: See Figure 1.1 for the Devon regions; the Exe estuary settlements have here been separated from the east Devon region.

[a]Each individual importer counted only once regardless of the number of times he or she imported wine during this period.

[b]Each cargo equals all the wine an importer brought in on one ship. Wine cargoes imported by partners were counted once for each partner but the cargoes of unnamed partners (such as mariners or *socii*) were only counted once.

[c]Wine cargoes of partners were split equally between the partners. The cargoes of *socii* of shipmasters who imported wine (twenty nine instances accounting for 169 tuns in 1381–91) were included in the shipmaster's region.

[d]Includes other English counties, Cornwall, Wales, and Ireland.

the western portion of which lay within Exeter's large hinterland. Similar developments occurred in other inland regions of Exeter's hinterland (east, mid, and Dartmoor Devon); they too sent an increasingly large number of importers to Exeter in the late middle ages.

At first glance, it appears that the Devon share of imports fell by about 12 per cent over the course of the fourteenth century, with only south Devon importers actually increasing their ownership of cargoes in this period (Table 6.4).[82] These figures are misleading, however,

[82] In 1302–20, Devon importers represented 50 per cent of individual importers and owned 73 per cent of the cargoes, compared to 1381–91 when they accounted for 44 per cent of importers and 61 per cent of the cargoes (Table 6.4).

Table 6.6. *Ownership (by percentage of total amounts imported) of selected imports at the port of Exeter, by importer's residence, 1381–91*

Residence	Wine	Iron	Salt[a]	Woad[b]	Madder	Alum[c]	Corn[d]	Herring	Linen cloth[e]
Exeter	43.6	50.8	11.2	67.0	39.0	13.9	11.4	38.1	19.1
Exe estuary	3.3	3.9	2.5	–	–	0.5	–	1.3	–
East Devon	4.5	3.8	1.6	–	–		1.4	5.8	–
South Devon	15.5	14.4	11.9	3.7	8.0	6.5	24.6	27.0	18.0
Other Devon	0.6	3.2	–	–	–	4.6	–	–	–
Somerset and Dorset	3.8	10.4	1.7	10.4	18.3	74.5	–	1.2	7.3
Other British Isles	1.6	0.5	25.0	6.4	19.0	–	4.9	5.6	–
Channel Islands	0.7	–	3.2	–	–	–	14.8	–	21.5
Continent	7.7	3.9	22.5	–	6.2	–	16.1	3.0	11.1
Unidentified	18.7	9.1	20.4	12.5	9.5	–	26.8	18.0	23.0
Total	100.0	100.0	100.0	100.0	100.0	100.0	100.0	100.0	100.0
Sums	4,991 tuns	216 tons	7,506 qtrs	435 qtrs	211 bales	216 cwt	528 qtrs	201 lasts	549 pieces

Source: PCA 1381/2–1390/1.

Notes: See Figure 1.1 for the Devon regions.

[a]The figure for the British Isles includes 15 muids of salt which at Exeter was equivalent to 5 quarters (Touchard 1967b: xx). Four cargoes of unspecified weight (3 Breton, 1 unidentified) were estimated to be 63 quarters each, the average size of Breton salt cargoes. All the Continental salt importers were from Brittany.

[b]Imported in tuns, pipes, quarters, bales, and sacks; bales could vary in weight so the figures offered here are in no way exact. Based on equivalent measures given in the customs accounts (PCA 1390/1; Touchard 1967b: xxvi–xxvii; Zupko 1985), the following was assumed: 1 tun = 2 pipes = 6 quarters = 24 cwt =6 bales = 9.6 sacks.

[c]Imported in tons, pipes, hogsheads, quintals, cwt, pounds, bales, and barrels; bales could vary in weight so the figures offered here are in no way exact. Based on equivalent measures given in the customs accounts (PCA 1360/1; Zupko 1985), the following equivalences were used: 1 ton = 2 pipes = 4 hogsheads = 4 barrels = 20 cwt = 20 quintals = 2160 pounds = 8 bales.

[d]Includes barley, beans, peas, rye, and (mostly) wheat.

[e]Imported in *cres*, seams, fardels, yards, hundreds (C), packs, ells, and pieces. Since the fardel could vary in size, the figures offered here are only estimates. It was assumed that all the linen was crescloth from Brittany so the following equivalences were employed (see PCA 1397/8; Touchard 1967a: 137; Touchard 1967b; xxviii): 1 piece = 25 *cres* = 100 ells = 100 yards = 1 C = 0.20 fardel = 0.10 seam = 0.10 pack. One of the continental cargoes was of unspecified size and is not included here. Bretons owned 92 per cent of the linen cloth listed under "Continent." About half of the Unidentified importers were also probably from Brittany; see Touchard 1967a: 137.

since they fail to account for the much larger percentage of unidentified importers in 1381–91 (31 per cent of the importers and 20 per cent of the cargoes). Five factors strongly suggest that at least three-quarters of the unidentified importers resided in Devon and that most probably came from inland locations in east Devon, mid Devon, and the Dartmoor borders region. One, the clerks writing the accounts did not record the residences of importers well known to them, a situation most likely to affect importers living in Exeter or its immediate hinterland of east Devon and the Exe estuary.[83] Scribes also tended to overlook the residences of importers who did not claim customs exemptions; since most inland towns in Devon did not enjoy such exemptions, the clerks rarely registered their importers' home residences.[84] Two, prosopographical evidence also points to Devon as the home of many in the unidentified group. Although the extant data are not precise enough to assign definite residences for these importers, the evidence (on their property ownership, commercial activity, public office, or jury service) does allow us to associate them with Devon, particularly the eastern and mid Devon regions.[85] Indeed, the difficulty of collecting enough data on these individuals to assign them definite residences is in itself an indication that they probably resided in smaller towns and conducted their affairs on a humbler scale than did the better-documented merchants in the larger towns.[86] Similarly, the smaller group of unidentified importers in 1302–20 reflects the greater numbers of highly visible urban merchants and importers from coastal settlements in this period. Three, very few of the unidentified importers had foreign names and almost all employed Devon ships to transport their goods, two characteristics that suggest homes in Devon rather than elsewhere. Four, the percentage of shipmaster- or mariner-importers from Devon declined significantly over the course of the fourteenth century (Table 6.4), implying that inland importers replaced them. This assumption is strengthened by the fact

[83] This trend is evident in both periods; see *Local PCA 1266–1321* and PCA passim. The quality and abundance of the documentation for Exeter is such that all its traders have certainly been identified, ensuring that few of the unidentified importers resided there.

[84] See above, pp. 196–9 for the exemptions allowed at Exeter. When inland importers did have their residences recorded in the accounts, it was usually because they claimed not to owe custom at Exeter; this was the situation for Taunton importers (Kowaleski 1993: 14, 38–9; PCA passim).

[85] Evidence on property ownership drawn from deeds and estate documents in the DRO, PRO, and BL; on commercial activity from the analyses of MCR and PCR debts and PRO CP 40, C131, and C241 debt analysis (above pp. 213–14 and below pp. 282–3 and Appendix 1); on public office from appointments as tax collectors and various county offices; on jury service from jury lists for hundred, county, and central courts (PRO KB 9, JUST 1 and JUST3).

[86] For the small size of Devon inland towns, see above, Table 2.1.

that very few of the unidentified importers were shipmasters. Although the declining presence of shipmaster-importers affected south Devon as much or more than the other regions, the better quality of surviving data for south Devon allows us to identify more of the importers from this region, suggesting that the bulk of the unidentified importers came from the less well-documented inland regions of east and mid Devon.[87] Five, the pattern of commercial activity among the unidentified importers closely paralleled that of importers from inland Devon regions. Both groups maintained a relatively low profile in the commercial life of the ports, appearing in the customs accounts only once or twice.[88] This pattern of activity was typical of the chapman or merchant of a small Devon market town who only occasionally ventured into maritime trade. The limited types and the small quantities of goods brought in by the unidentified and inland Devon importers were also similar; their percentage of the trade in goods like wine, iron, salt, some dyestuffs, corn, and herring was usually lower than their overall share of the cargoes (compare Tables 6.4 and 6.6).[89] Together these factors give us grounds for assuming that most of the large group of unidentified importers in 1381–91 came from inland locations in Exeter's hinterland.

If three-quarters of the unidentified importers and cargoes in each sample period are redistributed among the non-Exeter importers of Devon, then their share of the port trade at Exeter can be seen to have risen during the late middle ages. The percentage of Devon importers at Exeter would thus have climbed by 17 per cent and their share of cargoes by 3 per cent over the course of the fourteenth century. The more prominent position of Devon (and Somerset) importers probably resulted from rising prosperity and commercial development in these regions. For inland locations in Devon and Somerset, the upsurge was most likely generated by greater production in the cloth industry and by agricultural diversification.[90] For the coastal regions, particularly south Devon, the growth proceeded more from the development of

[87] H. R. Watkins' collection of sources in *Dartmouth* and *Totnes* means that the sources for two of the three largest towns in the region have long been available to historians. The high profile of south Devon port towns in the naval records (PRO E101, *Wardrobe book*), national customs accounts (PRO E122 and E101 Bordeaux wine accounts), and privateering records (*W.C. Chancery proc.*) of the period also furnishes extensive data on the shipowners, shipmasters, mariners, and traders of these ports; see also Kowaleski 1992.

[88] The average number of cargoes per unidentified importer was 1.2 and 1.6 for importers from east, south, mid, and Dartmoor Devon; for Exeter it was 4.4 and for the Exe estuary 2.2.

[89] The high percentage of linen cloth owned by unidentified importers (Table 6.6) was probably due to a small number of unidentified Breton and Channel Islands importers.

[90] See above, n. 81 and Chapter 1.

their fleets and their increasing role as carriers in the Atlantic trade.[91]

While Devon importers, particularly those from inland locations, saw their share of trade at the port of Exeter rise in the late fourteenth century, there is no getting around the fact that the portion controlled by Exeter merchants themselves declined substantially. The percentage of Exeter importers fell by 9 per cent, its merchants' share of cargoes by 19 per cent, and their portion of the wine tunnage by 16 per cent (Tables 6.5 and 6.6). These figures would not be affected, moreover, by redistributing the unidentified importers since the surviving documentation for Exeter is so rich that all its importers have certainly been identified.[92] It appears therefore that the growing presence of other Devon importers at Exeter, particularly those from coastal areas of south Devon and inland locations elsewhere (and in Somerset), cut into the control Exeter merchants were able to exercise over trade through their own port.

For several reasons, however, this situation should not be interpreted wholly as a sign of depression or economic crisis in Exeter. One, trade statistics for the local markets of Exeter show them to have been not only healthy but booming in the late fourteenth century; ale-brewing, hostelling, and the fish trade all operated at relatively higher levels of production than in most previous decades.[93] Obviously Exeter relied on more than maritime trade to maintain prosperity. Two, Exeter merchants had always been heavily oriented to serving markets in their hinterland, garnering profits from supplying its needs and channelling its goods overseas.[94] Economic development in their hinterland (as indicated in the higher profile of inland merchants in Exeter's late medieval port trade) would thus have benefited Exeter merchants as well as the hinterland's. Three, while the actual numbers of Exeter merchants involved in maritime trade certainly fell, the relative percentage of the town's population in maritime trade may have risen in the late fourteenth century, thus distributing the profits of maritime trade across a wider spectrum of urban society.[95] The average cargoes per importer decreased

[91] Above, pp. 29–36; Kowaleski 1992. Note also that importers from Newton Abbot, an inland town of south Devon located about 15 miles south-west of Exeter, also became more prominent at Exeter in the late fourteenth century, accounting for twenty eight cargoes in 1381–91.

[92] See below, Appendices 1 and 3, for these sources and the prosopographical analyses that have allowed virtually all Exeter householders to be identified, particularly in the late fourteenth century.

[93] See above, Table 3.2 and pp. 89–91, and below, pp. 307–12 for the fish trade.

[94] This theme is developed at greater length in the next section and in Chapter 7.

[95] See below, p. 252.

in the late fourteenth century, implying that profits may have been more evenly distributed.[96] Four, Exeter merchants actually expanded their control over several key commodities in the later period, taking advantage of the absence of Picard importers to win 67 per cent of the woad imports (compared to 12 per cent in the early part of the century) and capturing 51 per cent of the iron cargoes (when they had previously enjoyed only 35 per cent of such imports). Five, and most important, the Exeter merchants may have lost some ground to other Devon importers, but they still owned far more cargoes than importers from any other town or region (Table 6.4). Exeter importers each owned an average of 4.4 cargoes, almost twice as many as their closest rivals in the Exe estuary (2.2 cargoes), Somerset (2.6) and east Devon (1.8). South Devon importers may have outnumbered those from Exeter, but their share of cargoes (1.6) was considerably less. Exeter's portion of the wine trade also fell but its merchants still controlled 44 per cent of the wine tunnage, almost three times the amount brought in by any other group of importers (Table 6.5). This dominance in the wine trade, the port's single most valuable commodity, gave Exeter residents control over roughly 41 per cent of the value of goods imported into Exeter in 1381–91, a striking percentage given that they represented only 12 per cent of all importers (Tables 6.4 and 6.7).[97]

What do we know about these Exeter importers? In 1381–91, almost half were merchants, but 20 per cent were artisans, 11 per cent were innholders or taverners, 7 per cent were members of the clergy, and 4 per cent served in professional posts such as clerk or lawyer.[98] Merchants clearly dominated the trade, not only in terms of personnel but also in terms of merchandise since they controlled 75 per cent of the Exeter-owned cargoes. Artisanal importers usually sought merely to acquire the raw materials of their trade (although some also dabbled in the ubiquitous wine trade). Hence, the smith John Doccombe imported iron, Thomas le Glasiere shipped in 4 pipes of glass, the bowyer Thomas Pye imported bowstaves and tar, and the dyer Walter Hakeworthy

[96] In 1302–20, Exeter importers each owned an average of 6.4 cargoes compared to 4.4 cargoes in 1381–91 (see Table 6.4).

[97] The commodities listed in Tables 6.6 and 6.7 represented 81 per cent of all commodities imported at Exeter (Table 6.2).

[98] The following survey is based on a prosopographical analysis of the sixty nine Exeter residents who imported cargoes in PCA 1381/2–1390/1. There were thirty merchants and five others had "secondary" occupations as merchants; the occupations of seven men could not be identified. For Exeter importers in 1377, see above, pp. 108–10. Prosopographic analysis of the merchants for the earlier period remains to be done; the much larger number of Exeter importers in 1302–20, combined with the greater instability of surnames in this period and more spotty coverage of the freedom register, also make precision more difficult and the task more arduous.

Table 6.7. *Approximate customed values (in £) of selected imports at the port of Exeter, by importer's residence, 1381–91*

Residence	Wine £	Iron £	Salt £	Dyes £	Herring £	Linen Cloth £	Total Values £	%
Exeter	8,702	329	126	365	253	218	9,993	41.4
Exe estuary	652	26	28	–	9	–	715	3.0
East Devon	898	24	18	–	38	–	978	4.1
South Devon	3,094	93	134	28	179	206	3,734	15.5
Other Devon	116	21	–	–	–	–	137	.6
Somerset and Dorset	770	68	19	72	8	83	1,020	4.2
Other British Isles	323	3	281	54	37	–	698	2.9
Channel Islands	142	–	37	–	–	245	424	1.7
Continent	1,534	26	254	8	20	127	1,969	8.1
Unidentified	3,731	59	230	71	120	263	4,474	18.5
Total	19,962	649	1,127	598	664	1,142	24,142	100.0

Source: PCA 1381/2–1390/1.

Notes: See Figure 1.1 for the Devon regions. These figures represent at best only very rough estimates of the customed value (often lower than wholesale prices and always considerably below retail prices) as given in the royal customs accounts for Devon in the 1380s and 1390s. They do not take into account differences in quality and are further cast in doubt by the difficulty of calculating equivalences for the various measures used for dyestuffs (see notes to Table 6.6).

The following values were employed here: *wine*: £4 per ton (James 1971: 30); *iron*: £3 per ton (PRO E122/102/14); *salt*: 3*s* per quarter (PRO E122/102/14, 158/24; see also Bridbury 1955: 176); *woad*: 65*s* per pipe (an average of the 80*s* per pipe in PCA 1383/4 and PRO E122/102/14 and the 50*s* per pipe in E122/40/18); *madder*: 12*s* per bale (average of the 6*s* 4*d* per bale in PRO E122/40/18 and the 17*s* 6*d* per bale in E122/40/23); *herring*: 66*s* per last (PRO E122/40/23); *linen cloth*: 20*d* per cres (PRO E122/40/18 and 40/23) was the most common value employed.

No customed values could be found for alum, rye, and peas in these years so no total values for alum or corn could be calculated. The value of all the corn imported was, however, no greater than £90 while the value of the alum cargoes was probably £100–180.

brought in woad, madder, and alum.[99] Taverners, innholders, and the professionals concentrated on wine (and to a lesser extent herring) imports, while the clergy limited their imports to a few tuns of wine for their households or building materials for their churches. The vast majority of the Exeter importers also enjoyed the commercial and

[99] Doccombe: PCA 1390/1, 1395/6, 1398/9; Glasiere: PCA 1357/8; Pye (called Thomas Boghier): PCA 1395/6; Hakeworthy: PCA 1395/6, 1396/7. Pye/Boghier also imported fruit and wine.

political privileges of the town freedom; 82 per cent had joined the freedom by the time they started importing and almost all sought entry soon thereafter (since membership allowed them to avoid the import tolls).[100] The prevalence of rich merchants and freedom members was reflected in the high percentage of importers who served in the most powerful civic offices; 70 per cent eventually achieved oligarchic status, most in Rank A.[101]

While wealthy merchants of the oligarchy clearly dominated the import market, it is significant that artisans, Rank D men who held no civic office, and younger traders not yet accepted into the freedom handled almost 20 per cent of the Exeter cargoes. The demographic devastations of the late middle ages may have opened up opportunities in the import trade to some; in Exeter, the presence of such "new men" in the port trade was most visible in the 1350s and 1360s. Also influential in making the import trade accessible to a wider range of participants were the lower costs and risks associated with coastal trade. The relative stability of the coastal import trade, where importers were able to bypass many of the difficulties involved in purchasing goods abroad, attracted less well-established traders. In turn, investment in the coastal import trade offered these men the opportunity to better their lot by either bypassing merchant middlemen or adopting this lucrative role themselves. The social mobility which sometimes resulted can be seen in the political rise of the importers active in 1381–91. At the beginning of this period, about 50 per cent belonged to the oligarchy, but eventually 70 per cent were elected to one of the top municipal offices. This public recognition may have come in part because of the wealth and position these importers accrued through the profits of maritime trade.[102]

The varied backgrounds and potential for advancement of Exeter importers should not obscure, however, the extent to which an elite group of merchants dominated this trade. In 1381–91 only twenty men (33 per cent of the city's importers) owned 70 per cent of all the cargoes imported by Exeter merchants. Even this group had an internal hierarchy representing 15 per cent of Exeter importers (nine men, all but one Rank A oligarchs) who alone handled 44 per cent of all the

[100] This figure excludes the clergy who generally did not enter the freedom. Three of the men who joined later were apprentices who had not yet finished out their terms with their merchant-masters. Three men never appeared in the freedom lists, but two of these were professional clerks who resided in Exeter only for a short time.

[101] Compare this figure with the 21 per cent of householders in 1377 who achieved this rank (above, Table 3.4).

[102] For other evidence that some men climbed the social and political ladder with the help of their profits from maritime trade, see above, pp. 110–11.

cargoes and 46 per cent of wine (by volume) imported by Exeter residents. John Talbot, the second richest man in 1377 and the most active exporter in Exeter, imported twenty two cargoes (and seven different commodities) during this decade, considerably more than the 4.4-cargo average for all the city's importers. Adam Scut had eighteen cargoes, including 299 tuns of wine which alone represented about 14 per cent of all the wine imported by Exeter merchants during this decade. Scut and Talbot both specialized in wine and iron imports, the most common focus of the late medieval Exeter merchants. In the early fourteenth century, a similarly exclusive internal hierarchy existed; just under 11 per cent of the importers (the twenty one who owned fifteen or more cargoes apiece in 1302–20) controlled 41 per cent of all the cargoes. Their ranks included the ten-times mayor, Philip Lovecok, who owned sixty one cargoes in this ten-year period, including 1,928 tuns of wine and 745 quarters of grain, as well as herring, salt, wax, alum, canvas, iron, saffron, almonds, pitch, and salt-cellars. This impressive list indicates the grander scale of operations of Exeter's importers in the early fourteenth century.

Although the trading activities of late fourteenth-century Exeter importers rarely matched those of their early fourteenth-century counterparts (or those of the bigger London merchants), the goods handled by these Exeter merchants could represent a substantial investment.[103] Within the provincial sphere of Exeter, however, the sums invested in trading ventures were impressive, as indicated by the goods owned by Roger Plente, one of the foremost Exeter merchants. After Plente died (around 1375), his son claimed that Roger had in his possession 60 tuns of wine (worth £200), 50 quarters of salt (£134), iron, tin, and lead (£100), various spices (£100), a ship (£80), linen and wool cloths (£67), gold and silver money (£200), various items of plate and household utensils (£100), and livestock (£20).[104] If the wine was retailed at 6*d* per gallon (the going rate in Exeter), it alone could bring in £378 and thus a profit of £178. Other merchants also kept large amounts of wine and salt (up to 300 quarters in one case) in temporary storage at Exeter or Topsham; these stockpiled goods represented significant investments.[105] Only the wealthy could afford to trade on such a scale or to tie up their capital in such ventures. Some merchants invested so much capital in maritime trade that they literally had to wait until their ship came in to meet financial obligations. Such was the case with the

[103] For London, see James 1971: 196–217; Williams 1970: 152–4.

[104] *Year books of Richard II, 13 Richard II*: 11–12; the value of the salt seems inflated.

[105] For example, PRO JUST1/192, m. 2; PRO E159/171, Michaelmas recorda, m. 1d; PRO CP40/472, m. 199; MCR 1299/1300, m. 22; 1319/20, m. 14d; *CIM*, vol. 6: 75.

oligarchic merchant John Sleghe whose repayment schedule for a debt was predicated on the next arrival of the *Peter* of Exmouth, a ship carrying 600 quarters of salt he owned with three others.[106] Yet many Exeter merchants were probably shielded from the worst risks entailed in trade by sea since they rarely travelled abroad, preferring instead to concentrate on the inland distribution of imports (an emphasis noticeable in the few export goods held by Roger Plente). In contrast to their counterparts from Dartmouth and Plymouth, Exeter merchants rarely travelled to France for business purposes by the late fourteenth century (although such trips had been more common in the late thirteenth and early fourteenth centuries).[107] The financial risks faced by Exeter merchants were thus minimized by their concentration on the acquisition and redistribution of foreign goods by coastal trade.

Exeter importers favored wine above all other commodities, particularly in peacetime; in 1302–21, before the onset of the Hundred Years War, 81 per cent of all the Exeter importers owned cargoes of wine.[108] Even in the more troublesome decade of 1381–91, 84 per cent of all Exeter importers brought in wine cargoes, compared to 62 per cent of non-Exeter importers.[109] Since the value of the wine trade literally dwarfed all other imports (Table 6.7), the concentration of Exeter merchants on this commodity paid off handsomely, endowing the relatively small group of Exeter importers with control over some 41 per cent of the value of all goods shipped into the port.[110] This degree of control by such a small group of traders is impressive, especially when we also consider their domination of the local export trade.[111]

A closer look at the wine import trade illustrates the commercial options available to merchant-importers. Just under 40 per cent of the wine imported in the late fourteenth and early fifteenth centuries came directly to Exeter from France (Table 6.1); in these cases, it is likely that the importers or their agents had personal contact with wine dealers in Bordeaux or La Rochelle.[112] In the early fourteenth century, Exeter

[106] See MCR 1360/1, mm. 1, 7d; PCA 1360/1; and his entry in Table A3.1. For another example, see MCR 1291/2, m. 26.

[107] For Exeter merchants abroad, see MCR 1288/9, m. 19d; 1299/1300, m. 4; 1301/2, m. 37d; 1308/9, m. 45; 1309/10, m. 32d; 1317/18, m. 19d; 1354/5, m. 22d; 1387/8, m. 47; CRA 1392/3; PRO CP40/497, m. 143d.

[108] 160 of the 198 importers (Tables 6.4 and 6.5).

[109] Fifty eight of the sixty nine Exeter importers (Tables 6.4 and 6.5).

[110] The total value of goods imported through Exeter is impossible to calculate, but the commodities noted in Table 6.7 accounted for almost 80 per cent of all commodities (Table 6.2) arriving at Exeter during this period.

[111] See above, p. 234.

[112] For dealings by English merchants there, see James 1971: 160–76; for a Plymouth merchant in Bordeaux, see *Cal. P&MR London*, vol. 2: 245, 248–9.

merchants like Nicholas Busse and Thomas de Tetteburne themselves travelled to Gascony, but by the late fourteenth century, only the few Exeter merchants who owned ships, such as Roger Plente and Adam Scut, may have occasionally made such visits.[113] Plente's ship, the *George* of Exmouth, was annually so loaded down with wine on the autumn trip from Bordeaux that Plente had to purchase licences to discharge lower down the estuary since his ship could not make its way up the narrow channel to Topsham.[114] These direct importers always ranked among the port's top wine merchants; although representing only 28 per cent of wine importers, they brought in roughly 39 per cent of the wine in the last two decades of the century (Table 6.1). The annual imports of Plente and Scut averaged 30–33 tuns, sums that far exceeded the overall Exeter average of 4 tuns per year (although these amounts hardly compare to the 103 tuns annually brought in by Philip Lovecok in 1302–20).[115] Merchants from other Devon towns also occasionally imported wine directly from France to Exeter by the late fourteenth century; most were from port towns (such as Richard and Roger Neel of Topsham, John Baker of Dartmouth, and William Bentley of Plymouth) and only a few from inland towns (such as Gilbert Smyth and William Leg of Newton Abbot).[116] Breton and Guernsey shipmasters, as well as Gascon and Spanish merchants, also appeared as direct wine importers in Exeter although their share of the wine trade at Exeter was never great (Table 6.6).

Over 60 per cent of the wine imported to Exeter in the late fourteenth and early fifteenth centuries arrived not straight from overseas but via coastal craft from Dartmouth, Plymouth, Southampton, or other first ports of call for the wine ships (Table 6.1).[117] We can see the stops made by these ships on their way to Exeter by comparing the Bordeaux wine accounts with the Exeter local port customs accounts. In October of 1385, for example, the *St Mary* of Bayonne left Bordeaux with 144 tuns of wine owned by forty four merchants. Nineteen days later this ship showed up in Exeter with only 51 tuns of wine owned by one

[113] MCR 1305/6, m. 45; 1317/18, m. 19d. Plente's ship, n. 104, above. Scut's ship: *CIM*, vol. 7: 141. For their direct imports, see PRO E122/102/14, 40/18, 40/23.

[114] MCR 1365/6, m. 6d; 1366/7, m. 17d; 1367/8, m. 15d; 1368/9, m. 7d.

[115] Plente: PCA 1353/4–1371/2. Scut: PCA 1358/9–1399/1400; Lovecok: PCA 1302/3–1319/20. London vintners could bring in even larger cargoes to their port (James 1971: 161) .

[116] For this and the following, see PRO E122/102/14 (Neel, Breton shipmasters); 40/18 (Baker, Neel, Bentley); 40/23 (Neel, Smith, Guernsey, and Breton shipmasters); 40/15 and 40/26 (Leg, Smith, Spanish importers). For Gascon importers, see PRO E101/80/23.

[117] For this re-export trade, see James 1971: 180–7; pp. 226, 232–3, above.

importer, and with an added cargo of iron and steel.[118] Similarly, the *Trinity* of Dartmouth departed Bordeaux with over 83 tuns of wine but was customed at Exeter twenty five days later for only 4 tuns of wine, owned by two Exeter men whose names had not appeared on the list of importers at Bordeaux. Other ships carried cargoes into Exeter that were very similar to what they had held when leaving Bordeaux, but the importers' names had all changed, suggesting that the Exeter importers or their agents had purchased these cargoes in the English ports where the ships first docked.[119]

In the late middle ages, foreign goods often reached Exeter by coastal craft which came from Dartmouth and Plymouth.[120] The Mediterranean cargoes (including iron, oil, almonds, wax, fruit, and alum) brought to these two south Devon ports by Iberian ships proved especially attractive to Exeter traders since Spanish and Portuguese ships infrequently stopped at Exeter (Table 6.3).[121] The Exeter merchant John Westcote himself travelled to Dartmouth to buy 2,000 cwt of iron from John Boys, a Dartmouth shipmaster who then freighted the iron to Exeter in his ship.[122] In 1402, Simon Grendon, John Grilles, Roger Shaplegh, and five other Exeter merchants acquired 18 tuns of oil, 26 bales of almonds, 100 quintals of alum, and over 10 quintals of wax from various sellers at Dartmouth; all the goods came from a ship laden at Seville.[123] Coastal shipments from Plymouth were less frequent because it was much farther from Exeter than was Dartmouth. Yet Plymouth's role as the county's foremost bulking center for exports meant that it too shipped goods via coastal trade to Exeter, including canvas, lead, white glass from Rouen, and wine.[124]

The maritime orientation of these two towns (Dartmouth in particular was home to many shipowners, shipmasters, and mariners), combined with the limited market in their own hinterlands, encouraged Dartmouth

118 PRO E101/183/11 and PCA 1385/6 for this and the following.

119 For example, the *Grace Dieu* of Plymouth, *Petrock* of Dartmouth, *Trinity* of Exmouth, and *James* of Teignmouth in PCA 1385/6 and PRO E101/183/11.

120 Southampton was also an important source although it probably played a larger role in the earlier period when Hampshire ships were particularly prominent at Exeter (see Table 6.3). For the foreign trade at Dartmouth and Plymouth in the late fourteenth century, see above, pp. 231–2.

121 *W.C. Chancery proc.*, passim; PRO E122 passim; E101/40/2; *CIM*, vol. 3: 217–18; Childs 1978.

122 SQMT 1353; see also PRO E122/177/16 for other Exeter acquisitions of iron in Dartmouth.

123 *CIM*, vol. 7: 129.

124 *Local PCA 1266–1321*: 77; *Fabric accounts*: 98, 171; Kowaleski 1992: esp. Tables 7.1, 7.2.

and Plymouth traders to extend their commercial activities to other ports. Both their trade and activities as carriers increased dramatically over the course of the fourteenth century (Tables 6.3, 6.4) as these ports took advantage of their role in England's naval efforts during the Hundred Years War.[125] Their trade in certain commodities was particularly marked; they owned 24 per cent of all imported grain, over 17 per cent of all wine, and 16 per cent of all iron freighted to Exeter in 1381–91.[126] Most of the Dartmouth and Plymouth men who controlled these cargoes were rich, politically prominent merchants. Dartmouth importers like Richard Harry, John Hawley, William Knolle, and William Smale all served their town as mayor and also owned ships (Hauley possessed as many as twelve and William Smale had five).[127] Dartmouth shipmasters also did business at Exeter where they owned 18 per cent of the Dartmouth cargoes. Their ranks included Robert Forde, who was part-owner of the *Rose* of Dartmouth and also dabbled in the export trade, as well as Henry Galyman, who mastered at least nine different ships over his long career and imported small quantities of herring, iron, salt, and wine.[128] Shipmasters were also prominent among Plymouth importers although, like the Dartmouth shipmasters, their imports did not match those brought in by Plymouth merchants, many of whom also owned and mastered ships. The merchant Richard Rowe, for example, served as Plymouth's mayor and in numerous county offices, owned two ships, imported large quantities of wine at Exeter and Plymouth, and exported hake, dried merling, and cloth.[129] Rowe,

[125] In 1302–20, there were three ships from Plymouth and thirty five from Dartmouth; in 1381–91, there were sixty three from Dartmouth and thirty one from Plymouth; see also Kowaleski 1992.

[126] They owned 545 quarters of grain, 596½ tuns of wine, and 23½ tons of iron. In this period they represented 83 per cent of all south Devon importers and were thus largely responsible for that region's imports as portrayed in Tables 6.5, 6.6, and 6.7. With the exception of wine, imports by Dartmouth residents considerably outweighed those brought to Exeter by Plymouth traders.

[127] PCA passim. Two other major importers (John Monfort, who served as bailiff, and Alexander Juyl, who served as deputy aulnager and county tax collector) may also have been mayors but gaps in the record for the years they were active prevent an exact determination (PRO E159/179, Easter recorda, m. 7; *CFR, 1391–9*: 266). For offices, see *Dartmouth*: 182–4; Windeatt 1911: 134–7. For ships, see PRO E101/42/22 (Harry); *Dartmouth*: 58, 375, 380; *CCR 1385–9*: 271; *1392–6*: 174; PRO C47/6/4, roll 5; PRO E101/4 1/37–38, 42/22 (Hawley); *CIM*, vol. 7: 202 (Juyl); PRO E101/42/22 (Knolle); *CCR 1341–2*: 629; *1360–4*: 27 (Smale).

[128] Forde: PCA 1396/7, 1398/9; *CIM*, vol. 7: 376; *Dartmouth*: 382; PRO E122/40/18. Galyman made at least thirty three trips to Exeter (PCA 1356/7–1372/3), all in Dartmouth ships.

[129] PRO E159/175, Michaelmas recorda, m. 38d; PRO E122/40/23, 40/26; PCA 1383/4, 1390/1, 1396/7, 1399/1400; Bracken 1931: 277; Dunning and Stevenson 1940.

like several other prominent merchant/shipowners of Dartmouth and Plymouth, also profited greatly from privateering.[130]

A high percentage of the Exe estuary importers were also shipmasters; in the early fourteenth century their numbers were swelled by estuarine mariners who took advantage of portage provisions to import one tun or less of wine custom-free (Table 6.4).[131] Most came from Topsham and Kenton, and others from Powderham, Lympstone, and present-day Exmouth. Although Exe-estuary importers handled about 7 per cent of all cargoes in 1381–91, their actual share of the volume and value of trade was considerably lower (Tables 6.5, 6.6, 6.7), in part because shipmasters did not possess the capital or purely commercial interests of merchants. The Neel family of Topsham illustrates the mix of mercantile and maritime activities typical of many importers from the region. In the 1340s John Neel served as shipmaster of at least four different ships and occasionally imported small cargoes of wine; during the 1350s he mastered the *Chivaler* of Exmouth and began importing small quantities of herring, peas, iron, and canvas by coast.[132] Like most shipmasters of the day, he was also pressed into royal service, transporting troops to Gascony on at least two occasions.[133] In the 1360s he also began importing goods aboard ships he did not master and seems to have acquired his own ship, the *Margaret* of Exmouth, for which he also acted as master.[134] This ship, valued at £40 in 1395, was then owned by Roger Neel (probably John's son) and by Roger's son Richard Neel.[135] Like John, Roger was an active shipmaster, ordered by the Crown to perform naval service, and was at the helm of the *Margaret* on no fewer than twenty two trips to Exeter over the course of thirty years.[136] But his commercial activities were far more ambitious

Humphrey Passour (PCA 1360/1) and John Sampson (PCA 1356/7, 1368/9) also imported goods at Exeter, imported and exported goods at Plymouth (PRO E122/102/14, 158/34), were mayors of Plymouth (Bracken 1931: 277) and owned ships (PRO E101/42/22; PRO C47/30/8).

130 For the privateering of Rowe and others in Dartmouth and Plymouth, see Dunning and Stevenson 1940; Gardiner 1966; Pistono 1979; *W. C. Chancery proc.*, passim; Appleby 1992: 90–2. For how these activities channelled goods to Exeter, see *CIM*, vol. 3: 217–18; vol. 7: 129.

131 See Kowaleski 1993: 13, 18–20 for these mariners and portage. Note also that the tendency for medieval scribes to give "Exmouth" as the home port of any large ship coming from an estuarine settlement makes it difficult to specify the exact residence of many estuarine mariners and shipmasters.

132 PRO E122/158/10; PCA 1341/2–1359/60 passim.

133 Hewitt 1966: 183; PRO E101/36/20.

134 PCA 1361/2, 1366/7, 1368/9, 1370/1.

135 *CIM*, vol. 6: 75; vol. 7: 141; for their relationship, see ECL D&C 3550, f. 74.

136 PRO E101/41/30; PCA 1369/70–1398/9; he also served as shipmaster on three other ships for five voyages during this time.

and varied than John's had ever been. Although he continued to import goods on ships he mastered, he more often imported and exported goods on the ships of others.[137] Some of these ventures proved risky, since his failure to pay debts to such prominent Exeter merchants as Robert Wilford led to his outlawry.[138] He protested Wilford's suit on the grounds that he had been overseas (probably on a voyage transporting pilgrims to Santiago) and knew nothing of the complaint.[139] But Roger must have seen the problems that lay ahead since he had transferred most of what he owned (except for 300 quarters of salt he had stored in Topsham) to two men from Topsham and one from Exeter. Nor do these problems seem to have proved much of a setback since he and his son Richard continued to be very active players in the local land market, leasing large tracts of arable, pasture, and meadow in both Topsham and the neighboring manor of Cowick.[140] Indeed, the wealth they accumulated allowed the son Richard to bypass the maritime career of the older Neels. Unlike John and Roger, Richard never served as a shipmaster, but confined his activities to exports of small amounts of cloth, imports of salt and wine, and large-scale land transactions.[141]

Inland merchants also expanded their importing activities at Exeter during the late middle ages, although the exact scale of their imports at Exeter cannot be measured.[142] Traders from such mid Devon market towns as Chulmleigh and South Molton regularly visited Exeter, as did their east Devon counterparts from Crediton, Tiverton, Bradninch, Cullompton, Culmstock, Silverton, and Honiton, and merchants from the Dartmoor towns of Ashburton, Tavistock, and Okehampton.[143] Some of these merchants (mostly from east and mid Devon) occasionally exported cloth through Exeter or distributed local cloth in regional markets.[144] Most of these traders were wealthy members of their town's or even the region's elite. They included men such as John Prentis of Honiton, who imported wine and oil at Exeter on at least six occasions and was named a collector of the lay subsidy in Devon, as well as

[137] PCA 1367/8, 1382/3–1398/9; PRO E122/40/16, 40/23.

[138] *CIM*, vol. 6: 75–6; *CPR, 1391–6*: 399, 696; *CPR, 1396–9*: 36.

[139] *CPR, 1391–6*: 565; *CIM*, vol. 6: 75.

[140] DD 50104, 50107; W1258M/G6/50; ECL D&C 3550, f. 74; *CPR, 1396–9*: 108.

[141] PRO E122/40/18, 40/23; PCA 1389/90, 1392/3–1399/1400. For his land dealings, see above, n. 140.

[142] For the greater percentage of inland Devon merchants at Exeter, see the arguments made above, pp. 247–9.

[143] Only occasionally did north Devon importers (usually from Barnstaple) venture south to trade at Exeter. Between 1361 and 1396, eleven importers from Barnstaple appeared at Exeter, but only two in 1381–91 (PCA passim).

[144] For their exports, see below, p. 266; for their role in the local cloth trade, see above pp. 24–7.

Richard Chepman of Crediton, who brought in wine and iron and served as a local poll tax collector.[145] The east Devon importers focused mostly on herring, wine, iron, and salt, while those from mid Devon and the Dartmoor borders region emphasized alum, iron, and wine (Table 6.6). Fish imports also occasionally compelled inland merchants to enter the import trade, including John and William Grymell of Okehampton (just north of Dartmoor) and Richard Grymell of Winkleigh.[146] Despite the expanding presence of inland Devon importers at Exeter, however, these regions still relied heavily on the middleman services of Exeter merchants to purchase imports and handle cloth exports. It is to the paths whereby imported goods reached inland areas that we now turn our attention.

The inland distribution of imports

What happened to imported goods once they were unloaded at Topsham? Did the importers retail these items directly to consumers or sell them in bulk to other middlemen who handled retail distribution? How far inland did these imports travel? Which merchants supplied the inland towns with the foreign goods shipped to the port of Exeter? To what extent did the importer's residence or nature of the commodity influence how far inland imports might travel? Answers to these questions can be obtained more easily for the better-documented late fourteenth century when the extant sources facilitate prosopographical analysis of importers and traders in Exeter and its hinterland. In responding, we will also be able to delineate more clearly the size and scope of the port's hinterland, which extended eastwards into Somerset and Dorset, northwards to Exmoor, and westwards to Dartmoor.

A small percentage of importers, mostly clergy and gentry, brought goods in solely for their own consumption. This practice became more common in the late middle ages, perhaps because the rising price of wine and other imports made more households take advantage of the customs exemptions allowed on imports for personal use.[147] The amounts they imported were usually quite small; the canon Walter Levenant (one hogshead of wine), the dean of the cathedral (one pipe), the knight John Hill (one barrel), and the earl of Devon (1–4 tuns a year) were

[145] Prentis: *CFR 1391–9*: 266; PCA 1383/4, 1384/5, 1389/90; *Reg. Stafford*: 386. Chepman: PRO E179/95/55; PCA 1383/4, 1384/5, 1388/9.

[146] PCA 1392/3, 1393/4, 1394/5, 1395/6.

[147] No gentry and fourteen clerics imported in 1302–20, compared to seven gentry and six clergy in 1381–91. For this practice elsewhere, see James 1971: 178, 182–3.

typical examples.[148] Herring, fruit, fish, almonds, salt, wax, and wheat were also shipped in by these larger households. More exotic cargoes, such as the twenty iron swords owned by Earl Hugh Courtenay, were rare.[149] Some imports of building materials were also destined for personal or (in the case of religious institutions) corporate use. Examples include the roofing tiles imported by the prior of Plympton and vicar of Crediton, the regal boards shipped in by the local house of Dominicans, and the bell imported by the bishop of Exeter.[150]

Gentry and religious households were more likely, however, to buy wine and other imports from merchants than to engage directly in maritime trade themselves. Their purchases could be substantial, as was the Exeter canon John Cheyne's acquisition of 300 quarters of salt directly from an importer at Topsham.[151] The chief steward of the earl of Devon's household at Tiverton sent servants "to seek wine at Topsham," while the earl's bailiff at his manor of Topsham purchased salt, fish, and wheat from importers to send to Tiverton.[152] The bailiff of a gentry household at Porlock (34 miles north of Exeter near the Somerset coast) rode to Exeter and Topsham to buy wine for his mistress, a journey that took four days, but purchased fish at Exeter through purveying agents.[153] Other elite households sought wine, herring, salt, and other imports at Exeter and Topsham so often that their customary tenants owed carting duties to fetch such goods there. They included the Somerset households of the bishop of Winchester at Taunton (28 miles away) and a lay lord at Stogumber (30 miles away).

A second category of importers comprised those whose place of residence (outside the South-west) or whose occupation (shipmasters) made it unlikely that they would possess the necessary commercial connections or time to market their imports beyond the port itself. In the late thirteenth and early fourteenth centuries when foreign importers were more common at Exeter, they often compensated for their lack of knowledge about the local scene by employing local agents to market their goods. Thus Richard le Seler of Exeter sold 46 tuns of wine for Bruni le Carpenter of Bordeaux, while Serlo Taverner of Exeter contracted to receive 6*d* for every tun of wine he sold for a Gascon merchant

148 Levenant and Hill: PCA 1398/9; Dean: PCA 1384/5; Earl Hugh Courtenay: PCA 1358/9, 1359/60, 1365/6. One of the few exceptions was PCA 1418/19 when the earl of Devon imported 10 tuns of wine and the bishop of Exeter 17 tuns.

149 PCA 1359/60.

150 PCA 1356/7, 1366/7, 1396/7, 1418/19.

151 MCR 1392/3, m. 45.

152 W1258M/G6/50; BL Add. Ch. 64321, 64803.

153 Chadwyck Healy 1901: 431, 496.

and also brokered a corn sale for an importer from Sandwich.[154] Other foreigners, such as Peter le Monier and his brother James le Petit of Amiens, appointed young relatives to act as their agents in Exeter.[155] Neither foreign nor English importers from outside of Devon usually ventured inland to market their imports or engage in retail trade. Instead, like the Harwich merchants who sold wine to an Exeter taverner, they marketed their imports to other middlemen.[156] Sales in bulk, such as the over £40-worth of wheat and rye sold by a Winchelsea importer to an Exeter merchant, or the 12½ tuns of wine a Chichester importer released in one bargain, were the most convenient way for such out-of-towners to market their imports.[157] This was probably also the strategy followed by the Yarmouth herring merchants in the late middle ages when their representation at Exeter had grown quite small.[158] Since none of these men (nor any of the other herring importers from eastern England) was ever active at Exeter for more than one year, it is highly unlikely they had the commercial connections to do more than seek a buyer at Topsham as soon as their cargoes arrived. The fact that herring was often sold on board ship reinforces this impression.[159]

Shipmasters and mariners pursued many of the same options as foreign merchants and those from eastern England but operated on a far smaller scale. Crew members rarely imported more than one tun of wine and by the late fourteenth century even this limited activity had declined because of the rising costs of wine and freightage.[160] Shipmasters' wine imports were only slightly larger but they often accompanied these with other small imports, particularly if they were owner-operators of the ship. Shipmasters also frequently doubled as importers or agents for those who loaded cargoes on their vessels, especially in the later period when fewer foreign merchants travelled directly to Exeter.[161] By the late fourteenth century, shipmasters accounted for a larger percentage of importers (15 per cent) than earlier in the century when they represented only 8 per cent of importers and mariners 12 per cent. Even so, their share of the volume of trade was limited to less than 5 per cent of the iron, 6 per cent of the wine, 9

154 MCR 1319/20, m. 14d; 1289/90, m. 36; Roll 1, m. 4.

155 They appointed James's son, Thomas, for a period of three years (MCR 1314/15, m. 44d).

156 NQMT 1350. For the ubiquity of this practice in the wine trade, see James 1971: 180–90.

157 PRO E101/78/18; MCR 1320/1, m. 26d; *Local PCA 1266–1321*: 195.

158 In 1302–20 there were nineteen Yarmouth cargoes but in 1381–91, only one.

159 *Anglo-Norman custumal*: 37.

160 For this practice (called portage), see Kowaleski 1993: 13, 18.

161 See, for example, Wright 1862: 310; *Law merchant*, vol. 1: 116–21; Table 6.4, esp. notes b and c.

per cent of the salt, and 10 per cent of the linen cloth in 1381–91.[162] Their presence was important only when it came to fish (they owned 31 per cent of the cargoes), a business dominated largely by Cornish and Channel Island men, and corn (they owned 63 per cent of the cargoes and controlled 40 per cent of the amount imported). Sales by shipmasters were made mostly to merchant middlemen; shipmasters almost never appeared as retailers, except at their own home ports.[163] At Topsham even the Exe estuary shipmasters seem to have favored bulk sales to merchant middlemen over direct sales to consumers.[164]

Foreign and most English importers were also constrained by the city's prohibitions on trade by non-freedom members. They were forbidden to purchase any articles at Exeter or Topsham with the intention of reselling them later and were excluded from retailing any cloth and fish.[165] The authorities also attempted to discourage the use of local brokers to arrange for sales to third parties, probably because it was felt that such practices might raise prices.[166] Woad sales by non-freedom members were subject to the harshest restraints. While Exeter freemen could sell to anyone at any time, other importers had first to bring their woad to the city to be measured and assessed by the city's official woad assayers, then offer the woad for sale to city merchants alone for a period of forty days before being allowed to seek other buyers.[167] Efforts were made to extend these arrangements to potash and alum, but only the restrictions on woad sales prevailed into the late fourteenth century.[168] The cumulative effect of all these policies clearly favored local merchants and made it difficult for non-Exeter importers to compete equally once their goods reached the port. The Exeter triumph was complete by the late fourteenth century when hostile relations with most woad-producing areas in France terminated the direct imports of the Picard and Norman importers who had dominated woad imports during the late thirteenth and early fourteenth centuries (Table 6.6).

162 PCA 1381/2–1390/1; compare these figures with those in Table 6.6.

163 For example, the shipmaster William Elyot retailed wine in his home port of Brixham (PCA 1393/4, 1396/7, 1398/9; W1258M/X1, m. 3).

164 This was the case for Roger Neel; see MCR 1392/3, m. 45 for his sale of 200 quarters of salt; see also above, pp. 258–9. When shipmasters were litigants in debt cases at Exeter (MCR and PCR 1378/9–1387/8), the debts always involved other merchants and were for fairly large sums.

165 MCR 1301/2, m. 2d; *Anglo-Norman custumal*: 28; Rowe and Jackson 1973: xii–xiii.

166 MCR Roll 1, m. 4.

167 MCR 1289/90, mm. 10, 19; 1298/9, m. 33; 1328/9, m. 46d; 1334/5, m. 41d.

168 MCR 1285/6, m. 9. Woad assayers continued to be elected, but their work was considerably reduced as woad imports dwindled to a fraction of their earlier value (Table 6.2).

A third cateogory of importers – traders from Devon, Somerset, and Dorset – also had to deal with the favoritism shown to Exeter merchants, but could take advantage of their knowledge of local and regional markets and their more permanent ties to the community. Within this category, there were two sub-groups: those from port towns and those from inland locations. The maritime interests of the former often took such precedence that they rarely focused their energies on dealings beyond Topsham or Exeter. There were some exceptions, particularly among the Exe estuary importers who were operating at home on familiar territory. John Pomeroy of Topsham, for example, sold small amounts of oil and herring to the earl of Devon's Tiverton household and had dealings with other importers and traders from Dartmouth, Exeter, Teignmouth, and Tiverton.[169] On occasion modest importers from the smaller coastal locations, like Nicholas Flore of Paignton and John Certeyn of Dodbrooke, imported wine at Exeter and then retailed some in their home towns.[170] The few consumer sales made by port-town importers at Exeter usually involved building materials for religious institutions. The Dartmouth brazier/merchant John Brasyntere, for example, sold lead and 2,065 pounds of copper to the Exeter cathedral works for a new bell.[171] He shipped no fewer than nine bells to Exeter, along with other consignments of iron, lead, and copper that he probably sold in bulk, as indicated by the £19 debt the Exeter metalworker Robert Plomber owed him and the £7 promised him by the Exeter merchant John Clerk. Plomber was certainly a middleman and it was this type of sale that most importers from coastal locations pursued; like the second category of importers they quickly transferred their imports to local middlemen or other traders who gathered at the port. During the 1380s, for example, John Hawley of Dartmouth imported 11½ tuns of wine and 25 quarters of salt at Exeter and also made a sale of £8-worth of wine and another of £13 to Thomas Lomene of East Budleigh, sugggesting that his commercial activities in Exeter were limited to bulk sales made soon after his cargo was unloaded.[172]

Like importers from port towns, those from inland locations in Devon and its adjoining counties sold imports wholesale to traders, but they also carried on an active regional trade, offering goods to individual

[169] PCA 1361/2, 1368/9, 1370/1, 1384/5; BL Add. Ch. 64803; PRO CP40/509, m. 141.

[170] PCA 1385/6, 1394/5; W1258M/X1, mm. 3, 3d.

[171] PCA 1367/8, 1368/9, 1369/70, 1370/1, 1383/4, 1389/90, 1390/1; PRO E122/158/26; ECL D&C 2637, 2638, 2653; Scott 1968; and PCR 1–23 Ric. II, mm. 53, 90 for this and the following.

[172] PCA 1384/5, 1387/8, 1388/9; PCR 1–23 Ric. II, m. 70; PRO C241/175/50. Lomene also purchased £18-worth of goods from John Bonde, another importer (PCR 1–23 Ric. II, m. 71; PCA 1387/8).

consumers as well as to other merchants and middlemen in neighboring towns and villages. In 1381–91 the identifiable inland importers brought in at least 70 per cent of the alum, 21 per cent of the madder, 18 per cent of the iron, 8 per cent of the wine, and 4 per cent of the salt shipped to Exeter.[173] The Taunton merchants were the most prominent of these importers, accounting for almost 37 per cent of inland importers and 46 per cent of their cargoes. They imported most of the dyestuffs which the booming cloth industry in and near Taunton undoubtedly put to good use.[174] Taunton importers such as John Cullyng and William Marchaunt were clothiers who exported cloth from Exeter and were among their borough's foremost burgesses, serving in such county offices as poll tax collector.[175] Marchaunt also did business at Exeter with John Bovy, a prominent importer and citizen of Plymouth, as well as with William Taillor of Dunster who owed him £20.[176] Another Taunton importer, John Osbarn, left a list of his debts that shows his extensive commercial contacts throughout Somerset and Devon. They included £13 owed to him by Alexander Waleys, an A Rank oligarchic merchant of Exeter, along with debts of £5–52 from residents of Barnstaple, Crediton, and Bow in Devon, as well as Taunton, Lydeard, Ilchester, and Wellington in Somerset.[177]

Few of the Devon inland merchants imported goods as often or in such quantitites as Exeter merchants. Gilbert Smyth of Newton Abbot was one of the few who successfully competed with them, bringing in 152 tuns of wine in 1387–99 at Exeter (and at least another 10 tuns at Teignmouth), some directly from overseas.[178] He sold over £80-worth of wine to the Courtenay household at Tiverton, as well as sturgeon, one of the more expensive types of fish.[179] Given the scale of Smyth's importing activities, it is also likely that he distributed wine to taverners not only in his home town of Newton Abbot, but also in other small towns of east Devon. Another substantial inland merchant was Robert Bristowe of Chulmleigh (a small market town 20 miles north-west of

[173] These were the imports of the 6.5 per cent of identifiable importers from inland locations; as noted above (pp. 247–9) many of the importers in the unidentified group also probably came from inland towns and villages.

[174] See Gray 1924: 21–2, 30–4 and Pelham 1951: 248–56 for this industry.

[175] Cullyng: PCA 1384/5, 1386/7; PRO E122/40/18. Marchaunt: PCA 1365/6–1394/5; PRO E122/40/18. For their position at Taunton, see BL Harl. Ch. 49 B.46 and F.35, 53 E.25; Add. Ch. 25902; *CFR*, vol. 8: 388.

[176] MCR 1413/14, m. 28; PRO CP40/472, m. 81; 484, m. 415d; for Bovy, see also PRO E159/171 Hilary recorda, m. 1; PCR 1–23 Ric. II, m. 46; PCA 1396/7.

[177] PRO E143/16/1, no. 1; he was also appointed a subsidy collector in Somerset (*CFR*, vol. 9: 54, 147) and served as MP for Taunton (*CCR 1369–74*: 298).

[178] PCA 1386/7–1391/2, 1394/5, 1397/8–1399/1400; PRO E122/40/23, 40/26.

[179] CR 490; BL Add. Ch. 64321–22.

Exeter), who specialized in iron imports in exchange for which he exported local cloth to Spain.[180] He also made bulk purchases from the Exeter oligarch, John Smale.[181] Others who marketed cloth overseas or within the county while importing goods through Exeter included John Blackaller of Crediton, John Clayssh of South Molton, Richard Grymell of Winkleigh, John Grymell of Okehampton, and John Colyn of Culmstock.[182] All of these places were very small market towns in east and mid Devon; Culmstock was just a village, although it was located on the main road between Taunton and Exeter. Its native, John Colyn, was one of the more substantial clothiers in Devon.[183] Over a four-year period (1394–8), he aulnaged 530 straits or "narrow dozens," the coarse, relatively inexpensive cloth typical of Devon manufactures. Colyn was probably involved in all phases of cloth production; he served as pledge for Thomas Broun who leased the fulling mill and "Rackhay" at Culmstock, and imported madder (a red dye) at Exeter. Besides transacting business at Exeter, he also acquired much property in the city and its suburbs, including seven messuages, six gardens, 14 acres of land, meadow land, a grange, numerous shops, and various other tenements.[184] Colyn's acquisitions in Exeter point to the frequency of his dealings there and indicate the investments made by hinterland merchants in the urban center. Colyn's mercantile activites, as well as those of the other Devon and Somerset importers at Exeter who also participated in the cloth trade, suggest that these men were the forerunners of the well-known Devon clothiers whose activities some one hundred years later have drawn so much attention.[185]

Most inland merchants who participated in the port trade at Exeter were not involved in such large-scale transactions, nor did their trading efforts extend overseas or throughout the region. Instead, their distributing activities focused largely on their own home towns. Merchants like Raymond Goldsmith of Tiverton retailed wine at Tiverton that he had imported at Exeter, and probably sold some of it in bulk to taverners in Tiverton since he was the only one of five wine retailers at Tiverton

[180] PCA 1357/8, 1358/9, 1359/60, 1365/6; *CPR, 1361–4*: 480.

[181] *CPR, 1364–7*: 147.

[182] For cloth they had aulnaged, see PRO E101/338/11. For their other trade, see for Clayssh: PCA 1367/8, 1369/70; PRO E122/158/26; *CPR, 1361–4*: 480. Blackaller: PCA 1381/2, 1389/90, 1398/9. Grymells: PCA 1392/3, 1394/5. Colyn: n. 183, below.

[183] For this and the following, see PCA 1397/8; PRO E101/338/11; ECL D&C 4931, 5109; PRO E159/173, Michaelmas recorda, m. 3d.

[184] PCR 1–23 Ric. II, m. 42; MCR 1409/10, m. 22; 1412/13, m. 50; 1422/3, m. 24; Book 53A, ff. 85, 87.

[185] Carus-Wilson 1957 and 1963: 18–22.

in 1397 who ever imported wine at Exeter.[186] Indeed, of the fifteen wine retailers accused that year of breaking the assize of wine within a twenty-mile radius of Exeter, only three (Goldsmith, William Cokkeshead of Chulmleigh, and Richard atte Hille of Kennford) imported wine there in the 1390s.[187] Two others (John Potel of Bishop's Clyst and John Saltere of Chulmleigh) imported iron or oil at Exeter, so they probably made purchases from wine importers they met in the course of their business at the port. But the remaining eleven inland wine retailers must have acquired their wine from other importers, or from the middlemen with whom importers dealt.

The sources of supply for inland merchants obviously varied according to their means and the type of goods they wished to market. Wine, which usually arrived in large casks containing about 252 gallons, was so costly and fragile to transport overland that buyers usually sought wine at the closest port possible.[188] Availability and price were also key factors, particularly in the late middle ages when war greatly restricted the amount of wine carried to England. In the eyes of most inland merchants, the port of Exeter probably triumphed on all counts as a source of wine. The vast majority of Devon's inland towns had much easier overland access to Exeter than to its chief rivals, Dartmouth and Plymouth. Little competition was offered by other Devon ports. Seaton, Sidmouth, and Teignmouth in east Devon simply had too few residents with the necessary capital to finance such maritime ventures (as indicated by the very small amounts of wine arriving there). Barnstaple in north Devon presented more of a challenge, particularly in its own immediate hinterland. But Exeter-centered marketing even penetrated there; merchants from both South Molton (12 miles from Barnstaple but almost 25 miles from Exeter) and Chulmleigh (14 miles from Barnstaple, over 20 to Exeter) imported wine at Exeter, although it is likely that more of their business was channelled through Barnstaple.[189]

The Exeter advantage was the cheaper wine it could offer. Overseas freight charges added a significant amount to the price of wine in the late middle ages, and these charges were higher for destinations on the north Devon coast and Bristol Channel than for Exeter and other ports

[186] W1258M/X1, m. 8d (lists those who broke the assize of wine, probably by selling at prices higher than the set rate); PCA 1398/9; the PCA survive for all years from 1381/2–1399/1400.

[187] W1258M/X1 (assizes at port towns were omitted); PCA 1394/5, 1396/7, 1398/9.

[188] See James 1971: 147–9, for these costs.

[189] It is also possible that these merchants sold their Exeter imports at Exeter and never intended to cart them overland to their home towns.

along the south Devon coast.[190] If importers at Exeter purchased wine that had arrived by coast, they had to pay coastal freightage on top of overseas transport costs, but the former was negligible and the latter lower for Exeter's redistribution centers of Southampton, Dartmouth, and Plymouth than for any other English ports. Transportation costs for overland carriage are more difficult to assess because of differences in terrain, but do not seem to have been particularly high. In the early fourteenth century, a tun of wine could be transported overland in Devon for about 4.0*d* to 5.2*d* per mile.[191] Carting one tun of wine from Exeter to Torrington, about 31 miles away in north Devon, added one mark to the cost of the wine. Overland transport of other items also appears modest. In the 1330s, the Exeter cathedral works paid 3.4 per cent of the purchase price of 26 quintals of iron to cart it from Ottermouth to Exeter (roughly 11 miles away); in the 1340s, they paid 1.6 per cent of the purchase price of lead to cart it from Topsham to Exeter (about 4 miles).[192]

Lower costs were probably responsible for luring so many Taunton importers to Exeter, some 27 miles away. The closest port to Taunton was Bridgwater, less than 10 miles to its north. But Bridgwater's geographical position 16 miles down the winding and difficult Parret river, along with its dependence on its much larger neighbor, Bristol, inhibited the development of maritime trade there.[193] Taunton traders certainly sought wine at Bridgwater, but they also must have paid more dearly for wine there than at Exeter because of the higher freightage costs for wine shipped to Bristol and Bridgwater. One would think that the overland carriage costs from Exeter would compensate, but the 189 tuns of wine, 22½ tons of iron, and 126 quarters of salt imported at Exeter by Taunton merchants in 1381–91 suggest otherwise. The provisions made for customary carting services between Topsham and such Somerset locations as Taunton, Porlock, and Stogumber also imply that such journeys were readily undertaken, even though they required carts to cross the Brendon or Blackdown Hills.[194] Exeter was a significantly busier port than Bridgwater and could thus offer better bargains, better

[190] James 1971: 144, 151–5 for this and the following.

[191] Calculated from carriage costs to Bishop's Clyst (about 3 miles from Exeter), Crediton (almost 7 miles), Sidford (just under 14 miles), and Torrington (31 miles from Exeter) as given in *Fabric accounts*: 73, 113, 125 for the years 1316–20. Distances calculated as the crow flies. There seems to have been no price difference for transporting a tun or a pipe.

[192] *Fabric accounts*: 244, 268. For the even lower costs of carting grain, see Masschaele, 1993.

[193] Power and Postan 1966: 332; Powell 1907: 192–96; Taunton could be reached by boat from Bridgwater, but not easily.

[194] See n. 197, below.

facilities, and more diverse goods than the smaller port. Much the same argument can be made for why Taunton merchants did not use the port of Lyme Regis (about 22 miles south of Taunton); traffic there was also very light and merchants would also have to skirt the Blackdown Hills which lie between Taunton and the Dorset coast.[195]

The availability of goods was also a key factor in the decision of inland merchants to import goods through Exeter. Supplies of foreign dyestuffs must have been particularly decisive given the demand fostered by the growing Somerset and east Devon cloth industries. Exeter's regular coastal trade with Southampton was particularly crucial since Southampton, the first port of call for Italian trade in England, was probably the country's premier depot for foreign dyestuffs.[196] The Genoese, who monopolized the trade in alum, the preferred mordant in cloth dyeing, docked their ships almost exclusively at Southampton. Thus the easiest and cheapest access Taunton merchants had to supplies of alum was at Exeter, where they dominated its importation (Table 6.6). As their role in the import of iron and corn attests, Somerset merchants may also have enjoyed easier access to these goods at Exeter than at Bridgwater or Bristol since Exeter and its coastal redistribution areas lay on more convenient trade routes for these imports: iron came largely from Spain and corn from eastern England and northern France. Such goods certainly arrived in Bristol as well, but Taunton merchants would have had to pay higher overseas and overland carriage rates than they would at Exeter.

Availability and price must also explain why gentry households situated only a few miles from the north Somerset coast nonetheless chose to acquire imports at Exeter rather than at nearby ports like Minehead, Watchet, or Bridgwater. The early fourteenth-century custumal of a manor in Stogumber, less than 5 miles from the Bristol Channel, required its customary tenants to travel over 30 miles south to fetch herring and salt from Exeter or Lyme Regis.[197] In the early fifteenth century, the Lady Elizabeth Bonville sent her bailiff on a four-day trip over Exmoor to Exeter 34 miles away to obtain wine, even though her manor bordered Porlock Bay and Minehead was only 7 miles away.[198] The bailiff probably had instructions to buy a large quantity of wine since the Lady Elizabeth was in residence for the whole of the year. In the following year, however,

[195] Only one or two foreign ships stopped at Lyme every year in the late fourteenth century; PRO E122/102/14, 40/16, 40/26.

[196] Ruddock 1951: esp. 81–2, 213–14; Fryde 1974, 1976.

[197] Siraut 1985: 184; for customary carting services owed by Taunton tenants to Topsham to fetch wine, see *Customs of the manor of Taunton*: 32, 66.

[198] Chadwyck Healy 1901: 264, 431, 496 for this and the following.

she spent less time at Porlock and the bailiff went instead with a cart and two men to bring back a pipe of wine from nearby Dunster. Besides wine, the Porlock household also purchased sea fish such as conger, ling, and hake at Exeter, although an agent was employed for this purpose rather than sending the bailiff. These different types of expenditure show that magnate households could choose to bypass local middlemen in favor of acquiring expensive imports at entrepôts themselves; the lower prices they paid there must have compensated for the overland transport charges they then had to bear.[199]

When the bailiffs of magnate households came to Exeter to purchase imports, the chances were high that they made such purchases from Exeter importers who represented the fourth and most important category of importers. In both the early and late fourteenth century (when they owned 30 per cent of the cargoes), Exeter merchants controlled by far the largest share of trade at the port (Table 6.4). Most of their efforts concentrated on the wine trade where they were responsible for 44 per cent of all tunnage in 1381–91 (Table 6.5); they also possessed about 67 per cent of the woad imports, 51 per cent of the iron, and a hefty share of the madder and herring trades (Table 6.6). These figures do not, however, reveal the total scope of their involvement since they do not include the goods they handled as agents or purchased from other importers whose activities went no further than the port. In Exeter, as in other major ports, local merchants considerably augmented their distributive function by buying up imports from shipmasters, foreign merchants, and non-local traders who did not possess the time or local knowledge to market further the goods they brought to the port.[200] This is why Walter Launde of Winchelsea sold most of his cargo of wheat and rye to Nicholas de Lydford of Exeter, Adam Sage of Rouen made large sales to William Brewer and John de St Nicholas of Exeter, and various Bordeaux merchants sold wine to Exeter importers like Richard de Spaxton and others.[201]

Wine sales provide a good example of the marketing strategies pursued by the Exeter importers. Within the city proper, Exeter merchants dominated the supply of wine, keeping some for their own households,

[199] See also Dyer 1989a: 309–10 and James 1971: 180–3 on this point.

[200] At Exeter these purchases were often specifically noted in recognizances in the MCR; after the mid fourteenth century, the exact purpose of the recognizances was less frequently recorded, but the clustering of such obligations in the fall and spring months when the wine ships arrived suggests that they represented similar deals. For other ports, see James 1971: 183–7.

[201] MCR 1288/9, m. 33d; 1289/90, m. 9d; 1311/12, mm. 44–44d; 1313/14, m. 3d; 1320/1, m. 26d; *Local PCA 1266–1321*: 193. By the late fourteenth century, merchants increasingly recorded these arrangements as recognizances without specifying the details of bargains as they had done earlier (see n. 200, above).

retailing some directly to consumers at their taverns or inns,[202] selling in bulk to wealthier households[203] and to local taverners, or marketing casks to other Exeter middlemen for resale elsewhere.[204] In the late thirteenth and early fourteenth centuries, the biggest wine importers employed their own taverners but this practice had wholly ceased by the late fourteenth century, perhaps because of the shortage of wine and reduced urban population.[205] During the late fourteenth century, most Exeter taverners purchased wine from Exeter importers and only two (John Gaillard and John Piers) imported wine in excess of what they might have sold at their taverns.[206] Payments for bulk wine sales were frequently recorded in recognizances enrolled on the Exeter court rolls, but it is likely that many of these sales actually occurred some 4 miles away at Topsham since sellers had little incentive to pay for carting costs to Exeter unless they were sure customers would take possession there. Some sales probably took place on board ship, as was the norm for commodities like herring and fish.[207] Since wine ships generally arrived twice a year, once in late October or November with the vintage wines and again in the spring with reek wines, both buyers and sellers were well aware of when they should gather. Large consignments of wine were probably publicly advertised for sale at the port, particularly by foreign importers or shipmasters who did not want to tarry long at Exeter.[208] The biggest buyers of their wine were most likely Exeter merchants who, as indicated by the many cellars and selds they leased at Topsham, were the group best preparted to handle large quantities of wine on a regular basis.[209] The nine-week lease on a cellar at Topsham by the Exeter merchant Ives Birch may have been typical of the short-term leasing arrangments preferred by sellers who planned to sell their wine as quickly as possible and wished to avoid excessive storage costs.[210]

As the largest importers and bulk purchasers of wine, the Exeter merchants took a leading role in distributing wine to inland regions. Taverners in the small towns that dotted the hinterland provided perhaps

[202] For example, MCR 1376/7, m. 44; PCR 1–23 Ric. II, m. 44. See also Table A3.1, passim for merchants who ran taverns or inns.

[203] Debts arising from these sales, usually for 1 tun or less, appear as recognizances throughout the MCR; see also MCR 1386/7, m. 5; 1388/9, m. 40 (rider).

[204] MCR 1379/80, m. 27; PCR 1–23 Ric. II, mm. 28, 68; these cases show Exeter traders (none of whom ever imported wine) selling large quantities of wine.

[205] For example, *Reg. Bronescombe and Quivil*: 435; MCR 1291/2, m. 4d; 1300/1, mm. 23, 30; 1302/3, m. 7.

[206] In 1381–91, Piers imported only 18 tuns while Gaillard imported almost 117 tuns.

[207] *Anglo-Norman custumal*: 37; MCR 1392/3, m. 45.

[208] James 1971: 185.

[209] W1258M/G6/50; PRO JUST1/192, m. 2.

[210] MCR 1332/3, m. 38d.

their steadiest customers. Such purchases were behind the £35 10*s* debt owed by the taverner John Lyf of Sidmouth to Roger Plente of Exeter, the single largest importer of wine in the 1350s and 1360s.[211] The £10 owed by Jordan Ferror of Somerton (Somerset) to John Grey of Exeter for wine was enough to pay for 2 tuns, which was probably destined for retail sale.[212] Some Exeter merchants appear to have maintained longstanding relationships with inland taverners, as Henry Purpris of Exeter did with Elias William of Cadleigh, a village 10 miles north of the city.[213] Such regional sales by Exeter wine merchants had a long history. As early as 1238, Exeter merchants can be found selling wine at such inland market towns as Honiton, Bradninch, Barnstaple, and Tiverton; in 1249 at Bradninch, Tiverton, and Bampton; and in 1280 at South Molton, Okehampton, and Honiton.[214]

The Exeter merchants' penetration of the regional market in wine was paralleled in their transactions of other imported goods. John Talbot, one of the largest iron importers at Exeter, sold 17*s*-worth of iron to John Smyth of Broad Clyst, a village only a few miles away.[215] Imported iron was most likely what Adam Scut of Exeter sold to Nicholas Boys, a smith of Tiverton who owed Scut £6 and regularly worked for the Tiverton household of the earl of Devon, located 13 miles north of Exeter.[216] This same household also purchased imports directly from Exeter merchant-importers, including such expensive items as spices, linen cloth, furs, and wine.[217] Exeter importers distributed dyestuffs over a particularly wide territory. Robert Wilford, Exeter's biggest woad importer for the last three decades of the century, had extensive dealings with dyers and fullers throughout east Devon (in Cullompton and Ottery St Mary), south Devon (Dartmouth), Somerset (Broadway, Montacute, Honeycote, Taunton), and Dorset (Bridport).[218] The sums (including amounts up to £10 and £44) that these clothworkers owed Wilford indicate the large consignments that he provided them. Inland fullers like John Toukere of Cullompton relied on several different Exeter merchants to acquire dyestuffs and other goods; he owed large sums to Robert Wilford (60*s*) and John Talbot (50*s* 10*d* and 100

[211] PRO C241/157/19, 165/66.
[212] MCR 1389/90, m. 2.
[213] MCR 1302/3, m. 7.
[214] *Devon eyre*: 14, 26, 30, 60; PRO JUST1/186, mm. 10, 16, 18, 36d, 42d.
[215] PCA passim; PCR 1–23 Ric. II, m. 17.
[216] PRO CP40/490, m. 33d. For Boys' smithing, see CR 488; BL Add. Ch. 64319, 64803; and W1258M/X1 for his retail sales of wine. For Scut's imports, see PCA 1358/9–1399/1400; he specialized in wine and iron.
[217] BL Add. Ch. 64317, 64321–22; see also CR 1466 for other purchases in Exeter.
[218] PCA passim; PRO CP40/472, m. 180; CP40/497, m. 102; CP40/509, m. 151; C131/211/3 2.

marks), a smaller amount to Adam Scut (2*s* 10*d*), and unstated sums to Richard Bozoun and Robert Wilford.[219] Many of these sales probably took place in Exeter itself since both wealthy cloth exporters and more humble cloth retailers (including weavers, fullers, dyers, and tailors) regularly visited the city. Many of the retailers came from villages within 6 miles of Exeter (such as Stoke Canon, Heavitree, Upton Pyne, and Kenton), but others resided in small market towns within 15 miles (including Bradninch, Crediton, and Tiverton); some even came from as far away as Somerset (Taunton) and Dorset (Bridport).[220]

Foreign imports could also reach Exeter and its hinterland by overland trade. Lighter commodities such as spices, luxury fabrics, and some dyes, for example, often arrived via these routes from London, particularly in the late middle ages. Inland merchants from Devon took part in this trade, but Exeter traders like John Splot, who purchased madder and other merchandise from several London grocers, seem to have more often pursued this alternative.[221] Imported fabrics (such as silks, Cyprus lawns, fustians, and Flemish cloth) and costly imported furs also often reached Devon by overland routes.[222] These types of goods only occasionally appeared in the port trade in the late fourteenth century (Table 6.2). Imported goods also came to Exeter and its hinterland via overland trade from Southampton. In the first half of the fifteenth century, small amounts of alum and woad reached Exeter by packhorse from Southampton; a good deal more travelled by land carriage from Southampton to Taunton.[223] Merchants from Honiton and Barnstaple also transported some woad, alum, cloth, and other goods into and out of Southampton, mainly by packhorse.[224] The emphasis upon packhorses in the trade between Southampton and the South-west shows, however, how constrained this commerce was by the difficulties of overland travel

219 MCR 1379/80, m. 33; 1387/8, m. 28; PCR 1–23 Ric. II, mm. 31, 75, 78; PRO CP40/509, m. 36d.

220 They were all presented in the MT for retailing cloth in Exeter without freedom membership; see especially NQMT 1365, 1374–6; EQMT 1388–90.

221 MCR 1389/90, m. 2; 1390/1, mm. 14, 18. For London dealings with inland Devon merchants, see PRO C241/165/93; CP40/472, m. 190; CP40/484, m. 176d. Exeter merchants far outnumbered Devon inland traders in commercial dealings with Londoners as seen in the enrolled recognizances (PRO C131, C241 passim) and disputes that arose (PRO CP40 passim). Note also that goods could travel overland from Exeter to London with items such as linen cloth (Carus-Wilson 1963: 26–8).

222 For example, MCR 1303/4, m. 17d; 1396/7, m. 23d; 1422/3, m. 45d; Carus-Wilson 1963: 26–8; and below, p. 305. For furs, see above, p. 158.

223 Southampton Record Office SC.5/11, ff. 39, 48; *Brokage Book of Southampton from 1439–40*: 104 for Exeter; 28, 90, 121, 135, 148 for Taunton. See also *Brokage Book of Southampton, 1443–1444*: passim for Taunton.

224 *Brokage Book of Southampton from 1439–40*: xxxvi, 83, 104, 119, 154; *Brokage Book of Southampton, 1443–1444*: xxxiv, 28, 85, 313.

in the hilly regions of the South-west and points to the obvious advantages of sea transport, particularly for bulkier commodities.

Besides overland transport, maritime trade at ports other than Exeter also attracted some inland merchants, particularly those residing on the fringes of Exeter's hinterland and closer to other ports. Such was the case with Richard Sturion of Ashburton who imported wine at Exeter but graced Dartmouth more often with his maritime dealings.[225] Since he and Nicholas Sturion seem to have concentrated (unusually for Devon traders) more on exports (tin, cloth, and hides) than on imports, it is not surprising that they favored Dartmouth for its proximity and because of its position as a bulking center for Devon exports. Some of the wealthier inland merchants also travelled (or sent their agents) to redistribution ports like Southampton to acquire foreign imports. John Northmore of Tiverton, for example, had a wide variety of valuable goods stored at Southampton, including beaver, otter, squirrel, and Russian furs, linen cloth from Prussia, spruce boards, flax, iron, and dried fish.[226] He may have meant to ship these imports to Exeter but, in fact, most of these items were more exotic than the usual cargoes at Exeter. It is more likely that he intended to bypass Exeter in marketing these goods, perhaps by transporting them overland to Tiverton and other inland towns.

The geographic distribution of inland importers active at Exeter, combined with the geographic range of the commercial transactions of Exeter importers in these inland areas,[227] gives us a good idea of the hinterland serviced by the port of Exeter in the late fourteenth century (Figure 6.1). Most of the connections were to market towns, such as Moretonhampstead and Okehampton in the Dartmoor border region; Chulmleigh and South Molton in mid Devon; Crediton, Tiverton, Bradninch, and Honiton in east Devon; and Taunton and Chard in Somerset. Smaller towns and villages had fewer direct contacts with the port trade at Exeter, partly because of the lower demand for imported goods in these places and partly because they were probably

[225] PCA 1365/6; PRO E122/158/26, 40/26; Nicholas Sturion of Ashburton only traded at Dartmouth; PRO E122/40/18; E159/163, Trinity recorda, m. 17.

[226] PRO C131/197/10.

[227] The transactions of importers who resided in Exeter include all debts or pleas of account in which they appeared as creditors/plaintiffs in 7 rolls of the court of common pleas from 1378–88; CP40/463, mm. 158d, 162d; /472, mm. 14d, 180, 199, 199d; /480, m. 556; /484, m. 462; /490, mm. 33d, 121, 172d, 173, 180; /497, mm. 38, 79, 102, 124, 216, 255, 392; /509, m. 36d. In some instances when the defendant's place of residence was not stated in the court record, it proved possible to provide this information from the prosopographical data base; see Appendix 1.

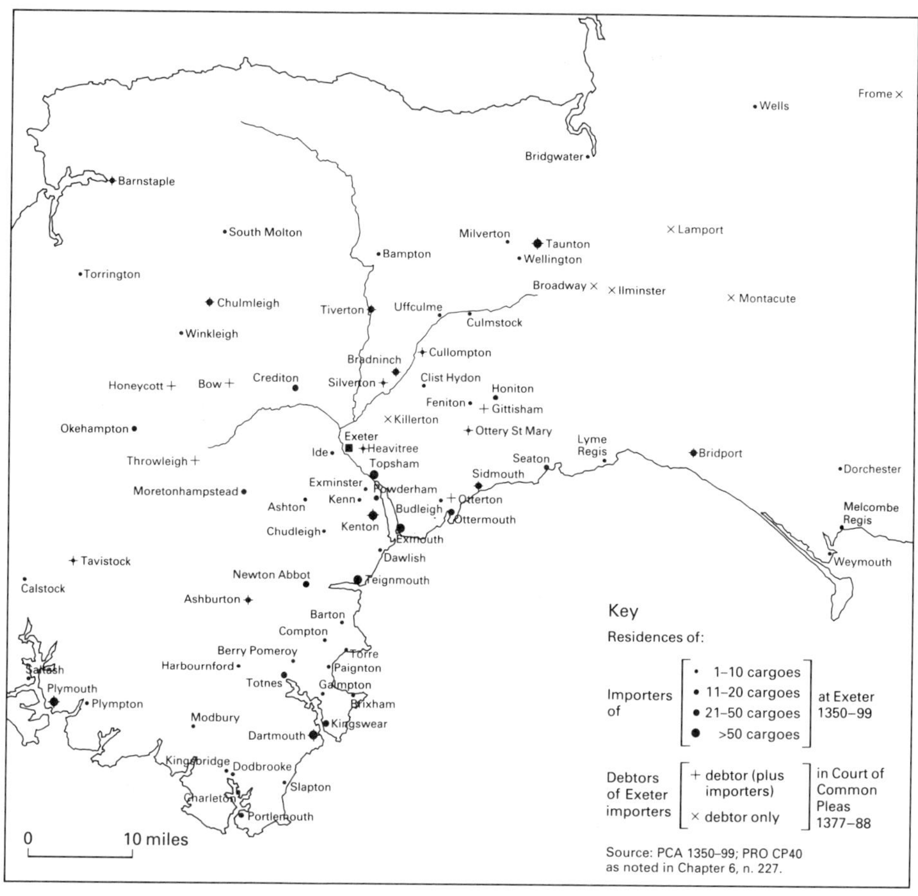

Figure 6.1 The hinterland of the port of Exeter in the late fourteenth century

supplied by importers and middlemen from the inland market towns. Places in Exeter's immediate hinterland of east Devon possessed the strongest links to Exeter and its importers. This eastern hinterland continued past the county border and well into Somerset. Dyestuffs channelled through the port promoted many of the ties with this region. To the north, Exeter's hinterland was limited both by low population density (especially once outside of the Exe valley or on the borders of Exmoor) and by the hinterland of the port of Barnstaple. Compared to Exeter's commercial ties to the east, which easily extended some 40 miles, those to the north and west did not stretch much further than 20 miles. But the hinterland was smallest to the south-west, ranging only so far as Newton Abbot (less than 15 miles away) and Ashburton (17 miles away). Here competition from Dartmouth was obviously a factor since these towns were closer to Dartmouth than to Exeter. They also had easy access to Teignmouth which, although not the port it had been in earlier decades, was nonetheless still a stopping-off point for coastal craft and some ships on the overseas routes.

Although the hinterland of Exeter was unquestionably larger and more populous than that of any other port in south-western England, it was considerably smaller than the hinterlands of Bristol and Southampton, which both abutted that of Exeter.[228] Southampton's immediate hinterland was bigger than Exeter's, stretching some 25 miles in each direction. Goods from Southampton also regularly reached inland destinations (including London) 50 miles or more away, in part because there were no intervening large moorlands, ranges of hills, or seas as in Devon. At Bristol, the town's easy connections to inland regions via the Avon and Severn rivers extended its hinterland well into Wiltshire and Gloucestershire. Although precise figures are hard to come by, it is clear that the volume of maritime trade at Exeter was significantly lower than at Southampton and Bristol. In the first two decades of the fifteenth century the annual average of wine imports at Exeter (even including coastal imports) was two to three times less than the tunnage arriving at the other two ports, while overseas cloth exports at Exeter were five to ten times lower.[229] The variety of imports at Exeter, at least up until the late fifteenth century, was also not on a par with the vast array of foreign goods unloaded at Bristol and Southampton, an indication of the less prosperous and populated inland regions served by Exeter.[230] Yet probably no other provincial ports enjoyed the volume of trade or extensive hinterlands of Bristol and Southampton, so in this Exeter was more typical of most second-rank provincial ports in England.

The extent to which the activities and profile of regional traders at other ports paralleled what we have seen for Exeter is still open to question. Further research should reveal which ports depended heavily on coastal trade and which ports (such as Southampton, Plymouth, and Dartmouth) may have been endowed by the customs accounts with deceptively high figures for overseas trade because of their position as

[228] For Southampton, Coleman 1960, esp. the maps; Coleman 1963; Platt 1973: 152–64. For Bristol, Carus-Wilson 1967c.

[229] James 1971: 108–10; Table 3.1, above; Carus-Wilson and Coleman 1963: 87–91.

[230] PCA passim; PRO E122 passim; *Local port book of Southampton 1435–6*; *Local port book of Southampton 1439–40*; Ruddock 1951; Carus-Wilson 1967c; *Bristol*; Sherborne 1965.

bulking and redistribution centers. The impressive degree of control exercised by Exeter's own merchants over incoming cargoes and overseas exports also needs to be measured against other ports. Certainly the low percentage of alien trade at Exeter must have given local merchants a larger share of the profits than they enjoyed at Southampton where aliens dominated the port trade to an unusual extent. But perhaps the much higher volume of trade through Southampton proved adequate compensation for the large share of foreign trade they lost to alien merchants. Even so, Southampton traders had stronger rivals in their hinterland than did the Exeter merchants.[231] Further prosopographical study of the importers at all provincial ports needs to be done before we can determine the relative role of the importers and exporters who operated there, although few ports probably experienced the extremes seen at Southampton (very high alien trade) and at Exeter (very low). With the expansion of England's cloth industry in the late middle ages, however, it is likely that other ports than Exeter witnessed growing activity by importers from inland towns and villages.

The demographic and wartime devastations of the mid fourteenth to mid fifteenth century severely cut into Exeter's maritime trade and led to transformations in the geographic distribution of ships visiting the port, the types of commodities imported, and the control exercised by importers from different regions. Exeter and its neighboring regions in Devon, Somerset, and Dorset were able to compensate for the loss of the Picard and Norman markets and commodities by focusing more on Breton, Gascon, and Iberian markets and products and by increasing trade with other English regions, particularly Cornwall. Wartime spending by the Crown at Dartmouth and Plymouth helped promote the fortunes of these south Devon towns, stimulating both their shipping industries and trading connections overseas. Although their shipping eventually edged out many east Devon vessels, the carrying trade of the Exe estuary ships remained stable and overall Devon carriers increased their domination of traffic at the port of Exeter and elsewhere. The widening mercantile activity of south Devon importers also helped to reduce the degree of control Exeter importers had enjoyed over their port's trade in the late thirteenth and early fourteenth centuries. This reduction, however, was partly compensated for by the increased opportunities available to Exeter merchants in their hinterland, which benefited from expansion in the cloth industry and agricultural diversification. Exeter merchants played a crucial role in linking their hinterland to overseas products and markets, sending dyestuffs and other goods

[231] Coleman 1963; Platt 1973: 155–63.

in return for cloth manufactures. Inland merchants also profited from these developments and by the late fourteenth century had begun to participate more directly in the port trade themselves. Commercial activity at the port of Exeter, therefore, was affected as much by developments within the town's hinterland as it was by occurrences overseas, showing once again the extent to which the marketing center of Exeter linked local, regional, and international trade. What remains to be determined is how the participants and commodities involved in the port trade functioned in relation to regional networks of trade in goods that did not arrive by sea, as well as the balance of control exercised by local and regional traders in overland trade.

7 Internal trade and the hinterland

Non-residents played an essential role in the commercial life of medieval Exeter. We have already seen how merchants from coastal settlements and inland locations imported goods at the port of Exeter and arranged for the transfer of regional products to overseas markets. Exeter merchants handled the single largest share of the port trade, but importers from elsewhere still owned roughly 70 per cent of the cargoes and 60 per cent of the value of goods imported in the late fourteenth century.[1] In addition to the port trade, the merchant staple at Exeter attracted many non-residents to the town because it provided a registry for bonds and debts made under statute merchant; about 85 per cent of the people who used the Exeter staple in the late fourteenth century resided outside of the city.[2] The frequency of commercial contact between Exeter and non-Exeter merchants and artisans is also evident in the debt litigation before the court of common pleas in Westminster: 84 per cent of Exeter debts there involved non-residents, as did all of the Exeter bonds made under statute merchant.[3] Even at a less exalted level of trade reliance upon outsiders was significant. No less than 35 per cent of the debt cases tried in the local Exeter courts included a non-resident as creditor or debtor; indeed, 5 per cent of the cases involved no Exeter inhabitant at all.[4] As we shall see, dependence on regional trade was also visible in the exchange of specific commodities in Exeter. Non-resident or "foreign" butchers, for example, accounted for roughly 46 per cent of the suppliers of hides and skins sold in late fourteenth-century Exeter, while non-resident tanners and leatherworkers comprised about 25 per cent of the buyers of these same items.[5] The role of outsiders in the

[1] See above, Chapter 6, esp. Tables 6.4 and 6.7.

[2] Based on all recognizances (sixty seven) made at Exeter found in the Chancery certificates of debt from 1370–87 (PRO C241/162–175), involving a total of 158 people.

[3] PRO CP40 cases as noted in Tables 7.1 and 7.2. They made twenty five of the bonds noted in PRO C241/162–175; see n. 2, above.

[4] Based on the 4,536 debts tried in MCR and PCR 1378–88; see below, pp. 347–9 for a discussion of this analysis.

[5] See below, pp. 300–3, 312–14 for this and the following.

exchange of fish was even more substantial; up to 80 per cent of those trading fish at Exeter lived outside the city, sometimes many miles away in Somerset and Dorset.

The following chapter will further examine Exeter's role as a regional center of commerce, building in particular upon the analyses of its position in the county hierarchy of markets and towns (Chapter 2) and in the distribution of goods imported by sea (Chapter 6). In order to define more precisely the nature and scope of Exeter's overland hinterland, this discussion will focus on two case studies: the marketing of pastoral products (livestock, meat, hides, and skins) and of fish in the late fourteenth century. Merchants exercised limited control over the distribution of these goods, in contrast to their dominance of the wine trade and other commodities traded by sea. Instead, artisans and retailers marketed most pastoral products and fish. By examining the occupations and status of the outsiders involved in these trades, and by comparing their residences in terms of agrarian/geographic region, distance from Exeter, and type of settlement, this chapter shows how different commodities affected the size and shape of the town's hinterland. The fish trade regularly attracted buyers from over 40 miles away in east Devon, Somerset, and Dorset, while traders of hides and skins usually came from villages and small towns located closer to Exeter, but with the pastoral orientation typical of the Dartmoor, mid Devon, and river valley regions of east Devon. Although not discussed here in detail, the trade in grain and cloth also shows many of the same trends found for the exchange of fish, pastoral products, and goods imported by sea.[6] As the cloth industry and pastoral agriculture expanded in Exeter's hinterland, commercial opportunities increased both for inland traders and for the Exeter merchants and traders with whom they conducted so much business. It was these industrial, agricultural, and commercial developments in the hinterland that largely account for Exeter's dramatic rise in wealth and population during the late middle ages, a period when many other English towns experienced economic crisis and decline.

Characterizing the commercial hinterland

Given the ubiquity of credit in medieval commerce, debt litigation provides one of the clearest pictures of the commercial world of medieval towns and their hinterlands. About 20 per cent of the creditors and

[6] The fourteenth-century grain trade of Exeter is analyzed in Kowaleski forthcoming. The growth of the south-western cloth trade has been traced by others (Hewitt 1911; Gray 1924; Pelham 1951: 250–5; Carus-Wilson 1963; Carus-Wilson and Coleman 1963; Bridbury 1982: 49–81); see also above, pp. 19–27.

debtors who came before the Exeter borough courts in the late fourteenth century resided outside of Exeter, a fairly high number when we remember the limited purview of borough courts and the favor they showed their own burgesses.[7] The transactions that brought non-residents into the borough courts were roughly the same as those that concerned local litigants. The variations that did exist, such as the tendency for non-residents to be less involved in disputes concerning unpaid rent, amercements, damages, and custom while they were more engaged in sales, bonds, and service debts, are not unexpected given their habitation elsewhere.[8] Indeed, the general similarity between the debts of residents and outsiders reflects the degree of commercial integration between Exeter and its surrounding towns and villages. It is also true, however, that larger debts with traders from further away or in different counties less often came before the borough courts because of their restricted jurisdictional sphere. In order to compensate for this limitation, the following analysis also considers the debts of Exeter residents tried before the court of common pleas in Westminster. Although the exact nature of the debts tried in this central court was rarely stated, the vast majority undoubtedly involved commercial transactions; merchants and artisan/retailers comprised 79 per cent of all litigants while the average debt of around £10 was typical of the bulk sales that dominated regional trade.[9]

Table 7.1 shows the regional distribution of the non-Exeter creditors and debtors. Not surprisingly, the majority (80 per cent) of the non-resident litigants in the local borough courts came from east Devon, the region wherein Exeter was located. East Devon (including the Exe estuary) was also the primary focus of the inland distribution of the port trade, as the previous chapter detailed. South Devon residents ranked a distant second, representing only 8 per cent of the litigants, but they appeared as creditors far more often than east Devon litigants. The more favorable balance of trade this implies reflects the important role played by south Devon shipmasters and merchants in supplying the port trade of Exeter.[10] Residents of the largely inland regions of Dartmoor, mid Devon, Somerset, and Dorset also appeared infrequently

[7] For the analysis of 4,536 debt cases in MCR and PCR 1378–88, upon which much of the following is based, see below, pp. 347–9. For borough courts, see above, pp. 216–20.

[8] See above, Table 5.1.

[9] See above, pp. 214–16 for further discussion of this source and analysis.

[10] Almost half of the south Devon litigants were involved in overseas enterprises. They included John Hawley (above, p. 264, esp. n. 172) and Thomas Ashheldon (PCR 1–23 Ric. II, m. 11; MCR 1379/80, m. 21; 1384/5, m. 6; PRO E122/158/26; *CPR, 1377–81*: 405), shipowner-merchants who appeared as creditors in the local courts.

Table 7.1. *Regional distribution of non-Exeter litigants in Exeter debt cases, 1377–88*

	Exeter borough courts		Court of common pleas
Region	Creditors in region %	All litigants %	All litigants %
East Devon	35	80.2	45
South Devon	44	8.0	20
Dartmoor and Borders	36	4.0	8
North and mid Devon	38	3.8	5
Somerset and Dorset	41	2.8	17
Other Counties	70	1.2	5
Total		100.0	100
(Total no.)	(291)	(798)	(60)
Unidentified	34	58.1	57

Source and note: MCR and PCR debt cases, 1378–88; including the unknowns (1,099), non-residents totaled 661 creditors and 1,236 debtors. PRO CP40/463, 472, 480, 484, 490, 497, 509 (all Devon and some London filazers); includes all debt (81) and account (22) cases involving Exeter residents. For the regions, see Figure 1.1.

as litigants at Exeter, but the high percentage of debtors from these regions shows that they may have been doing more buying (probably of imports) than selling in Exeter, or at least that they were at a disadvantage compared to the financial resources available in the city. Slightly more creditors (41 per cent) came from Somerset and Dorset and even more (70 per cent) from other counties, an indication perhaps of their more favorable balance of trade with Exeter. But these patterns might also reflect the difficulties faced by Exeter creditors in pursuing extra-county debtors; such creditors may have opted to sue these debtors in their own jurisdictions or at Westminster, thus reducing the number of debtors from outside of the county in the Exeter courts.

The geographic distribution of creditors and debtors in the court of common pleas was generally similar to the pattern observed for litigants in the local courts. The court's predilection for hearing cases involving larger sums and litigants from different jurisdictions and regions is reflected in the higher percentage of creditors and debtors from outside of Exeter's immediate hinterland of east Devon (Table 7.1).[11] Wherever Devon litigants in the central courts came from, however, they still appeared much more frequently as the debtors than the creditors of

[11] For litigation in this court, see Hastings 1947. Debts tried before the central courts were supposed to be over 40*s* (Beckerman 1975).

Exeter residents, yet another indication of how trade was weighted in favor of the urban regional center.[12] The situation for non-Devon litigants is harder to assess since source bias obscures cases in which they sued Exeter traders in the court of common pleas.[13] What is significant is that the proportion of litigants from non-Devon regions (mostly Somerset) was almost seven times larger in the central courts than in the local courts, suggesting that commerce between Exeter and Somerset was based on bulk sales. The greater buying power of Somerset merchants and clothiers and their need for the types of imported goods (particularly dyestuffs) that they could find at Exeter must have been largely responsible for this relationship.[14]

Regular commercial contact between Exeter and locations in Somerset and Dorset had been established from at least the thirteenth century. Traders from Bristol, Bridgwater, Taunton, Bruton, Lamport, Chard, Dorchester, and Bridport sold wool, horses, burel, and cloth at Exeter while others purchased potash, woad, cloth (including serge), hides, fish, and other items there in the thirteenth and early fourteenth centuries.[15] Exeter residents in turn frequented the fairs and markets of Somerset and Dorset to trade cloth, hides, skins, iron goods, rope, cart wheels, and ties in this period.[16] In the late fourteenth century, these commercial contacts intensified with the growth of cloth manufacturing in these counties. The greater involvement of inland merchants from east Devon and Somerset in both the import and export trade at Exeter was one manifestation of this intensification, as was the growing number of debts between traders from these regions.[17] Grain (especially wheat) from Somerset was marketed in Exeter during this period, while the expansion of the south Devon and Cornish fishing trade lured ever larger numbers of fish dealers from Dorset and Somerset to Exeter (Figure 7.1).[18] Somerset pottery, found in Exeter as early as the twelfth century, eventually came to dominate the city's ceramics market in the

[12] There were thirteen Devon (non-Exeter) creditors and thirty four debtors.

[13] Since only the Devon filazers and some London filazers of CP40 were examined, the analysis discriminates against non-Devon creditors who would have presented their complaints in the filazers of their own counties.

[14] For their involvement in the port trade, particularly dyestuffs, see above, pp. 244–5, 265.

[15] MCR 1287/8, m. 37d; 1289/90, m. 22d; 1295/6, m. 21d; 1300/1, m. 28; 1302/1, m. 10; 1303/4, m. 7d; 1304/5, m. 22d; 1315/16, m. 18; 1318/19, m. 52d; 1322/3, m. 36d; 1341/2, m. 44d; MT passim; *Local PCA 1266–1321*.

[16] *Fabric Accounts*: passim (for Bridport, Lopen, Petherton, and Taunton); above, pp. 56–7, esp. n. 54 (for Meriott, St Decuman, Tintinhull).

[17] Above, pp. 244–8, 259–60, Figure 6.1, and Table 7.1.

[18] For grain, see Kowaleski forthcoming and Figure 7.1, below. For fish, see below, pp. 312–18, esp. Table 7.6.

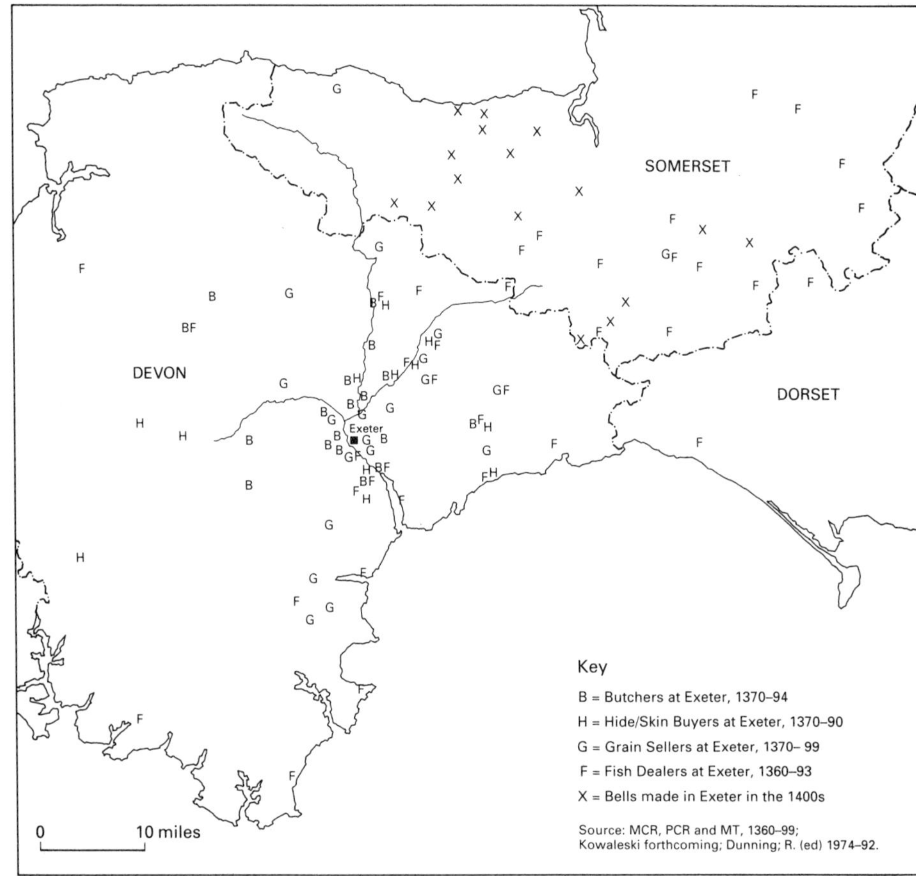

Figure 7.1 Inland trade and the hinterland of Exeter in the late fourteenth century

fifteenth century.[19] During the fifteenth century, bells manufactured in Exeter foundries also appeared in small parish churches all over Somerset and Dorset (Figure 7.1).[20] Given the distance between Exeter and these regions, their increased commercial contact in the late middle ages is particularly striking.

[19] Allan 1984: 8, 10–11, 31, 130, 133.

[20] These bells were at churches in Long Sutton, Yeovilton, Chaffcombe, Dowlish Wake, Brompton Regis, Brompton Ralph, Elworthy, Halse, West Quantoxhead, St Decuman, Bicknoller, Crowcombe, Huish Champflower, Over Stowey, Thurloxton, and Wambrook (Dunning 1974–85: vol. 3, 165, 175; vol. 4, 128, 156, 230; vol. 5, 18, 25, 63,

Just how important was distance in the economic relationship between the urban center and its hinterland? At what distance was the lure of the urban market center tempered by the difficulties and expense of travel and regional trade? One of the difficulties here is determining not only how much time journeys might have taken by various modes of transportation (on foot, on horse, accompanied with a loaded pack-horse, with a cart, driving livestock, or by river boat), but also how the business interests or economic means of travellers might have influenced their decision to undertake particular trips. In Devon, where in the words of one nineteenth-century man, "even five miles seems tantamount to a pilgrimage," few expected to complete a business journey to and from Exeter within one day if they lived more than 6 miles away.[21] This figure is also close to that suggested in the treatise by "Bracton" as a reasonable distance a trader might expect to travel to a local market and return home the same day. This same writer, however, implies that merchants with more wares to sell could not expect to return home the same day even if they lived within 6 miles from the market.[22]

Those travelling more than 25 miles to reach Exeter almost certainly anticipated an overnight stay in the town or along the way, thereby making travel and trade more expensive and perhaps more risky because conducted so far from familiar surroundings. The bailiff of Porlock in Somerset, about 35 miles north of Exeter on the other side of Exmoor, spent four days travelling to and from Exeter to purchase wine for his lady's household.[23] Round-trip journeys to fetch iron goods for the Exeter cathedral works at Lopen, about 34 miles away in Somerset, took three to four days with horses, including a day to get there, a day spent at Lopen, and another day or more for the return trip.[24] The travel times and plans of those from beyond 6 but less than 25 miles away are less certain. Chudleigh and Bradninch, for example, were both about 10 miles from Exeter. Yet travelers from Chudleigh had to hike up and over the Haldon Hills, wade through several streams

73, 80, 88, 135, 167). An Exeter freemason also helped construct a chapel in Croscombe in 1508–10 (*Churchwarden's accounts of Croscombe*: 29, 30, 32).

21 See also above, p. 49, for the difficulties of road travel in Devon. Other scholars also use 6–6 2/3 miles to measure a market's hinterland (Coates 1965: 106; Reed 1978: 567–9); some have used 5 miles for Devon (Shorter, Ravenhill, and Gregory 1969: 119–20).

22 *Bracton*, vol. III: 198–9; the clause reads "which ought to suffice for all except perhaps for those merchants who have stalls, who lay out and expose their ware for sale, for whom a longer sojourn in the market will be necessary." See also above, pp. 54–5.

23 Chadwyck Healy 1901: 431.

24 *Fabric accounts*: 82, 96, 141, 150.

Table 7.2. *Distribution of non-Exeter litigants in Exeter debt cases, by distance from Exeter, 1377–88*

	Exeter borough courts		Court of common pleas at Westminster
Distance from Exeter	Creditors in region %	All litigants %	All litigants %
Less than 6 miles	35	62.9	13
6–12 miles	28	15.2	42 (6–25 miles)
13–25 miles	42	10.1	
More than 25 miles	50	11.8	45
Total		100.0	100
(Total no.)	(291)	(798)	(60)
Unidentified	34	58.1	57

Source and note: MCR and PCR debt cases, 1378–88; including the unknowns (1,099), non-residents totaled 661 creditors and 1,236 debtors. PRO CP40/463, 472, 480, 484, 490, 497, 509 (all Devon and some London filazers); includes all debt (81) and account (22) cases involving Exeter residents.

and then make their way to Exe Bridge, the first crossing point of the Exe river. Few Chudleigh travellers on foot could have expected to return home the same day they set out for the market in Exeter. Indeed, the difficulties of travel from this region may explain why Chudleigh's Monday market was Exeter's closest rival in the hinterland. In contrast, travellers from Bradninch had no major hill ranges or rivers to cross and probably arrived in Exeter in considerably less time than it took those coming from Chudleigh.

Most of the outsiders (63 per cent) embroiled in debt litigation in the borough courts at Exeter came from the area within 6 miles of the town (Table 7.2). Many were frequent visitors to the town and would have been well known to borough residents.[25] Indeed, Exeter served as the local market for many of these people, a place where they could sell their produce and stock, purchase manufactured items such as cloth, and even hire themselves out for temporary work. Villeins from the manor of Pinhoe, a little less than 3 miles to the north-east, sold a whole range of produce in Exeter, including cheese, butter, eggs,

[25] For this reason, this distance group includes sixty creditors and 191 debtors whose exact place of residence could not be determined but whose frequent activity in Exeter (most were mentioned at least five times in the Exeter records over a ten-year span, almost always in reference to commercial matters) strongly suggests that they lived in the 6-mile area surrounding Exeter. This practice may have slightly inflated the number of people in this group, to the possible detriment of the 6–12 mile group.

Table 7.3. *Average debt amounts in debt cases in the Exeter borough courts, by creditors' and debtors' residence, 1378–88*

	Creditors		Debtors	
Residence	(No.)	Aver. debt	(No.)	Aver. debt
Distance from Exeter:				
Less than 6 miles	(64)	5*s* 1*d*	(112)	10*s* 1*d*
6–25 miles	(28)	70*s* 11*d*	(27)	21*s* 8*d*
More than 25 miles	(20)	92*s* 6*d*	(5)	151*s* 6*d*
Unidentified	(165)	12*s* 10*d*	(181)	30*s* 0*d*
Exeter residents:				
Oligarchy	(527)	17*s* 7*d*	(126)	28*s* 10*d*
Non-oligarchy	(1,062)	8*s* 3*d*	(1,461)	9*s* 2*d*

Source: MCR and PCR debt cases, 1378–88. See also Table 3.6, above.

wood, and even ale.[26] Topsham villeins like Geoffrey Paneys regularly marketed fish in Exeter while his more prosperous neighbor, the freeholder Roger Ewer, sold oxen, timber, and wine to Exeter residents and also provided carting services up to the town.[27] In return for these sales residents from the surrounding villages and farms could purchase imported or other goods in Exeter.[28] Aside from the natural lure of the goods and services a big town like Exeter could offer to inhabitants of its rural neighborhood, the absence of any other chartered market for miles around also brought many there to trade.[29]

The reliance of nearby residents on Exeter as a source of supply is reflected in their much more regular appearance as debtors than as creditors in the borough courts (Table 7.2). Their dependence on Exeter capital is particularly visible in the cash loans they took out from town residents, at a rate almost three times that of Exeter residents.[30] The substantially larger sums they owed as debtors than they could expect to collect as creditors points to their disadvantaged position in such transactions (Table 7.3). On the average they received about 3*s* less

[26] PRO SC2/168/1, mm. 10–10d; PCR 1–23 Ric. II, m. 34.

[27] Paneys: SQMT 1372–74, 1379–80, 1386–92; MCR 1391/2, m. 1; ECL D&C 1905. Ewer: MCR 1373/4, m. 20; 1390/1, m. 26; Misc. Roll 6, m. 34. For both: PRO SC2/168/43.

[28] See above, pp. 242, 272 for the distribution of imports, and below, pp. 294–301, 312–17 for fish and hides.

[29] See above, p. 60, esp. Figure 2.1.

[30] Only 7 per cent of Exeter debts involved cash loans (Table 5.1, above), compared to 20 per cent (nine of forty five) of the debts of creditors from within 6 miles away. Non-residents from farther away also borrowed money from burgesses, but the larger sums they obtained were more likely to be secured by a formal recognizance and eventually pursued in the central courts if left unpaid.

Table 7.4. *Court results for creditors and debtors in debt cases in the Exeter borough courts, by residence, 1378–88*

Distance from Exeter	Guilty	Plea not pursued	Licence of concord	False query	Failure to wage law	No information
Creditors						
Less than 6 miles (N=176)	19	33	18	8	3	19
6 miles or more (N=115)	24	20	10	6	1	39
Unidentified (N=370)	24	35	11	8	4	18
Debtors						
Less than 6 miles (N=326)	21	30	16	7	4	22
6 miles or more (N=181)	10	35	8	2	3	42
Unidentified (N=729)	15	37	14	5	2	27

Source: MCR and PCR debt cases, 1378–88. See Table 5.3 for rates of all non-Exeter litigants combined.

than even the non-oligarchic Exeter creditors, while as debtors they owed an average of 1*s* more. The amounts involved in their debts were typical of retail or moderate bulk purchases rather than any large-scale buying. Creditors and debtors from within 6 miles of Exeter also tended to experience less successful outcomes in their litigation, at times doing worse than even the lowest-ranked Exeter residents (Table 7.4). As creditors, for example, they failed to win guilty verdicts against their debtors more regularly than any other group. Their relative lack of success in the Exeter courts may have reflected their lower status and wealth. Almost half were artisan/retailers, 22 per cent followed agricultural pursuits, and fewer than 11 per cent were merchants.[31]

The commercial position of non-resident traders at Exeter became stronger the farther they had to travel from their homes to reach Exeter. The percentage of creditors generally increased with distance although the low number of creditors among those travelling only 6–12 miles to Exeter indicates the pervasive influence of Exeter capital and goods even beyond the city's immediate neighborhood (Table 7.2). Distance

[31] Occupations/status could be identified for 258 of these litigants; 123 were artisan/retailers, fifty eight followed agricultural pursuits, thirty one were of the professional class, twenty eight were merchants, thirteen were clergy, and five were gentry. For litigants from farther away, see below, p. 289.

also affected the amount of the debt which mounted the farther litigants lived from Exeter (Table 7.3). Regardless of distance, however, the balance of trade lay mostly in the hands of Exeter residents, since debtors usually owed more than creditors from the same distance group. Only for traders from the middle distances (6–25 miles) were creditors rather than debtors associated with the larger sums, suggesting that although fewer sellers from communities in this distance group found a market in the city, the one they did find could accommodate their bulk sales.

Those who resided farthest away (more than 25 miles) operated on a far grander scale than the other outsiders. Their debts were much more substantial on the average and many times higher than even those of the Exeter oligarchs (Table 7.3). These litigants obviously concentrated their efforts on bigger transactions and eschewed much involvement in retail trade at Exeter. They included men like Robert Leche of Dunster (over 35 miles away on the north Somerset coast), who prosecuted the Exeter spicer, John Syneet, for £14, and the Plymouth overseas merchant John Bovy who was sued by two men for £18.[32] Only those on a sound financial footing could afford to be involved in such expensive undertakings so far from home. These were the same type of people whose business called for them or their agents to travel and who had the wherewithal and knowledge to face the legal obstacles and unfriendly confines of a foreign court.[33] The greater mileage covered by traders who appeared before the central courts with Exeter residents also indicates how bulk sales dominated business dealings over the longer distances (Table 7.2). These litigants, whose debts averaged about £10, usually came from more than 6 miles away and over half were from places more than 25 miles from the town.

The status of individual creditors or debtors clearly influenced the distance they were willing to cover in commercial transactions. The inconvenience of leaving home and business, the difficulties and expense of travel, and the trouble of pleading in a foreign court all became more arduous the farther away one conducted commerce. Wealth and status allowed medieval people to face these problems more easily, although the sums involved had to be large enough to make such trouble worthwhile. Not unexpectedly, therefore, higher-status people were particularly well represented among the litigants from more than 25 miles away. Merchants accounted for 23 per cent, gentry for 11 per cent and clergy for 9 per cent of these creditors and debtors, proportions

[32] PCR 1–23 Ric. II, mm. 44, 46.
[33] For such obstacles, see above, pp. 215–16.

far in excess of their normal representation within the general population or even the local markets.[34] This trend was also evident in the debt disputes in the central courts where merchants comprised 39 per cent, gentry 5 per cent and clergy 6 per cent of all litigants.[35]

Many of the non-resident merchants active in Exeter trade were leading citizens of their own towns. John atte Forde of Tavistock (well over 30 miles away on the other side of Dartmoor) appeared in Exeter courts seven times in 1378–88, always as a creditor.[36] In Tavistock he was a prominent merchant, trading overseas and serving as both portreeve and MP for the borough of Tavistock. Thomas Lelya of Barnstaple, who was sued by the Exeter oligarch John Grey, served in both civic and county offices, was one of Barnstaple's biggest cloth merchants and exporters, and also regularly imported goods from overseas.[37] Merchants from Dartmouth and Plymouth who became involved in debt litigation at Exeter had similarly high economic and political profiles in their home towns.[38] The wealth and commercial success of these and other merchants enabled them to extend their networks of trade outside their own local markets. Similarly, Exeter merchants who traded at places more than 25 miles away from their home town tended to be prominent members of the merchant oligarchy.[39] This is not to imply, however, that only merchants conducted trade over longer distances; as discussed in the following sections, those whose occupational interests centered more on agrarian pursuits or on marketing items like fish also came from distant places to trade at Exeter.[40]

[34] Percentages based on ninety four litigants from more than 25 miles away. For comparisons, see above, Tables 4.1, 4.3. There may be some built-in bias in this description of occupational/status background since those of high status or high-profile commercial activity were more easily identified than those who were not. Yet the evidence concerning the status of traders in livestock, meat, hides, and fish (see below) shows that more ordinary traders and artisans could also be identified with the sources used in this study's prosopographical analyses.

[35] PRO CP40 as in Table 7.1; there were a total of 219 litigants.

[36] MCR 1381/2, m. 4; 1384/5, m. 47; 1385/6, m. 26; PCR 1–22 Ric. II, mm. 19, 84, 85. For his standing in Tavistock, see *Calendar of the Tavistock parish records*: 70–2, 109, 125. For his imports, see PCA 1370/1, 1372/3; he was also major cloth seller; PRO E101/338/11.

[37] PCR 1–23 Ric. II, m. 71; *CFR, 1377–83*: 338; *CPR, 1381–5*: 551; PRO E101/338/11; PRO E122/102/14, 40/26; PRO E159/167, Michaelmas recorda, m. 27.

[38] See above, pp. 257–8.

[39] For example, 65 per cent of the total 125 Exeter litigants in the central courts (PRO CP40 as in Table 7.1) were members of the Exeter merchant oligarchy.

[40] While very few of these traders were merchants or importers, they did tend to be substantial members of their own communities; see, for example, the discussion below regarding the status of some of the Devon butchers, tanners, and fish dealers involved in trade at Exeter. There is no reason to suppose that their Somerset counterparts were of a different status.

Gentry and aristocratic litigants would have been particularly well known to Exeter residents by virtue of their standing in the county community. Most distinguished was the earl of Devon, Edward Courtenay, who sued for debt recovery at Exeter three times in this period.[41] Other members of the local gentry who showed up in the borough courts included Edward's uncle, Sir Philip Courtenay; William Cary, steward to Bishop Brantingham and justice of the peace; Sir James Chuddlegh, a knight of the shire, justice of the peace, and escheator for Devon and Cornwall; and Nicholas Kirkham, a sheriff of Devon and county collector for both the poll tax and lay subsidy.[42] All of these men were important landowners who held positions of power in the Devon county community. They and other gentry litigants usually appeared as creditors (thirty four times) rather than debtors (fourteen times) and were probably compelled to frequent the Exeter courts because either their debtors were local residents or the debt had been contracted at the merchant staple in Exeter.[43]

Non-resident clerics involved in debt litigation at Exeter also enjoyed a relatively high status. They included heads of religious houses such as the prior of Plympton and the Cistercian abbots of Newenham and Buckfast, as well as vicars and rectors of such places as Littleham and Washford Pyne.[44] In contrast to the gentry, however, 67 per cent of the borough court appearances by non-resident clerical litigants were as debtors.[45] Their indebted state contrasts with that of Exeter clerics who surfaced as debtors only 44 per cent of the time and who paid much lower sums as debtors (average 7*s* 4*d*) compared to the non-resident clerics (average over 163*s*).[46] As creditors, non-resident clerics did just as poorly since they expected to recoup on the average only 8*s* 8*d*, three times less than what the Exeter clerics sued for. The small sums pursued by non-resident clerics in the borough courts may have been rent arrears from their properties in Exeter or other petty debts; for larger sums, they may have preferred to use other courts.[47] Their more frequent appearances as debtors reflected not only their attraction

41 MCR 1382/3, m. 41; 1385/6, m. 21.

42 MCR 1380/1, m. 3; 1382/3, m. 14; 1386/7, m. 24; PCR 1–23 Ric. II, m. 32. For their status, see Cherry 1983–5; Tyldesley 1978: esp. 83–6, 118, 121.

43 For recognizances made by the aristocracy and gentry at the Exeter staple in this period, see above, p. 213 and CR 543; BL Harleian Ch. 58 E.33; BL Add. Ch. 64322; PRO C267/6/33; there are also many examples in PRO C241 passim.

44 PCR 1–23 Ric. II, mm. 37, 67, 73; MCR 1379/80, m. 1; 1387/8, m. 9.

45 There were thirty nine non-resident clerical creditors and seventy nine debtors.

46 For Exeter clerics, see above, Table 4.4 and pp. 172–3. Debt amount known for fifteen non-resident clerical creditors and sixteen debtors.

47 In the central courts (PRO CP40 as in Table 7.1) clerical creditors (ten) outnumbered clerical debtors (four).

to the goods and services offered by the urban center, but also the central role enjoyed by Exeter in the religious life of the large diocese administered from the city. Exeter's other ecclesiastical institutions also played a part in forcing non-resident clerics into the local courts; it was, for example, the prior of the local Benedictine house of St Nicholas who was responsible for suing the abbot of Buckfast and one of his fellow monks.[48]

The wealth and influence of litigants who resided farther away from Exeter was also reflected in the outcomes of their borough court appearances. Creditors from more than 6 miles away won more guilty verdicts against their debtors, less often failed to follow up on their suits, and less often suffered fines for initiating a false query than their counterparts from closer to Exeter (Table 7.4). As debtors, they also enjoyed better outcomes; they were 11 per cent less likely to be convicted and 5 per cent more often benefited from having the suit against them dropped. Indeed, these non-resident litigants at times fared better than even most Exeter plaintiffs and defendants, notably in the limited guilty verdicts they received as debtors and the fewer times they were fined for not prosecuting cases or bringing a false complaint as creditors.[49] The very high number of their debts for which we know no outcome stems from the difficulties experienced by Exeter creditors in compelling these non-resident debtors to appear in the Exeter courts. Most such cases would have been tried in the debtor's home court or in the higher courts, particularly if the transaction involved larger sums and had been registered under statute merchant.[50]

Status, wealth, and business purpose were clearly crucial factors in determining the degree to which traders ventured outside the limited geographical sphere of their own settlements to pursue commercial opportunities.[51] Although the creditor/debtor ratio, debt amounts, court outcomes, and occupational profile of traders residing within 6 miles of Exeter indicate that they were engaged in different types of trade than that which took place over longer distances, this does not mean that they were uniformly subordinated to or exploited by Exeter traders. Instead, these indices signify the extent of their participation in the

[48] MCR 1387/8, m. 9.

[49] Compare these outcomes and those noted below for litigants from less than 6 miles away with those for non-oligarchic litigants from Exeter in Table 3.7, above.

[50] For cases that can be traced through the Exeter borough courts to the court of common pleas (PRO CP40) or in the Chancery certificates of debt (PRO C241), see above, pp. 213–14.

[51] In rural locations, most outsiders who appeared in village court rolls also came from the more prominent families in their own villages (Raftis 1965: 87–90; Hanawalt 1977: 410–11).

same local trade that dominated the concerns of the vast majority of Exeter residents who did not belong to the merchant oligarchy. In most of the measures of market participation presented here, people from within 6 miles ranked very close to the performance of Exeter artisan/retailers, while the debt profile of litigants from further away (particularly more than 12–25 miles distant) more closely resembled that of the oligarchic merchants.

The debt analysis also suggests that the regional networks of trade within 6 miles of Exeter were largely routed through the city and depended heavily on urban demand and urban capital. In effect, the local networks of trade of persons residing in villages around Exeter overlapped with the local markets of the urban center. Commercial dealings between Exeter residents and non-residents, however, also extended outside this immediate hinterland and into a zone that to the east reached at least 25 miles, taking advantage of their town's position as a port, and center of ecclesiastical, judicial, and administrative activities. Their influence was more restricted in other directions in part because of natural geography (the sea to the south, moors to the west and north) and because of competition from other port towns (particularly Dartmouth and Plymouth on the south Devon coast and Barnstaple on the north coast). What remains to be seen is how the regional networks of trade could vary according to the commodity being exchanged and how the various groups of artisan/retailers and agricultural occupations participated in these networks.

The trade in livestock, meat, hides, and skins

Rich in pastureland and rough moorland grazing, Devon was abundantly supplied with livestock; in the late middle ages, the county's demesne and tenant farmers also increasingly turned their attention to pastoral husbandry, particularly in Exeter's own region of east Devon.[52] The Dartmoor region had always emphasized pastoral activities; in the late fourteenth and early fifteenth centuries, well over 10,000 cattle were agisted on Dartmoor alone, including the stock of people who lived more than 20 miles away.[53] Some graziers pastured herds of as many as 300 cattle annually, although the average size of herds agisted by outsiders was closer to twenty eight.[54] Herds of cattle from many areas

[52] Fox 1991: 153–9; 315–21.

[53] For this and the following: Fox 1991: 319–20; 1989: 61–3; PRO SC2/166/45, esp. m. 13; see also DCO Min. Accts. 22 (1377/8).

[54] Based on agistments in east Dartmoor in 1413; PRO SC2/166/45. I am grateful to Harold Fox for pointing me to this source.

in Devon and Somerset also flocked to Exmoor for summer pasturing every year.[55] The movement of livestock could extend over considerable distances as cattle and other stock were sent to suitable pastures for rearing and fattening, or driven to market for sale. Livestock was often sold at regional fairs; transactions involving horses (including colts and draught horses), oxen, cows, and sheep (including lambs) were mentioned more often at Devon fairs than any other items.[56] Crediton hosted what may have been the premier livestock fair in medieval Devon; it and other important livestock fairs at Lydford (on the other side of Dartmoor), Holsworthy (in mid Devon), and Chudleigh were all visited by traders from Exeter.[57] Exeter residents also purchased livestock at Newton St Cyres, Cheriton Bishop, Sydenham Damarel (on the Devon/Cornwall border), and at Bodmin, located over 60 miles away in Cornwall.[58] Obviously the hinterland for livestock ranged much farther than that for products like grain, due in part to the lower costs of getting this mobile product to market.[59]

The regional dimension of the livestock trade is also evident in the large number of non-resident butchers who regularly worked in Exeter. Of a total of thirty six butchers active in the city in one year (1391/2), no fewer than seventeen came from other places, including Crockernwell and Moretonhampstead on the borders of Dartmoor, as well as Silverton, Tiverton, Clist St Michael, Brampford Speke, Nether Exe, Newton St Cyres, and Heghes in east Devon (see Figure 7.1).[60] This list, however, gives only a hint of the range of places from which butchers came to transact business in Exeter. In the three previous decades they had also arrived from Chulmleigh and Winkleigh in mid Devon, and Thorverton, Bickleigh, Ide, Exminster, Stoke Canon, Broadclyst, Withycombe Raleigh, and Ottery St Mary in east Devon.[61] All but Winkleigh and Chulmleigh were located within 15 miles of Exeter and most were nestled in the Culm, Exe, or Creedy river valleys where cattle were probably driven for fattening. It is likely that some of these outside butchers also operated as graziers, buying up stock in fairs or rural areas, fattening them on the rich meadows and pastures of their home villages, and then selling them at Exeter or other urban markets.

[55] Chanter 1907; MacDermot 1973; and below, n. 67.

[56] Above, p. 46; Misc. Roll 52, m. 7; CR 789; 4088M/Ashwater bailiff's accounts, 1467/8, 1476/7; see also Farmer 1991a: 377–87.

[57] MCR 1335/6, m. 4d; Misc. Roll 52, m. 7; see also above, p. 57.

[58] PCR 1–22 Ric. II, m. 46; MCR 1288/9, m. 7d; 1318/19, m. 29 (rider); 1320/1, m. 5d.

[59] For grain, see Kowaleski forthcoming and Figure 7.1.

[60] Book 53A, f. 76; SQMT 1391–92. For butcher-graziers in other towns, see below, n. 99.

[61] SQMT 1363, 1372–90; MCR 1360/1, m. 8d.

One of the places that graziers and butchers fattened their stock was the parish of Newton St Cyres, about 5 miles north-west of Exeter. The Creedy river and one of its tributaries cut right through the parish, creating large acreages of water meadow, while to the north and south lay more hilly areas containing much rough pastureland.[62] Most of the land belonged to Plympton priory, but a manor called Norton on the north side of the river was held by the dean and chapter of Exeter cathedral. Among the tenants of both manors was the butcher/grazier William Symond who sold hides in Exeter for over twenty years in the late fourteenth century.[63] In Newton St Cyres he was listed among the conventionary tenants (liable for work and service in various manorial offices) and held a cottage, two curtilages, and five parcels of land, one called a "park" and three others measuring one-half ferling, three acres, and three rods. He also kept pigs and leased lands in Norton, including a close called Norton marsh that bordered the river. His debts show he had dealings with the Exeter cordwainer John Boggebrook who probably bought hides from him, and with two other tenants of Newton St Cyres, John Wyger (one of the manorial reeves) and Andrew Paas.[64] Andrew Paas was a more substantial landowner than Wyger or Symond since he was the biggest lessor of demense land there, holding a meadow for the annual rent of 11*s* per year, a grange with land for 33*s* 4*d*, a "Deyhous" (dairy) for 12*d*, a garden for 4*s*, and a cottage with a curtilage. He too did business in Exeter, making at least two sales (one for sheep) to the Exeter butcher Simon Hony, selling a horse for 33*s* 4*d* to an Exeter dyer, and being sued by the skinner Peter Ponte for breaking a contract.[65] It is also possible that he maintained links with grazing areas in Dartmoor since he was involved in a debt dispute with Richard Colshull, the forester and bailiff of the north Dartmoor forest.[66] Although stock from Dartmoor could easily have been driven the 15 or so miles to Newton St Cyres for fattening, the manor also had links with the grazing lands of Exmoor, over 20 miles to its north. John Naterigg, one of the Prior's servants in 1385, had a few years earlier

[62] Reichel 1923: 151, 162, 174–5; Gover, Mawer, and Stenton 1931–2: 410–1; ECL D&C 5006; BL Harleian MS 4766.

[63] He appeared in the annual presentments (SQMT 1370–87) against those who sold hides outside the sanctioned marketplace in Exeter, a charge almost always made against butchers. For his landholdings, see ECL D&C 5006; BL Harleian MS 4766, ff. 3–6d.

[64] MCR 1384/5, m. 15b; 1386/7, m. 2; 1387/8, m. 6; PCR 1–23 Ric. II, m. 72; ECL D&C 2706.

[65] PCR 1–23 Ric. II, m. 27, 64, 78; MCR 1391/2, m. 41.

[66] *CPR 1396–9*: 298; DCO Min. Accts. 29 (1389/90). Since Paas served as the Duchy's collector of rents for Exeter castle in 1400, it is also possible that he came into contact with Colshull in this way (DCO Receivers' Accts. 201).

been accused of taking away seven oxen in that section of the "forest of Exmoor" located in the Somerset parish of Hawkridge.[67] He was found innocent of this charge, but it does show an interesting link between one of Devon's foremost grazing regions and an area known for fattening cattle and sending meatstock to urban markets like Exeter.

Even more active in Exeter were the two butchers Matthew Spencer and his son William, also from Newton St Cyres. They resided in the small tithing of Ford for which Matthew served as poll tax collector.[68] Like William Symond, they too were associated with the conventionary tenants; in 1408 William Spencer was listed as having recently held one-half ferling, two parcels of the rectory's land in Marlhull, and a cottage with a curtilage that Matthew had also once possessed.[69] In Exeter they were annually presented for selling meat without the hides attached, bringing animals to the city (or purchasing them there) but leaving blood and entrails behind after slaughtering them, or selling hides outside the sanctioned marketplace.[70] Matthew stopped coming to Exeter around 1382, but William continued to do business there, renting a place in the Fleshfold for 5*s* in 1392/3, the same year he was accused of taking part in a larger conspiracy to fix meat prices in the city.[71] He appeared only once as a creditor, but three times as a debtor: he owed 18*s* for oxen, 15*s* 11*d* to the butcher Henry Veisy, and sums of around 27*s* and 38*s* to two non-Exeter residents, amounts indicative of livestock purchases.[72]

Butchers from farther away also traded regularly in Exeter. From 1379 to 1391, Walter Hayward of Tiverton (13 miles north) sold livestock, meat, and hides in the city and made an agreement to supply an Exeter weaver with beef and pork.[73] Although he no longer appeared in the annual lists of fines assessed on butchers after 1391, he remained active in his own community, supplying the household of the earl of Devon at Tiverton with "victuals" (probably meat) for which he received part payments of £2 and £4 in the mid 1390s.[74] Such contracts to supply noble households could be lucrative; in 1383/4, the earl's household spent about £25 on thirty eight beef carcasses, twenty eight bacons, eighty sheep, and five boars.[75] Even supplying part of these amounts

[67] SRO DD/CN/Box5/12; PRO CP40/497, m. 145d; for Robert Naterigg's holdings in Newton St Cyres in 1408, see BL Harleian MS 4766, m. 4.

[68] PRO E179/95/55/2 (in 1377 the tithing had thirty four residents). For their activities in Exeter, see SQMT 1370–93.

[69] BL Harleian MS 4766, ff. 3–6 for this and the following.

[70] SQMT 1370–93.

[71] Book 53A, f. 76; MCR 1392/3, m. 21.

[72] PCR 1–23 Ric. II, mm. 66, 79; MCR 1387/8, m. 21; 1388/9, m. 5; 1389/90, m. 48.

[73] SQMT 1379–82, 1387–91; PCR 1–23 Ric. II, mm. 31–2.

[74] CR 500; BL Add. Ch. 64322.

[75] CR 491.

would require a butcher to become involved in the livestock trade. Butchers such as John Bochele and William Stoddon from the Dartmoor moorland parish of Moretonhampstead also practiced their trade in Exeter for at least fifteen years.[76] Stoddon had some involvement in the tin industry as well since he was taxed 13*d* in the tinner's subsidy of 1374. Other non-resident butcher-graziers at Exeter also appeared in this subsidy; Richard Rogge of Nether Exe (about 5 miles north of Exeter) was taxed 6*s*, strongly suggesting that he owned land in Dartmoor (well over 20 miles away) that he might have used to graze livestock he later sold in Exeter.[77] Butchers resident in Exeter also possessed ties with these livestock-rich moorland regions. The butcher John Hood, for example, extended pledging services to John Robyn of Moretonhampstead when he was in Exeter and also purchased oxen from a man in Dunscombe, a hamlet in Chudleigh located in the Haldon Hills.[78] Another Mortonhampstead resident, John Goldsmith, also had commercial dealings with an Exeter butcher named William Mannying.[79]

Urban markets exercised a strong influence on the trade in livestock, largely because of the urban demand for meat. Urban tastes also dictated the types of livestock brought to town for marketing; in the late middle ages lambs or young sheep were preferred to those of a more mature age, while beef was favored above all.[80] Over 70 per cent of the meat consumed (by weight) in late medieval Exeter was from cattle, mainly mature animals although veal was becoming more popular. Mutton (and goat) comprised under 20 per cent and pork around 10 per cent of meat consumed in the city. Pigs were often kept by Exeter households so urban residents probably relied less on butchers for pork than for other types of meat.[81] But since almost all cattle and sheep came to the city on the hoof for slaughter,[82] butchers enjoyed a central role in the livestock trade. Given the amount of pasture they leased in the city's suburbs and surrounding manors (particularly at Cowley, Heghes, Cowick, and Topsham, which all bordered the Exe river and were abundantly supplied with meadow land), Exeter butchers were also involved in fattening animals before slaughtering them for meat.[83] Their

[76] SQMT 1371–91; MCR 1387/8, m. 7; PRO E179/95/33 for this and the following.

[77] PRO E179/95/29. For his activities in Exeter, see SQMT 1376–81; MCR 1360/1, m. 8d; 1376/7, m. 23; 1379/80, m. 5; DCR 2–22 Ric. II, m. 6.

[78] PCR 1–23 Ric. II, mm. 25, 26, 29.

[79] PCR 1–23 Ric. II, m. 35.

[80] Maltby 1979: 40, 54, 59, 82–4, and 22, 31–2 for the following.

[81] The number of wandering pigs and sows attached to each household were listed every year in the mayor's tourn.

[82] Maltby 1979: 40, 54.

[83] See above, p. 137.

role as graziers also helps explain why butchers so frequently appeared as both buyers and sellers of livestock. Many of these deals involved fellow butchers such as when the Exeter butcher John Benet, after pasturing fourteen oxen for some time in the northern suburb of Duryard, sold them to Thomas Smyth, a butcher who lived in the western suburb of Exe Island.[84]

Like butchers resident in Exeter, those from outside the city conducted their trade on several different levels. They all certainly brought animals on the hoof to Exeter, selling some to butchers or other residents, and slaughtering others near the Fleshfold where a few of them maintained shops or stalls to sell meat.[85] The more occasional visitors may have come only to sell livestock as is suggested by the fines levelled against those who went out to intercept foreign butchers or others coming to town with livestock for sale. These illegal sales took place especially in the western suburbs, either outside the west gate or at Cowick Street on the western side of the river, both areas through which all those arriving from the livestock-rich mid Devon and moorland regions had to pass.[86] But foreign butchers also carried in ox and sheep carcasses (whole, halved, or quartered) from animals that had been killed elsewhere, something the civic authorities strongly discouraged because of the potential for spoilage, consumer fraud, and regrating that might lead to higher prices.[87] The varied interests of foreign butchers in Exeter were also reflected in the amounts of their debts there; their average debt was a little over 9*s* at a time when meat sales averaged only 4*s* 3*d* but livestock sales averaged five times that sum, almost 21*s*.[88]

It is also clear that urban demand for meat promoted the town as a regional center for the sale of livestock. Foreign butchers and other non-residents not only brought livestock to sell at Exeter but also came there to purchase animals. Livestock sales between two non-residents represent one example of this, such as the oxen sold by William Monk of Potheridge (27 miles away in mid Devon) to William Fodyng, butcher of Withycombe Raleigh, by Roger Ewer of Topsham to William Forst (for eight oxen), and by Robert Bryen to William Spencer of Newton St Cyres.[89] The butcher Robert Yurl of Silverton agreed to sell a cow for Walter Drascombe (an outsider who also sued two other butchers

[84] MCR 1379/80, m. 4.
[85] SQMT passim; Book 53A, f. 76.
[86] SQMT 1353, 1363, 1392.
[87] MCR 1360/1, m. 8d; 1379/80, m. 19; 1428/9, mm. 1, 12.
[88] Data from thirty four debt cases for meat, fifty one cases for livestock, and nineteen cases involving non-resident butchers (MCR and PCR debt cases, 1378–88).
[89] MCR 1388/9, m. 5; 1390/1, mm. 20, 26; 1391/2, m. 24.

for debt), but got into trouble when he sold it for a sum that was less than what Drascombe expected.[90] When not buying and selling among themselves, Exeter butchers generally purchased livestock from non-residents. Many of these purchases were quite small, suggesting that rural dwellers came to town with only one or two animals to sell. Examples of such sales to butchers include the one sheep sold by William Waleys, the ewe sold by Henry Carswill, or the two ewes sold by Richard Carswill.[91] But butchers invested a great deal in bulk transactions as well, particularly in exchanges made among themselves or with graziers. These include the sale of fourteen oxen by John Benet to his fellow butcher Thomas Smyth, the sale of three bullocks and two cows by Stephen Boghewode to the baker/hosteler John Brendon, and the 21*s* 4*d* owed by John Penkerigg for sheep (enough for at least ten) to Robert Brook, a cleric.[92] The better-off butchers also hired agents to acquire animals for them; William Boghewode, for example, gave £4 to Nicholas Golling to pay for cows and young steers from various men but had to sue Nicholas when he failed to render account.[93]

Unlike the grain hinterland which appears to have shrunk in the late middle ages, that for livestock probably expanded after the mid fourteenth century.[94] As standards of living rose and more land was given over to pastoral husbandry in the late fourteenth and fifteenth centuries, more livestock was brought to the town to satisfy the rising demand for meat.[95] The greater mobility and lower transport costs for livestock aided in enlarging the area from which livestock arrived, as did the increasingly strong regional specializations in Devon.[96] In Exeter this expansion was obvious in the much larger number of foreign butchers active in the city from the 1370s on and in the rebuilding of the Fleshfold in 1380/1 which doubled the space available to sell meat.[97] The total number of butchers trading livestock or selling meat in Exeter in the year 1392/3 was thirty six, almost half of whom (seventeen) lived elsewhere; nine of the seventeen also leased space in the Fleshfold. The regional livestock trade at other towns also grew during this period; at

[90] MCR 1380/1, m. 46; 1387/8, m. 33; PCR 1–23 Ric. II, m. 42.

[91] PCR 1–23 Ric. II, mm. 29, 68; Misc. Roll 55.

[92] PCR 1–23 Ric. II, mm. 20, 24; MCR 1379/80, m. 4.

[93] MCR 1374/5, mm. 25, 31. Boghewode farmed the meat custom and rented more stalls in the Fleshfold than anyone else (MCR 1364/5, m. 1d; 1366/7, m. 1d; 1368/9, m. 1d; 1372/3, m. 1d).

[94] For the grain hinterland, see Kowaleski forthcoming and Figure 7.1.

[95] For these trends, see Dyer 1981 and 1989b.

[96] For these specializations, see especially Fox 1991.

[97] SQMT passim; above, p. 183; Book 53A, f. 76. In 1392/3, twenty five men leased space in the Fleshfold, usually for 5*s* a year; all but two were butchers and nine resided outside of Exeter.

Winchester the mounting number of "foreign" butchers were accommodated in newly built stalls.[98] Their regular presence and growing representation at Exeter, Winchester, and Colchester reminds us of the dependence of urban markets on the products and skilled labor of the agricultural sector. Urban butchers also had ties to this sector through their leasing of rural pasture and meadow, their purchase of livestock on the hoof from graziers and farmers, and their business dealings with rural and small-town butchers. Indeed, the growing urban demand for meat in the late middle ages helped to stimulate the pastoral economy and create a new class of butcher-graziers whose wealth and regional commercial dealings rivaled those of many urban traders.[99]

Butchers also played a central role in the marketing of hides and skins, a trade which can be traced in the annual court presentments against those who sold raw hides and skins (mainly wool-fells) outside of the sanctioned marketplace.[100] The fines assessed were basically a type of licensing fee charged on the most active sellers of hides and skins. If each annual presentment is counted as a sale, then butchers were responsible for 95 per cent of all sales of hides and skins in 1370–90. More than half of these butchers resided outside of Exeter; most lived in communities within 12 miles of Exeter (Table 7.5). Butchers became involved in the hide and skin trade because the supply of raw hides and skins was largely dependent on the slaughter of animals for meat. Since hides from animals that died of natural causes did not make a satisfactory leather, the vast majority of hides came onto the market in towns where the greatest quantity of meat was consumed. Indeed, municipal ordinances actually required butchers to bring carcasses into the market with the hides and skins attached, in order to ensure quality, control prices, and make it easier for the authorities to collect tolls on the separate sale of all parts of the animal (meat, hides, horns, tallow).[101] They also aimed to prevent butchers from plucking and selling separately the valuable wool attached to sheepskins.

The buyers of hides and skins were a far more diverse group than the sellers. They can be identified through the annual presentments against those who purchased hides and skins outside the official marketplace or without belonging to the town freedom since this trade was

[98] Keene 1985: 258, 541. For Colchester, see Britnell 1986b: 131, 142, 198–200.

[99] On this point, see also Dyer 1972 and Watkin 1989 for the rise of yeomen graziers.

[100] MT (especially SQMT) 1370–90; see also Kowaleski 1990 for more on this analysis, including maps of the residences of buyers and sellers. There were a total of 577 presentments for ninety one different vendors.

[101] SQMT 1391–3; Jones 1976: 146.

Table 7.5. *Residences of dealers in hides and skins at Exeter, 1370–90*

		Purchases				Sales		
Distance from Exeter	Buyers (No.)	(No.)	%	% of known	Vendors (No.)	(No.)	%	% of known
Less than 6 miles	(2)	(18)	5	7	(15)	(117)	38	51
6–12 miles	(10)	(67)	19	28	(15)	(104)	34	46
13–25 miles	(19)	(140)	39	58	(2)	(7)	2	3
More than 25 miles	(1)	(16)	4	7	–	–	–	–
Unidentified	(23)	(121)	33	–	(17)	(81)	26	
Total non-residents	(55)	(362)	100	100	(49)	(309)	100	100
Exeter	(157)	(614)	63		(42)	(268)	46	

Source and note: SQMT 1370–90; presentments for 1373 and 1377 are missing. Buyers represent individuals who purchased raw hides and skins outside the sanctioned marketplace or without belonging to the freedom; purchases include the total number of presentments made for these "offenses." Vendors represent primarily butchers who sold raw hides or skins outside the appointed marketplace; sales include the total number of presentments.

supposed to be reserved for freedom members.[102] Like the fines assessed on sellers, these annual payments were essentially a licensing fee to pursue supposedly "illegal" activities. There were many more buyers than sellers; the former numbered 212 compared to only 91 individual vendors over this period (Table 7.5). Buyers came from more diverse occupations (at least twenty four different trades) in contrast to the overwhelming preponderence of butchers as sellers of hides and skins. Most of the buyers worked in the leather or skin trades; they included thirty shoemakers and saddlers, twenty four skinners, eleven glovers, pouchmakers, girdlers or others in the light leather crafts, fifteen butchers, nine innkeepers or taverners, seven cloth-workers and nine other crafts such as chandler and victualler.[103] This diversity of occupations reflects the large number of urban craftspeople involved in the working of leather. Indeed, almost 75 per cent of the leather and skin buyers resided in Exeter, compared to 46 per cent of the sellers.

[102] MT 1370–90; there were a total of 976 presentments representing 212 buyers. Since Exeter freemen who never purchased hides or skins in illegal places could avoid both of these fines, some buyers are probably not included here. This omission, however, merely intensifies the differences noted here between the many buyers resident in Exeter and the smaller group of sellers who tended to come from elsewhere.

[103] Occupations are known for 61 per cent of the 157 Exeter buyers but only 17 per cent of the 55 non-Exeter buyers.

While non-Exeter buyers represented about one-quarter of all customers of hides and skins, the intensity of their involvement was greater than that of residents since they were responsible for almost 40 per cent of the presentments. Non-resident buyers also travelled longer distances to get to Exeter than did the butchers-sellers (Table 7.5). Over 40 per cent of the non-resident buyers came from more than 12 miles away, a journey that must have taken some time to complete if loaded down with heavy hides. This regional marketing pattern stemmed in part from the substantial involvement of tanners, who alone accounted for at least one-third of all buyers of hides and who, unlike most of the other purchasers, usually lived outside of the city. Tanners may have preferred residences outside the larger towns for a variety of reasons. Many may have wished to avoid the increasingly restrictive regulation levied on their trade both by civic authorities anxious to control the smells and pollution generated by their work and by the other leather crafts who sought to control their own access to the essential raw material of their industry.[104] Proximity to running water and supplies of bark for tannin may have also been factors. Small-town and rural tanneries were certainly not unusual in medieval Devon; there were bark-grinding mills at Dartmoor-border locations in Tavistock and Okehampton, and four tanning pits on the riverbank at Bradninch in the Exe valley that the lord leased out every year.[105] Such rural tanneries had a long history in the county; as early as 1207 the men of Axmouth in east Devon paid 20*s* for the use of tanneries there.[106]

Bradninch tanners such as Adam Catour and John, Reginald, and Roger Tannere visited Exeter regularly to purchase hides, a trip of about 10 miles.[107] At least four tanners came from Tiverton, a very large parish 13 miles north of Exeter, situated on the border between east and mid Devon.[108] The Tiverton tanners not only purchased raw hides in Exeter, but they also sold their finished product there, as seen in the suit of the Exeter shoemaker, Henry Goldeford, against Thomas Doun of Tiverton for breaking an agreement to deliver tanned hides to him.[109] The tanner Matthew Michel from Matford, only 5 miles

[104] Kowaleski 1990: 60–8 for this and the following.

[105] Finberg 1969: 153–4. Okehampton: PRO C135/260/15; BL Add. Ch. 64663. Bradninch: DCO Min. Accts. 8, 10, 12, 14, 22, 25, 29; PRO SC11/802, m. 11 (under Bradninch).

[106] *Pipe roll*, vol. 60: 184.

[107] MCR 1360/1, m. 8d; SQMT 1371–87.

[108] John Christopher, John Ivoun (also called Ivo Tannere), Richard Lukeys, and Thomas Doun: SQMT 1370–87. For Lukeys' activities as a tanner, see also PRO JUST3/179, m. 2.

[109] MCR 1389/90, m. 49; SQMT 1374–89, 1392.

away, had even more regular (though just as unhappy) relationships with Exeter leatherworkers since he was sued for debt by the saddlers Richard Stoke and John Scarlet, the cordwainer John Boggebrook, and the currier Henry Orchard.[110]

What is especially noticeable, however, is the number of buyers who came to Exeter from the manors and small towns surrounding the livestock-rich region of Dartmoor. Over 20 per cent of the known non-resident hide and skin buyers at Exeter in 1370–90 came from South Zeal, Okehampton, and Tavistock on the borders of Dartmoor, a region that was not usually a part of Exeter's commercial hinterland.[111] With one exception, most of these buyers were probably tanners or dealers in hides rather than skins, as an accusation concerning a theft of two tanned hides from John Stondon's house in Okehampton suggests.[112] Several of the Okehampton buyers can be linked to their home communities where they seem to have enjoyed a relatively high status, as indicated by their appearances in land transactions and as witnesses to deeds made there.[113] John Stondon also served in the borough's top office as provost and was taxed 6*s* in one of the tinner's subsidies while Henry Sampson served as the town's chief poll tax collector in 1377.[114] With a tax-paying population of only 135 in 1377, Okehampton was a very small borough; the number of high-status hide dealers or tanners which it sent to Exeter in the space of twenty years points to how some of its residents capitalized on commercial opportunities linked to regional agricultural specialties.

It is also striking that tanners and hide dealers from livestock-rich areas like Okehampton and Tiverton travelled many miles to Exeter to acquire hides for their trade. This regional network of contacts clearly illustrates the pull of the urban marketplace, as well as the secondary character of the hide trade as a by-product of urban meat consumption. As the archaeological bone evidence shows, slaughtered cattle were in

[110] PCR 1–23 Ric. II, mm. 31, 34, 42, 82; MCR 1382/3, m. 41.

[111] They included Henry and John Breghe, Henry and John Sampson, and John Stondon of Okehampton; John atte Forde (a skinner) of Tavistock; and Roger Viel of South Zeal. Together they accounted for seven of the thirty two identifiable non-resident buyers and forty five of their 241 presentments (SQMT 1370–90; MCR 1360/1, m. 8d). At least two other buyers (Thomas Stondon and John Upright) also probably came from Okehampton but were not included in these figures. For Dartmoor's relationship to Exeter's hinterland, see above, Tables 6.4 and 7.1, and below, Table 7.7.

[112] PRO JUST1/1/192, m. 13d; the wording of the MT presentments also points to their dealing in hides rather than skins.

[113] John Breghe, Henry Breghe, Henry Sampson, and John Stondon; 314M/TF35, 36, 38, 46–49.

[114] 314M/TF46; PRO E179/95/22; E179/95/54.

good supply since almost three-quarters of the meat consumed by weight in late medieval Exeter was beef.[115] Thus the concentrated supply in towns of the essential raw material of the leather industry – hides and skins – channelled traders in these items, particularly tanners, to the urban marketplace and promoted networks of trade which extended out to towns and villages in the surrounding countryside. Similar marketing patterns were visible in other counties. In late fourteenth-century Lincolnshire, for example, tanners can be seen travelling regional circuits encompassing about 50 miles, buying up raw hides in a variety of marketplaces and selling them when tanned to urban and small-town leather craftspeople.[116] Rural and small-town tanners in Hampshire also made regular trips into Southampton to purchase raw hides, returning later with their tanned hides.[117]

Although the sale and purchase of hides was linked to that of skins in the court presentments, the marketing chain for the two differed in some significant ways. Unlike hides, which underwent a lengthy tanning process (up to a year) to render them strong and waterproof enough to be used in shoes, saddles, buckets, and other products made of heavy leather, skins could be made into leather in a matter of weeks by tawing with alum or oil. Tawed leather, which could easily be dyed, was made into gloves, leather garments, pouches, shoe uppers, and other products of the light leather industry. Most of the skins sold in Exeter were sheep skins (wool fells) followed by calf and lamb skins, although wolf and cat skins were also noted. The supply of raw skins was also more subject to seasonal variations than were hides since lamb and calf skins normally came onto the market in the spring.[118] Many skins were also tawed with the hair attached, thus making them part of the fur trade and the focus of the skinners' interests. The diverse groups involved in the skin trade can be seen in the occupational breakdown of the buyers noted above; excluding the butchers whose involvement in buying skins was marginal, 27 per cent of the buyers were skinners and 12 per cent were glovers or other users of light tawed leather.[119]

Many skinners also had commercial connections beyond the city. For those at the lower end of the trade such as Thomas Jesse, this merely entailed purchasing skins from outsiders such as John Bullok, who sold

[115] Maltby 1979: 22, 31–2.

[116] Kowaleski 1990: 62.

[117] Southampton Record Office SC5.5/1 (1430–1); *Brokage book of Southampton 1439–40* and *1443–44*; Kowaleski 1990: 62–3.

[118] Kowaleski 1990: 62–3; eighty five per cent of the skins brought into Southampton for three years in the mid-fifteenth century arrived between April and June.

[119] See above, p. 301.

him wolf and cat skins.[120] But wealthy oligarchic skinners maintained more lucrative commercial networks of trade over much greater distances; Walter Thomas, for example, regularly traded with London skinners who supplied him with costly imported furs, while other Exeter skinners traded skins in north Somerset.[121] In the late thirteenth and early fourteenth centuries Exeter skinners also traded furs and skins in London and were especially active at Winchester's international fair.[122] Their expensive product meant that their customers and market were also of a much higher status than that served by most leatherworkers. The A Rank skinner Nicholas Bynnecote counted among his clients William Speek, lord of Brampford Speke; the knights John FitzPayn (of Stoodleigh), Baldwin Malet (of Somerset), and Warin Lercedeken (of Haccombe); and the esquire and future sheriff Nicholas Kirkham (of Blagdon near Paignton), while the London skinner, John Manaton, served as one of his executors.[123]

Because of the links between the livestock, meat, and hide or skin trades, the commercial hinterland for all these products overlapped considerably. That for meat was the smallest because of the dangers of spoilage, although cured meats could be sent over greater distances as the number of imported "bacons" arriving every year at the port of Exeter attests.[124] The trade in livestock extended further because of the relative ease and cheapness with which animals could be moved, as indicated by inter-manorial stock transfers and the Devon practice of summering cattle on moorlands; trade over 20 and even 30 miles was not uncommon, particularly if we consider the popularity of regional fairs as selling points for livestock. In one instance, a herd of fifteen cows, oxen, and steers was driven from the Dartmoor parish of Moretonhampstead to Shaftesbury in Dorset, some 75 miles away.[125] This hinterland narrows if we consider only the livestock destined for urban tables since many of these animals had first been moved to lowland areas near towns for fattening. Normally there was a change of ownership at this time from rearer to butcher, or from grazier to butcher if the rearer sold first to graziers. Although some butchers active in Exeter came from 20 miles away or more, the vast majority lived within 12 miles of the city (Table 7.5). If we therefore consider the commercial hinterland to consist only of that region or distance over which the immediate

[120] MCR 1382/3, mm. 7, 8.
[121] See above, p. 158; EQMT 1365.
[122] MCR Roll 1, mm. 4d, 18, 28; 1290/1, m. 26d; 1302/3, m. 7; 1303/4, m. 8d.
[123] PCR 1–23 Ric. II, mm. 56, 63, 65, 66; MCR 1397/8, m. 38; Tyldesley 1978: 120–1; Cherry 1983–5: 262; Reichel 1935: 441.
[124] PCA passim; most probably came from the Channel Islands and France.
[125] MCR 1315/16, m. 37d.

seller of livestock travelled before coming to Exeter, then the hinterland ranged no farther than the homes of those butchers who brought livestock to the city for sale. But if we consider the marketing chain that livestock could travel before being slaughtered for meat, or the role Exeter played as a point of exchange for livestock that later travelled out of the city for work or consumption elsewhere, then the hinterland was much more extensive.

Most extensive of all was the hinterland for hides and skins. The tanners, skinners, and others who purchased these items journeyed over longer distances than did the vendors (Table 7.5). Their marketing chain also stretched further, from butcher-sellers (some resident in Exeter, some not), to out-of-town tanners in such places as Tiverton or Okehampton, and after tanning, back to the town for resale to members of the leather crafts, some of whom carried these tanned hides or tawed skins elsewhere for resale or manufacturing. Much of this trade was handled in the weekly or daily markets of market towns, but fairs also served as an important point of exchange. Hugh Tanner of Milverton (over 24 miles away in Somerset) sold 43 dozen calf skins at Exeter during the Lammas fair and Exeter cordwainers and others regularly purchased goat skins at the fair in St Decuman, over 30 miles away in north Somerset.[126] Overland transport of hides from Exeter could thus extend considerable distances. In one case three Exeter butchers were accused of buying sixty raw hides in Exeter and carrying them to Cornwall, a trip that would cover at least 40 miles and take them around Dartmoor and across the wide Tamar river.[127] In another instance, thirty five salted hides were to be carted from Exeter to Taunton, 28 miles north and over the Blackdown Hills.[128] For furs and skins tawed with the hair attached, even longer distances could be travelled, as the regular transactions between Exeter and London skinners show.

Some hides and skins also left Exeter via the port trade. Hide exports were a mainstay of Exeter trade in the late thirteenth and early fourteenth centuries, exported overseas to places like Rouen.[129] In the late fourteenth century, Exeter merchants such as Richard Bozoun occasionally exported hides overseas (he sent 103 in 1376), but more hides probably departed by coastal craft for re-export from Southampton or

126 Misc. Roll 40 (1415); MCR Roll 1, m. 25; MCR 1318/19, m. 4d compared with 1329/30, m. 24d and 1330/1, m. 6d.

127 MCR 1374/5, m. 10.

128 MCR Roll 1, m. 5.

129 PRO E122/40/1–1A, 40/3, 40/5, 40/7, 40/7A–B, 156/8; MCR Roll 1, m. 5.

other Devon and Cornwall ports.[130] The number of hides exported from England in the late middle ages was, however, markedly less than what had been conveyed overseas in the thirteenth and early fourteenth centuries.[131] This decline signaled not depression in the English leather trades, but rather, in a development analogous to that of the cloth industry, a relative increase in the manufacture and consumption of leather goods at home. The leather trades underwent substantial growth and diversification in the late middle ages, in part because of the expansion of cattle and sheep farming which produced a cheaper source of raw materials.[132] In the other direction, rising standards of living stimulated urban demand for meat and for leather products, thereby channelling hides and skins through the urban marketplace. Urban entrepôts like Exeter thus served as the vital link between local, regional, and even international marketing networks for both the raw materials and finished products of the industry. Few trades more clearly illustrate the dynamic interchange between town and country than the exchange of hides and skins.

The trade in fish

The trade in fish probably attracted more attention from Exeter's civic authorities than trade in any other item. Their efforts to control the marketing of fish reflected several concerns. First and foremost, they wanted to assure a steady and cheap supply of this vital foodstuff to Exeter's inhabitants. In a society whose religion dictated that fish replace meat on almost 150 days a year, fish constituted a very important part of the medieval diet. With its proximity to the sea and well-stocked rivers, Exeter enjoyed especially good access to supplies of fresh fish. This access, combined with its role as a regional entrepôt and its good overland connections to much of Devon, Somerset, and Dorset, also

[130] PRO E122/158/32; PRO E356/8, m. 51. For the re-export trade with Southampton and other Devon ports, see above, pp. 226, 232–3. Some of the 38,000 skins and 1,408 hides "imported" at Southampton in 1435–6 probably came from Exeter and its region (*Local port book of Southampton 1435–36*). For hides exported from Devon and Cornwall, see PRO E122 passim and the "Cokett" entries in the DCO Min. Accts. and relevant PRO SC6 Duchy accounts. In 1350/1, over 3,000 hides were exported from these ports (PRO SC6/817/1, m. 14).

[131] Newcastle exported over 15,000 hides a year in the late thirteenth century (Pelham 1951: 314–16). By the fifteenth century, hide exports had slowed to a trickle (Gray 1966: 4, 361, n. 6). Such exports also declined in Devon and Cornwall (PRO E122, SC6 Duchy accounts, and DCO Min. Accts. passim).

[132] This argument is developed at greater length in Kowaleski 1990.

made Exeter a natural marketing center for fish. The municipal government's second concern, therefore, was to regulate the large number of non-resident fish dealers drawn to Exeter, particularly when they infringed on the trading rights of freedom members. The dealers proved very difficult to control, however, in part because they were so mobile; fish were much easier to carry and conceal than livestock or hides, they easily spoiled and thus were brought in every day, and the regional networks of trade for fish (as we shall see) were much more extensive than for most other items. Third and last, the civic attention focused on the fish trade also reflected the substantial income that regulation of this trade generated for the city. In the last four decades of the fourteenth century annual revenues from the farm of the fish custom averaged about £11 and rose to £18 by the end of the fifteenth century; these sums totaled more than all the other customs put together.[133] Self-interest may thus have motivated some of Exeter's regulations concerning the fish trade.

From at least the thirteenth century the city tried to assert control over the fish trade along the 10-mile length of the Exe estuary. In the 1260s fines were levied on those who evaded custom on fish sales made at Topsham and Pratteshide; the city also attempted to establish its right to collect custom on the fish trade at the manor of Littleham (wherein lay the busy fish market at Exmouth) when it acquired the estuarine ferry there.[134] The city's efforts at Littleham and at Bradham, the manor just to its north, met with stiff resistance and little success. But the city persevered and pursued its claim in the central courts, finally winning the right in 1411 to collect custom on fish sold at Exmouth (a custom probably limited to toll on fish destined for Exeter).[135] At the rate of ½*d* per horseload, this toll was taken from at least 520 horseloads of fish sent through Exmouth to Exeter in 1411/12. On the western side of the river, similar tolls were collected on fish passing through Alphington on its way to Exeter by the end of the middle ages.[136] But the city's claims in Topsham ran into more trouble when the earls of Devon asserted their rights in this manor in

133 CRA passim; and see below, pp. 311–12. Additional profits accrued from sales of forfeited fish (ranging from 5–30*s* a year: MCR passim) and the annual fines assessed on those forestalling and regrating fish (9–25*s* a year: SQMT passim).

134 MCR Roll 1, m. 1; 1288/9, m. 39; Misc. Roll 2, nos. 34, 52. See also Jackson 1972: 62 for this and the following.

135 CRA 1410/11, 1411/12 et seq. *Citie of Excester*: 554, 567. See also Misc. Roll 48 (1493/4) for the collection of fish custom at *Checkstone* (Exmouth) recorded in an East Buddleigh account.

136 *Citie of Excester*: 554 for this toll in the sixteenth century. For the city's efforts to control the fish trade there and in Kennford in the fourteenth century, see below, n. 143.

the early fourteenth century.[137] The earls' construction of weirs on the Exe river also severely hurt the city's access to the valuable salmon fisheries in the Exe river.

The most persistent hurdle the city faced in gaining control of the fish trade concerned traders (called "fishers" in the local records, but actually more like fishmongers) who forestalled the Exeter market by going out to meet fishers travelling to Exeter to sell their catch. Some intercepted fishers in the southern suburbs near the estuary or in villages on the roads leading to south Devon, while others went down to the sea, purchased fish directly from fishers, and carried their purchases on packhorse back to the city for resale.[138] By reselling this fish (inevitably at higher prices) the forestallers also engaged in regrating, another practice the authorities wished to discourage. Regrating could double the price of fish; Henry Fisher purchased mackerel for ½*d* apiece from two men approaching Exeter from Slapton (a fishing village over 30 miles away on the south Devon coast) but sold them in Exeter at 1*d* apiece.[139] If the forestallers carried such fish out of town for resale elsewhere, the city lost in two ways: custom payments were evaded and the supplies available to local residents were diminished.[140] As a result, forestalling by interception before reaching the town was treated seriously, particularly when the forestallers showed up later in Exeter to sell this fish at inflated prices. The fines levied against those who engaged in this practice could be five to ten times higher than the usual charges assessed on forestallers, an indication of how damaging the municipal authorities considered this practice.[141] In one instance the offense was believed so harmful that several of the fishmongers lost their membership in the freedom.[142]

In the late fourteenth century, the interception of fish supplies became particularly acute to the south-west of the city, a reflection of the increasingly large amounts of sea fish coming from south Devon. Continual complaints were made against those who bought up fish at Alphington, Kennford, and the Haldon Hills (which border the western side of the lower Exe valley), all places which lay on the main roads between

[137] See above, pp. 223–4.
[138] MCR 1302/3, m. 4d; 1375/6, m. 43; 1376/7, m. 7.
[139] MCR 1379/80, m. 35; see also MCR 1303/4, m. 4d; 1334/5, m. 32d; 1379/80, m. 35; EQMT 1339.
[140] MCR 1334/5, m. 32d; NQMT 1409; Misc. Roll 2, no. 26.
[141] For example, Reginald Lil paid fines totaling 7*s* for these offenses at a time when most forestallers paid 3–6*d* (MCR 1376/7, mm. 9, 22; SQMT passim).
[142] MCR 1311/12, mm. 30d, 31d.

south Devon and Exeter.[143] Attempts to halt such forestalling extended the Exeter hand of law well outside its own jurisdiction, as seen in the presentments made against men like Walter Broun and Richard Modde of Alphington and Thomas Monk of Kennford for marketing fish even in their own villages, some 3 to 4 miles south-west of the city.[144] The increasingly frequent references to forestalling in these locations probably reflected a growth in fishing off the south Devon coast. Other evidence also points to an expansion of the fish trade in this period, rather than just a recovery after the crisis of the Black Death. Fish sellers from south Devon coastal communities such as Plympton, Yealmpton, Slapton, and Brixham began to appear more often at Exeter than they had in the late thirteenth and early fourteenth centuries.[145] In the late middle ages, the south Devon fishing grounds were also the richest in the county; fish tithes from south Devon coastal locations (especially near Start Bay and Tor Bay) were substantially larger than those collected elsewhere in the county.[146]

The expansion of the late medieval fishing trade off the southern coasts of Devon and Cornwall was also visible in the rising fish exports from these areas. At Exeter, fish imports from these regions grew tremendously in the 1390s and continued to mount in the fifteenth century; even in the last four decades of the fourteenth century over twenty different types of fish arrived there, most by coastal craft from south Devon and Cornwall.[147] Herring and hake were the biggest imports, followed by cod and conger eel. Much of the herring came from fishing grounds off the eastern coast of England, but some (probably an increasing amount) also came from the seas off Devon and Cornwall.[148]

[143] MCR 1367/8, m. 24d; 1376/7, mm. 5, 7, 9, 22; 1378/9, mm. 25, 24, 44; 1390/1, m. 5; 1403/4, mm. 5d, 38d. NQMT 1350; WQMT 1402.

[144] MCR 1378/9, m. 25; 1382/3, m. 16; SQMT 1390; WQMT 1402.

[145] Plympton: NQMT 1405. Yealmpton: SQMT 1387; PRO CP40/497, m. 406. Slapton: SQMT 1365; MCR 1379/80, m. 35. Brixham: SQMT 1384–90; 1414; MCR 1376/7, m. 22 (Reginald Lil).

[146] Russell 1951: 282 and above, p. 34.

[147] PCA passim. The types were cod, conger eel, common eel, dried fish (most probably cod and hake), hake, herring, lamprey, ling, mackerel, merling (whiting), mulwell, pike, pilchard, pollack, porpoise, ray, salmon, stockfish (probably cod), sturgeon, and whiting; they arrived fresh, dried, salted, or smoked. Bream and roach were imported in PCA 1345/6, 1348/9. For the much smaller fish imports (mostly herring from Yarmouth) in the earlier period, see above, Table 6.2. The fish remains from Exeter reflect an even wider diversity of fish although they show basically the same ranking (with the exception of herring since their small bones are less easily recovered and identified); see Wilkinson 1979: 74–81.

[148] For example, the *Julian* of Dartmouth's herring cargoes (PCA 1394/5, 1395/6, 1396/7) probably originated locally since the importers were mostly from south Devon and the cargo also included other items usually transhipped from south Devon ports. See also Southward, Boalch, and Maddock 1988 for herring and pilchard fishing off the Devon coast.

By the 1390s, however, herring was far outnumbered by imports of hake, cod, and other fish. Hake was found largely off the south Devon and Cornish coasts; cod was fished all around the south-western peninsula and off the coasts of Brittany and the Channel Islands; and conger was a specialty of the Channel Islands, Brittany, and Normandy, although much also arrived in Exeter on Cornish ships.[149] Conger must also have been available off the east Devon coast since it was specifically mentioned as part of the catch of the *rustici* of the prior of Otterton.[150] Fish from south Devon and Cornwall, however, dominated the maritime fish trade in late medieval Exeter. Ships from Portlemouth, Dartmouth, Brixham, and Paignton in south Devon, and Mousehole, Penzance, Looe, and Fowey in south Cornwall often arrived at the port of Exeter with large cargoes consisting only of fish that must have come from the rich fishing grounds near these ports.[151] By the second half of the fifteenth century, fish exports from Devon and Cornwall had surpassed those from the previously important east coast ports; hake, pilchard, herring, cod, and ray accounted for the bulk of these exports.[152]

This expansion of south Devon and Cornish fishing helped to promote Exeter as a regional center for the sale of fish. The success of the city's new fair (begun in 1374) on Ash Wednesday represents one way that Exeter capitalized on this development since much of the business of the fair concentrated on the trade in fish before the start of Lent.[153] During the late fourteenth century the number of non-resident fish traders visiting Exeter increased significantly, accelerating at an even faster pace during the first two decades of the fifteenth century. In the 1360s the fish custom levied on all outsiders was annually leased for just under £11, but by the 1410s it had swelled to almost £15 and reached £18 in 1500.[154] In the late 1360s annual presentments against forestallers and regrators of fish also began to appear in the south

149 PCA passim; Russell 1951; Wheeler 1969: 134, 230, 260–82; Litler 1979: esp. Map 1; Bolton 1968; Waquet 1913.

150 Oliver 1864: 255.

151 See especially PCA 1394/5–1398/9. These fish cargoes continued to dominate the fifteenth-century port trade (PCA passim).

152 Litler 1979: 227–36, 245–9 and Map 1. The reasons for this expansion need further study. Factors that played some role include the decline of the east coast ports and fishing grounds (especially in herring; see Heath 1968; Saul 1975; Bailey 1989), the discovery of new fishing grounds off the southern coasts of Devon and Cornwall, and increased consumption linked to rising standards of living. See also Southward, Boalch, and Maddock 1988, for how changes in water temperature affected the types and numbers of fish caught off the Devon coast.

153 See above, p. 66.

154 CRA passim; before the Black Death the fish custom averaged about £10 each year; from the 1420s–70s it held steady at about £14–15 but grew again in the next three decades, reaching £18 in 1500/1; see also Book 55, f. 48v for what was included in the farm (in 1477).

Table 7.6. *Residences of fish dealers at Exeter, 1370–90*

Distance from Exeter	Individuals (No.)	%	% of known	Presentments (No.)	%	% of known
Less than 6 miles	(9)	6	11	(33)	5	8
6–12 miles	(7)	4	9	(47)	6	11
13–25 miles	(24)	15	29	(105)	14	25
More than 25 miles	(42)	26	51	(231)	32	56
Unidentified	(79)	49	–	(310)	43	–
Total Non-Residents	(161)	100	100	(726)	100	100
Exeter	(36)	18		(215)	23	

Source and note: SQMT 1370–90 (presentments for forestalling and regrating fish). For 1377, see MCR 1377, see MCR 1376/7, mm. 5, 7, 11, 12, 23, 41; presentments for 1373 and 1383 are missing.

quarter mayor's tourn. An average of thirty nine persons were presented for forestalling and regrating fish each year in the 1370s; in the following decade the figure increased to fifty five and in the 1390s to seventy four.[155] These dealers handled mostly marine fish that reached Exeter overland rather than by sea. Over 80 per cent of these fish traders resided outside of Exeter, indicating the extent to which the local and regional fish trade in and near Exeter was in the hands of non-residents (Table 7.6).

The size and scope of the hinterland for fish can be illuminated by examining the annual presentments made against forestallers and regrators of fish in the mayor's tourn. Exeter residents played a relatively small role in this trade, accounting for only 18 per cent of the dealers, in contrast to the hide and skin trade where Exeter residents accounted for 74 per cent of the buyers and 46 per cent of the sellers. Non-resident fish dealers also conducted trade over much longer distances than did those who exchanged hides and skins (Tables 7.5 and 7.6). Only one hide/skin dealer resided more than 25 miles from Exeter but at least forty two (26 per cent) of the fish traders came from these greater distances. If only known residences

[155] SQMT 1370–99; the nature of the presentments changed in the next decade so no comparable figures are available. Like the presentments made against buyers and sellers of hides and skins, these for forestalling and regrating fish became a type of licensing fee to retail fish in the city, although the traders still had to pay custom on their sales and purchases. The presentments, however, only hint at the intensity of involvement of these fish dealers since they were made only once a year. It is reasonable to presume, however, that those whose names were entered year after year must have been more active than those who appeared only intermittently in the lists.

outside Exeter are considered, the disparity in the range of the marketing networks was even more marked; over half of these fish presentments involved dealers from more than 25 miles away, but less than 1 per cent of the hide/skin dealers.[156] The fish purchases of gentry households throughout England also point to the greater distances buyers were willing to travel to buy marine fish.[157] Exeter's reputation as a fish market lured purchasers from households at Dunster, Porlock, and Stogumber in north Somerset to buy fish, even though these places were situated only a few miles from the north Somerset coast.[158]

The regional direction of the trade in fish also differed from the orientations exhibited in the trade of the other commodities treated here. Most startling was the large number of traders from inland areas of Somerset and Dorset; in 1370–90, at least 26 per cent of the non-resident fish dealers (51 per cent of the known traders) recorded in the annual fish presentments came from these two counties. The largest number arrived from Somerset. Taunton, Lamport, and Crewkerne were each the homes of six fish dealers while three came from Martock, three from Shepton Beauchamp, and two each from Wells, Chard, and Ashill; others came from Yeovil, Bruton, Wellington, and Wincanton.[159] Fish dealers from south Dorset were less of a presence, probably because they had better access to supplies from coastal regions in their own county. Nonetheless, five different fish dealers at Exeter listed Bridport as their home and others came from Shaftesbury, Sherborne, and Salisbury.[160] Most of these locations in Somerset and Dorset were over 30 miles from Exeter and some, like Wells, Wincanton, and Shaftesbury, were more than 50 miles away. East Devon was also the home of many fish dealers active at Exeter, representing about 33 per cent of the non-resident fish dealers; most were from inland settlements located 10 to 20 miles from Exeter.[161]

[156] There is no reason to believe that the clerks of the mayor's tourn tended to register the residences of fish dealers at any greater rate than they cited the homes of those presented for marketing hides and skins. In several instances, the residences of Somerset fish dealers were omitted from the SQMT lists and were identifed only with the aid of stray references in the MCR and MT that linked them with the fish trade and their entries in the SQMT lists.

[157] Dyer 1989a: 307–8, 320–2.

[158] Chadwyck Healy 1901: 299, 496; Maxwell-Lyte 1909: 111; Siraut 1985: 184.

[159] Fish traders from these last two places were noted in SQMT 1369, 1391–93.

[160] Fish traders from these last two places were noted in MCR 1360/1, m. 1; 1367/8, m. 24d; SQMT 1369.

[161] Honiton (seven); Topsham (five); Clayhidon (four); Sidmouth (four); Bradninch (three); Colyford (two); Tiverton (two); Kennford (two); Sampford Peverel (two); Ottery St Mary (two); Lympstone (one); Kenton (one); Cullompton (one).

Although these Somerset, Dorset, and east Devon fish dealers occasionally retailed fish in Exeter, they came to the city primarily to purchase fish, as their frequent fines for intercepting supplies of fish coming to Exeter emphasize.[162] Although many varieties of freshwater fish were available at Exeter, most of these dealers were attracted to Exeter by its supplies of marine fish, including hake, mackerel, and haddock that were fished off the south Devon and Cornish coast, as well as conger, lamprey, ling, mulwell, merling, porpoise, and salmon.[163] Analysis of fish remains in Somerset towns reinforces this conclusion. Sea-fish bones completely dominated the deposits at medieval sites in both Taunton and Lamport, with hake (a large, deep-water fish primarily available off the south Devon coast) generally representing the most numerous species.[164] Indeed, the distribution of fish remains in both these places was remarkably similar to that found in Exeter, suggesting that they were supplied to a large extent by common sources.[165] Much of the fish carried out of Exeter to these regions was probably transported fresh, although some could have been preserved through salting or other methods. If properly packed in baskets and kept wet, fresh fish could be transported considerable distances overland.[166] Of the roughly £200-worth of (mostly marine) fish purchased in 1383/4 for the earl of Devon's household at Tiverton, over 20 miles from the sea, no less than 78 per cent of this sum was spent on fresh fish.[167]

The inland traders who came to Exeter for fish were often identified by local scribes with the occupational designation or surname of "Fisher." But they were not true fishermen; rather they served as intermediaries, buying up supplies in Exeter, selling some in Exeter and bringing the rest back to their home settlements for sale. Many, in fact, carried on other activities besides dealing in fish. At least three

[162] MCR 1376/7, m. 5; 1377/8, 13; 1378/9, m. 24; NQMT 1409; see also Misc. Roll 2, no. 26. Their appearances in debt cases were also more often linked to buying rather than selling, as were the other references to forestalling. Yet as the wording of the presentments in SQMT makes clear, they did sell (regrate) as well as buy (forestall) fish in Exeter.

[163] MCR 1343/4, m. 32d; 1375/6, m. 44; 1377/8, m. 13 (Kuske was from Somerset, Dyme from Lamport); 1379/80, m. 35 (Henry Fisher was from Taunton). For the other types, see MCR 1264/5, mm. 7, 12, 12d; 1334/5, m. 32d; 1360/1, m. 10; 1376/7, m. 21; for salmon, see below. For the availability of freshwater fish in Somerset, see Aston and Dennison 1988; Dennison and Iles 1988.

[164] Wheeler 1984; Grant 1988.

[165] Wilkinson 1979: 74–81; Grant 1988: 412. Obviously fish from the Bristol Channel could also have easily reached these towns; but the prevalence of hake, which was normally associated with fishing grounds off south Devon and Cornwall, suggests that much may also have been carried overland from Exeter and other markets in Devon.

[166] Litler 1979: 11.

[167] CR 491.

of the Somerset fish dealers (John Balchere, John Cokyll, and William Yonge) and one from Cullompton in east Devon (John Everard) also marketed grain, beans, and peas in Exeter.[168] Other fish dealers marketed cloth: Richard Grymell of Winkleigh and Geoffrey Wonston both aulnaged cloth and traded fish at Exeter.[169] William Grymell of Okehampton may have specialized in providing fish to inland regions since besides appearing as a fish regrator in Exeter he also imported pollack, conger, cod, ling, hake, herring, and other fish through the port of Exeter.[170] The varied commercial activities of these fish dealers suggest that they were small-town merchants or chapmen whose dealings in fish represented but one part of their commercial enterprises.

These Devon, Somerset, and Dorset fish dealers were crucial links in the marketing chain that connected Exeter to the small towns and villages in its hinterland. In their own settlements, these traders seem to have been fairly prominent although the scale of their commercial activities hardly matched that of the Exeter merchant oligarchs. One example is John Litele of Ottery St Mary (a manor and small market town about 12 miles away in east Devon) who marketed fish in Exeter for over twenty years.[171] On two occasions he was singled out for forestalling the market, once for buying up two sums of fish from a fisherman and reselling it too dearly to various men in the Exeter marketplace and once for purchasing fish in Henry Archer's tavern rather than in the sanctioned marketplace. Like other non-resident fish dealers, Litele probably seized the opportunity to sell some of the fish he had purchased in the urban marketplace, perhaps anticipating higher profits by doing so because of the demand generated by both consumers and traders there. His regular visits to Exeter also brought him into contact with such wealthy merchant oligarchs as John Nymet who sued him for an unpaid debt of 40*s*.[172] The nature of the debt was not recorded, but the payment could have been for one of Nymet's imports, perhaps some of the iron or wine in which he specialized. In Ottery St Mary, Litele also pursued agricultural interests, as seen in his agreement to deliver two young steers to a fellow tenant.[173] Litele was

168 SQMT 1372, 1384–93; NQMT 1402; WQMT 1403; MCR 1375/6, m. 5; 1392/3, m. 21.

169 PRO E101/338/11, mm. 1–1d, 5d–6d; SQMT 1393; MCR 1402/3, m. 38d; PRO CP40/509, m. 36d; PRO E368/167 Michaelmas recorda, m. 13d.

170 SQMT 1393; PCA 1392/3–1395/6. For his land transactions in Okehampton, see 314M/TF38.

171 SQMT 1369–79, 1385–93; NQMT 1392–3; MCR 1376/7, m. 23; 1392/3, m. 45 for this and the following.

172 PRO CP40/490, m. 173; for Nymet see below, Table A3.1 and PCA 1358/9–1390/1 passim for his imports.

173 CR 1288, esp. mm. 5, 6, 14 for this and the following.

also a man of some standing in his home community since he was elected an ale-taster (he also brewed) and served as a juror in an important case in the local court.

Once in Exeter, the non-resident fish dealers often made purchases through the services of local fishmongers or hostelers. Hostelers were particularly important in this trade, not surprising when we consider the overnight accommodation many of these non-resident fish dealers would require while in Exeter. As a result, several innkeepers became deeply involved in the fish trade. Hostelers like Walter Horrigg, Thomas Canun, Thomas Pode, John Sleghe, and John and Agnes Streyngher themselves forestalled and regrated fish, held illegal fish markets for "foreign" fish dealers in their inns, had regular commercial dealings with them, and sometimes farmed the city custom on fish.[174] Thomas Pode was one of the more active hosteler/fishmongers. Besides selling oysters, herring, and other types of fish, he dealt with such Exeter fishmongers as Henry Fisher (to whom he gave 40*s*-worth of fish to sell), John Frank, Henry Parlebien (whom he hired to work for him), Richard Walsshe, John Strange, William Hampton (for whom he acted as a pledge in a debt case), John Horn, and Thomas Canun.[175] He also did business with non-resident fish dealers like William Andrew of Bradninch (to whom he sold herring and loaned three horses), John Benet (who sold him salmon and *wallis*), John Cornissh fisher, John Tokere fisher (whom he owed 11*s*), and William Berlegh of Yealmpton (who owed him 44*s*).[176] Pode maintained commercial relationships over several years with some of these men (Henry Parlebien, John Frank, and William Andrew), suggesting regular or long-term business contacts. Other hostelers made similar arrangements. Walter Montagu, who also kept a tavern, contracted with John Blaycche to supply him with six seams of fish each week, taking for each seam 12*d* plus expenses.[177] A similar arrangement may have been behind the 16 marks owed to him and an Exeter merchant by Walter Fyssher of Sherborne.[178]

Much less is known about fishers who brought their catch to the city for sale since they were subject to few of the regulations that

[174] Fish marketing: SQMT 1368–90; MCR 1376/7, m. 7; 1378/9, m. 24; 1382/3, m. 16; 1387/8, m. 22 (rider); 1388/9, m. 17. Fish markets in inns: SQMT 1374–5; MCR 1375/6, m. 43; 1376/7, m. 7. Fish custom: MCR 1364/5, m. 1d; CRA 1380/1–1381/2. See also Table A3.1, below.

[175] MCR 1360/1, mm. 8, 18; 1367/8, m. 33d; 1378/9, m. 9; 1379/80, m. 33; 1382/3, mm. 16, 46; 1382/3, mm. 35, 36; 1384/5, m. 23; 1385/6, m. 52; PCR 1–23 Ric. II, mm. 13, 18, 19, 28, 38, 40; EQMT 1386; PRO CP40/497, m. 406.

[176] MCR 1377/8, m. 14; 1379/80, m. 21; 1389/90, m. 5; PCR 1–23 Ric. II, mm. 9, 21, 40; PRO CP40/497, m. 406.

[177] MCR 1360/1, mm. 25, 28.

[178] PRO C241/174/7.

covered the activities of retailers and buyers. It is possible that some of the forestallers and regrators listed in the annual mayor's tourn may have sold fish they actually caught themselves, but the wording of the presentments makes it difficult to discern who they might have been. Men from coastal settlements (Bridport in Dorset; Sidmouth in east Devon; Lympstone, Topsham, and Kenton in the Exe estuary; Brixham and Yealmpton in south Devon) accounted for only 12 per cent of the fish dealers and presentments in 1370–90. The four Sidmouth fish dealers were the most prominent but even their activities in Exeter focused largely on buying rather than selling fish. John Pigioun of Sidmouth, for example, was one of those who forestalled fish at Alphington, Kennford, and the Haldon Hills, suggesting that he came specifically to obtain the sea fish from south Devon that passed through these places on its way to the Exeter market.[179] He was also accused of forestalling and regrating fish in Sidmouth, another indication that he was a fishmonger, not a fisher.[180]

Although John Pigioun and other fish dealers from coastal settlements probably did not catch fish themselves, they may have owned fishing boats, hired fishing crews, and sold their catch. The commercial arrangements made by such Cornish fishermen as John Gundy of Mousehole in the late 1350s probably extended to Devon fishing ports as well.[181] Fishermen manned several boats owned by Gundy; their catch was divided up into shares that Gundy usually purchased after negotiating a price with them. Local residents and traders seem to have resented Gundy's claim on this fish and the deals he made with the fishers before they landed their catch. While Gundy was warned against depriving local consumers of fish, no such reprieve was given to the fish dealers who had to stand by and watch Gundy take advantage of his greater capital investment. Evidence regarding coastal fishing off Suffolk and North Yorkshire also suggests that boat owners rather than fishers enjoyed the largest profits from the fish trade.[182]

Some east Devon fishers did come to Exeter with fish to market, however; John Laneryng of Otterton carried two horseloads of fish to the city to sell and the custumal of his manor points to frequent fishing by his fellow tenants.[183] A south Devon man called Reginald of Brixham (one of the county's foremost fishing villages) may also have been a

179 MCR 1370/1, mm. 2d; 1376/7, m. 5; 1378/9, m. 24; 1403/4, m. 5d; SQMT 1369–90.
180 PRO SC6/829/1, 13.
181 *Register of the Black Prince*, vol. II: 93–4. For a York fishmonger who owned a fishing boat and hired a fisher to work for him, see *CIM*, vol 6: 76.
182 Heath 1968: 57–8 (esp. n. 18); Bailey 1990: 105–7.
183 MCR 1430/1, m. 5d; Oliver 1864: 254–5.

genuine fisher (or an investor in fishing enterprises) since he sold a very large amount of fish (12 seams) in the Exeter marketplace to a dealer who ran into trouble when he regrated portions of this purchase.[184] Most such fishers, however, probably lacked the time or inclination to travel to the urban marketplace on a regular basis, even though this was the situation that the unrealistic civic authorities tried to foster. Most of the fish trade was controlled by a series of middlemen who used their superior knowledge of the market to dominate the local and regional trade in this commodity. Fishers sold to fishmongers who frequently bought and sold from each other before making the final sale to consumers. These practices could involve fish dealers from many different counties. In one week, for example, the Exeter authorities cited sales of fish by Exeter "fishers" to men from Okehampton near Dartmoor, Salisbury in Dorset (80 miles away), and Taunton and Frome in Somerset (28 and 66 miles away); the Okehampton dealer then sold part of his purchase to a man from Malmesbury (85 miles away in Wiltshire), the Salisbury dealer sold some to a man from Warminster (70 miles away in Dorset), and the Taunton man sold some of his to a trader from Colyford in east Devon (20 miles away).[185] This example nicely illustrates the many hands through which fish could pass, as well as Exeter's role as a center for the regional marketing of fish.

Fish that arrived by sea at the port of Exeter (via Topsham) was marketed a little differently. Shipmasters owned about 32 per cent of these cargoes, more than twice the proportion of cargoes they normally handled.[186] Many clearly specialized in fish and may have been involved in sea-fishing themselves since fish was often the sole commodity carried on the ship and the shipmasters were the sole importers. Most of these shipmaster-importers came from Cornwall or south Devon (especially Portlemouth, Brixham, and Paignton). In contrast, all the Channel Island and Breton ships arriving with fish also carried other imports on board and the Yarmouth herring ships had several different importers. Fish caught in or near the Exe estuary was not registered in the customs accounts as imports; most was probably landed at

[184] MCR 1403/4, m. 38d; see also MCR 1404/5, m. 1d for his debt suit against a man from South Whimple in Broad Clyst. He may have been the Reginald Lil of Brixham who regularly marketed fish in Exeter (SQMT 1402; MCR 1376/7, mm. 9, 22).

[185] MCR 1305/6, m. 17d for this and the following. This example also shows that early fourteenth-century Exeter also served a center for the regional fish trade, although the trade did not seem as frequent or intense as it became in the late fourteenth and fifteenth centuries (above, pp. 310–12).

[186] In 1350–99, shipmasters owned about 15 per cent of the cargoes (Table 6.4, above). In 1370–99, shipmasters owned forty five of the 140 non-herring cargoes (PCA 1369/70–1398/9). For shipmaster-fishers elsewhere, see especially Bailey 1990.

Exmouth or estuarine fishing villages like Lympstone.[187] While Exeter merchants owned a hefty 35 per cent of the valuable herring imports, their share of the rest of the fish trade in the late fourteenth century was minuscule.[188] They concentrated their efforts largely on such "luxury" fish as salmon and sturgeon or the foreign imported varieties (such as conger) from Brittany; these fish cargoes were usually of secondary importance to the linen cloth or corn they brought in on the same ships. On occasion, Exeter merchants played a larger role in the fish export trade, however; the A Rank merchant Jordan de Venella agreed to sell a French importer 3 lasts of conger (priced at £50) in exchange for £35-worth of woad and a cash payment for the balance.[189]

Little freshwater fish was imported; most came from local rivers and ponds. Even so, the faunal remains at Exeter are composed almost exclusively of marine fish, indicating that freshwater fish was not a common part of the urban diet, in part because it could be expensive.[190] The salmon fisheries in the Exe river were among the most valuable in all of Devon and were frequently the subject of prolonged disputes and expensive court litigation between the city of Exeter and its main rivals in the region, the earls of Devon. The Courtenay earls of Devon, who owned the estuarine manors of Kenton, Exminister, and Topsham, as well as Exe Island (the western river-edge suburb of Exeter), reaped large profits from fisheries they helped create by constructing weirs on the river, a building effort that severely damaged the city's fishing sources.[191] By the late fourteenth century, the city had direct access only to the Exe river fishery in Duryard (the suburban manor to the north of the city). Salmon generated the largest profits for the city, but eels, grayling, lampreys, and trout were also sold.[192] From 1386/7 the city leased the Duryard fishery out to such men as Michael Bovy, one

[187] For the fish market at Exmouth, see below, p. 363. The use of this landing place for fish helps explain why Exeter was so anxious to gain control of the fish trade and customs in this area; see above, p. 308.

[188] In 1370–99 (PCA passim), they owned twelve (8.5 per cent) of the cargoes but the amounts they imported were much smaller than what the shipmasters or other fish importers brought in. For herring, see above, Tables 6.2, 6.6. and 6.7.

[189] MCR 1305/6, m. 22. Few fish exports show up in the Exeter export accounts (PRO E122 passim) but they could have exited on coastal craft and thus escaped registration in these accounts.

[190] Wilkinson 1979. The high cost of freshwater fish made the elite its biggest consumer (Dyer 1988).

[191] For these profits and the struggle over fishing rights, see *Citie of Excester*: 648–51; MCR 1303/4, m. 18d; W1258/G6/50; PRO SC6/827/39, SC6/828/4; PRO CP4O/509, m. 150d; Jackson 1972; and above, pp. 223–4.

[192] DRA 1377/8–1385/6 passim for salmon and eels. Grayling: DRA 1377/8, 1378/9; trout (*Trougheys*): DRA 1381/2; lampreys: DRA 1387/8.

of the local fishmonger/hostelers.[193] The salmon fisheries lower down the river also provided a livelihood to fishers from the surrounding area. Geoffrey Paneys, a Topsham villein, regularly sold fish in Exeter and served as an expert witness in a dispute over which parish had the right to tithe salmon taken near Countess Wear.[194] Geoffrey Stur, a free tenant of Topsham, also gave testimony at this inquest, only a year after he and John Stur had leased the tithes of the Topsham fishery from the dean and chapter for 106*s* 8*d*.[195] He and his relatives, John and Robert Stur of Topsham, all traded fish in Exeter, sometimes being fined for selling salmon in a tavern when they should have brought it to the Exeter marketplace for sale.[196] Salmon from other Devon rivers was also marketed in Exeter; John Taillor of Canon Teign (on the Teign river) sold four salmon to John Strange, an Exeter fishmonger who was fined for regrating them.[197]

Like the fishers and fishmongers of sea fish, these salmon fishers benefited from their proximity to waters abundantly endowed with this valuable and eminently tradeable commodity. What is particularly striking is the role Exeter played in this fish trade as a regional entrepôt. To a large extent the city enjoyed this position because of its geographical location; it not only had good connections to its own well-stocked estuary and to the sea, but its placement 10 miles inland also made it more accessible to inland traders than other seaports. Its position also allowed it to capitalize on the growth of sea fishing off the south Devon and Cornish coasts in the late fourteenth and fifteenth centuries. It was more convenient for buyers and sellers to meet at an established market and regional center like Exeter than for buyers to travel to various coastal areas or sellers to visit several different market towns. The customs assessed on fish at Exeter recognized the city's role in this trade as well. They specified that horseloads of fish arriving from the sea near east Devon (and channelled through Exmouth) or from south Devon (and carried through Alphington) had to pay custom, as did the loads of fish that then departed the city for inland locations such as

193 DCR 2–22 Richard II, m. 23; Book 53A, f. 76; SQMT 1387–90; NQMT 1391–3; MCR 1391/2, mm. 1, 3.

194 SQMT 1372, 1374, 1379–80, 1386–93; NQMT 1391; MCR 1379/80, m. 35 (jury); 1391/2, m. 1; 1392/3, m. 21; ECL D&C 1905; for his activities at Topsham, see also PRO SC2/168/43.

195 ECL D&C 1905; 3777, f. 53d; the agreement does not mention tithes but this must have been what the Sturs were leasing since that would have been the only claim the dean and chapter had in this fishery.

196 SQMT 1372, 1374, 1378; MCR 1373/4, m. 51; 1391/2, m. 1 (tavern); 1392/3, m. 45. For their activities at Topsham, see PRO SC6/168/43.

197 MCR 1377/8, m. 12; see also WW1258/G1/68 for salmon fishing in Christow, the parish wherein lies Canon Teign.

Crediton, Tiverton, or elsewhere.[198] In the late fourteenth century, "elsewhere" stretched very far indeed, well into the neighboring counties of Somerset and Dorset, to many of the same locations that were linked to Exeter through the trade in cloth, dyestuffs, wine, and the other items of long-distance and maritime commerce.

The size and range of an urban commercial hinterland in medieval England were determined by several different factors. Five in particular can be singled out: distance from the market center, terrain and the difficulties of transport, the status of the trader (in terms of wealth and occupation), the type of commodity being traded, and regional specializations. But distinguishing the relative importance of these factors is difficult since they often operated together. The weight assigned to each, moreover, will differ from town to town and region to region. In south-western England, the widely varying terrain and landscapes exercised a particularly potent effect. Moorlands, hill ranges, wide estuaries, and long coastlines all created difficulties for travellers and influenced how far traders were willing to journey. Geographical differences also dictated regional specializations which in turn influenced the types of goods traded. Items such as fish regularly drew traders to Exeter from much longer distances than did the trade in grain, meat, livestock, or hides and skins, while buyers of raw hides and skins travelled farther to trade at the town than did sellers of these goods. Importers of goods at the port of Exeter came from even farther away to acquire both the luxury and essential commodities imported there. By the same token, the direction of trade from the market center was also influenced by the nature of the commodity being traded. The growing cloth industries of east Devon and Somerset, for example, promoted the inland distribution of dyestuffs in these regions by Exeter merchants at the same time as importers from these areas also acquired imported dyestuffs and exported the woollen cloth manufactured in these regions.

Although the size and shape of Exeter's hinterland varied by commodity, some regions were more regularly linked to Exeter by commercial ties than others (Figure 7.1).[199] The networks of trade to east Devon were the strongest, but they also extended further east at least 25 miles and often beyond 40 miles into western Somerset and Dorset. To the north, the hinterland ranged well up the Exe valley to Bampton, Stoodleigh, and South Molton, and occasionally north of Exmoor for

[198] Book 55, f. 48v; *Citie of Excester*: 553–4, 567–8.
[199] See also Figure 6.1, above, for the following.

Table 7.7. *Regional distribution of non-resident and Exeter traders in selected commodities at Exeter, 1370–91 (by percentage of known residences)*

	Hides and skins		Fish	Wine	Madder
Region	Buyers/ purchases	Sellers/ sales	Dealers/ deals	Importers/ imports	Importers/ imports
East Devon	78/81	81/77	38/42	23/21	0
South Devon	0	0	6/4	46/41	15/16
Dartmoor and Borders	22/19	16/23	0	½/½	0
North and mid Devon	0	3/–	0	½/½	0
Somerset and Dorset	0	0	56/54	7/10	46/35
Other places	0	0	0	23/27	39/49
Total	100/100	100/100	100/100	100/100	100/100
(Total no.)	(32/241)	(32/228)	(82/416)	(193/1,882) tuns	(13/109) bales
Unidentified non-residents	11/12	19/14	40/33	33/19	16/10
Exeter	74/63	46/46	18/23	16/44	16/39

Source and note: For hides and skins, see Table 7.5; for fish, see Table 7.6; for wine and madder, see Table 6.6. Note that the figures for wine and madder are for the period 1381–91 and that East Devon includes the Exe estuary region.

gentry consumers. In general, however, Exmoor seems to have presented a formidable physical obstacle to more extensive commercial contacts to the north, while the convenience of trade through Barnstaple on the northern coast for residents of north and much of mid Devon limited the penetration of commercial influence in that direction. To the north-west and west, residents of Chulmleigh and Okehampton often appeared at Exeter but traders from beyond these small towns were less active at Exeter. Dartmoor probably hindered trade to the west and south although its pastoral economy did promote a livestock trade with Exeter that was visible in the attendance of Exeter traders at Dartmoor fairs, as well as in the regional exchange of meatstock, hides, and skins. To the south, Exeter's hinterland extended well down the coast to Dartmouth and Plymouth via maritime routes but was more limited overland. The main exception was fish from south Devon, large amounts of which seem to have arrived via overland routes as well as by sea.

Examining the size and range of Exeter's hinterland also points to the city's role in fostering inter-regional exchange (Table 7.7). The agricultural specializations of Devon regions, recently elucidated by Harold Fox,[200] were very much reflected in the regional networks of

[200] Fox 1991.

trade centered on Exeter. Trade with the Dartmoor border areas, for example, largely concentrated on the products of pastoral agriculture: hides, skins, and livestock. Even within Exeter's own region of east Devon, inter-regional trade on a smaller scale occurred as meatstock fattened in river-valley villages (such as Newton St Cyres, Nether Exe, and Brampford Speke) was sent to Exeter for slaughter while the raw hides and skins from these animals were carried out of Exeter to small-town market centers (such as Tiverton and Bradninch). Similarly, the grain-growing specialties of Devon agricultural regions were reflected in the malt and barley that arrived in Exeter from south Devon and the oats that came from mid and east Devon.[201]

Inter-regional trade in non-agricultural goods also took place at Exeter. Fish from south Devon and Cornwall represent perhaps the best example, drawing many traders from inland locations in east Devon, Somerset, and Dorset to the city. Exeter markets and traders also played an important part in the exchange of fish between the coastal and inland areas of its home region of east Devon. The town's role in inter-regional trade is also illustrated in the specialized imports channelled through Exeter's port, although here the distinction between those who were largely carriers (hence the substantial role of south Devon importers) and those who were supplying goods from or for their own regions should be kept in mind. The figures in Table 7.7 do illustrate, however, how maritime trade through Exeter funnelled imports such as wine and madder to certain regions. In some instances the demand was predicated on industrial specialization, as seen in the demand by Somerset and Dorset merchants and clothiers for madder. In turn, some of these same importers marketed their cloth overseas by exporting woollen cloth (mostly from Somerset not Dorset) through the port of Exeter. If the aulnage and export accounts survived in greater numbers and were of better quality, a similar exchange with cloth-producing areas in mid and north Devon might also be identified.

While Exeter traders and markets clearly exploited these regional specializations, their ability to shape the town's economic hinterland in the late fourteenth century was not particularly strong. With a population of only 3,100 in 1377, the city generated insufficient consumer demand to determine particular patterns of agricultural production or trade. Even in the early sixteenth century when its population reached 7,000, it is unlikely that Exeter consumer demand ever exercised a fraction of the impact of a large metropolis like London.[202] Instead, Exeter's late medieval prosperity rested largely on its role as the essential

[201] Kowaleski forthcoming.
[202] See, for example, Campbell, Galloway, Keene, and Murphy 1993.

link in a marketing chain that connected overseas and coastal commerce with inland networks of trade. The early emergence of strong regional specialties within its extended hinterland was especially influential in fostering inter-regional trade that often centered on Exeter. Together these roles allowed Exeter to profit in the late middle ages when pastoral husbandry expanded in mid, east, and Dartmoor Devon, when the fishing industry boomed off the south Devon and Cornish coasts, and when the cloth trade accelerated in parts of east Devon, Somerset, and Dorset.

Conclusion

For many centuries, Exeter was the premier market town in south-western England. Geographical location gave the town an early advantage; rather than being perched on the coast like most seaports, Exeter was situated 10 miles from the sea and 4 miles upstream from its outport of Topsham at the head of the Exe estuary. The town thus enjoyed good overland communications not only to its own fertile "red Devon" region in the Exe, Creedy, and Culm river valleys, but also to areas on the eastern and northern borders of Dartmoor, to mid Devon, and further east to the neighboring counties of Somerset and Dorset. Exeter also capitalized on its access to the sea, benefiting from coastal connections to English ports (especially those in Cornwall, Devon, Dorset, and Hampshire) and from overseas routes to the Atlantic coast of continental Europe. Exeter's emergence as an ecclesiastical center of a diocese encompassing all of Devon and Cornwall, and as an administrative center that hosted county and national courts, affirmed the value of its site and reflected its position in the regional marketing hierarchy. No other medieval town in south-western England boasted as many market days or fairs as Exeter. Its marketing dominance within Devon was particularly striking; the closest rival to its Friday market was over 40 miles away; the next Wednesday market was almost 18 miles distant, and even its Monday market had only one viable competitor within 10 miles. Although small by some standards (with a population of about 3,100 in 1377), Exeter's commercial, administrative, and ecclesiastical functions helped make it the largest town in south-western England during the middle ages.

In the eleventh and twelfth centuries, Exeter ranked among the foremost towns in England; chroniclers commented on its wealth and overseas trading connections while its contributions to royal aids and tallages placed it sixth or seventh among all English cities. During the thirteenth century, however, the town's fortunes declined as it lost its prominent position in tin exporting and faced mounting competition from port towns and cloth manufacturing elsewhere. Its relatively low ranking among English towns in assessed wealth in 1334 (twenty-fourth) and population in 1377 (twenty-first) perhaps reflect some of these difficulties. But this "decline" was probably more a function of faster growth in other towns than any economic crisis in Exeter; immigration to the town remained strong, Exeter emerged as the headport of England's largest customs jurisdiction, and in 1326 it was designated one of the country's nine wool staples. In the mid fourteenth century, visitations of the plague severely reduced its population and created labor shortages and vacant tenements, problems that faced all towns in this period. Less common were the wartime disruptions caused by the Hundred Years War on its overseas routes; these eventually altered some of the patterns of foreign trade at Exeter. Despite these difficulties, the local markets recovered and even grew from the 1370s on, as indicated in the town's increased fair revenues, customs farms, ale brewing, and building programs. Although more difficult times followed in the 1420s and 1430s, this period was more one of stagnation than real decline. By the 1440s, dramatic increases in cloth exports and maritime trade signaled a return to prosperity in Exeter. With the exception of a brief period in the 1450s–60s, this growth continued through the rest of the century. From the mid to the late fifteenth century, the city acquired several new fairs, profited from the growth of a cloth-finishing industry in its neighborhood, encouraged the development of craft guilds, and met its financial obligations more easily than most other English towns. By the end of the fifteenth century, Exeter's share of the national maritime trade in fish, tin, and cloth had increased significantly compared to its position one hundred years earlier. Indeed, from 1334 to 1525 the rate of economic growth in Exeter was greater than in any other English town. The population rose accordingly – from 3,100 in 1377 to about 7,000 in 1525.

Exeter's late-medieval prosperity can be understood only when placed in the context of developments in its surrounding regions. It is no coincidence that the county of Devon, like its chief city, enjoyed an unprecedented rate of economic growth during this same period. At the heart of this prosperity lay the agricultural, industrial, and maritime diversity that increasingly characterized south-western England during the late middle ages. Livestock husbandry became more important, benefiting from the county's large stretches of moorland and pastureland, while crop specializations – such as barley in south Devon and oats in mid Devon – became more marked. This diversification, combined with Devon's flexible system of convertible husbandry, tin fields, silver mines, and access to maritime activities such as fishing and seafaring, allowed the county's residents to adjust more easily to the demographic and agricultural crises of the fourteenth and fifteenth centuries. The growth of the cloth industry in Exeter's hinterland also played a central role in this adjustment since many of its manufactures were channelled through Exeter for finishing, sale, or export overseas. Exeter also capitalized on its ability to supply foreign dyestuffs, capital investment, and financial services to these regions. The expansion of tin mining in Dartmoor, the intensification of pastoral husbandry throughout most of Devon, and the boom in fishing off the south Devon and Cornish coasts in the late middle ages provided similar benefits. The prosperity generated by these developments also elevated consumption and stimulated demand in the hinterland, needs that trade through Exeter was best able to fulfill.

In order to understand more fully the nature of the dynamic relationship between the urban center and its surrounding regions, this study explores in detail the factors that determined the size and shape of Exeter's hinterland. The distances travelled by traders to the urban center offer one reflection of the size of the hinterland, although the difficulties of transport over Devon's rough and hilly terrain probably created more difficulties there than in the flatter Midlands. Those who resided within 6 miles of Exeter certainly expected to complete a journey to and from the town for business in one day. Many were peasants or manorial officials who so frequently visited the town that the boundaries between local and regional trade at this distance are almost impossible to distinguish. The situation for those residing from 6 to about 20 miles from Exeter is also difficult to measure; while a person mounted on horseback could easily cover 25 miles a day, travellers accompanied by packhorses or carts loaded with goods faced greater delays. Traders journeying more than 25 miles to Exeter confronted the most obstacles; most probably had to absorb the cost of staying there at least one night. The large number of inns in the town, along with the vital role played by innkeepers in fostering commercial exchange, also illustrate Exeter's ability to draw substantial numbers of traders and other visitors who came from more than 25 or 30 miles away.

The regional orientation of trade was the most important determinant of the shape of the hinterland; at Exeter, for example, traders from over 30 miles away in western Somerset were more common than Devon traders from similar distances in south Devon. The portability, supply, demand, and role in manufacturing of a region's products all helped to define the role played by Exeter in channelling the goods of one region to another. Exeter served as a particularly important marketing center for fish from south Devon, livestock from the Dartmoor region, and cloth from east Devon. Much of the fish was sold to inland traders who carried their purchases back to east Devon, Somerset, and parts of Dorset for sale. Much of the livestock was butchered for the table of Exeter residents but some was driven great distances or fattened in the rich pasturelands of nearby river valleys. After slaughter, the by-products were sold by butchers; the horns, tallow, and wool usually found a market in Exeter but the hides were often purchased by non-resident tanners from east Devon, mid Devon, and the Dartmoor borderlands. Many of the tanners then returned to Exeter to sell their finished product to the urban leather craftspeople who manufactured shoes, saddles, and other items that they eventually sold mainly in the local but occasionally in more distant markets. These examples show how the size and shape of the urban hinterland, as well as the personnel involved in their exchange, varied for different goods. Exeter's role in these regional networks of exchange was also promoted by its geographic location at the crossroads of several different regions which, by the late middle ages, had begun to develop distinctly different agricultural and industrial specializations. Although situated in east Devon, Exeter lies very near to the borders of mid Devon and Dartmoor and has easy access to south Devon ports via its coastal connections; this location helps to explain the crucial and ultimately very profitable role Exeter played in the increasingly prosperous commercial economy of south-western England.

Competition from other markets also helped to determine the shape and size of the urban hinterland. Because south Devon and south Dartmoor markets enjoyed easy access to maritime outlets at the nearby ports of Dartmouth and Plymouth, their trades less frequently employed Exeter markets than traders from east Devon and western Somerset who had fewer such maritime options. Exeter's commercial hinterland to the south and west was therefore always smaller than to the east. To the north Exeter's hinterland was also restricted by the rival seaport of Barnstaple, although Barnstaple's small size and orientation to the Bristol Channel meant that it never presented the challenge to Exeter offered by the better-situated south Devon ports. Besides distance from Exeter and access to maritime markets, natural features such as the sea to the south, Dartmoor to the west, Exmoor to the north, and the Brendon and Blackdown Hills to the north-east also affected the degree of competition offered by rival towns. The sea and Dartmoor seem to have presented the biggest deterrents, especially in the case of Dartmouth whose hinterland was always limited in size by the granite mass of Dartmoor.

The wealth, status, and occupation of traders at Exeter also influenced the size of the urban hinterland. Although drawn to Exeter in smaller numbers than those from within 6 miles of the city, traders from farther away tended to be wealthier, of higher status, and involved in transactions of substantially greater amounts. Many were merchants or clothiers from small towns who regularly traded through the port of Exeter. A substantial number, however, had no experience in maritime trade and, while of no mean status in their home communities, certainly did not possess the wealth and position of the overseas merchants and clothiers. Particularly noteworthy here are the tanners from Okehampton and Tiverton, the butchers and graziers of the Dartmoor borderlands and east Devon, and the fish and grain dealers from east Devon and Somerset. Attracted to Exeter because of specific business interests stemming from their occupational pursuits, these traders represented the fundamental links in the ties that commercially bound Exeter to the small towns of its wider hinterland.

Exeter's access to the sea helped to distinguish it from myriad other market towns in medieval England and more than any other factor explains its important role as a regional center of commerce. An analysis of the unusually complete series of local customs accounts extant for the port shows the impact of this role in some detail. At least 70 per cent of the importers and ships visiting Exeter in the late fourteenth and early fifteenth centuries used coastal rather than overseas routes; this finding makes it necessary to revise considerably upwards the previous low estimates of Exeter maritime trade which have been based on overseas trade alone. While native English cargoes accounted for much of this coastal trade, the greater part actually consisted of trans-shipments of foreign goods from redistribution centers like Southampton, Dartmouth, and Plymouth. Because coastal trade cost less and entailed fewer risks, Exeter's reliance on these routes enabled more traders to participate in maritime trade and acquire foreign goods. The customs accounts also point to the growing inter-dependence of Exeter and its hinterland in the late middle ages. Over the course of the fourteenth century, the percentage of Exeter merchants fell from 21 per cent to about 12 per cent of importers while their share of incoming cargoes dipped from almost half to 30 per cent. This decline did not, however, signal economic crisis in Exeter since indices of trends in its local markets show that this same period was actually one of mounting prosperity. The slack was taken up largely by importers from south Devon and from Exeter's own hinterland. The south Devon importers, like many importers from foreign and more distant English ports, probably sold the bulk of their imports to Exeter merchants who then handled their overland distribution. The rising percentage of inland importers from Exeter's hinterland, however, most likely handled overland distribution themselves. But these activities brought them to Exeter in greater numbers than before and made them increasingly reliant on Exeter for all types of business channelled through the city, especially the export trade which was dominated more than the import trade by wealthy merchants from Exeter itself.

The merchant oligarchs of medieval Exeter were small in number but exercised an inordinately powerful role in the import and export trades, the inland distribution of imports, and the supply of the local markets. Their distributive function was particularly visible in their sale of imported dyestuffs to dyers, fullers, and clothiers who resided in Exeter, east Devon, and Somerset. Exeter merchants also marketed much of the cloth produced in these areas; in 1399–1403, they were responsible for well over three-quarters of the cloth aulnaged at Exeter. The vast majority of the oligarchic merchants also participated in maritime trade and although their overall share of this trade had slipped by the end of the fourteenth century, they still controlled roughly 67 per cent of the valuable trade in woad, 51 per cent of iron imports, and 44 per cent of the all-important trade in wine (which alone accounted for almost half of the value of all imports). Their wealth, status, and dominance of local markets were especially evident in their frequent appearance as creditors in debt cases, the significantly higher sums involved in their transactions, and the much more favorable verdicts they received when they came before the local courts.

Besides the greater capital available to them, the merchant oligarchs also enjoyed political, legal, and commercial advantages that considerably lowered their costs of doing business. These advantages came largely from their membership in and control of the freedom of Exeter, an exclusive organization whose members benefited from toll exemptions throughout England, monopolies on many types of retail and wholesale trade in Exeter, legal privileges in pleading and essoins in the borough courts, and the sole right to elect all civic officials. These privileges were denied to the vast bulk of Exeter residents since fewer than one-quarter of all householders (and but 4 per cent of the total population) gained entry to the freedom. While the advantages enjoyed by freedom members were significant, unenfranchised traders in the late middle ages seem, however, to have increasingly found ways to avoid the worst effects of their status through the payment of small fines and even outright evasion. Many of the other arrangements employed by the wealthier oligarchs to reduce transaction costs (such as the use of credit, partnerships, and the enforcement machinery of the borough courts) were also available to unenfranchised traders, albeit on a smaller scale.

Although the merchant oligarchs exerted a disproportionate influence on Exeter commerce, the activities of retailers and artisans accounted for the bulk of trade carried on in the local markets. Victualling and hosteling were the primary activities of about one-third of all householders and, because victualling represented the most common by-occupation, ultimately engaged at least half of the urban workforce. Indeed, food and drink dominated local exchange, accounting for almost half of all debt litigation in the borough courts. Women especially focused their commercial interests on the victualling trades, through both their control of ale brewing (which was practiced by more than two-thirds of all households) and their activities as hawkers of fish, malt, dairy products, and other low-cost food items. Innkeepers also sold much food and drink and played a crucial intermediary role in regional trade because their inns functioned as convenient meeting and marketing points for out-of-towners. Other victualling occupations, notably the butchers and fish dealers, also regularly traded with outsiders and served as important links in the networks tying together local markets and regional trade.

In contrast, artisan/retailers often earned large portions of their income by working for others and were thus less visible in the commercial sphere. Some, especially the skinners and cloth workers at the upper ends of their trades, did venture outside the local markets, but most lacked the capital, freedom membership, or business interests to engage in such trade. The subordinate status of many of the clothing and textile workers was especially noticeable, a function perhaps of the increasing control exercised by the merchant clothiers who presided over all stages of the cloth-manufacturing process. The leather and skin trades ranked nearer the top of the artisanal occupations, but even wider variations in wealth and status occurred within their ranks than in other occupational groups. Metalworkers accounted for a relatively small number of householders but were distinguished by the large number of servants they employed and their occasional entry into maritime trade to acquire some of the raw materials of their trade. The relatively large building sector at Exeter owed its prominence to the on-going construction and maintenance of the cathedral.

Although this study focuses more on tracing the participants and commodities of exchange over several decades in one town than on detailing long-term economic developments over a large area, its findings on the relationship between market centers and their hinterlands point to useful avenues of inquiry for understanding such developments. The Braudelian model of commercial evolution cited at the beginning of this study, for example, needs to recognize the crucial role of the many smaller-scale shifts in local and regional economies that together engendered the larger changes we cite in textbooks. Commercialization had probably penetrated medieval English society to a far greater extent than Braudel's model or most early modern historians acknowledge.[1] This commercialization received a significant boost from the agricultural and industrial specialization that emerged early on in regions like south-western England; such commercialization helped both to shield these areas from the crises of the late middle ages and to promote faster economic growth there. While wealthy and privileged merchants exercised great influence in local and regional markets and dominated maritime trade, they were far outnumbered by legions of victuallers, artisans, and small-town traders who, despite the obstacles facing them, regularly went outside the boundaries of their local markets to participate in regional trade. These traders played an important role in linking the urban center with producers and consumers in the hinterland. Their commercial activities, more than those of the merchants, helped determine the shape of the hinterland because they responded more directly to the specializations of the surrounding regions. They also probably provided the greater fuel to commercial development as their regional exchanges intensified and became more frequent.

Local markets, with their emphasis upon supplying the necessities of life, played a limited role in stimulating economic change, particularly in a city as small as Exeter. But in a section of the country where very small towns were the norm, even the local markets of Exeter generated enough demand in certain goods (such as meat) to attract many traders to the city. These local markets also provided a forum for inter-regional trade, drawing, for example, livestock from pasture- and meadow-rich regions and channelling their by-products into the hands of urban craftspeople or rural artisans. In the case of such items as hides and grain, the overlapping networks of local and regional trade make it difficult to tell where one ended and the other began. Local merchants, retailers, and artisans played an essential role in providing goods and services to residents of the hinterland; in turn they profited from different goods and services furnished to them through these same networks of trade. Although Exeter's role as a center for inter-regional trade, along with its distant commercial ties overland and by sea set it apart from many other market towns, many aspects of its trade resembled those of market towns throughout England. In its internal organization of local markets, its commercial connections to inland

[1] See especially Britnell 1993 for other evidence on this point.

regions, and its position as a center of exchange for the surrounding countryside, Exeter can be compared to hundreds of other provincial market towns in the middle ages.

Appendix 1
Sources and methodology

Prosopographical analysis

The analyses contained in this book rely very heavily on the identification of individuals: their occupations, wealth, political status, commercial activities, and place of residence. To a large extent the methodology employed here is prosopographical in that I have aimed to create a collective biography of specific groups of people who lived or were commercially active in late fourteenth-century Exeter.[1] Ten such groups were singled out in particular. (1) Members of the late fourteenth-century oligarchy, represented by those men who held the highest political offices in the city, are analyzed in Chapter 3 with special attention paid to the relationship between their political and commercial privileges and activities. (2) The 525 identifiable householders who resided in Exeter in 1377 form the subject of a second analysis, presented in Chapter 4, which focuses on the inter-relationships between these householders' occupation, wealth, and commercial activities, as well as the implications of these relationships for the structure of the local economy. This study is described in more detail in Appendix 3. (3) Both the analysis of the oligarchy and that of the householders are supplemented by a third study that concentrates on the 7,457 Exeter creditors and debtors who appeared in the Exeter borough courts from 1378–88; this statistical analysis is described at length below. (4) The sixty eight cloth vendors listed in the Exeter aulnage accounts of 1399–1403 are also analyzed to illustrate the role of different occupations in the town's cloth industry.

These first four analyses center on people who resided in Exeter; the other six focus on groups wholly or partly comprised of non-Exeter residents, thus allowing some insight into the regional and international connections of Exeter traders and markets. (5) Chapter 6 focuses on the 1,523 importers (and their 3,573 cargoes) who participated in the

[1] For discussions of the prosopographical method, see Stone 1987; Beech 1976; Millet (ed.) 1985; Bulst and Genet (eds.) 1986.

import trade through the port of Exeter in two periods during the fourteenth century, 1302–20 and 1381–91; over 80 per cent of these importers lived outside of Exeter. (6) The 1,897 non-Exeter debtors and creditors (21 per cent of all litigants) who appeared in the debt cases pursued in the Exeter borough courts in 1378–88 are the basis of a study in Chapter 7 of regional traders active in Exeter. Their activities are compared to the (7) 204 creditors and debtors listed in the Chancery certificates of debt involving Exeter residents over the decade 1377–87 and the (8) 219 litigants appearing before the court of common pleas at Westminster in 1377–88. The last two groups are drawn from presentments made in the annual mayor's tourn from 1370 to 1390. (9) The first includes 976 presentments made against 212 different buyers of hides and skins at Exeter, and 577 presentments against ninety one sellers of the same items. About 37 per cent of the former and 54 per cent of the latter concerned non-resident traders. (10) The second contains 941 presentments naming 197 fish dealers, over 80 per cent of whom resided outside of Exeter. Both types of dealers were analyzed primarily in terms of their occupations and residences in order to illuminate the intersection of local and regional trade in the fish and hide trades in Chapter 7.

The reasons for selecting these groups and the problems involved in analyzing them (especially in terms of source bias) are for the most part considered in the chapters where the data on the groups are presented. These chapters, however, do not offer much discussion of the assumptions and guidelines I employed in matching distinguishing characteristics such as occupation or residence with particular individuals, nor do they dwell on the difficulties encountered in linking names to individuals across a wide variety of records. As prosopographical research becomes an increasingly important part of the historian's arsenal, it is essential for researchers to make these assumptions and guidelines clear to their audience. Failure to do so both hinders the comparability of data across studies and obscures the methodology employed. In this spirit, this appendix clarifies and briefly illustrates the sources and methodologies employed here. It also explains in detail the analysis of debts in Exeter courts in 1378–88, the single most important body of data in this study.

Sources

The success of the prosopographical method rests largely on the quality of the sources employed to identify individuals. For the medievalist, the survival rate of documentation and the type of information offered are the most important determinants of source quality. Although creative methodologies allow researchers to extract data that the original compilers of the source may not necessarily have intended to offer, the success of our ventures still hinges on whether our sources have survived the damage wrought by carelessness, damp, fire, and the like. Exeter has been exceptionally fortunate in the survival rate of its documentation. Perhaps its early status as an independent borough free from the tensions occasioned by the presence of an overlord, or its location in a county distant from the mainstream of English politics and troubles, helped in this regard. Certainly influential was the interest taken by the city's first chamberlain, John Hooker, an Elizabethan antiquarian who salvaged and calendared many of the town's ancient records.[2] Hooker also compiled, translated, and composed several documentary surveys and local histories, many now printed in *The description of the citie of Excester.*[3] His work on the city's archives was continued by Samuel Izacke, town clerk of Exeter from 1624–47, and his son Richard, who was appointed town chamberlain in 1653.[4] In the nineteenth century George Oliver and Stuart Moore also made important contributions with their histories and calendars of the city's ecclesiastical and administrative records.[5]

The prosopographical analyses focus on the late fourteenth century, a period when Exeter's documentation is particularly abundant, when surnames had become more stable, and when Exeter embarked on a long period of commercial prosperity. Following techniques developed by historians of rural communities, I began to build up a data bank of citations to all individuals who appeared in the late fourteenth-century documentation; the circumstances and people involved in each individual's appearance were recorded separately (along with the date and source) and all indexed alphabetically by name.[6] It soon became evident that only an army of researchers could employ this method for a relatively large town, let alone one blessed with the enormously rich records of Exeter, so the chronological focus of the survey was narrowed even further to concentrate on the twenty-year period from 1373 to

[2] For his life and writings, see Snow 1977: 3–28.

[3] Edited and published in 1919. His collections and writings on Exeter are described in HMCR, vol. 73: 340–81. See also Harte (no date); Blake 1915; Deakin 1980.

[4] Richard published *Remarkable antiquities of the city of Exeter* in 1677 and also compiled "Memorials of the city of Exeter" (DRO Book 53); both works borrowed heavily from Hooker's writings.

[5] Oliver 1861; S. Moore 1863–70, and 1873.

[6] This method owes much to that pioneered by J. A. Raftis. The best recent description of the method and its refinements may be found in Bennett 1987: 199–231. See also MacFarlane 1977, for a long discussion of data collection (aimed more, however, at early modern scholars with access to a team of workers).

1393.[7] Even greater selectivity was exercised for documents that fell outside the late fourteenth century although some sources, as indicated below, were exploited more fully than others because of the information they contained on commercial matters. For example, the identification of about 70 per cent of the 942 individual importers in the early fourteenth century required the collection of thousands of references from court rolls, civic elections, deeds, and lay subsidies in c. 1300–35. Despite these chronological and topical restrictions, over 105,000 references to individuals were ultimately collected for the data bank, about 35 per cent of which concerned non-Exeter residents.[8]

These references were culled from a wide variety of sources, all of which are listed in the bibliography of primary sources. Although it is not possible to describe all of these sources, it is worthwhile to discuss the more important series of local Exeter records which together form the foundation of this study and account for about 70 per cent of the references in the data bank.

Mayor's court rolls (MCR)

The mayor's court, which met every Monday in the Guildhall, was the busiest and most important of the borough's three courts.[9] A court of record, the mayor's court tried a wide variety of real and personal actions, crown and common pleas, including trespass, debt, assault, theft, and property and inheritance disputes. The clerks often gave the details of a case (including the outcome) in a superscript written over the main entry. In the 1380s, about 330 cases appeared each year. Anywhere from five to thirty new cases arose in each court during this decade but about 90 per cent of the cases were carried over from week to week; some continued for more than two years. The single most common plea was for debt (about 36 per cent), followed by trespass

[7] This choice was dictated by the years for which certain key sources survived, particularly the unique murage roll of 1377 (Misc. Roll 72), the mayor's tourn rolls, and the span of the extant port customs accounts (PCA), which survive with one gap from 1381–1433.

[8] These references were collected from 1978 to 1992; about half were recorded manually on 3 × 5 cards (often multiple references per card) and the rest were stored in various computer databases.

[9] Easterling (1931: xvi–xx) thinks the mayor's court may have originally been a hundred court. In the medieval period, it was usually termed "court of the city of Exeter"; only later was it called the "Mayor's Court." See also the brief remarks and examples in Wright 1862; HMCR vol. 73: 406–9; Parry 1936: 8, 43–8; Exeter City Library 1965; and Hooker's comments in *Citie of Excester*: 40, 777–81, 807–8, 827–8.

(34 per cent) which included both minor trespasses and major felonies.[10] Also enrolled (usually on the dorses) were final concords, testaments, freedom entries, recognizances, memoranda, the assize of bread, and other items of borough business. The municipal elections almost always appeared on the dorses of the first two membranes of each roll (elections were held on the Monday after Michaelmas), as did leases of the farms of city customs and pasture.[11]

There are 403 mayor's court rolls covering the years 1264 to 1701; from 1295/6 to 1508 there are only two years missing: 1383/4 and 1459/60. These court rolls are so voluminous that great selectivity had to be exercised when extracting data. For the decade from 1378/9 to 1387/8 all names enrolled in these courts were recorded with the pertinent information and filed in the data bank (the only exception being pledges who were indexed only when they were related to the pledgee or when their occupation was included). For 1373–77 and 1388–93, entries were made only when the details offered (on occupation, residence, spouses, kin, or commercial activities) were particularly full or not previously known. For other periods, the rolls were only sampled; while all the thirteenth- and fourteenth-century rolls were examined, only twelve of the ninety nine fifteenth-century rolls (which contain less detail than the earlier courts) were checked. Certain entries were, however, transcribed and included in the data bank over longer periods. These include all testaments 1290–1450, all final concords 1290–1430, all farms of customs and city pasture 1302–1499, all elections 1286–1405, and all freedom entries 1266–1500.[12]

Mayor's tourn (MT)

The mayor's tourn was a leet court which met once a year, usually in late October or November, but on occasion in December, January, or February. One tourn was held for each quarter of the city (corresponding to the north, south, east, and west gates). Juries of twelve men for each quarter made presentments (indictments tantamount to convictions

[10] Percentages taken from an analysis of all pleas (992) for a three-year period from 1385/6 to 1387/8, including 354 debt cases and 341 trespass pleas. Not included in the latter were the 112 jury presentments (11 per cent of the total) which usually concerned trespass cases.

[11] Therefore references in the text to elections or political offices usually cite only the year rather than membrane numbers of the MCR. A list detailing the membrane numbers where the elections may be found has been deposited in the DRO.

[12] For the final concords I sometimes relied on the abstracts made by the staff of the DRO (typescripts filed chronologically by parish) and by Staniforth and Juddery (1991) in *Exeter property deeds*. The freedom entries have been printed in *Exeter freemen*: 1–63.

in this court) that principally concerned market offenses. Many of these offenses had previously been noted in the mayor's court;[13] indeed, from the first appearance of the tourn in 1302 until about 1368, the tourns were usually enrolled on the dorses of membranes of the mayor's court rolls.[14] Many of the fines assessed in the tourn for market "offenses" had become in effect licensing fees or taxes to carry on these activities; the same names appeared in these lists of presentments year after year, often written down in the same order. This phenomenon may also be observed in other late medieval English towns and has encouraged historians to employ these lists to indicate trends within the local markets. Long-run counts of fines assessed on brewers, butchers, cooks, and vintners, for example, have been used to chart changes in the consumption of foodstuffs and thus, indirectly, fluctuations in the urban population and standard of living.[15] This study includes similar exercises; I tabulated all extant presentments for (1) brewing ale against the assize; (2) selling ale, wine, perry, and mead in false measures; and (3) selling oats in inns (*hostelaria*) in "false" measures from 1302 to 1459 when the series ends, although variations in the wording of presentments, the inclusion of suburban jurisdictions, and missing tourns for some quarters did not make it possible to include data for all years.[16] Other presentments were employed to help identify the occupational pursuits of both Exeter and non-resident traders, especially those in the leather, cloth, and victualling trades. All names from the tourns from 1370 to 1393 (averaging over 800 presentments each year) were included in the data bank. Only selected individuals and information were noted before and after this period.

Provosts' court rolls (PCR)

The third borough court was called the provosts' court because it was run by the provosts (later called stewards) of the city. This court

[13] For example, MCR Roll 1, mm. 9, 10d, list persons fined for breaking the assize of ale; MCR 1295/6, m. 16 contains lists of persons fined for, among other things, forestalling and regrating fish, poultry, and hides; MCR 1296/7, m. 6d contains a list of persons fined for failing to remove dung as ordered. For the first tourn, see MCR 1302/3, mm. 16d, 20d although the word "tourn" is a later insertion; mm. 4d, 5, 9, also contain relevant marketing fines.

[14] Separate rolls also exist for nine years between 1337 and 1366. The references to the MT in this study are usually listed according to the quarter of tourn and the year the tourn was held, regardless of whether the tourn appeared on the MCR or in a separate roll. I have deposited a finding list of mayor's tourns in the DRO.

[15] Keene 1985: 256–77; Britnell 1986b: 89–92, 193–200, 269–73, 276.

[16] The missing late fourteenth-century tourns are those for 1352, 1367, 1372, and 1377; part of the latter may be found on MCR 1376/7, m. 23. The tourns are particularly

exercised the same jurisdiction as the mayor's court in civil matters but did not possess its leet or criminal jurisdiction. Until 1373/4, its proceedings were usually entered onto the rolls of the mayor's court; thereafter they were kept separately.[17] In the 1370s and 1380s, over 80 per cent of the pleas heard in this court concerned debt; the remainder dealt primarily with minor cases of assault, broken contracts, detention of property and labor disputes. In the late fourteenth century, the court met about once every six weeks (more frequently in the summer and fall, less frequently in the winter and spring), yet forty to sixty new cases were presented at each court, and decisions were usually rendered within one or two court sessions. This relatively speedy justice may account for the lesser detail offered about each dispute compared to the information given in the mayor's court. All names that appeared in the pleadings for the ninety courts from 6 October 1377 to 7 January 1389 were extracted and filed in the data bank (except for pledges). The 3,583 debt pleas in this court from 1378–88 constituted 79 per cent of the total pleas in the debt analysis (see below).

Port customs accounts (PCA)

These are among the most valuable surviving records from medieval Exeter because they record all incoming ship traffic (customed or not), by coast or from overseas. Their evolution and contents are described in detail in an edition of the accounts from 1266–1321.[18] Until 1302 ship arrivals were often noted on the dorses of the mayor's court rolls; thereafter they were registered on separate rolls. The accounts list for each ship: the arrival date, the ship's name, type, home port and master; the importers, their custom status and custom owed (if any); and the type and quantity of goods they imported. Accounts survive for almost 75 per cent of the years from 1302 to 1498. All names,

detailed throughout the late fourteenth century but the quality of the series declined greatly in the fifteenth century because of administrative changes. The survival rate of the tourns also drops greatly from the 1420s on.

17 Separate rolls survive for 1337/8–1339/40, and from 1373/4 to 1701 with only about eight years missing between 1373 and 1500. PCR entries on the MCR were often enrolled with the marginal inscription *Provostria* and a notation on the days of the week; this led Hooker (*Citie of Excester*: 807–8) to believe that the provosts' court merely sat by adjournment of the mayor's court on days other than Monday. Yet the presiding officers of the two courts were different, the business of the provosts' court was almost entirely restricted to civil matters, and the same case never appeared in both courts (at least in the late fourteenth century). Closer scrutiny is needed to establish the relationship between the two courts over the course of the middle ages. Because of the ambiguities concerning this court, only proceedings from the separate rolls for the provosts' court are labelled PCR in the footnote references.

18 Kowaleski 1993.

ships, and imports in the mayor's-court entries of 1266–1302, the twelve accounts surviving for 1302–1321, and thirty seven accounts extant in 1345/6 –1399/1400 were included in a database.[19] Data concerning the number of ships entering the port and the wine tunnage imported were extracted for longer periods.[20]

City receiver's accounts (CRA)

These annual accounts enumerate the city's income and expenditure in detail. Extant from 1304, the earliest accounts have recently been edited.[21] From 1339/40 to 1517/18, only seventeen years are missing. A mine of information on the profits from customs farms, fairs, courts, port customs, and rents on city-owned properties, these accounts also include numerous payments and gifts made to local merchants, lawyers, and county gentry. Long sections detailing the construction work on the Guildhall, Fleshfold, marketplace, and other properties provide valuable information on the building and metal trades. Also useful are the lists of persons whose fines were excused because of their residence in one of the exempt jurisdictions. The data bank includes all names in these accounts from 1366/7 to 1400/1, and additional data and names were drawn from sample accounts in other periods.

Exe Bridge wardens' accounts (EBW)

Two bridge-wardens were elected each year to supervise both the upkeep of Exe Bridge and the properties it owned. These properties included those on the bridge itself, as well as the profitable Crikelpit mills outside the west gate on the Exe river. These accounts thus provide detailed information on the building, metal, and milling trades. They survive in an almost unbroken series from 1343 to 1711 with only two gaps before the sixteenth century (1346/7 and 1397/8). Names were extracted from the accounts between 1365/6 and 1398/9, but other years were only sampled.

19 An early version of this database (called EXCUST) is described in Kowaleski 1988. A similarly structured database (called NATCUST) includes over 2,300 names drawn from the PRO E122 accounts for Devon and most of Cornwall before 1400. Henri Touchard translated into French the accounts from 1381 to 1433 for his *thèse complémentaire* (1967b) but comparisons with the originals show a number of misreadings and omissions.

20 See Table 3.2, above.

21 See *Receivers' accounts* (eds. Margery Rowe and John Draisy 1989) for an excellent introduction to the series.

Duryard court rolls (DCR) and account rolls (DCA)

Located outside the city's north gate and bounded on the east by St Sidwell's fee, Duryard manor had belonged to the city since Anglo-Saxon times. Both the court rolls and account rolls of the manor survive from 1368. All names from the fifty three courts from 1368/9 to 1396/7 (which also contain a list of thirty eight free tenants in 1395/6 and annual rentals of pasture leases in the manor) were included in the data bank. All names from the account rolls were similarly extracted from 1368/9 to 1388/99 (when only one year is missing). Thereafter I mainly sampled the account rolls in order to trace the history of the city's mills and pasture lands in Duryard.

St Sidwell's fee court rolls, and dean and chapter rent rolls

St Sidwell's fee outside the east gate, owned by the dean and chapter of Exeter cathedral, was the city's largest suburb. The fee's court rolls are extant from 1320, but with many gaps. Only rolls within the target period of 1370–93 were included in the data bank.[22] Even more valuable were the dean and chapter's collectors' accounts of rents in Exeter which itemized all the rents paid by tenants in St Sidwell's fee, as well as offering considerable detail on the repairs made to various properties. All names (including many in the building trades) from the seven accounts between 1378/9 and 1395/6 were noted in the data bank.[23]

Other series in the Exeter cathedral library

The valuable records deposited in the Exeter cathedral library include those of the bishop, dean and chapter, and vicars choral: all include rentals, deeds, ministers' accounts, manorial court rolls, and account rolls for the properties these groups owned in Exeter, throughout Devon, and elsewhere.[24] The tithe accounts and manorial records offered particularly valuable data on rural society and agricultural production. Especially useful for the building and metal trades in Exeter were the cathedral fabric rolls which contain weekly accounts of the names and wages of all workers, along with lists of materials purchased and carting

[22] ECL D&C 4857–61 (1379/80, 1391–6); the series continues well into the fifteenth century. I also consulted the St Sidwell's court rolls in DRO CR 20,059 (1325), and Misc. Rolls 37, 38 (1327–41, 1341/2).

[23] ECL D&C 5150–56; this series begins in 1378/9 and continues into the fifteenth century.

[24] They are described in HMCR, vol. 55: 23–95, which is based on the even more useful "Calendar of the muniments and library of the dean and chapter of Exeter," a manuscript volume in the ECL compiled by Stuart A. Moore in 1873. The most up-to-date description of the various accounts may be found in Erskine 1962.

services. All names appearing on the twenty one rolls between 1371/2 and 1397/8 were included in the data bank,[25] as were all names from the surviving vicars choral quarterly account rolls of rents for Exeter.[26]

Linking names to individuals

Although medieval urban historians have had little to say about the issues involved in linking names to individuals, historians of rural communities in medieval England have for some time engaged in a lively exchange about the methodologies employed to identify individuals and reconstruct family groups from manorial records.[27] Many of their concerns about the quality of rural sources and the stability of rural surnames are, however, largely irrelevant for urban studies. As the description of sources above indicates, large boroughs generated many more different kinds of documents than did small villages. At the same time, their greater wealth and higher profiles as regional entrepôts, administrative capitals, or ecclesiastical centers made it more likely that their residents and activities appeared in county and national records. In short, urban historians have many more opportunities to identify individuals in many more sources.

The problems of surname stability and reliability are also less of an issue for this study. By the late fourteenth century, surnames were fairly stable in Exeter and other medieval towns. When aliases or alternative surnames were used, they were usually easily traced in the extant sources for Exeter. It was even possible to measure the frequency of such aliases among the 525 known Exeter householders in 1377. About 14 per cent of these householders were at one time or another identified by a surname different enough to lead an unwitting researcher to conclude that the surnames referred to two different people (if specific statements or substantial clues to the contrary had not existed in other sources).[28] This 14 per cent figure, however, probably exaggerates the degree to which aliases or unstable surnames might have impeded name

[25] ECL D&C 2636–57. For the years 1380/1–1397/8 I also consulted the transcripts compiled by D. F. Findlay for his 1939 doctoral dissertation. The earlier rolls (1279–1353) are printed in *Fabric accounts*.

[26] ECL V/C 3331 (1399). For the six accounts of 1386–1401, I used the abstract printed in DRO DD 22282.

[27] See, for example, Wrightson 1978; Razi 1979; Bennett 1983. See also the recent exchanges concerning the demographic possibilities of manorial court rolls in Poos and Smith 1984 and 1986; Razi 1985 and 1987.

[28] See Table A3.1 for a list. This figure does not include twenty two persons for whom an alias was possible but not verifiable nor the eight unidentifiable persons in the murage roll who were probably known under another name. If added to the known aliases, they would bring the total of alternative surnames to almost 20 per cent of the householders.

linkage in this study since the vast majority of any individual's appearances were made under only one surname. Moreover, 75 per cent of the alternative surnames were occupational and thus were easier to link with individuals than less distinguishing aliases.

The surname issue is also less of a problem for this study because I am not concerned, as the rural historians have been, with the reconstruction of families and family groups over time. The narrow chronological focus of the prosopographical analyses offered here (less than one generation in most instances) precludes many of the methodological questions over which the more demographically minded scholars of village life have argued. This does not mean that problems concerning the identification of individuals did not arise because they often did; it is that the problems were fewer and the tools to solve them more plentiful because of the coverage and depth of the sources for late fourteenth-century Exeter.[29]

The urban milieu and regional focus of this study did create two special difficulties regarding the identification of occupations and residences.[30] Obviously urban dwellers practiced a greater variety of occupations than did rural villagers; urban historians are thus much preoccupied with discovering and analyzing occupational structures. My own interest with this exercise is obvious in Chapter 4 and Tables A1.1 and A3.1. In an attempt to make clearer my assignment of occupational designations, I included with each occupational identification in my list of the 525 householders who resided in Exeter in 1377 (Table A3.1) a flag that noted the source of the occupational information. The murage roll of 1377 that formed the basis of this list only noted the occupations of twenty six of the 420 taxpayers. Most occupations were assigned on the basis of specific trade designations given for that person in another document (e.g., Edward Faireby "mason") or because an accumulation of evidence showed that the person engaged in activities associated with that occupation.

Because occupational assignments based on trade or craft activities could be somewhat subjective, I developed certain guidelines for matching an individual with a specific occupation. The most important factor in linking a person with an occupation was the frequency with which the person appeared in activities related to the craft. If a person was fined five or more times in a row for a trade-related marketing offense in the mayor's tourn and I had one other suggestive piece of evidence

[29] These problems are identical to those outlined in Bennett 1983; although she focuses on villagers and manorial records, her detailed and rigorous discussion of the problems involved in name linkage represents the best treatment of the subject. I have adhered as much as possible to the guidelines she suggests for linking the surnames of individuals.

[30] For occupations and occupational groups, see also above, Chapter 4, esp. pp. 120–6, and below, esp. Table A1.1. Residential designations are also considered below in the section on the debt analysis of 1378–88.

that corroborated this same trade, then I went ahead and assigned that occupation to the individual concerned. For example, Robert Taverner was presented for selling recooked fish and meat six times and for forestalling poultry four times. Since he also owned property in Cook Row and had dealings with a butcher, I was persuaded to label him a cook.[31] On rare occasions, I matched an occupation to an individual based on only one reference. William Whithiel, for example, claimed that he had broken his contract with Robert Fogeheler, a skinner, to taw 1,000 rabbit skins because Robert had failed to pay him weekly for his work as agreed upon.[32] This was Whithiel's sole appearance in the records I examined (suggesting that he was not an Exeter resident) so I had no way of corroborating the evidence that suggested he was a tawyer. But since it was highly unlikely that anyone but a tawyer would make such an agreement, I did not hesitate to assign him that occupation.

One of the biggest problems in making occupational identifications is the tendency for medieval people to practice more than one trade. The strategies adopted to take such multiple occupations into account are treated at greater length in Chapter 4, but it must be admitted that they are not wholly successful. In order to characterize the relationship between occupations and such factors as political rank, wealth, freedom membership, and commercial activity, it was necessary to identify one "primary" occupation and thereby exclude other activities the person may have carried on. The problem is made more acute because such information (in Exeter and most other medieval towns) is normally available only for the heads of households, rather than for all productive members of these households. In this study, occupations were designated primary ones when they seemed to take up most of the person's time and brought in the largest amount of income. If clerks went to the trouble to record a specific occupation for a person, then that trade was usually designated as the primary occupation.[33] Both the primary and secondary occupations of the 525 householders resident in Exeter in 1377 were noted in Table A3.1, along with a flag that records whether the occupations were surmised from the activities carried on by the person or from an occupational label assigned to the person in some document.

Residences were also hard to identify, particularly if a person lived outside of the city. Exeter householders were fairly easy to locate. If a

[31] SQMT 1378–83; 51/1/3/4; DD 23–24; MCR 1376/7, m. 1.
[32] MCR 1386/7, mm. 19, 20.
[33] For the changing meaning of such occupational labels and other problems involved in associating occupational terms with specific types of work, see the editors' essays in Corfield and Keene (eds.) 1990 and above, Chapter 4.

person showed up at least once in one of the mayor's tourn presentments that were made only on householders (breaking the assize of ale, letting pigs wander in the streets, leaving dung in the street, selling oats in one's inn, and holding a brothel), then they were considered city residents. Their dependents (spouses, servants, and most children) were also considered Exeter residents. The situation became more problematic, however, for residents who were not linked to these households or who lived in the exempt jurisdiction of Exe Island outside the west gate. Some who did not appear as householders could be identified in the records of the suburban and exempt jurisdictions or through an accumulation of references in deeds and commercial records that suggested residency.[34] But others clearly remain unlocated, particularly if they were servants, transients, or poor. These missing identifications do not really affect much of the analysis offered in the foregoing chapters, however, since these people had little impact on the commercial structure of Exeter. More serious was the inability to identify most of the 106 lay taxpayers in 1377 who resided in Exe Island, the exempt fee owned by the earl of Devon. The survival of some late-fourteenth-century deeds for Exe Island, as well as specific references to an "Exilond" residence for certain individuals helped, but it was still impossible to identify definitively all but five of the householders who lived there in 1377.[35]

Most difficult of all was the identification of non-Exeter residents who were included in the prosopographical studies with a regional focus. For the most part I relied solely on residential information given in the document undergoing analysis and did not presume to supply missing residential information unless I had concrete evidence tying the individual to his or her particular appearance in the document under discussion. The main exception to this conservative approach was the assignment of residences to the importers who appeared in the Exeter port customs accounts. Non-resident importers as a group were easy to distinguish from the Exeter importers, but the actual domicile of non-resident importers was stated for only about 13 per cent of them.[36] This figure underestimates the number of importers linked with residences,

[34] For the suburban and fee records, see above for the descriptions of the city receiver's accounts, Duryard records, and St Sidwell's documentation. Deeds, testaments, and the scribal notations of clerks in the MCR and MT were also very helpful in this regard.

[35] See below, p. 374, for a discussion of the Exe Island population and Table A3.1 for the five householders who resided there in 1377.

[36] Of the 333 identified non-Exeter importers in 1381–91 (above Table 6.4), 27 per cent had their residence noted at least once in the accounts. Although the accounts rarely specified Exeter as a domicile, it was relatively easy to identify the Exeter residents because they were mostly wealthy merchants and therefore prominent in freedom entries, election returns, debt cases, and other Exeter records.

however, because the clerks often indicated such residences only at the first appearance of the importer in the accounts. Thus I could assign a residence to subsequent appearances of the same importer with some confidence unless the importer went by a common name.[37] I also assumed that shipmasters and mariners (who owned 20 per cent of the cargoes) resided in the home port of their ships. Other details offered by the accounts also aided in assigning residences. For example, when Richard Sturion imported wine in 1365, he was termed *stannator* in the documents. A man by this name appeared in my data bank six other times between the dates 1365 and 1377; he lived in Ashburton (a stannary town), was taxed 11*d* and 3*s* in two different tinners' subsidies, and served as a poll tax collector for Ashburton.[38] Based on this information, I assigned Sturion the residence of Ashburton for the analysis of the port customs accounts.

The wealth and prominence of the vast majority of importers meant that they were likely to turn up in the lay subsidies, poll taxes, national customs accounts, estate records, deeds, and rentals that were among the many non-Exeter records I exploited for the data bank. Since the bulk of importers were urban residents, I made a special effort to include names from the borough records of the larger Devon towns and ports for the years 1290–1400. By carefully matching importers' names and other details in the accounts (date, custom status, trading partners, the ship's home port, the commodity imported, and the frequency of imports all provided clues to identity) with information in the data bank, I was eventually able to extend residential designations to the owners of about 85 per cent of the cargoes in 1302–20 and 80 per cent in 1381–91. The later importers were more difficult to identify because fewer came from Exeter, and more came from many different inland settlements rather than the smaller group of ports that served as the homes of most importers in the early fourteenth century.[39]

The analysis of Exeter debt cases, 1378–88

Because of the number of debt cases enrolled in their proceedings, borough court rolls provide the historian with an excellent opportunity

[37] For instance, there were at least five different John Bakers, two of whom the accounts identified as being from Dartmouth and Taunton. I did not venture, however, to assign these domiciles to other appearances by a John Baker.

[38] PRO E179/95/28, 33, 51; JUST3/15/6, m. 6 (a female servant stole goods worth a substantial sum from him); *Dartmouth*: 281; all of these references associated him with Ashburton. In addition there was a John (1332–73) and a Nicholas Sturion (1373–98) who were also prominent residents of Ashburton.

[39] See above, Table 6.4.

to examine local trade. Exeter possesses a particularly long and continuous series of three different court rolls, two of which routinely contained details of debt pleas. Working on the assumption that debt cases provide an accurate reflection of medieval commercial life, I extracted all debt cases (4,536) for the decade 1378/9–1387/8 (henceforth 1378–88) from the mayor's court rolls (953 pleas) and provosts' court rolls (3,583 pleas). These years were selected because the details offered about debt cases were particularly full during this decade and because subsidiary documentation used to help identify the debt litigants was best for this period.[40]

The debt pleas were transcribed and coded in 1979–80, analyzed with the aid of the computer software package SPSS, and discussed in my Ph.D. dissertation.[41] During the coding process I was able to add details concerning the political rank, occupation, and residence of many of the litigants, drawn from information stored in the data bank under these persons' names. This information was augmented by additions made to the data bank up to 1992, additions which in particular allowed for greater precision in the identification of occupations and residences.[42] Distinguishing Exeter inhabitants from non-residents was made easier by the rich body of source material in the data bank, particularly the household-related presentments made in the mayor's tourn. Political ranks were identified for all Exeter residents (with the aid of election returns in the MCR) and occupations for 78 per cent of the 7,457 Exeter litigants. Rather less data could be added for the non-Exeter residents because of the fewer references to these people in the data bank and because of the difficulties of name linkage. This problem was mitigated somewhat by the scribes' tendency to identify the residences (and more rarely the occupations) of outsiders, particularly for those who had travelled from farther away. Thus 42 per cent of the residences and 33 per cent of the occupations of the 1,897 non-Exeter litigants

[40] The only missing fourteenth-century MCR (1383/4) falls in the middle of the span. But because most of the debt pleas (79 per cent) were recorded in the PCR, and because the data pool examined was so big, this gap had very little effect on the analysis.

[41] Kowaleski 1982: 407–31 discusses the project in more detail than is offered here and includes a copy of the codebook used.

[42] These additions account for most of the differences (none of which changed my conclusions) between the figures offered in my dissertation and those offered here. The analysis offered here also includes eleven cases inadvertently left out of the 1982 analysis. For this study I also changed my method of assessing political rank. Instead of assigning litigants the highest political rank they attained, I here assigned them the rank they held when they actually appeared as a litigant. This latter method had the effect of softening, but not really altering the picture I presented (in Kowaleski 1982 and 1984) of the oligarchy's dominance of local markets.

could be identified.[43] No attempt was made to discern the political ranks of these outsiders for the database.

Why can debt cases be considered an accurate reflection of medieval commercial life? One may argue that such pleas represent only those commercial transactions that failed and hence are biased in favor of those who were unsuccessful. While this argument may be partially true for people who habitually appeared in court as debtors (which information in itself is valuable since it is worthwhile to discover the common characteristics of debtors), the frequency of any individual's appearance as a creditor (and even as a debtor) was primarily a function of that person's involvement in the local markets. Traders who maintained a busy, active profile in town trade inevitably surfaced in debt cases on a regular basis. Merchants, for example, appeared proportionately far more often in debt cases because they were more heavily involved in the trading activities that were at the heart of debt pleas. Similarly, merchants came into court more often as creditors than as debtors because they dominated the local markets with their greater capital, influence, and commercial privilege. But even artisans and other less commercially active people such as women and servants were represented in these debt cases. The ubiquity of credit amongst all levels of urban society ensured that most people appeared in debt court at some point, whether as a creditor or debtor.[44] This situation may have been especially true in the late fourteenth century when, as Richard Britnell argues, indebtedness increased as a result of economic development.[45]

The number of litigants who appeared in these proceedings also supports the assumption that borough debt cases reflected commercial life. Some 2,249 different adults (1,917 men, 332 women) appeared as a debtor or creditor in the two borough courts during this decade; over 1,700 of these people resided in Exeter at a time when the lay population of the town, including children, numbered about 3,100. Of the 420 householders listed in the 1377 murage roll, 339 appeared at least once as a debt litigant in 1378–88. Of those seventy eight who did not crop up in debt cases, most were either poorer artisans or women, and only fifteen were taxed more than 6*d*. This evidence reinforces the impression that appearances in debt cases correlated with degree of participation in local commerce.[46]

[43] They include 251 persons (60 creditors, 191 debtors) whose exact residence could not be determined but whose pattern of activity in Exeter indicates that they almost certainly lived within 6 miles of the city; see above, p. 286, n. 25.

[44] For the ubiquity of credit even in rural communities, see Clark 1981. See also above, pp. 202–12 for credit in Exeter.

[45] Britnell 1986b: 103.

[46] Chapter 5 discusses in more detail the use of credit and different causes for debt pleas.

Occupational groups in Exeter

In order to make sense of the occupational structure of medieval Exeter and to compare it with the occupational profile of those involved in the local and regional markets, it is necessary to arrange occupations into some sort of groups. This type of exercise has been attempted, with a fair amount of disagreement and varying results, by many other historians, particularly urban historians.[47] After some experimentation with occupational classifications that emphasize functions (e.g. distributors and retailers as opposed to artisan/retailers, or producers),[48] I have here opted to emphasize the more traditional method of grouping occupations by the nature of the raw materials or products with which their practitioners dealt.

The occupations listed below (Table A1.1) include non-residents and residents of Exeter (the former appearing in the analyses of Exeter debt cases, the port trade, and regional trade in hides and fish). Those occupations enclosed within round brackets could be included under more than one product classification, but for the sake of convenience were only counted as part of the classification (where they appear without parentheses) with which they were most closely connected in Exeter. Those occupations with distributive functions are marked with an asterisk (*). Merchants were distinguished primarily by their involvement in maritime trade, their participation in long-distance overland trade, wholesale or distributive trade, and the scale of their investments and financial undertakings. For more on the guidelines adopted to help identify occupations of individuals, see above (pp. 344–5).

[47] The various schemes are summarized in Patten 1977. See also Pound 1981; Goose 1982; Palliser 1983: 243–5, 392–3.

[48] Kowaleski 1982: 170–83; Kowaleski 1984: 370. This scheme followed the guidelines suggested in Patten 1977.

Table A1.1 *Occupations and occupational groups*

(1) Merchants
merchant*
shipmaster*
and *(2) Retailers and brokers*
broker
chandler
chapman
(huckster)
moneylender
retailer

(3) Victuallers
baker
brewer
butcher
cook
fisher
fishmonger
gardener
huckster
loder
miller
spicer
tapster
taverner
victualler
vintner*

(4) Hostelers

(5) Clothing trades
dressmaker
embroiderer
(girdler)
(hosier)
tailor
and *(6) Textile manufacture*
chaloner
clothworker
draper*
dyer
(embroiderer)
fuller
mercer*
shearman
tapicer
weaver

(7) Leather/skin trades
cordwainer
corveser
currier
furrier
girdler
glover
hosier
leatherseller*
leather-skinworker
leatherworker
parcheminer
pouchmaker
saddler
skinner
sutor
tanner
tawyer

(8) Metal trades
armourer
brazier
cardmaker
cutler
ferrour
furbisher
(girdler)
goldsmith
latoner
locksmith
lorimer
marshal
metalworker
pewterer
plumber
smith
spurrier

(9) Building trades
building worker/laborer
carpenter
couvreour
glazier
helier
lymer
mason
plasterer
(plumber)
sawyer
thatcher
tiler

Table A1.1. *cont.*

(10) Miscellaneous crafts	*(14) Professional and administrative*
candeler	bailiff
horner	castle gatekeeper
(piper)	clerk
roper	gatekeeper
soaper	lawyer
waxchandler	official
and *(11) Wood trades*	rentier
bowyer	schoolmaster
fletcher	town official
hooper	*(15) Clergy*
and *(12) Miscellaneous services*	abbot/prior
apprentice	bishop
barber	chaplain
(broker)	canon
launderer	monk
(loder)	parson
messenger	priest
(miller)	rector
piper	(schoolmaster)
pledger	vicar
porter	*(16) Gentry*
servant	earl
(shipmaster)	esquire
waite	gentry landowner
watercarrier	knight
and *(13) Agricultural*	
farmer	
(gardener)	
grazier	
peasant	
reeve	
shepherd	

Appendix 2
Markets and fairs in medieval Devon

The following table lists all the known fairs and markets in medieval Devon and serves as the basis of the discussion in Chapter 2. Thus far 113 markets occurring at 101 different places and 150 fairs at 101 locations have been identified within the administrative borders of medieval Devon (Thornecombe and Churchstanton are now in Somerset). The markets are mapped in Figure 2.1 and the fairs in Figure 2.2.[1] All known fairs are included in these figures,[2] but fish markets[3] and the deliberate replacement of one market day by another were not factored into any of the totals calculated for markets. Attempts to add an extra market day at a location were, however, counted in the totals. Also not included in these figures are occasional markets and fairs, such as those the bishop of Exeter tried to discourage from happening in the church and churchyard at Dotton in 1400.[4]

[1] These maps also contain references to the markets and fairs of Cornwall, Somerset, and Dorset. No accurate lists of the markets and fairs of these counties have been produced, so most were identified with the aid of references in Appendix XIX of Elton and Costelloe (eds.) 1889 and the *VCH* volumes for Somerset. Further research will undoubtedly turn up more references and should allow us to discover the market days of some of the early markets for which no data has yet been found. I am particularly grateful to Gilbert Stack for allowing me to see his unpublished list of Somerset fairs.

[2] Even fairs supposedly replaced by new grants have been counted in the totals because some may have continued despite the claims in the new grants to the contrary. For example, the grant of a Trinity fair at Bradworthy in 1236 (*CCR 1234–37*: 382) noted that it replaced the older St John the Baptist fair but this latter fair may still have been active in 1238 (*Devon eyre*: 47).

[3] Located at places where references to the regular sale of fish occurred but had no chartered market; Table A2.1 lists three such markets, probably only a fraction of the number of such places in Devon. In many cases there were probably regular markets held at these places as well. For example, references to the fish market at Exmouth (usually called 'Checkstone' in the middle ages) were in 1261 (Misc. Roll 2, no. 52) accompanied by a reference to a merchant selling goods there while archaeological evidence from the fifteenth century and references in the sixteenth and seventeenth centuries also point to the presence of a regular market there (Weddell 1986: 123). See also Brooking-Rowe 1906: 15 for a reference of c. 1340 to the *mercatum piscium* there.

[4] *Reg. Stafford*: 85–6. For the lordship and location of Dotton, see Orme 1987.

Frances Mace was the first to try to identify the fairs and markets of medieval Devon by listing all enrolled grants of Devon fairs and markets in the charter rolls from 1226 to 1417.[5] Some twenty five years later in 1952, W. G. Hoskins provided a map of markets and fairs in early fourteenth-century Devon, although he did not indicate the sources on which his information was based.[6] More recently, R. H. Britnell has noted, in his article on the proliferation of markets in medieval England, ninety four markets in Devon before 1349 which he identified from printed sources and Hoskins' map.[7] The table offered here identifies considerably more markets than this before 1349 (108) because a wider range of manuscript sources was consulted.

Many of the markets and fairs listed in the following table were identified with the help of the Public Record Office's card index of markets and fairs, which draws upon the charter rolls, close rolls, patent rolls, and fine rolls.[8] Roughly twenty seven of the markets and twenty eight of the fairs were identifed from other sources such as the pipe rolls, curia regis rolls, inquisitions post mortem, account rolls, and borough court rolls. Grants for these latter markets and fairs were sometimes enrolled at a later date in the charter rolls. Thus, although the market at Sampford Peverell was known to be in existence by 1220 when the owner of the market was sued by the lord of a neighboring market in the curia regis, no formal grant was enrolled for the market until 1335 when the owner also obtained a two-day fair at the feast of the Annunciation.[9] The late April–early May fair at Crediton was not sanctioned by charter until 1309 but was clearly in operation from at least 1291 when it was mentioned in the Exeter court rolls.[10] In other instances, there survives clear evidence of commercial activity at a place before any official market was sanctioned there. In 1238, for example, wine was sold at Bampton, Colyford, and Tiverton and cloth at South Molton even though chartered markets only appeared at these places

[5] She did so in Appendix C of her M.A. thesis (Mace 1925b).

[6] Hoskins 1952: map facing p. 225. See also the map of market towns and their five-mile hinterlands in Shorter, Ravenhill, and Gregory (eds.) 1969: 120, which is probably based on Hoskins' map.

[7] Britnell 1981b: 210; I am grateful to Richard Britnell for sending me his list of Devon markets and fairs.

[8] This card index was originally based on a list of charters concerning markets and fairs from 1199 to 1483 noted in a PRO index (Palmer's Index No. 93) and published as Appendix XIX to *First report of the royal commission on market rights and tolls* (1889). Appendix XI of this work lists markets and fairs in the quo warranto rolls.

[9] *Curia regis*, vol. 9: 305, 330; vol. 10: 96; vol. 13: 530; vol. 14: 1. *CCHR*, vol. 4: 344.

[10] MCR 1291/2, m. 18d; *CCHR*, vol. 3: 133.

many years later.[11] "Prescriptive" markets active before the thirteenth century were particularly likely to escape notice in any of the official sources. Older fairs or those that occurred in places with powerful political connections also frequently lacked formal charters of foundation. Indeed, only one of Exeter's seven fairs and one of the five fairs at Tiverton (the chief residence for the Courtenay earls of Devon during much of the middle ages) are known through official royal grants. These omissions suggest that historians should be wary of excessive reliance on royal grants, particularly the charter rolls, in identifying markets and fairs or determining their date of "foundation."

The sources listed in the table usually represent the first recorded notice of the fair or market. It is clear, however, that these documentary references could come decades, even centuries, after the market or fair actually began to take place. The first documented reference to a market in Exeter occurs only in 1213 (when the citizens were allowed to change their Sunday market to Monday), even though Exeter must have had a regular market by the end of the ninth century when a mint was established there.[12] Anglo-Saxon mints were also located at the *burhs* of Barnstaple, Lydford, and Totnes by the eleventh century so it has been assumed that they too possessed markets by this date.[13] More recently, Jeremy Haslam has argued that Plympton, Kingsbridge, and possibly Kingsteignton were also urban places by the beginning of the tenth century, implying that they were also sites of active trading by this time.[14] For these early markets, Domesday Book is not much help since it only recorded two markets in Devon: one at Okehampton and another at Otterton (although Sidmouth was most likely the actual location of this latter market).[15] When it is known that a market or fair was active before the year of the first recorded reference, the market flag (MF) or fair flag (FF) columns in the table record a "b" (for "by" this date). Markets known to exist in the twelfth century have a "p" (for "pre-1200") in the MF column, while the four Anglo-Saxon mints (Barnstaple, Exeter, Lydford, and Totnes) have an "m" (for "mint")

[11] *Devon eyre*: 20, 30, 33, 54; Table A2.1, below.

[12] *Rotuli litterarum clausarum*, vol. 1: 139; Maddicott 1989: 17. The first specific reference to the Wednesday and Friday markets was in 1281 (PRO JUST1/181, m. 35d and JUST1/186, m. 44d) even though these markets must have taken place for some time.

[13] Hill 1981: 131–2; Haslam 1984. The Source column for these places with early mints, however, lists the first documentary reference to the market and the MF column includes an "m."

[14] Haslam 1984. Similar "urban" settlements with trading functions may also have developed at Tavistock, Lifton, and Axminster; see Haslam 1984: 276.

[15] See below, Table A2.1, n. 14.

in this column.[16] This total is still likely to underestimate the number of pre-1200 markets since it does not include others, such as East Teignmouth, Kingsbridge, and Tiverton, for which we lack firm evidence to trace their twelfth-century activities.

An attempt has also been made to indicate in Table A2.1 which fairs and markets lasted into the late middle ages and beyond. Historians need to be more aware of which markets and fairs survived, the reasons for success or failure, or even, for that matter, what "survival" of a fair or market meant in medieval terms. For markets, inclusion in Alan Everitt's list of market towns from 1500 to 1700 was taken to be evidence of survival (noted by a "s" in the MF column).[17] In almost all instances, evidence from late medieval records was found to corroborate the continued existence of these markets. A few cases of late medieval markets known to be active in the fifteenth century but not included in Everitt's tabulation have also surfaced; these have been noted by an "a" in the MF column (for "active") but were not included in the calculations for "surviving" markets in Chapter 2.

Determining how long fairs survived is a much more difficult task. Those known to continue for at least several years after their date of "foundation" have a "c" (for "continued") in the fair flag (FF) column.[18] Those that were still going concerns in the late fourteenth and fifteenth centuries have been marked with an "a" in the FF column (for "active"). Fair profits enrolled in manorial or estate account rolls, extents in inquisitions post mortem, and incidental references to fairs in court rolls provided the bulk of these data on fair activity. Since such sources are not extant in very large numbers, nor are they always particularly reliable indicators of whether or not a fair was continuing to occur, an additional method had to be adopted to determine if a fair endured into the early modern period.[19] The benchmark chosen for survivability were two eighteenth-century lists of Devon fairs: a 1792 list noted in the report of the Royal Commission on market rights and tolls, and

[16] For the mints, see above, n. 13. The others were identified as pre-1200 foundations because of their borough status in the twelfth century, references to twelfth-century markets in legal disputes or in their later charters, or other indications of a pre-existing market. In Chapter 2, therefore, the pre-1200 markets were those with a foundation date earlier than 1200 or a "p" or "m" in the MF column.

[17] Everitt 1967: 470–2.

[18] This code was generally used for thirteenth-century evidence (such as the quo warranto proceedings, the hundred rolls, account rolls, and extents in the inquisitions post mortem) so fairs with only a "c" in the MF field were not considered to have survived into the early modern period.

[19] Extents, inquisitions, and account rolls of the thirteenth century, for example, were more careful to enroll fair profits than were those of later centuries.

Daniel Lysons' list of Devon fairs published in 1822.[20] Medieval fairs recorded in these lists were marked with an "s" in the FF column (for "survived"). This method has obvious drawbacks since both the list of 1792 and that of Lysons were far removed from the middle ages and many changes in the calendar of fair dates had occurred. Yet a reassuringly large number of these eighteenth-century survivals are also documented in late medieval sources, thus lending greater credibility to this method.[21] The discussion in Chapter 2 of "surviving" fairs thus refers to those with either an "a" or "s" in the FF column of Table A2.1.

Fair grants always referred to fairs by the saint's day or holy day upon which a fair was centered. This information is included in the table, along with the dedication of the local parish church, in order to see more clearly the correlation between pre-existing local celebrations and the timing of the fair. I have also noted dedications to a local abbey, priory, chapel, or even hospital when it appears that they may have affected the choice of fair dates.[22] The number of fair days are generally those given in the original grant even though it is evident that some fairs were reduced to fewer days in later years. The fair at Denbury, for example, was first granted for three days, but within four years was reduced to two, and by the end of the fifteenth century lasted only one day.[23] Undoubtedly many late medieval fairs followed a similar pattern. It is also unlikely that the county's longest fairs – those of eight or nine days' duration at Axminster, Colyton, Crediton, Modbury, and South Zeal – lasted, by the late middle ages, as long as their charters imply. On the other hand, several of the supposed one-day fairs, such as those at Exeter, Lydford, Sidmouth, and Tiverton, are listed as such only because of the brevity of the entry in the account or court rolls that recorded profits from these fairs; all of these fairs probably took place over more than one day.

[20] A fair was considered to have survived if the fair dates given in the Royal Commission report (Elton and Costelloe 1889: 153–7) or in Lysons (1822: xxxv–xxxviii) matched the fair dates of the medieval fair within three days. The relevance of these lists for the sixteenth century is reinforced by the data in Lysons' list of eighteenth-century and recently "disused" markets (pp. xxiv–xxxv) which generally paralleled markets listed by Everitt (1967) for the sixteenth century.

[21] Leland's *Itinerary* was also helpful in pointing to early modern survivals. Further information on the survival of fairs into the sixteenth century could undoubtedly be gained from the use of almanacs similar to those described by Hodgen (1942), although she notes only nine fairs in Devon from 1550 to 1600 in the almanacs she employed, clearly a goss underestimation.

[22] Identification of church dedications was based largely on information given in the gazetteer of Hoskins' *Devon* (1972) and supplemented by information in Oliver 1864; White 1850; Cherry and Pevesner 1989.

[23] Finberg 1969: 198–91 *CChR*, vol. 2: 331, 352.

Further research, particularly on the unpublished records of the thirteenth century, will probably turn up additional references to markets and fairs in Devon. Several historians, for example, have claimed that there was a market at Winkleigh and another fair at Modbury, although extensive searching has turned up no reference to them.[24] There is also no evidence that medieval markets existed at Lifton, Membury, North Bovey, or South Brent, although Everitt's list notes markets there between 1500 and 1700.[25] Markets have also not been discovered for several Devon boroughs; Lympstone, Newton Ferrers, and Winkleigh had neither markets nor fairs.[26] One borough that was actually a suburb of Totnes – Bridgetown Pomeroy – had a fair but no market.

The following list summarizes the codes used under each column heading (underlined) in Table A2.1:

MktDa (Market Day): A dash separating the market days (e.g. Su-S) indicates that the market day was moved from the first to the second day indicated.

MF (Market Flag) and *FF* (Fair Flag): the fair or market was
a= active in the late fourteenth to fifteenth centuries
b= active before date of documentary reference
c= continued for some years after foundation
l= grant limited to certain period (e.g. until king comes of age)
m= pre-1200 mint located here
n= new foundation that replaced the old one
p = market known to have existed pre-1200
r= replaced by another market or fair
s= survived into early modern period
x= probably failed

Fair Feast: v= vigil; f= feast; m= morrow

D: number of days over which the fair took place

Re (Region): N=north or mid Devon; S=south Devon; E= east Devon; D=Dartmoor and borderlands. See Figure 1.1 for these regions.

[24] Hoskins 1972: 516, for Winkleigh; Modbury Local History Society 1971: 28, for another fair in Modbury on the feast of St James. Hoskins may have had in mind the market at Hollacombe, a hamlet in Winkleigh parish.

[25] Everitt 1967: 471–2. See also Alan Dyer (1979) for an excellent discussion of the history of early modern markets.

[26] Compare Beresford and Finberg 1973: 86–101, with Table A2.1. All of these boroughs were extremely small; only the absence of a market at Winkleigh is surprising; perhaps the one founded at Hollacombe in that parish may have been used by Winkleigh

Source: Abbreviations for the sources are to be found in the Bibliography under Primary Sources; some are slightly shortened versions of the citations noted there. The "source" represents the first recorded reference to the fair or market; in some cases the day of the market or time of the fair is known from a later reference that is not given here.

Gr (Grantee): the status of the owner of the fair: C= corporate (city or vill); E=ecclesiastical; M=multiple (lay and ecclesiastical); R=royal; S=lay seigneurial. The first letter indicates the status of the owner at its foundation; the second indicates the owner in the fifteenth century. **E** designates markets and fairs owned by the bishop of Exeter; **S** indicates those owned wholly or in part by the earls of Devon.

residents. Further documentary research would probably turn up markets at all of these places.

Table A2.1. *Markets and fairs in medieval Devon*

Place	MktDa	Year MF	Fair Feast	Fair Dates	D	Year FF	Church dedication	Re	Source	Gr
Alphington	fish	1350 ba						E	NQMT 1350	S
Alvington, West	S	1272	vfm St Michael	28–30 Sep	3	1272	All Saints	S	CChR:2:p181	S
Ashburton	S	1155 bs					St Andrew	D	RegGran:2:1570	**E**
Ashburton			vfm St Lawrence	9–11 Aug	3	1309 s	St Lawrence chapel	D	CChR:3:p133	E
Ashburton			vfm St Martin	10–12 Nov	3	1313 s	St Andrew	D	CChR:3:p224	E
Ashprington	fish	1134 b					St David	S	Totnes Pr:p36	SE
Aveton Gifford			vfm Nativity St John Baptist	23–25 Jun	3	1290	St Andrew	S	CChR:2:p341	S
Aveton Gifford	T	1290	vfm Invention Cross	2–4 May	3	1290	St Andrew	S	CChR:2:p341	S
Awliscombe	W	1292	vfm St Michael	28–30 Sep	3	1292	St Michael	E	CChR:2:p423	S
Axminster	Su–S	1204 ps	vf+6 Nat St John Baptist	23–30 Jun	8	1215 s	Ss Mary and John Evangelist	E	RotCh:p139,217	SE
Aylesbeare[1]			f+3 St Osyth	7–10 Oct	4	1239	St Mary	E	CChR:1:p243	**S**
Aylesbeare			f+? St Osyth	3 June + ?	1	1239 bc	St Mary	E	CChR:1:p243	**S**
Bampton	W	1321 ns					St Michael	E	CChR:3:p436	S
Bampton	S	1267 pr	WThF Whitsuntide wk	May–Jun	3	1200 bs	St Michael	E	CChR:2:p80	S
Bampton			vfm St Luke	17–19 Oct	3	1258 ba	St Luke chapel	E	CChR:2:p12	E
Barnstaple	F	1274 ms					St Peter	N	Barn Rec:I:105	RS
Barnstaple[2]	W	1344 bs					St Peter	N	Barn.Rec:I:148	S
Barnstaple			vfm Nativity BVM	7–8 Sep	3	1154 ba	St Peter	N	NDRO Ath.Ms.27	S
Barnstaple			vf+2 St Mary Magdalene	21–24 Jul	4	1343 bx	St Mary Magdalene priory	N	CPR:1243:p90	C
Bere Alston	W	1295 s	vfm St Andrew	29 Nov–1 Dec	3	1295	St Andrew	S	CChR:2:p463	S
Bideford	F–W	1218 pr					St Mary	N	RLitC:1:p169	S
Bideford[3]	M	1272 s	vf+3 St Margaret	19–23 Jul	5	1272 cs	St Mary	N	CChR:2:p181	S
Bishop's Clyst	T	1309	vfm St Michael	28–30 Sep	3	1309	St Mary	E	CChR:3:p133	**E**
Bishop's Tawton			vf+2 St Lawrence	9–11 Aug	4	1399	St John Baptist	N	CChR:5:p375	**E**

Black Torrington	W	1219 c	vf Assumption BVM	14–15 Aug	2 1219 c	St Mary	N	RLitC:1:p.391	S
Bovey Tracy	Th	1219 bs				St Thomas Martyr	D	PipR:v80:p23	S
Bovey Tracy			vfm Translation of St Thomas	6–8 Jul	3 1260 ba	St Thomas Martyr	D	CChR:2:p181	S
Bow	Th	1259 s	vfm St Martin	10–12 Nov	3 1259 s	St Martin chapel	E	CChR:2:p19	S
Bradninch	S	1208 ps	3+f St Denis	6–9 Oct	4 1208 a	St Denis	E	RotCh:p183	S
Bradninch	Th	1239 x	vfm Trinity	May–Jun	3 1239 x	St Denis	E	CChR:1:p246	S
Bradworthy	W	1234 r	vfm Decollation St John Baptist	28–30 Aug	3 1234 cr	St John Baptist	N	CurReg:v15:227	S
Bradworthy	F	1236 n	vfm Trinity	May–Jun	3 1236 n	St John Baptist	N	CCR:1236:p382	S
Brendon	W	1221 l				St Brendan	N	PRO C60/16 m8	S
Brent Tor			vfm St Michael	28–30 Sep	3 1232 as	St Michael chapel	D	CChR:1:p157	E
Bridgetown Pomeroy			vfm St James	24–26 Jul	3 1267 s	St Mary	S	CChR:2:p76	S
Broadhembury	W	1290	vfm Assumption	14–16 Aug	3 1290	St Andrew	E	CChR:2:p371	E
Buckfastleigh	T	1353				St Mary abbey	D	CChR:5:p130	E
Buckfastleigh			f+2 St Bartholomew Ap	24–26 Aug	3 1460 s	Holy Trinity	D	CChR:6:p136	E
Buckland Brewer	W	1290	vfm Assumption	14–16 Aug	3 1290	Ss Mary and Benedict	N	CChR:2:p371	E
Buckland Monochorum	T	1318	vfm Nativitiy of St John Baptist	23–25 Jun	3 1318	St Andrew	D	CChR:3:p373	E
Canonsleigh	W	1286				St Mary	E	CChR:6:p291	E
Canonsleigh[4]			vf+3 St Theobald	29 Jun–3 Jul	5 1286 c	St Theobald chapel	E	CChR:2:p331	E
Chagford	Su–S	1220 ps				St Michael	D	CurReg:v8:p267	S
Chawleigh	Th	1254	vf+2 St Mary Magdalene	21–24 July	4 1254	St James	N	CPR:1254:338–9	**S**
Chillington			vfm SS Philip and James	31 Apr–2 May	3 1286	St Michael	S	Harl.Ch.58 I38	S
Chillington	T	1286	vfm St Michael	28–30 Sep	3 1286	St Michael	S	Harl.Ch.58 I38	S
Chittelhampton	Th	1218				St Urith	N	RLitC:1:p368	S
Chudleigh	M	1309 s	vfm St Barnabas	10–12 Jun	3 1309 as	St Martin	E	CChR:3:p133	**E**

Table A2.1. *Markets and fairs in medieval Devon (cont.)*

Place	MktDa	Year MF	Fair Feast	Fair Dates	D Year FF	Church dedication	Re Source	Gr
Chulmleigh	W?F?	1274 bs	f+ ? St Mary Magdalene	22–? Jul	1 1274 bs	St Mary Magdalene	N PRO C133/6/1m10	**S**
Churchstanton	W	1223 l				St Paul	E PRO C60/18 m3	S
Clovelly	W	1290	vfm All Saints	31 Oct–2 Nov	3 1290	All Saints	N CChR:2:p351	S
Cockington	M	1353	vfm Trinity	May–Jun	3 1353	Ss George and Mary	S CChR:5:p126	S
Colyford	Th	1274 ba				St Edmund chapel	E PRO C133/6/1	**S**
Colyton[5]	S?	1292 bs				St Andrew	E IPM:v3:p24	**S**
Colyton			octave+7 Michaelmas	7–14 Oct	8 1207 as	St Andrew	E RotCh:p169	S
Combe Martin	Th	1221 bs				St Peter ad Vincula	N PRO C60/16 m4	S
Combe Martin			vfm Pentecost	May–Jun	3 1222 ls	St Peter ad Vincula	N RLitC:1:p511	S
Crediton	Th	1231 s	vfm St Lawrence	9–11 Aug	3 1231 a	St Lawrence chapel	E CChR:1:p129	E
Crediton			m+8 Inv. Holy Cross	26 Apr–4 May	9 1291 ba	Holy Cross	E MCR 1291/2m18d	**E**
Crediton	T	1309	vf+7 Nativity BVM	7–15 Sep	9 1309 a	Holy Cross	E CChR:3:p133	**E**
Croyde	T	1253				St George	N CPR 1253:p296	
Cullompton[6]	Th	1257 s	vfm St John Baptist	28–30 Aug	3 1257	St Andrew	E CChR:2:p2	**S**
Cullompton	T	1318	vfm St George	22–24 Apr	3 1318	St Andrew	E CChR:3:p373	E
Dartmouth	W	1205 s				St Petrock	S Obl&Fn:p295	S
Dartmouth[7]			vfm St John Baptist	28–30 Aug	3 1231	St Petrock	S CChR:1:p128	S
Dartmouth	Th	1302 r?	vf St Margaret	19–20 Jul	2 1302	St Petrock	S CChR:3:p26	S
Denbury	W	1286	vfm Nativity BVM	7–9 Sep	3 1286 as	St Mary	S CChR:2:p331	E
Dodbrooke	W	1257 s	vf St Mary Magdalene	21–22 Jul	2 1257 c	St Thomas Martyr	S CChR:1:p456	E
Drewsteignton	M	1388				St Peter	D C143/407/23	S
Ermington	T&F	1304	vfm St John Baptist	28–30 Aug	3 1304	St Peter	S CChR:3:p40	S
Exeter[8]	Su–M	1213 ms					E Rot.ClausI:139	RC
Exeter	MWF	1281 bs				St Peter cathedral	E JUST1/181 m35d	RC
Exeter			vfm St Nicholas	5–7 Dec	3 1130 ba	St Nicholas priory	E MagRotSca:p153	RC
Exeter			vfm St Peter ad Vincula	31 Jul–2 Aug	3 1163 ba	St Peter cathedral	E PipeR:v7:p19	**SM**

Exeter			Whitmonday/Pentecost	May–Jun	7 1240 ba	St Peter cathedral	E	A–N Cust:p30	C
Exeter			Carniprivium	Feb–Mar	1 1374 ba	St Peter cathedral	E	MCR 1373/4m20d	C
Exeter			f St Thomas Apostle	21 Dec	1 1405 a	St Peter cathedral	E	CRA 1405/6	C
Exeter			Good Friday	Mar–Apr	1 1431 a	St Peter cathedral	E	CRA 1430/1	C
Exeter			vf St Mary Magdalene	21–22 Jul	2 1463 a	St Mary Magdalene hospital	E	CPR:1463:p400	C
Exmouth (Checkstone)	fish	1261 bc				St Margaret chapel	E	Misc.Ro.2 no52	S
Hartland	T	1281 bs	vf St Nectan	16–17 Jun	2 1281 ba	St Nectan	N	CChR:2:p253	S
Hartland			vfm St Andrew	29 Nov–1 Dec	3 1286 a	St Nectan	N	CChR:2:p329	S
Hatherleigh	Th	1219 s	vf Nativity St John Baptist	23–24 Jun	2 1219 s	St John Baptist	N	PRO C60/12 m2	E
Holcombe Rogus	F	1343	vf All Saints	31 Oct-1 Nov	2 1343	All Saints	E	CChR:5:p24	S
Hollacombe	M	1261	vfm Ascension	May	3 1261	St Petrock	N	CChR:2:p35	S
Holsworthy[9]	S	1185 bs	vfm Ss Peter and Paul	28–30 Jun	3 1185 ba	Ss Peter and Paul	N	L Day 1934 7–9	S
Honiton[10]	Su?–S	1220 bs				St Michael	E	CurReg:9:p305	**S**
Honiton			vfm All Saints	31 Oct–2 Nov	3 1220 r	All Saints chapel	E	PRO C60/12 m2	**S**
Honiton			vfm St Margaret	19–23 Jul	3 1247 ns	St Margaret chapel	E	CChR:1:p323	**S**
Honiton			MTW Whitsuntide	May–Jun	3 1257	St Michael	E	CChR:2:p2	**S**
Ilfracombe	S	1233 s	vfm Whitsuntide	May–Jun	3 1233 a?	Holy Trinity	N	CChR:1:p184	S
Ilfracombe	M	1272 n?	vfm Trinity	May–Jun	3 1272	Holy Trinity	N	CChR:2:p184	S
Ipplepen[11]			vfm Nativity St John Baptist	23–25 Jun	3 1317	St Andrew	S	CChR:1:p359	S
Ipplepen	Th	1317 bc	vfm St Andrew	29 Nov–1 Dec	3 1317	St Andrew	S	CChR:p359	S
Kennford	Th	1300 a?	vf St Mary Magdalene	21–22 Jul	2 1300	St Andrew	E	CChR:2:p488	**S**
Kenton	S	1230	vfm All Saints	30 Oct–2 Nov	3 1230	All Saints	E	CChR:1:p333	C
Kingsbridge[12]	F	1220 s				St Mary	S	PipR:v85:p85	E
Kingsbridge	S	1460 c	f+2 St Margaret	20–22 Jul	3 1460	St Edmund chapel	S	CChR:6:p136	E
Kingskerswell	T	1265	vfm St Giles	31 Aug–2 Sep	3 1265	St Mary	S	CChR:1:p89	S
Langford	Th	1333 x	vfm St James	23–25 Jul	3 1333 x	St Andrew	E	CChR:4:p302	S
Lydford	W	1199 ma				St Petrock	D	PipR:v12:p224	RC

Table A2.1. *Markets and fairs in medieval Devon (cont.)*

Place	MktDa	Year MF	Fair Feast	Fair Dates	D Year FF	Church dedication	Re	Source	Gr
Lydford			vfm St Petrock	3–5 Jun	3 1199 bc	St Petrock	D	CChR:2:p84	RC
Lydford			f+? St Bartholomew	24 Aug	1 1300 bs	St Petrock	D	IPM v3:456	S
Marwood			vfm St Michael	28–30 Sep	3 1293	St Michael	N	CChR:2:p433	S
Modbury	W–Th	1218 ps				St George	S	RLitC:1:p169	S
Modbury[13]			vf+7 St George	22–30 Apr	9 1238 bs	St George	S	Hoskins:p436	S
Moreleigh	T	1316	vf St Mary Magdalene	21–22 Jul	2 1316	All Saints	S	CChR:3:p306	S
Moretonhampstead	Su–S	1207 ps				St Andrew	D	RLitC:1:p82	**S**
Moretonhampstead			vf+3 All Saints	31 Oct–4 Nov	5 1207	St Andrew	D	RotCh:p166–7	S
Moretonhampstead			vfm St Andrew Apostle	29 Nov–1 Dec	3 1334 as	St Andrew	D	CChR:4:p312	**S**
Moretonhampstead			vfm St Margaret Virgin	19–21 Jul	3 1334 as	St Andrew	D	CChR:4:p312	**S**
Newport	M	1295	vfm Nativity St John Baptist	23–25 Jun	3 1295	St John Baptist chapel	N	CChR:2:p460	**E**
Newton Abbot	W–F	1221 ns	vfm St Leonard	5–7 Nov	3 1221 ns	St Leonard chapel	S	RLitCl:1p54,472	E
Newton Abbot	W	1221 br	vfm Nativity BVM	7–9 Sep	3 1221 br	St James	S	PipeR:v86:p72	RE
Newton Bushel	T	1246 a				All Saints	S	CChR:1:p311	S
Newton Bushel			1+vfm All Saints	29 Oct–2 Nov	4 1309	All Saints chapel	S	CChR:3:p127	S
Newton Bushel			1+vfm Ascension	May	4 1309 bc	St Mary chapel	S	CChR:3:p127	S
Newton Poppelford	T	1226 r?				St Mary	E	RLitC:2:p132	**S**
Newton Poppelford	Th	1254 a	vf+2 St Luke Evangelist	18–21 Oct	4 1254 as	St Mark chapel	E	CPR:1254:p338	**S**
North Molton	Su–Th	1218 ps	vfm Ascension of our Lord	May	3 1218 s	All Saints	N	RLitC:1:p366	S
North Molton			vfm All Saints	31 Oct–2 Nov	3 1270	All Saints	N	CChR:2:p150	S

North Tawton	W	1271 ps	vfm St Nicholas Confessor	5–7 Dec	3 1271	St Peter	N	CChR:2:p176	S
Northam			vf Decollation St John Baptist	28–29 Aug	2 1252	St Margaret	N	CChR:1:p408	E
Noss Mayo			vfm St John Baptist	23–25 June	3 1286	St Peter	S	Harl.Ch.58.I38	S
Noss Mayo	M&F	1286	vfm St Martin	10–12 Nov	3 1286	St Peter	S	Harl.Ch.58.I38	S
Okehampton	S	1086 bs					D	Domesday, 16:3	**S**
Okehampton			vf St James Apostle	24–25 Jul	2 1221 as	St James chapel	D	PipR:v86:p72	**S**
Otterton[14]	Su	1086 bx					E	Domesday,11:1	E
Ottery Saint Mary	T	1227 s	vfm Assumption	14–16 Aug	3 1227 as	St Mary	E	CChR:1:p46	E
Ottery Saint Mary			vfm Trinity	May–Jun	3 1378 as	St Mary	E	CChR:5:p243	E
Paignton	Th	1295 c	vfm Trinity	May–Jun	3 1295	St John	S	CChR:2:p460	E
Pilton	T	1344	fm St Matthew Apostle and Evangelist	21–22 Sep	2 1344	St Mary	N	CChR:5:p35	**E**
Plymouth	Th	1254 s	vfm St John Baptist	28–30 Aug	3 1254 c	St Andrew	S	CPR:1254:p263	E
Plymouth	W	1257 x	vfm Ascension	May	3 1257 a	St Andrew	S	CChR:2:p2	**S**
Plymouth			f+3 Conversion of St Paul	25–28 Jan	4 1440 b	St Andrew	S	CPR:1463:p309	C
Plymouth	M&Th	1440 bs	vfm+1? St Matthew Apostle	20–23 Sep	4 1440 b	St Andrew	S	CPR:1463:p309	C
Plympton Erle	S	1195 bs				St Thomas Martyr	S	PipR:v44:p131	**S**
Plympton Erle			vf Ss Peter and Paul	28–29 Jun	2 1195 br	Ss Peter and Paul pr	S	RLitC:1:p451	**SC**
Plympton Erle			f St Luke Evangelist	18 Oct	1 1221 na	St Luke chapel	S	RLitC:1:p451	**SC**
Plympton Erle			f+6 St John Baptist	29 Aug–4 Sep	7 1483 a	St Thomas Martyr	S	CChR:6:p257	C
Portlemouth, East			vfm St Peter ad Vincula	31 Jul–2 Aug	3 1280	St Winwaloe	S	CChR:1:p225	S
Portlemouth, East	M	1280	vfm Ss Peter and Paul	28–30 Jun	3 1280	St Winwaloe	S	CChR:2:p225	S
Rackenford	Th	1234	vfm All Saints	30 Oct–2 Nov	3 1234	All Saints	N	CChR:1:p193	S
Sampford Peverel	S	1220 bc				St John Baptist	E	CurReg:9:p305	S
Sampford Peverel			vf Annunciation	24–25 Mar	2 1335	St John Baptist	E	CChR:4:p344	S

Table A2.1. *Markets and fairs in medieval Devon (cont.)*

Place	MktDa	Year MF	Fair Feast	Fair Dates	D Year FF	Church dedication	Re Source	Gr
Sampford Peverel			2+f+2 St Alphege bp	17–21 Apr	5 1487 s	St John Baptist	E CPR:1487:p172	S
Sampford Peverel			2+f+2 Decollation St John Baptist	27–31 Aug	5 1487 s	St John Baptist	E CPR:1487:p172	S
Seaton[15]	W	1276 c	vfm St George Martyr	22–24 Apr	3 1276	St George	E CChR:2:p200	E
Sheepwash	M	1230 s	vfm St Lawrence	9–11 Aug	3 1230 s	St Lawrence	N CChR:1:p125	S
Sidbury	W	1291	vfm Nativity St Mary	7–9 Sep	3 1291 a	St Giles	E CChR:2:p403	E
Sidmouth[16]	Su-S	1220 ps				St Giles	E CurReg:9:p212	E
Sidmouth			St Giles	1 Sep	1 1281 ba	St Giles	E PRO J1/186 m36	E
Silverton			vf St Bartholomew Apostle	23–24 Aug	2 1272 bc	St Mary	E MiscR. 5 m36d	S
Silverton	S	1272 bc	fm St John Baptist	23–25 Jun	2 1272 bc	St Mary	E MiscR. 5 m36d	S
South Brent			2+f St Michael	27–29 Sep	3 1353 s	St Michael chapel	D CChR:5:p130	E
South Molton	S	1246 ps	vf+2 Assumption BVM	15–17 Aug	4 1246 a	St Mary Magdalene	N CChR:1:p307	S
South Molton			vfm Nativity St John Baptist	23–25 Jun	3 1490	St Mary Magdalene	N CChR:6:p269	S
South Tawton[17]	W	1204 s				St Andrew	D Rot de Lib:p85	S
South Zeal			vf+6 St Kalixtus	13–19 Oct	8 1299	St Andrew	D CChR:2:p479	S
South Zeal	Th	1299 a	vfm+5 Assumption	14–21 Aug	8 1299	St Mary chapel	D CChR:2:p479	S
Southbrook[18]			vfm St Martin	10–12 Nov	3 1267	St John Baptist	E CChR:2:p76	S
Southbrook	M	1267	vfm Holy Trinity	May–Jun	3 1267	St John Baptist	E CChR:2:p76	S
Stokeinteignhead	W	1310	vfm St Bartholomew	23–25 Aug	3 1310	St Andrew	S CChR:1:p137	S
Strete Raleigh	Th	1292	vfm Ascension	May	3 1292	St Mary	E CChR:2:p423	S
Tamerton Foliott	M	1270	vfm St Denis	18–20 Oct	3 1270	St Mary	S CChR:2:p148	S
Tamerton Foliott	W	1292	vfm Assumption	14–16 Aug	3 1292	St Mary	S CChR:2:428	S
Tavistock[19]	F	1105 bs				St Eustace	D Finberg 1947:355	E
Tavistock			vfm St Rumon	29–31 Aug	3 1116 a	St Rumon	D Dugdale:2:p496	E

Teignmouth, East	S	1220 ba				St Michael	E	PipR:v85:p85	E
Teignmouth, East			vfm St Michael	28–30 Sep	3 1253 cs	St Michael	E	CChR:1:p428	E
Teignmouth, West	Th	1256 c	vfm St James Apostle	24–26 Jul	3 1256 c	St James	E	CChR:2:p134	**E**
Thornecombe	W	1313 c	Easter Tuesday +5	Apr	6 1313 s	St Mary	E	CChR:3:p204	E
Tiverton	M	1257 bs	vfm St James	24–26 Jul	3 1257 c	St Peter	E	CChR:2:p2	**S**
Tiverton[20]			vfm? Translation St Thomas	6–8 Jul	3 1281 ba	St Peter	E	PRO J1/186m40d	**S**
Tiverton			vfm? St Andrew	30 Nov	3 1281 ba	St Peter	E	PRO J1/186m40d	**S**
Tiverton			vfm? St Giles	31 Aug–2 Sep	3 1281 bc	St Peter	E	PRO J1/186m40d	**S**
Tiverton			All Souls	1 Nov	1 1450 ba	St Peter	E	DRO CR 487	**S**
Topsham[21]	S	1300	vfm St Margaret Virgin	19–21 Jul	3 1257	St Margaret	E	CChR:2:pp2,488	**S**
Torrington, Great[22]	S	1221 ps	vfm St Michael	28–30 Sep	3 1221 ba	St Michael	N	CPR:1221:p292	S
Torrington, Little[23]			St Mary Magdalene?	22 July?	1 1209 b	Hospital of St Mary Magdalene	N	PipR:v24:p91	S
Totnes	S	1233 ms				St Mary	S	CurReg:15:p52	RS
Totnes[24]			vf Assumption BVM	14–15 Aug	2 1131 ba	St Mary	S	MagRotSca:p154	S
Uffculme			vfm St Peter ad Vincula	31 Jul–2 Aug	3 1267 cs	St Mary	E	CChR:2:p80	S
Uffculme	W	1267 c	vfm Ss Peter and Paul	28–30 Jun	3 1267 c	St Mary	E	CChR:2:p80	S
Werrington	S	1221 lx				Ss Martin and Giles	N	PipeR:v86:p72	E
Whitford	W	1342	f+3 St Peter ad Vincula	31 Jul–3 Aug	4 1342	St Michael	E	CChR:5:p10	S
Whitford			vf+3 Assumption	14–18 Aug	5 1346	St Michael	E	CChR:5:p51	S
Wiscombe[25]	W	1248 c	vfm St Matthew Apostle	20–22 Sep	3 1248 c	St Lawrence	E	CChR:1:p331	S
Witheridge	W	1248	vfm Nativity St John Baptist	23–25 Jun	3 1248 s	St John Baptist	N	CChR:1:p336	S
Woodbury	T	1286	vfm St Swithin	14–16 Jul	3 1286	St Swithun	E	CChR:2:p322	S

Table A2.1. *Markets and fairs in medieval Devon (cont.)*

[1] The 1239 grant allowed the fair owner to retain "the old fair held there on the feast of St Osyth in the summer." This implies that Aylesbeare held fairs on both feastdays of St Osyth: 3 June and 7 October. Although it has here been assumed that the fair profits at Aylesbeare in 1292 (*IPM*, vol. 3: 24) came from the older summer fair, it is also possible that they (1) belonged to the October fair or (2) belonged to the fair of Newton Popelford, a borough (also owned by the Courtenays) in the parish which received a market in 1226 and an October fair in 1254.

[2] The Wednesday market may date from before 1272 when Bideford added a new Monday market; this move may have been taken to avoid the competition provided by Barnstaple's Wednesday market. See also above, pp. 69–70.

[3] Bideford probably changed its Friday market to Wednesday because of competition from Barnstaple's market on that day (above, p. 69). The Monday market was the only one noted in 1274 (*Rotuli hundredorum*: 64), suggesting that the Wednesday market had lapsed by that time. By 1274, Bideford's fair had also been reduced to two days.

[4] The Canonsleigh cartulary (p. 11) states that this fair was granted on the vigil, feast, and morrow of Trinity and the two following days. Trinity was celebrated on the eighth Sunday after Easter and St Theobald's on 30 June (R.B.M. 1928: 125). The fair probably took place around the end of June, however, since Exeter cathedral made purchases at Canonsleigh (presumably at the fair) once at the end of June and once in the fifth week after Easter in late May (*Fabric accounts*: 83, 129).

[5] A market was noted at Colyton in 1292 (PRO C133/62/7 no. 9, extracted in *IPM*, vol. 3:24) and c. 1340 (PRO SC12/11/7, printed in Brooking-Rowe 1906: 13). No marketday was ever given and it is possible that the markets at Colyton and Colyford (a small borough in Colyton) were one and the same since the 1292 reference could be interpreted this way. The survey of c. 1340, however, notes markets in both places. The Colyton fair, one of the best known in Devon, was usually known as the St Calixtus fair because it ended on that feast day; by 1281 the fair reputedly ran for fifteen days (PRO JUST1/186 m. 34).

[6] The grant is for "Culmeton" which some have mistakenly taken to be Kilmington. Cullompton was obviously meant here since the grant was to Baldwin de Insula who died seised of the manor in 1262 (Reichel 1910: 230–1).

[7] There are two 1231 grants; one (*CCR 1227–31*: 471) mistakenly lists a Monday market rather than the Wednesday market noted in 1205 and in the other 1231 grant (*CChR*, vol. 1: 128). For the dispute between Totnes and Dartmouth which caused the temporary suspension of the Dartmouth market, see above, pp. 70–2. The Thursday market and fair granted in 1302 probably never got off the ground since they were never again mentioned in the sources.

[8] For an extended discussion of the markets and fairs of Exeter, see above, pp. 60–8.

[9] The first documented references I could find to the market and fair were in 1274 (*Rotuli hundredorum*: 64; PRO C133/6/6, the IPM of Henry de Tracy) when both had clearly been around for awhile. By 1238 Lydford men were complaining of tolls taken from them at Holsworthy (*Devon eyre*: 106–7). The market and fair were probably founded by Fulk Paynel who held the manor in the late twelfth century but fled the realm in 1185 (*Rotuli hundredorum*: 65; Sanders 1960: 5); this assumption is reinforced by the wording of the town crier's declaration of the fair that Fulk Paynel was the fair's founder (Day 1934: 7–9).

[10] The earl of Devon founded a borough here between 1194 and 1217 (Beresford 1967: 421) and by 1238 wine was being sold here (*Devon eyre*: 14). From 1217 to c. 1239, Fulk de Bréauté held Honiton as guardian of the future earl, Baldwin de Redvers, while he was a minor. In 1220 Fulk brought suits against the owners of markets in Sidmouth and Sampford Peverel (*Curia regis*, vol. 9: 305–6, 330; vol. 10: 96, 109, 177) for changing their Sunday markets to Saturday. The implication here is that these markets hurt one of Fulk's markets, which could only be that at Honiton. Note also that there is a tradition that the Honiton market was changed from Sunday to Saturday in the time of King John; the market was held on Saturday into the nineteenth century (Lysons 1822: xxxiv).

[11] Totnes complained (*Totnes*: 194) in about 1295 that the markets at Paignton and Ipplepen were harming its market, implying that Ipplepen had a market before 1317.

[12] The grant was for Churchstow, the manor wherein the new borough of Kingsbridge was located (*Rotuli hundredorum*: 79). It is uncertain whether the Saturday market granted in 1460 replaced or supplemented the earlier market. By the eighteenth century, the town had only a Saturday market (Lysons 1822: xxxiv).

[13] Modbury supposedly had two fairs (Hoskins 1972: 436; Amery 1933), one at the feast of St James, for which I have found no medieval evidence, and another at the feast of St George which was reputedly one of the largest fairs in medieval Devon. Since Modbury was rated a borough by 1238 (*Devon eyre*: 95) and had a market from the time of King Richard I (*Rotuli litterarum clausarum*, vol. 1: 169), it is likely that the fair also dates from an early period.

[14] It is highly likely that this market was in Sidmouth rather than Otterton. Both were held by the prior of Otterton and as late as 1281 (PRO JUST1/186, mm. 36, 39) Sidmouth's market was recorded as if it was in Otterton. The fact that the Sidmouth market originally met on Sunday (*Curia regis*, vol. 9: 212) and Sidmouth early on became a borough while Otterton remained a small village also suggests that Sidmouth, not Otterton, was the market referred to in Domesday Book. The Otterton market is thus not included in the calculations in Chapter 2.

[15] The charter records the fair as on the vigil, feast, and morrow of St Gregory martyr (PRO C53/64, m.1). This is probably a mistake for St George, to whom the Seaton parish church was dedicated, since there was no feast of St Gregory martyr celebrated in England.

[16] See above, n. 14.

[17] Everitt 1967: 471 says the South Tawton market survived into the sixteenth century, but he may have confused it with the market of the borough of South Zeal in South Tawton whose market was on Thursday; see Lysons 1822: xxxiv.

[18] The charter reads "Alebrook in co. Devon." This probably refers to Southbrook in Broad Clyst (Gover, Mawer, and Stenton 1932: 575) which was held by the Mortellis family (Reichel 1934b: 372–3) who acquired the grant.

[19] The original dedication of Tavistock abbey was to St Rumon (Finberg 1969: 1, 178).

[20] The 1281 record lists the three Tiverton fairs by their feast days and notes that they all lasted three days. It has here been assumed that they all followed the usual practice of occurring on the vigil, day, and morrow of the feast. The profits from all three were noted in an account roll of 1286 (PRO SC6/829/39) along with the St James fair.

[21] The fair claimed by Countess Amicia in 1245 as part of her manor of Topsham (*CCR 1242–47*: 340) probably refers to the Lammas fair of Exeter which the earls of Devon held with St Nicholas priory in Exeter (see above, pp. 62–5).

Table A2.1. *Markets and fairs in medieval Devon (cont.)*

[22] The borough was founded 1135–94 (Alexander and Hooper 1948: 9, 70) so the market probably dates from this time. For corn sold there c. 1182, see *Pipe roll*, vol. 32: 116. The 1221 grant gives William Brewer the borough and fair of Torrington for three years, implying the fair already existed. The Saturday market and Michaelmas fair were also noted in the 1554 charter of incorporation (PRO C66/890, mm. 6–7).

[23] Henry de la Pomeray received the fair at "Fordham" for the benefit of the hospital of St Peter and St Mary Magdalene. The place was Stoney Ford in Little Torrington (Reichel 1918: 366–7). The hospital was still there in the sixteenth century. In the absence of any other information, it has been assumed that the fair was held on the feast of St Mary Magdalene, the saint to whom the hospital was dedicated.

[24] In a law suit regarding tolls at Totnes in 1388 (*Year books of Richard II. 1387–88*: 176), it was claimed that there was a Saturday market and two fairs there. Only one fair is listed here, however, since I have been unable to find any evidence to corroborate the second fair despite the thorough survey of Totnes records published by *Totnes*. The reference may be to the July fair in Bridgetown Pomeroy, a suburb of Totnes.

[25] Another copy of this grant (DRO 123M/TB 433) is dated 1246.

Appendix 3
Population and households, Exeter 1377

The population of Exeter in 1377

Two different sources allow us to calculate the population of Exeter in 1377. The poll tax of 1377 records 1,560 lay taxpayers in Exeter along with another 106 lay taxpayers in the exempt jurisdiction of Exe Island outside the west gate.[1] This total of 1,666 lay taxpayers when multiplied by 1.75 to allow for those who evaded the tax or were under the age of fourteen, yields a figure of 2,916 lay residents, to which must be added another thirty "lay servants of the bishop,"[2] making for a lay population of 2,946 in Exeter in 1377.[3] If we add the clerical population, estimated at about 155, the total population for the city comes to 3,101.[4]

[1] PRO E359/8B, m.19d for Exeter; E179/95/52/46 for Exe Island in Wonford Hundred.

[2] PRO E179/95/34; since many of these servants were probably part of the bishop's itinerant household and unmarried, they are not included in the calculations adjusting for tax evasion and children. Table 2.1, above, includes these lay servants with the "clerical" population of Exeter.

[3] Not all agree about the size of the multiplier (covering both the population under fourteen and those who evaded the tax) to use when calculating total population from poll tax figures. J. C. Russell (1948: 142) employs a 1.5 multiplier, a figure now considered too low by most scholars (although Russell meant most of the multiplier to cover the population under fourteen). More recently Alan Dyer (1991: 72) has used a 1.9 multiplier. The 1.75 multiplier used here is lower than Dyer's figure, but higher than Russell's and Goldberg's 1.65 multiplier (Goldberg 1990a: 213, n. 42).

[4] For the large community attached to the cathedral chapter, see Orme 1981, 1983, and 1986: 31–42. In 1377, it included about seventy six clerics: eighteen canons, twenty vicars choral, fourteen annuellers, ten secondaries, and fourteen choristers. Not added to this clerical population are the estimated 108 servants, six for each canon's household (Orme 1986: 41), since they were presumably lay people taxed in the lay poll tax. The Franciscan and Dominican houses at Exeter (Little and Easterling 1927) included about fourteen friars and students at each in the late fourteenth century. The Benedictine priory of St Nicholas probably had only four monks during this period. At the Hospital of St John resided four priests, eight boys, and ten poor people, and at the leper house of St Mary Magdalene about ten lepers (Prof. Nicholas Orme, personal communication). Leaving out the poor lay people and lepers, clerics residing at the city's religious houses and hospitals amounted to some forty four people. The city's twenty parishes (Rose-Troup 1923) were probably short-staffed at this time so that cathedral clergy most likely filled in at several of the parishes; a rough estimate of fourteen parish priests seems the best guess here (Orme, personal communication). To

The second source for the population of Exeter in 1377 is the murage tax roll of the same date which lists the name, tax, and quarter of residence of 420 householders.[5] To these households should be added another 105 householders who were identified on the basis of additional information drawn largely from the mayor's tourn (the market court) which met annually for each quarter of the town and fined householders for such offenses as breaking the assize of ale, leaving refuse in the streets, allowing pigs to roam free, and a variety of other infractions. The survival of a continuous series of tourns in the late fourteenth century, combined with the tourn's predilection for fining householders for any offense committed by a member of their household, makes easier the task of identifying heads of household at any one time.[6]

The 105 householders who escaped the murage tax did so for one of three reasons. (1) Some may simply have evaded the tax although the number who successfully did so must have been small since local men assessed and systematically collected the tax by quarter. The fact that the funds collected were to be spent on a local project to benefit all residents (upkeep of the city walls and gates during a period of threatened invasion) may also have made evasion less likely. It was also the first (and only) such murage tax to be collected in the city so residents may not yet have had the experience or urge to evade the tax collectors. The relatively low amounts assessed on many residents (27 per cent paid 4*d* or less) may also have encouraged compliance.

(2) Another group of residents may have escaped the tax because they were too poor; the fact that some taxpayers had their tax wholly or partly excused because of poverty points to the collectors' awareness of a household's ability to pay.[7] These allowances based on poverty, coupled with the wording of the murage grant that the mayor and bailiffs "compel all lay residents and those who possess lands, tenements, goods and chattels therein, each according to the rate of his tenure and his condition and means to contribute to their repair," also illustrate why this tax can be used as a rough indicator of a householder's wealth

this must be added about twenty one unbeneficed chaplains and chantry priests (the 1419 clerical subsidy, PRO E179/24/80 and 27/319 lists twenty six in Exeter but five are also identified as annuellers). The estimated clerical population of Exeter permanently resident in 1377 was therefore about 155.

[5] Misc. Roll 72; see Kowaleski 1980 for the dating of this roll.

[6] See above, pp. 338–9 for a further discussion of the mayor's tourn. In 1378–88, about 850 people were presented each year in the tourns. Evidence drawn from testaments and records of property-holding was also useful in establishing residence in Exeter.

[7] Richard Beuman had 4*d* of his tax allowed "because he has nothing"; the 6*d* assessed on John Somerforde was respited "because he is poor"; 3*d* of John Peyntour's tax was allowed "because he has nothing and is unoccupied [*innocuous*]"; and the 6*d* assessed on John Graas was allowed "because it cannot be raised"; see Misc. Roll 72.

in 1377.[8] The exact basis of the tax assessment is, however, not clear, although similar murage taxes in Winchester and Canterbury at this time were assessed on landlords' rental values.[9] Yet the relatively large number of households (many of them demonstrably poor) included in the Exeter tax, along with the absence of any evidence concerning property-holding by well over one-third of them (despite a very good set of extant records for property ownership), suggest that the Exeter tax was assessed on a wider basis than elsewhere. The wording of the murage grant also quite explicitly includes goods and chattels, as well as lands and tenements.

(3) A third group of those who did not appear in the tax roll may have been liable, but avoided the tax because they lived in one of the exempt jurisdictions of St Stephen's fee (held by the bishop), St Nicholas' fee (owned by St Nicholas Priory), or Exe Island (a manor of the earl of Devon).[10] Yet many of the tenants of St Stephen's and St Nicholas' fees were recorded in the tax anyway. For example, Stephen Bolle was taxed 8*d* in the murage roll but a note at the bottom cancelled his payment with the remark "because he is in the fee of St Stephen." Memoranda added at the end of the sections listing residents of the east and south quarters also reported that over 9*s*-worth of tax assessed on other tenants of the bishop (presumably listed in the roll) were respited. Although no residents of St Nicholas' fee were singled out in the tax, many of them were also included in the assessments (see Table A3.1). Perhaps residents of these exempt jurisdictions who owned property within the city's jurisdiction were required to pay the tax despite their residence in an exempt jurisdiction. Others escaped the tax altogether; at least thirty two of the 105 householders not listed in the tax roll resided within these jurisdictions (Table A3.1).

[8] *CPR, 1377–81*: 3; see also *CPR, 1374–7*: 476. Although this wording might suggest that non-residents who owned property in Exeter were included, all taxpayers are known to have resided in Exeter or its suburbs.

[9] See Keene 1985: 44 and Butcher 1979b: 17–18.

[10] For more on the town's relationship to these franchises, their location, and toll privileges, see above, pp. 198–9. Residents of the largest jurisdiction, St Sidwell's fee in the eastern suburb, were clearly considered liable for the tax; see Kowaleski 1980 and Curtis 1932. A fifth fee was attached to the castle in the north-eastern section of the town. The records contain references to only three residents of this fee: Robert Parson, the castle gatekeeper (*CCR 1377–81*: 220–1; *1385–9*: 399; PCR 1–23 Ric. II, m. 12) who was probably not a permanent resident and so has not been included in the list of householders; William Stoddon (CRA 1405/6) who in 1377 lived elsewhere (Table A3.1); and John Eget, a city waite (musician) who may have been employed as an entertainer for castle visitors (CRA 1393/4, 1394/5, 1398/9). For the tenants of the fraternity of the tiny Kalendar fee (probably located near the vicars choral building on Kalendarhay), see above, p. 198, n. 106.

Five of the householders resident in exempt fees who did not pay the murage tax lived in the western surburb of Exe Island. Faced with the strident claims of the suburb's lord, the Courtenay earls of Devon, the city exercised no jurisdiction in Exe Island in the late fourteenth century.[11] As a result, it is very difficult to identify residents of this suburb. We do know, however, that 106 people were taxed there in the 1377 poll tax, amounting to a total population of about 186, a figure which in turn represented about forty one households. Since we can identify only five of these Exe Island households, it is necessary to add another thirty six households to the total of 525 identifiable households, thus making for a grand total of 561 households in Exeter and all of its suburbs in 1377.

This figure of 561 households must be very close to the actual number of households in Exeter in 1377. The excellent quality of the Exeter records, particularly the mayor's tourn with its wide scope and predilection for naming household heads and identifying them by their quarter of residence, has made the task of identifying households much easier. The relatively small size and weakness of most of the separate franchises in Exeter also helps since few of their residents escaped the eye of the Exeter courts or tax collectors. The figure of 561 households also yields a total population quite close to that derived from the poll tax of 1377. Using a household multiplier of 4.5 for these 561 households yields a total population of 2,525, a figure only 391 people less than the 2,916 lay residents calculated from the poll tax.[12] This 13 per cent margin of difference probably represents landless, poor people who were highly mobile and/or held low-paying unskilled jobs as occasional labourers.

Most calculations involving Exeter's population in this book will employ the figure derived from the household list, rather than the larger figure calculated from the poll tax returns, since the household list is

[11] For the city's battles against the earl on a variety of jurisdictional matters, see Book 60h, ff. 21v–31v; *Citie of Excester*: 388–95, 627–51; Jackson 1972; and above, p. 198.

[12] This multiplier is lower than the 5.0 used by some urban historians (Mols 1955: vol. 2, 100–9) but higher than the 3.8 calculated for Coventry in 1523 and several fifteenth-century Continental towns (Phythian-Adams 1979: 243–7). The higher figure is used here because Exeter in 1377 was relatively prosperous and probably growing while Coventry in 1523 was experiencing great economic and demographic distress. If a 3.8 multiplier was employed for the Exeter figures, the total households would number 569 (525 plus 44 unaccounted for Exe Island households), and the population would be 2,162; this falls short of the lay poll-tax population of 2,916 by 754 persons (198 households), suggesting that the list in Table A3.1 is missing (after excluding the 44 unidentified Exe Island households) 154 households or 585 people. Given the excellent coverage of the Exeter documentation in this period, this "missing" population seems unrealistically high and reinforces the use of a higher household multiplier.

based on the same data as those employed in the rest of the book. The poll tax figures will only be used when comparisons are made with other town populations also derived from the poll tax (e.g. Table 2.1).

Exeter households in 1377

The following table (Table A3.1) lists the 525 known householders in Exeter in 1377, omitting only the thirty one unidentified households in Exe Island outside the west gate. As noted above, 420 of these householders were named in the murage tax roll and the other 105 were identified from many other sources, especially the mayor's tourn rolls. Other sources that proved most useful in identifying the residents of exempt or suburban jurisdictions included the deeds and final concords enrolled in the mayor's court rolls, city receiver's accounts, the Duryard account rolls and court rolls, the dean and chapter's rent rolls, and St Sidwell's court rolls.

The content and codes in each of the columns are as follows. Note that a question mark (?) appearing in any field indicates inconclusive evidence that was never used in calculations.

Name: Surnames are noted exactly as they appeared in the murage roll; surnames of non-taxpayers are based on the most common spelling of their names. Forenames are generally anglicized.

Occupation: When someone practiced more than one occupation, the first listing represents the primary occupation or the occupation in which the householder was engaged in 1377. Secondary or subsequent occupations are listed after the slash. See Table 4.1 for a summary of these occupations. For a discussion of how occupational designations were made, see above, pp. 345–5.

Occ Fl: This occupational flag indicates the source and quality of the information concerning occupation. The codes refer to all occupations stated in the field unless separated by a slash which indicates that the code refers to the occupation that appears on the corresponding side of the slash.

m = occupation stated in the murage roll

d = occupation stated in another document

a = occupation surmised from activities carried on by householder (mostly from court roll evidence)

? = some, but not enough evidence exists for this occupation (not included in calculations of occupations)

?? = occupation surmised only from occupational surname (not included in calculations of occupations)

Su: Suburb the householder lived in, corresponding to the areas outside the city wall: N=North, S=South, E=East, W=West. Those living in the eastern suburb were tenants of St Sidwell's fee owned by the dean and chapter.

Qt: Quarter of residence of the householder; stated outright in the murage roll entries and indicated by mayor's tourn appearance for the other householders; codes as above for suburb.

Fe: Fee or exempt jurisdiction inhabited by the householder.

B = Bishop's fee, also called St Stephen's fee

E = Exe Island, outside the west gate, owned by earl of Devon

N= St Nicholas' fee, also called Harold's fee, owned by St Nicholas priory in Exeter

P: Political rank held by householder in 1377. See Chapter 3 for a full explanation of these ranks. See Tables 3.4 and 4.2 for summaries of political ranks in 1377. Together, Ranks A and B make up the ruling oligarchy, all of whom had to belong to the freedom of the city.

A = served as mayor, steward, receiver, or councillor

B = served as elector, warden of leper house, and no higher

C = served as gatekeeper, alderman, bailiff, and no higher

D = never served in city office

H: Highest political rank achieved by the householder. Codes as above for *P* with the addition of: W = female householder.

Tax: Murage tax paid in 1377, in pence. Two of the taxes (Crosman and Hodel) are illegible in the murage roll. This tax serves as a rough guide to wealth within the city. Some of the taxes were excused because of poverty, see above, pp. 372–3. See also Tables 3.4 and 4.2 for summaries of tax by political rank and occupational group.

Frdm: Year the householder entered the freedom, thereby gaining various economic, political, and legal privileges. Entries were recorded on the dorses of the mayor's court rolls which survive from 1295 to 1459 with only one gap (1383/4). They are printed in *Exeter freemen*. See also Tables 3.3, 3.4, and 4.2.

N: Note on freedom entry. In some instances, no record of the freedom entry survives but membership may be deduced from election to a political office for which freedom membership was a prerequisite. The date of the freedom entry (marked *) thus corresponds to the date of first election to such an office; actual admittance to the freedom probably pre-dated such an election by several years. Entries marked with ? represent questionable evidence concerning the freedom entry and were not used in calculations involving freedom members.

Br: The number of times between 1365 and 1393 that a householder was presented for brewing against the assize of ale. The maximum number of citations is twenty five since brewing fines are missing for three years (1367, 1373, 1377) of the twenty eight-year period surveyed. Brewing carried on by a widow or widower after the named householder died is included under the original householder's name. For summaries of brewing activity by occupation, see Table 4.4.

MT: Maritime trade activities (both coastal and foreign) of the householder as indicated by appearances in the Exeter local port customs accounts or the PRO E122 national port customs accounts. The gap from 1373/4 to 1380/1 in the local accounts and the poor coverage of the national accounts throughout the late fourteenth century means that no exact measure of maritime trade may be attempted. Thus the level of activity is indicated by:

+ = some activity in maritime trade; at least one cargo
++ = regular or frequent involvement in maritime trade
See Tables 3.4 and 4.2.

Sv: The number of servants known to have been employed by this household. These figures are suggestive only since they are gathered from stray references in the court rolls and are drawn primarily from the period 1370–90. They do not distinguish between resident and non-resident servants. See Table 4.2.

Alias: The alias under which the householder was also known. Aliases followed by ? are inconclusive so records under these names were not linked with those of the householder. The eight murage taxpayers for whom no information could be found are also noted in this field as "? (no other refs)."

Table A3.1 *Exeter householders in 1377*

Name	Occupation	Occ_Fl	Su	Qt	Fe	P	H	Tax	Frdm	N	Br	Ov	Sv	Alias
Aisshe, John	merchant/vintner	da		N		B	B	12	1350		11	++	1	
Aleyn, Henry	merchant/tailor	a		E		D	A	12	1378		1	++	4	
Aleyn, John	fuller	mda		S	B	D	D	4						Tokere, John
Ammary, Geoffrey	victualler	a		E		D	D	6	1370		1			
Archer, Henry	apprentice-merchant	da	N?	N		D	C		1380		8	++		
Armener, John	armourer	a		S		D	C	4			1			
Ayshewater, William	tailor	?		E		D	D	4						
Baby, William	mason	a		E		D	D	6			3		1	
Baillesford, William	spicer	d		E		C	A	12	1378		6		3	Spycer, William
Bailly, Alice				E		D	W	6						
Bakere, Andrew	baker	da		N		D	B	12	1380		14		1	Poleworthy, Andrew
Bakere, Hugh	baker	da		S	B	D	D	6			1			Conaunt, Hugh?
Bakere, John	baker/servant	da		N		D	D	4						Holewill, John
Bakere, Moses	baker	da		S	B	D	D	24			3		2	Brewer, Moses
Bakere, Richard				S		D	D	4			2			
Bakere, Richard	cook	da		S		D	D	6			1			Cook, Richard and Brewer, Richard
Bakere, Thomas	baker/hosteler	da/?		W		D	B	36	1378		14		2	Poleworthy, Thomas
Barbor, Helewisia				S	B	D	W				4			
Barbour, John	barber	da		E		D	D	12	1378		15		2	Dene, John
Barbour, Roger				E		D	D	6						
Barbour, Roger	saddler	ma		S		D	D	4			6			Shepton, Roger
Barry, Geoffrey	mason	da		E		D	D	6			13		2	
Battishull, Martin	merchant/clerk	da		N		A	A	48	1350		24	++	1	Clerk, Martin
Batyn, Robert	fisher	da		S		D	D	6		?	1		1	
Bealde, Richard	brazier	da		S		B	B	36	1364		24		2	
Beare, John			E	E		D	D				1			
Beauford, John			E?	E	B?	D	D	4			1			

Belchere, John	butcher	a		S		B	B	36	1360	*	17			
Belstoun, Walter	carpenter/sawyer	da		E		D	D	6					1	
Benet, William	carpenter	mda		S		D	D	6						
Berlegh, Sabina				S		D	W	2						
Berwyk, John	cordwainer	da		S		D	D	12	1378		6	+	2	
Beuman, John	glover	a		N		D	D	6					1	
Beuman, Richard	leatherworker	a	N	N	N	D	D	4						
Beyvyn, Robert				S		D	D	6						
Bluet, William	clothworker	a		N?		D	D		1382		4	+	1	
Bobham, John	tawyer	a	N	N	N	D	D	6					1	
Bochere, Benedict	butcher	da		E		C	B	36	1358		18			Shokebrook, Benedict
Bochere, Janekyn				S		D	D	4						?(no other refs)
Bochere, Nicholas	butcher	da		S		D	D	12	1380					Goldyng, Nicholas
Boggebrook, John	cordwainer/sutor	da		W		D	D	12	1378		5		3	
Bogheleghe, Richard	furrier	da	N	N	N	D	D	6					1	
Boghewode, Stephen	butcher	a		S		D	D	48	1356		15		1	
Boghiere, Alice				N		D	W	6			2		1	
Bole, John	shipmaster/merchant	da/a		S		A	A	18	1359		9	+		
Bolepitte, Richard				N		D	D	4	1369		12		1	
Bolle, John	butcher	a		S		D	D	6	1378		9			
Bolle, Stephen	butcher	a		S	B	D	D	8		?	3			
Bolle, Walter	hosteler/taverner	a	E	E		C	C	12	1387		25	+	1	
Bonevyll, Andrew	merchant/hosteler	a		W		B	B	40	1364		11	++		
Bony, Gregory				N		C	C	6			19			
Boor, Roger	weaver	mda		E		D	C	12	1378		16			
Botour, Henry				S		D	D	24	1366					
Boys, Walter	lawyer	?		N		A	A		1361		1			
Bozoun, John	lawyer	da		S		B	B		1362	*	9			
Bozoun, Richard	merchant/hosteler	da/a		S		A	A	30	1371		15	++	5	
Bozoun, Richard	fisher	da		E		D	D							
Bradecroft, Richard				S		B	B	24	1368		2			
Bradeleghe, William	building worker	a		E		D	D	4						

Table A3.1. *cont.*

Name	Occupation	Occ_Fl	Su	Qt	Fe	P	H	Tax	Frdm	N	Br	Ov	Sv	Alias
Bremelham, William	barber/hosteler	d/a		E		D	D	24			6		3	Barbor, William
Brendoun, John	baker/hosteler	da/a		N		D	D	12			2		1	
Brewere, Robert	servant/'prechour'	d		S	B	D	D							Prechour, Robert?
Brewere, Thomas	saddler	da		E		D	B	6	1378		16		3	Saddler, Thomas?
Brian, Robert	baker	?		E		D	D	4	1386		15		1	
Brideport, John	hosteler	a		W		D	D	6	1361		4		1	
Bridlegh, John	mason	da		E		D	D				10		1	
Bridleghe, John	merchant/draper	a		S		A	A	60	1364		16	+	3	
Britel, John	sutor/taverner	a		E		D	D	4			7			
Brokland, John				N		D	D	6					2	
Broun, Henry			E	E		D	D				8			
Broun, John	baker	mda		N		D	D	6	1342	?	2		2	
Broun, John	carpenter	mda		E		D	D	4			2			
Broun, Richard	carpenter	?	E	E		D	D				1			
Broun, Walter	carpenter	da		S	B?	D	D				1		1	Carpenter, Walter; Toly, Walter
Broun, William	hosteler/bailiff	a/da		W		D	C	18	1378		13			
Buchard, John				E		D	D	4						?(no other refs)
Bullokhurde, John				E		D	D	2						
Burnard, John	hosteler/farmer	a	E	E		D	D	4	1386		8		1	Burgeys, John?
Burnard, Richard				E		D	D	4			9			Burgeys, Richard
Bynnecote, Nicholas	skinner	da		S		A	A	30	1352		13		5	Pees, Nicholas
Byrche, Walter	cordwainer	da		S		D	D	6						
Byssham, John	clothworker	a	E	E		D	D	6			4			
Canne, Richard				S		D	D	12			2			
Canun, Thomas	hosteler/fisher	a/da	S	S		C	C	18			21		1	
Carbure, Robert				W		D	D	6						
Cardmaker, Thomas	retailer	a		N		D	B	12	1370				4	Newman, Thomas

Carpenter, Henry	carpenter	a		E		D	D				1		1	
Carpenter, Thomas	carpenter/servant	a/da		S		D	D	4			3			
Carsse, Alexander	butcher	a		S		D	D	4						
Cartere, Robert	carter	?	S	S	B	D	D	4			1			
Caubyn, Richard				E		D	D	6			4			
Chaloner, Thomas			S	S	B	D	D				9			
Chamberlayn, Richard				S		D	C	4			13		1	
Chepman, John	miller/loder	da		N		D	D	4						
Chilton, John	fuller	da		N		D	C	8	1378		2		5	
Chiseweye, John				N		D	D	6			17			
Chuddlegh, John	mason	da		E		D	D		1370		19			
Cobeleye, Thomas	hosteler	a		S		D	D	18	1368		14		2	
Cocheour, Hugh	tapicer	da		W		D	D	12			3		1	Watford, Hugh; Tapeser, Hugh
Cole, John	skinner	mda		N		D	D	18	1369		1		1	
Colmpton, John	fuller	da		W		D	D	6			6			
Comere, Robert	hosteler	a		S		B	B	12	1364		11			
Comere, William				S		B	B	18	1364		20			
Cook, Ralph				N		D	D	3			10			
Cook, Robert	smith/hosteler	mda/a		W		D	B	18	1378		16	+	3	Ferrour, Robert?
Cook, Walter	hosteler	a		E		D	D	6			24		1	
Cook, William	cook/servant	a/?	E	E		D	D	2			2			
Coppe, Stephen	bailiff/farmer	a	E	E		D	D				5			Wylcok, Stephen
Cornishe, John	shearman	mda		E		D	D	3			5			Shereman, John
Cornisshe, John jr.	hosteler/watercarrier	a/d		S		D	D	12			15			Waterlagger, John jr.
Cornisshe, John sr.	hosteler/watercarrier	a/d		W		D	D	6		9	1			Waterlagger, John sr.
Cornisshe, Richard			E	E		D	D	4			2		1	Waterlagger, Richard
Coscombe, William	town official/merchant	a		W		A	A	48	1363		25	+	1	
Cotelere, Stephen	cutler	a		W		D	D	6	1380		9			Carwythan, Stephen
Coulyng, John	tailor	da		S	B	D	D	6	1367		7		1	
Courtman, Walter				S	N?	D	D	12			4			
Cowhurde, William				E		D	D	2						?(no other refs)
Crewys, Claricia	victualler	a		S		D	W	4						

Table A3.1. *cont.*

Name	Occupation	Occ_Fl	Su	Qt	Fe	P	H	Tax	Frdm	N	Br	Ov	Sv	Alias
Cridia, John				S		D	D	4			5			
Criditon, Thomas	saddler/hosteler	da/a		E		D	D	6	1380		19			Kirton, Thomas
Criditon, William	lawyer	da		S		A	A	12	1361	*	15			
Cristowe, John	saddler	da		N		D	D	12	1380		2			
Crokkernewill, Walter	smith	a		W?	N	D	D				11		1	Crukerne, Walter
Crosman, Adam	building worker	a	E	E		D	D	...			1			
Crosse, John	weaver	ma		S		D	D	4				2		
Crosse, William	pewterer	d	E	E		D	D	4						Peuterer, William
Crouste, Christina	victualler	a		S		D	W							
Dalby, John	mason	a	E	E		D	D	6					1	
Danyel, Thomas				S		C	C	4			1			
Degher, Henry	miller/loder	a	N	N	N	C	C				13		1	
Deghere, John	dyer	a		W		D	D	24	1378			+	2	
Dene, John	leatherworker	a		S		D	D	6						
Dene, Nicholas	pouchmaker/girdler	da	N	N		B	B	12	1357		7			
Dene, Robert	cordwainer	da		S		B	B	60	1370	*	1		1	
Dirling, John	weaver	da		S		D	D	6			7		2	Webber, Dirling & Kene, Dirling
Doccombe, John	smith	da		N		D	D	6	1378		16	+	2	
Domet, John	merchant	a		S		D	B	24	1374		1	++		
Donstorre, Walter	skinner	d		E		B	B	24	1358		18		2	
Dony, Roger	goldsmith	d		N		D	D		1369		7			
Dook, John				S	B	D	D	12			2			
Doun, William	tailor	?		S	B	D	D	12			4			Doon, William
Drake, Lawrence	carpenter	da	S?	S	B?	D	D	12			1		1	
Dribel, Richard	carpenter	a		S		D	D	6						
Dudenay, Elena				S		D	W							

Dudenay, John			N?	N		D	D							
Duraunt, John				S		D	D	6			1			
Dygon, Richard	corveser/sutor	da	E	E		A	A	18	1349		15		1	Teyne, Richard
Dyshere, Richard	weaver			S		D	D	12	1378		5			Dycher, Richard
Egeleshale, William	victualler	?		E	B	D	D	6			12			
Ekesbonere, Matthew	spurrier	da		S		D	D	24	1372		16		3	Wrothe, Matthew
Estoun, Robert	skinner/merchant	da/a		S		D	A	12	1385	*	10	+	2	
Facy, Robert	carpenter	da	E	E		D	D	6	1392		5			Vacy, Robert
Faireby, Edward	mason	da		S		D	D	6			9			
Focregay, William	bailiff/hosteler/merchant	da		E		B	B	12	1340		19	+	1	
Foghelere, Richard	skinner	da		W		D	D	6			2		1	Skynnere, Richard
Folenorde, Adam	hosteler	a		W		D	D	4	1349		7			Voleforde, Adam
Forbor, Henry	hosteler/merchant	a		W		A	A	24	1339		14	+	1	
Forbour, Peter	furbisher	a		N		D	C	6			12		3	
Fouke, Walter	merchant	da		N		A	A	18	1364			++		
Founteyn, Thomas	waxchandler	a		S		D	D	6			5		1	
Frak, Robert	dyer	a	N	N		C	C	4			6			
Frank, John	fisher	mda		E		D	D	4			13			
Frank, Robert	cordwainer	da		S		D	D	12	1378		8		1	
Freman, William	hosteler	?	E	E		D	D	6			18			Flyker, William
Frensshe, Richard	brazier	da		S		B	B	24	1364		23		2	
Frere, William	smith	d		W		D	D	6						Smyth, William
Frome, John	fisher	?		S		D	D				1			Paart, John
Fustour, Roger				S		D	D	2			3			
Fyshe, John	miller/fisher	?	E	E		D	D	4			18			
Gerveys, William	rentier	a		N		A	A	24	1354		18		2	
Gibbe, John	fuller	da		S	B	D	D				22		1	
Gille, John	cordwainer	?		N		D	D	4						
Gist, John	merchant/draper	a/d		N		A	A	96	1337		12	++	1	
Gist, Walter	carpenter	da		N		D	D	12			8		3	
Glasiere, David	glazier	da		E		D	D	4			12			
Glasiere, Thomas	glazier	da		N		B	B	18	1362	*	11	+	3	Porter, Thomas?

Table A3.1. *cont.*

Name	Occupation	Occ_Fl	Su	Qt	Fe	P	H	Tax	Frdm	N	Br	Ov	Sv	Alias
Godman, Nicholas	chandler/taverner	a		E		D	B	12	1372				1	
Godyng, Roger	loder/leatherworker	da/a		N	N	D	D							
Golde, Adam	merchant	a		N		A	A	60	1362		21	++	4	
Golde, Walter			E	E		D	D	4			16			
Goldsmith, Philip	goldsmith	a		N		D	D		1382		3		1	Gernesie, Philip?
Goldsmyth, Joan	taverner/hosteler	a		S	B	D	W	4			10			Grey, Joan?
Goldsmyth, John	goldsmith	da		E		D	D	6			6		1	Grey, John
Goldsmyth, Robert	goldsmith	da		E		D	D	6						Cateneys, Robert
Goldwyr, Hugh			E?	E		D	D	4			1			
Goos, Raymond	merchant	a		N		A	A	48	1362		18	++		
Graas, John				S		D	D	6						
Grendel, John	building worker	?		E		D	D	3						
Grendel, William				E		D	D	3						
Grendson, Simon	merchant/draper	da		S		B	A	24	1376			++	4	
Grey, John	merchant	a		S		A	A	60	1362		1	++	3	
Grey, Roger	goldsmith	d		S	B	D	D							
Grilles, John	merchant/hosteler	a		W		D	A	24	1374		23	++	2	
Hadleghe, Peter	lawyer/hosteler	da		S		B	A	12	1370		18		1	Pledour, Peter
Hakeworthy, Walter	dyer	da	W	W	E	D	D					+	3	
Halewill, Hugh	carpenter	a	E	E		D	D	6						
Hamelyn, Richard	leatherworker	a	N	N		D	D							
Hamelyn, William	miller	da		E		D	D	3			1			Hamond, William?
Hamond, John	weaver	d	N	N		D	D	4						Milward, John, weaver?
Hamond, John	miller/loder	da	N?	N?	N?	D	D							Milward, John?
Hamond, Walter	miller/loder	da	N	N		D	D	4						
Hampton, William	fisher	da	S	S	B?	D	D				2			

Harepath, Isolda				W		D	W				8			
Haukyn, Matilda				W	N	D	W							
Haycombe, Robert	fuller	a		S		D	D	6			4			
Hayward, John	skinner	da		W		D	D	6						
Heliere, John	helier	da		S	B?	D	D	6			3			
Heliere, William	helier	da		E		D	D	4			2		2	
Herford, Agnes				N		D	W	6						?(no other refs)
Hethman, Richard	miller	da	N	N		D	D	12						
Hethman, Roger	hosteler/baker	a/d		W		C	B	24	1378		25		1	Candeler, Roger
Hille, John	lawyer	da	E	E		A	A		1372	⋆	3			
Hippestobbe, John				E		D	D	4						
Hodel, William	smith	da	E	E		D	C	...	1380		18		2	Russel, William?
Hoigge, Andrew	sutor	da		N		C	C	6						
Hoiggeslond, Geoffrey de			E	E		D	D	12			1			Pykebon, Geoffrey
Hopere, Geoffrey	butcher/victualler	da/a		S		D	D	6			10			
Hopere, John			E	E		C	C	6			2			
Hopere, John	skinner	md		E		B	B	48	1339		2			
Hopere, John	chandler	da		S		D	D				14			
Hopere, Michael	tailor	d	N	N		D	D	6						Taillor, Michael?
Hopere, Richard				E		D	D	3			1			
Hopere, Richard				N		D	D	6			15			
Hopere, Robert				S	B	D	D	6						
Hore, Roger	butcher	da		S?		D	C		1380		2		2	
Horlecumbe, Alexander				E		D	D	6			1			
Horrig, Walter	fisher/hosteler	da/a		S		D	D	12	1372		20		1	
Horrigg, Walter jr.	clothworker	a		S		D	D	6	1379		2			
Hotybake, Walter				W		D	D	12	1369		5		1	
Hull, Thomas atte	tailor	da		E		D	D	12			1		2	
Hulle, John	cordwainer	mda	E	E		D	C	6			16		3	
Hulle, Roger atte	merchant/cordwainer	da		S		D	B	40	1368		7	++	3	
Hurde, Geoffrey				E		D	D	2						?(no other refs)
Hurdying, Roger	smith/lorimer	d		S		D	D	4					1	

Table A3.1. *cont.*

Name	Occupation	Occ_Fl	Su	Qt	Fe	P	H	Tax	Frdm	N	Br	Ov	Sv	Alias
Hureward, John	skinner/servant	a		W		D	B	6	1398		4		1	
Hurtiland, William				N?		D	D							
Hydon, Richard				N?		D	D						1	
Irland, William				S		D	D	4			17			
Iwayn, John	tailor	da		S	B	D	D							
Jesse, Thomas	skinner	da		S		D	D							
Jetour, John	broker/pledger	a		E		D	C	4			1		1	
Joce, Henry	clothworker	?		W		D	D	6			2			
Johan, William	carpenter	mda		S		D	D	12			4		2	
Jonyng, John	glover	da	N	N		C	C	12	1350		1			
Joynguor, John	victualler	a		N		C	C				5			Gynguor, John
Kemystere, Joan	woolcomber	?		S	B	D	W							
Kiggel, John	skinner	da		W		D	C	6			20			
Kilrington, Sibilla	hosteler	a		S		D	W				5			Cornisshe, Sibila
Knyght, John	building worker	a		E		D	D				3			
Knyght, William	broker/moneylender	a		E		D	D	12			14		1	
Kyng, Adam	baker	mda		N		D	D	3			8			Baker, Adam
Kyng, John	weaver	mda		S		D	D	12	1380				1	
Lane, Thomas	hosteler/bailiff	a		W		D	B	18	1378		7		3	
Lane, William	carpenter	?		W	N	D	D				4		1	
Lange, Hawisia			N	N	N	D	W				8		1	
Lange, John	furrier	d		N	N?	D	D	6			3			
Lange, William	butcher/farmer	da/a		N		D	D				6		1	
Langeston, John	building worker	a		E		D	D	4			1			
Langetoft, Avicia				E		D	W	4						
Langford, Joan			N	N	N?	D	W				8		1?	
Large, Agatha	victualler	a		S		D	W	4						

Lavander, Thomas				S		D	D	4						
Leche, Thomas				S?		D	D							
Leman, William	clothworker	a		E		D	D	6			5		1	
Leye, Jordan atte	fuller	a		W	N	D	D	6			18		2	Toker, Jordan & Coydyngcote, Jordan
Litele, John	chapman/mercer	da		N		.D	B	24	1376		1	+	3	
Lodere, Stephen	miller/loder	a		W?		D	D							Mileward, Stephen?
Lorymere, Roger	lorimer/locksmith	a		S		D	D	18			6		1	Lokyer; Sporyer?
Loryng, Thomas	carpenter	da	E?	E		D	D	4						
Louche, William	merchant/hosteler	da/a		W		A	A	24	1362	*	24	++	1	Loude, William
Lovel, Richard	retailer/hosteler	da/a		N		D	C	6	1378		4			
Lucas, William	leatherworker	a		E		D	D	6						
Lyf, Joan	cook	a		S		D	W							
Lygha, Stephen	metalworker	a		W		D	D				7			
Lym, Henry				E		D	D	4			9			Lif, Henry?
Lymenere, Andrew	farmer/clothworker	a/?	E	E		D	D	12			4			
Lyncolne, Thomas				E		D	D	4			1			
Lyndeseye, Walter	hosteler	a		W		B	B	18	1363		5		1	
Lyoun, Robert	glazier	ma		S		D	D	4			1		1	Glasier, Robert?
Madeford, John	fletcher	d		S	B	D	D	6			1			Fletcher, John
Madeford, John jr.	fletcher	d		S	B	D	D	12						
Maiour, John	skinner/servant	d		S	B	D	D	4			3		1	Skinner, Maior
Manjoun, Matilda	retailer/victualler	a		S		D	W	4			16			
Mannyng, William	butcher	da		S		D	D	12	1380					
Marchaunt, Henry	baker's servant	da		S	B?	D	D	4						
Mareschal, Christina				N		D	W				9			
Mareschal, Petronilla			E	E		D	W				2			
Mareschal, Robert	marshal	da	E	E		C	C	18			12		2	Baker, Robert
Marleburgh, Matilda	retailer	a		W		D	W	4						
Martyn, John				E		D	D	3						
Maundevyll, Sibilla	taverner	a		E		D	W	36			7		1	

Table A3.1. *cont.*

Name	Occupation	Occ_Fl	Su	Qt	Fe	P	H	Tax	Frdm	N	Br	Ov	Sv	Alias
Mayoun, John	glover	da	N	N	N	C	C	4			3		1	
Medewyn, Richard			E	E		C	C	4			7		1	
Melbury, Robert	victualler	a		W		D	D	12	1372					
Merpole, John	marshal/ferrour	da		W		C	C				5			Marshal, John
Mewy, John	mason	da		E		D	D	4			2			Mason, John
Mey, John	metalwork	a		S		D	D	6						
Michel, Hervey			E	E		D	D				10			
Mileward, Geoffrey	miller	da		S		D	D	18						
Mileward, John	miller/loder	da		E?	N?	D	D				1		1	Lodere, John
Mileward, John	sutor/cordwainer	da		S		D	D	6						
Mileward, Richard	miller	a	N?	N	N	D	D							
Mileward, Walter	miller	da	N	N		D	D	4			2			
Milton, John	cook	a		S		D	D	6			1			
Monjoun, William	hosteler	a		W	N	D	D	12			19		1	
Monk, Peter				E		D	D	4						?(no other refs)
Monte, Adam	messenger/porter	a		E	B	D	D							
More, Nicholas atte	tanner	da	W?	W	N?	D	B	24	1381		5			
More, Thomas atte	tanner	da		W		D	D	18			2			
Morhay, Roger	weaver/hosteler	da/a		N	N	C	B	12	1378		16		2	
Moris, Alice				W		D	W	6						
Nelgable, Thomas	fishmonger/hosteler	da/?		N		D	D				1			
Nevyll, Robert	sutor/chapman	da		S		D	D	40	1380				3	
Nicol, Thomas	tailor/gatekeeper	da		S		D	C	12						
Norman, John	tailor/cook	da/a		S		D	D	4						
North, William	miller	da		S?		D	D							
Norton, William				E		B	B	12	1369		16		2	
Nowel, John	sawyer	a		W		D	D	6			2			

Nymet, John	merchant/cutler	da/d		E		A	A	84	1353		2	++	1	
Nyweton, John	tailor	mda	E	E		D	D	6			2			
Obelyn, William	skinner	da		E		D	D	4	1349					
Oke, William	merchant/mercer	a/da		E		D	A	12	1374		7	++	5	
Oldeston, Alexander				S		A	A		1349	*	13			Nayler, Alexander
Orchard, Henry	currier	da		S		D	D	12	1348		12			
Oreweye, Robert	fisher/victualler	da/a		S		D	D	12	1356		2			
Oteryton, Roger	cordwainer	da		S		D	D	24	1378		6		2	
Oteryton, William	metalworker	a		E		D	D	4						
Pafford, John	sutor	da		S		D	D	6			2			
Page, John	carpenter	da	E?	E		D	D				2			
Parlebien, Henry	fisher	a		S?		D	D							
Payn, William	gardener	d	E	E		D	D	3						
Payn, William	horner	da		N		D	D							Hornere, William
Pederton, John	carpenter	da	E	E		D	D	6			4		1	
Penkerigg, John	victualler	a	E?	E		D	D	4			7			
Peny, Walter				S	B	D	D							
Pestour, Richard			W	W	E	D	D							
Pestour, Roger	grazier/farmer	a	N	N		D	C	12					2	
Peuterer, Richard	pewterer/merchant	d/a		E		D	A	8	1370			+	3	Osbourne, Richard
Peyngtour, John				E		D	D	3						
Peytevyn, John	miller	d		E		D	D	2			2			
Peyton, John	weaver	d		S		D	D	12	1378		8			
Phelip, Andrew	furrier	?	E	E		D	D				1			Fursere, Andrew
Phelip, Geoffrey				S		D	D				1			
Phelip, John	furrier	d	N	N	N?	D	D	6			6			Fursere, Philip
Piers, John	taverner/merchant	da/a		S		B	A	24	1374		8	++		
Pipard, Roger				N		D	D	4			1			
Pippedene, John	clothworker	a		N		D	B		1379					
Placy, Henry	carpenter	da		N		D	D	12			15		1	
Plomere, Alice	hosteler	a		S		D	W	6			16			

Table A3.1. *cont.*

Name	Occupation	Occ_Fl	Su	Qt	Fe	P	H	Tax	Frdm	N	Br	Ov	Sv	Alias
Plomere, John	plumber	da		E		C	C	6	1367		16			
Plomere, Robert	plumber/farmer	da/a		E		C	B	12	1370		18		6	
Plym, Ralph	saddler	da		N		D	D	8	1381	?	1		1	
Pode, Thomas	fishmonger/hosteler	da/a		N		D	D	6			16		4	
Poleworthy, Robert	baker	da		E?	B	D	D				9			Bakere, Robert
Ponte, Peter	skinner/hosteler	a		W		D	D	12			12		6	
Ponton, John	clerk/merchant	da/?		W		D	A	24	1384	*	14			
Pope, Richard	glover	da	N?	N?		D	D							
Porter, Thomas	carpenter	mda	E	E		D	D	4			17			
Portisham, Joan	hosteler	a		S		D	W	4			10			
Pricchere, John				S		D	D							
Pricchere, Walter	building worker	?	E?	E		D	D	2						
Pye, Thomas	bowyer	mda	N	N		D	B	24	1369		2	+	2	Boghiere, Thomas
Pyn, Ralph				S		D	D	4	1342		5		1	
Pytman, John	weaver	da		S		D	D	6			4		1	
Raddych, William	leather-/skin-worker	a		S		D	D	18			5		1	
Radeslo, John	weaver	d		E		D	D	6					1	
Rede, John	merchant	da		N		A	A	120	1369		1	+		
Redham, Thomas				N		D	D	6						
Renebaud, John	hosteler/clothier	a/?		W		C	B	18	1360		25		1	
Rok, William	merchant/hosteler	a		E		A	A	40	1348		25	++	1	
Roland, Claricia				N	N	D	W				7			
Roof, John	glover/farmer	a	N	N	N	D	C	6						
Ropere, Robert	roper	a		S		D	D	12	1378		12			
Row, William	hosteler	a	E	E		D	D	6			23	+	4	
Russel, John	goldsmith	mda		N		D	B	24	1378		14		1	
Russel, John	merchant	da		W		A	A	48	1360		17	++	1	

Rye, John	hosteler/chandler	a		E		D	D	6	1390		17			
Rygoun, Thomas	sawyer	da		E		D	D	4			16		1	
Sachevyll, Henry	tailor	a		W		D	D	8	1378				1	
Sadelere, Edward				S	B	D	D							
Sadelere, Roger				E		D	D	6						
Sadelere, Walter	leatherworker	?		E		D	D	4			6		1	
Salesbury, John				N		D	D	6						
Sampforde, Walter	cordwainer	da		W		D	D	12	1378		4		2	
Sampson, Thomas	glover	da	N	N	N?	B	B	4	1350					
Sampson, William	leatherworker/glover	a/?		S		D	D	6		?	13		3	
Sanervay, William	miller	da	N	N	N	D	D				3			Mileward, William?
Scam, Henry	bailiff	da		N		C	A	18	1354		6			
Scare, Thomas	victualler/hosteler	a/?		W		D	D	18	1369		3			
Scarlet, John	brewer	da	E	E		C	C	12			24		1	
Scarlet, John	saddler	mda		S		D	D	12			2		3	
Scarlet, Margery				E		D	W				3			
Scut, Adam	merchant	a		S		A	A	84	1362		11	++	2	
Seger, John	helier	da	E	E		D	C				10		1	
Sele, Robert	tailor	da	N?	N	N	D	D				2			
Shephurde, John	miller	da	N	N	N	D	D				5		1?	
Shephurde, John	carpenter	da	E?	E		D	D							
Shepwaysshe, William	hosteler	a	N?	N	B	D	D	6			24		1	
Shereman, William				E		D	D	4						?(no other refs)
Shildoun, Juliana				E		D	W				2			
Shildoun, Walter	carpenter	a		S		D	D	4						Baker, Walter
Shildoun, William	baker	da		S	B	D	D	12			8		1	Baker, William
Shippestere, Joan	tailor/shipstere	a	N	N		D	W						1	
Skydemour, Robert	leatherworker	a		W		D	D	12						
Skynnere, John	skinner	da		E		D	B	12	1380				3	Leghe, John
Skyradon, Henry	leatherworker/hosteler	?		N?		D	D				6			
Skyradon, William	clothworker/weaver	a/?		W		D	B	18	1369		16		2	
Skyttisshs, William				S		D	D	8			4			

Table A3.1. *cont.*

Name	Occupation	Occ_Fl	Su	Qt	Fe	P	H	Tax	Frdm	N	Br	Ov	Sv	Alias
Sleghe, John	hosteler/helier	a/md	S	S	B?	D	D	12			2			Heliere, John
Sleghe, John sr.	merchant–retired	da		E		A	A		1335		8	++		
Sleghe, Robert	baker	d		S	B	D	D				21			
Smabbe, Jocelin	cordwainer	da		S		D	D	12					1	
Smyth, John	smith	da	N	N	N	C	C	12			4		1	Tadyford, John
Smyth, Richard	smith	da	S	S		D	C	4	1380		12		3	Carseys, Richard
Smyth, Thomas	butcher	da	W	W	E	D	B		1370		5		4	
Smythesheghes, Thomas	smith/merchant	da/a		E		B	A	24	1372		19	+	2	Ferrour, Thomas
Sodeen, John	clothworker	?	E	E		D	D				5			
Somer, John	hosteler	a		E		D	C	4			18		1	
Somer, Sarra				W		D	W	6						
Somerforde, John	fuller/victualler	a		S		D	D	12			6		1	
Sparke, John	hosteler	a		E		B	B	40	1366		1			
Spealte, Lawrence	smith	da	S	S		C	C	2			12			Smith, Lawrence
Splot, John	hosteler/cordwainer	a		W		D	C	40			19		1	
Sporiere, Geoffrey	spurrier	a		E		D	D	3			2			
Spray, Agnes	hosteler	a	N	N	N	D	W	6			11			
Sprite, Simon	saddler	ma		N		D	D	6	1391		6			
Spycer, Geoffrey				S		D	D	4						?(no other refs)
Spycer, Henry	skinner	da		E		D	D	6	1380		11		2	Skinner, Henry
Stayre, Richard	draper/merchant	a		E		A	A	24	1369		17	+	3	
Stephen, Claricia			N?	N	N?	D	W	2			5			
Stobbe, John	smith	d	N	N	N	C	C	12	1360		14		1	
Stoddon, William	currier	da		S		D	D	18	1378		12			
Stoke, John	plumber	a		N		D	D	6			6			
Stoke, Richard	saddler	mda		E		B	B	6	1350		15		2	
Stoke, Richard	skinner	mda		E		D	D	3						

Stoke, Robert	merchant–retired	da	E	E		A	A	12	1356	16	++	1	
Stokelond, John			S	S	B	D	D						
Stokleghe, Elena				S		D	W			10			
Storde, Maurice	farmer	a	E	E		D	D	12		11			
Strange, John	fisher/hosteler	da/?	S	S	B	D	D	6					
Streyngher, John	fisher/hosteler	da/a		S		D	D	6		14		2	
Sturre, John	hosteler	a	E	E		D	C	12		20			
Swan, Ralph	merchant/hosteler	a		S		D	A	12	1378	16	++		
Sydelyng, William	goldsmith	da		N		D	D	6				1	
Syneet, John	spicer	da		E		B	B	24	1374	1		3	
Taillor, Emma	hosier/tailor	a		W		D	W	12		1			Hosiere, Emma
Taillor, Hugh	tailor	da		E		D	D	6	1377	3		1	Broun, Hugh
Taillor, Robert	tailor	?		E		D	D	4		2			
Taillor, William				N		D	D	3				1	
Taillor, William	tailor	a	S?	S		D	D	6		3		1	Beare, William?
Talbot, John	merchant	a		N		A	A	160	1369	11	++	1	
Taverner, Alan	sutor	da		S		D	D	4					Suttore, Alan?
Taverner, Joan	cook	a		S		D	W	6					
Taverner, Robert	cook	a		S		D	D			3			
Thomas, John	miller	da	N?	N?		D	D						
Thomas, Walter	skinner/hosteler	da/a		W		B	B	42	1367	16	+	3	Skynnere, Walter
Thornyng, Hugh	bailiff of Duryard	a	E	E		B	B	12	1370	12	+		
Todebere, Thomas	tailor/tapicer	da		E		D	D	4		1			Taillor, Thomas
Tokere, Philip	fuller	da		W		D	D	6		1		2	
Tokere, William	fuller	a	E	E		D	D	4		5			
Tolk, Robert	clothworker	a	S	S		D	C	12		25			
Tolke, John	carpenter	ma	E	E		D	D	6		4		1	Tullok, John
Tolle, John	miller	da		S		D	D			1			
Totton, Joan				W		D	W	6					Tauton, Joan?
Toukere, Thomas	thatcher	d	N?	N	N	D	D			2			
Tresyny, Henry	weaver	a		S		D	D	12	1367				
Trevenour, Anastasia				E?		D	W			3			

Table A3.1. *cont.*

Name	Occupation	Occ_Fl	Su	Qt	Fe	P	H	Tax	Frdm	N	Br	Ov	Sv	Alias
Trosine, Thomas	cordwainer/corveser	da		N		D	D	12	1378		10			
Trote, Alice				E		D	W	4			3			
Truel, John	butcher	da		W		C	B	18	1364		13		3	
Tugg, John	clothworker/miller	a/da		S		D	D	6			8		3	
Tykerygg, Richard	cordwainer	da		N		D	B	12	1379	*	13		5	
Tyrel, John	fuller	da		N		D	D	12	1380		9		5	
Umfray, Matthew	sutor	da		E		D	D	3						
Uppedoune, William	merchant/hosteler	a	S	S		B	A	36	1369		19	+	1	Doune, William
Uppexe, Ralph	hosteler	?		S		B	B	12	1360	*	19		1	
Valence, Roger	leatherworker	a		N	N?	D	D	2						
Veisy, John	butcher	da		S		B	B	36	1366		19		1	
Viel, Richard	hosteler/leatherseller	a		W		D	D	12	1379		19	+	3	
Viene, John	saddler	d		N?		D	D				5			
Wallyng, William			S	S	B?	D	C				1			
Walsshe, Richard	fisher	a		N		D	D	6			16			
Walssheman, William	tailor/miller	da		E		D	D	12	1378		3		1	
Wandry, Richard	clothworker/shearman	a/?		S?	B?	D	D		1368		14		1	
Wandry, Thomas	merchant/clothier	a		N		D	A	24	1369		5	++	2	
Wappelood, John	shearman	da	W	W	E	D	D						2	Sherman, John
Wayte, Thomas	waite	da		N		D	D						1	
Webber, John	merchant	a		N		A	A	60	1362		12	++	3	
Webber, Luke	weaver	a		S		D	D	6					1	
Webber, Richard				S		D	D	6			2			
Webber, Thomas	merchant/clothier	a		N		A	A	36	1363		10	+	1	
Webber, Walter			E	E		D	D	4			12			
Webber, William	weaver	da	N	N		D	D	4					1	Herford, William
Webber, William	fuller	da		E		D	D	4			1		1	
Webber, Wylkyn	weaver	d		S		D	D	6						Flemming, William

Welfare, John	skinner	da		W	N	D	D	6			1			
Westecote, Henry	hosteler	a		W		B	A	40	1362		21		1	
Westecote, John	merchant	a		W		B	B	24	1349		14	++	3	
Westwode, John			N	N		D	D	2						
Whiteleghe, Baldwin	hosteler/tailor	a		S		B	A	24	1369		21		5	Taillor, Baldwin
Whitterne, Thomas				W		D	D	4			1			
Wilcock, John	miller/bailiff	da	N	N	N	D	D							Coppe, John
Wilde, Elena	hosteler	a	E	E		D	W	6			8			
Wille, John atte	fisher	da	E	E		D	D	24						
Wille, Robert atte	farmer	?	E	E		D	C	12			15			
Wille, William atte	bailiff	da		W		C	C	6						
Wode, Adam atte	leather-/skin-worker	a		E		C	C	12			24			
Wode, Walter atte				S		A	A	40	1350		11			
Wodeward, Nicholas			E?	E		D	D	4			3			
Wogwill, William	cordwainer	da		W		D	D	12	1368		8		2	
Workman, Nicholas				W	N	D	D							
Wycroft, John	hosteler	a		W		D	D				8	+		
Wygham, William	skinner	d	E	E		B	B	24	1340		18			
Wyke, Elena				S		D	W	12						
Wylde, Thomas	cordwainer/hosier	d/?		S		D	D	12	1377		3			
Wylde, Walter	smith/marshal	da		S		C	B	18	1380		23	+	3	Ferrour, Walter
Wylde, William			E	E		D	D	8						
Wylford, Robert	merchant	a		N		A	A	180	1364	*	8	++	7	
Wynd, Henry	metalworker	?		S?		D	D							
Wyndout, Robert	skinner	da		S		D	A	12	1369		5		3	
Wyndovere, Richard	hosteler/gatekeeper/ clothworker	a/da/a		W		C	C	24	1378		23		1	
Yevele, John	weaver	a		N		D	D	6			1		4	
Yunge, Nicholas	baker	da	W	W	E	D	D							
Yurl, Henry	helier/farmer	?	N	N		D	D	8			23			Helier, Henry?
Yurl, Thomas	helier/fuller	?	E?	E		D	D	12			18			

Bibliography

MANUSCRIPT SOURCES

Manuscript sources are cited in the footnotes and tables by the abbreviations given here. Unless stated otherwise, all document references in the footnotes and tables refer to records deposited in the Devon Record Office. Many of the Exeter city documents are described in Appendix 1.

(BL) British Library
Add. Ch.: Additional Charters
Add. Ms.: Additional Manuscripts
Cotton Claudius D. ii (Exeter city charter)
Cotton Vitellius D. ix (Cartulary of St Nicholas Priory)
Harley Manuscripts, Charters and Rolls

Corpus Christi College, Oxford
Kn. 3/1 (Langford account roll)

(DCO) Duchy of Cornwall Record Office
Min. Accts.: Ministers' Accounts (includes Havener's accounts)
Receivers' Accounts

(DRO) Devon Record Office
Exeter city documents:
Book 51 (Commonplace Book of John Hooker)
Book 53 (Izacke's "Memorials of the city of Exeter")
Book 53A (Cartulary of St John's Hospital)
Book 55 (Freemen's book)
Book 60h (Hooker's Journal and "History of the Manor of Exilond")
CRA: City receiver's accounts
DCR: Duryard court rolls
DRA: Duryard receiver's accounts
EBW: Exe Bridge wardens' accounts
ED/: Exeter deeds
Exeter city charters
MCR: Mayor's court rolls
Misc. Roll: Miscellaneous rolls 2 (Customs and precedents), 3 (Documents on disputes with the earls of Devon), 4 (Court roll extracts), 5 (Eyre roll, 1281–2), 6 (City building accounts), 7 (New conduit accounts), 12 (St Nicholas' fee court rolls), 37 and 38 (St Sidwell's fee court rolls), 40 (Pie powder court

roll), 48 (Reeve's accounts of East Budleigh), 49 (St Nicholas' fee rental), 52 (St Nicholas' fee receipts), 55 (St Nicholas priory and Lammas fair), 72 (Murage roll), 78 and 79 (Pleas regarding dispute with the earls of Devon), 83–90 and 98 (Extracts regarding dispute on fee farm and fair).
MT: Mayor's tourn
NQMT, SQMT, EQMT, WQMT: North, South, East, or West Quarter mayor's tourns
PCA: Port customs accounts
PCR: Provosts' court rolls
Transcripts 13–14, 20, 23, 26, 108
Devon county documents:
CR: Court rolls (and account rolls) 487, 490, 491, 500, 501, 789, 1288, 1466, 20,059
DD: Deeds and documents
M/: Deeds
W1258M/: Records of the Russell estate
Z 19/8/2: Moger's transcript of quo warranto proceedings for Devon
51/1/7: Deeds and papers deposited by Revd. J. A. Goundrey
123M/: Kingsbridge court rolls
314M/: Records of the Luxmoore estate
902M/: Stoke Fleming court rolls
1508M/: Records of the Courtenay of Powderham estate
4088M/: Records of the Cary estate

(ECL) Exeter Cathedral Library
While many ECL documents were used in the prosopographical analyses, only manuscripts cited in the footnotes are noted here.
D&C: Dean and chapter deeds, court rolls, account rolls
21–8, 119, 121, 216 (Deeds)
1905 (Tithe dispute)
2636–57 (Cathedral fabric rolls)
2706–13 (Debt rolls)
2857 (Manorial visitations)
2945 (Sidbury rental)
3550 (Chapter act book)
3683 (Miscellaneous books and rentals)
3773, 3777 (Accounts of ordinary and extraordinary receipts and payments)
4857–61 (St Sidwell's fee court rolls)
4931 (Culmstock court roll)
4993–4 (Ide court rolls)
5006 (Norton court roll)
5030–2 (Dawlish reeve's accounts)
5108–10 (Culmstock reeve's accounts)
5139 (Account roll)
5150–56 (Dean and chapter collectors' accounts of rents)
5232–38 (Sale of tithes)
V/C: Vicars choral deeds, court rolls, account rolls
3125 (Extract from Exeter mayor's court roll, 1321)

3158–9 (Deeds)
3331 (Quarterly account rolls of rents)
3351–3 (Woodbury tithe and manorial accounts)

(NDRO) North Devon Record Office
Ath. Ms: North Devon Athenaeum Manuscripts
Barnstaple court rolls

(PRO) Public Record Office
C1: Early Chancery proceedings
C47: Chancery miscellanea
C53: Chancery: Charter rolls
C60: Chancery: Fine rolls
C131: Chancery extents for debts
C133: Chancery inquisitions post mortem
C135: Chancery inquisitions post mortem
C241: Chancery certificates of statute merchant and statute staple
C258: Chancery files, writs certiorari
C260: Chancery recorda
C267: Chancery certificates of elections
CP40: Court of common pleas rolls
E101: Exchequer K. R. accounts various (Army, Navy, and Ordnance; Butlerage; France; Mines; Ulnage; Sheriff)
E122: Exchequer K. R. customs accounts
E143: Exchequer K. R. extents and inquisitions
E159: Exchequer K. R. memoranda rolls
E163: Exchequer K. R. miscellanea
E179: Exchequer K. R. lay subsidies and poll taxes
E356: Exchequer K. R. enrolled customs accounts
E358: Exchequer L.T.R. enrolled accounts miscellaneous
E359: Exchequer L.T.R. enrolled accounts of subsidies
E368: Exchequer L.T.R. memoranda rolls
E401: Exchequer of Receipt: Receipt rolls
JUST1: Justices Itinerant assize and eyre rolls
JUST3: Gaol delivery rolls
KB9: King's Bench ancient indictments
Palmer's Index No. 93 (of fairs and markets)
SC2: Court rolls
SC6: Ministers' accounts
SC8: Ancient petitions
SC11: Rentals and surveys
SC12: Rentals and surveys

(SRO) Somerset Record Office
DD/CN/Box 3, 5 (Records of Franceis estate)

Southampton Record Office
SC5. 5/1 (Brokage book, 1430–1)

PRINTED SOURCES

References to printed sources in the footnotes and tables are cited by title or by an abbreviation (as noted here preceding the bibliographic entry) and, where relevant, the volume and page numbers.

Anglo-Norman custumal of Exeter, ed. J. W. Schopp (History of Exeter Research Group, no. 2). Oxford, 1925.

Barnstaple records: Reprint of Barnstaple records, ed. J. R. Chanter and T. Wainright, 2 vols. Barnstaple, 1900.

Book of Margery Kempe, ed. S. B. Meech and H. E. Allen (Early English Text Society, no. 212). London, 1940.

Bracton: Henry Bracton. *Bracton on the laws and customs of England*, ed. George Woodbine, rev. and trans. Samuel E. Thorne, 4 vols. Cambridge, MA, 1968–77.

Bristol: The overseas trade of Bristol in the later middle ages, ed. E. M. Carus-Wilson (Bristol Record Society, 1937); reprint London, 1967.

Brokage book of Southampton from 1439–40, ed. Barbara D. M. Bunyard (Southampton Record Society, no. 40). Southampton, 1941.

Brokage book of Southampton, 1443–1444, ed. Olive Coleman (Southampton Records Series, vols. 4 and 6). Southampton, 1960–1.

Cal. P&MR London: Calendar of plea and memoranda rolls of London, vol. 2, *1364–1381*, ed. A. H. Thomas. Cambridge, 1929.

Calendar of Letter-Books of the City of London, Letter-Book L, ed. R. R. Sharpe. London, 1912.

Calendar of the Tavistock parish records, ed. R. N. Worth. Plymouth, 1887.

Cartulary of Canonsleigh Abbey, ed. Vera C. M. London (Devon and Cornwall Record Society, new ser., vol. 8). Torquay, 1965.

CChR: Calendar of charter rolls preserved in the Public Record Office. Henry III–Henry VIII, 6 vols. London, 1903–27.

CCR: Calendar of close rolls preserved in the Public Record Office, Edward I–Henry VII, 47 vols. London, 1892–1963.

CFR: Calendar of fine rolls preserved in the Public Record Office, Edward I–Henry VII, 22 vols. London, 1911–63.

Chronicle of Richard of Devizes of the Time of King Richard the First, ed. J. T. Appleby. London, 1963.

Chronicon Adae de Usk A.D. 1377–1404, ed. Edward Maunde Thompson. London, 1876.

Church-wardens' accounts of Croscombe, Pilton, Yatton, Tintinhull, Morebath, and St. Michael's, Bath ranging from A.D. 1349 to 1560, ed. Edmund Hobhouse (Somerset Record Society, vol. 4). Yeovil, 1890.

CIM: Calendar of inquisitions miscellaneous, 7 vols. London, 1916–69.

Citie of Excester: John Vowell alias Hoker, *The description of the Citie of Excester*, ed. Walter J. Harte, J. W. Schopp, and H. Tapley-Soper (Devon and Cornwall Record Society, vol. 12). Exeter, 1919.

CPR: Calendar of patent rolls preserved in the Public Record Office, Edward I–Henry VII, 48 vols. London, 1894–1916.

Curia regis rolls. 17 vols. London, 1923–91.

Customs of the manors of Taunton: The medieval customs of the manors of Taunton and Bradford on Tone, ed. T. J. Hunt (Somerset Record Society, vol. 66). Yeovil, 1962.

Dartmouth. vol. I – Pre-Reformation, ed. Hugh R. Watkin (Parochial Histories of Devonshire, no. 5). Exeter, 1935.

Devon eyre: Crown pleas of the Devon eyre of 1238, ed. Henry Summerson (Devon and Cornwall Record Society, new ser., vol. 28). Exeter, 1985.

Devon fines: Devon feet of fines, vol. I, *Richard I–Henry III*, ed. Oswald J. Reichel (Devon and Cornwall Record Society, vol. 6). Exeter, 1912.

Diplomatarium anglicum aevi saxonici, ed. Benjamin Thorpe. London, 1865.

Domesday Book, Devon, ed. Caroline and Frank Thorn, 2 parts (History from the sources, vol. 9). Chichester, 1985.

Ecclesiastical history: Orderic Vitalis, *The ecclesiastical history of Orderic Vitalis*, vol. II, ed. Marjorie Chibnall. Oxford, 1969.

English gilds, ed. Toulmin Smith and Lucy Toulmin Smith (Early English Text Society, original ser., no. 40). Oxford, 1870.

English historical documents, c. 500–1042, ed. Dorothy Whitelock. Oxford, 1955.

Exeter freemen 1266–1967, ed. Margery M. Rowe and Andrew M. Jackson (Devon and Cornwall Record Society, extra ser., no. 1). Exeter, 1973.

Exeter property deeds 1150–1450, ed. P. R. Staniforth and J. Z. Juddery, 4 vols (Exeter Museums Archaeological Field Unit, Report Nos. 91.45–91.48). Exeter, 1991.

Fabric accounts: Accounts of the fabric of Exeter cathedral, 1279–1353, ed. Audrey M. Erskine, 2 vols. (Devon and Cornwall Record Society, new ser., vols. 24 and 26). Exeter, 1981, 1983.

Feudal aids, vol. 1. London, 1899.

Gesta Stephani: The deeds of Stephen (1135–54), ed. K. R. Potter. Oxford, 1976.

Great Red Book of Bristol. Text. Part I, ed. E.W.W. Veale (Bristol Record Society, vol. 4). Bristol, 1933.

HMCR, vol. 55: *The records of the dean and chapter of Exeter*, comp. Reginald L. Poole (Royal Commission on Historical Manuscripts, Reports on collections, vol. 55, part IV). London, 1907.

HMCR, vol. 73: *The records of the city of Exeter*, comp. J. H. Wylie (Royal Commission on Historical Manuscripts, Reports on collections, vol. 73). London, 1916.

IPM: Calendar of inquisitions post mortem, 16 vols. London, 1904–74.

Issue roll of Thomas de Brantingham, Bishop of Exeter, Lord High Chancellor, containing payments out of the revenue, 44 Edward III, 1370, ed. F. Devon. London, 1835.

Itineraries: William Worcestre. *Itineraries*, ed. John H. Harvey. Oxford, 1969.

Itinerary: The itinerary of John Leland, ed. Lucy Toulmin Smith, 5 vols. Carbondale, IL, 1964.

Law merchant: Select cases concerning law merchant, ed. Charles Gross and Hubert Hall, 3 vols. (Selden society, vols. 23, 46, 49). London, 1908–32.

Lay subsidy 1332: The Devonshire lay subsidy of 1332, ed. Audrey M. Erskine (Devon and Cornwall Record Society, new ser., vol. 14). Torquay, 1969.

Lay subsidy 1334: The lay subsidy of 1334, ed. Robin E. Glasscock. London, 1974.

Little Red Book of Bristol, vol. 2, ed. Francis B. Bickley. Bristol, 1900.

Local PCA 1266–1321: The local port customs accounts of the city of Exeter, 1266–1321, ed. Maryanne Kowaleski (Devon and Cornwall Record Society, new ser., vol. 36). Exeter, 1993.

Local port book of Southampton 1435–36, ed. Brian Foster (Southampton records series, vol. 7). Southampton, 1963.

Local port book of Southampton 1439–40, ed. Henry S. Cobb (Southampton records series, vol. 5). Southampton, 1961.

London assize of nuisance, 1301–1431: a calendar, ed. Helena M. Chew and William Kellaway (London Record Society, no. 10). London, 1973.

Magnus rotulus scaccarii de anno 31º Henrici I, ed. J. Hunter. London, 1833.

Min. Accts. Cornwall: Ministers' accounts of the earldom of Cornwall 1296–1297, ed. L. Margaret Midgley, 2 vols. (Camden society, 3rd. ser., vols. 66 and 68). London, 1942–45.

Moore, Stuart A. (comp.) 1863–70. Calendar of the records and muniments belonging to the corporation of the city of Exeter. Manuscript volume in the Devon Record Office.

Moore, Stuart A. (comp.) 1873. Calendar of the muniments and library of the dean and chapter of Exeter. Manuscript volume in the Exeter Cathedral Library.

Oak Book of Southampton, ed. P. Studer, 2 vols. (Southampton Records Series, vols. 10 and 11). Southampton, 1910–11.

Pipe roll: Publications of the Pipe Roll Society, 89 vols. London, 1884–1990.

Pipe roll, 1155–58: The great rolls of the pipe for the second, third and fourth years of the reign of king Henry the second, 1155–1158, ed. J. Hunter. London, 1844.

Pipe roll, 1188–89: The great roll of the pipe for the first year of the reign of king Richard the first, 1188–1189, ed. J. Hunter. London, 1844.

Placitorum abbreviatio, Richard I–Edward II, ed. G. Rose and W. Illingworth. London, 1811.

Quo warranto: Placita de quo warranto, ed. W. Illingworth and J. Caley. London, 1818.

Receivers' accounts: The receivers' accounts of the city of Exeter 1304–1353, ed. M. M. Rose and J. M. Draisy (Devon and Cornwall Record Society, new ser., vol. 32). Exeter, 1989.

Records of the city of Norwich, ed. William Hudson and J. C. Tingey, 2 vols. Norwich, 1906–10.

Reg. Brantingham: The register of Thomas de Brantingham, bishop of Exeter, 1370–1394, ed. F. C. Hingeston-Randolph, 2 vols. London, 1901–6.

Reg. Bronescombe and Quivil: The registers of Walter Bronescombe (A.D. 1257–1280) and Peter Quivil (A.D. 1280–1291) bishops of Exeter, ed. F. C. Hingeston-Randolph. London and Exeter, 1889.

Reg. Grandisson: The register of John Grandisson, bishop of Exeter, 1327–1369, ed. F. C. Hingeston-Randolph, 3 vols. London and Exeter, 1894–9.

Reg. Lacy: The Register of Edmund Lacy, bishop of Exeter, 1420–1455, Registrum Commune, ed. G. R. Dunstan, 5 vols. (Canterbury and York Society, vols. 60–63 and 66; Devon and Cornwall Record Society, new ser., vols. 7, 10, 13, 16 and 18), 1963–72.

Reg. Stafford: The register of Edmund Stafford, 1395–1419, ed. F. C. Hingeston-

Randolph. London and Exeter, 1886.

Register of the Black Prince: Register of Edward the Black Prince, 4 vols. London, 1930–33.

Rotuli chartarum in Turri Londinensi asservati, 1199–1216, ed. T. D. Hardy. London, 1837.

Rotuli de liberate ac de misis et praestitis, regnante Johanne, ed. T. D. Hardy. London, 1844.

Rotuli de oblatis et finibus in turri Londinensi asservati, 1200–1205: also 1417–1418, ed. T. D. Hardy. London, 1835.

Rotuli hundredorum, ed. W. Illingworth and J. Caley, 2 vols. London, 1812–18.

Rotuli litterarum clausarum in turri Londiensi asservati, ed. T. D. Hardy, 2 vols. London, 1833–44.

Rotuli parliamentorum, 6 vols. London, 1783.

Rotulus cancellarii vel antigraphum magni rotuli pipae de 3° anno regis Johannis, ed. J. Hunter. London, 1833.

Select cases before the king's council 1243–1482, ed. I. S. Leadam and J. F. Baldwin (Selden Society, vol. 36). Cambridge, MA, 1918.

Somerset coroner's roll: Douglas Stevens. A Somerset coroner's roll, 1315–1321, *Somerset & Dorset Notes & Queries,* 31 (1985): 451–72.

Totnes: The history of Totnes Priory and medieval town, ed. Hugh R. Watkin, 3 vols. Torquay, 1914–17.

Tudor Exeter tax assessments 1489–1595, ed. Margery Rowe (Devon and Cornwall Record Society, new ser., vol. 22). Torquay, 1977.

Wardrobe book: The wardrobe book of William de Norwell 12 July 1338 to 27 May 1340, ed. Mary Lyon, Bryce Lyon, Henry S. Lucas. Brussels, 1983.

W.C. Chancery proc.: Calendar of early Chancery proceedings relating to West Country shipping 1388–1493, ed. Dorothy A. Gardiner (Devon and Cornwall Record Society, new ser., vol. 21). Torquay, 1976.

Wassom, John M. (ed.) *Devon* (Records of early English drama). Toronto, 1986.

Year books of Richard II. 11 Richard II. 1387–88, ed. Isabel D. Thornley. London, 1937.

Year books of Richard II. 13 Richard II. 1389–1390, ed. T.F.T. Plucknett. London, 1929.

SECONDARY SOURCES

Alcock, N. W. 1966. The medieval buildings of Bishop's Clyst. *TDA*, 98: 133–53.

1970. An east Devon manor in the later middle ages. Part I: 1370–1420. The manor farm. *TDA*, 102: 141–88.

Alexander, J. J. 1928. Exeter members of parliament. Part II. 1377 to 1537. *TDA*, 60: 183–214.

Alexander, J. J. and Hooper, W. R. 1948. *The history of Great Torrington in the county of Devon.* Sutton.

Allan, John 1984. *Medieval and post-medieval finds from Exeter, 1971–1980.* Exeter.

A note on the building stones of the Cathedral. In *Medieval art and architecture at Exeter cathedral*, ed. Francis Kelly, pp. 10–18. Leeds.

Allan, John, Henderson, Christopher, and Higham, Robert 1984. Saxon Exeter. In *Anglo-Saxon towns of southern England*, ed. Jeremy Haslam, pp. 385–414. Chichester.

Amery, Fabyan 1933. Country fairs and revels. *TDA*, 65: 128–30.

Appleby, John C. 1992. Devon privateering from early times to 1688. In *A new maritime history of Devon*, vol. I, eds. M. Duffy, S. Fisher, B. Greenhill, D. Starkey, and J. Youings, pp. 90–7. London and Exeter.

Aston, M. and Dennison, E. 1988. Fishponds in Somerset. In *Medieval fish, fisheries and fishponds in England*, ed. Michael Aston, pp. 391–416. Oxford.

Attreed, Lorraine 1984. The English royal government and its relations with the boroughs of Norwich, York, Exeter and Nottingham, 1377–1509. Unpublished Ph.D. thesis. Harvard University.

Bailey, Mark 1989. The concept of the margin in the medieval English economy. *EcHR*, 2nd ser., 42: 1–17.

1990. Coastal fishing off south east Suffolk in the century after the Black Death. *Proceedings of the Suffolk Institute of Archaeology and History*, 37: 102–14.

Bailey, Stanley J. 1932. Assignment of debts in England from the twelfth to the twentieth century, II. *Law Quarterly Review*, 48: 248–71.

Baker, Robert L. 1961. *The English customs service, 1307–1343: A study of medieval administration.* Philadelphia.

Barlow, Frank 1972. Leofric and his times. In *Leofric of Exeter*, ed. Frank Barlow *et al.*, pp. 1–16. Exeter.

1979. *The English church, 1000–1066*, 2nd edn. London.

Barlow, Frank, Biddle, Martin, von Feilitzen, Olof, and Keene, D. J. 1976. *Winchester in the early middle ages: an edition and discussion of the Winton Domesday*. Oxford.

Barron, Caroline 1970. Ralph Holland and the London radicals, 1438–1444. In *The medieval town: a reader in English urban history 1200–1540*, ed. Richard Holt and Gervase Rosser, pp. 160–83. London.

Bateson, Mary 1906. Introduction. *Borough customs* (Selden Society, vol. 21), pp. xv–clvi. London.

Beale, P. B. 1969. The freshwater fisheries of Exeter and district. In *Exeter and its region*, ed. Frank Barlow, pp. 90–6. Exeter.

Beardwood, Alice 1931. *Alien merchants in England 1350–1377*. Cambridge, MA.

1939. Introduction. *The statute merchant roll of Coventry 1392–1416* (Dugdale Society, vol. 17), pp. vii–xxvi. London.

Beckerman, J. S. 1975. The forty-shilling jurisdictional limit in medieval English personal actions. In *Legal history studies 1972*, ed. Dafydd Jenkins, pp. 110–17. Cardiff.

Beech, George 1976. Prosopography. In *Medieval studies: an introduction*, ed. James M. Powell, pp. 151–84. Syracuse.

Bennett, Judith M. 1983. Spouses, siblings and surnames: reconstructing families from medieval village court rolls. *Journal of British Studies*, 23: 26–46.

1986. The village ale-wife: women and brewing in fourteenth-century England. In *Women and work in pre-industrial Europe*, ed. Barbara Hanawalt, pp. 20–36. Bloomington.

1987. *Women in the medieval English countryside.* Oxford.
forthcoming. *Ale, beer and brewsters in England: Women's work in a changing world, c. 1300–1600.*

Benton, G. M. 1934. Archaeological notes: irregular markets held at Fingringhoe, etc., *temp.* Henry VI. *Transactions of the Essex Archaeological Society*, n. s., 21: 137–9.

Beresford, M. W. 1967. *New towns of the middle ages,* reprint, 1988. London.
1981. English medieval boroughs: a hand-list: revisions, 1973–81. *Urban History Yearbook:* 59–65.

Beresford, M. W. and Finberg, H.P.R. 1973. *English medieval boroughs: a hand-list.* Newton Abbot.

Beveridge, William H. 1929. A statistical crime of the seventeenth century. *Journal of Economic and Business History,* 1: 503–33.

Biddick, Kathleen 1985. Medieval English peasants and market involvement. *Journal of Economic History,* 45: 823–31.
1987. Missing links: taxable wealth, markets, and stratification among medieval English peasants. *Journal of Interdisciplinary History,* 18: 277–98.
1989. *The other economy: pastoral husbandry on a medieval estate.* Berkeley.

Bidwell, P. T. 1979. *The legionary bath-house and basilica and forum at Exeter.* Exeter.
1980. *Roman Exeter: fortress and town.* Exeter.

Blake, D. W. 1974. Bishop Leofric. *TDA*, 106: 47–57.

Blake, William 1915. Hooker's Synopsis Chorographical of Devonshire. *TDA*, 47: 334–48.

Blanchard, Ian 1972. The miner and the agricultural community in late medieval England. *Agricultural History Review*, 20: 93–106.
1974. Rejoinder: Stannator fabulosus. *Agricultural History Review*, 22: 62–74.

Blaylock, S. R. 1990. Exeter Guildhall. *PDAS*, 48: 123–78.

Bolton, Brenda 1968. Esperkeria congrorum. *Reports and Transactions of la Société guernesiaise,* 18: 288–96.

Bonney, Margaret 1990. *Lordship and the urban community: Durham and its overlords, 1250–1540.* Cambridge.

Born, Anne 1986. *A history of Kingsbridge and Salcombe.* Chichester.

Bracken, C. W. 1931. *A History of Plymouth.* Plymouth.

Braudel, Fernand 1981–84. *Civilization and capitalism 15th–18th century,* trans. Sian Reynolds, 3 vols. New York.

Brentano, L. 1870. On the history and development of gilds and the origin of trade-unions. In *English gilds,* ed. Lucy Toulmin Smith and Toulmin Smith (Early English Text Society, no. 40), pp. xlix–cxcix. London.

Bridbury, A. R. 1955. *England and the salt trade in the later middle ages* Oxford.
1975. *Economic growth: England in the later middle ages,* 2nd edn. New York.
1982. *Medieval English clothmaking: an economic survey.* London.

Britnell, R. H. 1978. English markets and royal administration before 1200. *EcHR*, 2nd ser., 31: 183–96.
1981a. Essex markets before 1350. *Essex Archaeology and History,* 3rd ser., 13: 15–21.
1981b. The proliferation of markets in England, 1200–1349. *EcHR*, 2nd ser., 34: 209–21.

1986a. Colchester courts and court records, 1310–1525. *Essex Archaeology and History*, 3rd ser., 17: 133–40.

1986b. *Growth and decline in Colchester, 1300–1525*. Cambridge.

1987. *Forstall*, forestalling and the Statute of Forestallers. *English Historical Review*, 102: 89–102.

1993. *The commercialisation of English society 1000–1500*. Cambridge.

Brooking-Rowe, J. B. 1906. *A history of Plympton Erle*. Exeter.

Bulst, Neithard and Genet, Jean-Philippe (eds.) 1986. *Medieval lives and the historian: studies in medieval prosopography*. Kalamazoo.

Burrow, Ian 1977. The town defences of Exeter. *TDA*, 109: 13–40.

Bush, Henry 1828. *Bristol town duties*. Bristol.

Butcher, A. F. 1979a. Canterbury's earliest rolls of freemen admissions, 1297–1363: a reconsideration. In *A Kentish miscellany*, ed. F. Hull, pp. 1–26. London.

1979b. Rent and the urban economy: Oxford and Canterbury in the later middle ages. *Southern History*, 1: 11–41.

1984. English urban history and the revolt of 1381. In *The English rising of 1381*, ed. R. H. Hilton and T. H. Aston, pp. 84–111. Cambridge.

Campbell, B.M.S. 1988. Towards an agricultural geography of medieval England. *Agricultural History Review*, 36: 87–98.

forthcoming. Intensive pastoral husbandry in medieval England: a Norfolk perspective. In *The salt of common life: essays in honor of J. Ambrose Raftis*, ed. Edwin DeWindt. Kalamazoo.

Campbell, Bruce M.S., Galloway, James A., Keene, Derek, and Murphy, Margaret 1993. *A medieval capital and its grain supply: agrarian production and distribution in the London region circa 1300* (Historical Geography Research Group, Research Paper Series, no. 30). London.

Carus-Wilson, E. M. 1941. An industrial revolution of the thirteenth century. *EcHR*, 11: 39–60.

1953. La guède française en Angleterre: un grand commerce du moyen âge. *Revue du nord*, 35: 89–105.

1957. The significance of the secular sculptures in the Lane Chapel, Cullompton. *Medieval archaeology*, 1: 104–57.

1959. The woollen industry before 1500. In *Victoria county history of Wiltshire*, vol. 4, ed. R. B. Pugh, pp. 115–47. London.

1963. *The expansion of Exeter at the close of the middle ages*. Exeter.

1967a. The aulnage accounts: a criticism. In *Medieval merchant venturers*, 2nd edn., pp. 279–91. London. First published in *EcHR*, 1st ser., 2 (1929).

1967b. The effects of the acquisition and of the loss of Gascony on the English wine trade. In *Medieval merchant venturers*, 2nd edn., pp. 265–78. London. First published in *Bulletin of the Institute of Historical Research*, 21 (1947).

1967c. The overseas trade of Bristol in the fifteenth century. In *Medieval merchant venturers*, 2nd edn., pp. 1–97. London. First published in *Studies in English trade in the fifteenth century*, eds. Eileen Power and M. M. Postan, 1933.

1967d. Trends in the export of English woollens in the fourteenth century. In *Medieval merchant venturers*, 2nd edn., pp. 239–64. London. First published in *EcHR*, 2nd ser., 3: 162–79.

Carus-Wilson, E. M. and Coleman, Olive 1963. *England's export trade 1275–1547*. Oxford.

Cate, James Lea 1938. The church and market reform in England during the reign of Henry III. In *Medieval and historiographical essays in honor of James Westfall Thompson*, ed. James Lea Cate and Eugene N. Anderson, pp. 27–65. Chicago.

Chanter, J. F. 1907. The swainmote courts of Exmoor, and the Devonshire portion and purlieus of the forest. *TDA*, 39: 267–301.

Chartres, J. A. 1977. *Internal trade in England 1500–1700*. London.

Cherry, Bridget and Pevesner, Nikolaus 1989. *Devon* (The buildings of England). London.

Cherry, Martin 1979. The Courtenay earls of Devon: the formation and disintegration of a late medieval aristocratic affinity. *Southern History*, 1: 71–90.

1981. The struggle for power in mid-fifteenth-century Devonshire. In *Patronage, the crown and the provinces in later medieval England*, ed. Ralph A. Griffiths, pp. 123–44. Gloucester.

1983–5. The liveried personnel of Edward Courtenay, earl of Devon, 1384–5. *DCNQ*, 35: 151–9, 189–93, 219–25, 258–63, 302–10.

Childs, Wendy R. 1978. *Anglo-Castilian trade in the later middle ages*. Manchester.

1986. Channel Island shipping as recorded in the English customs accounts, 1300–1500. In *A people of the sea: the maritime history of the Channel Islands*, ed. A. G. Jamieson, pp. 44–58. London.

1992. Devon's overseas trade in the late middle ages. In *A new maritime history of Devon*, vol. I, ed. M. Duffy, B. Greenhill, S. Fisher, and J. Youings, pp. 79–89. Exeter and London.

Chope, R. Pearse 1912a. The aulnager in Devon. *TDA*, 45: 568–96.

1912b. The silver mines in Devonshire. *DCNQ*, 7: 54–7.

1919. Devonshire wool. *DCNQ*, 10: 290–1.

Clark, E.A.G. 1960. *The ports of the Exe estuary 1660–1860*. Exeter.

Clark, Elaine 1977. Medieval debt litigation: Essex and Norfolk, 1270–1490. Unpublished Ph.D. thesis. University of Michigan.

1981. Debt litigation in a late medieval English vill. In *Pathways to medieval peasants*, ed. J. A. Raftis, pp. 247–79. Toronto.

Clarke, Kate M. 1912. The records of St. Nicholas' priory, Exeter. *TDA*, 44: 192–205.

Clarkson, L. A. 1960. The organization of the English leather industry in the late sixteenth and seventeenth centuries. *EcHR*, 2nd ser., 13: 245–53.

Coates, Bryan E. 1965. The origin and distribution of markets and fairs in medieval Derbyshire. *Derbyshire Archaeological Journal*, 85: 92–111.

Cobb, Henry S. 1961. Introduction. In *The local port book of Southampton for 1439–40* (Southampton Records Series, vol. 5), pp. xi–lxx. Southampton.

1973. Local port customs accounts prior to 1550. In *Prisca munimenta*, ed. F. Ranger, pp. 215–28. London.

Coleman, Olive 1960. Introduction. *The brokage book of Southampton, 1443–1444*, vol. 1 (Southampton Records Series, vol. 4). Southampton.

1963. Trade and prosperity in the fifteenth century: some aspects of the trade of Southampton. *EcHR*, 2nd ser., 16: 9–22.

Conyers, Angela 1973. Introduction. *Wiltshire extents for debts Edward I–*

Elizabeth I (Wiltshire Record Society, vol. 28), pp. 1–16. Devizes.

Corfield, Penelope J. and Keene, Derek (eds.) 1990. *Work in towns 850–1850.* Leicester.

Curtis, Muriel 1932. *Some disputes between the city and cathedral authorities of Exeter* (History of Exeter Research Group, no. 5). Manchester.

Darby, H. C. 1977. *Domesday England.* Cambridge.

Darby, H. C., Glasscock, R. E., Sheail, J., and Versey, G. R. 1979. The changing geographical wealth in England: 1086–1334–1525. *Journal of Historical Geography,* 5: 247–62.

Day, John 1987. The great bullion famine of the fifteenth century. In *The medieval market economy,* pp. 1–54. Oxford.

Day, W. I. Leeson 1934. *Holsworthy.* Torquay.

Deakin, Q. E. 1980. John Hooker's 'Description of Excester': a comparison of the manuscripts. *TDA*, 34: 229–38, 264–71.

Dendy, F. W. 1905. Purchases at Corbridge fair in 1298. *Archaeologia Aeliana,* 3rd ser., 2: 1–9.

Dennison, E. and Iles, R. 1988. Medieval fishponds in Avon. In *Medieval fish, fisheries and fishponds in England,* ed. Michael Aston, vol. 2, pp. 205–28. Oxford.

Devon Archaeological Society 1990. Excavations at Lower Coombe street, Exeter. *Devon Archaeological Society Newsletter,* 46: 8–9.

Dobson, R. B. 1973. Admissions to the freedom of the city of York in the later middle ages. *EcHR*, 2nd ser., 26: 1–22.

1984. The risings in York, Beverley and Scarborough, 1380–1381. In *The English rising of 1381,* ed. R. H. Hilton and T. H. Aston, pp. 112–42. Cambridge.

Dunning, M. and Stevenson, J. 1940. Richard Rowe of Plymouth, a fifteenth-century sea-dog. *DCNQ*, 21: 145–51.

Dunning, R. (ed.) 1974–85. *Victoria county history of Somerset,* vols. 3–5. London.

Dyer, Alan 1979. The market towns of south England. *Southern History,* 1: 123–34.

1991. *Decline and growth in English towns, 1400–1600.* London.

Dyer, Christopher 1972. A small landowner in the fifteenth century. *Midland History,* 1: 1–14.

1981. *Warwickshire farming 1349–c.1540: preparations for agricultural revolution* (Dugdale Society Occasional Papers, no. 27). Oxford.

1988. The consumption of fresh-water fish in medieval England. In *Medieval fish, fisheries and fishponds in England,* ed. Michael Aston, vol. 1, pp. 27–38. Oxford.

1989a. The consumer and the market in the later middle ages. *EcHR*, 2nd ser., 42: 305–27.

1989b. *Standards of living in the later middle ages: social change in England c.1200–1520.* Cambridge.

1989c. 'The retreat from marginal land': the growth and decline of medieval rural settlements. In *The rural settlements of medieval England,* eds. M. Aston, D. Austin, and C. Dyer, pp. 45–57. Oxford.

1990. Dispersed settlements in medieval England. A case study of Pendock, Worcestershire. *Medieval Archaeology,* 34: 97–121.

1992. The hidden trade of the middle ages: evidence from the West Midlands of England. *Journal of Historical Geography*, 18: 141–57.

Dymond, Robert 1880. The old inns and taverns of Exeter. *TDA*, 12: 387–416.

Easterling, R. C. 1931. Introduction. In B. Wilkinson, *The mediaeval council of Exeter*, pp. xiii–xxxiv. Manchester.

1938. List of civic officials in the twelfth and thirteenth centuries, c. 1100–1300. *TDA*, 70: 455–94.

Elton, Charles I. and Costelloe, B.F.C. (eds.) 1889. *First report of the Royal Commission on Market Rights and Rolls*. London.

Erskine, A. M. and Portman, D. 1960. The history of an Exeter tenement (229 High Street). *TDA*, 92: 142–57.

Erskine, Audrey M. 1962. The medieval financial records of the cathedral church of Exeter. *Journal of the Society of Archivists*, 2: 254–66.

1983. Introduction. *The accounts of the fabric of Exeter cathedral, Part 2: 1328–1353* (Devon and Cornwall Record Society, new ser., vol. 26). Torquay.

Everitt, Alan 1967. The marketing of agricultural produce. In *The agrarian history of England and Wales*, vol. 4, *1500–1640*, ed. Joan Thirsk, pp. 466–592. Cambridge.

Exeter City Library 1965. *Exeter borough courts: an exhibition of city archives*. Exeter.

Farmer, David L. 1989. Two Wiltshire manors and their markets. *Agricultural History Review*, 37: 1–11.

1991a. Marketing the produce of the countryside, 1200–1500: an essay. In *The agrarian history of England and Wales, III, 1348–1500,* ed. E. Miller, pp. 324–430. Cambridge.

1991b. Prices and wages, 1350–1500. In *The agrarian history of England and Wales, III, 1348–1500,* ed. E. Miller, pp. 431–525. Cambridge.

Finberg, H.P.R. 1947. Some early Tavistock charters. *English Historical Review*, 62: 352–77.

1950. The customs of Stokenham. *DCNQ*, 25: 69–70.

1952a. The borough of Tavistock. In *Devonshire studies*. eds. H.P.R. Finberg and W. G. Hoskins, pp. 172–97. Oxford.

1952b. The open field in Devon. In *Devonshire studies,* eds. H.P.R. Finberg and W. G. Hoskins, pp. 265–88. Oxford.

1957. The genesis of the Gloucestershire towns. In *Gloucestershire studies,* ed. H.P.R. Finberg, pp. 52–88. Leicester.

1969. *Tavistock abbey: a study in the social and economic history of Devon*. Newton Abbot.

Findlay, D. F. 1939. The fabric rolls of Exeter cathedral, 1370–1520. Unpublished Ph.D. thesis. University of Leeds.

Flower, C. T. (ed.) 1944. Introduction. *The curia regis rolls 1199–1230 A.D.* (Selden Society, vol. 62), London.

Fox, H.S.A. 1972. Field systems of east and south Devon. Part I: east Devon. *TDA*, 104: 81–135.

1975. The chronology of enclosure and economic development in medieval Devon. *EcHR*, 2nd ser., 28: 181–202.

1986. Exeter, Devonshire, *circa* 1420. In *Local maps and plans from medieval England*, ed. R. A. Skelton and P.D.A. Harvey, pp. 163–9. Oxford.

1989. Peasant farmers, patterns of settlement and *pays*: transformations in the landscapes of Devon and Cornwall during the later middle ages. In *Landscape and townscape in the south west*, ed. Robert Higham, pp. 41–73. Exeter.

1991. Devon and Cornwall. In *The agrarian history of England and Wales, III, 1348–1500,* ed. E. Miller, pp. 152–74, 303–23, 722–43. Cambridge.

forthcoming. Medieval rural industry and mining. In *An historical atlas of South-West England,* ed. R.J.P. Kain and W. Ravenhill. Exeter.

Fraser, Constance 1969. The pattern of trade in the north-east of England, 1265–1350. *Northern History,* 4: 44–66.

Fryde, E. B. 1974. Italian maritime trade with medieval England (c.1270–c.1530). *Recueils de la société Jean Bodin,* 32: 291–337.

1976. The English cloth industry and the trade with the Mediterranean c.1370-c.1530. *Produzione, commercio et consumo dei panni di lana*, pp. 243–63. Florence.

Gardiner, Dorothy A. 1966. John Hawley of Dartmouth. *TDA*, 98: 173–205.

Gasquet, F. A. 1908. *The Black Death of 1348 and 1349*, 2nd edn. London.

Gilchrist, Roberta 1988. A reappraisal of Dinas Powys: local exchange and specialized livestock production in 5th- to 7th-century Wales. *Medieval Archaeology,* 32: 50–62.

Gill, Crispin 1966. *Plymouth, a new history: ice age to the Elizabethans.* Newton Abbot.

1987. Plymouth's Sutton Pool. In *A living from the sea,* ed. M. G. Dickinson, pp. 3–13. Exeter.

Glasscock, R. E. 1973. England *circa* 1334. In *A new historical geography of England*, ed. H. C. Darby, pp. 136–85. Cambridge.

Goldberg, P.J.P. 1986a. Female labour, service and marriage in the late medieval urban North. *Northern History*, 22: 18–38.

1986b. Marriage, migration, servanthood and life-cycle in Yorkshire towns of the later middle ages: some York cause paper evidence. *Continuity and Change*, 1: 141–69.

1988. Women in fifteenth-century town life. In *Towns and townspeople in the fifteenth century,* ed. John A. F. Thomson, pp. 107–28. Gloucester.

1990a. Urban identity and the poll taxes of 1377, 1379, and 1381. *EcHR*, 2nd ser., 43: 194–216.

1990b. Women's work, women's role, in the late-medieval North. In *Profit, piety and the professions in later medieval England,* ed. M. A. Hicks, pp. 34–50. Gloucester.

1992. *Women, work, and life cycle in a medieval economy: women in York and Yorkshire c. 1300–1520.* Oxford.

Goodfellow, Peter 1988. Medieval markets in Northamptonshire. *Northamptonshire Past and Present,* 7: 305–23.

Goose, Nigel 1982. English pre-industrial urban economies. *Urban History Yearbook:* 24–30.

Gover, J.E.B., Mawer, A., and Stenton, F.M. 1931–2. *The place-names of Devon,* 2 vols. (English Place-name Society, vols. 8–9), Cambridge.

Grant, E. 1988. Marine and river fishing in medieval Somerset: fishbone evidence from Langport. In *Medieval fish, fisheries and fishponds in England,* vol. 2, ed. Michael Aston, pp. 409–16, Oxford.

Gray, H. L. 1924. The production and exportation of English woollens in the fourteenth century. *EHR*, 39: 13–35.

1966. English foreign trade from 1446 to 1482. In *Studies in English trade in the fifteenth century*, ed. Eileen Power and M. M. Postan, pp. 1–38. New York.

Green, Alice Stopford 1894. *Town life in the fifteenth century*, 2 vols. London.

Gross, Charles 1890. *The gild merchant*, 2 vols. Oxford.

Hallam, H. E. 1981. *Rural England 1066–1348*. Glasgow.

Hanawalt, Barbara 1977. Community conflict and social control: crime and justice in the Ramsey abbey villages. *Mediaeval Studies*, 39: 402–23.

1979. *Crime and conflict in English communities, 1300–1348*. Cambridge, MA.

Harte, Walter J. (no date). *Gleanings from the Common Place Book of John Hooker, relating to the city of Exeter (1485–1590)*. Exeter.

Haslam, Jeremy 1984. The towns of Devon. In *Anglo-Saxon towns in southern England*, ed. Jeremy Haslam, pp. 249–83. Chichester.

Hastings, Margaret 1947. *The court of common pleas in fifteenth century England*. Ithaca.

Hatcher, John 1969. A diversified economy: later medieval Cornwall. *EcHR*, 2nd ser., 22: 208–27.

1970. *Rural economy and society in the Duchy of Cornwall 1300–1500*. Cambridge.

1973. *English tin production and trade before 1550*. Oxford.

1974. Myths, miners, and agricultural communities. *Agricultural History Review*, 22: 54–61.

1988. South-western England. In *The agrarian history of England and Wales, II, 1042–1350*, ed. H. E. Hallam, pp. 234–45, 383–98, 675–85. Cambridge.

Healy, Charles E. H. Chadwyck 1901. *The history of part of west Somerset*, London.

Heath, Peter 1968. North sea fishing in the fifteenth century: the Scarborough fleet. *Northern History*, 3: 53–69.

Heaton, Herbert 1965. *The Yorkshire woollen and worsted industries from the earliest times up to the industrial revolution*, 2nd edn. Oxford.

Henderson, C. G. and Bidwell, P. T. 1982. The Saxon minster at Exeter. In *The early church in western Britain and Ireland*, ed. Susan M. Pearce (BAR British series, no. 102), pp. 145–75. Oxford.

Henderson, Christopher 1988. Exeter (Isca Dumnoniorum). In *Fortress into city*, ed. Graham Webster, pp. 91–119. London.

Henry, Robert L. 1926. *Contracts in the local courts of medieval England*. London.

Hewitt, Ethel M. 1911. Textiles. In *Victoria county history of Somerset*, vol. 2, ed. W. Page, pp. 405–24. London.

Hewitt, H. J. 1958. *The Black Prince's expedition of 1355–1357*. Manchester.

1960. Medieval Plymouth. *Annual Report and Transactions of the Plymouth Institution*, 23: 48–52.

Hewitt, J. 1966. *The organization of war under Edward III, 1338–62*. Manchester.

Higham, R. A. 1977. Excavations at Okehampton castle, Devon. Part 1: the motte and keep. *PDAS*, 35: 3–42.

Higham, R. A., Allan, J. P., and Blaylock, S. R. 1982. Excavations at Okehampton castle, Devon: part 2: the bailey. *PDAS*, 40: 19–151.

Hill, David 1981. *An atlas of Anglo-Saxon England*. Toronto.

Hill, Francis 1965. *Medieval Lincoln*. Cambridge.

Hilton, R. H. 1967. Some problems of urban real property in the middle ages.

In *Socialism, capitalism and economic growth,* ed. C. H. Feinstein, pp. 326–37. Cambridge.

1982. Lords, burgesses and hucksters. *Past and Present,* 97: 3–15.

1984. Small town society in England before the Black Death. *Past and Present,* 105: 53–78.

1985. Medieval market towns and simple commodity production. *Past and Present,* 109: 3–23.

1990. Women traders in medieval England. In *Class conflict and the crisis of feudalism,* 2nd edn. London.

Hindle, B. P. 1976. The road network of medieval England and Wales. *Journal of Historical Geography,* 2: 207–21.

Hockey, S. F. 1968. Otterton priory and Mont St. Michel its Mother-House. *DCNQ,* 31: 1–10.

Hodgen, Margaret Traube 1942. Fairs of Elizabethan England. *Economic Geography,* 18: 389–400.

Hodges, R. and Mainman, A. 1984. The Saxo-Norman imported pottery. In *Medieval and post-medieval finds from Exeter, 1971–1980,* ed. J. P. Allan, pp. 13–18. Exeter.

Hohenberg, Paul M. and Lees, Lynn Hollen 1985. *The making of urban Europe 1000–1900.* Cambridge, MA.

Holden, E. W. 1989. Slate roofing in medieval Sussex. *Sussex Archaeological Collections,* 127: 73–88.

Holt, Richard 1985. Gloucester in the century after the Black Death. *Transactions of the Bristol and Gloucestershire Archaeological Society,* 103: 149–61.

1988. *The mills of medieval England.* Oxford.

Hoskins, W. G. 1935. *Industry, trade, and people in Exeter, 1688–1800.* Manchester.

1947. Chagford and Moreton markets. *DCNQ,* 23: 21–2.

1952. The wealth of medieval Devon. In *Devonshire Studies,* ed. W. G. Hoskins and H.P.R. Finberg, pp. 212–49. London.

1963a. *Provincial England.* London.

1963b. *Two thousand years in Exeter,* reprint 1974. Chichester.

1970. *The westward expansion of Wessex* (Dept. of English Local History Occasional Papers, no. 13). Leicester.

1972. *Devon,* new edn. Newton Abbot.

Hudson, William and Tingey, John Cottingham 1910. Introduction. *The records of the city of Norwich,* vol. II, pp. i–cxlviii. Norwich and London.

Hunt, T. J. 1957. Some notes on the cloth trade in Taunton in the thirteenth century. *Somersetshire Archaeological and Natural History Society Proceedings,* 101: 89–107.

Izacke, Richard 1724. *Remarkable antiquities of the city of Exeter,* 2nd edn. London.

Jackson, A. M. 1972. Medieval Exeter, the Exe and the earldom of Devon. *TDA,* 104: 57–79.

James, M. K. 1971. *Studies in the medieval wine trade.* Oxford.

Joce, T. J. 1912. The Exeter and Dartmouth road. *TDA,* 44: 597–604.

1918. The original main road west of Exeter. *TDA,* 50: 411–16.

Jones, Philip E. 1976. *The butchers of London.* London.

Jope, E. M. and Dunning, G. C. 1954. The use of blue slate for roofing in medieval England. *Antiquaries Journal*, 34: 209–17.

Juddery, J. Z., Staniforth, P. R., and Stoyle, M. 1989. *Exeter city defences: expenditure on the walls and gates recorded in the Receivers' accounts 1339–1450* (Exeter Museums Archaeological Field Unit, Report no. 89.09). Exeter.

Keene, Derek 1985. *Survey of medieval Winchester*. Oxford.

1989a. Medieval London and its region. *The London Journal*, 14: 99–111.

1989b. The property market in English towns A.D. 1100–1600. In *D'une ville à l'autre: structures matérielles et organisation de l'espace dans les villes européennes (xiiie–xvie siècle)*, ed. Jean-Claude Maire Vigueur, pp. 201–26. Rome.

1990. Shops and shopping in medieval London. In *Medieval art, architecture and archaeology in London*, ed. Lindy Grant, pp. 29–46. London.

Kelly, Serena, Rutledge, Elizabeth, and Tillyard, Margot 1983. *Men of property: an analysis of the Norwich enrolled deeds 1285–1311*, ed. Ursula Priestly. Norwich.

Kermode, Jennifer I. 1991. Money and credit in the fifteenth century: some lessons from Yorkshire. *Business History Review*, 65: 475–501.

Kingsford, C. L. 1925. *Prejudice and promise in fifteenth-century England*. Oxford.

Kowaleski, Maryanne 1980. Taxpayers in late fourteenth century Exeter: the 1377 murage roll. *DCNQ*, 34: 217–22.

1982. Local markets and merchants in late fourteenth-century Exeter. Unpublished Ph.D. thesis. University of Toronto.

1984. The commercial dominance of a medieval provincial oligarchy: Exeter in the late fourteenth century. *Mediaeval Studies*, 46: 355–84.

1985. The 1377 Dartmouth poll tax. *DCNQ*, 35: 286–95.

1986. Women and work in a market town: Exeter in the late fourteenth century. In *Women and work in pre-industrial Europe*, ed. Barbara Hanawalt, pp. 145–64. Bloomington.

1988. The Exeter port customs project. *Computing and History Today*, 3: 24–7.

1990. Town and country in late medieval England: the hide and leather trade. In *Work in towns 850–1850*, eds. Penelope J. Corfield and Derek Keene, pp. 57–73. Leicester.

1992. Port towns in fourteenth-century Devon. In *A new maritime history of Devon*, vol. I, ed. M. Duffy, B. Greenhill, S. Fisher, D. Starkey, and J. Youings, pp. 62–72. London.

1993. Introduction. In *The local port customs accounts of the city of Exeter 1266–1321* (Devon and Cornwall Record Society, new ser., vol. 36). Exeter.

forthcoming. The grain trade in fourteenth-century Devon. In *The salt of common life: essays in honor of J. Ambrose Raftis*, ed. E. B. DeWindt. Kalamazoo.

Laithwaite, Michael 1971. Two medieval houses in Ashburton. *PDAS*, 29: 181–94.

Langdon, John 1984. Horse hauling: a revolution in vehicle transport in twelfth- and thirteenth-century England? *Past and Present*, 103: 37–66.

1986. *Horses, oxen and technological innovation: the use of draught animals in English farming from 1066–1500*. Cambridge.

Lega-Weekes, Ethel 1903. Neighbors of North Wyke. Part III. In South

Tawton. *TDA*, 35: 497–538.

1912. An account of the hospitium de le Egle, some ancient chapels in the Close, and some persons connected therewith. *TDA*, 44: 480–511.

1914. Athelstan's dyke, Exeter. *DCNQ*, 8: 210–21.

1915. *Some studies in the topography of the cathedral close Exeter*. Exeter.

Legett, Jennifer I. 1972. The 1377 poll tax return for the city of York. *Yorkshire Archaeological Journal*, 43: 128–46.

Levitan, Bruce 1989. Bone analysis and the urban economy: examples of selectivity and a case for comparison. In *Diet and craft in towns*, ed. D. Serjeantson and T. Waldron, pp. 161–88. Oxford.

Lewis, G. R. 1908. *The stannaries: a study of the medieval tin miners of Devon and Cornwall*. Cambridge, MA.

Lipson, E. 1959. *Economic history of England*, vol. I, *The middle ages*, 12th edn. London.

Litler, Alison S. 1979. Fish in English economy and society down to the Reformation. Unpublished Ph.D. thesis. University of Wales, Swansea.

Little, A. G. and Easterling, R. C. 1927. *The Franciscans and Dominicans of Exeter* (History of Exeter Research Group, no. 3). Exeter.

Lloyd, T. H. 1982. *Alien merchants in England in the high middle ages*. New York.

Lysons, Daniel 1822. *Magna Britannia*, vol. 6, *Topographical and historical account of Devonshire*. London.

MacCaffrey, Wallace T. 1975. *Exeter, 1540–1640: the growth of an English country town*, 2nd edn. Cambridge, MA.

MacDermot, Edward T. 1973. *A history of the forest of Exmoor*, revised edn. Newton Abbot.

Mace, Frances A. 1925a. Devonshire ports in the fourteenth and fifteenth centuries. *Transactions of the Royal Historical Society*, 4th ser., 8: 98–126.

1925b. The trade and industry of Devonshire in the later middle ages. Unpublished M.A. thesis. University of London.

Macfarlane, Alan 1977. *Reconstructing historical communities*. Cambridge.

Maddicott, J. R. 1989. Trade, industry and the wealth of King Alfred. *Past and Present*, 123: 1–51.

1992. Trade, industry and the wealth of King Alfred: a reply. *Past and Present*, 135: 164–88.

Madox, Thomas 1726: *Firma burgi*. London.

Maltby, Mark 1979. *Faunal studies on urban sites: the animal bones from Exeter, 1971–1975*. Sheffield.

Marshall, William 1796. *Rural economy of the West of England*, 2 vols., reprint 1970. London.

Masschaele, James 1992. Market rights in thirteenth-century England. *English Historical Review*, 107: 78–89.

1993. Transport costs in medieval England. *Economic History Review*, 46: 266–79.

Mastoris, S. N. 1986. Regulating the Nottingham markets: new evidence from a mid-thirteenth century manuscript. *Transactions of the Thoroton Society*, 90: 79–83.

Maxwell-Lyte, H. C. 1909. *A history of Dunster*. London.

McClenaghan, Barbara 1924. *The Springs of Lavenham and the Suffolk cloth trade in the XV and XVI centuries.* Ipswich.

McClure, Peter 1979. Patterns of migration in the late middle ages: the evidence of English place-name surnames. *EcHR*, 2nd ser., 32: 167–82.

McCutcheon, K. L. 1940. *Yorkshire fairs and markets to the end of the eighteenth century* (Thoresby Society, vol. 39). Leeds.

McDonnell, John 1988. The role of transhumance in northern England. *Northern History*, 24: 1–17.

McGovern, William M. 1968. Contract in medieval England: wager of law and the effect of death. *Iowa Law Review*, 54: 19–62.

McIntosh, Marjorie Keniston 1986. *Autonomy and community: the royal manor of Havering, 1200–1500.* Cambridge.

McLean, Teresa 1980. *Medieval English gardens.* London.

Millet, Hélène (ed.) 1985. *Informatique et prosopographie: actes du table ronde de CNRS.* Paris.

Milsom, S.F.C. 1966. Account stated in the action of debt. *Law Quarterly Review*, 82: 535–45.

1981. *Historical foundations of the common law*, 2nd edn. London.

Modbury Local History Society 1971. *A history of Modbury.* Plymouth.

Mollat, Michel 1952. *Le commerce maritime normand à la fin de moyen âge.* Paris.

Mols, Roger 1955. *Introduction à la démographie historique des villes d'Europe du XIVe au XVIIIe siècle*, vol. 2. Louvain.

Moore, Ellen Wedemeyer 1985. *The fairs of medieval England: an introductory study.* Toronto.

Morgan, F. W. 1940. The Domesday geography of Devon. *TDA*, 72: 305–31.

Morley, Beric M. 1983. Leigh Barton, Churchstow, south Devon. *PDAS*, 41: 81–106.

Morris, Percy 1932. Report on the underground passages in Exeter. *Proceedings of the Devon Archaeological Exploration Society*, 1: 191–200.

Munro, J. H. 1978. Wool-price schedules and the qualities of English wools in the later middle ages c. 1270–1499. *Textile History*, 9: 119–69.

1983. Bullion flows and monetary contraction in late-medieval England and the Low Countries. In *Precious metals in the later medieval and early modern worlds*, ed. J. F. Richards, pp. 97–158. Durham, NC.

Nelson, Janet L. 1992. Debate: trade, industry and the wealth of King Alfred. *Past and Present*, 135: 151–63.

Nicholls, Laura M. 1960. The trading communities of Totnes and Dartmouth in the late fifteenth and early sixteenth centuries. Unpublished M.A. thesis. University of Exeter.

1964. The lay subsidy of 1523. *University of Birmingham Historical Journal*, 9: 1–29.

Nightingale, Pamela 1990. Monetary contraction and mercantile credit in later medieval England. *EcHR*, 2nd ser., 43: 560–75.

North, D. C. 1985. Transaction costs in history. *Journal of European Economic History*, 14: 557–83.

North, Douglass C. and Thomas, Robert Paul 1973. *The rise of the western world: a new economic history.* Cambridge.

O'Donnell, John 1971. Market centres in Herefordshire, 1200–1400. *Transactions of the Woolhope Naturalists' Field Club*, 40: 186–94.

Oliver, George 1861. *History of the city of Exeter*. Exeter.

1864. *Monasticon diocesis Exoniensis*. Exeter and London.

Oppenheim, M. 1968. *The maritime history of Devon*. Exeter.

Orme, Nicholas 1981. The medieval clergy of Exeter cathedral. I. The vicars and annuellars. *TDA*, 113: 79–102.

1983. The medieval clergy of Exeter cathedral. II. The secondaries and choristers. *TDA*, 115: 79–100.

1986. *Exeter cathedral as it was, 1050–1550*. Exeter.

1987. The 'lost' parish of Dotton. *DCNQ*, 36:1: 1–5.

1991. The charnel chapel of Exeter cathedral. In *Medieval art and architecture at Exeter cathedral*, ed. Francis Kelly, pp. 162–71. Leeds.

Palliser, David 1983. *The age of Elizabeth: England under the later Tudors 1547–1603*. London.

1988. Urban decay revisited. In *Towns and townspeople in the fifteenth century*, ed. John A.F. Thomson, pp. 1–21. Gloucester.

Palliser, D. M. and Pinnock, A. C. 1971. The markets of medieval Staffordshire. *North Staffordshire Journal of Field Studies*, 11: 49–63.

Palmer, Robert C. 1993. *English law in the age of the Black Death, 1348–1381*. Chapel Hill and London.

Parry, H. Lloyd 1936. *The history of the Exeter guildhall and the life within*. Exeter.

1941. The government of Exeter – a survey. *TDA*, 73: 29–50.

1960. *St. Nicholas Priory Exeter: historical summary*, revised by Joyce Youings. Exeter and London.

Patten, John 1977. Urban occupations in pre-industrial England. *Transactions of the Institute of British Geographers*, new ser., 2: 296–313.

Pelham, R. A. 1951. Medieval foreign trade: eastern ports. In *An historical geography of England before 1800*, ed. H. C. Darby, pp. 298–329. Cambridge.

Penn, Simon 1983. The origins of Bristol migrants in the early fourteenth century: the surname evidence. *Bristol and Gloucestershire Archaeological Society Transactions*, 101: 123–30.

Peter, Richard and Peter, Otho Bathhurst 1885. *The histories of Launceston and Dunheved*. Plymouth.

Phelps Brown, E. H. and Hopkins, Sheila V. 1956. Seven centuries of the prices of consumables compared with builders' wage-rates. *Economica*, 92; reprinted in Henry Phelps Brown and Sheila V. Hopkins, *A perspective of wages and prices*, pp. 13–59. London.

Phythian-Adams, Charles 1979. *Desolation of a city: Coventry and the urban crisis of the late middle ages*. Cambridge.

Pickard, Ransom 1947. *The population and epidemics of Exeter*. Exeter.

Pistono, Stephen P. 1979. Henry IV and John Hawley, privateer, 1399–1408. *TDA*, 111: 145–63.

Platt, Colin 1973. *Medieval Southampton: the port and trading community, A.D. 1000–1600*. London.

1976. *The English medieval town*. New York.

Poos, L. R. and Smith, R. M. 1984. Legal windows onto historical populations? Recent research on demography and the manor court in medieval England.

Law and History Review, 2: 128–52.
1986. Shades still on the window: a reply to Zvi Razi. *Law and History Review*, 3: 409–29.
Porter, J. H. 1984. Teign oyster beds. *DCNQ*, 35: 174–80.
Portman, D. 1966. *Exeter houses 1400–1700*. Exeter.
Postan, M. M. 1973a. Credit in medieval trade. In *Medieval trade and finance*, pp. 1–27. Cambridge. First printed in *EcHR*, 1, 1928.
1973b. Partnership in English medieval commerce. In *Medieval trade and finance*, pp. 65–91. First printed in *Rivista della Societa*, 11, 1957.
1973c. Private financial instruments in medieval England. In *Medieval trade and finance*, pp. 28–64. Cambridge. First printed in *Vierteljahrschrift für Social- und Wirtschaftsgeschchte*, 13, 1930.
Postles, David 1984. Customary carrying services. *Journal of Transport History*, 3rd ser., 5: 1–15.
1987. Markets for rural produce in Oxfordshire, 1086–1350. *Midland History*, 12: 14–26.
Postles, David with Richard McKinley 1994. *The surnames of Devon* (English Surnames series). Leicester.
Pound, J. F. 1966. The social and trade structure of Norwich 1525–1575. *Past and Present*, 34: 49–69.
1981. The validity of the freemen's lists: some Norwich evidence. *EcHR*, 2nd ser., 34: 48–59.
Pound, John 1988. *Tudor and Stuart* Norwich. Chichester.
Powell, Arthur Herbert 1907. *The ancient borough of Bridgewater*. Bridgewater.
Power, Eileen 1941. *The wool trade in English medieval history*. Oxford.
Power, Eileen and Postan, M. M. (eds.) 1933. *Studies in English trade in the fifteenth century*, reprint, 1966. New York.
Putnam, Bertha 1908. *The enforcement of the Statutes of Labourers during the first decade after the Black Death*. New York.
R.B.M. 1928. Medieval fairs, duration of. *DCNQ*, 15: 125–7.
R.B.M. 1929. Denizens, 1436. *DCNQ*, 15: 236–9.
Radford, Cecily 1950. Three centuries of playgoing in Exeter. *TDA*, 82: 241–69.
Radford, G. H. (Mrs) 1903. Nicholas Radford 1385(?)–1455. *TDA*, 35: 251–78.
1912. The fight at Clyst in 1455. *TDA*, 44: 252–65.
Raftis, J. A. 1965. Social structure in five east Midland villages. *EcHR*, 2nd ser., 18: 81–99.
1982. *A small town in late medieval England: Godmanchester 1278–1400*. Toronto.
1990. *Early Tudor Godmanchester: survivals and new arrivals*. Toronto.
Ramsay, G. D. 1965. *The Wiltshire woollen industry in the sixteenth and seventeenth centuries*, 2nd edn. London.
Rappaport, Steve 1991. Reconsidering apprenticeship in sixteenth-century London. In *Renaissance society and culture: essays in honor of Eugene F. Rice, Jr.*, ed. John Monfasani and Ronald G. Musto, pp. 239–61. New York.
Rawcliffe, Carole 1991. 'That kindliness should be cherished more, and discord driven out': the settlement of commercial disputes by arbitration in later medieval England. In *Enterprise and individuals in fifteenth-century England*,

ed. Jennifer Kermode, pp. 99–117. Wolfeboro Falls, NH.

Razi, Zvi 1979. The Toronto school's reconstitution of medieval peasant society: a critical view. *Past and Present,* 85: 141–57.

1985. The use of manorial court rolls in demographic analysis: a reconsideration. *Law and History Review,* 3: 191–200.

1987. The demographic transparency of manorial court rolls. *Law and History Review,* 5: 523–35.

Reed, Michael 1978. Markets and fairs in medieval Buckinghamshire. *Records of Buckinghamshire,* 20: 563–85.

Reichel, Oswald J. 1897. Extracts from the pipe rolls of Henry II relating to Devon. *TDA*, 29: 453–509.

1910. The hundred of Sulfretona or Hairidge in early times. *TDA*, 42: 215–57.

1918. Extracts from the Hundred Rolls of 3 Edward I. *TDA*, 50: 353–81.

1923. The manor and hundred of Crediton. *TDA*, 54: 146–81.

1934a. The hundred of Cliston in early times. In *The Hundreds of Devon,* supplement 7, pp. 363–85. Exeter

1934b. The hundred of Colyton in early times. In *The Hundreds of Devon,* supplement 7, pp. 333–62. Exeter.

1935. The hundred of Braunton in early times. In *The Hundreds of Devon,* supplement 8, pp. 387–459. Torquay.

Reynolds, Susan 1969. The forged charters of Barnstaple. *English Historical Review,* 84: 699–720.

1977. *An introduction to the history of English medieval towns.* Oxford.

Rich, E. E. 1934. Introduction. *The staple court book of Bristol* (Bristol Record Society, vol. 5), pp. 1–91. Bristol.

Roberts, Michael 1990. Women and work in sixteenth-century English towns. In *Work in towns 850–1850,* eds. Penelope J. Corfield and Derek Keene, pp. 86–102. Leicester.

Roncière, Charles de la 1976. *Florence: centre économique régional au xiv*[e] *siècle.* Aix-en-Provence.

Rose-Troup, Frances 1912. The Kalenders and the Exeter trade-gilds before the Reformation. *TDA*, 44: 406–30.

1923. *Lost chapels of Exeter* (History of Exeter Research Group, no. 1). Exeter.

1928. Bishop Grandisson: student and art-lover. *TDA*, 60: 239–75.

Ross, Alan S. C. 1956. The assize of bread. *EcHR*, 2nd ser., 9: 332–42.

Rosser, Gervase 1989. *Medieval Westminster 1200–1540.* Oxford.

Rowe, Margery M. 1977. Introduction. *Tudor Exeter tax assessments 1489–1595* (Devon and Cornwall Record Society, new ser., vol. 22), pp. v–xvii. Exeter.

Rowe, Margery M. and Cochlin, John 1964. *Mayors of Exeter from the 13th century to the present day.* Exeter.

Rowe, Margery M. and Draisy, John M. 1989. Introduction. *The receivers' accounts of the city of Exeter 1304–1353* (Devon and Cornwall Record Society, new ser., vol. 32), pp. vii–xxxi. Exeter.

Rowe, Margery M. and Jackson, Andrew M. 1973. Introduction. *Exeter freemen 1266–1967* (Devon and Cornwall Record Society, extra ser., vol. 1), pp. xi–xxxv. Exeter.

Ruddock, A. 1951. *Italian merchants and shipping in Southampton, 1270–1600* (Southampton Records Series, vol. 1). Southampton.

1946. Alien hosting in Southampton in the fifteenth century. *EcHR*, 1st ser., 16: 30–7.

Runyan, Timothy J. 1986. Ships and fleets in Anglo-French warfare, 1337–1360. *American Neptune*, 46: 91–8.

Russell, J. C. 1948. *British medieval population*. Albuquerque.

1972. *Medieval regions and their cities*. Bloomington.

Russell, Percy 1950. *Dartmouth: a history of the port and town*. London.

1951. Some historical notes on the Brixham fisheries. *TDA*, 83: 278–97.

1960. *A history of Torquay*. Torquay.

1964. *The good town of Totnes*, 2nd impression with Introduction by E. N. Masson Phillips, 1984. Exeter.

Rutledge, Elizabeth 1988. Immigration and population growth in early fourteenth-century Norwich: evidence from the tithing rolls. *Urban History Yearbook:* 15–30.

Sabine, E. L. 1933. Butchering. *Speculum*, 8: 335–52.

Salter, T.R. 1985. The urban hierarchy in medieval Staffordshire. *Journal of Historical Geography*, 11: 115–37.

Salusbury, G. T. 1948. *Street life in medieval England*, 2nd edn. Oxford.

Salzman, L. F. 1928. The legal status of markets. *Cambridge Historical Journal*, 2: 205–12.

1931. *English trade in the middle ages*. Oxford.

1950. Mines and stannaries. In *The English government at work, 1327–1336*, vol. 3, ed. James F. Willard, William A. Morris, and William H. Dunham, pp. 67–104. Cambridge, MA.

1964. *English industries of the middle ages*, new edn. London.

Sanders, I. J. 1960. *English baronies: a study of their origin and descent 1086–1322*. Oxford.

Saul, A. 1975. Great Yarmouth in the fourteenth century: a study in trade, society and politics. Unpublished Ph.D. thesis. Oxford.

Schofield, R. S. 1965. The geographical distribution of wealth in England, 1334–1649. *EcHR*, 2nd ser., 18: 483–510.

Schopp, J. W. 1925. Introduction. *The Anglo-Norman custumal of Exeter* (History of Exeter Research Group, no. 2), pp. 5–23. Oxford.

Scott, J.G.M. 1968. Casting a bell for Exeter cathedral 1372. *TDA*, 100: 191–203.

Seebohm, Mabel E. 1952. *The evolution of the English farm*, 2nd edn. London.

Seward, David 1970. The Devonshire cloth industry in the early seventeenth century. In *Industry and society in the south-west*, ed. Rogert Burt (Exeter papers in economic history), pp. 29–50. Exeter.

Shaw, David Gary 1993. *The creation of a community: the city of Wells in the middle ages*. Oxford.

Sheldon, Gilbert 1928. *From trackway to turnpike: an illustration from east Devon*. Oxford.

Sherborne, J. W. 1965. *The port of Bristol in the middle ages*. Bristol.

1967. The Hundred Years' War. The English navy: shipping and manpower

1369–1389. *Past and Present*, 37: 163–75.

Sherwell, J. W. 1937. *The history of the guild of saddlers of the city of London*, rev. edn. London.

Shiel, Norman, 1980. The Saxon and medieval mint. In *Exeter coinage*, ed. J. Andrews, W. Elston, and N. Shiel, pp. 9–17. Exeter.

Shorter, A. H., Ravenhill, W.L.D., and Gregory, K. J. (eds.) 1969. *Southwest England*. London.

Singer, Barbara 1980. The recovery of market toll at common law. *The Irish Jurist*, 1978, new ser., 13: 348–71.

Siraut, M. C. 1985. Stogumber. In *The Victoria history of the county of Somerset*, ed. R. W. Dunning, vol. 5, pp. 177–89. London.

Smith, Carol A. 1974. Economics of marketing systems: models from economic geography. *Annual Review of Anthropology*, 3: 167–201.

(ed.) 1976. *Regional analysis*, 2 vols. New York.

Snow, Vernon F. 1977. *Parliament in Elizabethan England: John Hooker's 'Order and Usage'*. New Haven.

Southward, Alan, Boalch, Gerald, and Maddock, Linda 1988. Climatic change and the herring and pilchard fisheries of Devon and Cornwall. In *Devon's coastline and coastal waters: aspects of man's relationship to the sea*, ed. David J. Starkey, pp. 33–57. Exeter.

Stephens, W. B. 1958. *Seventeenth-century Exeter: a study of industrial and commercial development, 1625–1688* (History of Exeter Research Group, no. 9). Exeter.

Stoljar, S. J. 1964: The transformations of account. *Law Quarterly Review*, 80: 203–24.

Stone, Lawrence 1987. Prosopography. In *The past and the present revisited*, pp. 45–73. New York. First published in *Daedulus*, 1971.

Stoyle, Mark, Juddery, J. Z. and Staniforth, P. R. forthcoming. *The medieval aqueducts of Exeter* (Exeter Museums Archaeological Field Unit Report). Exeter.

Swanson, Heather 1983. *Building craftsmen in late medieval York* (Borthwick papers, no. 63). York.

1988. The illusion of economic structure: craft guilds in late medieval English towns. *Past and Present*, 121: 29–48.

1989. *Medieval artisans*. Oxford.

1990. Artisans in the urban economy: the documentary evidence from York. In *Work in towns 850–1850*, eds. Penelope J. Corfield and Derek Keene, pp. 42–56. Leicester.

Tait, James 1936. *The medieval English borough: studies on its origins and constitutional history*. Manchester.

Thirsk, Joan (ed.) 1967. *The agrarian history of England and Wales, IV, 1500–1640*. Cambridge.

Thomas, A. H. 1924. Introduction. *Calendar of early mayor's court rolls, 1298–1307*, pp. vii–xlv. London.

1926. Introduction. *Calendar of plea and memoranda rolls 1381–1412*, pp. vii–xli. London.

1943. Introduction. *Calendar of plea and memoranda rolls 1413–1437*, pp. vii–xli. London.

Thrupp, Sylvia 1933. *A short history of the worshipful company of bakers of London.* London.

1948. *The merchant class of medieval London, 1300–1500.* Ann Arbor.

1957. A survey of the alien population of England in 1440. *Speculum,* 32: 262–73.

Tingey, J. C. 1911. The grants of murage to Norwich, Yarmouth, and Lynn. *Norfolk Archaeology,* 18: 129–48.

Titow, J. Z. 1987. The decline of the fair of St Giles, Winchester, in the thirteenth and fourteenth century. *Nottinghamshire Medieval Studies,* 31: 58–75.

Todd, Malcolm 1987. *The south-west to AD 1000.* New York.

Touchard, Henri 1967a. *Le commerce maritime breton à la fin du moyen âge.* Paris.

1967b. Les douanes municipales d'Exeter (Devon). Publication des roles de 1381 à 1433. Thèse complémentaire pour le Doctorat ès lettres. Université de Paris.

1973. Le commerce maritime d'Exeter au début du xve siècle. In *Économies et sociétés au moyen âge: mélanges offerts à Edouard Perroy,* pp. 531–7. Paris.

Toulson, Shirley 1983. *Lost trade routes* (Shire Album, no. 108). Aylesbury.

Triffit, John 1983. Urban leadership and the struggle for control in towns. Unpublished paper delivered at the Pre-modern towns conference, 2 December 1983, as reported in Richard Rodger (comp.) "Conference reports," *Urban History Yearbook,* 1985: 77.

Tuck, J. A. 1985. War and society in the medieval North. *Northern History,* 21: 33–52.

Tupling, G. H. 1936. An alphabetical list of the markets and fairs of Lancashire recorded before the year 1701. *Transactions of the Lancashire and Cheshire Antiquarian Society,* 51: 86–110.

Turner, H. L. 1971. *Town defences in England and Wales (900–1500).* London.

Tyldesley, C. J. 1978. The county and local community in Devon and Cornwall from 1377 to 1422. Unpublished Ph.D. thesis. University of Exeter.

Ugawa, K. 1962. The economic development of some Devon manors in the thirteenth century. *TDA,* 44: 630–83.

Unwin, George 1927. The history of the cloth industry in Suffolk. In *Studies in economic history: collected papers of George Unwin,* ed. R. H. Tawney, pp. 262–301. London.

1938. *The gilds and companies of London,* 3rd edn. London.

Unwin, Tim 1981. Rural marketing in medieval Nottinghamshire. *Journal of Historical Geography,* 7: 231–51.

Veale, E. W. W. 1933. Introduction. *The great red book of Bristol* (Bristol Record Society, vol. 4), pp. 9–32. Bristol.

Veale, Elspeth 1966. *The English fur trade in the later middle ages.* Oxford.

Walford, Cornelius 1880. Early laws and customs in Great Britain regarding food. *Transactions of the Royal Historical Society,* 8: 70–157.

Walker, Hilda H. 1972. The history of Kingskerswell, a medieval market town. *PDAS,* 30: 195–215.

Waquet, H. 1913. Les pêcheurs des Cornouaille. *Bullétin de la société archéologie Finisterre,* 11: 249–60.

Waterer, J. W. 1946. *Leather in life, art and industry.* London.

Watkin, A. 1989. Cattle grazing in the forest of Arden in the later middle ages. *Agricultural History Review,* 37: 12–25.

Weddell, Peter J. 1985. The excavation of medieval and later houses at Wolborough Street, Newton Abbot. *PDAS*, 43: 77–109.

1986. The excavation of medieval and later houses and St Margaret's chapel at Exmouth 1982–1984. *PDAS*, 44: 107–41.

Wedemeyer [Moore], Ellen 1970. Social groupings at the fair of St Ives (1275–1302). *Mediaeval Studies,* 32: 27–59.

Welldon Finn, R. 1967. Devonshire. In *The Domesday geography of South-West England.* ed. H. C. Darby and R. Welldon Finn, pp. 223–95. Cambridge.

Welsford, A. E. 1984. *John Greenway 1460–1529. Merchant of Tiverton and London,* Tiverton.

Wheeler, Alwyne 1969. *The fishes of the British Isles and North-West Europe.* East Lansing, MI.

1984. Fish bones. In *The archaeology of Taunton: excavation and fieldwork to 1980,* ed. Peter Leach, pp. 193–4. Gloucester.

White, William 1850. *History, gazetteer and directory of Devonshire,* reprint 1968. New York.

Wilkinson, B. 1931. *The mediaeval council of Exeter* (History of Exeter Research Group, no. 4). Manchester.

Wilkinson, M. 1979. The bird and fish remains. In *Faunal studies of urban sites: the animal bones from Exeter 1971–1975,* ed. Mark Maltby, pp. 66–81. Sheffield.

Willan, T. S. 1976. *The inland trade: studies in English internal trade in the sixteenth and seventeenth centuries.* Manchester.

Willard, James F. 1933. Taxation boroughs and parliamentary boroughs, 1294–1336. In *Historical essays in honour of James Tait,* ed. J. G. Edwards, V. H. Galbraith, and E. F. Jacob, pp. 417–35. Manchester.

Williams, D. T. 1951. Medieval foreign trade: western ports. In *An historical geography of England before A.D. 1800,* ed. H. C. Darby, pp. 266–97. Cambridge.

Williams, Gwyn A. 1970. *Medieval London: from commune to capital.* London.

Windeatt, Edward 1911. The borough of Clifton-Dartmouth-Hardness and its mayors and mayoralties. *TDA*, 43: 120–48.

Wolff, Philippe 1950. English cloth in Toulouse (1380–1450). *EcHR*, 2nd ser., 2: 290–4.

Woodward, D. M. 1970. Freemen's rolls. *Local Historian,* 9: 89–95.

Worth, R. N. 1894. Early days in South Molton. *TDA*, 26: 122–32.

1931. *A history of Plymouth.* Plymouth.

Wright, T. 1862. The municipal archives of Exeter. *Journal of the British Architectural Association,* 18: 306–17.

Wrightson, Keith 1978. Medieval villagers in perspective. *Peasant studies,* 7: 203–17.

Youings, Joyce 1952. The city of Exeter and the property of the dissolved monasteries. *TDA*, 84: 122–41.

1965. Monastic wool sales. *DCNQ*, 30: 70–2.

1967. King James's charter to Tiverton, 1615. *TDA*, 99: 147–63.

1968. *Tuckers Hall Exeter: the history of a provincial city company through five centuries.* Exeter.

1970. Tuckers Hall Exeter: some early gild ordinances. *DCNQ*, 31: 235–8.

Young, Edward H. 1931. *Okehampton* (Devonshire Association, Parochial histories of Devonshire, no. 1). Exeter.

Zupko, Ronald E. 1985. *Dictionary of weights and measures for the British Isles.* Philadelphia.

Index

Unless noted otherwise, all places are in Devon.